HOLGER SPAMANN &

JENS FRANKENREITER

CORPORATIONS

CORPORATIONS

By Holger Spamann & Jens Frankenreiter

Independently published on KDP.

COLOPHON

The serif font used in this book is EQUITY.

The sans serif font is CONCOURSE.

Both were designed by Matthew Butterick.

ISBN-13: 979-8856103198

Third Edition, August 2023.

About This Book

This book is a print edition of materials initially created and made available by Holger Spamann on H2O, an online learning and content platform, now updated to a third edition jointly by Holger Spamann and Jens Frankenreiter. The online version, including access to the full text of the cases presented herein, is available at https://opencasebook.org/casebooks/261-corporations.

A few notes on the book's formatting:

1. Original source materials, including cases, are presented in sans serif font, e.g.:

    "Two cases pitting the directors of Atlas Corporation against that company's largest (9.1%) shareholder, Blasius Industries, have been consolidated and tried together."

2. Footnotes in sans serif font are taken from the original case.

3. Materials written by the authors are presented in serif font, e.g.:

    "Formally speaking, a corporation is nothing but an abstraction to which we assign rights and duties."

4. Additional notes or annotations by the authors appear in several formats in the text. Some are included as footnotes, in serif font. Others are inline comments, in which case they presented in grey and generally preceded by "eds," e.g., [eds: the buyer could then merge with Transunion]. Others are presented as sidenotes, also in grey, with the location to which they refer marked with a diamond, e.g., ◆. ◆Example of a sidenote.

5. Elided text—parts of cases that have been removed by the authors—is indicated by [...]. In several cases, text has been removed and replaced with abbreviated summaries, which is indicated with [bracketed sans serif text].

Contents

Authors' Note—Hints for Readers

We wrote this book as the basis for a first course in corporate law. We provide extensive introductions and explanations to situate the cases and other materials.

We strongly encourage you to read the cases from two related but quite different perspectives. The first is the usual, legal perspective. Almost all the cases in this book are seminal cases familiar to all corporate law practitioners. They "lay down the law." You can read them for what the law is, for what it could have been, and for how judges chose between the various paths open to them.

The second perspective is less obvious but ultimately even more important. The *facts* of the cases demonstrate how corporate actors use the building blocks of the corporate form to achieve various goals—they illustrate corporate law's transactional nature. There are infinite permutations of the various building blocks, so we can't show all. But we have endeavored to include a good selection of standard transactional scenarios—buy-and sell-side M&A, share reclassifications (*Zuckerberg*), executive compensation (*Disney*), dividends (*Sinclair*), jostling for control of the board (*Blasius* and others), control conflicts in private corporations (*Coster*; *eBay*), etc.—and moves (voting, written consent, unilateral board action, enlarging the board, issuing new stock, merger, asset sale, etc.). Most court opinions evaluate these maneuvers or some small part of them under equitable principles. But you should also pay attention to the maneuvers themselves. They are what most corporate lawyers do in practice (even if most maneuvers do not end up in court). This is a fundamental difference from other areas of law where lawyers mostly get involved at the back end, so to speak.

A separate reason to pay great attention to the facts is that much of corporate law consists of broad standards that take on real meaning only in their application. Understanding the law often requires reading the full facts. The judges clearly considered these factual details important, even on appeal, and so should you!

With one exception, all cases in these materials are Delaware or federal cases. Delaware law is the dominant corporate law of the United States. In the U.S., each state has its own corporate law, and the applicable law is the law of the state of incorporation. Corporations are free to incorporate where they want, in return for paying incorporation tax ("franchise tax") in that jurisdiction. Delaware has attracted more than half of all public corporations and many private corporations in the U.S. (Delaware derives a third of its state revenue from the franchise tax!) Furthermore, Delaware is also the model followed by many other states. As a result, we see no point in teaching you other states' law. We occasionally use other countries' laws to expose you to alternative arrangements; the variance between countries is much larger than between U.S. states.

For similar reasons, we teach only corporations proper. We do not cover partnerships, limited liability companies (LLCs), or the many other entity forms now available. These other forms are undoubtedly important in practice. But an introductory course cannot teach the nuanced differences between these forms, many of which lie in tax law. So we only give you a brief warning about involuntary partnerships in the first class. However, there are substantial commonalities between the various entity forms. If you understand corporate law and the underlying business problems, you will easily learn the other forms when the need arises.

I am very grateful to Molly Eskridge, Scott Hirst, Zoe Piel, and Mengjie Zou for their amazing help in putting together the first and second editions, and to Jordi Weinstock for the wonderful cover. —HS

We are very grateful to Molly Eskridge for her great editorial help with the third edition and to Heiko Strubel for help in redesigning the cover. —HS & JF

Glossary

Bylaws = a corporation's secondary governing document (cf. DGCL 109(b)). The charter can provide, and usually does provide, that the board can amend the bylaws without shareholder consent (DGCL 109(a); contrast the charter itself, which can only be amended by board and shareholders jointly, DGCL 242(b)).

Certificate of incorporation = a corporation's founding and primary governing document (cf. DGCL 102).

Charter = certificate of incorporation.

Common stock / share = see share.

Debt holders = creditors.

DGCL = Delaware General Corporation Law, i.e., the basic Delaware statute. As a guide to this important statute, you might want to consult simplifiedcodes.com.

Dividends = an official distribution of cash or other assets to all shareholders of one class. Even though dividends are generally the only way shareholders as a group get a return on their investment (individual shareholders can also sell their shares, but that only puts the buyer of the shares into the seller's shoes), dividends are in the board's discretion (DGCL 170(a)).

Equity; equity capital = the excess of assets over liabilities, if any (or equivalently, non-debt financing).

Equity holders = shareholders. The term derives from the fact that roughly speaking, equity is available for distribution to shareholders.

Limited liability = no liability (of shareholders). The expression "limited" comes from the observation that shareholders stand to lose whatever they put into the corporation, as this is available to satisfy the corporations' creditors' claims. However, shareholders have no liability beyond that, absent pathological circumstances.

Merger = the fusion of two corporations into one (cf. DGCL 251).

Preferred stock / share = stock with special rights ("preferences"), generally with respect to dividends. A standard term is that preferred shares are entitled to a certain dividend per year, payable if and when a dividend will be paid to common stockholders. In return, preferred shares often do not carry voting rights.

Public corporation = a corporation whose stock is publicly traded, usually on a regulated stock exchange such as the New York Stock Exchange.

Share = an interest in the corporation with rights that are defined by the corporation's charter. Unlike debt, shares do not provide a right to fixed payouts. Rather, the board decides if and when shareholders will receive so-called dividends. The default rule is that each share provides one vote (cf. DGCL 212) and equal dividend rights; such shares are called "common shares" or "common stock."

Stock = a synonym or collective term for shares (as in "twenty shares of the corporation's stock").

Part I: Introduction

Chapter 1. Foundations and Background

A. The Corporation

1. What is a corporation?

Formally speaking, a corporation is nothing but an **abstraction** to which we assign rights and duties. It exists independently of humans in the sense that it has indefinite life, and its assets and obligations are legally separate from those of any humans involved in its founding or administration. Today in the United States, anyone—a single individual, group, or another corporation or other entity—can create a corporation in a day for a couple hundred dollars in registration fees (e.g., using incorporate.com).

The corporate abstraction is an extraordinarily useful and widely used device for organizing relationships between various people and different assets. Most importantly, a group of people can pool their assets by transferring them to a corporation that will act as a single contracting interface with third parties (and with the owners among themselves, for that matter). Or a single person can set up multiple corporations to hold different assets and to enter into contracts relating to those assets. You can and should, therefore, also think of the corporation as a **contracting technology**. It facilitates contracting by partitioning and pooling assets.

Of course, being an abstraction rather than a real person, the corporation cannot exercise its rights, discharge its duties, or consume its profits by itself. Human beings must act on its behalf and ultimately consume its profits, if any. Humans can be involved directly, or through a chain of corporations (e.g., corporation A's sole shareholder is corporation B, whose shareholders are human beings). The basic **default governance** is simple: (common) shareholders elect the board of directors (cf. DGCL 211(b)), which formally manages the corporation (DGCL 141(a)), mostly by appointing the chief executive officer and other top management (cf. DGCL 142(a)), who in turn act on behalf of the corporation in day-to-day matters. As to consuming the profits, the board may decide to distribute available funds to shareholders—or not (cf. DGCL 170(a)). By default, each share confers one vote and the right to equal distributions per share (cf. DGCL 212(a) - the more shares you own, the more votes you have and the more of any distribution you get. Corporate law fills in the details: what if the board is unfaithful to shareholder interest? What if shareholders have divergent interests? Are there any other interests to be taken into account?

Technically, the corporation is not the only abstraction available for asset pooling and partitioning. There are **variants** such as the limited liability company (LLC) that have all or most of the features discussed here, and are subject to very similar rules. From the perspective of this introductory course, the differences are minor, and hence not covered.

2. What the corporation is not

The corporation is **not a person** like a human being. To be sure, we sometimes refer to corporations as "legal persons" (cf. 1 U.S.C. §1). But you should realize that this is just legalistic shorthand to emphasize the fact that a corporation can be the object and subject of legal claims. It does not mean that a corporation is a person in the sense that it has the same rights and obligations as human beings. Or have you ever heard of a corporation being drafted into military service? Or invoking a human right not to be tortured? As Chief Justice Roberts quipped in an opinion denying that AT&T could suffer "an unwarranted invasion of personal privacy" (*FCC v. AT&T*, 131 S.Ct. 1177, 1185 (2011)): "We trust that AT&T will not take it personally."

The corporation is also **not the same as a business**. A corporation may "own" a business, but they are not the same thing. A business is a collection of assets and a set of real world activities. A corporation is an abstract legal reference point to which we assign those assets. (Another formal note: In most jurisdictions, one technically cannot own a "business." Rather, one owns the assets that form the business, which include not only chattel and real property but also contracts, intellectual property, etc.)

3. Example 1: Olivia's Pizza

To make this more concrete, think of your local pizza store. Perhaps it is called "Olivia's Pizza," and Olivia indeed runs the place. You might think that Olivia is the "owner" of the store. In all likelihood, however, the formal "owner" of the pizza place — or rather the contracting party on the relevant contracts — is actually a corporation. The corporation might be called "Olivia's Pizza Place Inc.," or "XYZ Corp." for that matter. XYZ Corp. might be (a) the lessee under any lease contract for the store building or other leased items, (b) the employer of any employees, (c) the owner of any real estate or chattel such as the pizza oven or the store sign, and (d) the contracting party with the payment system operator (so your payment for the pizza might show up under "XYZ Corp." on your credit card statement).

Of course, Olivia might be XYZ Corp.'s sole shareholder, director, and chief executive officer (CEO). As shareholder, Olivia would elect the board (here a single director), which in turn appoints the CEO. As CEO and director, Olivia would then have plenary power to administer the business. And as shareholder, she might receive any profits as dividend. For many practical purposes, it is thus irrelevant if Olivia owns the store outright or through a corporation. So what's the point of incorporating?

One benefit of incorporating can be convenience in contracting in certain transactions. If Olivia ever wanted to sell the pizza place after incorporating, she would just sell the corporation — a **single asset** (or to be more precise, all her shares in the corporation, still just one collection of a uniform asset). By contrast, as a single owner, she would have to transfer all the assets individually.

Another convenience is that incorporating changes the default rule from unlimited liability to **limited liability**. The default rule for corporations is that shareholders, directors, and corporate officers are not liable for corporate debts (but they do stand to lose any assets they invested in the corporation as shareholders: hence the expression "limited liability" rather than "no liability"). By contrast, the default rule for single owners is the same as that for any other individual debt: full liability except for protection under the bankruptcy code. It is extremely important that you realize these are only default rules. Contracts can and often do transform limited liability into unlimited liability and vice versa. For example, a no-recourse mortgage contractually limits the borrower's liability to the value of the underlying real estate. Most importantly for present purposes, controlling shareholders such as Olivia often contractually guarantee particular corporate debts such as bank loans (i.e., they contractually promise to pay the corporate debt if the corporation does not). In contractual relationships, the legal concept of "limited liability" is thus neither necessary nor sufficient to provide actual limited liability for shareholders; it merely facilitates it. The situation is different (and controversial) for most tort liability, as most tort creditors never consented, even implicitly, to the limited liability arrangement.

Questions

1. Do you, as a customer of Olivia's Pizza, consent to Olivia's limited liability?
2. Does it matter, legally or as a policy matter?

3. What if Olivia herself negligently dropped a piece of glass onto your pizza — is she still protected by limited liability?

4. Should she be?

Another benefit is **entity shielding**. Entity shielding refers to a liability barrier in the opposite direction: Olivia's personal creditors cannot demand payment or seize any assets from XYZ Corp. The personal creditors can only seize Olivia's shares in XYZ Corp. Entity shielding is extremely useful because it allows those interacting with XYZ Corp. to focus their attention on the pizza store's assets and financial prospects, and not worry about Olivia's other businesses. Imagine for example that Olivia also runs a construction business in a different city. Without entity shielding, creditors from the construction business might seize assets of the pizza store, and vice versa. As a consequence, the two businesses' financial health could not be assessed independently of each other. By contrast, with entity shielding, a bank making a loan to develop the pizza store need only assess the financial prospects of the pizza store, i.e., XYZ Corp. And if the construction business does fail, XYZ Corp. can nevertheless continue business as usual. Entity shielding is more than a mere convenience in that it cannot be accomplished by contracting in the technical sense of the term (i.e., as opposed to the broader set of voluntary arrangements discussed below, which include corporate charters). That being said, the law also provides entity shielding to other entities such as partnerships.

One can neatly summarize limited liability and entity shielding with the simple legal construction of the corporation as a separate **"legal person."** "Naturally," one might say, separate persons are not liable for each other's debts. Importantly, however, the legal construction is only a convenient summary of policy choices that must be grounded elsewhere. For there is nothing natural about declaring the corporation a separate legal person in the first place (nor, for that matter, would there be anything natural about the opposite arrangement, in particular holding investors liable for all debts of the business). It is a convenient fiction, and the law does not adhere to it strictly. We will encounter exceptions in corporate law (notably "piercing the veil"), and there are many more in tax, antitrust, etc. See generally Felix Cohen, *Transcendental Nonsense and the Functional Approach*, 35 COLUM. L. REV. 809 (1935).

4. Example 2: Apple Inc.

We have just argued that the corporation can be useful for small, single-owner-manager businesses such as Olivia's Pizza. But the corporation's full advantages only come into play in larger businesses with multiple shareholder-investors, many or most of whom have no direct involvement in management – i.e., there is **separation of ownership and control**. Almost all large firms are organized as corporations. And the majority of economic activity is bundled in large firms.

Think of Apple Inc. When its legendary co-founder and CEO Steve Jobs died, from a legal perspective all that happened was that the board of Apple Inc. had to appoint a new CEO. By contrast, if Steve Jobs had been the single owner of Apple, the entire business would have been part of his estate, presumably with deleterious consequences. Similarly, if the board of Apple Inc. decides to replace the CEO, it does so by simple resolution — it does not need to expropriate the old CEO.

Even more important than independence from its managers, Apple is independent from its shareholders, and the shareholders are excluded from management. Think of Apple Inc.'s millions of shareholders. Imagine the mayhem if any one of them could demand participation in Apple's management, or liquidation and distribution of Apple's assets. Or if the creditors of any one shareholder could demand payment from Apple, even just for a limited amount, and seize Apple's assets to the extent the payment is not forthcoming. And of course it would be impossible for Apple to enter into a contract or file a suit if this required the signatures of all its shareholders, just as no plaintiff could sue "Apple" if it required naming every single shareholder as a defendant. In other words, Apple Inc. as we know it could not exist without the convenience of a single fictitious "legal person," restricting shareholder involvement in management, and entity shielding.

Many think that Apple Inc. and other large corporations also could not exist without limited liability. The argument is that shareholder liability would deter wealthy investors (who are the ones most likely to be sued), would make the corporation's credit-worthiness dependent on its fluctuating shareholder base, and would interfere with diversification (the strategy to invest in many different assets so as to not put all eggs into one basket). There is reason to doubt this common wisdom, however. Limited liability distorts shareholders' incentives because they (fully) benefit from the upside but do not (fully) bear the downside of risky investments. And the problems of unlimited shareholder liability may be minor if liability is proportional to the number of shares held. Empirically, California provided for proportional shareholder liability until 1931, and American Express was organized with unlimited shareholder liability until 1965. It appears that shareholders largely viewed the shift to limited liability with indifference both in California and in American Express.

Back to indefinite life, and the inability of individual shareholders to demand liquidation. If an Apple shareholder wants to cash out, he or she can simply sell the shares. The default rule is that **shares are freely transferable**. This default rule complements indefinite life. It reconciles the corporation's need for continuity with individual shareholders' need for liquidity, i.e., the ability to convert their investment to cash. In smaller corporations, particularly family firms, however, the charter or shareholder agreements sometimes restrict transferability of shares. And even if sale is not restricted, there is often no market for a small corporation's shares at a price that fully reflects the corporation's value. In these cases, liquidity can be a major source of disagreement between shareholders.

In general, multi-member organizations also have governance problems that Olivia's Pizza does not have. (We write "organizations" because the problems are not specific to corporations.) When the only shareholder (Olivia) is also the only director, the only manager, and the only employee, there are no conflicts to resolve. But when there are millions of shareholders or more generally investors, a multi-member board, dozens of managers, and thousands of employees, conflicts abound. Millions are not necessary for conflicts to arise, however. The conflicts can be even more acrimonious when there are only two shareholders. Mitigating these conflicts is the main preoccupation of corporate law and of this course.

5. The broader picture

Before embarking on our study of conflict mitigation, here are a couple more basic facts to round out the corporate picture.

(a) Holdings and subsidiaries

Large businesses are usually not one but many corporations. Usually, a so-called "holding company" sits at the top of a pyramid of several layers of fully-owned subsidiary corporations. That is, the holding company owns 100% of the shares of several direct subsidiaries. These direct subsidiaries in turn own 100% of the shares of some other, indirect subsidiaries. And so on. This is a further illustration of the point that a corporation and a business are not the same thing.

Some advantages of the subsidiary structure are similar to the advantages of incorporating Olivia's Pizza. Others include tax considerations and regulatory requirements. For example, Apple Inc. became infamous for its use of Irish subsidiaries to "manage" its corporate tax liability. And yet, the relevant part of its corporate structure (see https://goo.gl/5w8qJQ at 20) appeared simple compared to the full network of subsidiaries of, e.g., JP Morgan (https://goo.gl/sxx1FU), which comprises hundreds of subsidiaries.

In this course, we usually focus on the top level holding company because that is where the governance problems arise.

(b) Partnerships and other entity types

You may wonder what would happen if a multi-person firm did *not* incorporate. The answer is that "the association of two or more persons to carry on as co-owners a business for profit forms a partnership, whether or not the persons intend to form a partnership," unless the association was specifically formed under a separate statute such as the DGCL (which will generally require at least a registration). See section 202 of the Uniform Partnership Act of 1997; cf. section 6(1) of the Uniform Partnership Act of 1914.

This is a very dangerous default rule. Absent agreement to the contrary, (1) all partners have unlimited liability for partnership debt, (2) all partners have equal rights to participate in management, (3) any partner may be able to demand dissolution at any time, and (4) partnership interests are not transferable. It is a recipe for disaster.

You might now wonder how businesses could even operate before incorporation became generally available in the 19th century. There are three answers: First, some were lucky or corrupt enough to procure a special corporate charter from the queen/king or legislature (by "special act" or "private law"). Second, some businesses may indeed not have commenced or grown beyond a certain point because the corporate form was not available. Third, and most importantly, the partnership rules described above are merely the default rules. They can and usually are heavily tailored in the partnership agreement, provided that the partners are aware that they are forming a partnership.

For example, the partnership agreements of contemporary law firm partnerships reserve management to a committee, and provide for a regulated cash-out without dissolution if a partner wants to exit the partnership. The one thing that the partnership agreement cannot exclude in a traditional partnership is unlimited liability. To limit liability in a practical way, the law firm must choose a different entity type, as most large firms have done by now. In the past, before incorporation became freely available in England in the middle of the 19th century, English solicitors tailored trusts to approximate a corporation with limited liability.

(c) Contractual freedom

There is a more general theme here. Almost everything in U.S. corporate law can be modified by contract, at least if we understand contract in a broader sense to include charters and bylaws. For example, the charter can create separate classes of stock with different voting and distribution rights (DGCL 151(a), 212(a)). Even if a rule is mandatory on its face, like unlimited liability for partners in general partnerships, one can usually circumvent it by choosing an economically equivalent but legally different transaction or entity type, such as the limited liability partnership (LLP). See generally Bernard Black, *Is Corporate Law Trivial?*, 84 Nw. U. L. Rev. 542 (1990).

We will discuss the normative sense or nonsense of this state of affairs towards the end of the course. Until then, it is important to keep in mind that any judicial or legislative decision we read is contingent on the particular contractual arrangements chosen by the individuals involved. More to the point, as a budding corporate lawyer, you should always be thinking: what clause or arrangement could have avoided this problem?

Questions

1. Some large law firms choose to remain general partnerships. Can you guess why? (Do you know an example of a firm that's a general partnership?)
2. Which of the elements of the corporation could not have been provided by a simple contract between the participants (shareholders, managers, etc.)? In other words, if there were no corporate, partnership, or other organizational law but merely contract law, what would be missing?

B. Agency Law Primer

We take a brief detour into agency law. One of agency law's two components is the legal attribution of the actions of one person (the "agent") to another (the "principal") in relationship to third parties. This explains why agency law is often taught alongside corporate law. Being an abstraction, a corporation needs someone else to act on its behalf, i.e., as its agent. Corporate officers—e.g., the CEO—are legally agents of the corporation, as are the many other people acting for the corporation. Agency law provides the legal basis why actions of the CEO or a store clerk can establish liability between the corporation and some third party, both in contract and in tort. Agency law's second component is rules for the "internal" relationship between agent and principal, which is relevant for a corporation's relationships with its employees etc. and refined into special corporate law rules for corporate officers and directors covered extensively later in the book.

Agency law is state law, but the leading source of agency law is actually the Restatement of Agency (Third), a summary of the various state laws published by the American Law Institute. The Restatement is not binding law but it is highly influential in practice.

Formally, agency is the fiduciary relationship that arises when one person (the principal) agrees with another person (the agent) that the agent shall act on the principal's behalf and subject to the principal's control (Restatement (Third) of Agency § 1). The agency relationship therefore exists by **consent**: both principal and agent must consent to create it, and if either wishes to terminate the agency relationship, then the relationship is terminated. In addition, if the parties have agreed to what is in substance an agency relationship, a court will treat it as such, even if the parties do not recognize that they have created an agency relationship, or even if they wish to avoid doing so.

The formal definition also notes a core feature of agency: it is a "**fiduciary relationship**" in which the agent owes the principal fiduciary duties. The concept of fiduciary duties is one of the most fundamental in corporate law, because a corporation's officers and directors owe the corporation special fiduciary duties that pervasively regulate their conduct. In general, fiduciary duties mean that the fiduciary (here the agent) must act loyally to serve the interests of the recipient of the fiduciary duty (here the principal). Agents owe specific fiduciary duties of care, loyalty, and obedience. The duty of care requires agents to act with the competence that a reasonable person would exercise in similar circumstances. The duty of loyalty requires agents to serve the principal's interests rather than their own. The duty of obedience requires agents to act in accordance with the instructions of the principal.

The law also holds a **principal responsible to third parties** for various acts of the agent. Here, we will discuss the principal's liability for contracts the agent enters into and torts the agent commits. Whether a principal is obligated by a **contract** an agent enters depends on the extent to which the agent was acting with *authority*. There are two main forms of authority. First, **actual authority** exists when the *agent* reasonably believes, based on the *principal's conduct*, that the principal wants the agent to so act. Practically speaking, this is by far the most common form of authority in real life: In most agency relationships, agents understand and follow the wishes of their principal. They will enter contracts if, and only if, the principal wants them to contract. These agents act with actual authority. Second, **apparent authority** exists when a *third party* reasonably believes the agent to possess authority to enter a contract based on the third party's perception of the *principal's conduct*. Even if an agent enters into a contract without authority, a principal can still be liable for it when the principal later approves of the contract (called "**ratification**"), or if the principal is aware a third party entered a contract because he or she believed the principal was bound by it and the principal caused such belief or did not take reasonable steps to notify the third party of the actual facts (called "**estoppel**").

The principal is always liable for an agent's **torts** if the principal specifically instructed the agent to perform the tortious act (though this is not the typical scenario). Otherwise, the principal's liability in tort depends mostly on the type of agent. A principal is generally *not liable* for torts committed by an **independent contractor**, unless the principal was negligent in selecting the contractor. A principal *is liable* for the torts committed by an **employee** when the employee is acting *within the scope* of his or her employment. Whether an agent is an independent contractor or an employee depends on the principal's level of control over the agent's performance of the task. If the principal exercises considerable control, then the agent is generally an employee. Otherwise, the agent is an independent contractor. A current controversy is whether Uber drivers are independent contractors or employees. The liability for employees is "strict" meaning that the principal is liable for the tort regardless of how much care the principal exercised in trying to avoid torts by an employee, and a tort does not fall outside the scope of employment simply because the employee disregarded instructions. This doctrine of principal liability is called "vicarious liability" or "respondeat superior."

An **agent** is also **personally liable** for any *torts* the agent commits. However, plaintiffs will generally prefer to sue the principal rather than (or in addition to) the agent, because principals usually have far more money than their agents, especially when the principal is a large corporation. Sometimes, the agent may also be obligated under a *contract* that the agent enters into for the principal. The agent is *not* obligated under the contract in the standard case where the third party knows the actual identity of the principal on whose behalf the agent acts (a "disclosed principal"); only the principal and the third party are parties to the contract. However, if the third party knows that there is a principal, but not the actual identity of the principal, then the principal is said to be an "unidentified principal." In this case, the principal and the third party are again parties to the contract, but the agent is also a party. If the third party does not even know that the person they are contracting with is an agent acting on another's behalf then the principal is said to be an "undisclosed principal." For example, if a celebrity wanted to buy a house but did not want her neighbors to know, she might have an agent buy the house for her, so that her neighbors remained unaware that she was the ultimate buyer, i.e., the undisclosed principal. In this case, the third party and the agent are parties to the contract, and the principal is too unless the contract specifically excludes the principal.

C. Pizza Shop Exercise

Here is a little problem to warm up and introduce some basics of agency and partnership. Before attempting the problem, please read (!): Uniform Partnership Act (1914) §§ 6(1), 7(4), 9(1), 13, 15, 21(1), 29, 31(1)(b), 37, 38(1); Restatement of the Law (Third) Agency §§ 1.01, 1.04(7), 2.01, 2.03, 2.05, 3.01, 3.03, 4.01(1), 4.02(1), 6.01, 7.03, 8.01-03.

1. Litigator's perspective

Louis comes to you in distress. He tells you the following:

> Kathryn and I have been operating a pizza shop here in Cambridge for years. From a business perspective, we are doing extremely well. Personally, however, things have not been going so well lately. We have been fighting a lot. Today, I received a letter from Kathryn's attorney 'demanding and declaring that the business be dissolved and all assets liquidated to pay off the debt.' I have no idea what that means but I guess it's serious?
>
> 'All assets' is a fancy term, too! It is essentially one big pizza oven that we bought a year ago. We lease the store and our three delivery cars. We just renewed the leases a year ago for a five-year term. They all include penalties for early resolution, and they are not assignable. I reckon the penalties would collectively amount to $50,000 if we had to terminate the contracts now! And that oven, there's a problem there if we have to sell it now, too: it was custom-fit to our location, so I doubt we'd get more than $50,000 for it. But we still have that bank loan for about $100,000 that we used to finance it.
>
> Is that all? Well, actually, there is another issue that came up right after I received the letter. That guy Steve – he generally buys our veggies and stuff. Goes to the wholesalers every week, they know he works for us. He gets the stuff, they debit our account, and we pay them by check later. Of course, after I got the letter, I told him not to buy anything today – who knows if we'll ever need it! But he just goes off and buys everything – and then crashes the car on the way back! Apparently he did major damage because now I am getting all these phone calls from various people and their attorneys demanding that I

pay some crazy amounts. But I didn't drive that car, or put in those orders. Why should I pay for them?

And I sure hope I can keep the shop running. At least I don't want to be saddled with that bank loan if we do have to close.

Questions

1.   What do you think? Is there anything else you need to know?

2. Transactional View

We just looked at Louis and Kathy's pizza shop from a litigator's perspective. Most of the work of corporate lawyers, however, is to avoid disputes arising in the first place, in particular to design procedures that will resolve conflicts without litigation. So let's travel back in time six years.

Kathy and Louis ask you to set up the legal side of a pizza shop they envision. Louis has been working as a baker in a local bakery for many years. He will give up his job to become the pizza shop's general manager and, for the time being, only full-time employee. Kathy runs a marketing agency that does lots of business with mostly upscale restaurants. She will work on generating demand for the pizza shop in her spare time, while continuing to run her agency.

Kathy and Louis are childhood friends. They still spend a lot of time together. The idea for the pizza shop started at a recent dinner where they were both unhappy with the pizza. They concluded that they could do this better, and that there would be demand for better pizza in Cambridge. Over the next couple weeks, they worked out a business plan. They believe the pizza shop will be quite profitable.

They initially thought that Louis should set up the shop by himself, and that Kathy would just help out with the initial marketing. The problem is, however, that Louis doesn't have the cash to make the required investments. To be more exact, Louis is totally broke. A bank is willing to lend $100,000 to buy the pizza oven (the single biggest expense), taking a security interest in the oven. But the bank is not willing to lend unsecured for the initial operating expenses (supplies, drivers' salaries, etc.). Kathy and Louis are confident that the store will be profitable eventually. But they reckon it will take a couple months to get there. In the meantime, expenses will need to be paid, including Louis's living expenses.

As a solution, Kathy offers to invest some of her retirement savings in the pizza shop. The number they envision – roughly their estimate of six months of expenses –

is $60,000. She and Louis also hope that Kathy may eventually join the business full time if things go well – in the long run, they dream of developing a chain.

Questions

1. Can you ethically represent both Kathy and Louis in this matter?

2. How would you advise Kathy and Louis to structure their business relationship? What eventualities should they prepare for? To make this more concrete, assume the only reasonable entity choice is a corporation (in reality, they might use an LLC). Which, if any, provisions would you advise they write into the charter or into the bylaws?

Read: Apple charter (Appendix 1); DGCL 102(b)(1), 109, 141(a)/(b), 212, 216, 242, and 275(a)/(b) (for present purposes, it is sufficient to read the simplified versions at simplifiedcodes.com)

Skim: Apple bylaws (Appendix 2).

Optional: Take a glance at DGCL 273 (joint venture dissolution) and 341 et seq. (close corporations).

D. The Really Big Picture – and Basic Corporate Finance

Note: This section matters as much for terminology as for substance. If you have no background in business and finance, you should read it extremely carefully and look up any terms that you do not understand after reading twice.

As already mentioned above, the corporation is the vehicle of choice for pooling the resources of many investors. Before studying this vehicle in detail, it is worth zooming out for a moment to appreciate why these details matter—a lot!

1. The basic corporate investment relationship

The corporation is at the center of an elaborate system that matches cash-rich investors to cash-poor firms, and thereby enables life as we know it. On one side are **savers** who invest. For the time being, you can think of such savers as yourself when you start saving for retirement, usually through a tax-deferred plan like a 401(k). Savers invest first and foremost to **transfer value through time**, from today to the future: you put money into your 401(k) today and get it out when you retire in 40 years or so. On the other side are **firms** (or, in the beginning, a simple entrepreneur). Firms also wish to transfer value through time, but in the opposite direction, i.e., from the future to today: the firm expects to generate lots of cash in the future and offers to share it in return for financing today, without which it would not be able to generate the future cash in the first place ("Have idea, need money!").

To be sure, individual savers and entrepreneurs could decide to go it alone and put only their own money into a small-scale self-financed business. But in most industries, the investment required for efficient production far exceeds the wealth of individuals and thus requires **pooling resources**. For example, Apple has in excess of $300 billion in assets, financed by countless investors. Even if an individual could afford to finance an entire firm, it is generally preferable to spread the individual's wealth over many firms so as not to put all eggs into one basket, i.e., to reduce risk through **diversification**.

The importance of large-scale matching of savers and firms cannot be overstated. Without it, life as we know it would be impossible. There would be no personal computers, no smart phones, no cars (electric or not), and no electric skateboards. Nor should we take this matching for granted. In the U.S. and some other developed economies, the system matches savers and firms without much friction (cost): many firms can finance themselves on a grand scale at reasonable rates, and a great number of savers can expect returns not much below the rates paid by the firms. Elsewhere in the world, the spread between what savers get and what firms must pay is large, firms often find it hard to impossible to obtain funding at all, and saving is a treacherous affair. Given the enormous temptations for the recipients of financing not to pay it back, it is easy to see why the system might not work ("Tens of trillions of dollars entrusted to money-driven, focused people by naïve and absent-minded savers – what could go wrong?"). The astonishing thing is that it works so well in some parts of the world – and corporate law has a large part in that.

2. Investors, intermediaries, and the lifecycle of firms

In fact, the system achieves nothing short of a miracle once you consider that the typical retirement plan saver invests the money for decades and never looks closely at what firms do with the money or even which firms have the money (more on this below). Firms, on the other hand, come and go and mutate all the time, as new ideas are born and old ones adapt or disappear. Throughout this lifecycle of firms, investors have to make important decisions or risk wasting their money on bad firms or being taken to the cleaners by the firms' managers or other investors. Fortunately, most of these decisions are made by professional investment managers—intermediaries—to whom the ultimate investors like us have entrusted their savings, relying on a well-functioning legal system and other institutions to ensure that we will eventually get our money back, and more.

A thumbnail sketch of a firm's lifecycle might be: In the beginning, an entrepreneur solicits financing from so-called **venture capital funds (VCs)** that specialize in early-stage financing. 90% of early stage companies fail. The VCs make their money off of the 10% that do not and reach the next stage: a "trade sale" to another company, or an **initial public offering (IPO)** of the corporation's stock to investors at large by means of registration with the S.E.C. and listing on a stock exchange. Depending on how the business develops, the corporation might later offer more stock to the public in a so-called **secondary equity offering (SEO)**, be acquired by another company, acquire other companies, or go bankrupt – or all of the above in various permutations.♦ Along the way, the corporation holds numerous shareholder votes and investor calls, engages in all sorts of financing transactions, and, last but decidedly not least, runs its business. This happens at tens of thousands of firms. Meanwhile, all that the ultimate investors are doing is to put their money into a bank account, annuity contract, retirement plan, etc., wait a couple decades, and leave the rest to financial intermediaries.

♦ Note in this regard that bankruptcy usually means restructuring or sale rather than liquidation, and firms not only buy but also sell a/k/a "spin off" subsidiaries and other parts of their business. For example, United Airlines was founded as Boeing Air Transport by William Boeing in 1927, merged with his Boeing Airplane Company in 1929, and spun out as United Airlines in 1934; it filed for bankruptcy in 2002, emerged from bankruptcy in 2006, and merged with Continental Airlines in 2013.

Such intermediaries include **banks and insurance companies**. Banks use funds received as deposits or savings to make loans. Insurance companies offer annuity products by taking savers' premia and investing them in firms; they also invest premia received from other insurance clients. Prudential regulation generally prohibits banks and insurance companies from investing in stocks, however, and thus they will feature less prominently in this course.

Retail investors' main way to invest in stocks and bonds (= tradeable debt) is through **mutual funds**. As the name suggests, mutual funds pool individual investor' funds and invest them in a pre-specified type of assets (e.g., S&P 500 stocks); each individual investor owns a share of the fund. By size, mutual funds are the big dog among intermediaries, especially in stocks: as of 2017, U.S. mutual funds had almost 20 trillion U.S. dollars under management. However, mutual funds are not the most active participants in corporate governance, nor are they present in all types of firms. This is largely because, in the name of investor protection, the Investment Company Act and the Investment Advisers Act, respectively, impose considerable restrictions on mutual funds and their management companies (like Fidelity or Vanguard). In particular, mutual funds must offer daily redemption at the fund's then-current net asset value (NAV), which makes it difficult to impossible for mutual funds to invest in illiquid assets, i.e., assets that do not trade in thick markets and hence cannot be sold quickly except at a major discount. Mutual funds therefore mostly invest in public securities, i.e., securities that are registered with the S.E.C. and, usually, admitted to trading on a trading venue such as a stock exchange. Moreover, mutual funds' diversification requirement and prohibition of performance fees makes it relatively unattractive for mutual fund managers to expend resources on effecting change at individual firms in the fund's portfolio.

Private funds—funds open only to select investors—are not subject to these restrictions and are thus present in all asset classes. They provide high-powered incentives to their managers for active management, and thus generate a disproportionate amount of trading and engagement. One small but important group of private funds are the aforementioned VCs. A larger group of private funds called **private equity (PE)** buys mature companies (usually using plenty of additional debt financing), holds and reshapes them for a couple years, and then resells them. Both VCs and private equity funds have investment horizons of at least several years up to a decade and require their own investors to commit their capital for similar periods. All other private funds go by the catch-all name **hedge funds**. Their investment strategies and horizons differ greatly. Of particular importance for this course, so-called **activist** hedge funds seek to profit from changing the way a public company conducts its business, having taken a sizeable equity stake in the company that will increase in value if the company improves. **Merger arbitrage** hedge funds specialize in buying the equity of corporations that have announced to merge.

Investors in private funds include institutional investors such as public and private pension funds (e.g., CalPERS), endowments (e.g., Harvard's), and sovereign wealth funds (e.g., Saudi Arabia's). (The teams managing institutional investors are themselves intermediaries for the ultimate beneficiaries, such as employees and retirees.) Other investors in private funds are wealthy individuals, particularly ultra wealthy individuals who often have their own wealth management teams ("family offices"). In this connection, it is worth pointing out that the "savers" that invest their money in firms are not the average Joe: in the U.S., the top 1% own one third of all equity in public firms, and the top 10% own four fifths (these numbers include indirect ownership through pension funds etc.).

3. Capital structure and corporate governance

As hinted above, there are two broad categories of financial claims that investors acquire in firms, in return for their investment: debt and equity. **Debt** is an IOU—a fixed claim. It includes loans from banks and others, as well as publicly traded debt securities called *bonds*. These payment claims can be enforced in court: creditors can sue for payment, and seize the corporation's assets if payment is not forthcoming. **Equity** (a/k/a shares, stock), on the other hand, provides no right to payment but usually provides voting rights to elect the corporation's board, which *may* determine to pay money to equity holders as a dividend or to buy back their stock.

If the corporation cannot pay its creditors—i.e., if it is *insolvent*—, unpaid creditors or the corporation itself may petition the bankruptcy court to open a **bankruptcy** procedure. Bankruptcy does not mean that the business of the corporation is liquidated. Rather, bankruptcy is a collective proceeding to settle various investors' claims, while preserving the business's going concern value, if any (potentially simply by selling the business, and then dividing the sale price between existing claimants). The most important tool of bankruptcy law is its *automatic stay* of individual proceedings, which prevents inefficient liquidation by individual creditors racing to grab the corporation's assets and explains the expression "filing for bankruptcy *protection*." In bankruptcy, claimants are supposed to be paid in order of their seniority (see below). In particular, equity holders are supposed to get paid only after all creditors have been paid in full. Hence equity holders are often referred to as the corporation's *residual claimants*.

Debt and equity come in various flavors, including hybrids. This is especially true for debt. Not only do debt claims come in different maturities and with different ancillary rights, such as creditor undertakings to do or not to do something (**covenants**). Importantly, debt claims also differ in their **seniority**. Some creditors—so-called juniors—may contractually agree to subordination to certain other creditors—so-called seniors—in bankruptcy, i.e., to receive payment only after the latter have been paid in full. (Bankruptcy law itself also contains some seniority rules for special groups of creditors.) The debtor may grant a **security interest** in particular assets (e.g., a mortgage) to so-called secured creditors, which enables the secured creditors to obtain satisfaction of their claim from the sale of the asset prior to any other creditors, provided certain formalities, usually including a filing, have been complied with. (Security interests are also called collateral.) The debt contract may provide that the debt is **convertible** into equity at the election of the creditor and/or the corporation. The debt may also be issued together with **options**—known as **warrants** when issued by the corporation—, i.e., rights to purchase stock of the corporation at a pre-specified price (cf. DGCL 157).

Equity tends to be less varied, and most corporations only have one class of common stock. Of late, however, many prominent tech corporations such as Google, Facebook, or Snap have gone public with two or more different classes of stock ("**dual class**") to preserve the founders' control: one high-voting class reserved to the founders, and one low- or even non-voting class for outside investors. Many corporations also issue so-called **preferred stock**, which tends to have no voting rights but a dividend preference, i.e., the right to receive some specified minimum amount of dividends before any dividends can be paid to common stockholders (cf. DGCL 151(c)/(d)). Anything goes under Delaware corporate law: DGCL 151(a)). Voting and other rights may even be extended to creditors (DGCL 221).

A very important point is that the so-called **capital structure** formed by the combination of different claims on the corporation is just that: a structure to raise capital and ultimately to divide the returns, if any. There is nothing essential or even permanent about any of the claims or the investors who hold them. The same investors often hold different parts of the capital structure, such as debt and equity, simultaneously or at different points in time. Investors may trade in an out of the corporations' claims at any time (at least if they are traded in a liquid market). The corporation frequently extinguishes some claims by paying or buying them back and creates others by selling them in return for new investment. For example, the corporation may borrow money to buy back stock ("leveraged recapitalization"), issue stock to pay off debt, repay one loan by taking on another ("refinancing"), or offer to exchange one type of stock for another. (However, sensibly enough, shares owned by the corporation itself—"treasury shares"—do not have voting rights etc., see DGCL 160(c).)

Does capital structure matter? It obviously matters for the pricing of individual claims, as investors only pay for what they get. But what the corporation gives to holders of one claim it cannot give to another, and in light of the previous paragraph, the value of individual claims is hardly of deep interest (except, of course, to those buying or holding those claims!). The real question is whether the total value of all claims that the corporation can sell, and hence the total amount of financing it can raise, depends on the way the claims are delineated by contract, charter, and law? Specifically, does it matter which part of the dollars taken in by the firm (cash flows) go to which investors under which circumstances (**cash flow rights**), and what rights do those investors have to influence the decisions taken by the firm (**control rights**)?

Modigliani and Miller's famous benchmark result in corporate finance is that if the firm's cash flows were fixed and some other conditions held, it would not matter what sort of financial claims the firm issued – the total value of the claims would always be the same. As Miller once explained this proposition, it does not matter how you slice a pizza – it will always be the same amount of pizza. A corporation, however, is not a pizza: its cash flows depend crucially on how it is managed, which in turn depends on how it is governed, i.e., who has which control rights and how they exercise them. Cash flow rights provide incentives to exercise control rights in a certain manner. These incentives can be more or less aligned with increasing the value of the pie (or size of the pizza, if you will). The division and bundling of cash flow and control rights thus matters a great deal.

Corporate and bankruptcy law have some role in the division and bundling of rights, but most of it is done by **contract writ large**, including the corporate charter. This is inevitable because businesses differ and hence need different governance terms adjusted to the business. In particular, businesses differ in the amount of debt they can service. Debt offers important advantages. First, it is tax advantaged: interest is tax deductible, while dividends are not. Second, debt is less information-sensitive: creditors only need to assess the corporation's ability to repay the loan rather than the corporation's full potential. Last but not least, creditors' return expectations are backed up by a hard legal claim and its threat of judicial enforcement and bankruptcy, whereas shareholders are at the mercy of the board. This last feature, however, also makes debt inflexible: it will lead to costly litigation, bankruptcy, or even liquidation whenever the actual cash flows fall short of projected cash flows, or at least give creditors the ability to extract concessions in renegotiating the debt. That is why only stable businesses with predictable cash flows tend to use a lot of debt, while more volatile businesses, particularly startups, rely mostly or exclusively on equity financing. Most of this course will be concerned with the ways in which corporate law seeks to ensure that shareholders will get a return even though they lack a hard claim to repayment.

A final note on capital structure and corporate governance is that every possible arrangement is a compromise, and perfection is impossible. Ex ante, every participant in the business would agree that the goal is to maximize the size of the total pie (or pizza, if you prefer) because that will enable everyone to get a bigger slice (the division can be adjusted by side payments). Once the business gets under way, however, whoever has control over a decision will be tempted to **(ab-)use that control to get a bigger slice**, even if doing so reduces the size of the total pie. For example, managers may favor growing the business beyond the efficient size if they enjoy the greater power and prestige that comes from running a bigger firm. Creditors may favor inefficient liquidation if continuation, while profitable in expectation, is also risky, such that creditors stand to lose but not much to gain from continuation (remember that creditors' claims are fixed!). Inversely, shareholders may favor inefficient continuation if continuation, while unprofitable in expectation, presents at least the possibility of a positive outcome whereas the liquidation proceeds would go fully or mostly to creditors. The point is that as soon as people pool resources, conflicts of interest are unavoidable. The goal is to mitigate such conflicts; they cannot be eliminated.

4. Valuation

> *Note:* This subsection is conceptually denser and more algebraic than anything else in this course. You may find it challenging on first reading.

Above, we said tongue-in-cheek that the value of individual claims does not matter in the big scheme of things. Of course, to individual investors, the value of their claim is all that matters. And because of that, understanding how different actions affect the value of individual claims is crucial to understand the incentives of those holding those claims.

To value a claim, one usually starts with the claim's **expected future cash flows**. Expected cash flows are the probability-weighted average of the cash flows that the investor will receive in all the conceivable scenarios. For example, if the investment will return either $2 million or nothing with equal probability, the expected cash flows are 50% × $2 million + 50% × 0 = $1 million. In the real world, estimating expected cash flows requires understanding the business and the capital structure, particularly—for debt—the seniority structure and security interests. Usually, such estimates are fraught with very considerable uncertainty, especially for equity (cf. discussion of information-sensitivity above).

The next step is to **discount** the future cash flows **to present value** for the time value of money and a risk premium, to name only the most important ones. The **time value of money** arises from the simple fact that in the world we live in, all investors have the alternative to put their money into other investments that are expected to pay back the same amount of money *plus a positive return* in the future. In particular, investors have the alternative to invest in U.S. government bonds that will pay back the same amount of money plus interest with certainty.[1] Thus, to persuade investors

---

[1] Well, actually, the government bond also pays you a compensation for expected inflation. But we'll assume our business's outcomes are measured in nominal terms, so including an inflation premium is appropriate.

to give their money to the corporation, the corporation has to offer more than the interest paid by the government. How much more? That depends on the risk of the corporation's claim. Risk in this context does not mean the probability of non-payment per se: that is already accounted for in the calculation of *expected* future cash flows. Rather, risk here means the variance or volatility of the expected cash flows. For example, for their retirement, most people would rather have $1 million for sure rather than a 50/50 chance of $2 million or nothing (note that the expected cash flows are the same, namely 50% × $2 million + 50% × 0 = 100% × $1 million). That said, investors can diversify away most risk by investing small amounts in many different assets rather than everything in one asset. By and large, investors thus receive a **risk premium** only for **systematic risk**, i.e., risk that is undiversifiable because it is likely to hit all assets at the same time, such as a global recession. (Of course, individual investors would prefer to receive premia for all sorts of things, but in a competitive financial market, investors compete away most other premia – ultimately, the **expected return** on an investment is set by the supply and demand for capital.)

⬧ At the limit, if the success of the firm were purely idiosyncratic—e.g., it depends on whether or not a patent will be upheld in court—, then the appropriate risk premium would be zero, and our firm would be worth $100/(1+1%+0%)=$99.01.

Let us consider an extremely stylized example. Imagine we knew for certain that a firm will be in operation for only one year, after which it will liquidate all its assets and distribute them to its investors. Imagine further that we magically know that there are only three possible outcomes, all equally likely: after liquidation but before distribution, the firm will hold (1) $0, (2) $100, or (3) $200. What is this firm worth? Start with the expected future cash flows: $\frac{1}{3}×\$0+\frac{1}{3}×\$100+\frac{1}{3}×\$200=\$100$. To discount those future cash flows to present value, we need to know the time value of money and the firm-specific risk premium. As mentioned above, the time value of money is what you could earn on a government bond of the same duration.° Let's assume the government currently offers 1% on a one year bond. What is the right risk premium? It depends on the firm! The more the success of the firm is correlated with the health of the economy, the higher the risk premium. How high? It depends on what financial markets demand—or equivalently, what investors can get elsewhere—, which in practice we would estimate by looking at similar firms. Imagine we found the right premium to be 10%. In that case, our firm would be worth $100/(1+1%+10%)=$90.09.⬧

⬧⬧ Nor did the creditor necessarily invest $100: $100 is merely the **face value** of the claim, i.e., the promised amount. In fact, given the time value of money, the investor presumably invested less than $100!

Having valued the firm as a whole, let us value individual claims on it. Imagine the firm is organized as a corporation and only has two claimants: a creditor owed $100, and a shareholder.

Let us start with the creditor and observe that the creditor's claim is not necessarily worth $100—the corporation has promised $100, but whether it will pay that much is an entirely different question, and how to value those payments yet another.♦♦ Concretely, the corporation will not be able to pay anything to the creditor in case 1 where it ends up holding $0 (perhaps *the shareholder* would be able to pay, but, because of limited liability, the shareholder will not need to pay and presumably won't). In the other two cases 2 and 3, the corporation will be able to pay $100 but will not pay more than that (in case 3, it *could* pay more but it won't because the creditor only has a fixed claim for $100). Thus, the expected cash flows to the creditor are $\frac{1}{3} \times \$0 + \frac{1}{3} \times \$100 + \frac{1}{3} \times \$100 = \$66.67$. As to the appropriate discount rate, observe that the creditor's claim is less volatile than the firm as a whole: in two out of three states, the creditor gets the same amount of money. The appropriate risk premium will thus be lower than for the firm as a whole (which was 10%); assume it is 7%. The time value of money is still 1%. Thus, the creditor's claim is worth $\$66.67/(1\%+7\%)=\$61.73$.

Meanwhile, the shareholder as residual claimant gets whatever is left over after paying the creditor, which is nothing in cases 1 and 2 and $100 in case 3, for an expected cash flow of $\frac{1}{3} \times \$0 + \frac{1}{3} \times \$0 + \frac{1}{3} \times \$100 = \$33.33$ (alternatively, we could have found this number by subtracting the creditor's expected cash flows from those of the corporation as a whole). The shareholder's claim is riskier than the firm as a whole because the shareholder will only be paid in the best possible case; let us assume the appropriate risk premium is 16.5%. Then, the shareholder's claim is worth $\$33.33/(1\%+16.5\%)=\$28.37$.[2]

For obvious reasons, the valuation approach exposited above is called **discounted cash-flow analysis (DCF)**. An alternative to DCF is to use **comparables**: one calculates some valuation ratio (or "multiple") for comparable claims, and then assumes that the same ratio will hold for the claim under examination. For example, to

---

[2] In this example, the value of the creditor's claim and the value of the shareholder's claim add up to the value of the firm as a whole. This might appear unsurprising because the two claims are the only claims on the firm, and value cannot evaporate or appear from out of nowhere. Notice, however, that the algebraic equivalence depended on the risk premia: it would not hold with different risk premia (e.g., a lower risk premium for equity). Modigliani and Miller, mentioned above, are famous for showing that, under certain conditions, risk premia must be such that the equivalence does hold. As also mentioned above, however, Modigliani-Miller is merely a benchmark result. In reality, risk premia may not obey the equivalence exactly. More importantly, Modigliani-Miller applies to fixed cash flows; if capital structure influences cash flows, then all bets are off. In the example above, an important omission was taxes: the mix of debt and equity generally influences tax burdens, and it would not even make sense to value "the firm" without taking into account its financing and associated expected taxes.

value the shares of company A (say, Pepsi), one might look at comparable company B (say, Coca-Cola), calculate the ratio of company B's stock price to B's current earnings per share (EPS; roughly, firm profits divided by number of shares outstanding), and then calculate company A's share value as A's EPS times B's share value divided by B's EPS, *on the assumption* that A and B should have the same price/EPS multiple. (Thus, if Coca-Cola's share is worth $150, Coca-Cola's EPS is $10 per share, and Pepsi's EPS is $8 per share, then Pepsi's share is worth $8 × $150/$10 = $120, as valued by EPS multiple.) The advantage of the comparables approach to valuation is that it avoids the difficult task of estimating company A's expected cash flows. The disadvantage is that one must not only assume that company B is already correctly valued, but also that both companies will develop in parallel from their current starting point. The latter assumption is never exactly true and even the approximation may be very bad. In practice, most valuations triangulate from a combination of DCF and multiple comparable firms.

Finally, knowing a claim's present value, or PV, is not enough to make an investment decision. At the risk of stating the obvious, the price of the claim also matters. The investment is appealing only if the *net* **present value (NPV)**, i.e., PV minus price, is positive.

E. Securities Law Primer

State corporate law is very closely intertwined with federal securities law. The link is so close that it is worth giving you a very brief introduction of some elements that will come up again and again in this course. (In other countries, these elements might be included in "corporate law." The distinction is artificial.)

Securities are, roughly, tradable investments such as shares and bonds (tradable debt claims). For our purposes, the relevant statutes are the Securities Act of 1933, and the Securities Exchange Act of 1934 ("Exchange Act"). Both grant broad powers to the U.S. Securities and Exchange Commission (SEC). In particular, the SEC has promulgated very detailed rules implementing the securities laws.

The **Securities Act** is chiefly concerned with the initial disclosure upon a first sale of a security to the public in a so-called registration statement. We will therefore encounter it less often.

The **Exchange Act,** on the other hand, is ubiquitous. Among other things, it regulates ongoing corporate disclosure, and trading in corporate securities. Most provisions of the Exchange Act apply only to "registered securities," which include all securities that are publicly traded on a stock exchange or elsewhere. This excludes securities of private companies, i.e., companies whose securities are not marketed to the public, and in particular not traded on a stock exchange. Private companies include not only small firms but also some large ones like Uber (as of December 2017).

In terms of **disclosure**, the Exchange Act requires, inter alia, the following filings with the SEC, who makes them publicly available on **EDGAR:**

- **Annual** disclosure of the corporation's financial and business situation on **Form 10-K**. This disclosure is quite comprehensive. For example, corporations have to disclose audited financial statements and many details about their executive compensation arrangements.
- **Quarterly** disclosure on **Form 10-Q**. Less comprehensive than 10-K.
- **Ad hoc** disclosure of certain specified events such as a merger on **Form 8-K**.
- **Proxy statements**, i.e., comprehensive disclosure from anyone soliciting shareholder votes, including the corporation itself – see the shareholder voting part of the course.
- Anyone proposing certain important transactions must disclose background, terms, and plans – details when we get there.
- **Ownership interests** above 5% on **Schedule 13D**.
- **Trades by corporate insiders** (directors, officers, and anyone owning 10% or more of a corporation's stock) (Exchange Act §16(a)).

Since 2000, SEC **Regulation FD** (for "fair disclosure") additionally provides, in the SEC's own words, that "when an issuer discloses material nonpublic information to certain individuals or entities—generally, securities market professionals, such as stock analysts, or holders of the issuer's securities who may well trade on the basis of the information—the issuer must make public disclosure of that information."

The Securities Laws and the SEC's rules thereunder also provide private and public remedies for false or misleading statements. The most important provision is SEC **Rule 10b-5**, a broad anti-fraud rule implementing section 10(b) of the Exchange Act. Courts have implied a private right of action under this and similar rules, which sustain an industry of securities class action lawyers. We will deal with rule 10b-5 and others when we cover securities trading in Part IV: of the course.

F. Alphabet/Google Exercise

- Read the Wikipedia excerpts on Alphabet/Google below and look up any terms that you do not know (most were explained in the previous sections!).
- Find out who Alphabet's major stockholders are, both in terms of (a) voting rights and (b) cash-flow rights.[*]
    - What are their stakes worth, approximately, given Alphabet's current stock price?
    - Beyond their names, who are they, i.e., what is their economic role? To the extent they are businesses, not individuals, what is their business model?
- As you know from the last question, voting rights and cash flow rights do not go hand in hand in Alphabet. In particular, Class A and Class B shares have equal cash flow rights but unequal voting rights. This is laid down in certain provisions of Alphabet's charter. Which ones? (You can find the Alphabet charter in the SEC database with a little effort, or with no effort on the Alphabet investor relations webpage.)
- Since 2014, Google/Alphabet's charter also authorizes Class C shares. What voting and cash flow rights do they have? Why do you think Google/Alphabet created this additional class?
- In 2006, Google bought YouTube for around $1.5 billion. Find out how Google paid the YouTube sellers. (It's ok to Google this one.)

1. Google: Excerpt from Wikipedia Entry[3]

Google LLC . . . is an American multinational technology company focusing on artificial intelligence, online advertising, search engine technology, cloud computing, computer software, quantum computing, e-commerce, and consumer electronics. It has been referred to as "the most powerful company in the world" and one of the world's most

---

[*] There are two ways to find out who those major stockholders are. One possibility is to Google them. A more reliable method is to look up Alphabet's proxy statement in the SEC's public database. Go to SEC.gov, select Filings/Company_Filings_Search, search for Alphabet Inc. or its ticker GOOG, and then for its latest form DEF 14A (April 2023), which lists common stock ownership under that heading. One big advantage of this method is that it also works for much less famous public companies.

[3] Entry on "Google," accessed 6/6/2023, footnotes removed; reproduced under Creative Commons license CC-BY-SA (http://creativecommons.org/licenses/by-sa/3.0/).

valuable brands due to its market dominance, data collection, and technological advantages in the area of artificial intelligence. Its parent company Alphabet is considered one of the Big Five American information technology companies, alongside Amazon, Apple, Meta, and Microsoft.

Google was founded on September 4, 1998, by computer scientists Larry Page and Sergey Brin while they were PhD students at Stanford University in California. Together they own about 14% of its publicly listed shares and control 56% of its stockholder voting power through super-voting stock. The company went public via an initial public offering (IPO) in 2004. In 2015, Google was reorganized as a wholly owned subsidiary of Alphabet Inc. Google is Alphabet's largest subsidiary and is a holding company for Alphabet's internet properties and interests. Sundar Pichai was appointed CEO of Google on October 24, 2015, replacing Larry Page, who became the CEO of Alphabet. On December 3, 2019, Pichai also became the CEO of Alphabet.

The company has since rapidly grown to offer a multitude of products and services beyond Google Search, many of which hold dominant market positions. These products address a wide range of use cases, including email (Gmail), navigation (Waze & Maps), cloud computing (Cloud), web browsing (Chrome), video sharing (YouTube), productivity (Workspace), operating systems (Android), cloud storage (Drive), language translation (Translate), photo storage (Photos), video calling (Meet), smart home (Nest), smartphones (Pixel), wearable technology (Pixel Watch & Fitbit), music streaming (YouTube Music), video on demand (YouTube TV), artificial intelligence (Google Assistant), machine learning APIs (TensorFlow), AI chips (TPU), and more. Discontinued Google products include gaming (Stadia), Glass, Google+, Reader, Play Music, Nexus, Hangouts, and Inbox by Gmail.

Google's other ventures outside of Internet services and consumer electronics include quantum computing (Sycamore), self-driving cars (Waymo, formerly the Google Self-Driving Car Project), smart cities (Sidewalk Labs), and transformer models (Google Brain).

Google and YouTube are the two most visited websites worldwide followed by Facebook and Twitter. Google is also the largest search engine, mapping and navigation application, email provider, office suite, video sharing platform, photo and cloud storage provider, mobile operating system, web browser, ML framework, and AI virtual assistant provider in the world as measured by market share. On the list of most valuable brands, Google is ranked second by Forbes and fourth by Interbrand. It has received significant criticism involving issues such as privacy concerns, tax avoidance, censorship, search neutrality, antitrust and abuse of its monopoly position.

History

Early years

Google began in January 1996 as a research project by Larry Page and Sergey Brin when they were both PhD students at Stanford University in California. ...

While conventional search engines ranked results by counting how many times the search terms appeared on the page, they theorized about a better system that analyzed the relationships among websites. They called this algorithm PageRank; it determined a website's relevance by the number of pages, and the importance of those pages that linked back to the original site. ...

Page and Brin originally nicknamed the new search engine "BackRub", because the system checked backlinks to estimate the importance of a site. ...

Eventually, they changed the name to Google; the name of the search engine was a misspelling of the word googol, a very large number written 10100 (1 followed by 100 zeros), picked to signify that the search engine was intended to provide large quantities of information.

Google was initially funded by an August 1998 investment of $100,000 from Andy Bechtolsheim, co-founder of Sun Microsystems. **...**

Google received money from [three] other angel investors in 1998: [Bechtolsheim's co-founder David Cheriton,] Amazon.com founder Jeff Bezos, and entrepreneur Ram Shriram. ...

After some additional, small investments through the end of 1998 to early 1999, a new $25 million round of funding was announced on June 7, 1999, with major investors including the venture capital firms Kleiner Perkins and Sequoia Capital. ...

[Following the closing of the $25 million financing round, Sequoia encouraged Brin and Page to hire a CEO. Brin and Page ultimately acquiesced and hired Eric Schmidt as Google's first CEO in August 2001.

In October 2003, while discussing a possible initial public offering of shares (IPO), Microsoft approached the company about a possible partnership or merger. The deal never materialized. In January 2004, Google announced the hiring of Morgan Stanley and Goldman Sachs Group to arrange an IPO.][4]

Initial public offering

On August 19, 2004, Google became a public company via an initial public offering. At that time Larry Page, Sergey Brin, and Eric Schmidt agreed to work together at Google for 20 years, until the year 2024. The company offered 19,605,052 shares at a price of $85 per share. Shares were sold in an online auction format using a system built by Morgan Stanley and Credit Suisse, underwriters for the deal. The sale of $1.67 billion gave Google a market capitalization♦ of more than $23 billion. ...

♦ Market cap(italization) = number of shares outstanding × price per share. By this measure, Alphabet/Google is currently the 4th largest company in the world, with a market capitalization of $1.603 trillion as of 6/6/2023.

[There were concerns that Google's IPO would lead to changes in company culture. Reasons ranged from shareholder pressure for employee benefit reductions to the fact that many company executives would become instant paper millionaires. As a reply to this concern, co-founders Brin and Page promised in a report to potential investors that the IPO would not change the company's culture.][5]

The stock performed well after the IPO, with shares hitting $350 for the first time on October 31, 2007, primarily because of strong sales and earnings in the online advertising market. The surge in stock price was fueled mainly by individual investors, as opposed to large institutional investors and mutual funds. GOOG shares split into GOOG class C shares and GOOGL class A shares. The company is listed on the NASDAQ stock exchange under the ticker symbols GOOGL and GOOG, and on the Frankfurt Stock Exchange under the ticker symbol GGQ1. These ticker symbols now refer to Alphabet Inc., Google's holding company, since the fourth quarter of 2015.

---

[4] This insert is from the separate Wikipedia entry on "History of Google." For copyright, see previous note.

[5] Like the previous insert, this one is from the Wikipedia entry on "History of Google."

Chapter 2. The Basic Corporate Law Problem & Solutions

A. The Basic Problem

The basic corporate governance problem is how to control those who have been entrusted with the assets assembled in the corporation: managers and directors.

This economic problem is called an *"agency problem"*: how to ensure that the "agents" (managers/directors) act in furtherance of the "principals'" (shareholders') interests rather than the agents' own interest? If this agency problem cannot be addressed satisfactorily, investors will not be willing to put their money into corporations, and the wealth generating machine matching savers and businesses to finance investment won't work (see The Really Big Picture above).

(NB: the economic terminology of "agent" and "principal" employed in this section is related to, but much broader than, the legal terminology in the law of agency. Legally, managers are agents for the corporation, not for shareholders, and directors aren't legal agents for anybody - in particular, they are not subject to shareholder directives. From an economic perspective, however, the corporation is a fiction — a convenient way of describing relationships between human beings. In this perspective, directors and managers ultimately work for shareholders and hence are shareholders' agents in an economic, though not legal, sense.)

Importantly, it is not a solution to completely forgo the use of agents. In reality, it is essential for large organizations to maintain a centralized management with the flexibility and discretion to guide the course of business as they see fit, especially when responding to novel circumstances or unforeseen challenges. To appreciate this point, consider the alternative: Were shareholders required to approve every single decision made by the organization—whether pursuing a new business venture, or deciding to defend the corporation against a potentially expensive lawsuit—the logistical inefficiency and administrative burden would be simply overwhelming. Obtaining shareholder approval would consume an inordinate amount of time, leading to delays and potentially missed opportunities. Furthermore, shareholders (especially passive investors without any experience in an industry) may not possess the expertise or experience necessary to make informed decisions on certain complex business matters. This scenario could expose the corporation to unnecessary risk and jeopardize its viability.

Accordingly, the solution to agency problems cannot be to not employ agents at all. Instead, the trick is to devise appropriate controls.

B. The Basic Partial Solutions: Basic Corporate Law

U.S. corporate law offers two basic solutions to the corporate agency problem: shareholder voting, and fiduciary duties enforced by shareholder lawsuits. Here we offer a first tour d'horizon of these and other basic building blocks of corporate law, before delving into them in much more detail later in the book.

Even in this brief tour, you will see that U.S. corporate law generally sets only **default rules**. Charter provisions and other contractual or quasi-contractual arrangements can supplement or alter all or most of these rules. Indeed, "contractual" arrangements pervade corporate law, from the definition of shareholder rights and allocation of management power in the corporate charter, to bylaws on voting, to executive compensation contracts. Read: DGCL 102(b)(1), 151(a), 141(a), 242(a), 242(b)(1) and 109.

1. Shareholder voting

Shareholders' most visible protection is their right to vote on certain important corporate decisions. In particular, shareholders **elect**, and can remove, **directors**, who in turn appoint management (cf. DGCL 211(b), 141(k), 142(b)). Thus, shareholders at least get to choose their "agents." Shareholders also vote to approve **fundamental changes**, such as charter amendments (cf. DGCL 242(b)) or mergers (cf. DGCL 252(c)). Other matters *may* be submitted to a shareholder vote.

Notably, this "shareholder democracy" isn't truly democratic. First, the default rule in corporations is one vote per share ("**one share one vote**"), rather than one vote per shareholder (cf. DGCL 212(a)). Second, the corporate charter can authorize the issue of shares with different voting rights (DGCL 151(a)), which corporations such as Alphabet/Google, Facebook, and other so-called **dual-class** companies have done: their founders hold high-voting stock, whereas outside investors hold low- or non-voting stock, such that the founders can maintain control even after selling a majority of the equity (measured by cash flow rights) to outside investors. Finally, incumbents enjoy a large advantage because they control the voting process (dates etc.) and because only they can use corporate funds for their campaign: challengers generally have to pay their own costs.

The corporation must hold at least an **annual meeting** of stockholders, DGCL 211(b). Under the default rules, only the board can call additional meetings (DGCL 211(a)(1)); shareholders may act instead by **written consent** (DGCL 228), but even that possibility is usually excluded in the charters of public corporations. Meetings can be in person or online (DGCL 211(a)(1)).

A peculiarity of corporate voting is that voting rights are determined on the "**record date**," 10-60 days *before* the actual vote (DGCL 213). At least in practice, one keeps one's voting rights even if one sells the shares in between. (Any problem with this?)

By default, there are **annual elections** for all board seats. Under DGCL 141(d), however, the charter or a qualified bylaw can provide that as few as one third of the seats are contestable each year, i.e., that directors hold staggered terms of up to three years. This so-called "**staggered board**" probably seems like technical minutiae to you now. But it turns out to be an extremely important provision because it may critically delay anybody's attempt to take control of the board. An important complementing rule is that unlike annually-elected boards, staggered boards are subject to removal only for cause (DGCL 141(k)(1); cf. DGCL 141(k)(2) for the case of cumulative voting).

Unless otherwise provided in the charter or the statute, a majority of the shares entitled to vote constitutes a **quorum** (DGCL 216.1), and the **requisite majority** for a resolution to pass is the affirmative vote of a majority of the shares present (DGCL 216.2). The default for director elections is different (plurality voting, DGCL 216.3), but most large corporations have instituted some form of majority voting rule for director elections in their bylaws or charter. This matters mostly when shareholders express their dissatisfaction through a "withhold campaign" against a particular director. Under the default rule, the director could be elected with a single vote (if running unopposed, as is the norm). A more radical but rare deviation from the default rule is cumulative voting. See DGCL 214 for the technical details. Roughly, cumulative voting ensures proportional representation. Cf. *eBay v. Newmark* later in the book.

In large corporations, few shareholders attend shareholder meetings in person, be it physically or online. Most vote by "**proxy**": a power of attorney to vote a shareholder's shares (cf. DGCL 212(b)). The proxy is usually given on a standard form—the "**proxy card**"—furnished by those who solicit proxies, nowadays mostly electronically. For most meetings, the only soliciting party is the board, acting for (and with all expenses paid for by) the corporation. The board solicits proxies to ensure a quorum, to prevent a "coup" by a minority stockholder, and because the stock-exchange rules require it (see, e.g., NYSE Listed Company Manual 402.04). The board decides which proposals and nominees to include on the corporation's proxy card, except as mandated by the federal proxy rules covered below. Rarely, "dissidents" solicit their own proxies in opposition to the incumbent board, usually in order to elect their own candidates to the board. This is called a **proxy fight** or proxy contest. The challenger generally bares their own cost, which largely explains why proxy fights are rare.

Proxy solicitations are heavily regulated by the **SEC's proxy rules** (Regulation 14A promulgated under section 14 of the Securities Exchange Act). For a first course on corporations, you only need to know the following:

1. Before any proxy solicitation commences, a **proxy statement** must be filed with the SEC (rule 14a-6(b)). In contested matters, a preliminary proxy statement must be filed 10 days before any solicitation commences (rule 14a-6(a)).

2. The **content and form** of the proxy materials are heavily regulated (rules 14a-3, 14a-4, and 14a-5, and Schedule 14A). Virtually everything you see in an actual proxy statement is prescribed by the rules.

3. **"Proxy" and "solicitation"** are defined extremely broadly (rule 14a-1(f) and (l)(1)). Accordingly, the sweep of the proxy rules is very wide. In fact, in the past, the proxy rules impeded even conversations among shareholders about their votes. Certain exceptions to the definitions (particularly rule 14a-1(l)(2)(iv)) or requirements (particularly rules 14a-2(a)(6) and 14a-2(b)(1)-(3)) are therefore extremely important — you should read them.

4. Rule 14a-8 requires corporations to include certain **shareholder proposals** in the corporation's proxy materials. Under the rule, corporations must include in their proxy certain precatory resolutions and bylaw amendments sponsored by shareholders. By contrast, the rule does not cover director nominations or anything else that would affect "the upcoming election of directors" (see rule 14a-8(i)(8)). You should read the rule — unlike the rest of the proxy rules, it's written in plain English.

5. In 2021, the SEC adopted the so-called **universal proxy** rule 14a-19. It provides that in proxy fights, every proxy card must list and allow voting for each individual candidate, no matter who nominated the candidate or who solicits the proxy. Prior to 2021, people would solicit proxies using proxy cards that only allowed voting for the soliciting party's candidates, and did not permit pick-and-choose among all candidates. Note that a challenger still needs to file a proxy statement, solicit proxies, and bear the associated costs to force the corporation to put the challenger's candidates onto the corporation's (universal) proxy. Please read this rule, too.

6. There is a special anti-fraud provision (rule 14a-9).

2. Fiduciary Duties and the Right to Sue

The second set of protections that shareholders have are fiduciary duties. Directors and managers hold their corporate powers as fiduciaries, i.e., for the sole benefit of "the corporation and its shareholders." As fiduciaries, directors and managers owe a duty of **care** and a duty of **loyalty** to "the corporation and its shareholders."

Fiduciary duties are creations of **equity** in the technical sense of having been developed in courts of equity rather than courts of law. While courts of law and equity were merged into courts of general jurisdiction almost everywhere in the 19th century, this was not the case in Delaware. The Delaware Chancery Court technically remains a court of equity. Delaware judges like to emphasize this fact and the critical role of equity in constraining legal powers, which are not to be used for "inequitable purposes." In the memorable words of the Delaware Supreme Court:

> [I]nequitable action does not become permissible simply because it is legally possible.
>
> —*Schnell v. Chris-Craft Industries, Inc.*, 285 A.2d 437, 439 (Del. 1971).

In fact, as you will see, corporate law, or at least the Delaware variety, imposes so few legal limits—in the technical sense, excluding equity—that fiduciary duties are the only true limit on what is possible. In almost all the cases you will read, corporate fiduciaries do something that is legal under the statute, but the question is whether it complies with the fiduciaries' fiduciary duties.

Crucially, U.S. courts liberally grant shareholders standing to enforce these duties in court, including through **derivative suits**:

> The derivative action developed in equity to enable shareholders to sue in the corporation's name where those in control of the company refused to assert a claim belonging to it. The nature of the action is two-fold. First, it is the equivalent of a suit by the shareholders to compel the corporation to sue. Second, it is a suit by the corporation, asserted by the shareholders on its behalf, against those liable to it.
>
> —*Aronson v. Lewis*, 473 A.2d 805, 811 (Del. 1984).

3. Other shareholder rights

In addition to voting rights and standing to sue, shareholders also have the right to access certain corporate **information**. This is an important ancillary right because both shareholder voting and derivative suits require information to work well. DGCL 220 allows shareholders "to inspect for any proper purpose … [t]he corporation's … books and records," and Delaware courts have interpreted this very broadly, even including internal emails in some circumstances. Furthermore, publicly traded corporations must make extensive affirmative disclosures under the securities laws.

Finally, shareholders can **sell** their stock. This is important for individual shareholders' liquidity, i.e., shareholders' ability to convert the value of their corporate investment into cash when necessary. However, this so-called Wall Street Walk is useless, at least by itself, as a protection against bad management. If the corporation has bad management, its value to shareholders will be less than it could be, and its stock price will be discounted to reflect this. So a shareholder can sell, but that just locks in the loss from bad management; it does not fix it. (By analogy, an arson victim's right to sell the land with the burnt ruins hardly compensates the victim for, nor prevents, the arson.) Selling is useful only in as much as it enables a *buyer* to amass a large enough position from which to challenge the sitting board using the first two tools (voting and suing).

4. HLS Inc. Exercise

Let us work through a few hypotheticals to illustrate how basic corporate statutory rules operate. These scenarios will highlight the grotesque outcomes that these rules alone would countenance and thus demonstrate the importance of fiduciary duties.

HLS Inc. has a single class of stock and three shareholders owning one third each: John M., John G., and Kristen S. Each shareholder is also a member of the current board. John M. currently serves as CEO. HLS Inc. generates about $10 million in annual profits; it has traditionally paid out all profits to the three shareholders every year.

Consider the following questions – what is the answer under the Delaware statute, not considering fiduciary duties (which will [fortunately] change many of the answers)?

1. Imagine that HLS Inc. is only subject to Delaware default rules, i.e., it does not have divergent charter provisions. Can John G. and Kristen S.

do any or all of the following, in their capacity as shareholders and/or board members:

- Remove John M. from his position as CEO and his directorship, and instead elect their friend Jeannie S. — who does not own any stock in HLS Inc. — as a director and CEO.

- Issue new stock only to themselves and/or Jeannie S. at a low price.

- Cancel John M.'s stock.

- Pay dividends only to themselves (and Jeannie S. if she has become a shareholder).

- Stop paying dividends and instead pay out the profits as remuneration for "director services" and/or "CEO services" to themselves and/or Jeannie S., as applicable.

2. Now imagine that HLS Inc. has a staggered/classified board such that only one of the three directors is up for reelection each year (DGCL 141(d)). Does this possibly change any of your answers to Question 1?

3. Now imagine that HLS Inc. does not have a staggered board but dual class stock: John M. owns 50 shares of class A stock that has 10 votes per share, and John G. and Kristen S. each own 50 shares of class B stock that has 1 vote per share. Does this possibly change any of your answers to Question 1?

C. Variations on the Basic Problem

1. The board as a monitor

So far, we have framed the basic problem of corporate governance as how to control managers *and* the board. An important tool of corporate governance, however, is control of managers *by* the board. Arguably, the primary role of a board composed mostly of outside members (i.e., non-management) is to select, monitor, and thus control managers. It is now standard or even legally required for public corporations' boards to consist mostly of independent directors, i.e., directors who do not have other relationships with the corporation, especially not a role in management. That being said, in U.S. corporations, it is still customary for CEOs and other top managers to sit on the board and even to chair it.

Some countries go even further and fully separate outside directors and management. Under the so-called two-tier system, a "supervisory board" composed exclusively of outside directors is superimposed on the "management board" composed of top managers. Shareholders elect the supervisory board, which in turn appoints and monitors the management board. (In some jurisdictions the supervisory board is self-nominating or partially elected by the corporation's employees.)

But while directors may indeed monitor management, this only shifts the basic problem one level up: how can we control those who have been entrusted with this monitoring role? *Quis custodiet ipsos custodes?* (Who monitors the monitors?)

2. Dominant shareholders

Monitoring the monitor is a particularly acute problem with respect to large, dominant shareholders. Most public corporations around the world have a dominant shareholder. In the U.S. and in the U.K., dispersed ownership is the norm but far from universal. On the positive side, dominant shareholders help overcome shareholders' collective action problem in monitoring managers and the board. On the flip side, however, dominant shareholders may attempt to extract a disproportionate share for themselves. Delaware limits such minority abuse by imposing fiduciary duties on "controlling shareholders." Other jurisdictions impose super-majority requirements, or outright prohibit certain transactions, etc.

In general, a shareholder needs to own close to 50% of the outstanding stock to **control** the corporation. ("close to" because some other shareholders tend not to vote, such that the controlling stockholder can command a majority of the stock *voted* at the meeting even though owning less than a majority of the stock *outstanding*.) However, if the corporation issues multiple classes of stock with differentiated voting rights ("dual class stock"), a shareholder can control (by owning the high-voting stock) even while owning only a small fraction of the cash flow rights (cf. Google Exercise above, and "Shareholder Democracy" below). This exacerbates the conflict of interest with the other shareholders: the lower the controlling shareholder's proportional economic stake in the corporation, the higher the controlling shareholder's gain from diverting value from the corporation into the controlling shareholder's own pockets (cf. Some (Not So) Fictitious Examples in the Duty of Loyalty section below).

Many non-U.S. jurisdictions prohibit dual class stock, but dominant shareholders employ a **pyramid** structure to achieve a very similar result. To wit, the dominant shareholder will be the majority shareholder of corporation A, which is in turn the majority shareholder of corporation B, which may be a majority shareholder of corporation C, and so on. In such a structure, the dominant shareholder controls each of the layers even though economically the dominant shareholder only receives much less than 50% of the cash flows from the lower layers. For example, if the dominant shareholder owns 50.01% of the stock of A, which owns 50.01% of B, which owns 50.01% of C, then the dominant shareholder indirectly controls C even though the dominant shareholder will receive only 50.01% × 50.01% × 50.01% = 12.51% of any dividend paid by C and passed through B and A to their respective shareholders. In the U.S., pyramids are tax-disadvantaged because each layer is subject to corporate income tax (such that multiplying layers means multiplying tax), and for this and perhaps other reasons virtually inexistent. (For the avoidance of doubt: U.S. corporations do employ holding structures where the top-level corporation owns several subsidiaries, which may own sub-subsidiaries and so on, but all the subsidiaries are wholly-owned by their respective parent(s), such that control and cash flow rights go hand in hand; the IRS exempts such wholly-owned structures from multiple taxation.)

3. Protecting other constituencies

We defer until the end of the book the question of whether corporate law does or should protect constituencies other than shareholders (often called "stakeholders"), such as creditors, workers, or customers. For the time being, we just note that the question is not whether stakeholders should be protected at all, but whether they should be protected by the tools of corporate law—that is, beyond the level of protection afforded by contract (loan agreements, employment contracts, collective bargaining, etc.), and by other branches of law (employment law, labor law, consumer law, etc.).

4. Enforcement

Enforcement and its problems are of paramount importance for corporate law. At the extreme, if general law enforcement were too weak, managers could, for example, simply abscond with the corporation's money. No fiduciary duties, shareholder litigation, or shareholder voting could protect against this. Fortunately, criminal law enforcement in the U.S. is strong enough that outright fraud and theft are not the most pressing concerns and can be mostly ignored in this course.

In the more subtle form of inadministrability, however, enforcement problems are key to understanding the rationale behind much of corporate law — and indeed behind much of law generally. Administrability refers to courts' ability to administer the laws as written. The problem is that courts often lack the requisite information. For this reason, many superficially appealing rules do not work as intended. For example, it is certainly desirable that managers always do only what is best for shareholders, or at least what they think is best for shareholders, and that they do so flawlessly or at least to the best of their abilities. Formally speaking, that is indeed more or less what fiduciary duties require of managers. That does not mean, however, that it is realistic to think that courts could actually enforce such a standard. Courts may not know what action was best for shareholders, much less what the managers truly thought was best for shareholders. Nor can courts easily know whether managers gave their best efforts or loyalty. Courts will inevitably misjudge many careful, loyal actions as disloyal or careless, and vice versa — even after costly and lengthy litigation.

Faced with such difficulties, it may be best to forego costly judicial review altogether unless a transaction raises a red flag. The reddest of red flags is when the decision would financially benefit the decision-makers or their affiliates more than (other) shareholders. That, in a nutshell, is the approach taken in Delaware and other U.S. states and epitomized by the **business judgment rule**. We will dive deep into the details later. For now, here is the scoop in the words of the seminal case, *Aronson v. Lewis*:

> The business judgment rule is an acknowledgment of the managerial prerogatives of Delaware directors under Section 141(a). It is a presumption that in making a business decision the directors of a corporation acted on an informed basis, in good faith and in the honest belief that the action taken was in the best interests of the company. Absent an abuse of discretion, that judgment will be respected by the courts. ...
>
> [However, the rule's] protections can only be claimed by disinterested directors . ... From the standpoint of interest, this means that directors can neither appear on both sides of a transaction nor expect to derive any personal financial benefit from it in the sense of self-dealing . ... See 8 Del.C. § 144(a)(1).
>
> [Moreover], to invoke the rule's protection directors have a duty to inform themselves, prior to making a business decision, of all material information reasonably available to them. Having become so informed, they must then act with requisite care in the discharge of their duties. While the Delaware cases use a variety of terms to describe the

applicable standard of care, our analysis satisfies us that under the business judgment rule director liability is predicated upon concepts of gross negligence.

— *Aronson v. Lewis,* 473 A.2d 805, 812 (Del. 1984) (footnotes and internal references omitted).

More generally, many rules of corporate law are decidedly second-best. That is, they are optimal only in recognition of the difficulties of enforcing any alternative rule. Agency problems can be reduced. They can never be eliminated.

Part II: Fiduciary Duties

Chapter 3. The Duty of Loyalty

This chapter begins our exploration of fiduciary duties. As previously mentioned, fiduciary duties originate in equity and comprise the duty of loyalty and the duty of care. This chapter focuses on the duty of loyalty; Chapter 5 considers the duty of care.

Both duties apply equally to directors and officers (*Gantler v. Stephens*, Del. 2009). Controlling stockholders are subject to fiduciary duties as well and generate some of the most important duty-of-loyalty cases (*cf. Sinclair* in this section and *Weinberger* and *MFW* in the M&A part of the course).

As a first approximation, the duties of care and loyalty target what their names imply: the duty of care demands that the fiduciary act with appropriate care, while the duty of loyalty demands that the fiduciary act loyally, i.e., guided by the interests of the principal. In other words, the former addresses simple mistakes, while the latter addresses conflicts of interest, i.e., self-dealing. Delaware courts vigilantly police self-dealing but are unreceptive to claims of honest mistakes.

♦ The controller's agreed share is the controller's percentage of the cash flow rights according to the corporation's charter and other relevant contracts.

(Minority) Shareholders' interests are most at risk in transactions between the corporation and its controllers, be it management or large shareholders. The risk is obvious: the controllers may attempt to extract more than their agreed share♦ of the corporation's value for themselves, at the expense of (minority) shareholders.

1. Some (not so) fictitious examples

Here are three typical ways controlling shareholders do it. We will illustrate using a fictitious oil company, OilCo, with a controlling stockholder, Mikhail. Mikhail owns 50% of OilCo, and 100% of another fictitious company, Honeypot.

1. The first thing Mikhail can do is to have OilCo sell its oil to Honeypot at below-market prices. For example, if the market price of oil is $16 per barrel, Mikhail might arrange for OilCo to sell its oil to Honeypot for $10. For every barrel of oil, this redistributes $3 from minority shareholders to Mikhail. Why? Because if OilCo had sold its oil on the market instead, it would have received $16 per barrel. These $16 would have been shared equally between Mikhail and the

minority shareholders. Each would have received $8. But when OilCo instead sells to Honeypot for $10 per barrel, minority shareholders get only $5 (half of $10). The difference of $3 is captured by Mikhail: per barrel of oil, he gets $5 as a shareholder of OilCo and $6 as the sole shareholder of Honeypot (because Honeypot buys for $10 and sells for $16, generating a $6 profit), or a total of $11. The use of artificially inflated or deflated prices to shift value from one company to another is called a **transfer pricing** scheme. It is also used for tax avoidance purposes.

2. Mikhail can also have OilCo issue new shares to himself or to Honeypot at low prices. For example, imagine that OilCo owns oil fields worth $100 m(illion), and that OilCo has one million shares outstanding. That means each share is worth $100 (assuming no transfer pricing scheme), and Mikhail's 50% stake and the 50% minority shares as a group each comprise 500,000 shares worth $50 million in total. Mikhail now has OilCo issue 100 million shares to himself at $0.01 per share for an overall price of $1 million. This means three things. First, OilCo is now worth $101 million: In addition to the $100 million oil field, it now has the $1 million cash that Mikhail put in for the new shares. Second, Mikhail now owns almost the entire company, owning 100.5 million out of 101 million shares (99.5%). Third, the transaction earned him $49.5 million: Before the transaction, Mikhail owned OilCo shares worth $50m (50% × $100m). After buying the new shares, Mikhail now owns shares worth $100.5m (99.5% × $101m). Thus, Mikhail spent $1m to increase his OilCo holding by $50.5m ($100.5m – $50m), generating a pure profit of $49.5m ($50.5m – $1m). Mikhail's gain is the minority shareholders' loss: they lost $49.5 million in this **dilution** of their share.

3. Finally, Mikhail can also dispense with the minority altogether by selling OilCo's assets to Honeypot for a low price. To wit, he could have OilCo sell its oil fields to Honeypot for less than their $100 million value. This is another transfer pricing scheme, but executed on OilCo's productive assets rather than its products, and hence also known as **asset stripping**. As with other transfer pricing schemes, it

can also be done in reverse: Mikhail could have OilCo buy an asset from Honeypot at an inflated price.

None of these schemes is fictitious at all. For example, they are stylized versions of what Mikhail Khodorkovsky and all the other Russian oligarchs are said to have done to the oil companies they came to control in Russia in the 1990s. Russian corporate law erected barriers to such self-dealing. But corrupt, scared, or just plain incompetent courts breached those barriers. It is a vivid illustration of the importance of the general "legal infrastructure" for the enforcement of corporate law. See generally Bernard Black, Reinier Kraakman, & Anna Tarassova, *Russian Privatization and Corporate Governance: What Went Wrong?*, 52 STAN. L. REV. 1731 (2000).

2. The U.S. approach

Now back to the U.S., where we nowadays take a functioning "legal infrastructure" for granted. What protections does it offer against minority expropriation?

First, public corporations are prohibited from making loans to its directors or officers (section 13(k) of the Exchange Act, as amended by section 402 of the Sarbanes-Oxley Act of 2002). More importantly (because loans are only one form of self-dealing among many), public corporations must disclose all self-dealing transactions in an amount above $120,000 in their annual report (item 404 of the SEC's Regulation S-K). Managers or a controlling shareholder may choose to not comply with this rule, but only at the risk of becoming the target of an SEC enforcement action.

The only provision of the DGCL that explicitly addresses self-dealing is DGCL 144. On its face, DGCL 144 merely declares that transactions between the corporation and its officers and directors are *not* void or voidable *solely* because of the conflict of interest, *provided* the transaction fulfills *one* of the three conditions in subparagraphs (a)(1)-(3). This statutory text implies that transactions not fulfilling *either* of these conditions *are* automatically void or voidable. But the text leaves open the possibility that some conflicted transactions might be void or voidable even though they do fulfill one of the three conditions of DGCL 144(a)(1)-(3).

Notwithstanding, Delaware courts do treat the three conditions as individually sufficient and jointly necessary for the permissibility of self-dealing by directors and officers. That is, self-dealing by officers and directors is beyond judicial reproach if and only if it has been approved in good faith by a majority of fully informed, disinterested directors or shareholders, or it is otherwise shown to be "entirely fair." The courts do not derive this formulation from DGCL 144, however, but from "equitable principles." Moreover, *controlling shareholders* are subject to more stringent review: their self-dealing is always reviewed for "entire fairness;" approval by a "well-functioning committee of independent directors" or by fully informed disinterested shareholders merely shifts the burden of proof (subject to the recent doctrinal-transactional innovation of *Kahn v. MFW*, covered in the M&A part of the course).

What is "entire fairness"? It is not clear anybody knows. The Delaware Supreme Court essentially refuses to define it. In the authoritative words of *Weinberger* (covered in the M&A part below):

> The concept of fairness has two basic aspects: fair dealing and fair price. The former embraces questions of when the transaction was timed, how it was initiated, structured, negotiated, disclosed to the directors, and how the approvals of the directors and the stockholders were obtained. The latter aspect of fairness relates to the economic and financial considerations of the [transaction], including all … elements that affect the intrinsic or inherent value of [the object of the transaction]. … However, the test for fairness is not a bifurcated one as between fair dealing and price. All aspects of the issue must be examined as a whole since the question is one of entire fairness.
>
> —*Weinberger v. UOP*, 457 A.2d 701, 711 (Del. 1983).

Presumably the message to fiduciaries is: if you are self-interested, then you better pay top dollar and generally go out of your way to show you treated the corporation fairly (or, if you are a mere director or officer, you get absolution from the independent directors or shareholders).

Before diving into the details of this self-dealing jurisprudence, consider a preliminary question: why permit any self-dealing? Delaware law can be characterized as an attempt to differentiate self-dealing that expropriates shareholders, from self-dealing that does not. It is likely that courts will make mistakes, however, and that some expropriation will slip through the judicial cracks. For instance, the transactions at issue in *Sinclair* (the oil sales), *Weinberger*, and *Americas Mining* later in the book resemble the three Mikhail examples above. While they were ultimately caught, the controlling shareholders in these Delaware corporations must have thought they might get away with the expropriation. And sometimes, they arguably do (cf. *Dorsey* below).

Questions

1. Why not seal those cracks by prohibiting all self-dealing? The potential harm from self-dealing is great. What is the redeeming benefit, if any?

A. Guth v. Loft (Del. 1939) [Pepsi]

Guth is the mother of all Delaware duty of loyalty cases. The decision introduces the basic idea that it is incumbent on the fiduciary to prove that the fiduciary acted "in the utmost good faith" (or, in modern parlance, with "entire fairness") to the corporation in spite of the fiduciary's conflict of interest. As mentioned above, approval by a majority of fully informed, disinterested directors or shareholders can absolve the fiduciary or at least shift the burden of proof. In *Guth*, however, the Court of Chancery had found that Guth had not obtained such approval from his board.

The decision deals with two separate aspects of Guth's behavior. The corporate resources that Guth used for his business, such as Loft's funds and personnel, clearly belonged to Loft, and there was little question that Guth had to compensate Loft for their use. The contentious part of the decision deals with a difficult line-drawing problem: which transactions come within the purview of the duty of loyalty in the first place?

Questions

1. Surely fiduciaries must retain the right to self-interested behavior in some corner of their life. Where is the line?

2. In particular, which business opportunities are "corporate opportunities" belonging to the corporation, and which are open to the fiduciaries to pursue for their own benefit? Cf. DGCL 122(17).

3. And why does it matter here, seeing that *some* of Guth's actions clearly were actionable self-dealing? Hint: Which remedy is available for which action?

5 A.2d 503

GUTH et al.

v.

LOFT, Inc.

Supreme Court of Delaware.

April 11, 1939.

[...]

For convenience, Loft Incorporated, will be referred to as Loft; the Grace Company, Inc., of Delaware, as Grace; and Pepsi-Cola Company, a corporation of Delaware, as Pepsi.

Loft filed a bill in the Court of Chancery against Charles G. Guth, Grace and Pepsi seeking to impress a trust in favor of the complainant upon all shares of the capital stock of Pepsi registered in the name of Guth and in the name of Grace (approximately 91% of the capital stock), to secure a transfer of those shares to the complainant, and for an accounting.

The cause was heard at great length by the Chancellor who, on September 17, 1938, rendered a decision in favor of the complainant in accordance with the prayers of the bill. Loft, Inc., v. Guth, Del.Ch., 2 A.2d 225. An interlocutory decree, and an interlocutory order fixing terms of stay and amounts of supersedeas bonds, were entered on October 4, 1938; and, thereafter, an appeal was duly prosecuted to this Court.

The essential facts, admitted or found by the Chancellor, briefly stated, are these: Loft was, and is, a corporation engaged in the manufacturing and selling of candies, syrups, beverages and foodstuffs, having its executive offices and main plant at Long Island City, New York. In 1931 Loft operated 115 stores largely located in the congested centers of population along the Middle Atlantic seaboard. While its operations chiefly were of a retail nature, its wholesale activities were not unimportant, amounting in 1931 to over $800,000. It had the equipment and the personnel to carry on syrup making operations, and was engaged in manufacturing fountain syrups to supply its own extensive needs. It had assets exceeding $9,000,000 in value, excluding goodwill; and from 1931 to 1935, it had sufficient working capital for its own cash requirements.

Guth, a man of long experience in the candy, chocolate and soft drink business, became Vice President of Loft in August, 1929, and its president in March 1930.

Grace was owned by Guth and his family. It owned a plant in Baltimore, Maryland, where it was engaged in the manufacture of syrups for soft drinks, and it had been supplying Loft with "Lady Grace Chocolate Syrup".

In 1931, Coca-Cola was dispensed at all of the Loft Stores, and of the Coca-Cola syrup Loft made large purchases, averaging over 30,000 gallons annually. The cost of the syrup was $1.48 per gallon. Guth requested the Coca-Cola Company to give Loft a jobber's discount in view of its large requirements of syrups which exceeded greatly the purchases of some other users of the syrup to whom such discount had been granted. After many conferences, the Coca-Cola Company refused to give the discount. Guth became incensed, and contemplated the replacement of the Coca-Cola beverage with some other cola drink. On May 19, 1931, he addressed a memorandum to V. O. Robertson, Loft's vice-president, asking "Why are we paying a full price for Coca-Cola? Can you handle this, or would you suggest our buying Pebsaco (Pepsi-Cola) at about $1.00 per gallon?" To this Robertson replied that Loft was not paying quite full price for Coca-Cola, it paying $1.48 per gallon instead of $1.60, but that it was too much, and that he was investigating as to Pepsi-Cola.

Pepsi-Cola was a syrup compounded and marketed by National Pepsi-Cola Company, controlled by one Megargel. The Pepsi-Cola beverage had been on the market for upwards of twenty five years, but chiefly in southern territory. It was possessed of a secret formula and trademark. This company, as it happened, was adjudicated a bankrupt on May 26, 1931, upon a petition filed on May 18, the day before the date of Guth's memorandum to Robertson suggesting a trial of Pepsi-Cola syrup by Loft.

[506] Megargel was not unknown to Guth. In 1928, when Guth had no connection with Loft, Megargel had tried unsuccessfully to interest Guth and one Hoodless, vice-president and general manager of a sugar company, in National Pepsi-Cola Company. Upon the bankruptcy of this company Hoodless, who apparently had had some communication with Megargel, informed Guth that Megargel would communicate with him, and Megargel did inform Guth of his company's bankruptcy and that he was in a position to acquire from the trustee in bankruptcy, the secret formula and trademark for the manufacture and sale of Pepsi-Cola.

In July, 1931, Megargel and Guth entered into an agreement whereby Megargel would acquire the Pepsi-Cola formula and trademark; would form a new corporation, with an authorized capital of 300,000 shares of the par value of $5, to which corporation Megargel would transfer the formula and trademark; would keep 100,000 shares for himself, transfer a like number to Guth, and turn back 100,000 shares to the company as treasury stock, all or a part thereof to be sold to provide working capital. By the agreement between the two Megargel was to receive $25,000 annually for the first six years, and, thereafter, a royalty of 2 1/2 cents on each gallon of syrup.

Megargel had no money. The price of the formula and trademark was $10,000. Guth loaned Megargel $12,000 upon his agreement to repay him out of the first $25,000 coming to him under the agreement between the two, and Megargel made a formal assignment to Guth to that effect. The $12,000 was paid to Megargel in this way: $5000 directly to Megargel by Guth, and $7,000 by Loft's certified check, Guth delivering to Loft simultaneously his two checks aggregating $7000. Guth also advanced $426.40 to defray the cost of incorporating the company. This amount and the sum of $12,000 were afterwards repaid to Guth.

Pepsi-Cola Company was organized under the laws of Delaware in August, 1931. The formula and trademark were acquired from the trustee in bankruptcy of National Pepsi-Cola Company, and its capital stock was distributed as agreed, except that 100,000 shares were placed in the name of Grace.

At this time Megargel could give no financial assistance to the venture directly or indirectly. Grace, upon a comparison of its assets with its liabilities, was insolvent. Only $13,000 of Pepsi's treasury stock was ever sold. Guth was heavily indebted to Loft, and, generally, he was in most serious financial straits, and was entirely unable to finance the enterprise. On the other hand, Loft was well able to finance it.

Guth, during the years 1931 to 1935 dominated Loft through his control of the Board of Directors. He has completely controlled Pepsi. Without the knowledge or consent of Loft's Board of Directors he drew upon Loft without limit to further the Pepsi enterprise having at one time almost the entire working capital of Loft engaged therein. He used Loft's plant facilities, materials, credit, executives and employees as he willed. Pepsi's payroll sheets were a part of Loft's and a single Loft check was drawn for both.

An attempt was made to keep an account of the time spent by Loft's workmen on Pepsi's enterprises, and in 1935, when Pepsi had available profits, the account was paid; but no charge was made by Loft as against Pepsi for the services rendered by Loft's executives, higher ranking office employees or chemist, nor for the use of its plant and facilities.

[...]

Guth claimed that he offered Loft the opportunity to take over the Pepsi-Cola enterprise, frankly stating to the directors that if Loft did not, he would; but that the Board declined because Pepsi-Cola had proved a failure, and that for Loft to sponsor a company to compete with Coca-Cola would cause trouble; that the proposition was not in line with Loft's business; that it was not equipped to carry on such business on an extensive scale;

and that it would involve too great a financial risk. Yet, he claimed that, in August, 1933, the Loft directors consented, without a vote, that Loft should extend to Guth its facilities and resources without limit upon Guth's guarantee of all advances, and upon Guth's contract to furnish Loft a continuous supply of syrup at a favorable price. The guaranty was not in writing if one was made, and the contract was not produced.

[...]

The Chancellor found that Guth had never offered the Pepsi opportunity to Loft; [...] that Guth's use of Loft's money, credit, facilities and personnel in the furtherance of the Pepsi venture was without the knowledge or authorization of Loft's directors; that Guth's alleged personal guaranty to Loft against loss resulting from the venture was not in writing, and otherwise was worthless; that no contract existed between Pepsi and Loft whereby the former was to furnish the latter with a constant supply of syrup for a definite time and at a definite price; that as against Loft's contribution to the Pepsi-Cola venture, the appellants had contributed practically nothing; that after the repayment of the sum of $12,000 which had been loaned by Guth to Megargel, Guth had not a dollar invested in Pepsi stock; that Guth was a full time president of Loft at an attractive salary, and could not claim to have invested [508] his services in the enterprise; that in 1933, Pepsi was insolvent; that Loft, until July, 1934, bore practically the entire financial burdens of Pepsi, but for which it must have failed disastrously to the great loss of Loft.

[...]

By the decree entered the Chancellor found, inter alia, that Guth was estopped to deny that opportunity of acquiring the Pepsi-Cola trademark and formula was received by him on behalf of Loft, and that the opportunity was wrongfully appropriated by Guth to himself; that the value inhering in and represented by the 97,500 shares of Pepsi stock standing in the name of Guth and the 140,000 shares standing in the name of Grace, were, in equity, the property of Loft; that the dividends declared and paid on the shares of stock were, and had been, the property of Loft; and that for all practical purposes Guth and Grace were one.

The Chancellor ordered Guth and Grace to transfer the shares of stock to Loft; [...]

LAYTON, Chief Justice, delivering the opinion of the Court:

In the Court below the appellants took the position that, on the facts, the complainant was entitled to no equitable relief whatever. In this Court, they seek only a modification of the Chancellor's decree, not a reversal of it. They now contend that the question is one of equitable adjustment based upon the extent and value of the respective contributions of the appellants and the appellee. This change of position is brought about, as it is said, because of certain basic fact findings of the Chancellor which are admittedly unassailable in this Court. The appellants accept the findings of fact; but they contend that the Chancellor's inferences from them were unwarrantable in material instances [...]

Corporate officers and directors are not permitted to use their position of trust and confidence to further their private interests. While technically not trustees, they stand in a fiduciary relation to the corporation and its stockholders. A public policy, existing through the years, and derived from a profound knowledge of human characteristics and motives, has established a rule that demands of a corporate officer or director, peremptorily and inexorably, the most scrupulous observance of his duty, not only affirmatively to protect the interests of the corporation committed to his charge, but also to refrain from doing anything that would work injury to the corporation, or to deprive it of profit or advantage which his skill and ability might properly bring to it, or to enable it to make in the reasonable and lawful exercise of its powers. The rule that requires an undivided and unselfish loyalty to the corporation demands that there shall be no conflict between duty and self-interest. The occasions for the determination of honesty, good faith and loyal conduct are many and varied, and no hard and fast rule can be formulated. The standard of loyalty is measured by no fixed scale.

If an officer or director of a corporation, in violation of his duty as such, acquires gain or advantage for himself, the law charges the interest so acquired with a trust for the benefit of the corporation, at its election, while it denies to the betrayer all benefit and profit. The rule, inveterate and uncompromising in its rigidity, does not rest upon the narrow ground of injury or damage to the corporation resulting from a betrayal of confidence, but upon a broader foundation of a wise public policy that, for the purpose of removing all temptation, extinguishes all possibility of profit flowing from a breach of the confidence imposed by the fiduciary relation. Given the relation between the parties, a certain result follows; and a constructive trust is the remedial device through which precedence of self is compelled to give way to the stern demands of loyalty. [...]

The rule, referred to briefly as the rule of corporate opportunity, is merely one of the manifestations of the general rule that demands of an officer or director the utmost good faith in his relation to the corporation which he represents.

It is true that when a business opportunity comes to a corporate officer or director in his individual capacity rather than in his official capacity, and the opportunity is one which, because of the nature of the enterprise, is not essential to his corporation, and is one in which it has no interest or expectancy, the officer or director is entitled to treat the opportunity as his own, and the corporation has no interest in it, if, of course, the officer or director has not wrongfully embarked the [511] corporation's resources therein. Colorado & Utah Coal Co. v. Harris et al., 97 Colo. 309, 49 P.2d 429; Lagarde v.

Anniston Lime & Stone Co., 126 Ala. 496, 28 So. 199; Pioneer Oil & Gas Co. v. Anderson, 168 Miss. 334, 151 So. 161; Sandy River R. Co. v. Stubbs, 77 Me. 594, 2 A. 9; Lancaster Loose Leaf Tobacco Co. v. Robinson, 199 Ky. 313, 250 S.W. 997. But, in all of these cases, except, perhaps, in one, there was no infidelity on the part of the corporate officer sought to be charged. In the first case, it was found that the corporation had no practical use for the property acquired by Harris. In the Pioneer Oil & Gas Co. case, Anderson used no funds or assets of the corporation, did not know that the corporation was negotiating for the oil lands and, further, the corporation could not, in any event have acquired them, because their proprietors objected to the corporation's having an interest in them, and because the corporation was in no financial position to pay for them. In the Stubbs case, the railroad company, desiring to purchase from Porter such part of his land as was necessary for its right of way, station, water-tank, and woodshed, declined to accede to his price. Stubbs, a director, made every effort to buy the necessary land for the company and failed. He then bought the entire tract, and offered to sell to the company what it needed. The company repudiated expressly all participation in the purchase. Later the company located its tracks and buildings on a part of the land, but could not agree with Stubbs as to damages or terms of the conveyance. Three and one-half years thereafter, Stubbs was informed for the first time that the company claimed that he held the land in trust for it. In the Lancaster Loose Leaf Tobacco Co. case, the company had never engaged in the particular line of business, and its established policy had been not to engage in it. The only interest which the company had in the burley tobacco bought by Robinson was its commissions in selling it on its floors, and these commissions it received. In the Lagarde case, it was said that the proprietorship of the property acquired by the Legardes may have been important to the corporation, but was not shown to have been necessary to the continuance of its business, or that its purchase by the Legardes had in any way impaired the value of the corporation's property. This decision is, perhaps, the strongest cited on behalf of the appellants. With deference to the Court that rendered it, a different view of the correctness of the conclusion reached may be entertained.

On the other hand, it is equally true that, if there is presented to a corporate officer or director a business opportunity which the corporation is financially able to undertake, is, from its nature, in the line of the corporation's business and is of practical advantage to it, is one in which the corporation has an interest or a reasonable expectancy, and, by embracing the opportunity, the self-interest of the officer or director will be brought into conflict with that of his corporation, the law will not permit him to seize the opportunity for himself. And, if, in such circumstances, the interests of the corporation are betrayed, the corporation may elect to claim all of the benefits of the transaction for itself, and the law will impress a trust in favor of the corporation upon the property, interests and profits so acquired. [...]

But, there is little profit in a discussion of the particular cases cited. In none of them are the facts and circumstances comparable to those of the case under consideration. The question is not one to be decided on narrow or technical grounds, but upon broad considerations of corporate duty and loyalty.

[...]

Duty and loyalty are inseparably connected. Duty is that which is required by one's station or occupation; is that which one is bound by legal or moral obligation to do or refrain from doing; and it is with [512] this conception of duty as the underlying basis of the principle applicable to the situation disclosed, that the conduct and acts of Guth with respect to his acquisition of the Pepsi-Cola enterprise will be scrutinized. Guth was not merely a director and the president of Loft. He was its master. It is admitted that Guth manifested some of the qualities of a dictator. The directors were selected by him. Some of them held salaried positions in the company. All of them held their positions at his favor. Whether they were supine merely, or for sufficient reasons entirely subservient to Guth, it is not profitable to inquire. It is sufficient to say that they either wilfully or negligently allowed Guth absolute freedom of action in the management of Loft's activities, and theirs is an unenviable position whether testifying for or against the appellants.

Prior to May, 1931, Guth became convinced that Loft was being unfairly discriminated against by the Coca-Cola Company of whose syrup it was a large purchaser, in that Loft had been refused a jobber's discount on the syrup, although others, whose purchases were of far less importance, had been given such discount. He determined to replace Coca-Cola as a beverage at the Loft stores with some other cola drink, if that could be accomplished. So, on May 19, 1931, he suggested an inquiry with respect to desirability of discontinuing the use of Coca-Cola, and replacing it with Pepsi-Cola at a greatly reduced price. Pepsi-Cola was the syrup produced by National Pepsi-Cola Company. As a beverage it had been on the market for over twenty-five years, and while it was not known to consumers in the area of the Loft stores, its formula and trademark were well established. Guth's purpose was to deliver Loft from the thraldom of the Coca-Cola Company, which practically dominated the field of cola beverages, and, at the same time, to gain for Loft a greater margin of profit on its sales of cola beverages. Certainly, the choice of an acceptable substitute for Coca-Cola was not a wide one, and, doubtless, his experience in the field of bottled beverages convinced him that it was necessary for him to obtain a cola syrup whose formula and trademark were secure against attack. Although the difficulties and dangers were great, he concluded to make the change. Almost simultaneously, National Pepsi-Cola Company, in which Megargel was predominant and whom Guth knew, went into bankruptcy; and Guth was informed that the long established Pepsi-Cola formula and trademark could be had at a small price. Guth, of course, was Loft; and Loft's determination to replace Coca-Cola with some other cola beverage in its many stores was practically co-incidental with the opportunity to acquire the Pepsi-Cola formula and trademark. This was the condition of affairs when Megargel approached Guth. Guth contended that his negotiation with Megargel in 1931 was but a continuation of a negotiation begun in 1928, when he had no connection with Loft; but the Chancellor found to the contrary, and his finding is accepted.

It is urged by the appellants that Megargel offered the Pepsi-Cola opportunity to Guth personally, and not to him as president of Loft. The Chancellor said that there was no way of knowing the fact, as Megargel was dead, and the benefit of his testimony could not be had; but that it was not important, for the matter of consequence was how Guth received the proposition.

It was incumbent upon Guth to show that his every act in dealing with the opportunity presented was in the exercise of the utmost good faith to Loft; and the burden was cast upon him satisfactorily to prove that the offer was made to him individually. Reasonable inferences, drawn from acknowledged facts and circumstances, are powerful factors in arriving at the truth of a disputed matter, and such inferences are not to be ignored in considering the acts and conduct of Megargel. He had been for years engaged in the manufacture and sale of a cola syrup in competition with Coca-Cola. He knew of the difficulties of competition with such a powerful opponent in general, and in particular in the securing of a necessary foothold in a new territory where Coca-Cola was supreme. He could not hope to establish the popularity and use of his syrup in a strange field, and in competition with the assured position of Coca-Cola, by the usual advertising means, for he, himself, had no money or resources, and it is entirely unbelievable that he expected Guth to have command of the vast amount of money necessary to popularize Pepsi-Cola by the ordinary methods. He knew of the difficulty, not to say impossibility, of inducing proprietors of soft drink establishments to use a cola drink utterly unknown [513] to their patrons. It would seem clear, from any reasonable point of view, that Megargel sought to interest someone who controlled an existing opportunity to popularize his product by an actual presentation of it to the consuming public. Such person was Guth, the president of Loft. It is entirely reasonable to infer that Megargel approached Guth as president of Loft, operating, as it did, many soft drink fountains in a most necessary and desirable territory where Pepsi-Cola was little known, he well knowing that if the drink could be established in New York and circumjacent territory, its success would be assured. Every reasonable inference points to this conclusion. What was finally agreed upon between Megargel and Guth, and what outward appearance their agreement assumed, is of small importance. It was a matter of indifference to Megargel whether his co-adventurer was Guth personally, or Loft, so long as his terms were met and his object attained.

Leaving aside the manner of the offer of the opportunity, certain other matters are to be considered in determining whether the opportunity, in the circumstances, belonged to

Loft; and in this we agree that Guth's right to appropriate the Pepsi-Cola opportunity to himself depends upon the circumstances existing at the time it presented itself to him without regard to subsequent events, and that due weight should be given to character of the opportunity which Megargel envisioned and brought to Guth's door.

The real issue is whether the opportunity to secure a very substantial stock interest in a corporation to be formed for the purpose of exploiting a cola beverage on a wholesale scale was so closely associated with the existing business activities of Loft, and so essential thereto, as to bring the transaction within that class of cases where the acquisition of the property would throw the corporate officer purchasing it into competition with his company. This is a factual question to be decided by reasonable inferences from objective facts.

[...]

The appellants suggest a doubt whether Loft would have been able to finance the project along the lines contemplated by Megargel, viewing the situation as of 1931. The answer to this suggestion is two-fold. The Chancellor found that Loft's net asset position at that time was amply sufficient to finance the enterprise, and that its plant, equipment, executives, personnel and facilities, supplemented by such expansion for the necessary development of the business as it was well able to provide, were in all respects adequate. The second answer is that Loft's resources were found to be sufficient, for Guth made use of no other to any important extent.

Next it is contended that the Pepsi-Cola opportunity was not in the line of Loft's activities which essentially were of a retail nature. It is pointed out that, in 1931, the retail stores operated by Loft were largely located in the congested areas along the Middle Atlantic Seaboard, that its manufacturing [514] operations were centered in its New York factory, and that it was a definitely localized business, and not operated on a national scale; whereas, the Megargel proposition envisaged annual sales of syrup at least a million gallons, which could be accomplished only by a wholesale distribution. Loft, however, had many wholesale activities. Its wholesale business in 1931 amounted to over $800,000. It was a large company by any standard. It had an enormous plant. It paid enormous rentals. Guth, himself, said that Loft's success depended upon the fullest utilization of its large plant facilities. Moreover, it was a manufacturer of syrups and, with the exception of cola syrup, it supplied its own extensive needs. The appellants admit that wholsesale distribution of bottled beverages can best be accomplished by license agreements with bottlers. Guth, president of Loft, was an able and experienced man in that field. Loft, then, through its own personnel, possessed the technical knowledge, the practical business experience, and the resources necessary for the development of the Pepsi-Cola enterprise.

[...]

It is urged that Loft had no interest or expectancy in the Pepsi-Cola opportunity. That it had no existing property right therein is manifest; but we cannot agree that it had no concern or expectancy in the opportunity within the protection of remedial equity. Loft had a practical and essential concern with respect to some cola syrup with an established formula and trademark. A cola beverage has come to be a business necessity for soft drink establishments; and it was essential to the success of Loft to serve at its soda fountains an acceptible five cent cola drink in order to attract into its stores the great multitude of people who have formed the habit of drinking cola beverages. When Guth determined to discontinue the sale of Coca-Cola in the Loft stores, it became, by his own act, a matter of urgent necessity for Loft to acquire a constant supply of some satisfactory cola syrup, secure against probable attack, as a replacement; and when the Pepsi-Cola opportunity presented itself, Guth having already considered the availability of the syrup, it became impressed with a Loft interest and expectancy arising out of the circumstances and the urgent and practical need created by him as the directing head of Loft.

As a general proposition it may be said that a corporate officer or director is entirely free to engage in an independent, competitive business, so long as he violates no legal or moral duty with respect to the fiduciary relation that exists between the corporation and himself. The appellants contend that no conflict of interest between Guth and Loft resulted from his acquirement and exploitation of the Pepsi-Cola opportunity. They maintain that the acquisition did not place Guth in competition with Loft any more than a manufacturer can be said to compete with a retail merchant whom the manufacturer supplies with goods to be sold. However true the statement, applied generally, may be, we emphatically dissent from the application of the analogy to the situation of the parties here. There is no unity between the ordinary manufacturer and the retailer of his goods. Generally, the retailer, if he [515] becomes dissatisfied with one supplier of merchandise, can turn to another. He is under no compulsion and no restraint. In the instant case Guth was Loft, and Guth was Pepsi. He absolutely controlled Loft. His authority over Pepsi was supreme. As Pepsi, he created and controlled the supply of Pepsi-Cola syrup, and he determined the price and the terms. What he offered, as Pepsi, he had the power, as Loft, to accept. Upon any consideration of human characteristics and motives, he created a conflict between self-interest and duty. He made himself the judge in his own cause. This was the inevitable result of the dual personality which Guth assumed, and his position was one which, upon the least austere view of corporate duty, he had no right to assume. Moreover, a reasonable probability of injury to Loft resulted from the situation forced upon it. Guth was in the same position to impose his terms upon Loft as had been the Coca-Cola Company. If Loft had been in servitude to that company with respect to its need for a cola syrup, its condition did not change when its supply came to depend upon Pepsi, for, it was found by the Chancellor, against Guth's contention, that he had not given Loft the protection of a contract which secured to it a constant supply of Pepsi-Cola syrup at any definite price or for any definite time.

It is useless to pursue the argument. The facts and circumstances demonstrate that Guth's appropriation of the Pepsi-Cola opportunity to himself placed him in a competitive position with Loft with respect to a commodity essential to it, thereby rendering his personal interests incompatible with the superior interests of his corporation; and this situation was accomplished, not openly and with his own resources, but secretly and with the money and facilities of the corporation which was committed to his protection.

[...]

Upon a consideration of all the facts and circumstances as disclosed we are convinced that the opportunity to acquire the Pepsi-Cola trademark and formula, goodwill and business belonged to the complainant, and that Guth, as its President, had no right to appropriate the opportunity to himself.

[...]

B. Sinclair Oil Corp. v. Levien (Del. 1971)

Questions

1. As we learned in *Guth* and the introductory notes, the standard of review for self-dealing — "utmost good faith" or "intrinsic fairness" or, nowadays, "entire fairness" — is demanding. It is, thus, extremely important to determine which transactions count as self-dealing. What is *Sinclair*'s answer?

2. Do you agree with it?

3. May *Sinclair*'s answer condone abuse of minority stockholders?

4. What would happen if *Sinclair* had accepted the plaintiff's broader view, not just in the short run but also in the long run (when a corporate group has time to restructure)?

280 A.2d 717 (1971)

SINCLAIR OIL CORPORATION, Defendant Below, Appellant,

v.

Francis S. LEVIEN, Plaintiff Below, Appellee.

Supreme Court of Delaware.

June 18, 1971.

Henry M. Canby, of Richards, Layton & Finger, Wilmington, and Paul W. Williams, Floyd Abrams and Eugene R. Scheiman of Cahill, Gordon, Sonnett, Reindel & Ohl, New York City, for appellant.

Richard F. Corroon, Robert K. Payson, of Potter, Anderson & Corroon, Leroy A. Brill of Bayard, Brill & Handelman, Wilmington, and J. Lincoln Morris, Edward S. Cowen and Pollock & Singer, New York City, for appellee.

WOLCOTT, C. J., CAREY, J., and CHRISTIE, Judge, sitting. [719]

WOLCOTT, Chief Justice.

This is an appeal by the defendant, Sinclair Oil Corporation (hereafter Sinclair), from an order of the Court of Chancery, 261 A.2d 911 in a derivative action requiring Sinclair to account for damages sustained by its subsidiary, Sinclair Venezuelan Oil Company (hereafter Sinven), organized by Sinclair for the purpose of operating in Venezuela, as a result of dividends paid by Sinven, the denial to Sinven of industrial development, and a breach of contract between Sinclair's wholly-owned subsidiary, Sinclair International Oil Company, and Sinven.

Sinclair, operating primarily as a holding company, is in the business of exploring for oil and of producing and marketing crude oil and oil products. At all times relevant to this litigation, it owned about 97% of Sinven's stock. The plaintiff owns about 3000 of 120,000 publicly held shares of Sinven. Sinven, incorporated in 1922, has been engaged in petroleum operations primarily in Venezuela and since 1959 has operated exclusively in Venezuela.

Sinclair nominates all members of Sinven's board of directors. The Chancellor found as a fact that the directors were not independent of Sinclair. Almost without exception, they were officers, directors, or employees of corporations in the Sinclair complex. By reason of Sinclair's domination, it is clear that Sinclair owed Sinven a fiduciary duty. Getty Oil Company v. Skelly Oil Co., 267 A.2d 883 (Del.Supr. 1970); Cottrell v. Pawcatuck Co., 35 Del. Ch. 309, 116 A.2d 787 (1955). Sinclair concedes this.

The Chancellor held that because of Sinclair's fiduciary duty and its control over Sinven, its relationship with Sinven must meet the test of intrinsic fairness. The [720] standard of intrinsic fairness involves both a high degree of fairness and a shift in the burden of proof. Under this standard the burden is on Sinclair to prove, subject to careful judicial scrutiny, that its transactions with Sinven were objectively fair. Guth v. Loft, Inc., 23 Del.Ch. 255, 5 A.2d 503 (1939); Sterling v. Mayflower Hotel Corp., 33 Del.Ch. 293, 93 A.2d 107, 38 A. L.R.2d 425 (Del.Supr.1952); Getty Oil Co. v. Skelly Oil Co., supra.

Sinclair argues that the transactions between it and Sinven should be tested, not by the test of intrinsic fairness with the accompanying shift of the burden of proof, but by the business judgment rule under which a court will not interfere with the judgment of a board of directors unless there is a showing of gross and palpable overreaching. Meyerson v. El Paso Natural Gas Co., 246 A.2d 789 (Del.Ch. 1967). A board of directors enjoys a presumption of sound business judgment, and its decisions will not be disturbed if they can be attributed to any rational business purpose. A court under such circumstances will not substitute its own notions of what is or is not sound business judgment.

We think, however, that Sinclair's argument in this respect is misconceived. When the situation involves a parent and a subsidiary, with the parent controlling the transaction and fixing the terms, the test of intrinsic fairness, with its resulting shifting of the burden of proof, is applied. Sterling v. Mayflower Hotel Corp., supra; David J. Greene & Co. v. Dunhill International, Inc., 249 A.2d 427 (Del.Ch.1968); Bastian v. Bourns, Inc., 256 A.2d 680 (Del.Ch.1969) aff'd. Per Curiam (unreported) (Del.Supr.1970). The basic situation for the application of the rule is the one in which the parent has received a benefit to the exclusion and at the expense of the subsidiary.

Recently, this court dealt with the question of fairness in parent-subsidiary dealings in Getty Oil Co. v. Skelly Oil Co., supra. In that case, both parent and subsidiary were in the business of refining and marketing crude oil and crude oil products. The Oil Import Board ruled that the subsidiary, because it was controlled by the parent, was no longer entitled to a separate allocation of imported crude oil. The subsidiary then contended that it had a right to share the quota of crude oil allotted to the parent. We ruled that the business judgment standard should be applied to determine this contention. Although the subsidiary suffered a loss through the administration of the oil import quotas, the parent gained nothing. The parent's quota was derived solely from its own past use. The past use of the subsidiary did not cause an increase in the parent's quota. Nor did the parent usurp a quota of the subsidiary. Since the parent received nothing from the subsidiary to the exclusion of the minority stockholders of the subsidiary, there was no self-dealing. Therefore, the business judgment standard was properly applied.

A parent does indeed owe a fiduciary duty to its subsidiary when there are parent-subsidiary dealings. However, this alone will not evoke the intrinsic fairness standard. This standard will be applied only when the fiduciary duty is accompanied by self-dealing — the situation when a parent is on both sides of a transaction with its subsidiary. Self-dealing occurs when the parent, by virtue of its domination of the subsidiary, causes the subsidiary to act in such a way that the parent receives something from the subsidiary to the exclusion of, and detriment to, the minority stockholders of the subsidiary.

We turn now to the facts. The plaintiff argues that, from 1960 through 1966, Sinclair caused Sinven to pay out such excessive dividends that the industrial development of Sinven was effectively prevented, and it became in reality a corporation in dissolution.

From 1960 through 1966, Sinven paid out $108,000,000 in dividends ($38,000,000 [721] in excess of Sinven's earnings during the same period). The Chancellor held that Sinclair caused these dividends to be paid during a period when it had a need for large amounts of cash. Although the dividends paid exceeded earnings, the plaintiff concedes that the payments were made in compliance with 8 Del.C. § 170, authorizing payment of dividends out of surplus or net profits. However, the plaintiff attacks these dividends on the ground that they resulted from an improper motive — Sinclair's need for cash. The Chancellor, applying the intrinsic fairness standard, held that Sinclair did not sustain its burden of proving that these dividends were intrinsically fair to the minority stockholders of Sinven.

Since it is admitted that the dividends were paid in strict compliance with 8 Del.C. § 170, the alleged excessiveness of the payments alone would not state a cause of action. Nevertheless, compliance with the applicable statute may not, under all circumstances, justify all dividend payments. If a plaintiff can meet his burden of proving that a dividend cannot be grounded on any reasonable business objective, then the courts can and will interfere with the board's decision to pay the dividend.

Sinclair contends that it is improper to apply the intrinsic fairness standard to dividend payments even when the board which voted for the dividends is completely dominated. In support of this contention, Sinclair relies heavily on American District Telegraph Co. [ADT] v. Grinnell Corp., (N.Y.Sup.Ct.1969) aff'd. 33 A.D.2d 769, 306 N.Y.S.2d 209 (1969). Plaintiffs were minority stockholders of ADT, a subsidiary of Grinnell. The plaintiffs alleged that Grinnell, realizing that it would soon have to sell its ADT stock because of a pending anti-trust action, caused ADT to pay excessive dividends. Because the dividend payments conformed with applicable statutory law, and the plaintiffs could not prove an abuse of discretion, the court ruled that the complaint did not state a cause of action. Other decisions seem to support Sinclair's contention. In Metropolitan Casualty Ins. Co. v. First State Bank of Temple, 54 S.W.2d 358 (Tex.Civ.App.1932), rev'd. on other grounds, 79 S.W.2d 835 (Sup.Ct. 1935), the court held that a majority of interested directors does not void a declaration of dividends because all directors, by necessity, are interested in and benefited by a dividend declaration. See, also, Schwartz v. Kahn, 183 Misc. 252, 50 N.Y.S. 2d 931 (1944); Weinberger v. Quinn, 264 A.D. 405, 35 N.Y.S.2d 567 (1942).

We do not accept the argument that the intrinsic fairness test can never be applied to a dividend declaration by a dominated board, although a dividend declaration by a dominated board will not inevitably demand the application of the intrinsic fairness standard. Moskowitz v. Bantrell, 41 Del.Ch. 177, 190 A.2d 749 (Del.Supr. 1963). If such a dividend is in essence self-dealing by the parent, then the intrinsic fairness standard is the proper standard. For example, suppose a parent dominates a subsidiary and its board of directors. The subsidiary has outstanding two classes of stock, X and Y. Class X is owned by the parent and Class Y is owned by minority stockholders of the subsidiary. If the subsidiary, at the direction of the parent, declares a dividend on its Class X stock only, this might well be self-dealing by the parent. It would be receiving something from the subsidiary to the exclusion of and detrimental to its minority stockholders. This self-dealing, coupled with the parent's fiduciary duty, would make intrinsic fairness the proper standard by which to evaluate the dividend payments.

Consequently it must be determined whether the dividend payments by Sinven were, in essence, self-dealing by Sinclair. The dividends resulted in great sums of money being transferred from Sinven to Sinclair. However, a proportionate share of this money was received by the minority shareholders of Sinven. Sinclair received nothing from Sinven to the exclusion of its [722] minority stockholders. As such, these dividends were not self-dealing. We hold therefore that the Chancellor erred in applying the intrinsic fairness test as to these dividend payments. The business judgment standard should have been applied.

We conclude that the facts demonstrate that the dividend payments complied with the business judgment standard and with 8 Del.C. § 170. The motives for causing the declaration of dividends are immaterial unless the plaintiff can show that the dividend payments resulted from improper motives and amounted to waste. The plaintiff contends only that the dividend payments drained Sinven of cash to such an extent that it was prevented from expanding.

The plaintiff proved no business opportunities which came to Sinven independently and which Sinclair either took to itself or denied to Sinven. As a matter of fact, with two minor exceptions which resulted in losses, all of Sinven's operations have been conducted in Venezuela, and Sinclair had a policy of exploiting its oil properties located in different countries by subsidiaries located in the particular countries.

From 1960 to 1966 Sinclair purchased or developed oil fields in Alaska, Canada, Paraguay, and other places around the world. The plaintiff contends that these were all opportunities which could have been taken by Sinven. The Chancellor concluded that Sinclair had not proved that its denial of expansion opportunities to Sinven was intrinsically fair. He based this conclusion on the following findings of fact. Sinclair made no real effort to expand Sinven. The excessive dividends paid by Sinven resulted in so great a cash drain as to effectively deny to Sinven any ability to expand. During this same period Sinclair actively pursued a company-wide policy of developing through its subsidiaries new sources of revenue, but Sinven was not permitted to participate and was confined in its activities to Venezuela.

However, the plaintiff could point to no opportunities which came to Sinven. Therefore, Sinclair usurped no business opportunity belonging to Sinven. Since Sinclair received nothing from Sinven to the exclusion of and detriment to Sinven's minority stockholders, there was no self-dealing. Therefore, business judgment is the proper standard by which to evaluate Sinclair's expansion policies.

Since there is no proof of self-dealing on the part of Sinclair, it follows that the expansion policy of Sinclair and the methods used to achieve the desired result must, as far as Sinclair's treatment of Sinven is concerned, be tested by the standards of the business judgment rule. Accordingly, Sinclair's decision, absent fraud or gross overreaching, to achieve expansion through the medium of its subsidiaries, other than Sinven, must be upheld.

Even if Sinclair was wrong in developing these opportunities as it did, the question arises, with which subsidiaries should these opportunities have been shared? No evidence indicates a unique need or ability of Sinven to develop these opportunities. The decision of which subsidiaries would be used to implement Sinclair's expansion policy was one of business judgment with which a court will not interfere absent a showing of gross and palpable overreaching. Meyerson v. El Paso Natural Gas Co., 246 A.2d 789 (Del.Ch.1967). No such showing has been made here.

Next, Sinclair argues that the Chancellor committed error when he held it liable to Sinven for breach of contract.

In 1961 Sinclair created Sinclair International Oil Company (hereafter International), a wholly owned subsidiary used for the purpose of coordinating all of Sinclair's foreign operations. All crude purchases by Sinclair were made thereafter through International.

On September 28, 1961, Sinclair caused Sinven to contract with International whereby Sinven agreed to sell all of its [723] crude oil and refined products to International at specified prices. The contract provided for minimum and maximum quantities and prices.

The plaintiff contends that Sinclair caused this contract to be breached in two respects. Although the contract called for payment on receipt, International's payments lagged as much as 30 days after receipt. Also, the contract required International to purchase at least a fixed minimum amount of crude and refined products from Sinven. International did not comply with this requirement.

Clearly, Sinclair's act of contracting with its dominated subsidiary was self-dealing. Under the contract Sinclair received the products produced by Sinven, and of course the minority shareholders of Sinven were not able to share in the receipt of these products. If the contract was breached, then Sinclair received these products to the detriment of Sinven's minority shareholders. We agree with the Chancellor's finding that the contract was breached by Sinclair, both as to the time of payments and the amounts purchased.

Although a parent need not bind itself by a contract with its dominated subsidiary, Sinclair chose to operate in this manner. As Sinclair has received the benefits of this contract, so must it comply with the contractual duties.

Under the intrinsic fairness standard, Sinclair must prove that its causing Sinven not to enforce the contract was intrinsically fair to the minority shareholders of Sinven. Sinclair has failed to meet this burden. Late payments were clearly breaches for which Sinven should have sought and received adequate damages. As to the quantities purchased, Sinclair argues that it purchased all the products produced by Sinven. This, however, does not satisfy the standard of intrinsic fairness. Sinclair has failed to prove that Sinven could not possibly have produced or someway have obtained the contract minimums. As such, Sinclair must account on this claim.

Finally, Sinclair argues that the Chancellor committed error in refusing to allow it a credit or setoff of all benefits provided by it to Sinven with respect to all the alleged damages. The Chancellor held that setoff should be allowed on specific transactions, e. g., benefits to Sinven under the contract with International, but denied an over all setoff against all damages claimed. We agree with the Chancellor, although the point may well be moot in view of our holding that Sinclair is not required to account for the alleged excessiveness of the dividend payments.

We will therefore reverse that part of the Chancellor's order that requires Sinclair to account to Sinven for damages sustained as a result of dividends paid between 1960 and 1966, and by reason of the denial to Sinven of expansion during that period. We will affirm the remaining portion of that order and remand the cause for further proceedings.

C. Hypo: Board Service?

Imagine you are the in-house lawyer for a real estate developer, Rosalind Franklin Broes. Broes is doing business through RFB Condominiums Inc. ("RFBC"), a Delaware corporation. Broes is RFBC's sole shareholder and president. You are technically an employee of RFBC. RFBC develops and administers condo complexes in the Midwestern United States, mainly in Michigan.

Broes now wants your opinion on the following issue. One of RFBC's bankers, John Cash of Big Bank, has asked Broes to join the board of another real estate developer, CIS Inc., also a Delaware corporation. CIS is an erstwhile competitor of RFBC. It has been in chapter 11 for the last two years, however, and lost or sold most of its properties and contracts during that time. When it emerges from bankruptcy next month, it will only have interests in Texas. Cash sits on CIS's creditor committee on behalf of Big Bank, a major creditor of CIS. Cash would like to get Broes's experience onto CIS's board.

Broes is concerned that service on CIS's board will expose her to conflicts of interest. She has shared these concerns with Cash. In Cash's view, the concerns are unfounded. After all, he, Cash, also has access to much confidential information from both CIS and RFBC in his role as their banker. Besides, he argues, CIS and RFBC will no longer be operating in the same areas. Lastly, even if CIS wanted to expand back into the Midwest, Cash points out that CIS would find it very difficult to do so under the restrictive post-bankruptcy loan covenants that prohibit most acquisitions or additional financing.

Broes is still worried though. She looked around the internet, and what she found did not reassure her. The most famous description of the duty of loyalty sounds rather ominous to her. It was penned by Judge Benjamin Cardozo, then Chief Judge of the New York Court of Appeals, in *Meinhard v. Salmon*, 249 N.Y. 458 (1928):

> Joint adventurers, like copartners, owe to one another, while the enterprise continues, the duty of the finest loyalty. Many forms of conduct permissible in a workaday world for those acting at arm's length, are forbidden to those bound by fiduciary ties. A trustee is held to something stricter than the morals of the market place. Not honesty alone, but the punctilio of an honor the most sensitive, is then the standard of behavior. As to this there has developed a tradition that is unbending and inveterate. Uncompromising rigidity has been the attitude of courts of equity when petitioned to undermine the rule of undivided loyalty by the 'disintegrating erosion' of particular exceptions

... Only thus has the level of conduct for fiduciaries been kept at a level higher than that trodden by the crowd. It will not consciously be lowered by any judgment of this court.

Broes says she definitely does not want to sink to the "level ... trodden by the crowd," but she isn't quite sure what "the punctilio of an honor the most sensitive" demands of her.

Questions

1. Can she or can she not serve on CIS's board without getting into trouble?

2. What would you advise Broes to do?

Chapter 4. The Duty of Care

Is there room for liability — and thus judicial involvement — in corporate decision-making, outside of self-dealing? Applying the business judgment rule, Delaware courts hardly ever sanction managers and boards absent self-dealing. Nor do other states' courts. In a well-known case, the New York Supreme Court absolved American Express's board of liability even though they had forgone an $80 million tax benefit (in today's money) without any convincing countervailing benefit. Some have called this area of the law the "law of director non-liability."

This raises two questions: Why no liability? And if there truly is no liability, why not say so outright and save the expense and distraction of litigation?

Importantly, the cases in this area still involve conflicts of interest, albeit of a subtler kind than the outright financial or similarly strong conflicts giving rise to claims of self-dealing. Boards' and managers' interests diverge from shareholders' interests at least inasmuch as the former have to do all the work but surrender most of the benefits to the latter, incentive compensation notwithstanding. As you read the cases, you should be on the lookout for more specific conflicts.

A. Smith v. Van Gorkom (Del. 1985)

This is the one case where Delaware courts imposed monetary liability on disinterested directors for breach of the duty of care. It caused a storm. Liability insurance rates for directors skyrocketed. The Delaware legislature intervened by enacting DGCL 102(b)(7), which allows exculpatory charter provisions to eliminate damages for breaches of the duty of care (see next section). Such charter provisions are now standard. Even without them, however, it is unlikely that a Delaware court would impose liability on these facts today. The courts seem to have retrenched — not in their doctrine but in how they apply it. *Cf. Disney* below.

You should, therefore, read the case not as an exemplary application of the duty of care, but as a policy experiment that showed that corporate law practitioners and lawmakers regard monetary damages on these facts as undesirable. Why?

Background: the Acquisition Process (more in M&A, infra)

The case involves the acquisition of the Trans Union Corporation by Marmon Group, Inc. As is typical, the acquisition is structured as a merger. The acquired corporation (the "target") merges with the acquiror (the "buyer") or one of the buyer's subsidiaries. In the merger, shares in the target are extinguished. In exchange, target shareholders receive cash or other consideration (usually shares in the buyer).

Under most U.S. statutes such as DGCL 251, the merger generally requires a merger agreement between the buyer and the target to be approved by the boards and a majority of the shareholders of each corporation. This entails two important consequences.

First, the board controls the process because only the board can have the corporation enter into the merger agreement. This is one example of why it is at least misleading to call shareholders the "owners of the corporation."

Two, in public corporations, the requirement of shareholder approval means that several months will pass between signing the merger agreement and completion of the merger. This is the time it takes to convene the shareholder meeting and solicit proxies in accordance with the applicable corporate law and SEC proxy rules. Of course, many things can happen during this time. In particular, other potential buyers may appear on the scene.

Questions

1. According to the majority opinion, what did the directors do wrong? In other words, what should the directors have done differently? Why did the business judgment rule not apply?

2. What are the dissenters' counter-arguments?

3. How do you think directors in other companies reacted to this decision — what, if anything, did they most likely do differently after *Van Gorkom*?

488 A.2d 858 (1985)

Alden SMITH and John W. Gosselin, Plaintiffs Below, Appellants,

v.

Jerome W. VAN GORKOM, Bruce S. Chelberg, William B. Johnson, Joseph B. Lanterman, Graham J. Morgan, Thomas P. O'Boyle, W. Allen Wallis, Sidney H. Bonser, William D. Browder, Trans Union Corporation, a Delaware corporation, Marmon Group, Inc., a Delaware corporation, GL Corporation, a Delaware corporation, and New T. Co., a Delaware corporation, Defendants Below, Appellees.

Supreme Court of Delaware.

Submitted: June 11, 1984.

Decided: January 29, 1985.

[...]

William Prickett (argued) and James P. Dalle Pazze, of Prickett, Jones, Elliott, Kristol & Schnee, Wilmington, and Ivan Irwin, Jr. and Brett A. Ringle, of Shank, Irwin, Conant & Williamson, Dallas, Tex., of counsel, for plaintiffs below, appellants.

Robert K. Payson (argued) and Peter M. Sieglaff of Potter, Anderson & Corroon, Wilmington, for individual defendants below, appellees.

Lewis S. Black, Jr., A. Gilchrist Sparks, III (argued) and Richard D. Allen, of Morris, Nichols, Arsht & Tunnell, Wilmington, for Trans Union Corp., Marmon Group, Inc., GL Corp. and New T. Co., defendants below, appellees.

Before HERRMANN, C.J., and McNEILLY, HORSEY, MOORE and CHRISTIE, JJ., constituting the Court en banc. [863]

HORSEY, Justice (for the majority):

This appeal from the Court of Chancery involves a class action brought by shareholders of the defendant Trans Union Corporation ("Trans Union" or "the Company"), originally seeking rescission of a cash-out merger of Trans Union into the defendant New T Company ("New T"), a wholly-owned subsidiary of the defendant, Marmon Group, Inc. ("Marmon"). Alternate relief in the form of damages is sought against the defendant members of the Board of Directors of Trans Union, [864] New T, and Jay A. Pritzker and Robert A. Pritzker, owners of Marmon.

Following trial, the former Chancellor granted judgment for the defendant directors by unreported letter opinion dated July 6, 1982. Judgment was based on two findings: (1) that the Board of Directors had acted in an informed manner so as to be entitled to protection of the business judgment rule in approving the cash-out merger; and (2) that the shareholder vote approving the merger should not be set aside because the stockholders had been "fairly informed" by the Board of Directors before voting thereon. The plaintiffs appeal.

Speaking for the majority of the Court, we conclude that both rulings of the Court of Chancery are clearly erroneous. Therefore, we reverse and direct that judgment be entered in favor of the plaintiffs and against the defendant directors for the fair value of the plaintiffs' stockholdings in Trans Union, in accordance with *Weinberger v. UOP, Inc.,* Del.Supr., 457 A.2d 701 (1983).

We hold: (1) that the Board's decision, reached September 20, 1980, to approve the proposed cash-out merger was not the product of an informed business judgment; (2) that the Board's subsequent efforts to amend the Merger Agreement and take other curative action were ineffectual, both legally and factually; and (3) that the Board did not deal with complete candor with the stockholders by failing to disclose all material facts, which they knew or should have known, before securing the stockholders' approval of the merger.

I.

The nature of this case requires a detailed factual statement. The following facts are essentially uncontradicted:

-A-

Trans Union was a publicly-traded, diversified holding company, the principal earnings of which were generated by its railcar leasing business. During the period here involved, the Company had a cash flow of hundreds of millions of dollars annually. However, the Company had difficulty in generating sufficient taxable income to offset increasingly large investment tax credits (ITCs). Accelerated depreciation deductions had decreased available taxable income against which to offset accumulating ITCs. The Company took these deductions, despite their effect on usable ITCs, because the rental price in the railcar leasing market had already impounded the purported tax savings.♦

♦ In other words, Transunion's "problem" was that it could not make full use of the available massive tax breaks. These tax breaks would reduce the corporate income tax. But Transunion benefitted from so many tax breaks that it was already not paying corporate income tax. The remaining tax breaks were thus "wasted," unless Transunion could persuade Congress to pay out those breaks in cash (i.e., to allow income taxes to be negative in this case -- from the Treasury to firms) or find other taxable income to use the tax breaks on.

In the late 1970's, together with other capital-intensive firms, Trans Union lobbied in Congress to have ITCs refundable in cash to firms which could not fully utilize the credit[, but without any success.]

Beginning in the late 1960's, and continuing through the 1970's, Trans Union pursued a program of acquiring small companies in order to increase available taxable income. In July 1980, Trans

Union Management prepared [and presented to the board] the annual revision of the Company's Five Year Forecast [...] The report projected an annual income growth of about 20%. The report also concluded that Trans Union would have about $195 million in spare cash between 1980 and 1985 [...] The report referred to the ITC situation as a "nagging problem" [...]The report then listed four alternative uses of the projected 1982-1985 equity surplus: (1) stock repurchase; (2) dividend increases; (3) a major acquisition program; and (4) combinations of the above. The sale of Trans Union was not among the alternatives. The report [...] concluded: "As a result, we have sufficient time to fully develop our course of action."

-B-

On August 27, 1980, Van Gorkom met with Senior Management of Trans Union. Van Gorkom reported on his lobbying efforts in Washington and his desire to find a solution to the tax credit problem more permanent than a continued program of acquisitions. Various alternatives were suggested and discussed preliminarily, including the sale of Trans Union to a company with a large amount of taxable income. [Eds: The buyer could then merge with Transunion and, under applicable IRS rules and certain conditions, apply the tax credits of the former Transunion to the combined taxable income of the merged entities.]

Donald Romans, Chief Financial Officer of Trans Union, stated that his department had done a "very brief bit of work on the possibility of a leveraged buy-out."♦

* A leveraged buyout (LBO) is a purchase financed largely with debt. The debt is usually secured by the purchased corporation's assets. LBOs became frequent and spectacularly large in the 1980s. For the LBO to succeed post-acquisition, the target corporation must produce high and steady cash flows to service the high levels of debt incurred. Otherwise, the target will end up in bankruptcy. We will discuss these issues in much greater detail when we discuss Unocal later in the course.

This work had been prompted by a media article which Romans had seen regarding a leveraged buy-out by management. The work consisted of a "preliminary study" of the cash which could be generated by the Company if it participated in a leveraged buyout. As Romans stated, this analysis "was very first and rough cut at seeing whether a cash flow would support what might be considered a high price for this type of transaction."

On September 5, at another Senior Management meeting which Van Gorkom attended, Romans again brought up the idea of a leveraged buy-out as a "possible strategic alternative" to the Company's acquisition program. Romans and Bruce S. Chelberg, President and Chief Operating Officer of Trans Union, had been working on the matter in preparation for the meeting. According to Romans: They did not "come up" with a price for the Company. They merely "ran the numbers" at $50 a share and at $60 a share with the "rough form" of their cash figures at the time. Their "figures indicated that $50 would be very easy to do but $60 would be very difficult to do under those figures." This work did not purport to establish a fair price for either the Company or 100% of the stock. It was intended to determine the cash flow needed to service the debt that would "probably" be incurred in a leveraged buyout, based on "rough calculations" without "any benefit of experts to identify what the limits were to that, and so forth." These computations were not considered extensive and no conclusion was reached.

At this meeting, Van Gorkom stated that he would be willing to take $55 per share for his own 75,000 shares. He vetoed the suggestion of a leveraged buy-out by Management, however, as involving a potential conflict of interest for Management. Van Gorkom, a certified public accountant and lawyer, had been an officer of Trans Union [866] for 24 years, its Chief Executive Officer for more than 17 years, and Chairman of its Board for 2 years. It is noteworthy in this connection that he was then approaching 65 years of age and mandatory retirement.

For several days following the September 5 meeting, Van Gorkom pondered the idea of a sale. He had participated in many acquisitions as a manager and director of Trans Union and as a director of other companies. He was familiar with acquisition procedures, valuation methods, and negotiations; and he privately considered the pros and cons of whether Trans Union should seek a privately or publicly-held purchaser.

Van Gorkom decided to meet with Jay A. Pritzker, a well-known corporate takeover specialist and a social acquaintance. However, rather than approaching Pritzker simply to determine his interest in acquiring Trans Union, Van Gorkom assembled a proposed per share price for sale of the Company and a financing structure by which to accomplish the sale. Van Gorkom did so without consulting either his Board or any members of Senior Management except one: Carl Peterson, Trans Union's Controller. Telling Peterson that he wanted no other person on his staff to know what he was doing, but without telling him why, Van Gorkom directed Peterson to calculate the feasibility of a leveraged buy-out at an assumed price per share of $55. Apart from the Company's historic stock market price,[5] and Van Gorkom's long association with Trans Union, the record is devoid of any competent evidence that $55 represented the per share intrinsic value of the Company.

Having thus chosen the $55 figure, based solely on the availability of a leveraged buy-out, Van Gorkom multiplied the price per share by the number of shares outstanding to reach a total value of the Company of $690 million. Van Gorkom told Peterson to use this $690

---

[5] The common stock of Trans Union was traded on the New York Stock Exchange. Over the five year period from 1975 through 1979, Trans Union's stock had traded within a range of a high of $39½ and a low of $24¼. Its high and low range for 1980 through September 19 (the last trading day before announcement of the merger) was $38¼-$29½.

million figure and to assume a $200 million equity contribution by the buyer. Based on these assumptions, Van Gorkom directed Peterson to determine whether the debt portion of the purchase price could be paid off in five years or less if financed by Trans Union's cash flow as projected in the Five Year Forecast, and by the sale of certain weaker divisions identified in a study done for Trans Union by the Boston Consulting Group ("BCG study"). Peterson reported that, of the purchase price, approximately $50-80 million would remain outstanding after five years. Van Gorkom was disappointed, but decided to meet with Pritzker nevertheless.

Van Gorkom arranged a meeting with Pritzker at the latter's home on Saturday, September 13, 1980. Van Gorkom prefaced his presentation by stating to Pritzker: "Now as far as you are concerned, I can, I think, show how you can pay a substantial premium over the present stock price and pay off most of the loan in the first five years. * * * If you could pay $55 for this Company, here is a way in which I think it can be financed."

Van Gorkom then reviewed with Pritzker his calculations based upon his proposed price of $55 per share. Although Pritzker mentioned $50 as a more attractive figure, no other price was mentioned. However, Van Gorkom stated that to be sure that $55 was the best price obtainable, Trans Union should be free to accept any better offer. Pritzker demurred, stating that his organization would serve as a "stalking horse" for an "auction contest" only if Trans Union would permit Pritzker to buy 1,750,000 shares of Trans Union stock at market price which Pritzker could then sell to any higher bidder. After further discussion on this point, Pritzker told Van Gorkom that he would give him a more definite reaction soon.

[867] On Monday, September 15, Pritzker advised Van Gorkom that he was interested in the $55 cash-out merger proposal and requested more information on Trans Union. Van Gorkom agreed to meet privately with Pritzker, accompanied by Peterson, Chelberg, and Michael Carpenter, Trans Union's consultant from the Boston Consulting Group. The meetings took place on September 16 and 17. Van Gorkom was "astounded that events were moving with such amazing rapidity."

On Thursday, September 18, Van Gorkom met again with Pritzker. At that time, Van Gorkom knew that Pritzker intended to make a cash-out merger offer at Van Gorkom's proposed $55 per share. Pritzker instructed his attorney, a merger and acquisition specialist, to begin drafting merger documents. There was no further discussion of the $55 price. However, the number of shares of Trans Union's treasury stock to be offered to Pritzker was negotiated down to one million shares; the price was set at $38-75 cents above the per share price at the close of the market on September 19. At this point, Pritzker insisted that the Trans Union Board act on his merger proposal within the next three days, stating to Van Gorkom: "We have to have a decision by no later than Sunday [evening, September 21] before the opening of the English stock exchange on Monday morning." Pritzker's lawyer was then instructed to draft the merger documents, to be reviewed by Van Gorkom's lawyer, "sometimes with discussion and sometimes not, in the haste to get it finished."

On Friday, September 19, Van Gorkom, Chelberg, and Pritzker consulted with Trans Union's lead bank regarding the financing of Pritzker's purchase of Trans Union. The bank indicated that it could form a syndicate of banks that would finance the transaction. On the same day, Van Gorkom retained James Brennan, Esquire, to advise Trans Union on the legal aspects of the merger. Van Gorkom did not consult with William Browder, a Vice-President and director of Trans Union and former head of its legal department, or with William Moore, then the head of Trans Union's legal staff.

On Friday, September 19, Van Gorkom called a special meeting of the Trans Union Board for noon the following day. He also called a meeting of the Company's Senior Management to convene at 11:00 a.m., prior to the meeting of the Board. No one, except Chelberg and Peterson, was told the purpose of the meetings. Van Gorkom did not invite Trans Union's investment banker, Salomon Brothers or its Chicago-based partner, to attend.

Of those present at the Senior Management meeting on September 20, only Chelberg and Peterson had prior knowledge of Pritzker's offer. Van Gorkom disclosed the offer and described its terms, but he furnished no copies of the proposed Merger Agreement. Romans announced that his department had done a second study which showed that, for a leveraged buy-out, the price range for Trans Union stock was between $55 and $65 per share. Van Gorkom neither saw the study nor asked Romans to make it available for the Board meeting.

Senior Management's reaction to the Pritzker proposal was completely negative. No member of Management, except Chelberg and Peterson, supported the proposal. Romans objected to the price as being too low; he was critical of the timing and suggested that consideration should be given to the adverse tax consequences of an all-cash deal for low-basis shareholders; and he took the position that the agreement to sell Pritzker one million newly-issued shares at market price would inhibit other offers, as would the prohibitions against soliciting bids and furnishing inside information [868] to other bidders. Romans argued that the Pritzker proposal was a "lock up" and amounted to "an agreed merger as opposed to an offer." Nevertheless, Van Gorkom proceeded to the Board meeting as scheduled without further delay.

Ten directors served on the Trans Union Board, five inside (defendants Bonser, O'Boyle, Browder, Chelberg, and Van Gorkom) and five outside (defendants Wallis, Johnson,

Lanterman, Morgan and Reneker). All directors were present at the meeting, except O'Boyle who was ill. Of the outside directors, four were corporate chief executive officers and one was the former Dean of the University of Chicago Business School. None was an investment banker or trained financial analyst. All members of the Board were well informed about the Company and its operations as a going concern. They were familiar with the current financial condition of the Company, as well as operating and earnings projections reported in the recent Five Year Forecast. The Board generally received regular and detailed reports and was kept abreast of the accumulated investment tax credit and accelerated depreciation problem.

Van Gorkom began the Special Meeting of the Board with a twenty-minute oral presentation. Copies of the proposed Merger Agreement were delivered too late for study before or during the meeting. He reviewed the Company's ITC and depreciation problems and the efforts theretofore made to solve them. He discussed his initial meeting with Pritzker and his motivation in arranging that meeting. Van Gorkom did not disclose to the Board, however, the methodology by which he alone had arrived at the $55 figure, or the fact that he first proposed the $55 price in his negotiations with Pritzker.

Van Gorkom outlined the terms of the Pritzker offer as follows: Pritzker would pay $55 in cash for all outstanding shares of Trans Union stock upon completion of which Trans Union would be merged into New T Company, a subsidiary wholly-owned by Pritzker and formed to implement the merger; for a period of 90 days, Trans Union could receive, but could not actively solicit, competing offers; the offer had to be acted on by the next evening, Sunday, September 21; Trans Union could only furnish to competing bidders published information, and not proprietary information; the offer was subject to Pritzker obtaining the necessary financing by October 10, 1980; if the financing contingency were met or waived by Pritzker, Trans Union was required to sell to Pritzker one million newly-issued shares of Trans Union at $38 per share.

Van Gorkom took the position that putting Trans Union "up for auction" through a 90-day market test would validate a decision by the Board that $55 was a fair price. He told the Board that the "free market will have an opportunity to judge whether $55 is a fair price." Van Gorkom framed the decision before the Board not as whether $55 per share was the highest price that could be obtained, but as whether the $55 price was a fair price that the stockholders should be given the opportunity to accept or reject.

Attorney Brennan advised the members of the Board that they might be sued if they failed to accept the offer and that a fairness opinion was not required as a matter of law.

Romans attended the meeting as chief financial officer of the Company. He told the Board that he had not been involved in the negotiations with Pritzker and knew nothing about the merger proposal until [869] the morning of the meeting; that his studies did not indicate either a fair price for the stock or a valuation of the Company; that he did not see his role as directly addressing the fairness issue; and that he and his people "were trying to search for ways to justify a price in connection with such a [leveraged buy-out] transaction, rather than to say what the shares are worth." [...]

Romans told the Board that, in his opinion, $55 was "in the range of a fair price," but "at the beginning of the range."

[...]

The Board meeting of September 20 lasted about two hours. Based solely upon Van Gorkom's oral presentation, Chelberg's supporting representations, Romans' oral statement, Brennan's legal advice, and their knowledge of the market history of the Company's stock,[9] the directors approved the proposed Merger Agreement. However, the Board later claimed to have attached two conditions to its acceptance: (1) that Trans Union reserved the right to accept any better offer that was made during the market test period; and (2) that Trans Union could share its proprietary information with any other potential bidders. While the Board now claims to have reserved the right to accept any better offer received after the announcement of the Pritzker agreement (even though the minutes of the meeting do not reflect this), it is undisputed that the Board did not reserve the right to actively solicit alternate offers.

The Merger Agreement was executed by Van Gorkom during the evening of September 20 at a formal social event that he hosted for the opening of the Chicago Lyric Opera. Neither he nor any other director read the agreement prior to its signing and delivery to Pritzker.

* * *

On Monday, September 22, the Company issued a press release announcing that Trans Union had entered into a "definitive" Merger Agreement with an affiliate of the Marmon Group, Inc., a Pritzker holding company. Within 10 days of the public announcement, dissent among Senior Management over the merger had become widespread. Faced with

---

[9] The Trial Court stated the premium relationship of the $55 price to the market history of the Company's stock as follows:

> * * * the merger price offered to the stockholders of Trans Union represented a premium of 62% over the average of the high and low prices at which Trans Union stock had traded in 1980, a premium of 48% over the last closing price, and a premium of 39% over the highest price at which the stock of Trans Union had traded any time during the prior six years.

threatened resignations of key officers, Van Gorkom met with Pritzker who agreed to several modifications of the Agreement. Pritzker was willing to do so provided that Van Gorkom could persuade the dissidents to remain on the Company payroll for at least six months after consummation of the merger.

Van Gorkom reconvened the Board on October 8 and secured the directors' approval of the proposed amendments — sight unseen. The Board also authorized the employment of Salomon Brothers, its investment [870] banker, to solicit other offers for Trans Union during the proposed "market test" period.

The next day, October 9, Trans Union issued a press release announcing: (1) that Pritzker had obtained "the financing commitments necessary to consummate" the merger with Trans Union; (2) that Pritzker had acquired one million shares of Trans Union common stock at $38 per share; (3) that Trans Union was now permitted to actively seek other offers and had retained Salomon Brothers for that purpose; and (4) that if a more favorable offer were not received before February 1, 1981, Trans Union's shareholders would thereafter meet to vote on the Pritzker proposal.

It was not until the following day, October 10, that the actual amendments to the Merger Agreement were prepared by Pritzker and delivered to Van Gorkom for execution. As will be seen, the amendments were considerably at variance with Van Gorkom's representations of the amendments to the Board on October 8; and the amendments placed serious constraints on Trans Union's ability to negotiate a better deal and withdraw from the Pritzker agreement. Nevertheless, Van Gorkom proceeded to execute what became the October 10 amendments to the Merger Agreement without conferring further with the Board members and apparently without comprehending the actual implications of the amendments.

* * *

Salomon Brothers' efforts over a three-month period from October 21 to January 21 produced only one serious suitor for Trans Union — General Electric Credit Corporation ("GE Credit"), a subsidiary of the General Electric Company. However, GE Credit was unwilling to make an offer for Trans Union unless Trans Union first rescinded its Merger Agreement with Pritzker. When Pritzker refused, GE Credit terminated further discussions with Trans Union in early January.

In the meantime, in early December, the investment firm of Kohlberg, Kravis, Roberts & Co. ("KKR"), the only other concern to make a firm offer for Trans Union, withdrew its offer under circumstances hereinafter detailed. [Eds: KKR is one the oldest, largest, and most successful private equity / LBO firms.]

On December 19, this litigation was commenced and, within four weeks, the plaintiffs had deposed eight of the ten directors of Trans Union, including Van Gorkom, Chelberg and Romans, its Chief Financial Officer. On January 21, Management's Proxy Statement for the February 10 shareholder meeting was mailed to Trans Union's stockholders. On January 26, Trans Union's Board met and, after a lengthy meeting, voted to proceed with the Pritzker merger. The Board also approved for mailing, "on or about January 27," a Supplement to its Proxy Statement. The Supplement purportedly set forth all information relevant to the Pritzker Merger Agreement, which had not been divulged in the first Proxy Statement.

* * *

On February 10, the stockholders of Trans Union approved the Pritzker merger proposal. Of the outstanding shares, 69.9% were voted in favor of the merger; 7.25% were voted against the merger; and 22.85% were not voted.

II.

We turn to the issue of the application of the business judgment rule to the September 20 meeting of the Board.

[...]

Under Delaware law, the business judgment rule is the offspring of the fundamental principle, codified in 8 *Del.C.* § 141(a), that the business and affairs of a Delaware corporation are managed by or under its board of directors. *Pogostin v. Rice,* Del.Supr., 480 A.2d 619, 624 (1984); *Aronson v. Lewis,* Del.Supr., 473 A.2d 805, 811 (1984); *Zapata Corp. v. Maldonado,* Del.Supr., 430 A.2d 779, 782 (1981). In carrying out their managerial roles, directors are charged with an unyielding fiduciary duty to the corporation and its shareholders. *Loft, Inc. v. Guth,* Del.Ch., 2 A.2d 225 (1938), *aff'd,* Del.Supr., 5 A.2d 503 (1939). The business judgment rule exists to protect and promote the full and free exercise of the managerial power granted to Delaware directors. *Zapata Corp. v. Maldonado, supra* at 782. The rule itself "is a presumption that in making a business decision, the directors of a corporation acted on an informed basis, in good faith and in the honest belief that the action taken was in the best interests of the company." *Aronson, supra* at 812. Thus, the party attacking a board decision as uninformed must rebut the presumption that its business judgment was an informed one. *Id.*

The determination of whether a business judgment is an informed one turns on whether the directors have informed themselves "prior to making a business decision, of all material information reasonably available to them."

Under the business judgment rule there is no protection for directors who have made "an unintelligent or unadvised judgment." [...] A director's duty to inform himself in preparation for a decision derives from the fiduciary capacity in which he serves the corporation and its stockholders. [...] Since a director is vested with the responsibility for the management of the affairs of the corporation, he must execute that duty with the recognition that he acts on behalf of others. Such obligation does not tolerate faithlessness or self-dealing. But fulfillment of the fiduciary function requires more than the mere absence of bad faith or fraud. Representation of the financial interests of others imposes on a director an affirmative duty to protect those interests and to proceed with a critical eye in assessing information of the type and under the circumstances present here. [...]

Thus, a director's duty to exercise an informed business judgment is in [873] the nature of a duty of care, as distinguished from a duty of loyalty. Here, there were no allegations of fraud, bad faith, or self-dealing, or proof thereof. Hence, it is presumed that the directors reached their business judgment in good faith [...] and considerations of motive are irrelevant to the issue before us.

The standard of care applicable to a director's duty of care has also been recently restated by this Court. In *Aronson, supra,* we stated:

> While the Delaware cases use a variety of terms to describe the applicable standard of care, our analysis satisfies us that under the business judgment rule director liability is predicated upon concepts of gross negligence. (footnote omitted)

473 A.2d at 812.

We again confirm that view. We think the concept of gross negligence is also the proper standard for determining whether a business judgment reached by a board of directors was an informed one.

[...]

III.

[...]

the question of whether the directors reached an informed business judgment in agreeing to sell the Company, pursuant to the terms of the September 20 Agreement presents, in reality, two questions: (A) whether the directors reached an informed business judgment on September 20, 1980; and (B) if they did not, whether the directors' actions taken subsequent to September 20 were adequate to cure any infirmity in their action taken on

September 20. We first consider the directors' September 20 action in terms of their reaching an informed business judgment.

-A-

On the record before us, we must conclude that the Board of Directors did not reach an informed business judgment on September 20, 1980 in voting to "sell" the Company for $55 per share pursuant to the Pritzker cash-out merger proposal. Our reasons, in summary, are as follows:

The directors (1) did not adequately inform themselves as to Van Gorkom's role in forcing the "sale" of the Company and in establishing the per share purchase price; (2) were uninformed as to the intrinsic value of the Company; and (3) given these circumstances, at a minimum, were grossly negligent in approving the "sale" of the Company upon two hours' consideration, without prior notice, and without the exigency of a crisis or emergency.

As has been noted, the Board based its September 20 decision to approve the cash-out merger primarily on Van Gorkom's representations. None of the directors, other than Van Gorkom and Chelberg, had any prior knowledge that the purpose of the meeting was to propose a cash-out merger of Trans Union. No members of Senior Management were present, other than Chelberg, Romans and Peterson; and the latter two had only learned of the proposed sale an hour earlier. Both general counsel Moore and former general counsel Browder attended the meeting, but were equally uninformed as to the purpose of the meeting and the documents to be acted upon.

Without any documents before them concerning the proposed transaction, the members of the Board were required to rely entirely upon Van Gorkom's 20-minute oral presentation of the proposal. No written summary of the terms of the merger was presented; the directors were given no documentation to support the adequacy of $55 price per share for sale of the Company; and the Board had before it nothing more than Van Gorkom's statement of his understanding of the substance of an agreement which he admittedly had never read, nor which any member of the Board had ever seen.

Under 8 *Del.C.* § 141(e), "directors are fully protected in relying in [875] good faith on reports made by officers." [...] The term "report" has been liberally construed to include reports of informal personal investigations by corporate officers, *Cheff v. Mathes,* Del.Supr., 199 A.2d 548, 556 (1964). However, there is no evidence that any "report," as defined under § 141(e), concerning the Pritzker proposal, was presented to the Board on September 20.[16] Van Gorkom's oral presentation of his understanding of the terms of the proposed Merger Agreement, which he had not seen, and Romans' brief oral statement of his preliminary study regarding the feasibility of a leveraged buy-out of Trans Union do not qualify as § 141(e) "reports" for these reasons: The former lacked substance because Van Gorkom was basically uninformed as to the essential provisions of the very document about which he was talking. Romans' statement was irrelevant to the issues before the Board since it did not purport to be a valuation study. At a minimum for a report to enjoy the status conferred by § 141(e), it must be pertinent to the subject matter upon which a board is called to act, and otherwise be entitled to good faith, not blind, reliance. Considering all of the surrounding circumstances — hastily calling the meeting without prior notice of its subject matter, the proposed sale of the Company without any prior consideration of the issue or necessity therefor, the urgent time constraints imposed by Pritzker, and the total absence of any documentation whatsoever — the directors were duty bound to make reasonable inquiry of Van Gorkom and Romans, and if they had done so, the inadequacy of that upon which they now claim to have relied would have been apparent.

The defendants rely on the following factors to sustain the Trial Court's finding that the Board's decision was an informed one: (1) the magnitude of the premium or spread between the $55 Pritzker offering price and Trans Union's current market price of $38 per share; (2) the amendment of the Agreement as submitted on September 20 to permit the Board to accept any better offer during the "market test" period; (3) the collective experience and expertise of the Board's "inside" and "outside" directors; and (4) their reliance on Brennan's legal advice that the directors might be sued if they rejected the Pritzker proposal. We discuss each of these grounds *seriatim*:

(1)

A substantial premium may provide one reason to recommend a merger, but in the absence of other sound valuation information, the fact of a premium alone does not provide an adequate basis upon which to assess the fairness of an offering price. Here, the judgment reached as to the adequacy of the premium was based on a comparison between the historically depressed Trans Union market price and the amount of the Pritzker offer. Using market price as a basis for concluding that the premium adequately reflected the

---

[16] In support of the defendants' argument that their judgment as to the adequacy of $55 per share was an informed one, the directors rely on the BCG study and the Five Year Forecast. However, no one even referred to either of these studies at the September 20 meeting; and it is conceded that these materials do not represent valuation studies. Hence, these documents do not constitute evidence as to whether the directors reached an informed judgment on September 20 that $55 per share was a fair value for sale of the Company.

true value [876] of the Company was a clearly faulty, indeed fallacious, premise, as the defendants' own evidence demonstrates.

The record is clear that before September 20, Van Gorkom and other members of Trans Union's Board knew that the market had consistently undervalued the worth of Trans Union's stock, despite steady increases in the Company's operating income in the seven years preceding the merger. [...] Yet, on September 20, Trans Union's Board apparently believed that the market stock price accurately reflected the value of the Company for the purpose of determining the adequacy of the premium for its sale.

In the Proxy Statement, however, the directors reversed their position. There, they stated that, although the earnings prospects for Trans Union were "excellent," they found no basis for believing that this would be reflected in future stock prices. With regard to past trading, the Board stated that the prices at which the Company's common stock had traded in recent years did not reflect the "inherent" value of the Company. [...] By their own admission they could not rely on the stock price as an accurate measure of value. Yet, also by their own admission, the Board members assumed that Trans Union's market price was adequate to serve as a basis upon which to assess the adequacy of the premium for purposes of the September 20 meeting.

The parties do not dispute that a publicly-traded stock price is solely a measure of the value of a minority position and, thus, market price represents only the value of a single share. Nevertheless, on September 20, the Board assessed the adequacy of the premium over market, offered by Pritzker, solely by comparing it with Trans Union's current and historical stock price. [...]

Indeed, as of September 20, the Board had no other information on which to base a determination of the intrinsic value of Trans Union as a going concern. As of September 20, the Board had made no evaluation of the Company designed to value the entire enterprise, nor had the Board ever previously considered selling the Company or consenting to a buy-out merger. Thus, the adequacy of a premium is indeterminate unless it is assessed in terms of other competent and sound valuation information that reflects the value of the particular business.

Despite the foregoing facts and circumstances, there was no call by the Board, either on September 20 or thereafter, for any valuation study or documentation of the $55 price per share as a measure of the fair value of the Company in a cash-out context. It is undisputed that the major asset of Trans Union was its cash flow. Yet, at no time did the Board call for a valuation study taking into account that highly significant element of the Company's assets.

We do not imply that an outside valuation study is essential to support an informed business judgment; nor do we state that fairness opinions by independent investment bankers are required as a matter of law. Often insiders familiar with the business of a going concern are in a better position than are outsiders to gather relevant information; and under appropriate circumstances, such directors may be fully protected in relying in good faith upon the valuation reports of their management. [877] *See 8 Del.C.* § 141(e). *See also Cheff v. Mathes, supra.*

Here, the record establishes that the Board did not request its Chief Financial Officer, Romans, to make any valuation study or review of the proposal to determine the adequacy of $55 per share for sale of the Company. On the record before us: The Board rested on Romans' elicited response that the $55 figure was within a "fair price range" within the context of a leveraged buy-out. No director sought any further information from Romans. No director asked him why he put $55 at the bottom of his range. No director asked Romans for any details as to his study, the reason why it had been undertaken or its depth. No director asked to see the study; and no director asked Romans whether Trans Union's finance department could do a fairness study within the remaining 36-hour period available under the Pritzker offer.

Had the Board, or any member, made an inquiry of Romans, he presumably would have responded as he testified: that his calculations were rough and preliminary; and, that the study was not designed to determine the fair value of the Company, but rather to assess the feasibility of a leveraged buy-out financed by the Company's projected cash flow, making certain assumptions as to the purchaser's borrowing needs. Romans would have presumably also informed the Board of his view, and the widespread view of Senior Management, that the timing of the offer was wrong and the offer inadequate.

The record also establishes that the Board accepted without scrutiny Van Gorkom's representation as to the fairness of the $55 price per share for sale of the Company — a subject that the Board had never previously considered. The Board thereby failed to discover that Van Gorkom had suggested the $55 price to Pritzker and, most crucially, that Van Gorkom had arrived at the $55 figure based on calculations designed solely to determine the feasibility of a leveraged buy-out.[19] No questions were raised either as to

---

[19] As of September 20 the directors did not know: that Van Gorkom had arrived at the $55 figure alone, and subjectively, as the figure to be used by Controller Peterson in creating a feasible structure for a leveraged buy-out by a prospective purchaser; that Van Gorkom had not sought advice, information or assistance from either inside or outside Trans Union directors as to the value of the Company as an entity or the fair price per share for 100% of its stock; that Van Gorkom had not consulted with the Company's investment bankers or other financial analysts; that Van Gorkom had not consulted with or confided in any officer or director of the Company except Chelberg; and that Van Gorkom had deliberately chosen

the tax implications of a cash-out merger or how the price for the one million share option granted Pritzker was calculated.

We do not say that the Board of Directors was not entitled to give some credence to Van Gorkom's representation that $55 was an adequate or fair price. Under § 141(e), the directors were entitled to rely upon their chairman's opinion of value and adequacy, provided that such opinion was reached on a sound basis. Here, the issue is whether the directors informed themselves as to all information that was reasonably available to them. Had they done so, they would have learned of the source and derivation of the $55 price and could not reasonably have relied thereupon in good faith.

None of the directors, Management or outside, were investment bankers or financial analysts. Yet the Board did not consider recessing the meeting until a later hour that day (or requesting an extension of Pritzker's Sunday evening deadline) to give it time to elicit more information as to the sufficiency of the offer [...]

Thus, the record compels the conclusion that on September 20 the Board lacked valuation information adequate to reach an informed business judgment as to the fairness of $55 per share for sale of the Company.[20]

(2)

This brings us to the post-September 20 "market test" upon which the defendants ultimately rely to confirm the reasonableness of their September 20 decision to accept the Pritzker proposal. In this connection, the directors present a two-part argument: (a) that by making a "market test" of Pritzker's $55 per share offer a condition of their September 20 decision to accept his offer, they cannot be found to have acted impulsively or in an uninformed manner on September 20; and (b) that the adequacy of the $17 premium for sale of the Company was conclusively established over the following 90 to 120 days by the most reliable evidence available — the marketplace. Thus, the defendants impliedly contend that the "market test" eliminated the need for the Board to perform any other form of fairness test either on September 20, or thereafter.

Again, the facts of record do not support the defendants' argument. There is no evidence: (a) that the Merger Agreement was effectively amended to give the Board freedom to put Trans Union up for auction sale to the highest bidder; or (b) that a public auction was in fact permitted to occur. The minutes of the Board meeting make no reference to any of

---

to ignore the advice and opinion of the members of his Senior Management group regarding the adequacy of the $55 price.

[20] For a far more careful and reasoned approach taken by another board of directors faced with the pressures of a hostile tender offer, see *Pogostin v. Rice, supra* at 623-627.

this. Indeed, the record compels the conclusion that the directors had no rational basis for expecting that a market test was attainable, given the terms of the Agreement as executed during the evening of September 20. [...]

Van Gorkom, conceding that he never read the Agreement, stated that he was relying upon his understanding that, under corporate law, directors always have an inherent right, as well as a fiduciary duty, to accept a better offer notwithstanding an existing contractual commitment by the Board. [...]

The defendant directors assert that they "insisted" upon including two amendments to the Agreement, thereby permitting a market test: (1) to give Trans Union the right to accept a better offer; and (2) to reserve to Trans Union the right to distribute proprietary information on the Company to alternative bidders. Yet, the defendants concede that they did not seek to amend the Agreement to permit Trans Union to solicit competing offers.

[...]

The defendants attempt to downplay the significance of the prohibition against Trans Union's actively soliciting competing offers by arguing that the directors "understood that the entire financial community would know that Trans Union was for sale upon the announcement of the Pritzker offer, and anyone desiring to make a better offer was free to do so." Yet, the press release issued on September 22, with the authorization of the Board, stated that Trans Union had entered into "definitive agreements" with the Pritzkers; and the press release did not even disclose Trans Union's limited right to receive and accept higher offers. Accompanying this press release was a further public announcement that Pritzker had been granted an option to purchase at any time one million shares of [880] Trans Union's capital stock at 75 cents above the then-current price per share.

Thus, notwithstanding what several of the outside directors later claimed to have "thought" occurred at the meeting, the record compels the conclusion that Trans Union's Board had no rational basis to conclude on September 20 or in the days immediately following, that the Board's acceptance of Pritzker's offer was conditioned on (1) a "market test" of the offer; and (2) the Board's right to withdraw from the Pritzker Agreement and accept any higher offer received before the shareholder meeting.

(3)

The directors' unfounded reliance on both the premium and the market test as the basis for accepting the Pritzker proposal undermines the defendants' remaining contention that the Board's collective experience and sophistication was a sufficient basis for finding that it reached its September 20 decision with informed, reasonable deliberation. [...].

(4)

Part of the defense is based on a claim that the directors relied on legal advice rendered at the September 20 meeting by James Brennan, Esquire, who was present at Van Gorkom's request. [...]

Several defendants testified that Brennan advised them that Delaware law did not require a fairness opinion or an outside valuation of the Company before the Board could act on the Pritzker proposal. If given, the advice was correct. However, that did not end the matter. Unless the directors had before them adequate information regarding the intrinsic value of the Company, upon which a proper exercise of business judgment could be made, mere advice of this type is meaningless; and, given this record of the defendants' failures, it constitutes no defense here.[22]

[...]

A second claim is that counsel advised the Board it would be subject to lawsuits if it rejected the $55 per share offer. It is, of course, a fact of corporate life that today when faced with difficult or sensitive issues, directors often are subject to suit, irrespective of the decisions they make. However, counsel's mere acknowledgement of this circumstance cannot be rationally translated into a justification for a board permitting itself to be stampeded into a patently unadvised act. While suit might result from the rejection of a merger or tender offer, Delaware law makes clear that a board acting within the ambit of the business judgment rule faces no ultimate liability. *Pogostin v. Rice, supra.* Thus, we cannot conclude that the mere threat of litigation, acknowledged by counsel, constitutes either legal advice or any valid basis upon which to pursue an uninformed course.

[...]

-B-

We now examine the Board's post-September 20 conduct for the purpose of determining first, whether it was informed and not grossly negligent; and second, if informed, whether it was sufficient to legally rectify and cure the Board's derelictions of September 20.[23]

---

[22] Nonetheless, we are satisfied that in an appropriate factual context a proper exercise of business judgment may include, as one of its aspects, reasonable reliance upon the advice of counsel. This is wholly outside the statutory protections of 8 *Del.C.* § 141(e) involving reliance upon reports of officers, certain experts and books and records of the company.

[23] As will be seen, we do not reach the second question.

(1)

First, as to the Board meeting of October 8 [... T]he primary purpose of the October 8 Board meeting was to amend the Merger Agreement, in a manner agreeable to Pritzker, to permit Trans Union to conduct a "market test." Van Gorkom understood that the proposed amendments were intended to give the Company an unfettered "right to openly solicit offers down through January 31." Van Gorkom presumably so represented the amendments to Trans Union's Board members on October 8. In a brief session, the directors approved Van Gorkom's oral presentation of the substance of the proposed amendments, [883] the terms of which were not reduced to writing until October 10. But rather than waiting to review the amendments, the Board again approved them sight unseen and adjourned, giving Van Gorkom authority to execute the papers when he received them.[25]

[...]

The October 10 amendments to the Merger Agreement did authorize Trans Union to solicit competing offers, but the amendments had more far-reaching effects. The most significant change was in the definition of the third-party "offer" available to Trans Union as a possible basis for withdrawal from its Merger Agreement with Pritzker. Under the October 10 amendments, a better *offer* was no longer sufficient to permit Trans Union's withdrawal. Trans Union was now permitted to terminate the Pritzker Agreement and abandon the merger only if, prior to February 10, 1981, Trans Union had either consummated a merger (or sale of assets) with a third party or had entered into a "definitive" merger agreement more favorable than Pritzker's and for a greater consideration — subject only to stockholder approval. Further, the "extension" of the market test period to February 10, 1981 was circumscribed by other amendments which required Trans Union to file its preliminary proxy statement on the Pritzker merger proposal by December 5, 1980 and use its best efforts to mail the statement to its shareholders by January 5, 1981. Thus, the market test period was effectively reduced, not extended. [...]

In our view, the record compels the conclusion that the directors' conduct on October [884] 8 exhibited the same deficiencies as did their conduct on September 20. The Board

---

[25] We do not suggest that a board must read *in haec verba* every contract or legal document which it approves, but if it is to successfully absolve itself from charges of the type made here, there must be some credible contemporary evidence demonstrating that the directors knew what they were doing, and ensured that their purported action was given effect. That is the consistent failure which cast this Board upon its unredeemable course.

permitted its Merger Agreement with Pritzker to be amended in a manner it had neither authorized nor intended. [...]

We conclude that the Board acted in a grossly negligent manner on October 8 [...]

(2)

Next, as to the "curative" effects of the Board's post-September 20 conduct, we review in more detail the reaction of Van Gorkom to the KKR proposal and the results of the Board-sponsored "market test." [Eds: The KKR proposal, an alternative to the Pritzker sale, was orchestrated by Trans Union's senior officers, excluding Van Gorkom. Van Gorkom dismissed the KKR proposal from the start due to his interpretation of its financing condition as weak, even though the Pritzker agreement contained a similar condition. KKR withdrew the proposal when one of the TransUnion managers, who was supposed to be part of the management group involved in the deal, abruptly withdrew after Van Gorkom had spoken to him (Van Gorkom, however, denied influencing this outcome). The court also recounts how GE Credit Corporation, seemingly prepared to offer a higher price for TransUnion, withdrew its interest after Pritzker refused to extend the negotiation deadline, thereby leaving insufficient time for GE to make an offer. Based on these circumstances, the court concludes that the market test was essentially meaningless.]

(3)

Finally, we turn to the Board's meeting of January 26, 1981. The defendant directors rely upon the action there taken to refute the contention that they did not reach an informed business judgment in approving the Pritzker merger. [Eds: The Supreme Court's answer: too little, too late.]

* * *

Upon the basis of the foregoing, we hold that the defendants' post-September conduct did not cure the deficiencies of their September 20 conduct; and that, accordingly, the Trial Court erred in according to the defendants the benefits of the business judgment rule.

[...]

V.

The defendants ultimately rely on the stockholder vote of February 10 for exoneration. [...]

The settled rule in Delaware is that "where a majority of fully informed stockholders ratify action of even interested directors, an attack on the ratified transaction normally must fail." [...]

In *Lynch v. Vickers Energy Corp., supra,* this Court held that corporate directors owe to their stockholders a fiduciary duty to disclose all facts germane to the transaction at issue in an atmosphere of complete candor. [...] "[G]ermane" means material facts.

[...] Trans Union's stockholders were not fully informed of all facts material to their vote on the Pritzker Merger [...] We list the material deficiencies in the proxy materials:

(1) The fact that the Board had no reasonably adequate information indicative of the intrinsic value of the Company, [...]

(2) We find false and misleading the Board's characterization of the Romans report in the Supplemental Proxy Statement. The Supplemental Proxy stated:

> At the September 20, 1980 meeting of the Board of Directors of Trans Union, Mr. Romans indicated that while he could not say that $55,00 per share was an unfair price, he had prepared a preliminary report which reflected that the value of the Company was in the range of $55.00 to $65.00 per share.

Nowhere does the Board disclose that Romans stated to the Board that his calculations were made in a "search for ways to justify a price in connection with" a leveraged buy-out transaction, "rather than to say what the shares are worth," and that he stated to the Board that his conclusion thus arrived at "was not the same thing as saying that I have a valuation of the Company at X dollars." [...]

(3) We find misleading the Board's references to the "substantial" premium offered. [... T]he Board did not disclose its failure to assess the premium offered in terms of other relevant valuation techniques, thereby rendering questionable its determination as to the substantiality of the premium over an admittedly depressed stock market price.

(4) [...] The directors disclosed that Van Gorkom suggested the $55 price to Pritzker. But the Board misled the shareholders when they described the basis of Van Gorkom's suggestion as follows:

> Such suggestion was based, at least in part, on Mr. Van Gorkom's belief that loans could be obtained from institutional lenders (together with about a $200 million [892] equity contribution) which would justify the payment of such price, ...

Although by January 26, the directors knew the basis of the $55 figure, they did not disclose that Van Gorkom chose the $55 price because that figure would enable Pritzker to both finance the purchase of Trans Union through a leveraged buy-out and, within five years, substantially repay the loan out of the cash flow generated by the Company's operations.

(5) The Board's Supplemental Proxy Statement, mailed on or after January 27 [eds: belatedly furnished all or most of the missing information. Nevertheless, the Supreme Court found that it fell short of the required "complete candor" because it did not explicitly say that the board already possessed much of this information when mailing the original proxy statement].

* * *

For the foregoing reasons, we conclude that the director defendants breached their fiduciary duty of candor by their failure to make true and correct disclosures of all information they had, or should have had, material to the transaction submitted for stockholder approval.

VI.

To summarize: we hold that the directors of Trans Union breached their fiduciary duty to their stockholders (1) by their failure to inform themselves of all information reasonably available to them and relevant to their decision to recommend the Pritzker merger; and (2) by their failure to disclose all material information such as a reasonable stockholder would consider important in deciding whether to approve the Pritzker offer.

We hold, therefore, that the Trial Court committed reversible error in applying the business judgment rule in favor of the director defendants in this case.

On remand, the Court of Chancery shall conduct an evidentiary hearing to determine the fair value of the shares represented by the plaintiffs' class, based on the intrinsic value of Trans Union on September 20, 1980. Such valuation shall be made in accordance with *Weinberger v. UOP, Inc., supra* at 712-715. Thereafter, an award of damages may be entered to the extent that the fair value of Trans Union exceeds $55 per share.

* * *

REVERSED and REMANDED for proceedings consistent herewith.

McNEILLY, Justice, dissenting:

The majority opinion reads like an advocate's closing address to a hostile jury. And I say that not lightly. Throughout the [894] opinion great emphasis is directed only to the negative, with nothing more than lip service granted the positive aspects of this case. In my opinion Chancellor Marvel (retired) should have been affirmed. [...]

The majority has spoken and has effectively said that Trans Union's Directors have been the victims of a "fast shuffle" by Van Gorkom and Pritzker. That is the beginning of the majority's comedy of errors. The first and most important error made is the majority's assessment of the directors' knowledge of the affairs of Trans Union and their combined ability to act in this situation under the protection of the business judgment rule.

Trans Union's Board of Directors consisted of ten men, five of whom were "inside" directors and five of whom were "outside" directors. The "inside" directors were Van Gorkom, Chelberg, Bonser, William B. Browder, Senior Vice-President-Law, and Thomas P. O'Boyle, Senior Vice-President-Administration. At the time the merger was proposed the inside five directors had collectively been employed by the Company for 116 years and had 68 years of combined experience as directors. The "outside" directors were A.W. Wallis, William B. Johnson, Joseph B. Lanterman, Graham J. Morgan and Robert W. Reneker. With the exception of Wallis, these were all chief executive officers of Chicago based corporations that were at least as large as Trans Union. The five "outside" directors had 78 years of combined experience as chief executive officers, and 53 years cumulative service as Trans Union directors.

[...]

Directors of this caliber are not ordinarily taken in by a "fast shuffle". [...] These men knew Trans Union like the back of their hands and were more than well qualified to make on the spot informed business judgments concerning the affairs of Trans Union including a 100% sale of the corporation. Lest we forget, the corporate world of then and now operates on what is so aptly referred to as "the fast track". These men were at the time an integral part of that world, all professional business men, not intellectual figureheads.

The majority of this Court holds that the Board's decision, reached on September 20, 1980, to approve the merger was not the product of an informed business judgment. [...] I disagree.

At the time of the September 20, 1980 meeting the Board was acutely aware of Trans Union and its prospects. The problems created by accumulated investment tax credits and accelerated depreciation were discussed repeatedly at Board meetings, and all of the directors understood the problem thoroughly. Moreover, at the July, 1980 Board meeting the directors had reviewed Trans Union's newly prepared five-year forecast, and at the August, 1980 meeting Van Gorkom presented the results of a comprehensive study of Trans Union made by The Boston Consulting Group. This study was prepared over an 18 month period and consisted of a detailed analysis of all Trans Union subsidiaries [...]

At the September 20 meeting Van Gorkom reviewed all aspects of the proposed transaction and repeated the explanation of the Pritzker offer he had earlier given to senior management. Having heard Van Gorkom's explanation of the Pritzker's offer, and Brennan's explanation of the merger documents the directors discussed the matter. Out of this discussion arose an insistence on the part of the directors that two modifications to the offer be made. First, they required that any potential competing bidder be given access to the same information concerning Trans Union that had been provided to the Pritzkers. Second, the merger documents were to be modified to reflect the fact that the directors could accept a better offer and would not be required to recommend the Pritzker offer if a better offer was made. [...]

The majority of this Court holds that the Board's decision, reached on September 20, 1980, to approve the merger was not the product of an *informed* business judgment. [...] I disagree.

At the time of the September 20, 1980 meeting the Board was acutely aware of Trans Union and its prospects. [...]

At the September 20 meeting Van Gorkom reviewed all aspects of the proposed transaction and repeated the explanation of the Pritzker offer he had earlier given to senior management. Having heard Van Gorkom's explanation of the Pritzker's offer, and Brennan's explanation of the merger documents the directors discussed the matter. Out of this discussion arose an insistence on the part of the directors that [...] the merger documents were to be modified to reflect the fact that the directors could accept a better offer and would not be required to recommend the Pritzker offer if a better offer was made. [...]

At a subsequent meeting on October 8, 1981 the directors, with the consent of the Pritzkers, amended the Merger Agreement so as to establish the right of Trans Union to *solicit* as well as to receive higher bids [...]

Following the October 8 board meeting of Trans Union, the investment banking firm of Salomon Brothers was retained by the corporation to search for better offers than that of the Pritzkers, Salomon Brothers being charged with the responsibility of doing "whatever possible to see if there is a superior bid in the marketplace over a bid that is on the table for Trans Union". In undertaking such project, it was agreed that Salomon Brothers would be paid the amount of $500,000 to cover its expenses as well as a fee equal to 3/8ths of 1% of the aggregate fair market value of the consideration to be received by the company in the case of a merger or the like, which meant that in the event Salomon Brothers should find a buyer willing to pay a price of $56.00 a share instead of $55.00, such firm would receive a fee of roughly $2,650,000 plus disbursements.

[...] As matters transpired, no firm offer which bettered the Pritzker offer of $55 per share was ever made. [...]

I have no quarrel with the majority's analysis of the business judgment rule. It is the application of that rule to these facts which is wrong. An overview of the entire record, rather than the limited view of bits and pieces which the majority has exploded like popcorn, convinces me that the directors made an informed business judgment which was buttressed by their test of the market.

[...]

CHRISTIE, Justice, dissenting:

I respectfully dissent.

Considering the standard and scope of our review under *Levitt v. Bouvier*, Del. Supr., 287 A.2d 671, 673 (1972), I believe that the record taken as a whole supports a conclusion that the actions of the defendants are protected by the business judgment rule. [...] I also am satisfied that the record supports a conclusion that the defendants acted with the complete candor required by *Lynch v. Vickers Energy Corp.*, Del.Supr., 383 A.2d 278 (1978). Under the circumstances I would affirm the judgment of the Court of Chancery.

[...]

B. DGCL 102(b)(7)

After the *Smith v. Van Gorkom* shock of 1985, the Delaware legislature promptly enacted DGCL 102(b)(7) in 1986 (emphasis added):

> the certificate of incorporation may ... contain ... [a] provision **eliminating** ... the personal liability of a **director** ... for **monetary damages** for breach of fiduciary duty ..., [**except**]:
>
> (i) For any breach of the director's **duty of loyalty** ...;
>
> (ii) for acts or omissions not in **good faith** or which involve **intentional misconduct** or a **knowing violation of law**;
>
> (iii) under § 174 of this title [**unlawful dividends**]; or

(iv) for any transaction from which the director derived an **improper personal benefit**.

Other states followed suit, and such "102(b)(7) waivers" are now standard in corporate charters. In 2022, Delaware amended the section to include officers in direct shareholder actions (i.e., *not* in derivative actions or actions prosecuted by the corporation itself), and many corporations have already amended their charters to avail themselves of this opportunity.

Questions

1. The big question, already posed for *Smith v. Van Gorkom* above, is why such waivers are almost universally accepted. What is so bad about director (and officer) liability for breach of the duty of care? Keep in mind that adopting a 102(b)(7) waiver requires shareholder approval (DGCL 242(b)(1)), and that investors can choose not to invest in corporations that have a waiver.

2. Which (aspects of) fiduciary duties can be eliminated by the waiver, and which cannot?

3. How do "duty of loyalty," "good faith," (absence of) "intentional misconduct," and (absence of) "improper personal benefit" differ from one another? All or some of these arguably mean the same thing, but DGCL 102(b)(7)'s separate mentions arguably imply that they do not. You do not need to think too hard about this at this point, but understanding the tension will facilitate your understanding of *Disney*'s struggle with this question.

C. In re Walt Disney Co. Derivative Litigation (Del. 2006)

After *Smith v. Van Gorkom*, *Disney* is the closest Delaware courts have come to imposing monetary liability on disinterested directors after trial on the merits. The litigation was heavily colored by Disney's 102(b)(7) waiver, which Disney and most other large corporations had adopted after *Van Gorkom*. The Delaware Supreme Court, however, chose first to make an affirmative finding that the defendants met even the default standard of due care.

Questions

As you read that part of the opinion (chiefly IV.A.1), ask yourself why the court reached the opposite result from *Van Gorkom*:

1. Did the court apply different law, i.e., did it overrule *Van Gorkom*, explicitly or implicitly?

2. Did the case present materially different facts? The *Disney* court certainly paints a more favorable picture of the board process than the *Van Gorkom* court. But were the processes substantively different? Imagine you are the plaintiffs' lawyer (or a judge in the *Van Gorkom* majority) and try to recast the *Disney* facts in a light less favorable to the defendants.

In answering the last question, consider the following questions about executive compensation, which is at issue in *Disney*:

3. Executive pay is high. In particular, the median CEO of an S&P 500 company is paid around $15 million per year, over 250 times the median wage in the United States. Why?

4. Much of executive pay is in the form of restricted stock (i.e., stock that the executive is not allowed to sell for a number of years) and stock options (i.e., the right to acquire the corporation's stock in the future at a specified price). Why?

5. Why did Disney's board offer even more than this to Ovitz (which alternatives did it consider)? And what incentives were generated by the structure of Ovitz's compensation package?

The *Disney* court next addresses "good faith," which is a necessary condition for liability protection under DGCL 102(b)(7) (as well as for indemnification under DGCL 145(a) and (b)).

6. How does the court interpret "good faith"?

7. How does "good faith" relate to the duty of care and the duty of loyalty?

8. Was addressing both "good faith" and the default standard of due care necessary for the court's decision of the case? If not, why did it?

906 A.2d 27 (2006)

In re the WALT DISNEY COMPANY DERIVATIVE LITIGATION.
William Brehm [et al.], Plaintiffs Below, Appellants,

v.

Michael D. Eisner, Michael S. Ovitz, Stephen F. Bollenbach, Sanford M. Litvack, Irwin Russell, Roy E. Disney, Stanley P. Gold, Richard A. Nunis, Sidney Poitier, Robert A.M. Stern, E. Cardon Walker, Raymond L. Watson, Gary L. Wilson, Reveta F. Bowers, Ignacio E. Lozano Jr., George J. Mitchell, Leo J. O'Donovan, Thomas S. Murphy and The Walt Disney Company, Defendants Below, Appellees.

No. 411, 2005.

Supreme Court of Delaware.

Submitted: January 25, 2006.

Decided: June 8, 2006.

Joseph A. Rosenthal and Norman M. Monhait, Esquires, of Rosenthal, Monhait, Gross & Goddess, P.A., Wilmington, Delaware; Seth D. Rigrodsky, Esquire, of Milberg Weiss Bershad & Schulman LLP, Wilmington, Delaware; Of Counsel: Steven G. Schulman (argued), Joshua H. Vinik, Jennifer K. Hirsh, John B. Rediker and Laura H. Gundersheim, Esquires, of Milberg Weiss Bershad & Schulman LLP, New York, New York; for Appellants.

Lawrence C. Ashby, Richard D. Heins and Philip Trainer, Jr., Esquires, of Ashby & Geddes, P.A., Wilmington, Delaware; Of Counsel: Gary P. Naftalis (argued), Michael S. Oberman, Paul H. Schoeman and Shoshana Menu, Esquires; of Kramer Levin Naftalis & Frankel, LLP, New York, New York; for Appellee Eisner.

David C. McBride and Christian Douglas Wright, Esquires, of Young Conaway Stargatt & Taylor, LLP, Wilmington, Delaware; Of Counsel: Mark H. Epstein (argued), Bart H. Williams and Jason L. Haas, Esquires, of Munger, Tolles & Olson LLP, Los Angeles, California; for Appellee Ovitz.

Jesse A. Finkelstein, Gregory P. Williams (argued), Anne C. Foster, Lisa A. Schmidt, Evan O. Williford, and Michael R. Robinson, Esquires, of Richards, Layton & Finger, P.A.,

Wilmington, Delaware; [35] for Appellees Bollenbach, Russell, Nunis, Poitier, Stern, Walker, Watson, Wilson, Bowers, Lozano, Mitchell, O'Donovan, and Murphy.

Robert K. Payson, Stephen C. Norman and Kevin R. Shannon, Esquires, of Potter Anderson & Corroon LLP, Wilmington, Delaware; for Appellee Litvack.

A. Gilchrist Sparks, III and S. Mark Hurd, Esquires, of Morris, Nichols, Arsht & Tunnell, Wilmington, Delaware; Of Counsel: Stephen D. Alexander and Susan C. Chun, Esquires, of Bingham McCutchen LLP, Los Angeles, California; for Appellees Disney and Gold.

Andre G. Bouchard and Joel Friedlander, Esquires, of Bouchard Margules & Friedlander, Wilmington, Delaware; for Appellee The Walt Disney Company.

Before STEELE, Chief Justice, HOLLAND, BERGER, JACOBS and RIDGELY, Justices, constituting the Court en Banc. [34]

JACOBS, Justice.

In August 1995, Michael Ovitz ("Ovitz") and The Walt Disney Company ("Disney" or the "Company") entered into an employment agreement under which Ovitz would serve as President of Disney for five years. In December 1996, only fourteen months after he commenced employment, Ovitz was terminated without cause, resulting in a severance payout to Ovitz valued at approximately $130 million.

In January 1997, several Disney shareholders brought derivative actions in the Court of Chancery, on behalf of Disney, against Ovitz and the directors of Disney who served at the time of the events complained of (the "Disney defendants"). The plaintiffs claimed that the $130 million severance payout was the product of fiduciary duty and contractual breaches by Ovitz, and breaches of fiduciary duty by the Disney defendants, and a waste of assets. After the disposition of several pretrial motions and an appeal to this Court, the case was tried before the Chancellor over 37 days between October 20, 2004 and January 19, 2005. In August 2005, the Chancellor handed down a well-crafted 174 page Opinion and Order, determining that "the director defendants did not breach their fiduciary duties or commit waste." The Court entered judgment in favor of all defendants on all claims alleged in the amended complaint.

The plaintiffs have appealed from that judgment, claiming that the Court of Chancery committed multitudinous errors. We conclude, for the reasons that follow, that the Chancellor's factual findings and legal rulings were correct and not erroneous in any respect. Accordingly, the judgment [36] entered by the Court of Chancery will be affirmed.

I. THE FACTS

We next summarize the facts as found by the Court of Chancery that are material to the issues presented on this appeal. The critical events flow from what turned out to be an unfortunate hiring decision at Disney, a company that for over half a century has been one of America's leading film and entertainment enterprises.

In 1994 Disney lost in a tragic helicopter crash its President and Chief Operating Officer, Frank Wells, who together with Michael Eisner, Disney's Chairman and Chief Executive Officer, had enjoyed remarkable success at the Company's helm. Eisner temporarily assumed Disney's presidency, but only three months later, heart disease required Eisner to undergo quadruple bypass surgery. Those two events persuaded Eisner and Disney's board of directors that the time had come to identify a successor to Eisner.

Eisner's prime candidate for the position was Michael Ovitz, who was the leading partner and one of the founders of Creative Artists Agency ("CAA"), the premier talent agency whose business model had reshaped the entire industry. By 1995, CAA had 550 employees and a roster of about 1400 of Hollywood's top actors, directors, writers, and musicians. That roster generated about $150 million in annual revenues and an annual income of over $20 million for Ovitz, who was regarded as one of the most powerful figures in Hollywood.

Eisner and Ovitz had enjoyed a social and professional relationship that spanned nearly 25 years. Although in the past the two men had casually discussed possibly working together, in 1995, when Ovitz began negotiations to leave CAA and join Music Corporation of America ("MCA"), Eisner became seriously interested in recruiting Ovitz to join Disney. Eisner shared that desire with Disney's board members on an individual basis.[4]

A. Negotiation Of The Ovitz Employment Agreement

Eisner and Irwin Russell, who was a Disney director and chairman of the compensation committee, first approached Ovitz about joining Disney. Their initial negotiations were unproductive, however, because at that time MCA had made Ovitz an offer that Disney could not match. The MCA-Ovitz negotiations eventually fell apart, and Ovitz returned

---

[4] The Disney board of directors at that time and at the time the Ovitz Employment Agreement was approved (the "old board") consisted of Eisner, Roy E. Disney, Stanley P. Gold, Sanford M. Litvack, Richard A. Nunis, Sidney Poitier, Irwin E. Russell, Robert A.M. Stern, E. Cardon Walker, Raymond L. Watson, Gary L. Wilson, Reveta F. Bowers, Ignacio E. Lozano, Jr., George J. Mitchell, and Stephen F. Bollenbach. The board of directors at the time Ovitz was terminated as President of Disney (the "new board") consisted of the persons listed above (other than Bollenbach), plus Leo J. O'Donovan and Thomas S. Murphy. Neither O'Donovan nor Murphy served on the old board.

to CAA in mid-1995. Business continued as usual, until Ovitz discovered that Ron Meyer, his close friend and the number two executive at CAA, was leaving CAA to join MCA. That news devastated Ovitz, who concluded that to remain with the company he and Meyer had built together was no longer palatable. At that point Ovitz became receptive to the idea of joining Disney. Eisner learned of these developments [37] and re-commenced negotiations with Ovitz in earnest. By mid-July 1995, those negotiations were in full swing.

Both Russell and Eisner negotiated with Ovitz, over separate issues and concerns. From his talks with Eisner, Ovitz gathered that Disney needed his skills and experience to remedy Disney's current weaknesses, which Ovitz identified as poor talent relationships and stagnant foreign growth. Seeking assurances from Eisner that Ovitz's vision for Disney was shared, at some point during the negotiations Ovitz came to believe that he and Eisner would run Disney, and would work together in a relation akin to that of junior and senior partner. Unfortunately, Ovitz's belief was mistaken, as Eisner had a radically different view of what their respective roles at Disney should be.

Russell assumed the lead in negotiating the financial terms of the Ovitz employment contract. In the course of negotiations, Russell learned from Ovitz's attorney, Bob Goldman, that Ovitz owned 55% of CAA and earned approximately $20 to $25 million a year from that company. From the beginning Ovitz made it clear that he would not give up his 55% interest in CAA without "downside protection." Considerable negotiation then ensued over downside protection issues. During the summer of 1995, the parties agreed to a draft version of Ovitz's employment agreement (the "OEA") modeled after Eisner's and the late Mr. Wells' employment contracts. As described by the Chancellor, the draft agreement included the following terms:

> Under the proposed OEA, Ovitz would receive a five-year contract with two tranches of options. [...]
>
> The proposed OEA sought to protect both parties in the event that Ovitz's employment ended prematurely [... I]f Disney fired Ovitz for any reason other than gross negligence or malfeasance, Ovitz would be entitled to a non-fault payment (Non-Fault Termination or "NFT"), which consisted of his remaining salary, $7.5 million a year for unaccrued bonuses, the immediate vesting of his first tranche of options and a $10 million cash out payment for the second tranche of options.

As the basic terms of the OEA were crystallizing, Russell prepared and gave Ovitz and Eisner a "case study" to explain those terms. In that study, Russell also expressed his concern that the negotiated terms represented an extraordinary level of executive compensation. Russell acknowledged, however, that Ovitz was an "exceptional corporate executive" and "highly successful and unique entrepreneur" who merited "downside protection and upside opportunity." Both would be required to enable Ovitz to adjust to the reduced cash compensation he would receive [38] from a public company, in contrast to the greater cash distributions and other perquisites more typically available from a privately held business. But, Russell did caution that Ovitz's salary would be at the top level for any corporate officer and significantly above that of the Disney CEO. [...]

To assist in evaluating the financial terms of the OEA, Russell recruited Graef Crystal, an executive compensation consultant, and Raymond Watson, a member of Disney's compensation committee and a past Disney board chairman who had helped structure Wells' and Eisner's compensation packages. [...]

On August 10, Russell, Watson and Crystal met. They discussed and generated a set of values using different and various inputs and assumptions [...]. Two days later, Crystal faxed to Russell a memorandum concluding that the OEA would provide Ovitz with approximately $23.6 million per year for the first five years, or $23.9 million a year over seven years if Ovitz exercised a two year renewal option. Those sums, Crystal opined, would approximate Ovitz's current annual compensation at CAA.

[After some back and forth between the three, Crystal] revised his original letter, adjusting the value of the OEA (assuming a two year renewal) to $24.1 million per year. Up to that point, only three Disney directors—Eisner, Russell and Watson— [39] knew the status of the negotiations with Ovitz and the terms of the draft OEA.

While Russell, Watson and Crystal were finalizing their analysis of the OEA, Eisner and Ovitz reached a separate agreement. Eisner told Ovitz that: (1) the number of options would be reduced [...]; and (2) Ovitz would join Disney only as President, not as a co-CEO with Eisner. After deliberating, Ovitz accepted those terms, and that evening Ovitz, Eisner, Sid Bass[10] and their families celebrated Ovitz's decision to join Disney.

Unfortunately, the celebratory mood was premature. The next day, August 13, Eisner met with Ovitz, Russell, Sanford Litvack (an Executive Vice President and Disney's General Counsel), and Stephen Bollenbach (Disney's Chief Financial Officer) to discuss the decision to hire Ovitz. Litvack and Bollenbach were unhappy with that decision, and voiced concerns that Ovitz would disrupt the cohesion that existed between Eisner, Litvack and Bollenbach. Litvack and Bollenbach were emphatic that they would not report to Ovitz, but would continue to report to Eisner. Despite Ovitz's concern about his "shrinking

---

[10] Sid Bass was one of Disney's largest individual shareholders.

authority" as Disney's future President, Eisner was able to provide sufficient reassurance so that ultimately Ovitz acceded to Litvack's and Bollenbach's terms.

On August 14, Eisner and Ovitz signed a letter agreement (the "OLA"), which outlined the basic terms of Ovitz's employment, and stated that the agreement (which would ultimately be embodied in a formal contract) was subject to approval by Disney's compensation committee and board of directors. Russell called Sidney Poitier, a Disney director and compensation committee member, to inform Poitier of the OLA and its terms. Poitier believed that hiring Ovitz was a good idea because of Ovitz's reputation and experience. Watson called Ignacio Lozano, another Disney director and compensation committee member, who felt that Ovitz would successfully adapt from a private company environment to Disney's public company culture. Eisner also contacted each of the other board members by phone to inform them of the impending new hire, and to explain his friendship with Ovitz and Ovitz's qualifications.

[40] That same day, a press release made the news of Ovitz's hiring public. The reaction was extremely positive: Disney was applauded for the decision, and Disney's stock price rose 4.4 % in a single day, thereby increasing Disney's market capitalization by over $1 billion.

Once the OLA was signed, Joseph Santaniello, a Vice President and counsel in Disney's legal department, began to embody in a draft OEA the terms that Russell and Goldman had agreed upon and had been memorialized in the OLA. In the process, Santaniello concluded that the $50 million guarantee created negative tax implications for Disney, because it might not be deductible. Concluding that the guarantee should be eliminated, Russell initiated discussions on how to compensate Ovitz for this change. What resulted were several amendments to the OEA to replace the back-end guarantee. [...]

On September 26, 1995, the Disney compensation committee (which consisted of Messrs. Russell, Watson, Poitier and Lozano) met for one hour to consider, among other agenda items, the proposed terms of the OEA. A term sheet was distributed at the meeting, although a draft of the OEA was not. The topics discussed were historical comparables, such as Eisner's and Wells' option grants, and also the factors that Russell, Watson and Crystal had considered in setting the size of the option grants and the termination provisions of the contract. Watson testified that he provided the compensation committee with the spreadsheet analysis that he had performed in August, and discussed his findings with the committee. Crystal did not attend the meeting, although he was available by telephone to respond to questions if needed, but no one from the committee called. After Russell's and Watson's presentations, Litvack also responded to substantive questions. At trial Poitier and Lozano testified that they believed they had received sufficient information from Russell's and Watson's presentations to exercise their judgment in the best interests of the Company. The committee voted unanimously to approve the OEA terms, subject to "reasonable further negotiations within the framework of the terms and conditions" described in the OEA.

[41] Immediately after the compensation committee meeting, the Disney board met in executive session. The board was told about the reporting structure to which Ovitz had agreed, but the initial negative reaction of Litvack and Bollenbach to the hiring was not recounted. Eisner led the discussion relating to Ovitz, and Watson then explained his analysis, and both Watson and Russell responded to questions from the board. After further deliberation, the board voted unanimously to elect Ovitz as President.

At its September 26, 1995 meeting, the compensation committee determined that it would delay the formal grant of Ovitz's stock options until further issues between Ovitz and the Company were resolved. That was done, and the committee met again, on October 16, 1995, to discuss stock option-related issues. The committee approved amendments to the Walt Disney Company 1990 Stock Incentive Plan (the "1990 Plan"), and also approved a new plan, known as the Walt Disney 1995 Stock Incentive Plan (the "1995 Plan"). [...] After approving those Plans, the committee unanimously approved the terms of the OEA and the award of Ovitz's options under the 1990 Plan.

B. Ovitz's Performance As President of Disney

Ovitz's tenure as President of the Walt Disney Company officially began on October 1, 1995, the date that the OEA was executed. When Ovitz took office, the initial reaction was optimistic, and Ovitz did make some positive contributions while serving as President of the Company. [42] By the fall of 1996, however, it had become clear that Ovitz was "a poor fit with his fellow executives." By then the Disney directors were discussing that the disconnect between Ovitz and the Company was likely irreparable and that Ovitz would have to be terminated.

The Court of Chancery identified three competing theories as to why Ovitz did not succeed:

> First, plaintiffs argue that Ovitz failed to follow Eisner's directives, especially in regard to acquisitions, and that generally, Ovitz did very little. Second, Ovitz contends Eisner's micromanaging prevented Ovitz from having the authority necessary to make the changes that Ovitz thought were appropriate. In addition, Ovitz believes he was not given enough time for his efforts to bear fruit. Third, the remaining defendants simply posit that Ovitz failed to transition from a private to a public company, from the "sell side to the buy side," and otherwise did not adapt to the Company culture or fit in with other executives. In the end, however, it makes no difference why Ovitz was not as

successful as his reputation would have led many to expect, so long as
he was not grossly negligent or malfeasant.

Although the plaintiffs attempted to show that Ovitz acted improperly (*i.e.*, with gross negligence or malfeasance) while in office, the Chancellor found that the trial record did not support those accusations. Rejecting the plaintiffs' first factual claim that Ovitz was insubordinate, the Court found that although many of Ovitz's efforts failed to produce results, that was because his efforts often reflected a philosophy opposite to "that held by Eisner, Iger, and Roth." That difference did not mean, however, "that Ovitz intentionally failed to follow Eisner's directives or that [Ovitz] was insubordinate."

The Chancellor also rejected the appellants' second claim—that Ovitz was a habitual liar. The Court found no evidence that Ovitz ever told a material falsehood or made any false or misleading disclosures during his tenure at Disney. Lastly, the Chancellor found that the record did not support, and often contradicted, the appellants' third claim—that Ovitz had violated the Company's policies relating to expenses and to reporting gifts he received while President of Disney.

Nonetheless, Ovitz's relationship with the Disney executives did continue to deteriorate through September 1996. In mid-September, Litvack, with Eisner's approval, told Ovitz that he was not working out at Disney and that he should start looking for a graceful exit from Disney and a new job. Litvack reported this conversation to Eisner, who sent Litvack back to Ovitz to make it clear that Eisner no longer wanted Ovitz at Disney and that Ovitz should seriously consider other opportunities, including one then developing at Sony. Ovitz responded by telling Litvack that he was not leaving and that if Eisner wanted him [43] to leave Disney, Eisner could tell him that to his face.

On September 30, 1996, the Disney board met. During an executive session of that meeting, and in small group discussions where Ovitz was not present, Eisner told the other board members of the continuing problems with Ovitz's performance. On October 1, Eisner wrote a letter to Russell and Watson detailing Eisner's mounting difficulties with Ovitz, including Eisner's lack of trust of Ovitz and Ovitz's failures to adapt to Disney's culture and to alleviate Eisner's workload. Eisner's goal in writing this letter was to prevent Ovitz from succeeding him at Disney. Because of that purpose, the Chancellor found that the letter contained "a good deal of hyperbole to help Eisner 'unsell' Ovitz as his successor." Neither that letter nor its contents were shared with other members of the board.

Those interchanges set the stage for Ovitz's eventual termination as Disney's President.

C. Ovitz's Termination At Disney

After the discussions between Litvack and Ovitz, Eisner and Ovitz met several times. During those meetings they discussed Ovitz's future, including Ovitz's employment prospects at Sony. [However, Eisner's attempts to tell Ovitz that he was no longer welcome at Disney and to look for opportunities elsewhere were not very successful. For example, he left one] meeting believing that "Ovitz just would not listen to what he was trying to tell him and instead, Ovitz insisted that he would stay at Disney, going so far as to state that he would chain himself to his desk."

During this period Eisner was also working with Litvack to explore whether they could terminate Ovitz under the OEA for cause. If so, Disney would not owe Ovitz the NFT payment. From the very beginning, Litvack advised Eisner that he did not believe there was cause to terminate Ovitz under the OEA. Litvack's advice never changed.

At the end of November 1996, Eisner again asked Litvack if Disney had cause to fire Ovitz and thereby avoid the costly NFT payment. Litvack proceeded to examine that issue more carefully. He studied the OEA, refreshed himself on the meaning of "gross negligence" and "malfeasance," and reviewed all the facts [44] concerning Ovitz's performance of which he was aware. Litvack also consulted Val Cohen, co-head of Disney's litigation department and Joseph Santaniello, in Disney's legal department. Cohen and Santaniello both concurred in Litvack's conclusion that no basis existed to terminate Ovitz for cause. Litvack did not personally conduct any legal research or request an outside opinion on the issue, because he believed that it "was not a close question, and in fact, Litvack described it as "a no brainer.'" Eisner testified that after Litvack notified Eisner that he did not believe cause existed, Eisner "checked with almost anybody that [he] could find that had a legal degree, and there was just no light in that possibility. It was a total dead end from day one." Although the Chancellor was critical of Litvack and Eisner for lacking sufficient documentation to support his conclusion and the work they did to arrive at that conclusion, the Court found that Eisner and Litvack "did in fact make a concerted effort to determine if Ovitz could be terminated for cause, and that despite these efforts, they were unable to manufacture the desired result."[28]

Litvack also believed that it would be inappropriate, unethical and a bad idea to attempt to coerce Ovitz (by threatening a for-cause termination) into negotiating for a smaller NFT package than the OEA provided. The reason was that when pressed by Ovitz's attorneys, Disney would have to admit that in fact there was no cause, which could subject

---

[28] *Id.* The Chancellor found Litvack's testimony on this issue especially persuasive because "[i]n light of the hostile relationship between Litvack and Ovitz, I believe that if Litvack thought it were possible to avoid paying Ovitz the NFT payment, that out of pure ill-will, Litvack would have tried almost anything to avoid the payment." *Id.* at ___, *20, n. 269.

Disney to a wrongful termination lawsuit. Litvack believed that attempting to avoid legitimate contractual obligations would harm Disney's reputation as an honest business partner and would affect its future business dealings.

The Disney board next met on November 25. By then the board knew Ovitz was going to be fired, yet the only action recorded in the minutes concerning Ovitz was his renomination to a new three-year term on the board. Although that action was somewhat bizarre given the circumstances, Stanley Gold, a Disney director, testified that because Ovitz was present at that meeting, it would have been a "public hanging" not to renominate him. An executive session took place after the board meeting, from which Ovitz was excluded. At that session, Eisner informed the directors who were present that he intended to fire Ovitz by year's end, and that he had asked Gary Wilson, a board member and friend of Ovitz, to speak with Ovitz while Wilson and Ovitz were together on vacation during the upcoming Thanksgiving holiday.[30]

Shortly after the November 25 board meeting and executive session, the Ovitz and Wilson families left on their yacht for a Thanksgiving trip to the British Virgin Islands. Ovitz hoped that if he could manage [45] to survive at Disney until Christmas, he could fix everything with Disney and make his problems go away. Wilson quickly dispelled that illusion, informing Ovitz that Eisner wanted Ovitz out of the Company. At that point Ovitz first began to realize how serious his situation at Disney had become. Reporting back his conversation with Ovitz, Wilson told Eisner that Ovitz was a "loyal friend and devastating enemy," and he advised Eisner to "be reasonable and magnanimous, both financially and publicly, so Ovitz could save face."

After returning from the Thanksgiving trip, Ovitz met with Eisner on December 3, to discuss his termination. Ovitz asked for several concessions, all of which Eisner ultimately rejected. Eisner told Ovitz that all he would receive was what he had contracted for in the OEA.

[...]

On December 11, Eisner met with Ovitz to agree on the wording of a press release to announce the termination, and to inform Ovitz that he would not receive any of the additional items that he requested [...] After his December 11 meeting with Eisner, Ovitz never returned to Disney.

---

[30] The Court of Chancery found that at least Eisner, Gold, Bowers, Watson, and Stern were present at that executive session. The Court also found that the record was in conflict as to whether any details of the NFT and the termination for cause question were discussed.

Ovitz's termination was memorialized in a letter, dated December 12, 1996, that Litvack signed on Eisner's instruction. The board was not shown the letter, nor did it meet to approve its terms. A press release announcing Ovitz's termination was issued that same day. Before the press release was issued, Eisner attempted to contact each of the board members by telephone to notify them that Ovitz had been officially terminated. None of the board members at that time, or at any other time, objected to Ovitz's termination, and most, if not all, of them thought it was the appropriate step for Eisner to take. Although the board did not meet to vote on the termination, the Chancellor found that most, if not all, of the Disney directors trusted Eisner's and Litvack's conclusion that there was no cause to terminate Ovitz, and that Ovitz should be terminated without cause even though that involved making the costly NFT payment.

[46] A December 27, 1996 letter from Litvack to Ovitz, which Ovitz signed, memorialized the termination [...] Shortly thereafter, Disney paid Ovitz what was owed under the OEA for an NFT, minus a holdback of $1 million pending final settlement of Ovitz's accounts. One month after Disney paid Ovitz, the plaintiffs filed this action.

II. SUMMARY OF APPELLANTS' CLAIMS OF ERROR

As noted earlier, the Court of Chancery rejected all of the plaintiff-appellants' claims on the merits and entered judgment in favor of the defendant-appellees on all counts. On appeal, the appellants claim that the adverse judgment rests upon multiple erroneous rulings and should be reversed [...] In Part III, we analyze the claims relating to Ovitz. In Part IV, we address the claims asserted against the Disney defendants.

III. THE CLAIMS AGAINST OVITZ

The appellants argue that the Chancellor erroneously rejected their claims against Ovitz on two distinct grounds. We analyze them separately.

A. Claims Based Upon Ovitz's Conduct Before Assuming Office At Disney

First, appellants contend that the Court of Chancery erred by dismissing their claim, as a summary judgment matter, that Ovitz had breached his fiduciary duties to Disney by negotiating and entering into the OEA. On summary judgment the Chancellor determined that Ovitz had breached no fiduciary duty to Disney, because Ovitz did not become a fiduciary until he formally assumed office on October 1, 1995, by which time the essential terms of the NFT provision had been negotiated. Therefore, the Court of Chancery held, Ovitz's pre-October 1 conduct was not constrained by any fiduciary duty standard.

That ruling was erroneous, appellants argue, because even though Ovitz did not formally assume the title of President until October 1, 1995, he became a *de facto* fiduciary before then. [...]

[T]he *de facto* officer argument lacks merit, both legally and factually. A *de facto* officer is one who actually assumes possession of an office under the claim and color of an election or appointment and who is actually discharging the duties of that office, but for some legal reason lacks *de jure* legal title to that office. Here, Ovitz did not assume, or [49] purport to assume, the duties of the Disney presidency before October 1, 1995. [...]

B. Claims Based Upon Ovitz's Conduct During His Termination As President

The appellants' second claim is that the Court of Chancery erroneously concluded that Ovitz breached no fiduciary duty, including his duty of loyalty, by receiving the NFT payment upon his termination as President of Disney. The Chancellor found:

> Ovitz did not breach his fiduciary duty of loyalty by receiving the NFT payment because he played no part in the decisions: (1) to be terminated and (2) that the termination would not be for cause under the OEA. Ovitz did possess fiduciary duties as a director and officer while these decisions were made, but by not improperly interjecting himself into the corporation's decisionmaking process nor manipulating that process, he did not breach the fiduciary duties he possessed in that unique circumstance. Furthermore, Ovitz did not "engage" in a transaction with the corporation—rather, the corporation imposed an unwanted transaction upon him.

> Once Ovitz was terminated without cause (as a result of decisions made entirely without input or influence from Ovitz), he was contractually entitled, without any negotiation or action on his part, to receive the benefits provided by the OEA for a termination without cause, benefits for which he negotiated at arm's length *before* becoming a fiduciary.

[...]

The Court made no error in arriving at that determination and we uphold it.

IV. THE CLAIMS AGAINST THE DISNEY DEFENDANTS

We next turn to the claims of error that relate to the Disney defendants. Those claims are subdivisible into two groups: (A) claims arising out of the approval of the OEA and of Ovitz's election as President; and (B) claims arising out of the NFT severance payment to Ovitz upon his termination. We address separately those two categories and the issues that they generate.

A. Claims Arising From The Approval Of The OEA And Ovitz's Election As President

As earlier noted, the appellants' core argument in the trial court was that the Disney defendants' approval of the OEA and election of Ovitz as President were not entitled to business judgment rule protection, because those actions were either grossly negligent or not performed in good faith. The Court of Chancery rejected these arguments, and held that the appellants had failed to prove that the Disney defendants had breached any fiduciary duty.

For clarity of presentation we address the claimed errors relating to the fiduciary duty of care rulings separately from those that relate to the directors' fiduciary duty to act in good faith. [52]

1. The Due Care Determinations

The plaintiff-appellants advance five contentions to support their claim that the Chancellor reversibly erred by concluding that the plaintiffs had failed to establish a violation of the Disney defendants' duty of care. [...]

To the extent that these claims attack legal rulings of the Court of Chancery we review them *de novo*. To the extent they attack the Court's factual findings, those findings will be upheld where they are based on the Chancellor's assessment of live testimony. The issue these claims present is whether the Court of Chancery legally (and reversibly) erred in one or more of the foregoing respects. We conclude that the Chancellor committed no error.

(a)

[...]

(b) RULING THAT THE FULL DISNEY BOARD WAS NOT REQUIRED TO CONSIDER AND APPROVE THE OEA

The appellants next challenge the Court of Chancery's determination that the full Disney board was not required to consider and approve the OEA [...]

As the Chancellor found, under the Company's governing documents the board of directors was responsible for selecting the corporation's officers, but under the compensation committee charter, the committee was responsible for establishing and approving the salaries, together with benefits and stock options, of the Company's CEO and President. The compensation committee also had the charter-imposed duty to "approve employment contracts, or contracts at will" for "all corporate officers who are members of the Board of Directors regardless of salary." That is exactly what occurred here. The full board ultimately selected Ovitz as President, [54] and the compensation committee considered and ultimately approved the OEA, which embodied the terms of Ovitz's employment, including his compensation.

The Delaware General Corporation Law (DGCL) expressly empowers a board of directors to appoint committees and to delegate to them a broad range of responsibilities, which may include setting executive compensation. Nothing in the DGCL mandates that the entire board must make those decisions. At Disney, the responsibility to consider and approve executive compensation was allocated to the compensation committee, as distinguished from the full board. The Chancellor's ruling—that executive compensation was to be fixed by the compensation committee—is legally correct.

[...] [55]

(c)

[...]

(d) HOLDING THAT THE COMPENSATION COMMITTEE MEMBERS DID NOT FAIL TO EXERCISE DUE CARE IN APPROVING THE OEA

The appellants next challenge the Chancellor's determination that although the compensation committee's decision-making process fell far short of corporate governance "best practices," the committee members breached no duty of care in considering and approving the NFT terms of the OEA. That conclusion is reversible error, the appellants claim, because the record establishes that the compensation committee members did not properly inform themselves of the material facts and, hence, were grossly negligent in approving the NFT provisions of the OEA.

The appellants advance five reasons why a reversal is compelled: (i) not all committee members reviewed a draft of the OEA; (ii) the minutes of the September 26, 1995 compensation committee meeting do not recite any discussion of the grounds for which Ovitz could receive a non-fault termination; (iii) the committee members did not consider any comparable employment agreements or the economic impact of extending the exercisability of the options being granted to Ovitz; (iv) Crystal did not attend the September 26, 1995 committee meeting, nor was his letter distributed to or discussed with Poitier and Lozano; and (v) Poitier and Lozano did not review the spreadsheets generated by Watson. These contentions amount essentially to an [56] attack upon underlying factual findings that will be upheld where they result from the Chancellor's assessment of live testimony.

Although the appellants have balkanized their due care claim into several fragmented parts, the overall thrust of that claim is that the compensation committee approved the OEA with NFT provisions that could potentially result in an enormous payout, without informing themselves of what the full magnitude of that payout could be. Rejecting that claim, the Court of Chancery found that the compensation committee members were adequately informed. The issue thus becomes whether that finding is supported by the evidence of record. We conclude that it is.

In our view, a helpful approach is to compare what actually happened here to what would have occurred had the committee followed a "best practices" (or "best case") scenario, from a process standpoint. In a "best case" scenario, all committee members would have received, before or at the committee's first meeting on September 26, 1995, a spreadsheet or similar document prepared by (or with the assistance of) a compensation expert (in this case, Graef Crystal). Making different, alternative assumptions, the spreadsheet would disclose the amounts that Ovitz could receive under the OEA in each circumstance that might foreseeably arise. One variable in that matrix of possibilities would be the cost to Disney of a non-fault termination for each of the five years of the initial term of the OEA. The contents of the spreadsheet would be explained to the committee members, either by the expert who prepared it or by a fellow committee member similarly knowledgeable about the subject. That spreadsheet, which ultimately would become an exhibit to the minutes of the compensation committee meeting, would form the basis of the committee's deliberations and decision.

Had that scenario been followed, there would be no dispute (and no basis for litigation) over what information was furnished to the committee members or when it was furnished. Regrettably, the committee's informational and decisionmaking process used here was not so tidy. That is one reason why the Chancellor found that although the committee's process did not fall below the level required for a proper exercise of due care, it did fall short of what best practices would have counseled.

The Disney compensation committee met twice: on September 26 and October 16, 1995. The minutes of the September 26 meeting reflect that the committee approved the terms of the OEA (at that time embodied in the form of a letter agreement), except for the option grants, which were not approved until October 16—after the Disney stock incentive plan had been amended to provide for those options. At the September 26 meeting, the compensation committee considered a "term sheet" which, in summarizing the material terms of the OEA, relevantly disclosed that in the event of a non-fault termination, Ovitz would receive: (i) the present value of his salary ($1 million per year) for the balance of the contract term, (ii) the present value of his annual bonus payments (computed at $7.5 million) for the balance of the contract term, (iii) a $10 million termination fee, and (iv) the acceleration of his options for 3 million shares, [57] which would become immediately exercisable at market price.

Thus, the compensation committee knew that in the event of an NFT, Ovitz's severance payment alone could be in the range of $40 million cash, plus the value of the accelerated options. Because the actual payout to Ovitz was approximately $130 million, of which roughly $38.5 million was cash, the value of the options at the time of the NFT payout would have been about $91.5 million. Thus, the issue may be framed as whether the compensation committee members knew, at the time they approved the OEA, that the value of the option component of the severance package could reach the $92 million order of magnitude if they terminated Ovitz without cause after one year. The evidentiary record shows that the committee members were so informed.

On this question the documentation is far less than what best practices would have dictated. There is no exhibit to the minutes that discloses, in a single document, the estimated value of the accelerated options in the event of an NFT termination after one year. The information imparted to the committee members on that subject is, however, supported by other evidence, most notably the trial testimony of various witnesses about spreadsheets that were prepared for the compensation committee meetings.

The compensation committee members derived their information about the potential magnitude of an NFT payout from two sources. The first was the value of the "benchmark" options previously granted to Eisner and Wells and the valuations by Watson of the proposed Ovitz options. [...]

The committee's second source of information was the amount of "downside protection" that Ovitz was demanding. Ovitz required financial protection from the risk of leaving a very lucrative and secure position at CAA, of which he was a controlling partner, to join a publicly held corporation [58] to which Ovitz was a stranger, and that had a very different culture and an environment which prevented him from completely controlling his destiny. The committee members knew that by leaving CAA and coming to Disney, Ovitz would be sacrificing "booked" CAA commissions of $150 to $200 million—an amount that Ovitz demanded as protection against the risk that his employment relationship with Disney might not work out. [...]

It is on this record that the Chancellor found that the compensation committee was informed of the material facts relating to an NFT payout. If measured in terms of the documentation that would have been generated if "best practices" had been followed, that record leaves much to be desired. The Chancellor acknowledged that, and so do we. But, the Chancellor also found that despite its imperfections, the evidentiary record was sufficient to support the conclusion that the compensation committee had adequately informed itself of the potential magnitude of the entire severance package, including the options, that Ovitz would receive in the event of an early NFT.

The OEA was specifically structured to compensate Ovitz for walking away from $150 million to $200 million of anticipated commissions from CAA over the five-year OEA contract term. This meant that if Ovitz was terminated without cause, the earlier in the contract term the termination occurred the larger the severance amount would be to replace the lost commissions. Indeed, because Ovitz was terminated after only one year, the total amount of his severance payment (about $130 million) closely approximated the lower end of the range of Ovitz's forfeited commissions ($150 million), less the compensation Ovitz received during his first and only year as Disney's President. Accordingly, the Court of Chancery had a sufficient evidentiary basis in the record from which to find that, at the time they approved the OEA, the compensation committee members were adequately informed of the potential magnitude of an early NFT severance payout.

Exposing the lack of merit in appellants' core due care claim enables us to address more cogently (and expeditiously) the appellants' fragmented subsidiary arguments. First, the appellants argue that not all members of the compensation committee reviewed the then-existing draft of the OEA. The Chancellor properly found that that was not required, because in this case the compensation committee was informed of the substance of the OEA.

Second, appellants point out that the minutes of the September 26 compensation committee meeting recite no discussion of the grounds for which Ovitz could receive a non-fault termination. But the term sheet did include a description of the consequences of a not-for-cause termination, and the Chancellor found that although "no one on the committee recalled any discussion concerning the meaning of gross [59] negligence or malfeasance," those terms "were not foreign to the board of directors, as the language was standard, and could be found, for example, in Eisner's, Wells', Katzenberg's and Roth's employment contracts."

Third, contrary to the appellants' position, the compensation committee members did consider comparable employment agreements. [...]

Fourth, the appellants stress that Crystal did not make a report in person to the compensation committee at its September 26 meeting. Although that is true, it is undisputed that Crystal was available by phone if the committee members had questions that could not be answered by those who were present. Moreover, Russell and Watson related the substance of Crystal's analysis and information to the committee. The Court of Chancery noted (and we agree) that although it might have been the better course of action, it was "not necessary for an expert to make a formal presentation at the committee meeting in order for the board to rely on that expert's analysis.…." Nor did the Chancellor find merit to the appellants' related argument that two committee members, Poitier and Lozano, were not entitled to rely upon the work performed by Russell, Watson and Crystal in August and September 1995, without having first seen all of the written materials generated during that process or having participated in the discussions held during that time. In reaching a contrary conclusion, the Chancellor found:

> The compensation committee reasonably believed that the analysis of the terms of the OEA was within Crystal's professional or expert competence, and together with Russell and Watson's professional competence in those same areas, the committee relied on the information, opinions, reports and statements made by Crystal, even if Crystal did not relay the information, opinions, reports and statements in person to the committee as a whole. Crystal's analysis was not so deficient that the compensation committee would have reason to question it. Furthermore, Crystal appears to have been selected with reasonable care, especially in light of his previous engagements with the Company in connection with past executive compensation contracts that were structurally, at least, similar to the OEA. For all these reasons, the compensation committee also is entitled to the protections of 8 *Del. C.* § 141(e) in relying upon Crystal.

The Chancellor correctly applied Section 141(e) in upholding the reliance of Lozano and Poitier upon the information that Crystal, Russell and Watson furnished to [60] them. [...]

Finally, the appellants contend that Poitier and Lozano did not review the spreadsheets generated by Watson at the September 26 meeting. The short answer is that even if Poitier and Lozano did not review the spreadsheets themselves, Russell and Watson adequately informed them of the spreadsheets' contents. [...]

For these reasons, we uphold the Chancellor's determination that the compensation committee members did not breach their fiduciary duty of care in approving the OEA.

(e) HOLDING THAT THE REMAINING DISNEY DIRECTORS DID NOT FAIL TO EXERCISE DUE CARE IN APPROVING THE HIRING OF OVITZ AS THE PRESIDENT OF DISNEY

The appellants' final claim in this category is that the Court of Chancery erroneously held that the remaining members of the old Disney board had not breached their duty of care in electing Ovitz as President of Disney. This claim lacks merit, because the arguments appellants advance in this context relate to a different subject—the approval of the OEA, which was the responsibility delegated to the compensation committee, not the full board.

The appellants argue that the Disney directors breached their duty of care by failing to inform themselves of all material information reasonably available with respect to Ovitz's employment agreement. We need not dwell on the specifics of this argument, because in substance they repeat the gross negligence claims previously leveled at the compensation committee—claims that were rejected by the Chancellor and now also by this Court. [61] The only properly reviewable action of the entire board was its decision to elect Ovitz as Disney's President. In that context the sole issue, as the Chancellor properly held, is "whether [the remaining members of the old board] properly exercised their business judgment and acted in accordance with their fiduciary duties when they elected Ovitz to the Company's presidency." The Chancellor determined that in electing Ovitz, the directors were informed of all information reasonably available and, thus, were not grossly negligent. We agree.

The Chancellor found and the record shows the following: well in advance of the September 26, 1995 board meeting the directors were fully aware that the Company needed—especially in light of Wells' death and Eisner's medical problems—to hire a "number two" executive and potential successor to Eisner. There had been many discussions about that need and about potential candidates who could fill that role even before Eisner decided to try to recruit Ovitz. Before the September 26 board meeting Eisner had individually discussed with each director the possibility of hiring Ovitz, and Ovitz's background and qualifications. The directors thus knew of Ovitz's skills, reputation and experience, all of which they believed would be highly valuable to the Company. The directors also knew that to accept a position at Disney, Ovitz would have to walk away from a very successful business—a reality that would lead a reasonable person to believe that Ovitz would likely succeed in similar pursuits elsewhere in the industry. The directors also knew of the public's highly positive reaction to the Ovitz announcement, and that Eisner and senior management had supported the Ovitz hiring. Indeed, Eisner, who had long desired to bring Ovitz within the Disney fold, consistently vouched for Ovitz's qualifications and told the directors that he could work well with Ovitz.

The board was also informed of the key terms of the OEA (including Ovitz's salary, bonus and options). Russell reported this information to them at the September 26, 1995 executive session, which was attended by Eisner and all non-executive directors. Russell also reported on the compensation committee meeting that had immediately preceded the executive session. And, both Russell and Watson responded to questions from the board. Relying upon the compensation committee's approval of the OEA and the other information furnished to them, the Disney directors, after further deliberating, unanimously elected Ovitz as President.

Based upon this record, we uphold the Chancellor's conclusion that, when electing Ovitz to the Disney presidency the remaining Disney directors were fully informed of all material facts, and that the appellants [62] failed to establish any lack of due care on the directors' part.

2. The Good Faith Determinations

The Court of Chancery held that the business judgment rule presumptions protected the decisions of the compensation committee and the remaining Disney directors, not only because they had acted with due care but also because they had not acted in bad faith. That latter ruling, the appellants claim, was reversible error because the Chancellor formulated and then applied an incorrect definition of bad faith.

In its Opinion the Court of Chancery defined bad faith as follows:

> Upon long and careful consideration, I am of the opinion that the concept of *intentional dereliction of duty,* a *conscious disregard for one's responsibilities,* is an appropriate (although not the only) standard for determining whether fiduciaries have acted in good faith. Deliberate indifference and inaction *in the face of a duty to act* is, in my mind, conduct that is clearly disloyal to the corporation. It is the epitome of faithless conduct.

[...]

The appellants essentially concede that their proof of bad faith is insufficient to satisfy the standard articulated by the Court of Chancery. That is why they ask this Court to treat a failure to exercise due care as a failure to act in good faith. Unfortunately for appellants, that "rule," even if it were accepted, would not help their case. If we were to conflate these two duties and declare that a breach of the duty to be properly informed violates the duty to act in good faith, the outcome would be no different, because, as the Chancellor and we now have held, the appellants failed to establish any breach of the duty of care. To say it differently, even if the Chancellor's definition of bad faith were erroneous, the error would not be reversible because the appellants cannot satisfy the very test they urge us to adopt.

For that reason, our analysis of the appellants' bad faith claim could end at this point. In other circumstances it would. This case, however, is one in which the duty to act in good faith has played a prominent role, yet to date is not a well-developed area of our corporate fiduciary law. Although the good faith concept has recently been the subject of considerable scholarly writing, which includes articles [64] focused on this specific case, the duty to act in good faith is, up to this point relatively uncharted. Because of the increased recognition of the importance of good faith, some conceptual guidance to the corporate community may be helpful. For that reason we proceed to address the merits of the appellants' second argument.

The precise question is whether the Chancellor's articulated standard for bad faith corporate fiduciary conduct—intentional dereliction of duty, a conscious disregard for one's responsibilities—is legally correct. In approaching that question, we note that the Chancellor characterized that definition as *"an* appropriate *(although not the only)* standard for determining whether fiduciaries have acted in good faith." That observation is accurate and helpful, because as a matter of simple logic, at least three different categories of fiduciary behavior are candidates for the "bad faith" pejorative label.

The first category involves so-called "subjective bad faith," that is, fiduciary conduct motivated by an actual intent to do harm. That such conduct constitutes classic, quintessential bad faith is a proposition so well accepted in the liturgy of fiduciary law that it borders on axiomatic. We need not dwell further on this category, because no such conduct is claimed to have occurred, or did occur, in this case.

The second category of conduct, which is at the opposite end of the spectrum, involves lack of due care—that is, fiduciary action taken solely by reason of gross negligence and without any malevolent intent. In this case, appellants assert claims of gross negligence to establish breaches not only of director due care but also of the directors' duty to act in good faith. Although the Chancellor found, and we agree, that the appellants failed to establish gross negligence, to afford guidance we address the issue of whether gross negligence (including a failure to [65] inform one's self of available material facts), without more, can also constitute bad faith. The answer is clearly no.

From a broad philosophical standpoint, that question is more complex than would appear, if only because (as the Chancellor and others have observed) "issues of good faith are (to a certain degree) inseparably and necessarily intertwined with the duties of care and loyalty...." But, in the pragmatic, conduct-regulating legal realm which calls for more precise conceptual line drawing, the answer is that grossly negligent conduct, without more, does not and cannot constitute a breach of the fiduciary duty to act in good faith. The conduct that is the subject of due care may overlap with the conduct that comes within the rubric of good faith in a psychological sense, but from a legal standpoint those duties are and must remain quite distinct. Both our legislative history and our common law jurisprudence distinguish sharply between the duties to exercise due care and to act in good faith, and highly significant consequences flow from that distinction.

The Delaware General Assembly has addressed the distinction between bad faith and a failure to exercise due care (*i.e.*, gross negligence) in two separate contexts. The first is Section 102(b)(7) of the DGCL, which authorizes Delaware corporations, by a provision in the certificate of incorporation, to exculpate their directors from monetary damage liability for a breach of the duty of care. That exculpatory provision affords significant protection to directors of Delaware corporations. The statute carves out several exceptions, however, including most relevantly, "for acts or omissions not in good faith...." Thus, a corporation can exculpate its directors from monetary liability for a breach of the duty of care, but not for conduct that is not in good faith. To adopt a definition of bad faith that would cause a violation of the duty of care automatically to become an act or omission "not in good faith," would eviscerate the protections accorded to directors by the General Assembly's adoption of Section 102(b)(7).

A second legislative recognition of the distinction between fiduciary conduct that is grossly negligent and conduct that is not in good faith, is Delaware's indemnification statute, found at 8 *Del. C.* § 145. To oversimplify, subsections (a) and (b) of that statute permit a corporation to indemnify (*inter alia*) any person who is or was a director, officer, employee or agent of the corporation against expenses (including attorneys' fees), judgments, fines and amounts paid in settlement of specified actions, suits or proceedings, where (among other things): (i) that person is, was, or is threatened to be made a party to that action, suit or proceeding, and (ii) that person "acted in good faith and in a manner the person reasonably believed to be in or not opposed to the best interests of the [66] corporation...." Thus, under Delaware statutory law a director or officer of a corporation can be indemnified for liability (and litigation expenses) incurred by reason of a violation of the duty of care, but not for a violation of the duty to act in good faith.

Section 145, like Section 102(b)(7), evidences the intent of the Delaware General Assembly to afford significant protections to directors (and, in the case of Section 145, other fiduciaries) of Delaware corporations. To adopt a definition that conflates the duty of care with the duty to act in good faith by making a violation of the former an automatic violation of the latter, would nullify those legislative protections and defeat the General Assembly's intent. There is no basis in policy, precedent or common sense that would justify dismantling the distinction between gross negligence and bad faith.

That leaves the third category of fiduciary conduct, which falls in between the first two categories of (1) conduct motivated by subjective bad intent and (2) conduct resulting from gross negligence. This third category is what the Chancellor's definition of bad faith—intentional dereliction of duty, a conscious disregard for one's responsibilities—is intended to capture. The question is whether such misconduct is properly treated as a non-exculpable, non-indemnifiable violation of the fiduciary duty to act in good faith. In our view it must be, for at least two reasons.

First, the universe of fiduciary misconduct is not limited to either disloyalty in the classic sense (*i.e.,* preferring the adverse self-interest of the fiduciary or of a related person to the interest of the corporation) or gross negligence. Cases have arisen where corporate directors have no conflicting self-interest in a decision, yet engage in misconduct that is more culpable than simple inattention or failure to be informed of all facts material to the decision. To protect the interests of the corporation and its shareholders, fiduciary conduct of this kind, which does not involve disloyalty (as traditionally defined) but is qualitatively more culpable than gross negligence, should be proscribed. A vehicle is needed to address such violations doctrinally, and that doctrinal vehicle is the duty to act in good faith. [...]

Second, the legislature has also recognized this intermediate category of fiduciary misconduct, which ranks between conduct involving subjective bad faith and gross negligence. Section 102(b)(7)(ii) of the DGCL expressly denies money damage exculpation for "acts or omissions not in good faith or which involve intentional misconduct or a knowing violation of law." By its very terms that provision distinguishes between "intentional misconduct" and a "knowing violation of law" (both examples of subjective bad faith) on the one hand, and "acts...not in good faith," on the other. Because the statute exculpates directors only for conduct amounting to gross negligence, the statutory denial of exculpation for "acts...not in good faith" must encompass the intermediate category of misconduct captured by the Chancellor's definition of bad faith.

For these reasons, we uphold the Court of Chancery's definition as a legally appropriate, although not the exclusive, definition of fiduciary bad faith. We need go no further. To engage in an effort to craft (in the Court's words) "a definitive and categorical definition of the universe of acts that would constitute bad faith" would be unwise and is unnecessary to dispose of the issues presented on this appeal.

Having sustained the Chancellor's finding that the Disney directors acted in good [68] faith when approving the OEA and electing Ovitz as President, we next address the claims arising out of the decision to pay Ovitz the amount called for by the NFT provisions of the OEA.

B. Claims Arising From The Payment Of The NFT Severance Payout To Ovitz

The appellants advance three alternative claims (each accompanied by assorted subsidiary arguments) whose overall thrust is that even if the OEA approval was legally valid, the NFT severance payout to Ovitz pursuant to the OEA was not. Specifically, the appellants contend that: [...] (2) because Ovitz could have been terminated for cause, Litvack and Eisner acted without due care and in bad faith in reaching the contrary conclusion; and (3) the business judgment rule presumptions did not protect the new Disney board's acquiescence in the NFT payout, because the new board was not entitled to rely upon Eisner's and Litvack's contrary advice. Appellants urge that in rejecting these claims the Court of Chancery committed reversible error. We disagree.

[...]

2. In Concluding That Ovitz Could Not Be Terminated For Cause, Did Litvack or Eisner Breach Any Fiduciary Duty?

[...]the Chancellor determined independently, as a matter of fact and law, that (1) Ovitz had not engaged in any conduct as President that constituted gross negligence or malfeasance—the standard for an NFT under the OEA; and (2) in arriving at that same conclusion in 1996, Litvack and Eisner did not breach their fiduciary duty of care or their duty to act in good faith.

[...]

the appellants' true quarrel is with the factual findings that underlie the Court's legal conclusion. The appellants are unable, however, to show that those findings, all of which are based on extensive trial testimony, witness credibility determinations, and highly textured treatment in the Post-trial Opinion, are in any way wrong.

[...] As to Litvack, the Court of Chancery held:

> I do not intend to imply by these conclusions that Litvack was an infallible source of legal knowledge. Nevertheless, Litvack's less astute moments as a legal counsel do not impugn his good faith or preparedness in reaching his conclusions with respect to whether Ovitz could have been terminated for cause....

[...] With respect to Eisner, the Chancellor found [...]

> that Eisner's actions in connection with the termination are, for the most part, consistent with what is expected of a faithful fiduciary.[...]

Even though the Chancellor found much to criticize in Eisner's "imperial CEO" style of governance, nothing has been shown to overturn the factual basis for the Court's conclusion that, in the end, Eisner's conduct satisfied the standards required of him as a fiduciary.

3. Were The Remaining Directors Entitled To Rely Upon Eisner's And Litvack's Advice That Ovitz Could Not Be Fired For Cause?

The appellants' third claim of error challenges the Chancellor's conclusion that the remaining new board members could rely upon Litvack's and Eisner's advice that Ovitz could be terminated only without cause. The short answer to that challenge is that, for the reasons previously discussed, the advice the remaining directors received and relied upon was accurate. Moreover, the directors' reliance on that advice was found to be in good faith. Although formal board action was not necessary, the remaining directors all supported the decision to terminate Ovitz based on the information given by Eisner and Litvack. The Chancellor found credible the directors' testimony that they believed that Disney would be better off without Ovitz, and the appellants offer no basis to overturn that finding.

* * * *

To summarize, the Court of Chancery correctly determined that the decisions of the Disney defendants to approve the OEA, to hire Ovitz as President, and then to terminate him on an NFT basis, were protected business judgments, made without any violations of fiduciary duty. [...]

V. THE WASTE CLAIM

The appellants' final claim is that even if the approval of the OEA was protected by the business judgment rule presumptions, the payment of the severance amount to Ovitz constituted waste. [...]

To recover on a claim of corporate waste, the plaintiffs must shoulder the burden of proving that the exchange was "so one sided that no business person of ordinary, sound judgment could conclude that the corporation has received adequate consideration." A claim of waste will arise only in the rare, "unconscionable case where directors irrationally squander or give away corporate assets." This onerous standard for waste is a corollary of the proposition that where business judgment presumptions are applicable, the board's decision will be upheld unless it cannot be "attributed to any rational business purpose."

The claim that the payment of the NFT amount to Ovitz, without more, constituted waste is meritless on its face, because at the time the NFT amounts were paid, Disney was contractually obligated to pay them. The payment of a contractually obligated amount cannot constitute waste, unless the contractual obligation is itself wasteful. Accordingly, the proper focus of a waste analysis must be whether the amounts required to be paid in the event of an NFT were wasteful *ex ante*.

Appellants claim that the NFT provisions of the OEA were wasteful because they incentivized Ovitz to perform poorly in order to obtain payment of the NFT provisions. [...]

Specifically, the OEA gave Ovitz every incentive to leave the Company before serving out the full term of his contract. The appellants urge that although the OEA may have induced Ovitz to join Disney as President, no contractual safeguards were in place to retain him in that position. In essence, appellants claim that the NFT provisions of the OEA created an irrational incentive for Ovitz to get himself fired.

[75] That claim does not come close to satisfying the high hurdle required to establish waste. The approval of the NFT provisions in the OEA had a rational business purpose: to induce Ovitz to leave CAA, at what would otherwise be a considerable cost to him, in order to join Disney. The Chancellor found that the evidence does not support any notion that the OEA irrationally incentivized Ovitz to get himself fired. Ovitz had no control over whether or not he would be fired, either with or without cause. To suggest that at the time he entered into the OEA Ovitz would engineer an early departure at the cost of his extraordinary reputation in the entertainment industry and his historical friendship with Eisner, is not only fanciful but also without proof in the record. Indeed, the Chancellor found that it was "patently unreasonable to assume that Ovitz intended to perform just poorly enough to be fired quickly, but not so poorly that he could be terminated for cause."

We agree. Because the appellants have failed to show that the approval of the NFT terms of the OEA was not a rational business decision, their waste claim must fail.

VI. CONCLUSION

For the reasons stated above, the judgment of the Court of Chancery is affirmed.

D. Marchand v. Barnhill (Del. 2019)

The business judgment rule applies only to actions, not omissions (*Aronson v. Lewis*, 473 A.2d 805, 813 (Del. 1984)). For omissions, however, the standard of liability itself is deferential to directors. Delaware courts require "bad faith conduct ... to establish director oversight liability"—i.e., liability for omissions—and "the fiduciary duty violated by that conduct is the duty of loyalty" (*Stone v. Ritter*, 911 A.2d 362, 370 (Del. 2006)). Doctrinally then, you might say that the duty of care does not compel any action—inaction violates a duty only if it rises to the level of disloyalty. Specifically, under the so-called *Caremark* standard,

> the necessary conditions predicate for director oversight liability [are]: (a) the directors utterly failed to implement any reporting or information system or controls, *or* (b) having implemented such a system or controls, consciously failed to monitor or oversee its operations ... In either case, ... liability requires ... that the directors knew that they were not discharging their fiduciary obligations.

> — *Stone v. Ritter*, 911 A.2d 362, 370 (Del. 2006).

As always, the devil is in the details of how the doctrine is applied. For the longest time, Delaware courts had dismissed all *Caremark* claims. This changed with *Marchand v. Barnhill* (Del. 2019). Consider the following questions:

1. Facially, what is more deferential to corporate directors: the business judgment rule, or *Caremark*? Does the outcome in *Marchand* comport with your answer?

2. Can a *Caremark* violation be exculpated under DGCL 102(b)(7)?

3. Is it relevant for the outcome or reasoning in *Marchand* that the corporation harmed third parties (customers) and/or that it may have broken the law (e.g., FDA food safety regulations) as a result of the directors' alleged lack of oversight?

212 A.3d 805 (2019)

Jack L. MARCHAND II, Plaintiff Below, Appellant,

v.

John W. BARNHILL, Jr., Greg Bridges, Richard Dickson, Paul A. Ehlert, Jim E. Kruse, Paul W. Kruse, W.J. Rankin, Howard W. Kruse, Patricia I. Ryan, Dorothy McLeod MacInerney and Blue Bell Creameries USA, Inc., Defendants Below, Appellee.

No. 533, 2018.

Supreme Court of Delaware.

[...]

Upon appeal from the Court of Chancery. REVERSED and REMANDED.

[...]

Before STRINE, Chief Justice; VALIHURA, VAUGHN, SEITZ, and TRAYNOR, Justices, constituting the Court en Banc.

STRINE, Chief Justice:

Blue Bell Creameries USA, Inc., one of the country's largest ice cream manufacturers, suffered a *listeria* outbreak in early 2015, causing the company to recall all of its products, shut down production at all of its plants, and lay off over a third of its workforce. Blue Bell's failure to contain *listeria* 's spread in its manufacturing plants caused *listeria* to be present in its products and had sad consequences. Three people died as a result of the *listeria* outbreak. Less consequentially, but nonetheless important for this litigation, stockholders also suffered losses because, after the operational shutdown, Blue Bell suffered a liquidity crisis that forced it to accept a dilutive private equity investment.

Based on these unfortunate events, a stockholder brought a derivative suit ... against Blue Bell's directors claiming breaches of the defendants' fiduciary duties. The complaint alleges ... that the directors breached their duty of loyalty under *Caremark*.[1]

The defendants moved to dismiss the complaint [...] The Court of Chancery granted the motion [...] [T]he Court of Chancery held that the plaintiff did not plead any facts to support "his contention that the [Blue Bell] Board 'utterly' failed to adopt or implement any reporting and compliance systems." Although the plaintiff argued that Blue Bell's board had no supervisory structure in place to oversee "health, safety and sanitation controls and compliance," the Court of Chancery reasoned that "[w]hat Plaintiff really attempts to challenge is not the existence of monitoring and reporting controls, but the effectiveness of monitoring and reporting controls in particular instances," and "[t]his is not a valid theory under ... *Caremark* ."

In this opinion, we reverse [...] [T]he complaint alleges particularized facts that support a reasonable inference that the Blue Bell board failed to implement any system to monitor Blue Bell's food safety performance or compliance. Under *Caremark* and this Court's opinion in *Stone v. Ritter*, directors have a duty "to exercise oversight" and to monitor the corporation's operational viability, legal compliance, and financial performance. A board's "utter failure to attempt to assure a reasonable information and reporting system exists" is an act of bad faith in breach of the duty of loyalty.

As a monoline company that makes a single product-ice cream-Blue Bell can only thrive if its consumers enjoyed its products and were confident that its products were safe to eat. That is, one of Blue Bell's central compliance issues is food safety. Despite this fact, the complaint alleges that Blue Bell's board had no committee overseeing food safety, no full board-level process to address food safety issues, and no protocol by which the board was expected to be advised of food safety reports and developments. Consistent with this dearth of any board-level effort at monitoring, the complaint pleads particular facts supporting an inference that during a crucial period when yellow and red flags about food safety were presented to management, there was no equivalent reporting to the board and the board was not presented with any material information about food safety. Thus, the

---

[1] In re Caremark Int'l Inc. Derivative Litig., 698 A.2d 959 (Del. Ch.1996) (Allen, C.); [...]

complaint alleges specific facts that create a reasonable inference that the directors consciously failed "to attempt to assure a reasonable information and reporting system exist[ed]."

I. Background

A. Blue Bell's History and Operating Environment

i. History

Founded in 1907 in Brenham, Texas, Blue Bell Creameries USA, Inc. ("Blue Bell"), a Delaware corporation, produces and distributes ice cream under the Blue Bell banner [...]

ii. The Regulated Nature of Blue Bell's Industry

As a U.S. food manufacturer, Blue Bell operates in a heavily regulated industry. Under federal law, the Food and Drug Administration ("FDA") may set food quality standards, require food manufacturing facilities to register with the FDA, prohibit regulated manufacturers from placing adulterated food into interstate commerce, and hold companies liable if they place any adulterated foods into interstate commerce in violation of FDA rules. Blue Bell is "required to comply with regulations and establish controls to monitor for, avoid and remediate contamination and conditions that expose the Company and its products to the risk of contamination."

Specifically, FDA regulations require food manufacturers to conduct operations "with adequate sanitation principles"[22] and, in line with that obligation, "must prepare ... and implement a written food safety plan."[23] As part of a manufacturer's food safety plan, the manufacturer must include processes for conducting a hazard analysis that identifies possible food safety hazards, identifies and implements preventative controls to limit potential food hazards, implements process controls, implements sanitation controls, and monitors these preventative controls. Appropriate corporate officials must monitor these preventative controls.

Not only is Blue Bell subject to federal regulations, but it must also adhere to various state regulations. At the time of the *listeria* outbreak, Blue Bell operated in three states, and each had issued rules and regulations regarding the proper handling and production of food to ensure food safety.[25]

---

[22] 21 C.F.R. § 110.80
[23] *Id.* § 117.3.
[25] *Id.*

B. Plaintiff's Complaint

With that context out of the way, we briefly summarize the plaintiff's well-pled factual allegations and the reasonable inferences drawn from them.

The complaint starts by observing that, as a single-product food company, food safety is of obvious importance to Blue Bell. But despite the critical nature of food safety for Blue Bell's continued success, the complaint alleges that management turned a blind eye to red and yellow flags that were waved in front of it by regulators and its own tests, and the board-by failing to implement any system to monitor the company's food safety compliance programs-was unaware of any problems until it was too late.

i. The Run-Up to the *Listeria* Outbreak

According to the complaint, Blue Bell's issues began to emerge in 2009. At that time, Paul Kruse, Blue Bell's President and CEO, and his cousin, Paul Bridges, were responsible for the three plants Blue Bell operated in Texas, Oklahoma, and Alabama. The complaint alleges that, despite being responsible for overseeing plant operations, Paul Kruse and Bridges failed to respond to signs of trouble in the run up to the *listeria* outbreak. From 2009 to 2013 several regulators found troubling compliance failures at Blue Bell's facilities:

> • In July 2009, the FDA's inspection of the Texas facility revealed "two instances of condensation, one from a pipe carrying liquid caramel [that] was dripping into three gallon cartons waiting to be filled, and one dripping into ice cream sandwich wafers." The FDA reported these observations directly to Paul Kruse, who assured the FDA that "condensation is treated by Blue Bell as a serious concern."

> • In March 2010, the Alabama Department of Health inspected the Alabama plant and "found equipment left on the floor and a ceiling in disrepair in the container forming room."

> • Two months later, in May 2010, the FDA returned to the Texas plant "and observed ten violations that were cited to Paul Kruse including, again, a condensation drip." While the condensation drip persisted from the FDA's last inspection of the Texas plant, the FDA also observed "ripped and open containers of ingredients, inconsistent hand-washing and glove use and a spider and its web near the ingredients."

> • In July 2011, an inspection by "the Alabama Department of Public Health cited drips from a ceiling unit and pipelines, standing water, open tank lids and unprotected measuring cups."

• Nine months later, in March 2012, an inspection of the Oklahoma facility revealed the plant's " '[f]ailure to manufacture foods under conditions and controls necessary to minimize contamination' and '[f]ailure to handle and maintain equipment, containers and utensils used to hold food in [sic] manner that protects against contamination.'"

• That same month, in March 2012, "[t]he Alabama Department of Public Health required five changes" to the Alabama facility, "including instructions to clean various rooms and items, make repairs and [sic] after fruit processing to prevent contamination." A year later, "in March 2013, the Alabama Department of Public Health again ordered cleaning and repairs and observed an uncapped fruit tank." The Alabama Department of Public Health made similar observations in a July 2014 inspection.

Regulatory inspections during this time were not the only signal that Blue Bell faced potential health safety risks. In 2013, "the Company had five positive tests" for *listeria*, and in January 2014, "the Company received a presumptive positive *[l]isteria* result reports from the third party laboratory for the [Oklahoma] facility on January 20, 2014 and the samples reported positive for a second time on January 24, 2014."

Although management had received reports about *listeria* 's growing presence in Blue Bell's plants, the complaint alleges that the board never received any information about *listeria* or more generally about food safety issues. Minutes from the board's January 29, 2014 meeting "reflect no report or discussion of the increasingly frequent positive tests that had been occurring since 2013 or the third party lab reports received in the preceding two weeks." Board meeting minutes from February and March likewise reflect no board-level discussion of *listeria*.

During the rest of 2014, Blue Bell's problems accelerated, but the board remained uninformed about Blue Bell's problems. In April, "[t]he Company received further positive *[l]isteria* lab tests regarding [the Oklahoma facility]." That same month, the company had three "positive coliform tests far above the known legal regulator limits." Yet, minutes from the April board meeting reflected no discussion of *listeria*. Instead, the minutes note only that the Oklahoma and Alabama facilities' "plant operations were discussed briefly" and that Bridges also discussed "a good report from the TCEQ [Texas Commission on Environmental Quality]."

Over the course of 2014, Blue Bell received ten positive tests for *listeria*. According to the complaint, these positive tests "included repeated positive results from the Company's third party laboratory in 2014, on consecutive samples, evidencing the inadequacy of the Company's remedial methods to eliminate the contamination."

Despite management's knowledge of the growing problem, the complaint alleges that this information never made its way to the board, and the board continued to be uninformed about (and thus unaware of) the problem. Minutes from the board's 2014 meetings are bereft of reports on the *listeria* issues. Only during the September meeting is sanitation discussed, when Bridges informed the board that "[t]he recent Silliker audit [Blue Bell's third-party auditor for sanitation issues in 2014] went well." This lone reference to a third-party audit is the only instance, until the *listeria* outbreak forced the recall of Blue Bell's products, of *any* board-level discussion regarding food safety.

At this stage of the case, we are bound to draw all fair inferences in the plaintiff's favor from the well-pled facts. Based on this chronology of events, the plaintiffs have fairly pled that:

• Blue Bell had no board committee charged with monitoring food safety;

• Blue Bell's full board did not have a process where a portion of the board's meetings each year, for example either quarterly or biannually, were specifically devoted to food safety compliance; and

• The Blue Bell board did not have a protocol requiring or have any expectation that management would deliver key food safety compliance reports or summaries of these reports to the board on a consistent and mandatory basis. In fact, it is inferable that there was no expectation of reporting to the board of any kind.

In short, the complaint pleads that the Blue Bell board had made no effort at all to implement a board-level system of mandatory reporting of any kind.

ii. The *Listeria* Outbreak and the Board's Response

Blue Bell's *listeria* problem spread in 2015. Starting in January 2015, one of Blue Bell's product tests had positive coliform levels above legal limits. The same result appeared in February 2015. And by this point, the problem spread to Blue Bell's products and spiraled out of control.

On February 13, 2015, "Blue Bell received notification that the Texas Department of State Health Services also had positive tests for [*l*]*isteria* in Blue Bell samples." The Texas Department of State Health Services was alerted to these positive tests by the South Carolina Health Department. Company swabs at the Texas facility on February 19 and 21, 2015 tested positive for *listeria*. Yet despite these reports to management, Blue Bell's board was not informed by management about the severe problem. The board met on February 19, 2015, following Blue Bell's annual stockholders meeting, but there was no *listeria* discussion.

Four days later, Blue Bell initiated a limited recall. Two days after that, Blue Bell's board met, and Bridges reported that "[t]he FDA is working with Texas health inspectors regarding the Company's recent recall of products. More information is developing and should be known within the next days or weeks." Despite two years of evidence that *listeria* was a growing problem for Blue Bell, this is the first time the board discussed the issue, according to the complaint and the incorporated board minutes. Instead of holding more frequent emergency board meetings to receive constant updates on the troubling fact that life-threatening bacteria was found in its products, Blue Bell's board left the company's response to management.

And the problem got worse, with awful effects. "In early March 2015, health authorities reported that they suspected a connection between human [*l*]*isteria* infections in Kansas and products made by Blue Bell's [Texas] facility." The outbreak in Kansas matched a *listeria* strain found in Blue Bell's products in South Carolina. And by March 23, 2015, Blue Bell was forced to recall more products. Two days later, Blue Bell's board met and adopted a resolution "express[ing] support for Blue Bell's CEO, management, and employees and encourag[ing] them to ensure that everything Blue Bell manufacture[s] and distributes is a wholesome and good testing [sic] product that our consumers deserve and expect."

Blue Bell expanded the recall two weeks later, and less than a month later, on April 20, 2015, Blue Bell "instituted a recall of all products." By this point, the Center for Disease Controls and Prevention ("CDC") had begun an investigation and discovered that the source of the *listeria* outbreak in Kansas was caused by Blue Bell's Texas and Oklahoma plants. Ultimately, five adults in Kansas and three adults in Texas were sickened by Blue Bell's products; three of the five Kansas adults died because of complications due to *listeria* infection. The CDC issued a recall to grocers and retailers, alerting them to the contamination and warning them against selling the products.

After Blue Bell's full product recall, the FDA inspected each of the company's three plants. Each was found to have major deficiencies. In the Texas plant, the FDA found a "failure to manufacture foods under conditions and controls necessary to minimize the potential for growth of microorganisms," inadequate cleaning and sanitizing procedures, "failure to maintain buildings in repair sufficient to prevent food from coming [sic] adulterated," and improper construction of the building that failed to prevent condensation from occurring. Likewise, at the Oklahoma facility, "[t]he FDA found that the Company had been receiving increasingly frequent positive [*l*]*isteria* tests at [the Oklahoma facility] for over three years," failed "to manufacture and package foods under conditions and controls necessary to minimize the potential growth of microorganisms and contamination," failed to perform testing to ferret out microbial growth, implemented inadequate cleaning and sterilization procedures, failed to provide running water at an appropriate temperature to sanitize equipment, and failed to store food in clean and sanitized portable equipment.

Although the Alabama facility fared better, the FDA still found contamination and several issues, including the "failure to perform microbial testing where necessary to identify possible food contamination," "failure to maintain food contact surfaces to protect food from contamination by any source," and inadequate construction of the facility such that condensation was likely. Most of these findings, the complaint alleges, are unsurprising because similar deficiencies were found by the FDA and state regulators in the run up to the *listeria* outbreak, yet according to the FDA's inspection after the fact, it appeared that neither management nor the board made progress on remedying these deficiencies.

After the fact, various news outlets interviewed former Blue Bell employees who "claimed that Company management ignored complaints about factory conditions in [the Texas facility]." One former employee "reported [that] spilled ice cream was left to pool on the floor, 'creating an environment where bacteria could flourish.'" Another former employee described being "instructed to pour ice cream and fruit that dripped off his machine into mix to be used later."

iii. The Aftermath of the *Listeria* Outbreak

With its operations shuttered, Blue Bell faced a liquidity crisis. Blue Bell initially sought a more traditional credit facility to bridge its liquidity, but after Blue Bell director W.J. Rankin informed his brother-in-law, Bill Reimann, about Blue Bell's liquidity crunch, Blue Bell ended up striking a deal with Moo Partners, a fund controlled by Sid Bass and affiliated with Reimann. Moo Partners provided Blue Bell with a $125 million credit facility and purchased a $100 million warrant to acquire 42% of Blue Bell at $50,000 per share. As part of Moo Partners's investment conditions, Blue Bell also amended its certificate of incorporation to grant Moo the right to appoint one member of Blue Bell's board who would be entitled to one-third of the board's voting power (or five votes based on a then-10-member board).

After investing in Blue Bell, Moo named Reimann to Blue Bell's board, expanding the board to 11 members with Reimann possessing five votes. In February 2016, Reimann suggested that the board separate the roles of CEO and Chairman (both held by Paul Kruse). The board voted to follow Reimann's recommendation at its February 18th meeting, but after Paul Kruse disagreed with the recommendation and threatened to resign as President and CEO if the split occurred, the board held another vote in which all members, except Reimann and Rankin, voted to restore the position of CEO and Chairman of the board.

C. The Court of Chancery Dismisses the Case

After requesting Blue Bell's books and records through a § 220 request, the plaintiff, a Blue Bell stockholder, sued Blue Bell's [...] board derivatively, asserting [a] claim[] based on ... the board's violation of its duty of loyalty, under *Caremark*, by failing to implement any reporting system and therefore failing to inform itself about Blue Bell's food safety compliance. The Court of Chancery dismissed [...], holding that the plaintiff failed to [meet Delaware's pleading standard for derivative actions, cf. chapter 5].

[...] The Court of Chancery [...] rejected the plaintiff's [...] claim that Blue Bell's directors breached their duty of loyalty under *Caremark* by failing to "institute a system of controls and reporting" regarding food safety. In support of this claim, the plaintiff asserted, based on the facts alleged in the complaint and reasonable inferences from those facts, that: (1) the Blue Bell board had no committee overseeing food safety; (2) Blue Bell's board did not have any reporting system in place about food safety; (3) management knew about the growing *listeria* issues but did not report those issues to the board, further evidence that the board had no food safety reporting system in place; and (4) the board did not discuss food safety at its regular board meetings.

Rejecting the plaintiff's *Caremark* claim, the Vice Chancellor started by observing that "[d]espite the far-reaching regulatory schemes that governed Blue Bell's operations at the time of the [*l*]*isteria* contamination, the Complaint contains no allegations that Blue Bell failed to implement the monitoring and reporting systems required by the FDCA [Federal Food, Drug, and Cosmetic Act], FDA regulations or state statutes (or that it was ever cited for such a failure)." In fact, the Court of Chancery concluded that "documents incorporated by reference in the Complaint reveal that Blue Bell distributed a sanitation manual with standard operating and reporting procedures, and promulgated written procedures for processing and reporting consumer complaints." And at the board level, the Vice Chancellor noted that "[b]oth Bridges and Paul Kruse ... provided regular reports regarding Blue Bell operations to the ... Board," including reports about audits of Blue Bell's facilities.

Based on Blue Bell's compliance with FDA regulations, ongoing third-party monitoring for contamination, and consistent reporting by senior management to Blue Bell's board on operations, the Court of Chancery concluded that there was a monitoring system in place. At bottom, the Court of Chancery opined that "[w]hat Plaintiff really attempts to challenge is not the *existence* of monitoring and reporting controls, but the *effectiveness* of monitoring and reporting controls in particular instances." That, the Court of Chancery held, does not state a *Caremark* claim. As a result, the court held that demand was not excused as to the *Caremark* claims and dismissed the complaint.

The plaintiff timely appealed from that dismissal.

II. Analysis

We review a motion to dismiss for failure to [meet the pleading standard] *de novo*. [...]

Although *Caremark* claims are difficult to plead and ultimately to prove out, we nonetheless disagree with the Court of Chancery's decision to dismiss the plaintiff's claim against the Blue Bell board.

Under *Caremark* and *Stone v. Ritter*, a director must make a good faith effort to oversee the company's operations. Failing to make that good faith effort breaches the duty of loyalty and can expose a director to liability. In other words, for a plaintiff to prevail on a *Caremark* claim, the plaintiff must show that a fiduciary acted in bad faith-"the state of mind traditionally used to define the mindset of a disloyal director."

Bad faith is established, under *Caremark*, when "the directors [completely] fail[ ] to implement any reporting or information system or controls[,] or ... having implemented such a system or controls, consciously fail[ ] to monitor or oversee its operations thus disabling themselves from being informed of risks or problems requiring their attention."[102] In short, to satisfy their duty of loyalty, directors must make a good faith effort to implement an oversight system and then monitor it.

As with any other disinterested business judgment, directors have great discretion to design context- and industry-specific approaches tailored to their companies' businesses and resources. But *Caremark* does have a bottom-line requirement that is important: the board must make a good faith effort-*i.e.*, try-to put in place a reasonable board-level system of monitoring and reporting. Thus, our case law gives deference to boards and has dismissed *Caremark* cases even when illegal or harmful company activities escaped detection, when the plaintiffs have been unable to plead that the board failed to make the required good faith effort to put a reasonable compliance and reporting system in place.[105]

For that reason, our focus here is on the key issue of whether the plaintiff has pled facts from which we can infer that Blue Bell's board made no effort to put in place a board-level compliance system. That is, we are not examining the effectiveness of a board-level

---

[102] *Stone*, 911 A.2d at 370-72.

[105] *See, e.g., Stone*, 911 A.2d at 372-73 (dismissing a Caremark claim despite the fact that the company violated the Bank Secrecy Act and was fined $50 million); In re General Motors Derivative Litig., 2015 WL 3958724, at *1, *17 (Del. Ch. 2015) (dismissing a Caremark claim despite the fact that the company's actions "led to monetary loss on the part of the corporation, via fines, damages and punitive damages from lawsuits; reputational damage; and most distressingly, personal injury and death to GM customers"); In re Citigroup Inc. S'holder Derivative Litig., 964 A.2d at 127 (dismissing a Caremark claim despite the fact that the company suffered billions of dollars in losses because of its exposure to subprime mortgages).

compliance and reporting system after the fact. Rather, we are focusing on whether the complaint pleads facts supporting a reasonable inference that the board did not undertake good faith efforts to put a board-level system of monitoring and reporting in place.

Under *Caremark*, a director may be held liable if she acts in bad faith in the sense that she made no good faith effort to ensure that the company had in place any "system of controls." Here, the plaintiff did as our law encourages and sought out books and records about the extent of board-level compliance efforts at Blue Bell regarding what has to be one of the most central issues at the company: whether it is ensuring that the only product it makes-ice cream-is safe to eat.[107] Using these books and records, the complaint fairly alleges that before the *listeria* outbreak engulfed the company:

- no board committee that addressed food safety existed;

- no regular process or protocols that required management to keep the board apprised of food safety compliance practices, risks, or reports existed;

- no schedule for the board to consider on a regular basis, such as quarterly or biannually, any key food safety risks existed;

- during a key period leading up to the deaths of three customers, management received reports that contained what could be considered red, or at least yellow, flags, and the board minutes of the relevant period revealed no evidence that these were disclosed to the board;

- the board was given certain favorable information about food safety by management, but was not given important reports that presented a much different picture; and

- the board meetings are devoid of any suggestion that there was any regular discussion of food safety issues.

And the complaint goes on to allege that after the *listeria* outbreak, the FDA discovered a number of systematic deficiencies in all of Blue Bell's plants-such as plants being constructed "in such a manner as to [not] prevent drip and condensate from contaminating food, food-contact surfaces, and food-packing material"-that might have been rectified

---

[107] Though, to be fair and completely accurate, Blue Bell does make a few other related products, such as frozen yogurt.

had any reasonable reporting system that required management to relay food safety information to the board on an ongoing basis been in place.

In sum, the complaint supports an inference that no system of board-level compliance monitoring and reporting existed at Blue Bell. Although *Caremark* is a tough standard for plaintiffs to meet, the plaintiff has met it here. When a plaintiff can plead an inference that a board has undertaken no efforts to make sure it is informed of a compliance issue intrinsically critical to the company's business operation, then that supports an inference that the board has not made the good faith effort that *Caremark* requires.

In defending this case, the directors largely point out that by law Blue Bell had to meet FDA and state regulatory requirements for food safety, and that the company had in place certain manuals for employees regarding safety practices and commissioned audits from time to time. In the same vein, the directors emphasize that the government regularly inspected Blue Bell's facilities, and Blue Bell management got the results.

But the fact that Blue Bell nominally complied with FDA regulations does not imply that the *board* implemented a system to monitor food safety *at the board level*. Indeed, these types of routine regulatory requirements, although important, are not typically directed at the board. At best, Blue Bell's compliance with these requirements shows only that management was following, in a nominal way, certain standard requirements of state and federal law. It does not rationally suggest that the board implemented a reporting system to monitor food safety or Blue Bell's operational performance. The mundane reality that Blue Bell is in a highly regulated industry and complied with some of the applicable regulations does not foreclose any pleading-stage inference that the directors' lack of attentiveness rose to the level of bad faith indifference required to state a *Caremark* claim.

In answering the plaintiff's argument, the Blue Bell directors also stress that management regularly reported to them on "operational issues." This response is telling. In decisions dismissing *Caremark* claims, the plaintiffs usually lose because they must concede the existence of board-level systems of monitoring and oversight such as a relevant committee, a regular protocol requiring board-level reports about the relevant risks, or the board's use of third-party monitors, auditors, or consultants.[112] For example, in *Stone v.*

---

[112] See, e.g., City of Birmingham Ret. Sys. v. Good , 177 A.3d 47, 59 (Del. 2017) (affirming the Court of Chancery's dismissal of a Caremark claim because "reports to the board showed that the board 'exercised oversight by relying on periodic reports' from the officers" and that board presentations "identified issues with the coal ash disposal ponds, but also informed the board of the actions taken to address the regulatory concerns"); Stone , 911 A.2d at 372-73 (affirming the Court of Chancery's dismissal of a Caremark claim, in part, because an outside auditor's report "reflect[s] that the Board received and approved relevant policies and procedures, delegated to certain employees and departments the responsibility for filing [suspicious activity reports] and monitoring compliance, and exercised

Ritter , although the company paid $50 million in fines related "to the failure by bank employees" to comply with "the federal Bank Secrecy Act," the"[b]oard dedicated considerable resources to the [Bank Secrecy Act] compliance program and put into place numerous procedures and systems to attempt to ensure compliance." Accordingly, this Court affirmed the Court of Chancery's dismissal of a *Caremark* claim. Here, the Blue Bell directors just argue that because Blue Bell management, in its discretion, discussed general operations with the board, a *Caremark* claim is not stated.

But if that were the case, then *Caremark* would be a chimera. At every board meeting of any company, it is likely that management will touch on some operational issue. Although *Caremark* may not require as much as some commentators wish, it does require that a board make a good faith effort to put in place a reasonable system of monitoring and reporting about the corporation's central compliance risks. In Blue Bell's case, food safety was essential and mission critical. The complaint pled facts supporting a fair inference that no board-level system of monitoring or reporting on food safety existed.

If *Caremark* means anything, it is that a corporate board must make a good faith effort to exercise its duty of care. A failure to make that effort constitutes a breach of the duty of loyalty. Where [...] a plaintiff [...] plead[s] facts supporting a fair inference that no reasonable compliance system and protocols were established as to the obviously most central consumer safety and legal compliance issue facing the company, that the board's lack of efforts resulted in it not receiving official notices of food safety deficiencies for several years, and that, as a failure to take remedial action, the company exposed consumers to *listeria*-infected ice cream, resulting in the death and injury of company customers, the plaintiff has met his onerous pleading burden and is entitled to discovery to prove out his claim.

---

oversight by relying on periodic reports from them"); In re General Motors Derivative Litig. , 2015 WL 3958724, at *14 (Del. Ch. 2015) (dismissing a Caremark claim where "GM had a system for reporting risk to the Board, but in the Plaintiffs' view it should have been a better system"); In re Citigroup Inc. S'holder Derivative Litig. , 964 A.2d 106, 127 (Del. Ch. 2009) (dismissing a Caremark claim because "[p]laintiffs do not contest that Citigroup had procedures and controls in place that were designed to monitor risk"); Desimone v. Barrows , 924 A.2d 908, 940 (Del. Ch. 2007) (dismissing a Caremark claim premised on the plaintiff's allegations that a properly formed and well-functioning audit committee must have known about options backdating despite the fact that management intentionally kept this information from the audit committee); Guttman v. Huang , 823 A.2d 492, 506-07 (Del. Ch. 2003) (dismissing a Caremark claim because the plaintiff failed to plead any particularized facts about the audit committee's lack of reporting or information systems).

III. Conclusion

We therefore reverse the Court of Chancery's decision and remand for proceedings consistent with this opinion.

Chapter 5. Shareholder Litigation

It is often said that corporate fiduciary duties are a U.S. specialty. It would be more accurate to say that shareholder litigation is the U.S. specialty. Fiduciary duties or something resembling them exist in all corporate laws that we know of. Most jurisdictions, however, severely limit shareholder litigation that could enforce these duties, relying instead on prohibitions, shareholder approval requirements, or perhaps even criminal law enforcement. Not so the U.S., particularly Delaware.

U.S. law provides two avenues for shareholders to enforce fiduciary duties in court: the direct action, and the derivative action. The direct action is a suit in the shareholder-plaintiff's own right (usually brought as a class action in the name of all such shareholders), whereas the derivative action is a suit on behalf of the corporation. The test for distinguishing **direct vs. derivative actions** in Delaware is

(1) who suffered the alleged harm (the corporation or the suing stock-holders, individually); and (2) who would receive the benefit of any recovery or other remedy (the corporation or the stock-holders, individually)?

— *Tooley v. DLJ*, 845 A. 2d 1031, 1033 (Del. 2004).

In practice, this means that shareholders can sue directly over mergers and other transactions that affect their status as shareholders, but not over transactions such as executive compensation that affect shareholders merely financially. For example, of the shareholder suit cases you have read so far, *Van Gorkom* was a direct (class) action, while *Sinclair*, *Disney*, and *Marchand* were derivative actions. The distinction matters because the demand requirement and the powers of the special litigation committee (see section A. below) apply only to derivative suits.

Like most litigation, shareholder litigation presents an obvious **dilemma**. On the one hand, fiduciary duties are toothless without shareholder litigation to enforce them. That is why courts encourage it with generous fee awards (see *Americas Mining* below). On the other hand, litigation is extremely expensive, especially the corporate sort. In particular, defendants can incur substantial costs in discovery even if the case never goes to trial, let alone results in a verdict for the plaintiff. In fiduciary duty suits, the main cost is the disruption caused by depositions of directors and managers and, more generally, their distraction from ordinary business. Opportunistic plaintiffs may threaten such litigation costs to extract a meritless settlement.

In other words, Delaware's reliance on fiduciary duties creates a conundrum: how to encourage meritorious suits while discouraging deleterious nuisance suits. Meritorious suits are necessary to enforce fiduciary duties and allow the courts to flesh out their content, whereas nuisance suits can be a costly drag on the system. Do the procedural peculiarities introduced in this section succeed in sorting the good shareholder litigation from the bad?

5.1 Derivative Actions: Demand Futility Test and SLCs

Two important filters apply only to derivative actions, not direct actions: The "demand futility" test, and dismissal by a special litigation committee (SLC) of the board. In theory, both can lead to dismissal at any stage of a derivative action. In practice, the demand futility test is invoked virtually exclusively at the motion to dismiss stage, and SLCs tend to be formed after the motion to dismiss was denied, often prompting a stay of discovery until the SLC has given its recommendation.

The **term "demand futility"** derives from the somewhat quaint idea that, in principle, a dissatisfied shareholder should first ask the board to bring the lawsuit, i.e., make a "demand" on the board. The shareholder should be allowed to sue in the corporation's name only (a) after the board wrongfully rejects the shareholder's demand or (b) if a demand seems "futile" because the board is hopelessly conflicted. In practice, it is very rare for plaintiffs to make a formal demand, and even rarer for boards to accede to it. If the board were inclined to sue, it would not need the shareholder's reminder, and in the practically relevant case where the board or some of its members are the potential defendant, the board will be very much not inclined to sue. The shareholder thus has little to gain from making a demand, but a lot to lose because Delaware courts consider a demand a concession that demand was not futile, i.e., that the board is impartial with respect to the suit. The only option for a shareholder whose demand was rejected would be to challenge the board's procedure in rejecting the demand—a near impossible task under the business judgment rule. Thus, shareholders just sue, alleging demand futility.

Substantively, the demand futility test lets a shareholder derivative suit proceed only if a majority of the board appears partial as to the outcome of the suit. But the test of partiality is not mechanical. Most importantly, merely naming a director as defendant is *not* enough to disqualify that director. Nor is it enough to make abstract allegations. Rather, the shareholder-plaintiff must allege *particularized facts* that allow a reasonable inference that a director breached his or her duty, has a self-interest in the underlying transaction, or is connected to someone ticking either of these boxes.

Crucially, this means the derivative plaintiff must be in possession of at least some pertinent incriminating facts before even being allowed to enter discovery. In the case of a derivative action against the entire board for violation of their duties, the demand futility test is thus a **heightened pleading standard**: the derivative complaint must allege particularized facts that suggest they may actually be liable. To meet this standard, would-be derivative plaintiffs make copious "books and records" requests under section 220 of the DGCL, often leading to separate "220 litigation" before a derivative lawsuit is even filed.

Demand futility is litigated in virtually every derivative action because defendants virtually always move to dismiss the complaint for failure to plead demand futility.

By contrast, **special litigation committees** are a rarer beast. This is in part because an SLC is unnecessary if the derivative action is dismissed for failure to plead demand futility, as most are. If the derivative action is not dismissed, boards often form an SLC composed of disinterested and independent directors and vested with the power to terminate the lawsuit should the continuation of the latter not serve the company's best interests. This forces courts into a balancing act:

> If, on the one hand, corporations can consistently wrest bona fide derivative actions away from well-meaning derivative plaintiffs through the use of the committee mechanism, the derivative suit will lose much, if not all, of its generally-recognized effectiveness as an intra-corporate means of policing boards of directors. If, on the other hand, corporations are unable to rid themselves of meritless or harmful litigation and strike suits, the derivative action, created to benefit the corporation, will produce the opposite, unintended result. [...]

> The context here is a suit against directors where demand on the board is excused. We think some tribute must be paid to the fact that the lawsuit was properly initiated. [... W]e have to be concerned about the creation of an 'Independent Investigation Committee' [...] years later, after the election of [some] new outside directors [who compose the committee]. Situations could develop where such motions could be filed after years of vigorous litigation for reasons unconnected with the merits of the lawsuit.

> Moreover, notwithstanding our conviction that Delaware law entrusts the corporate power to a properly authorized committee, we must be mindful that directors are passing judgment on fellow directors in the

same corporation and fellow directors, in this instance, who designated them to serve both as directors and committee members. The question naturally arises whether a 'there but for the grace of God go I' empathy might not play a role.

[...] We thus steer a middle course [...]

After an objective and thorough investigation of a derivative suit, an independent committee may cause its corporation to file a pretrial motion to dismiss in the Court of Chancery. The basis of the motion is the best interests of the corporation, as determined by the committee. The motion should include a thorough written record of the investigation and its findings and recommendations. [...] The Court should apply a two-step test to the motion.

First, the Court should inquire into the independence and good faith of the committee and the bases supporting its conclusions. Limited discovery may be ordered to facilitate such inquiries. The corporation should have the burden of proving independence, good faith and a reasonable investigation, rather than presuming independence, good faith and reasonableness. [...]

The second step provides, we believe, the essential key in striking the balance between legitimate corporate claims as expressed in a derivative stockholder suit and a corporation's best interests as expressed by an independent investigating committee. The Court should determine, applying its own independent business judgment, whether the motion should be granted. [...] The Court of Chancery of course must carefully consider and weigh how compelling the corporate interest in dismissal is when faced with a non-frivolous lawsuit. The Court of Chancery should, when appropriate, give special consideration to matters of law and public policy in addition to the corporation's best interests.

—*Zapata Co. v. Maldonado*, 430 A.2d. 779, 786-789 (Del. 1981) (footnotes and internal references omitted).

Questions

1. What is worse for derivative plaintiffs: dismissal because demand was not futile or later dismissal upon recommendation of an SLC?

2. What do you think the *Zapata* court means by the Chancery Court's "own independent business judgment"?

A. United Food and Com. Workers Union v. Zuckerberg

Zuckerberg is now the authoritative statement of the demand futility test. It merged separate formulations of the test adopted in two prior precedents, *Aronson* and *Rales*, and decided the important question of the role of exculpated claims for demand futility purposes.

Questions

1. What is the three-part test adopted in *Zuckerberg*?

2. What is the role of exculpated claims for demand futility according to *Zuckerberg*? What alternative role did the plaintiff argue for? Does it even matter given that, by definition, exculpated claims cannot give rise to liability?

262 A.3d 1034 (2021)

UNITED FOOD AND COMMERCIAL WORKERS UNION AND PARTICIPATING FOOD INDUSTRY EMPLOYERS TRI-STATE PENSION FUND, Plaintiff-Below, Appellant,

v.

Mark ZUCKERBERG, Marc Andreessen, Peter Thiel, Reed Hastings, Erskine B. Bowles, and Susan D. Desmond-Hellmann, Defendants-Below, Appellees and

Facebook, Inc., Nominal Defendant-Below, Appellee.

No. 404, 2020.

Supreme Court of Delaware.

Submitted: June 30, 2021.

Decided: September 23, 2021.

Court Below: Court of Chancery of the State of Delaware.

Upon appeal from the Court of Chancery. AFFIRMED.

P. Bradford deLeeuw, Esquire, DELEEUW LAW LLC, Wilmington, Delaware; Robert C. Schubert, Esquire, Willem F. Jonckheer, Esquire (argued), SCHUBERT JONCKHEER & KOLBE LLP, San Francisco, California; James E. Miller, Esquire, SHEPHERD FINKELMAN MILLER & SHAH, LLP, Chester, Connecticut; Attorneys for Appellant United Food and Commercial Workers Union and Participating Food Industry Employers Tri-State Pension Fund.

Kevin R. Shannon, Esquire, Berton W. Ashman, Jr., Esquire, Tyler J. Leavengood, Esquire, POTTER ANDERSON & CORROON LLP, Wilmington, Delaware; William Savitt, Esquire (argued), Ryan A. McLeod, Esquire, Anitha Reddy, Esquire, Kevin M. Jonke, Esquire, WACHTELL, LIPTON, ROSEN & KATZ, New York, New York; Attorneys for Appellees Marc L. Andreessen, Erskine B. Bowles, Susan D. Desmond-Hellman, Reed Hasting, and Peter Thiel.

Raymond J. DiCamillo, Esquire, Kevin M. Gallagher, Esquire, RICHARDS, LAYTON & FINGER, P.A., Wilmington, Delaware; George M. Garvey, Esquire, Laura Lin, Esquire,

MUNGER, TOLLES & OLSON LLP, Los Angeles, California; Attorneys for Appellee Mark Zuckerberg.

David E. Ross, Esquire, Garrett B. Moritz, Esquire, R. Garrett Rice, Esquire, ROSS ARONSTAM & MORITZ LLP, Wilmington, Delaware; Attorneys for Appellee Facebook, Inc.

Before SEITZ, Chief Justice; VALIHURA, VAUGHN, TRAYNOR, and MONTGOMERY-REEVES, Justices, constituting the Court en banc.

[1039] MONTGOMERY-REEVES, Justice:

In 2016, the board of directors of Facebook, Inc. ("Facebook") voted in favor of a stock reclassification (the "Reclassification") that would allow Mark Zuckerberg —Facebook's controller, chairman, and chief executive officer—to sell most of his Facebook stock while maintaining voting control of the company. Zuckerberg [1040] proposed the Reclassification to allow him and his wife to fulfill a pledge to donate most of their wealth to philanthropic causes. With Zuckerberg casting the deciding votes, Facebook's stockholders approved the Reclassification.

Not long after, numerous stockholders filed lawsuits in the Court of Chancery, alleging that Facebook's board of directors violated their fiduciary duties by negotiating and approving a purportedly one-sided deal that put Zuckerberg's interests ahead of the company's interests. The trial court consolidated more than a dozen of these lawsuits into a single class action. At Zuckerberg's request and shortly before trial, Facebook withdrew the Reclassification and mooted the fiduciary-duty class action. Facebook spent more than $20 million defending against the class action and paid plaintiffs' counsel more than $68 million in attorneys' fees under the corporate benefit doctrine.

Following the settlement, another Facebook stockholder—the United Food and Commercial Workers Union and Participating Food Industry Employers Tri-State Pension Fund ("Tri-State")—filed a derivative complaint in the Court of Chancery. This new action rehashed many of the allegations made in the prior class action but sought compensation for the money Facebook spent in connection with the prior class action.

Tri-State did not make a litigation demand on Facebook's board. Instead, Tri-State pleaded that demand was futile because the board's negotiation and approval of the Reclassification was not a valid exercise of its business judgment and because a majority of the directors were beholden to Zuckerberg. Facebook and the other defendants moved to dismiss Tri-State's complaint under Court of Chancery Rule 23.1, arguing that Tri-State did not make demand or prove that demand was futile. [...]

In October 2020, the Court of Chancery dismissed Tri-State's complaint under Rule 23.1. The court held that *exculpated* care claims do not excuse demand [...] because they do not expose directors to a substantial likelihood of liability. The court also held that the complaint failed to raise a reasonable doubt that a majority of the demand board lacked independence from Zuckerberg. [...]

Tri-State has appealed the Court of Chancery's judgment. For the reasons provided below, this Court affirms the Court of Chancery's judgment. [...]

I. RELEVANT FACTS AND PROCEDURAL BACKGROUND

A. The Parties and Relevant Non-Parties

Appellee Facebook is a Delaware corporation with its principal place of business in California. Facebook is the world's largest social media and networking service and one of the ten largest companies by market capitalization.

Appellant Tri-State has continuously owned stock in Facebook since September 2013.

Appellee Mark Zuckerberg founded Facebook and has served as its chief executive officer since July 2014. Zuckerberg controls a majority of Facebook's voting power and has been the chairman of Facebook's board of directors since January 2012.

Appellee Marc Andreessen has served as a Facebook director since June 2008. Andreessen was a member of the special committee that negotiated and recommended that the full board approve the Reclassification. In addition to his work as a Facebook director, Andreessen is a cofounder and general partner of the venture capital firm Andreessen Horowitz.

Appellee Peter Thiel has served as a Facebook director since April 2005. Thiel voted in favor of the Reclassification. In addition to his work as a Facebook director, Thiel is a partner at the venture capital firm Founders Firm.

Appellee Reed Hastings began serving as a Facebook director in June 2011 and was still a director when Tri-State filed its complaint. Hastings voted in favor of the Reclassification. In addition to his work as a Facebook director, Hastings founded and serves as the chief executive officer and chairman of Netflix, Inc. ("Netflix").

Appellee Erskine B. Bowles began serving as a Facebook director in September 2011 and was still a director when Tri-State [1042] filed its complaint. Bowles was a member of the special committee that negotiated and recommended that the full board approve the Reclassification.

Appellee Susan D. Desmond-Hellman began serving as a Facebook director in March 2013 and was still a director when Tri-State filed its complaint. Desmond-Hellman was the chair of the special committee that negotiated and recommended that the full board approve the Reclassification. In addition to her work as a Facebook director, Desmond-Hellman served as the chief executive officer of the Bill and Melinda Gates Foundation (the "Gates Foundation") during the events relevant to this appeal.

Sheryl Sandberg has been Facebook's chief operating officer since March 2018 and has served as a Facebook director since January 2012.

Kenneth I. Chenault began serving as a Facebook director in February 2018 and was still a director when Tri-State filed its complaint. Chenault was not a director when Facebook's board voted in favor of the Reclassification in 2016.

Jeffery Zients began serving as a Facebook director in May 2018 and was still a director when Tri-State filed its complaint. Zients was not a director when Facebook's board voted in favor of the Reclassification in 2016.

B. Zuckerberg Takes the Giving Pledge

According to the allegations in the complaint, in December 2010, Zuckerberg took the Giving Pledge, a movement championed by Bill Gates and Warren Buffet that challenged wealthy business leaders to donate a majority of their wealth to philanthropic causes. Zuckerberg communicated widely that he had taken the pledge and intended to start his philanthropy at an early age.

In March 2015, Zuckerberg began working on an accelerated plan to complete the Giving Pledge by making annual donations of $2 to $3 billion worth of Facebook stock. Zuckerberg asked Facebook's general counsel to look into the plan. Facebook's legal team cautioned Zuckerberg that he could only sell a small portion of his stock—$3 to $4 billion based on the market price—without dipping below majority voting control. To avoid this problem, the general counsel suggested that Facebook could follow the "Google playbook" and issue a new class of non-voting stock that Zuckerberg could sell without significantly diminishing his voting power. The legal team recommended that the board form a special committee of independent directors to review and approve the [1043] plan and noted that litigation involving Google's reclassification resulted in a $522 million settlement. Zuckerberg instructed Facebook's legal team to "start figuring out how to make this happen."

C. The Special Committee Approves the Reclassification

At an August 20, 2015 meeting of Facebook's board, Zuckerberg formally proposed that Facebook issue a new class of non-voting shares, which would allow him to sell a substantial amount of stock without losing control of the company. Zuckerberg also disclosed that he had hired Simpson Thacher & Bartlett LLP ("Simpson Thacher") to give him personal legal advice about "what creating a new class of stock might look like."

A couple of days later, Facebook established a special committee, which was composed of three purportedly-independent directors: Andreessen, Bowles, and Desmond-Hellman (the "Special Committee"). The board charged the Special Committee with evaluating the Reclassification, considering alternatives, and making a recommendation to the full board. The board also authorized the Special Committee to retain legal counsel, financial advisors, and other experts.

Facebook management recommended and the Special Committee hired Wachtell, Lipton, Rosen & Katz ("Wachtell") as the committee's legal advisor. Before meeting with the Special Committee, Wachtell called Zuckerberg's contacts at Simpson Thacher to discuss the potential terms of the Reclassification. Simpson Thacher rejected as non-starters several features from the Google playbook, such as a stapling provision that would have required Zuckerberg to sell a share of his voting stock each time that he sold a share of the non-voting stock, and a true-up payment that would compensate Facebook's other stockholders for the dilution of their voting power. By the time Wachtell first met with the Special Committee, the key contours of the Reclassification were already taking shape, and the Special Committee anticipated that the Reclassification would occur. Thus, the Special Committee focused on suggesting changes to the Reclassification rather than considering alternatives or threatening to reject the plan.

Following the recommendation of Bowles, the Special Committee hired Evercore Group L.L.C. ("Evercore") as its financial advisor. Evercore was founded by Roger Altman, a personal friend of Bowles who had helped him with various political efforts. Evercore's team leader observed that it had been hired "in the second inning" and that negotiations were well underway before it began to advise the Special Committee on the Reclassification.

[1044] As the negotiations progressed, the Special Committee largely agreed to give Zuckerberg the terms that he wanted and did not consider alternatives or demand meaningful concessions. For example, the Special Committee did not ask Zuckerberg to revisit any of the terms that Simpson Thacher identified as non-starters and did not try to place restrictions on Zuckerberg's ability to sell as much stock as he wanted, for whatever purpose, on any timetable that he desired. Similarly, the Special Committee asked for only small concessions from Zuckerberg, such as a sunset provision that was designed to discourage Zuckerberg from leaving the company despite the absence of any demonstrable reason to believe that Zuckerberg would step away from his existing Facebook duties.

On November 9, 2015, Zuckerberg publicly reaffirmed the Giving Pledge. The next day, Zuckerberg circulated a draft announcement within Facebook that would disclose his intent to begin making large annual donations to complete the pledge. Zuckerberg asked for feedback on the announcement from various people, including Desmond-Hellman. Zuckerberg also informed Bowles and Andreessen of his planned announcement. Bowles and Andreessen told Zuckerberg that they were "proud" of him for taking the Giving Pledge and announcing his plan to begin donating his wealth to philanthropic causes. Zuckerberg also told Warren Buffett, Bill Gates, and Melinda Gates of his planned announcement. Melinda Gates forwarded an email that she received from Zuckerberg to Desmond-Hellman, adding a smiley-face emoji. At that time, Desmond-Hellman was the chief executive officer of the Gates Foundation.

A few weeks later, Zuckerberg published a post on his Facebook page announcing that he planned to begin making large donations of his Facebook stock. The post noted that Zuckerberg intended to "remain Facebook's CEO for many, many years to come" and did not mention that his plan hinged on the Special Committee's approval of the Reclassification. The Special Committee did not try to use the public announcement as leverage to extract more concessions from Zuckerberg.

Throughout the negotiations about the Reclassification, Andreessen engaged in facially dubious back-channel communications with Zuckerberg about the Special Committee's deliberations. For example, during a March 2016 teleconference with the Special Committee, Zuckerberg pushed for an eight-year leave of absence. [1045] Andreessen sent Zuckerberg text messages during the meeting that provided live updates on which lines of argument were working and which were not. When confronted with these text messages later on, Desmond-Hellmann agreed that it appeared Andreessen had been "coaching" Zuckerberg through the negotiations.

On April 13, 2016, the Special Committee recommend that the full board approve the Reclassification. The next day, Facebook's full board accepted the Special Committee's recommendation and voted to approve the Reclassification. Zuckerberg and Sandberg abstained from voting on the Reclassification.

D. Facebook Settles a Class Action Challenging the Reclassification

On April 27, 2016, Facebook revealed the Reclassification to the public. The announcement was timed to coincide with the company's best-ever quarterly earnings report. Evercore's project leader, Altman, sent Desmond-Hellmann an email remarking, "Anytime [Facebook] announces earnings like that, no one will care about an equity recapitalization."

On April 29, 2016, the first class action was filed in the Court of Chancery challenging the Reclassification. Several more similar complaints were filed, and in May 2016 the Court of Chancery consolidated thirteen cases into a single class action (the "Reclassification Class Action").

On June 20, 2016, Facebook held its annual stockholders meeting. Among other things, the stockholders were asked to vote on the Reclassification. Zuckerberg voted all of his stock in favor of the plan. Including Zuckerberg's votes, a majority of Facebook's stockholders approved the Reclassification. More than three-quarters of the minority stockholders voted against the Reclassification.

On June 24, 2016, Facebook agreed that it would not go forward with the Reclassification while the Reclassification Class Action was pending. The Court of Chancery certified the Reclassification Class Action in April 2017 and tentatively scheduled the trial for September 26, 2017. About a week before the trial was scheduled to begin, Zuckerberg asked the board to abandon the Reclassification. The board agreed, and the next day Facebook [1046] filed a Form 8-K with the Securities and Exchange Commission disclosing that the company had abandoned the Reclassification and mooted the Class Action. The Form-8K also disclosed that despite abandoning the Reclassification, Zuckerberg planned to sell a substantial number of shares over the coming 18 months.

In a companion Facebook post, Zuckerberg explained that he "knew [the Reclassification] was going to be complicated and [that] it wasn't a perfect solution." The post continued, "Today I think we have a better one" that would allow Zuckerberg and his wife to "fully fund [our] philanthropy and retain voting control of Facebook for 20 years or more." The post also clarified that this new plan would not "change [our] plans to give away 99% of our Facebook shares during our lives. In fact, we now plan to accelerate our work and sell more of those shares sooner." By January 3, 2019, Zuckerberg had sold about $5.6 billion worth of Facebook stock without the Reclassification.

E. Tri-State Files a Class Action Seeking to Recoup the Money that Facebook Spent Defending and Settling the Reclassification Class Action

Facebook spent about $21.8 million defending the Reclassification Class Action, including more than $17 million on attorneys' fees. Additionally, Facebook paid $68.7 million to the plaintiff's attorneys in the Reclassification Class Action to settle a claim under the corporate benefit doctrine.

On September 12, 2018, Tri-State filed a derivative action in the Court of Chancery seeking to recoup the money that Facebook spent defending and settling the Reclassification Class Action. The complaint asserted a single count alleging that Zuckerberg, Andreessen, Thiel, Hastings, Bowles, and Desmond-Hellmann (collectively, the "Director Defendants") breached their fiduciary duties of care and loyalty by improperly negotiating and approving the Reclassification. When Tri-State filed its complaint, Facebook's board was composed of nine directors: Zuckerberg, Andreessen, Bowles, Desmond-Hellman, Hastings, Thiel, Sandberg, Chenault, and Zients (collectively, the "Demand Board").

The complaint alleged that demand was excused as futile under Court of Chancery Rule 23.1 because "the Reclassification was not the product of a valid exercise of business judgment" and because "a majority of the Board face[d] a substantial likelihood of liability[] and/or lack[ed] independence." Facebook and the Director Defendants moved to dismiss the complaint under Court of Chancery Rule 23.1 for failing to comply with the demand requirement.

On October 26, 2020, the Court of Chancery issued a memorandum opinion dismissing the complaint for failing to comply with Rule 23.1. The court held that demand was required because the complaint [1047] did not contain particularized allegations raising a reasonable doubt that a majority of the Demand Board received a material personal benefit from the Reclassification, faced a substantial likelihood of liability for approving the Reclassification, or lacked independence from another interested party.

Tri-State appeals the Court of Chancery's judgment dismissing the derivative complaint under Rule 23.1 for failing to make a demand on the board or plead with particularity facts establishing that demand would be futile.

II. STANDARD OF REVIEW

"[O]ur review of decisions of the Court of Chancery applying Rule 23.1 is *de novo* and plenary."

III. ANALYSIS

"A cardinal precept" of Delaware law is "that directors, rather than shareholders, manage the business and affairs of the corporation." This precept is reflected in Section 141(a) of the Delaware General Corporation Law ("DGCL"), which provides that "[t]he business and affairs of every corporation organized under this chapter *shall be managed by or under the direction of a board of directors* except as may be otherwise provided in this chapter or in [a corporation's] certificate of incorporation." The board's authority to govern corporate affairs extends to decisions about what remedial actions a corporation should take after being harmed, including whether the corporation should file a lawsuit against its directors, its officers, its controller, or an outsider.

"In a derivative suit, a stockholder seeks to displace the board's [decision-making] authority over a litigation asset and assert the corporation's claim." Thus, "[b]y its very nature[,] the derivative action" encroaches "on the managerial freedom of directors" by seeking to deprive the board of control over a corporation's litigation asset. "In order for a stockholder to divest the directors of their authority to control the litigation asset and bring a derivative action on behalf of the corporation, the stockholder must" (1) make a demand on the company's board of directors or (2) show that demand would be futile. The demand requirement is a substantive requirement that "`[e]nsure[s] that a stockholder exhausts his intracorporate remedies,' `provide[s] a safeguard against strike suits,' and `assure[s] that the stockholder affords the corporation the opportunity to address an alleged wrong without litigation and to control any litigation which does occur.'"

[1048] Court of Chancery Rule 23.1 implements the substantive demand requirement at the pleading stage by mandating that derivative complaints "allege with particularity the efforts, if any, made by the plaintiff to obtain the action the plaintiff desires from the directors or comparable authority and the reasons for the plaintiff's failure to obtain the action or for not making the effort." To comply with Rule 23.1, the plaintiff must meet "stringent requirements of factual particularity that differ substantially from … permissive notice pleadings." When considering a motion to dismiss a complaint for failing to comply with Rule 23.1, the Court does not weigh the evidence, must accept as true all of the complaint's particularized and well-pleaded allegations, and must draw all reasonable inferences in the plaintiff's favor.

The plaintiff in this action did not make a pre-suit demand. Thus, the question before the Court is whether demand is excused as futile. This Court has articulated two tests to determine whether the demand requirement should be excused as futile: the *Aronson* test and the *Rales* test.[104] [... T]he Court of Chancery has recognized that the broader reasoning of *Rales* encompasses *Aronson*, and therefore the *Aronson* test is best understood as a special application of the *Rales* test.

While Delaware law recognizes that there are circumstances where making a demand would be futile because a majority of the directors "are under an influence which sterilizes their discretion" [1049] and "cannot be considered proper persons to conduct litigation on behalf of the corporation," the demand requirement is not excused lightly because derivative litigation upsets the balance of power that the DGCL establishes between a corporation's directors and its stockholders. Thus, the demand-futility analysis provides an important doctrinal check that ensures the board is not improperly deprived of its decision-making authority, while at the same time leaving a path for stockholders to file a

---

[104] *Aronson*, 473 A.2d at 805; *Rales*, 634 A.2d at 927.

derivative action where there is reason to doubt that the board could bring its impartial business judgment to bear on a litigation demand.

[...]

A. Exculpated Care Violations Do Not Satisfy *Aronson's* Second Prong

[...]

Facebook's charter contains a Section 102(b)(7) clause; as such, the Director Defendants face no risk of personal liability from the allegations asserted in this action. Thus, Tri-State's demand-futility allegations raise the question whether a derivative plaintiff can rely on exculpated care violations to establish that demand is futile under the second prong of the *Aronson* test. [...]

1. The second prong of *Aronson* focuses on whether the directors face a substantial likelihood of liability

[...]

Tri-State's argument hinges on the plain language of *Aronson's* second prong, which focuses on whether "the challenged transaction was ... the product of a valid business judgment":

> [I]n determining demand futility, the Court of Chancery ... must decide whether, under the particularized facts alleged, a reasonable doubt is created that: (1) the directors are disinterested and independent and (2) the challenged transaction was otherwise the product of a valid business judgment. Hence, the Court of Chancery must make two inquiries, one into the independence and disinterestedness of the directors and the other into the substantive nature of the challenged transaction and the board's approval thereof.

Later opinions issued by this Court contain similar language that can be read to suggest that *Aronson's* second prong focuses on the propriety of the challenged transaction. These passages do not address, however, why *Aronson* used the standard of review as a proxy for whether the board could impartially consider a litigation demand. The likely answer is that, before the General Assembly adopted Section 102(b)(7) in 1995, rebutting the business judgment rule through allegations of care violations exposed directors to a substantial likelihood of liability. Thus, even if the demand board was independent and disinterested with respect to the challenged transaction, the litigation presented a threat that would "sterilize [the board's] discretion" with respect to a demand.

Aronson supports this conclusion. For example, in *Aronson* the Court noted that, although naming directors as defendants is not enough to establish that demand would be futile, "in rare cases a *transaction* may be so egregious on its face that board approval cannot meet the test of business judgment, and a *substantial likelihood of liability* therefore exists.... [I]n that context demand is excused." This passage [1052] helps to illuminate the connection that the Court drew between rebutting the business judgment rule and the board's ability to consider a litigation demand. At that time, if the business judgment rule did not apply, allowing the derivative litigation to go forward would expose the directors to a substantial likelihood of liability for breach-of-care claims supported by well-pleaded factual allegations. It is reasonable to doubt that a director would be willing to take that personal risk. Thus, demand is excused.

On the other hand, if the business judgment rule would apply, allowing the derivative litigation to go forward would expose the directors to a minimal threat of liability. A remote threat of liability is not a good enough reason to deprive the board of control over the corporation's litigation assets. Thus, demand is required.

Although not unanimous, the weight of Delaware authority since the enactment of Section 102(b)(7) supports holding that exculpated care violations do not excuse demand under *Aronson's* second prong. [...]

This Court's opinion in *In re Cornerstone Therapeutics, Inc. Stockholder Litigation,* changed the landscape even more. Before *Cornerstone,* there was some uncertainty about how to apply a Section 102(b)(7) provision when deciding a motion to dismiss under Court of Chancery Rule 12(b)(6). Some courts held that an exculpation clause could warrant dismissing a complaint alleging care claims. Others, particularly where the entire fairness standard of review might apply, ruled that more factual development was needed [1054] to determine whether the director's breach would be exculpated. Thus, a complaint alleging exculpated care violations *might* compromise a director's ability to impartially consider a litigation demand by exposing them to the distraction of protracted litigation, public scrutiny, and potential reputational harm, even if the risk was low that the director would be found liable for breaching their fiduciary duties.

Cornerstone eliminated any uncertainty and held that where a corporation's charter contains a Section 102(b)(7) provision, "[a] plaintiff seeking only monetary damages must plead non-exculpated claims against a director who is protected by an exculpatory charter provision to survive a motion to dismiss, regardless of the underlying standard of review for the board's conduct." Thus, under current law a Section 102(b)(7) provision removes the threat of liability and protracted litigation for breach of care claims. As such, *Cornerstone* eliminated "any continuing vitality from *Aronson's* use of the standard of review for the challenged transaction as a proxy for whether directors face a substantial likelihood of liability sufficient to render demand futile."

Accordingly, this Court affirms the Court of Chancery's holding that exculpated care claims do not satisfy *Aronson's* second prong. [...]

2. Tri-State's other arguments do not change the analysis

Tri-State raises a few more counterarguments that do not change the Court's analysis.

[1055] First, Tri-State argues that construing the second prong of *Aronson* to focus on whether directors face a substantial likelihood of liability erases any distinction between the two prongs of the *Aronson* test. The argument goes like this. If directors face a substantial likelihood of liability for approving the challenged transaction, then they are interested with respect to the challenged transaction. The first prong of *Aronson* already addresses whether directors are interested in the challenged transaction. Thus, construing the second prong to require a substantial risk of liability makes it redundant. This argument misconstrues *Aronson*. The first prong of *Aronson* focuses on whether the directors had a personal interest in the challenged transaction (i.e., a personal financial benefit from the challenged transaction that is not equally shared by the stockholders). This is a different consideration than whether the directors face a substantial likelihood of liability for approving the challenged transaction, even if they received nothing personal from the challenged transaction. The second prong excuses demand in that circumstance. Thus, the first and second prongs of *Aronson* perform separate functions, even if those functions are complementary.

Second, Tri-State argues that this holding places an unfair burden on plaintiffs and will fail to deter controllers from pressuring boards to approve unfair transactions. Although not entirely clear, Tri-State appears to argue that because the entire fairness standard of review applies *ab initio* to a conflicted-controller transaction, demand is automatically excused under *Aronson's* second prong. As the Court of Chancery noted below, some cases have suggested that demand is automatically excused under *Aronson's* second prong if the complaint raises a reasonable doubt that the business judgment standard of review will apply, even if the business judgment rule is rebutted for a reason unrelated to the conduct or interests of a majority of the directors on the demand board. The Court of Chancery's case law developed in a different direction, however, concluding that demand is not futile under the second prong of *Aronson* simply because entire fairness applies *ab initio* to a controlling stockholder transaction. As the Court of Chancery has explained, the theory that demand should be excused simply because an alleged controlling stockholder stood on both sides of the transaction is "inconsistent with Delaware Supreme Court authority that focuses the test for demand futility exclusively on the ability of a corporation's board of directors to impartially consider a demand to institute litigation on behalf of the corporation—including litigation implicating the interests of a controlling stockholder."

Further, Tri-State's argument presumes that a stockholder has a general right to control corporate claims. Not so. The directors are tasked with managing the affairs of the corporation, including whether [1056] to file action on behalf of the corporation. A stockholder can only displace the directors if the stockholder alleges with particularity that "the directors are under an influence which sterilizes their discretion" such that "they cannot be considered proper persons to conduct litigation on behalf of the corporation." As such, enforcing the demand requirement where a stockholder has only alleged exculpated conduct does not "undermine shareholder rights;" instead, it recognizes the delegation of powers outlined in the DGCL.

Finally, Tri-State's argument collapses the distinction between the board's capacity to consider a litigation demand and the propriety of the challenged transaction. It is entirely possible that an independent and disinterested board, exercising its impartial business judgment, could decide that it is not in the corporation's best interest to spend the time and money to pursue a claim that is likely to succeed. Yet, Tri-State asks the Court to deprive directors and officers of the power to make such a decision, at least where the derivative action would challenge a conflicted-controller transaction. This rule may have its benefits, but it runs counter to the "cardinal precept" of Delaware law that independent and disinterested directors are generally in the best position to manage a corporation's affairs, including whether the corporation should exercise its legal rights.[...]

3. This Court adopts the Court of Chancery's three-part test for demand futility

This issue raises one more question—whether the three-part test for demand futility the Court of Chancery applied below is consistent with *Aronson, Rales,* and their progeny. [... B]ecause the three-part test is consistent with and enhances *Aronson, Rales,* and their progeny, the Court need not overrule *Aronson* to adopt this refined test, and cases properly construing *Aronson, Rales,* and their progeny remain good law.

Accordingly, from this point forward, courts should ask the following three questions on a director-by-director basis when evaluating allegations of demand futility:

> (i) whether the director received a material personal benefit from the alleged misconduct that is the subject of the litigation demand;
>
> (ii) whether the director faces a substantial likelihood of liability on any of the claims that would be the subject of the litigation demand; and
>
> (iii) whether the director lacks independence from someone who received a material personal benefit from the alleged misconduct that

would be the subject of the litigation demand or who would face a substantial likelihood of liability on any of the claims that are the subject of the litigation demand.

If the answer to any of the questions is "yes" for at least half of the members of the demand board, then demand is excused as futile. [...]

B. The Complaint Does Not Plead with Particularity Facts Establishing that Demand Would Be Futile

The second issue on appeal is whether Tri-State's complaint pleaded with particularity facts establishing that a litigation demand on Facebook's board would be futile. The Court resolves this issue by applying the three-part test adopted above on a director-by-director basis.

The Demand Board was composed of nine directors. Tri-State concedes on appeal that two of those directors, Chenault and Zients, could have impartially considered a litigation demand. And Facebook does not argue on appeal that Zuckerberg, Sandberg, or Andreessen could have impartially [1060] considered a litigation demand. Thus, in order to show that demand is futile, Tri-State must sufficiently allege that two of the following directors could not impartially consider demand: Thiel, Hastings, Bowles, and Desmond-Hellmann.

Tri-State concedes on appeal that neither Thiel, Hastings, Bowles, nor Desmond-Hellmann had a personal interest in the Reclassification. This eliminates the possibility that demand could be excused under the first prong of the demand-futility test, as none of the remaining four directors obtained a material personal benefit from the alleged misconduct that is the subject of the litigation demand.

Similarly, there is no dispute that Facebook has a broad Section 102(b)(7) provision; and Tri-State concedes on appeal that the complaint does not plead with particularity that Thiel, Hastings, Bowles, or Desmond-Hellmann committed a *non-exculpated* breach of their fiduciary duties with respect to the Reclassification. This eliminates the possibility that demand could be excused under the second prong of the demand-futility test, as none of the remaining four directors would face a substantial likelihood of liability on any of the claims that would be the subject of the litigation demand.

This leaves one unanswered question: whether the complaint pleaded with particularity facts establishing that two of the four remaining directors lacked independence from Zuckerberg.

"The primary basis upon which a director's independence must be measured is whether the director's decision is based on the corporate merits of the subject before the board, rather than extraneous considerations or influences." Whether a director is independent "is a fact-specific determination" that depends upon "the context of a particular case." To show a lack of independence, a derivative complaint must plead with particularity facts creating "a reasonable doubt that a director is ... so `beholden' to an interested director ... that his or her `discretion would be sterilized.'"

"A plaintiff seeking to show that a director was not independent must satisfy a materiality standard." The [1061] plaintiff must allege that "the director in question had ties to the person whose proposal or actions he or she is evaluating that are sufficiently substantial that he or she could not objectively discharge his or her fiduciary duties." In other words, the question is "whether, applying a subjective standard, those ties were *material*, in the sense that the alleged ties could have affected the impartiality of the individual director." "Our law requires that all the pled facts regarding a director's relationship to the interested party be considered in full context in making the, admittedly imprecise, pleading stage determination of independence." And while "the plaintiff is bound to plead particularized facts in ... a derivative complaint, so too is the court bound to draw all inferences from those particularized facts in favor of the plaintiff, not the defendant, when dismissal of a derivative complaint is sought."

"A variety of motivations, including friendship, may influence the demand futility inquiry. But, to render a director unable to consider demand, a relationship must be of a bias-producing nature." Alleging that a director had a "personal friendship" with someone else, or that a director had an "outside business relationship," are "insufficient to raise a reasonable doubt" that the director lacked independence. "Consistent with [the] predicate materiality requirement, the existence of some financial ties between the interested party and the director, without more, is not disqualifying."

Like the Court of Chancery below, we hold that Tri-State failed to raise a reasonable doubt that either Thiel, Hastings, or Bowles was beholden to Zuckerberg.[188]

1. Hastings

The complaint does not raise a reasonable doubt that Hastings lacked independence from Zuckerberg. [...]

---

[188] Because the complaint failed to raise a reasonable doubt that Hastings, Thiel, or Bowles were not independent, this Opinion need not address whether Desmond-Hellmann was beholden to Zuckerberg.

2. Thiel

The complaint does not raise a reasonable doubt that Thiel lacked independence from Zuckerberg. According to the complaint, Thiel was not independent because:

- "Thiel was one of the early investors in Facebook," is "its longest-tenured board member besides Zuckerberg," and "has ... been instrumental to Facebook's business strategy and direction over the years."

- "Thiel has a personal bias in favor of keeping founders in control of the companies they created...."

- The venture capital firm at which Thiel is a partner, Founders Fund, "gets `good deal flow'" from its "high-profile association with Facebook."

- "According to Facebook's 2018 Proxy Statement, the Facebook shares owned by the Founders Fund (i.e., by [1063] Thiel and Andreessen) will be released from escrow in connection with" an acquisition.

- "Thiel is Zuckerberg's close friend and mentor."

- In October 2016, Thiel made a $1 million donation to an "organization that paid [a substantial sum to] Cambridge Analytica" and "cofounded the Cambridge Analytica-linked data firm Palantir." Even though "[t]he Cambridge Analytica scandal has exposed Facebook to regulatory investigations" and litigation, Zuckerberg did not try to remove Thiel from the board.

- Similarly, Thiel's "acknowledge[ment] that he secretly funded various lawsuits aimed at bankrupting [the] news website Gawker Media" lead to "widespread calls for Zuckerberg to remove Thiel from Facebook's Board given Thiel's apparent antagonism toward a free press." Zuckerberg ignored those calls and did not seek to remove Thiel from Facebook's board.

These allegations do not raise a reasonable doubt that Thiel is beholden to Zuckerberg. The complaint does not explain why Thiel's status as a long-serving board member, early investor, or his contributions to Facebook's business strategy make him beholden to Zuckerberg. And for the same reasons provided above, a director's good faith belief that founder controller maximizes value does not raise a reasonable doubt that the director lacks independence from a corporation's founder.

While the complaint alleges that Founders Fund "gets `good deal flow'" from Thiel's "high-profile association with Facebook," the complaint does not identify a single deal that flowed to—or is expected to flow to—Founders Fund through this association, let alone any deals that would be material to Thiel's interests. The complaint also fails to draw any connection between Thiel's continued status as a director and the vesting of Facebook stock related to the acquisition. And alleging that Thiel is a personal friend of Zuckerberg is insufficient to establish a lack of independence.

The final pair of allegations suggest that because "Zuckerberg stood by Thiel" in the face of public scandals, "Thiel feels a sense of obligation to Zuckerberg." These allegations can only raise a reasonable doubt about Thiel's independence if remaining a Facebook director was financially or personally material to Thiel. As the Court of Chancery noted below, given Thiel's wealth and stature, "[t]he complaint does not support an inference that Thiel's service on the Board is financially material to him. Nor does the complaint sufficiently allege that serving as a Facebook director confers such cachet that Thiel's independence is compromised." Accordingly, this Court affirms the Court of Chancery's holding that the complaint does not raise a reasonable doubt about Thiel's independence.

3. Bowles

The complaint does not raise a reasonable doubt that Bowles lacked independence [1064] from Zuckerberg. [...]

IV. CONCLUSION

For the reasons provided above, the Court of Chancery's judgment is affirmed.

B. City of Coral Springs Police Officers' Pension Plan v. Dorsey

Dorsey nicely illustrates the joint operation of substantive standards of review and the demand futility test.

Questions

1. If the case had reached the merits, what would have been the standard of review applicable to (a) Dorsey and (b) the other directors? Would they have made it easy or hard to win for the plaintiff?

2. Would the outcome of the case have changed if Dorsey had owned not around 50% but 1% or 80% of Block's voting power? If the transaction had been a purchase not of Jay-Z's business but of Dorsey's other business or house or whatever?

3. What if the transaction at issue had been a squeeze-out merger (infra Part III:Chapter 7), i.e., a transaction where Dorsey uses his voting power to convert other shareholders' shares into cash such that Dorsey remains as the sole owner of Block?

4. Based on your previous answers, would you be concerned about litigation risk (a) as a controlling stockholder doing whatever you want or (b) as an outside director who thinks you are doing your job?

5. In light of the foregoing questions, do you think the demand futility test is appropriate, too strict, or too lenient?

CITY OF CORAL SPRINGS POLICE OFFICERS' PENSION PLAN,
derivatively on behalf of BLOCK, INC., Plaintiff,

v.

JACK DORSEY, ROELOF BOTHA, AMY BROOKS, PAUL DEIGHTON, RANDY GARUTTI, JIM MCKELVEY, MARY MEEKER, ANNA PATTERSON, LAWRENCE SUMMERS, DAVID VINIAR, and DARREN WALKER, Defendants, and BLOCK, INC., Nominal Defendant.

C.A. No. 2022-0091-KSJM.

Court of Chancery of Delaware.

Submitted: January 10, 2023.

Decided: May 9, 2023.

Thomas Curry, Tayler D. Bolton, SAXENA WHITE P.A., Wilmington, Delaware; David Wales, Sara DiLeo, SAXENA WHITE P.A., White Plains, New York; Adam Warden, Jonathan Lamet, SAXENA WHITE P.A., Boca Raton, Florida; *Counsel for Plaintiff City of Coral Springs Police Officers' Pension Plan.*

Raymond J. DiCamillo, Kevin M. Gallagher, RICHARDS, LAYTON & FINGER, P.A., Wilmington, Delaware; Colin B. Davis, Katie Beaudin, GIBSON DUNN & CRUTCHER LLP, Irvine, California; Brian M. Lutz, GIBSON DUNN & CRUTCHER LLP, San Francisco, California; Lissa M. Percopo, GIBSON DUNN & CRUTCHER LLP, Washington, D.C.; *Counsel for Defendants Jack Dorsey, Roelof Botha, Amy Brooks, Paul*

Deighton, Randy Garutti, Jim McKelvey, Mary Meeker, Anna Patterson, Lawrence Summers, David Viniar, and Darren Walker, and Nominal Defendant Block, Inc.

MEMORANDUM OPINION

McCORMICK, C.

The plaintiff, a stockholder of Block, Inc., filed this derivative suit challenging Block's acquisition of TIDAL—a music streaming company associated with rapper, producer, and entrepreneur Shawn Carter. Block facilitates payment processing and helps individuals transfer money electronically; it had never ventured into the music streaming industry and, at the time it acquired TIDAL, had no plans to do so. The idea for the acquisition came to Jack Dorsey—Block's founder, CEO, and Chairman—when he was summering with Carter in the Hamptons. From his Hamptons retreat, Dorsey joined a videoconference meeting of Block's board and proposed that Block acquire TIDAL. The board formed a transaction committee to consider the proposal.

Over the ensuing months, the committee learned that TIDAL was failing financially, losing its major contracts, and facing an ongoing criminal investigation. The committee also learned that Carter personally loaned TIDAL $50 million to help the troubled company through its difficulties and that Dorsey was the sole Block management member in support of the acquisition. Despite the obvious problems with the deal, the committee approved the transaction for $306 million. It seemed, by all accounts, a terrible business decision.

Under Delaware law, however, a board comprised of a majority of disinterested and independent directors is free to make a terrible business decision without any meaningful threat of liability, so long as the directors approve the action in good faith.

The defendants moved to dismiss the complaint for failure to plead demand futility. That motion hinges on whether the plaintiff adequately alleges that the committee members would face a substantial likelihood of liability for approving the transaction. The plaintiff did not meet that pleading burden. The case is dismissed.

I. FACTUAL BACKGROUND

The facts are drawn from the Verified Stockholder Derivative Complaint (the "Complaint") and documents it incorporates by reference, including meeting minutes and associated materials that were referenced or quoted in the Complaint.

A. Block And Its Board

Block, a California-based company, offers products and services that help businesses facilitate payment processing and help individuals transfer money electronically. Block's net income in 2019 and 2020 was $375.4 million and $213.1 million, respectively.

Dorsey founded Block and took the Company public in 2015. He is Block's President and CEO, and he serves as Chairman of Block's Board of Directors (the "Board"). According to Block's public filings, Dorsey held between 48.08% and 51.32% of the Company's total stockholder voting power at relevant times.

At the time of the acquisition, the Board comprised eleven members: Dorsey and Defendants Roelof Botha, Amy Brooks, Paul Deighton, Randy Garutti, Jim McKelvey, Mary Meeker, Anna Patterson, Lawrence Summers, David Viniar, and Darren Walker (collectively, "Defendants").

B. Carter's Acquisition And Attempted Revamp Of TIDAL

Carter, known professionally as "Jay-Z," is a rapper, record producer, and entrepreneur. In 2015, a group of recording artists led by Carter acquired a Norwegian music streaming company, formerly called Aspiro, for $56 million and rebranded it as TIDAL. Carter spearheaded these efforts and served as the public face of TIDAL. He also held a 27% stake in the company. Along with his partners, Carter launched a campaign for TIDAL to break into the music streaming industry as an artist-friendly platform.

[...]

C. Dorsey Proposes That Block Acquire TIDAL.

Dorsey and Carter are friends. They share interests in cryptocurrency and philanthropy. Dorsey publicly supported Carter's acquisition of TIDAL in 2015, tweeting, "I appreciate & respect people who depart from their strengths and take on new challenges. Been using Tidal & digging it!" In April 2020, they jointly issued grants for COVID-19 relief totaling $6.2 million. Dorsey donated $10 million to Carter's nonprofit, Reform Alliance, in May 2020.

While their families were summering together in the Hamptons, Dorsey and Carter began discussing a potential acquisition of TIDAL by Block. On August 25, 2020, Dorsey joined the Board's regularly scheduled meeting by videoconference from the Hamptons. During the meeting, Dorsey raised the idea that Block acquire TIDAL. The meeting minutes reflect the Board's discussion of strategic rationales, proposed valuations, and the Company's potential integration strategies. The Board then "instructed management to continue to evaluate such transactions including through additional due diligence and negotiation of a letter of intent." The Board resolved to establish a transaction committee to review any potential acquisition of TIDAL by unanimous written consent (the "Transaction Committee").

The proposed Transaction Committee members were four independent directors: Botha, Brooks, Meeker, and Walker (the "Committee Defendants"). [...] Two days later [...] the Transaction Committee was officially formed.

Meanwhile, Dorsey drafted and submitted a non-binding letter of intent for Block to purchase TIDAL for $554.8 million.

D. The Transaction Committee's First Meeting

The Transaction Committee convened by videoconference for its first meeting on September 29, 2020. The meeting lasted 35 minutes. Dorsey and members of Block's legal team attended the meeting and were present for its duration. [...]

E. The Transaction Committee's Second Meeting

Block management provided the Transaction Committee with its fourth written report on October 14, 2020. Management reported that TIDAL had only amassed 2.1 million paying subscribers and that growing this number would prove difficult Management reasoned that "Spotify is synonymous with music streaming," and Apple Music and Amazon Music had largely captured the remaining market share. The report also apprised the board that TIDAL had generated negative EBITDA of $39 million in 2019 and of Carter's $50 million loan to the company [to salvage the company].

Management further revealed that TIDAL operated under semi-formal or expired arrangements with these labels, capitalizing on the influence of the prominent artists who were partial owners of TIDAL. The report warned that TIDAL's relationships with these labels could sour following an acquisition by Block.

The report highlighted other potential risks in an acquisition, such as the ongoing criminal probe by the Norwegian government and a federal lawsuit brought by artists alleging that TIDAL had withheld their owed royalties. TIDAL's relationships with its artists were also faltering, and rapper Kanye West had withdrawn from his exclusive streaming arrangement with TIDAL for one of his albums due to piracy issues.

Management set an "[e]xpected purchase price" of $550-750 million. They reached this conclusion based on: comparables analyses with Spotify, Apple Music, and Amazon Music; comparables analyses with private precedent transactions; discounted cash flows analysis derived from TIDAL's management forecasts; and TIDAL's representations that it was in discussions with an undisclosed third party for a loan that valued TIDAL at $500-600 million.

The Transaction Committee convened for its second meeting on October 20, 2020. […] The October 20 meeting lasted an hour, and Dorsey was present for the entirety of the meeting. […]

The Transaction Committee updated the full Board at its regularly scheduled meeting the next day, October 21. […] The Transaction Committee's update was one of 14 items of business discussed at the October 21 Board meeting.

F. Block And TIDAL Agree On A Term Sheet.

On November 10, 2020, Block entered a term sheet to purchase a majority interest in TIDAL. A few days later, Dorsey and Carter were spotted vacationing together in Hawaii.

The Transaction Committee did not convene again until January 22, 2021. The meeting lasted an hour […]

G. The Transaction Committee Approves The Acquisition.

Without any further meetings, the Transaction Committee approved the acquisition by unanimous written consent on February 25, 2021. The Company announced the deal on March 4, after which its stock price decreased by 7%. In an 8-K filed two days later, the Company reported that it would pay consideration of approximately $306 million, subject to adjustments, for an ownership stake of approximately 87.5%.

Block closed the deal on April 30, 2021. In its 10-Q filed on November 4, 2021, Block disclosed that, after adjustments, it ultimately paid $237.3 million for an ownership interest of 86.23%. […] After the transaction closed, Carter joined the Board as a twelfth member.

Also in February 2021, Dorsey and Carter continued to partner in their personal lives, creating an endowment to fund bitcoin development in India and Africa. Their joint contributions to this endowment totaled $23.6 million.

H. This Litigation

Plaintiff City of Coral Springs Police Officers' Pension Plan ("Plaintiff") is a beneficial owner of Block common stock. Before filing this action, Plaintiff made a demand for books and records pursuant to 8 *Del. C.* § 220, and Block produced documents in response.

Plaintiff filed this derivative action on January 27, 2022. The Complaint asserts two causes of action challenging the TIDAL acquisition as a breach of fiduciary duty— Count I against Dorsey as a controller and Count II against the directors on the Board at the time the transaction was approved. Defendants moved to dismiss the Complaint. The motion was fully briefed, and the court heard oral argument on January 10, 2023.

II. LEGAL ANALYSIS

Defendants moved to dismiss the Amended Complaint pursuant to Court of Chancery Rules 23.1 and 12(b)(6). Because the Rule 23.1 motion results in dismissal, the court does not reach the Rule 12(b)(6) motion.

[…]

Under Rule 23.1, […s]tockholders choosing to allege demand futility must meet the "heightened pleading requirements," alleging "particularized factual statements that are essential to the claim." "[…] conclusory allegations are not considered as expressly pleaded facts or factual inferences."

[…] When conducting a demand futility analysis under *Zuckerberg*, Delaware courts ask, on a director-by-director basis:

> (i) whether the director received a material personal benefit from the alleged misconduct that is the subject of the litigation demand;
>
> (ii) whether the director faces a substantial likelihood of liability on any of the claims that would be the subject of the litigation demand; and
>
> (iii) whether the director lacks independence from someone who received a material personal benefit from the alleged misconduct that would be the subject of the litigation demand or who would face a substantial likelihood of liability on any of the claims that are the subject of the litigation demand.[36]

"If the answer to any of the questions is `yes' for at least half of the members of the demand board, then demand is excused as futile." […]

As of the date when Plaintiff filed their complaint, the Board comprised twelve directors: Dorsey, Carter, the Committee Defendants, and the remaining six Defendants (Deighton,

---

[36] United Food & Com. Workers Union & Participating Food Indus. Empls. Tri-State Pension Fund v. Zuckerberg, 262 A.3d 1034, 1059 (Del. 2021) […].

Garutti, McKelvey, Patterson, Summers, and Viniar). To defeat Defendants' Rule 23.1 motion, Plaintiff must impugn the impartiality of at least six directors under *Zuckerberg*.

Generally, demand futility is assessed on a claim-by-claim, or Count-by-Count, basis. In this case, however, the two Counts are based on the same factual predicate— the Board's approval of the TIDAL acquisition. The sole distinction is in named defendants—Dorsey in Count I and the rest of the Board who approved the transaction in Count II. Because the difference in defendants does not alter the outcome, this decision consolidates the analysis of the two Counts.

Plaintiff focuses its arguments on Carter, Dorsey, and the four Committee Defendants. Plaintiff argues that: Carter is disqualified because he received a material personal benefit from the TIDAL acquisition; Dorsey's relationship with Carter made him incapable of impartially considering a demand concerning the TIDAL acquisition; and the Committee Defendants face a substantial likelihood of liability from claims challenging the TIDAL acquisition.

The analysis as to Carter and Dorsey goes Plaintiff's way. Defendants concede that Carter is interested in the transaction. And there are good arguments that Dorsey lacks independence from Carter for the purpose of the TIDAL acquisition. When supported by specific factual allegations, "professional or personal friendships, which may border on or even exceed familial loyalty and closeness, may raise a reasonable doubt whether a director can appropriately consider demand." [...] It is reasonably conceivable that Dorsey used corporate coffers to bolster his relationship with Carter. But the court need not delve too deeply into this issue, because Plaintiff has failed to meet its burden as to the remaining ten directors.

Plaintiff argues that demand is futile as to the Committee Defendants because they face a substantial likelihood of liability from the subject matter of the litigation demand. Where, as here, the corporation's certificate of incorporation exculpates its directors from liability to the fullest extent permitted by law, the substantial-likelihood standard requires that a plaintiff "plead particularized facts providing a reason to believe that the individual director was self-interested, beholden to an interested party, or acted in bad faith." A stockholder need not show a probability of success to meet the substantial-likelihood standard; the standard requires only a showing that "the claims have some merit."

Plaintiff does not argue that the Committee Defendants acted in a self-interested manner or that they were beholden to an interested party. Rather, Plaintiff argues that the Committee Defendants failed to act in good faith when approving the TIDAL acquisition. Although a keen mind can rightly perceive a distinction between acting "not in good faith" and acting "in bad faith," Delaware courts have used the phrases interchangeably in this context, and this decision follows suit.

Delaware courts have declined to offer an exhaustive definition of bad faith. "To engage in an effort to craft . . . `a definitive and categorical definition of the universe of acts that would constitute bad faith' would be unwise." The Delaware Supreme Court has described a non-exhaustive set of circumstances forming a failure to act in good faith:

A failure to act in good faith may be shown, for instance, where the fiduciary intentionally acts with a purpose other than that of advancing the best interests of the corporation, where the fiduciary acts with the intent to violate applicable positive law, or where the fiduciary intentionally fails to act in the face of a known duty to act, demonstrating a conscious disregard for his duties. There may be other examples of bad faith yet to be proven or alleged, but these three are the most salient.

Pleading a failure to act in good faith requires the plaintiff to "plead particularized facts that demonstrate that the directors acted with scienter, *i.e.,* that they had `actual or constructive knowledge' that their conduct was legally improper." That is, to allege a lack of good faith, a plaintiff must allege that the actor knew that he was acting "inconsistent with his fiduciary duties." "Gross negligence, without more, is insufficient to get out from under an exculpated breach of the duty of care."

Generally, this court is not in the business of second-guessing board decisions made by disinterested and independent directors. Of course, there are some business decisions that are so suspect that it is reasonably conceivable that the decision makers were not acting to advance the best interest of the corporation. Two cases relied on by the parties in briefing help delineate the boundaries of this principle—*Disney*, denying a motion to dismiss where the plaintiff adequately alleged that the board acted in bad faith, and *McElrath*, granting a motion to dismiss where the plaintiff failed to adequately allege that the board acted in bad faith.

In *Disney*, a stockholder sued Disney's departing CEO, Eisner, and its board for breach of fiduciary duty in connection with the hiring and firing of Eisner's longtime friend Ovitz as President. The narrative set out in the *Disney* complaint was quite stark. As alleged, Eisner "unilaterally" made the hiring decision.[52] The board did not receive any presentations on the terms of the employment contract, did not ask questions about the proposed agreement, received only a summary of the employment agreement's terms, approved the hire while the employment agreement was still a "work in progress," did not engage in further review once it had authorized the hire, and did not retain any outside experts to

---

[52] *Disney*, 825 A.2d at 287.

consult on the agreement. Negotiation of the unresolved employment terms took place solely between Eisner, Ovitz, and their attorneys. The compensation committee followed up with meetings to receive updates on the negotiations but did not otherwise engage in the process. The final agreement differed vastly from the initial summary that the board had approved. And when Eisner terminated Ovitz a year later, the employment agreement allowed Ovitz to reap substantial exit benefits, which the board permitted without further investigation.

On these facts, then-Chancellor Chandler denied the defendants' motion to dismiss for failure to plead demand futility, holding that the plaintiff had adequately pled that the directors failed to act in good faith. The well-pled allegations portrayed more than mere negligent or grossly negligent conduct, and instead suggested "that the defendant directors *consciously and intentionally disregarded their responsibilities,* adopting a `we don't care about the risks' attitude concerning a material corporate decision." Put differently, the facts as alleged gave rise to the inference that the directors "*knew* that they were making material decisions without adequate information and without adequate deliberation, and that they simply did not care if the decisions caused the corporation and its stockholders to suffer injury or loss." The Chancellor weighed the board's "ostrich-like" approach and concluded that the plaintiff had adequately alleged that "the defendant directors' conduct fell outside the protection of the business judgment rule," and that conclusion was sufficient to render demand futile under the second prong of *Aronson*.

Distinguishable allegations resulted in a different outcome in *McElrath*.[57] There, a stockholder challenged Uber's acquisition of a self-driving car project from Google. Uber's CEO, Travis Kalanick, negotiated the acquisition. Uber's diligence materials included a report from a computer forensic investigation firm finding that some of the target's employees had retained confidential information from Google following their departure. When the misuse of confidential information was later revealed, Uber suffered financially and reputationally. The plaintiff brought derivative claims against Kalanick and the directors who approved the transaction. To plead bad faith as to a majority of the board, the plaintiff constructed a narrative that the board was on notice that Kalanick might ignore intellectual property issues because Kalanick's prior business had been sued for copyright violations, Uber had a practice of hiring employees from competitors to steal trade secrets, and the merger agreement contained an abnormal indemnification clause that prevented Uber from seeking indemnification from the target's employees for non-compete and infringement claims.

---

[57] *McElrath*, 224 A.3d at 995.

The defendants moved to dismiss the complaint for failure to plead demand futility, and Vice Chancellor Glasscock granted the motion. The Delaware Supreme Court affirmed on appeal, identifying a number of factors that made it unreasonable to infer that Uber's board acted in bad faith. The high court observed that "[b]y any reasonable measure, the Uber board of directors approved a flawed transaction," but that did not give rise to a "real threat of personal liability" sufficient to disqualify a majority of the board for Rule 23.1 purposes. In reaching this conclusion, the court observed that the board did more than just rubberstamp the deal: they heard a presentation summarizing the transaction, reviewed the risk of litigation with Google, discussed due diligence, and asked questions. When the board asked questions about diligence and litigation risk, they received answers indicating that the risk was present, but not necessarily prevalent enough to kill the deal, and the board concluded that the diligence was "okay." The high court rejected the appellant's appeal to *Disney* by noting important distinctions—unlike the board in *Disney*, the Uber directors heard a presentation from the CEO on the transaction, met to consider the acquisition, and enlisted the assistance of outside counsel and an investigative firm to help with due diligence. The high court affirmed this court's dismissal based on the plaintiff's failure to show that the directors faced a substantial likelihood of liability.

Here, as in *McErath*, it is clear that the TIDAL acquisition was a "flawed" business decision "[b]y any reasonable measure." The question is whether, as in *Disney,* Plaintiff adequately alleged that the majority of the board acted in bad faith when approving it.

Plaintiff's counsel took an admirable stab at packaging the facts of this case into the mold of *Disney*. As Plaintiff tells it, Dorsey pulled some Eisner-level moves by pushing the deal forward singlehandedly, with the Transaction Committee playing an "ostrich-like" role. Plaintiff alleges that Dorsey caused Block to submit a letter of intent to purchase TIDAL before the Transaction Committee was even formed. The Transaction Committee then allowed Dorsey to handle negotiations. After discussing the opportunity for only thirty-five minutes during their first meeting in September, the Transaction Committee encouraged Dorsey to move forward. In advance of its second meeting in October, management provided a report that showed just how dire TIDAL's market position looked.

To be sure, the Transaction Committee asked many questions throughout the process, and Plaintiff concedes this much. Plaintiff argues, however, that the court should not credit the Transaction Committee for asking questions given the answers it received. As Plaintiff sees it, the problem was not that the Transaction Committee failed to ask questions—it is that the answers did not seem to matter.

Before its October meeting, the Transaction Committee asked whether any other members of senior management supported the acquisition; in response, the committee learned that there were none, aside from Dorsey. The Transaction Committee asked whether the artist commitments, which formed the basis for at least half of management's valuation of TIDAL, were legally enforceable; in response, the committee learned that Block would have "no recourse" if the artists decided to walk away. The Transaction Committee asked for near- and long-term plans for integrating TIDAL into Block's business; in response, the committee learned that management had not created these plans and that this remained "one of the biggest risks."

After the October meeting, the Transaction Committee went dark for three months while Dorsey negotiated the purchase price. Ultimately, without any further meetings, the Transaction Committee approved the acquisition by unanimous written consent.

Although the facts emphasized by Plaintiff do not generate tremendous confidence in the Transaction Committee's process, they fall short of supporting an inference of bad faith. Effectively, Plaintiff asks the court to presume bad faith based on the merits of the deal alone. Plaintiff does not allege that the Transaction Committee lacked a business reason for wanting to acquire TIDAL—the presentation materials show management's strategic goals for expanding Block into the music industry. Plaintiff does not attempt allege that any of the Committee Defendants were in any way beholden to Dorsey. Plaintiff acknowledge that the Committee Defendants did not sit idly by while Dorsey presented They asked many appropriate questions before the October 20 meeting, and they asked many appropriate follow-up questions in advance of the next meeting on January 22. The Transaction Committee were presented with over twenty single-spaced slides providing management's detailed answers to each of these questions. Over the course of negotiations, and even inexplicably after the deal was publicly announced, the purchase price dropped considerably.

On these facts, the Transaction Committee's actions more closely resemble those in *McElrath* than *Disney*. Plaintiff has alleged sufficient facts to make a reasonable person question the business wisdom of the TIDAL acquisition, but Plaintiff has failed to plead that the Committee Defendants acted in bad faith and thus faced a substantial likelihood of liability for that decision.

Plaintiff's allegations as to the remaining six non-Committee Defendant directors are even more attenuated. Plaintiff's only allegations as to those defendants are that they failed to meaningfully supervise the Transaction Committee's process. According to Plaintiff, the rest of the Board should have intervened to stop the TIDAL acquisition. Because Plaintiff has not adequately alleged that the Transaction Committee's approval of the TIDAL acquisition rose to the level of bad faith, it is difficult to imagine how the Board's lack of "supervision" of that process did so. Plaintiff's allegations as to the remaining directors fail.

III. CONCLUSION

Ultimately, the demand requirement is a manifestation of the business judgment rule, which exists in part to "free fiduciaries making risky business decisions in good faith from the worry that if those decisions do not pan out in the manner they had hoped, they will put their personal net worths at risk." In this case, the demand requirement operates as intended. Because Plaintiff failed to adequately allege with particularity facts giving rise to a reasonable doubt that a majority of the Board was disinterested or lacked independence with respect to the TIDAL acquisition, Plaintiff failed to plead that demand was futile. Defendants' motion to dismiss pursuant to Rule 23.1 is granted.

C. Demand Hypotheticals

The demand futility test can be confusing (even though it is ultimately very simple!). Let's practice.

SUTOCS Inc. ("SUTOCS") is a Delaware corporation with nine board members. In all the hypotheticals, shareholder Merrick files a derivative action against SUTOCS as nominal defendant and the respective principal defendants mentioned below. Merrick has not made a prior demand on the board. In each hypothetical, the question is if demand is excused as futile.

1. Merrick names as principal defendant X Corporation ("X"), alleging a damages claim.

2. Merrick names as principal defendants three former directors of SUTOCS, alleging a damages claim.

3. Merrick names as principal defendants the nine current directors of SUTOCS, alleging "breach of fiduciary duty."

4. Merrick names as principal defendants the nine current directors of SUTOCS, alleging they paid themselves vacations, excessive salaries, etc. from SUTOCS's accounts; Merrick lists the vacations, their costs, and the salaries, as well as comparison salaries at other firms and minutes from the SUTOCS board meetings approving these expenses.

5. Merrick names as principal defendants the nine current directors of SUTOCS, alleging that they approved a $30 billion acquisition agreement without reading it, without involving lawyers, bankers, or other advisors in the process, and while being very drunk on a beach;

Merrick also alleges that a standard valuation method suggests SUTOCS should have paid $5 billion less in the deal.

6. Same as 4., but since the board meetings and payments in question, five of the nine directors have been replaced by new directors who did not participate in the meetings and did not receive any of the money.

7. Same as 6., but the five new board members are employees of another corporation owned by some of the nine principal defendants.

5.2 Rules Applicable to All Shareholder Litigation

D. Indemnification and Insurance

Disney made it quite clear that the risk of liability for unconflicted directors is now modest at best even under the default rules: the business judgment rule provides robust protection to directors (and arguably officers). If the corporation's charter has a 102(b)(7) waiver, as most do, the risk of liability for directors (but not officers) is even less. Finally, derivative suits face the formidable hurdle of the demand requirement and perhaps a special litigation committee.

Nevertheless, directors and officers still face residual risk, in particular from litigation costs. Moreover, directors and officers may be the target of third-party litigation in relation to their corporate office: for example, the directors might be the target of an SEC enforcement action or an employee lawsuit as a result of their board service, whether or not such actions have a legally sound basis. For this reason, directors and officers should (and do) require that corporations indemnify and insure them extensively, even in advance of the final disposition of proceedings, which can take years (and generate hefty expenses in the interim). Please (re-)read Article IV of Apple's charter, Article X of Apple's bylaws, and the law firm advice to prospective directors at http://perma.cc/4QGU-M4FL. Under DGCL 145, corporations are allowed (subsections (a)-(b), (e)-(f)) and sometimes required (subsection (c)) to provide such indemnification and insurance. As a result, outside directors virtually never have to pay anything out of their own pockets in corporate lawsuits; *see* Bernard Black, Brian Cheffins, & Michael Klausner, *Outside Director Liability*, 58 STAN. L. REV. 1055 (2006).

Questions

1. Which liabilities and expenses are indemnifiable under DGCL 145? Which are insurable?

2. What does your answer to the preceding question imply for directors' and officers' incentives to settle a derivative action?

3. Why do directors and officers insist on insurance, i.e., why are they still worried in spite of the business judgment rule, 102(b)(7) waivers, and generous indemnification promises?

4. What is the point of liability, if any, if all of the foregoing neutralizes it?

E. Americas Mining Corp. v. Theriault (Del. 2012) (Attorney's fees)

To generate a substantial amount of shareholder litigation, merely allowing shareholders suits, direct or derivative, is not sufficient. Somebody needs to have an incentive to bring the suit. If shareholder-plaintiffs only recovered their pro rata share of the recovery (indirectly in the case of a derivative suit), incentives to bring suit would be very low and, in light of substantial litigation costs, usually insufficient. Litigation would be hamstrung by the same collective action problem as proxy fights. Under the *common fund doctrine*, however, U.S. courts award a substantial part of the recovery to the plaintiff or, in the standard case, to the plaintiff lawyer. As *Americas Mining* shows, that award can be very substantial indeed. Note that we excerpt only the passages relevant to the attorney fee award. The case in the court below was *In re Southern Peru* (Del. Ch. 2011).

The litigation incentives generated by such awards strike some as excessive. For a while, virtually every M&A deal attracted shareholder litigation, albeit mostly with much lower or no recovery. Corporations tried various tactics to limit the amount of litigation they face, prompting recent amendments of the DGCL (sections 102(f) and 115 – read!).

Questions

1. How does the court determine the right amount of the fee award? What criteria does it use, and what purposes does it aim to achieve? Are the criteria well calibrated to the purposes?

2. Who is opposing the fee award, and why?

3. Are the damage and fee awards sufficient to deter fiduciary duty violations similar to those at issue in this case?

51 A.3d 1213 (2012)

AMERICAS MINING CORPORATION, et al., Defendants Below, Appellants,

v.

Michael THERIAULT, as Trustee for the Theriault Trust, Plaintiff Below, Appellee.

Southern Copper Corporation, formerly known as Southern Peru Copper Corporation, Nominal Defendant Below, Appellant,

v.

Michael Theriault, as Trustee for the Theriault Trust, Plaintiff Below, Appellee.

Nos. 29, 2012, 30, 2012.

Supreme Court of Delaware.

Submitted: June 7, 2012.

Decided: August 27, 2012.

Reargument Denied: September 21, 2012.

[1218] S. Mark Hurd, Esquire and Kevin M. Coen, Esquire, Morris, Nichols, Arsht & Tunnell LLP, Wilmington, Delaware, and Bruce D. Angiolillo, Esquire (argued), Jonathan K. Youngwood, Esquire, Craig S. Waldman, Esquire, and Daniel J. Stujenske, Esquire, Simpson, Thacher & Bartlett LLP, New York, New York, for appellants, Americas Mining Corporation, Germán Larrea Mota-Velasco, Genaro Larrea Mota-Velasco, Oscar Gonzalez Rocha, Emilio Carrillo Gamboa, Jaime Fernando Collazo Gonzalez, Xavier Garcia de Quevedo Topete, Armando Ortega Gómez, and Juan Rebolledo Gout.

Stephen E. Jenkins, Esquire (argued), Richard L. Renck, Esquire, Andrew D. Cordo, Esquire and F. Troupe Mickler, IV, Esquire, Ashby & Geddes, Wilmington, Delaware, for appellant, Nominal Defendant Southern Copper Corporation, formerly known as Southern Peru Copper Corporation.

Ronald A. Brown, Jr., Esquire (argued) and Marcus E. Montejo, Esquire, Prickett, Jones & Elliott, P.A., Wilmington, Delaware, and Kessler Topaz Meltzer & Check, LLP, Radnor, Pennsylvania, for appellee.

Before STEELE, Chief Justice, HOLLAND, BERGER and RIDGELY, Justices and VAUGHN, President Judge, constituting the Court en Banc.

HOLLAND, Justice, for the majority:

This is an appeal from a post-trial decision and final judgment of the Court of Chancery awarding more than $2 billion in damages and more than $304 million in attorneys' fees. The Court of Chancery held that the defendants-appellants, Americas Mining Corporation ("AMC"), the subsidiary of Southern Copper Corporation's ("Southern Peru") controlling shareholder, and affiliate directors of Southern Peru (collectively, the "Defendants"), breached their fiduciary duty of loyalty to Southern Peru and its minority stockholders by causing Southern Peru to acquire the controller's 99.15% interest in a Mexican mining company, Minera México, S.A. de C.V. ("Minera"), for much more than it was worth, *i.e.*, at an unfair price[, in 2004.]

The Plaintiff challenged the transaction derivatively on behalf of Southern Peru. The Court of Chancery found the trial evidence established that the controlling shareholder, Grupo México, S.A.B. de C.V. ("Grupo Mexico"), through AMC, "extracted a deal that was far better than market" from Southern Peru due to the ineffective operation of a special committee (the "Special Committee"). To remedy the Defendants' breaches of loyalty, the Court of Chancery awarded the difference between the value Southern Peru paid for Minera ($3.7 billion) and the amount the Court of Chancery determined Minera was worth ($2.4 billion). The Court of Chancery awarded damages in the amount of $1.347 billion plus pre- and post-judgment interest, for a total judgment of $2.0316 billion. The Court of Chancery also awarded the Plaintiff's counsel attorneys' fees and expenses in the amount of 15% of the total judgment, which amounts to more than $304 million. [...]

ATTORNEYS' FEE AWARD

The Plaintiff petitioned for attorneys' fees and expenses representing 22.5% of the recovery plus post-judgment interest. The Court of Chancery awarded 15% of the $2.031 billion judgment, or $304,742,604.45, plus post-judgment interest until the attorneys' fee and expense award is satisfied ("Fee Award"). The Court of Chancery found that the Fee Award "fairly implements the most important factors our Supreme Court has highlighted under *Sugarland*, including the importance of benefits," and "creates a healthy incentive for plaintiff's lawyers to actually seek real achievement for the companies that they represent in derivative actions and the classes that they represent in class actions."

On appeal, the Defendants contend "the Court of Chancery abuse[d] its discretion by granting an unreasonable fee award of over $304 million that pays the Plaintiff's counsel over $35,000 per hour worked and 66 times the value of their time and expenses." [...]

Common Fund Doctrine

Under the common fund doctrine, "a litigant or a lawyer who recovers a [1253] common fund for the benefit of persons other than himself or his client is entitled to a reasonable attorney's fee from the fund as a whole." The common fund doctrine is a well-established basis for awarding attorneys' fees in the Court of Chancery. It is founded on the equitable principle that those who have profited from litigation should share its costs.

"Typically, successful derivative or class action suits which result in the recovery of money or property wrongfully diverted from the corporation ... are viewed as fund creating actions." In this case, [...] the $2.031 billion judgment resulted in the creation of a common fund. Accordingly, Plaintiff's counsel, whose efforts resulted in the creation of that common fund, are entitled to receive a reasonable fee and reimbursement for expenses from that fund. [...]

Sugarland

Factors Applied

The determination of any attorney fee award is a matter within the sound judicial discretion of the Court of Chancery. In this case, the Court of Chancery considered and applied each of [...]

> [t]he aptly-named *Sugarland* factor[s], perhaps never more aptly-named than today, [...]

Benefit Achieved

With regard to the first and most important of the *Sugarland* factors, the benefit achieved, the Court of Chancery found that "[t]he plaintiffs here indisputably prosecuted this action through trial and secured an immense economic benefit for Southern Peru." The Court of Chancery stated that "this isn't small and this isn't monitoring. This isn't a case where it's rounding, where the plaintiffs share credit." The Court of Chancery concluded that "anything that was achieved ... by this litigation [was] by these plaintiffs." With pre-judgment interest, the benefit achieved through the litigation amounts to more than $2 billion. Post-judgment interest accrues at more than $212,000 per day. The extraordinary benefit that was achieved in this case merits a very substantial award of attorneys' fees.

The Defendants take issue with the fact that the Fee Award was based upon the total damage award, which included pre-judgment interest. They contend that including such interest in the damage award is reversible error because the Plaintiff took too long to litigate this matter. The record reflects that the Court of Chancery considered the slow pace of the litigation in making the Fee Award. In response to the Defendants' [1256] arguments, the trial judge stated: "I'm not going to ... exclude interest altogether. I get that argument.... The interest I awarded is fairly earned by the plaintiffs. It's a lower amount. And, again, I've taken that [pace of litigation] into account by the percentage that I'm awarding." The Court of Chancery's decision to include pre-judgment interest in its determination of the benefit achieved was not arbitrary or capricious, but rather was the product of a logical and deductive reasoning process.

Difficulty and Complexity

The Court of Chancery carefully considered the difficulty and complexity of the case. It noted that the Plaintiff's attorneys had succeeded in presenting complex valuation issues in a persuasive way before a skeptical court:

> They advanced a theory of the case that a judge of this court, me, was reluctant to embrace. I denied their motion for summary judgment. I think I gave [Plaintiff's counsel] a good amount of grief that day about the theory. I asked a lot of questions at trial because I was still skeptical of the theory. It faced some of the best lawyers I know and am privileged to have come before me, and they won....
>
> I think when you talk about *Sugarland* and you talk about the difficulty of the litigation, was this difficult? Yes, it was. Were the defense counsel formidable and among the best that we have in our bar? They were. Did the plaintiffs have to do a lot of good work to get done and have to push back against a judge who was resistant to their approach? They did.

The Plaintiff's attorneys established at trial that Southern Peru had agreed to overpay its controlling shareholder by more than fifty percent ($3.7 billion compared to $2.4 billion). In doing so, the Court of Chancery found that the Plaintiff had to "deal with very complex financial and valuation issues" while being "up against major league, first-rate legal talent." This factor supports a substantial award of attorneys' fees.

Contingent Representation

The Plaintiff's attorneys pursued this case on a contingent fee basis. They invested a significant number of hours and incurred more than one million dollars in expenses. The

Defendants litigated vigorously and forced the Plaintiff to go to trial to obtain any monetary recovery. Accordingly, in undertaking this representation, the Plaintiff's counsel incurred all of the classic contingent fee risks, including the ultimate risk — no recovery whatsoever. The Court of Chancery acknowledged that the fee award was "going to be a lot per hour to people who get paid by the hour," but that in this case, the Plaintiff's attorneys' compensation was never based on an hourly rate. Therefore, the Court of Chancery found that an award representing 15% of the common fund was reasonable in light of the absolute risk taken by Plaintiff's counsel in prosecuting the case through trial on a fully contingent fee basis.

Standing and Ability of Counsel

The Court of Chancery acknowledged that it was familiar with Plaintiff's counsel and had respect for their skills and record of success. The Defendants do not contest the skill, ability or reputation of the Plaintiff's counsel. They argue, however, that the Court of Chancery "should have weighed more heavily Plaintiff's counsel's undoubted ability against the causal manner in which this case was litigated." The record does not support that argument.

[1257] First, the Court of Chancery credited the Defendants' arguments that a rescission-based remedy was inappropriate because of the Plaintiff's delay in litigating the case. Second, the Court of Chancery noted that the record could justify a much larger award of attorneys' fees, but it ultimately applied a "conservative metric because of Plaintiff's delay." Accordingly, the record reflects that the Court of Chancery's Fee Award took into account the length of time involved in getting this case to trial.

Time and Effort of Counsel

The effort by the Plaintiff's attorneys was significant. The Plaintiff's attorneys reviewed approximately 282,046 pages in document production and traveled outside the United States to take multiple depositions. They also engaged in vigorously contested pretrial motion practice. They invested their firms' resources by incurring over a million dollars of out-of-pocket expenses. Most significantly, however, the Plaintiff's attorneys took this case to trial and prevailed. We repeat the Court of Chancery's statement: "anything that was achieved ... by this litigation [was] by [the Plaintiff's attorneys]."

The primary focus of the Defendants' challenge to the Court of Chancery's Fee Award is on the hourly rate that it implies, given that Plaintiff's counsel spent 8,597 hours on this case. They argue that the Court of Chancery abused its discretion by failing to consider the hourly rate implied by the Fee Award as a "backstop check" on the reasonableness of the fee. The Court of Chancery recognized the implications of this argument: "I get it. It's approximately — on what I awarded, approximately $35,000 an hour, if you look at it that way." However, the Court of Chancery did not look at it that way.

Sugarland does not require, as the Defendants argue, courts to use the hourly rate implied by a percentage fee award, rather than the benefit conferred, as the benchmark for determining a reasonable fee award. To the contrary, in *Sugarland,* this Court refused to adopt the Third Circuit's lodestar approach, which primarily focuses on the time spent. [...]

Instead, we held that the [1258] *benefit achieved* by the litigation is the "common yardstick by which a plaintiff's counsel is compensated in a successful derivative action." [...]

The Defendants' alternative to their hourly argument is a challenge to the fairness of the percentage awarded by the Court of Chancery. The Defendants contend that the Court of Chancery erred by failing to apply a declining percentage analysis in its fee determination. According to the Defendants, this Court's decision in *Goodrich v. E.F. Hutton Group, Inc.* supports the *per se* use of a declining percentage. We disagree.

In *Goodrich,* we discussed the declining percentage of the fund concept, noting that the Court of Chancery rightly "acknowledged the merit of the emerging judicial consensus that the percentage of recovery awarded should "decrease as the size of the [common] fund increases.'" We also emphasized, however, that the multiple factor *Sugarland* approach to determining attorneys' fee awards remained adequate for purposes of applying the equitable common fund doctrine. Therefore, the use of a declining percentage, in applying the *Sugarland* factors in common fund cases, is a matter of discretion and is not required *per se*. [...]

Fee Award Percentage Discretionary

In determining the amount of a reasonable fee award, our holding in *Sugarland* assigns the greatest weight to the benefit achieved in the litigation. When the benefit is quantifiable, as in this case, by the creation of a common fund, *Sugarland* calls for an award of attorneys' fees based upon a percentage of the benefit. The *Sugarland* factor that is given the greatest emphasis is the size of the fund created, because a "common fund is itself the measure of success ... [and] represents the benchmark from which a reasonable fee will be awarded."

Delaware case law supports a wide range of reasonable percentages for attorneys' fees, but 33% is "the very top of the range of percentages." The Court of Chancery has a history of awarding lower percentages of the benefit where cases have settled before trial. When a case settles early, the Court of Chancery tends to award 10-15% of the monetary benefit conferred. When a case settles after the plaintiffs have engaged in meaningful litigation efforts, typically including [1260] multiple depositions and some level of motion practice, fee awards in the Court of Chancery range from 15-25% of the monetary benefits conferred. "A study of recent Delaware fee awards finds that the average amount of fees awarded when derivative and class actions settle for both monetary and therapeutic consideration is approximately 23% of the monetary benefit conferred; the median is 25%." Higher percentages are warranted when cases progress to a post-trial adjudication.

The reasonableness of the percentage awarded by the Court of Chancery is reviewed for an abuse of discretion. The question presented in this case is how to properly determine a reasonable percentage for a fee award in a megafund case. A recent study by the economic consulting firm National Economic Research Associates ("NERA") demonstrates that overall as the settlement values increase, the amount of fee percentages and expenses decrease. The study reports that median attorneys' fees awarded from settlements in securities class actions are generally in the range of 22% to 30% of the recovery until the recovery approaches approximately $500 million. Once in the vicinity of over $500 million, the median attorneys' fees falls to 11%.

Appellate courts that have examined a "megafund rule" requiring a fee percentage to be capped at a low figure when the recovery is quite high, have rejected it as a blanket rule. It is now accepted that "[a] mechanical, a *per se* application of the [1261] "megafund rule' is not necessarily reasonable under the circumstances of a case." For example, although the Third Circuit recognized that its jurisprudence confirms the use of a sliding scale as "appropriate" for percentage fee awards in large recovery cases, it has held that trial judges are not required to use a declining percentage approach in every case involving a large settlement. [...]

In *Goodrich,* [...] We reasoned that "[t]he adoption of a mandatory methodology or particular mathematical model for determining attorney's fees in common fund cases would be the antithesis of the equitable principles from which the concept of such awards originated." [...]

Fee Award Reasonable Percentage

The percentage awarded as attorneys' fees from a common fund is committed to the sound discretion of the Court of Chancery. [...]

We review an award of attorneys' fees for an abuse of discretion. [...]

In this case, the Court of Chancery carefully weighed and considered all of the *Sugarland* factors. The record supports its factual findings and its well-reasoned decision that a reasonable attorneys' fee is 15% of the benefit created. [...]

Conclusion

The judgment of the Court of Chancery, awarding more than $2 billion in damages [1263] and more than $304 million in attorneys' fees, is affirmed.

BERGER, Justice, concurring and dissenting:

I concur in the majority's decision on the merits, but I would find that the trial court did not properly apply the law when it awarded attorneys' fees, and respectfully dissent on that issue.

The majority finds no abuse of discretion in the trial court's decision to award more than $304 million in attorneys' fees. The majority says that the trial court applied the settled standards set forth in *Sugarland Industries, Inc. v. Thomas,* and that this Court may not substitute its notions of what is right for those of the trial court. But the trial court did not apply *Sugarland,* it applied its own world views on incentives, bankers' compensation, and envy.

To be sure, the trial court recited the *Sugarland* standards. Its analysis, however, focused on the perceived need to incentivize plaintiffs' lawyers to take cases to trial. The trial court hypothesized that a stockholder plaintiff would be happy with a lawyer who says, "If you get really rich because of me, I want to get rich, too." Then, the trial court talked about how others get big payouts without comment, but that lawyers are not viewed the same way:

> [T]here's an idea that when a lawyer or law firms are going to get a big payment, that there's something somehow wrong about that, just because it's a lawyer. I'm sorry, but investment banks have hit it big.... They've hit it big many times. And to me, envy is not an appropriate motivation to take into account when you set an attorney fee.

The trial court opined that a declining percentage for "mega" cases would not create a healthy incentive system, and that the trial court would not embrace such an approach. Rather, the trial court repeatedly pointed out that "plenty of market participants make big fees when their clients win," and that if this were a hedge fund manager or an investment bank, the fee would be okay. In sum, the trial court said that the fundamental test for reasonableness is whether the fee is setting a good incentive, and that the only basis for reducing the fee would be envy. That is not a decision based on *Sugarland.*

[...]

F. Court Scrutiny of Settlement

Settlements of class and derivative actions require court approval under Del. Ch. Rules 23(e) and 23.1(c), respectively. In the 2015 *Riverbed* opinion, Vice-Chancellor Glasscock explained the rationale for this requirement in the context of a class action:

> Settlements in class actions present a well-known agency problem: A plaintiff's attorney may favor a quick settlement where the additional effort required to fully develop valuable claims on behalf of the class may not generate an additional fee as lucrative to the plaintiff's attorney as accepting a quick and moderate fee, then pursuing other interests. The interest of the principal—the individual plaintiff/stockholder—is often so small that it serves as scant check on the perverse incentive described above, notwithstanding that the aggregate interest of the class in pursuing litigation may be great—the very problem that makes class litigation appropriate in the first instance.
>
> —*In re Riverbed Tech., Inc. S'holders Litig.*, 2015 WL 5458041, at *7 (Del. Ch. Sept. 17, 2015).

In particular, as class representatives, plaintiff attorneys have the power to forfeit claims on behalf of the entire class in a settlement. Plaintiff attorneys are thus in a position to "sell" shareholder claims—possibly below value but keeping the "price" (fees) for themselves:

> In combination, the incentives of the litigants may be inimical to the class: the individual plaintiff may have little actual stake in the outcome, her counsel may rationally believe a quick settlement and modest fee is in his best financial interest, and the defendants may be happy to "purchase," at the bargain price of disclosures of marginal benefit to the class and payment of the plaintiffs' attorney fees, a broad release from liability.
>
> —Id., at *9.

In spite of these concerns, Delaware courts long approved settlements containing broad releases of shareholder claims in return for moderate corporate disclosures and six-figure attorney fees. This spurred a practice that Chancellor Bouchard described in the seminal *Trulia* opinion:

Today, the public announcement of virtually every transaction involving the acquisition of a public corporation provokes a flurry of class action lawsuits alleging that the target's directors breached their fiduciary duties by agreeing to sell the corporation for an unfair price. On occasion, although it is relatively infrequent, such litigation has generated meaningful economic benefits for stockholders when, for example, the integrity of a sales process has been corrupted by conflicts of interest on the part of corporate fiduciaries or their advisors.[17] But far too often [892] such litigation serves no useful purpose for stockholders. Instead, it serves only to generate fees for certain lawyers who are regular players in the enterprise of routinely filing hastily drafted complaints on behalf of stockholders on the heels of the public announcement of a deal and settling quickly on terms that yield no monetary compensation to the stockholders they represent.

In such lawsuits, plaintiffs' leverage is the threat of an injunction to prevent a transaction from closing. Faced with that threat, defendants are incentivized to settle quickly in order to mitigate the considerable expense of litigation and the distraction it entails, to achieve closing certainty, and to obtain broad releases as a form of "deal insurance." These incentives are so potent that many defendants self-expedite the litigation by volunteering to produce "core documents" to plaintiffs' counsel, obviating the need for plaintiffs to seek the Court's permission to expedite the proceedings in aid of a preliminary injunction application and thereby avoiding the only gating mechanism (albeit one friendly to

---

[17] Some examples of adjudicated cases of this type arising from acquisitions of public corporations include: *In re Rural/Metro Corp. S'holders Litig.*, 102 A.3d 205, 263 (Del. Ch.2014) (finding after trial that class suffered damages of $91 million, of which the board's financial advisor was liable for 83%, based on aiding and abetting fiduciary breaches in sale of corporation), *aff'd sub nom. RBC Capital Mkts., LLC v. Jervis*, 129 A.3d 816, 2015 WL 7721882 (Del. Nov. 30, 2015); *In re Dole Food Co., Inc. S'holder Litig.*, 2015 WL 5052214, at *47 (Del. Ch. Aug. 27, 2015) (finding after trial that certain directors were liable for $148 million in damages, based on fiduciary breaches in going-private transaction); *In re Emerging Commc'ns, Inc. S'holders Litig.*, 2004 WL 1305745, at *43 (Del. Ch. May 3, 2004) (finding after trial that certain defendants were liable to stockholders for damages of $27.80 per share for fiduciary breaches in going-private transaction). *See also In re Jefferes Grp., Inc. S'holders Litig.*, 2015 WL 1414350 (Del. Ch. Mar. 26, 2015) (ORDER) (approving settlement for $70 million (net of attorneys' fees) to resolve allegations involving conflicts of interest in the sale of Jefferies Group to Leucadia National Corporation); *In re Del Monte Foods Co. S'holder Litig.*, Cons.C.A. No. 6027-VCL, 2011 WL 6008590 (Del. Ch. Dec. 1, 2011) (ORDER) (approving $89 million settlement of stockholder suit alleging fiduciary duty violations in connection with leveraged buy-out).

plaintiffs[18]) the Court has to screen out frivolous cases and to ensure that its limited resources are used wisely.

Once the litigation is on an expedited track and the prospect of an injunction hearing looms, the most common currency used to procure a settlement is the issuance of supplemental disclosures to the target's stockholders before they are asked to vote on the proposed transaction. The theory behind making these disclosures is that, by having the additional information, stockholders will be better informed when exercising their franchise rights. Given the Court's historical practice of approving disclosure settlements when the additional information is not material, and indeed may be of only minor value to the stockholders, providing supplemental disclosures is a particularly easy "give" for defendants to make in exchange for a release.

Once an agreement-in-principle is struck to settle for supplemental disclosures, the litigation takes on an entirely different, non-adversarial character. Both sides of the caption then share the same interest in obtaining the Court's approval of the settlement. The next step, after notice has been provided to the stockholders, is a hearing in which the Court must evaluate the fairness of the proposed settlement. Significantly, in advance of such hearings, the Court receives briefs and affidavits from plaintiffs extolling the value of the supplemental disclosures and advocating for approval of the proposed settlement, but rarely receives any submissions expressing an opposing viewpoint.

—*In re Trulia, Inc. S'holders Litig.*, 129 A.3d 884, 891-3 (Del Ch. 2016).

Notice that Chancellor Bouchard does not mention any submissions from defendants in the fairness hearing. That is because the defendants, too, wanted to settle the lawsuit—and obtain the release! In essence, there had developed a practice—or at least a perception of a practice—where defendants and certain plaintiff attorneys colluded at the expense of shareholders at large: the plaintiff attorney got a fee and

---

[18] Stockholder plaintiffs who seek expedition benefit from the most favorable standard available under our law for assessing the merits of a claim—"colorability"—and from the sensible policy of this Court to attempt to resolve disclosure claims before stockholders are asked to vote. [...]

defendants got a broad release, while shareholders lost potentially valuable claims in return for useless disclosures. Chancellor Bouchard essentially put an end to this practice in Delaware with the following announcement:

> Based on these considerations, this opinion offers the Court's perspective that disclosure claims arising in deal litigation optimally should be adjudicated outside of the context of a proposed settlement so that the Court's consideration of the merits of the disclosure claims can occur in an adversarial process without the defendants' desire to obtain an often overly broad release hanging in the balance. The opinion further explains that, to the extent that litigants continue to pursue disclosure settlements, they can expect that the Court will be increasingly vigilant in scrutinizing the "give" and the "get" of such settlements to ensure that they are genuinely fair and reasonable to the absent class members.

—Id., at 887.

Predictably, plaintiff attorneys then attempted to sue in other fora, namely federal courts or other states' courts (e.g., where the corporation is headquartered), while corporations attempted to cut off such attempts through forum selection clauses (*cf.* DGCL 115).

Part III: Mergers & Acquisitions

"Mergers & acquisitions," or M&A for short, denotes the buying, selling, and joining of entire corporations or at least business units. The size and complexity of such transactions generate much attention and fee income. More to the point, these transactions implicate many areas of corporate law, which make them a great training ground for us. Last but not least, acquisitions can be an important governance device if better-managed firms "take over" worse-managed firms.

Chapter 6. Introduction to M&A

A. Background

1. Importance

(a) Importance for the firm

Acquisitions are the single most important event in most corporations' existences. On a formal level, the corporation may cease to exist after the acquisition (see transactional technique below).

More importantly, however, most acquisitions profoundly affect the substantive organization of the business. This is especially so for the acquired firm (the "target"). The target's management will usually leave (or be made to leave) following the acquisition. Often, business units are sold or shut down. But acquisitions tend to be major events for the acquirer as well, because the acquirer's business may grow and change dramatically through the transaction.

Acquisitions are routine events only if the acquirer is much bigger than the target. (For example, big pharmaceutical companies frequently buy small biotechs or other startups to add to their technology portfolio.)

(b) Importance for the social allocation of productive capacity

In a broader social perspective, acquisitions reallocate large pools of assets to different management and possibly different economic tasks (e.g., Google's acquisition of Motorola; Facebook's acquisition of Instagram).

Oftentimes, the capital structure of the corporation changes dramatically as well. This is particularly so in acquisitions or divestitures by so called "financial acquirers" — mainly private equity funds (acquirers who do not have a stand-alone line of business but specialize in acquiring and then improving existing companies).

(c) Importance for corporate governance

From the perspective of corporate governance, the most important aspect of acquisitions may be their role as a governance device.

Takeovers have a direct effect on governance when a better-governed firm takes over a worse-governed firm. After the takeover, both firms' assets will be managed under the former's better governance structure.

But takeovers also have an indirect effect on governance. The *threat* of a takeover may incentivize boards to do a better job. If they don't, the corporation's stock price may fall below potential. This may create an opportunity for a potential acquirer to take over the firm at a profit. While this indirect effect is hard to measure, it may well be more important than the direct effect.

(d) Hostile takeovers and takeover defenses

To be sure, the threat of a takeover would be empty if takeovers only occurred with the approval of the current management (so-called "friendly takeovers"). This is why "hostile takeovers" — takeovers without the approval of current management — deserve special attention as a potentially potent governance device.

By definition, target management opposes hostile takeovers. Over time, target managers and their advisers have devised various "takeover defenses" to fend off such "attacks." The defenses may be justified because hostile takeovers and the threat thereof can be abused to disrupt the target's business. The defenses can also be an important bargaining tool to get a better price for target shareholders. At the same time, target management may use defenses merely to perpetuate itself in office and to blunt the governance mechanism of hostile takeovers. We will study an important string of cases struggling with the double-edged nature of takeover defenses— "entrenchment" on the one hand and legitimate protection of corporate interests on the other.

2. Transactional technique: mergers in a technical sense

Most acquisitions are structured to involve a "merger" in a technical legal sense. In this sense, it would be more accurate to speak of "acquisitions by way of merger" instead of "mergers and acquisitions."

A merger in this legal sense is the fusion of two corporations into one (cf. DGCL subchapter 9, especially sections 251, 259-261). The target merges with the acquirer or, more frequently, a wholly-owned subsidiary of the acquirer. The acquirer thus obtains control over the target's assets directly (if the target merges with the acquirer) or indirectly (if the target merges into the acquirer's subsidiary). The target shareholders obtain the merger consideration for their shares, if they have not already sold them earlier.

Because a merger tends to be such an important transaction, it generally requires approval by the board and a majority of the shareholders (DGCL 251(b)/(c)). Furthermore, shareholders can request to receive the "fair value" of their shares as appraised by the Chancery Court rather than the merger consideration (appraisal, cf. DGCL 262). There are, however, numerous exceptions and conditions – see Delaware Merger ABC below.

The shareholder approval requirement has major implications for deal structure and timing even if a clear majority of shareholders approves of the deal when it is signed. Properly calling a shareholder meeting and soliciting proxies takes time – usually several months. (You wouldn't know this from DGCL 213(a) and 222 alone, but you need to factor in the time it takes to clear the proxy statement with the SEC [again, not a statutory or regulatory requirement but everybody does it] and then to solicit the proxies – at least 50% of the shareholder need to approve, DGCL 251(c).) Many things can happen between signing and shareholder vote. Most importantly, a new bidder may arrive on the scene—usually to the (then) delight of the seller and dismay of the buyer.

Question

1. Why do sellers tend to like the appearance of other bidders whereas bidders dread them?

A partial alternative is to structure the deal as a tender offer, i.e., an offer to all shareholders to sell ("tender") their shares to the bidder at the price announced by the offeror (and, in a friendly deal, agreed by the target corporation's board). Under SEC rules, a tender offer must be open for at least 20 business days (rule 14e-1, see below), but it can still be quicker than calling a shareholder meeting. The tender offer is only a partial alternative because not all of the shares will be tendered, and so the offeror will have to conduct a follow-up merger to "squeeze out" (see below) the remaining shareholders. (But see now DGCL 251(h), which greatly facilitates the post-tender squeeze-out—more on this below.)

(a) Mergers vs. asset sales

The use of the merger technique is a choice of convenience (and possibly tax and accounting considerations, but those are beyond this course). The alternative to a merger is an asset sale, as in *Hariton* v. *Arco Electronics* below.

The hassles of asset sales

In an asset sale, the target transfers its assets individually to the acquirer. The sales contract must carefully describe all assets and employ transfer mechanisms compliant with the applicable transfer rules, which differ by asset type (e.g., personal property, real property, contracts, negotiable instruments, etc.). If the sales contract fails to do so, the acquirer will not obtain ownership rights in all the assets. Moreover, some assets cannot be transferred in this way without the affirmative approval of some third party. In particular, by default, contracts cannot be transferred without the approval of the contract counterparty. All of this makes asset sales extremely cumbersome. (Unless, of course, the assets are shares in one or more subsidiaries. That sort of asset sale would be very simple.)

An asset sale does have two potential advantages. First, dissenting shareholders do not get appraisal rights (cf. DGCL 262 and *Hariton* v. *Arco Electronics* below). Second, the acquirer does not automatically assume all the liabilities of the target. In practice, however, a variety of rules limit the importance of this second point. Some liabilities automatically transfer with ownership of the asset (such as environmental cleanup obligations). Further, a variety of rules covered later in the class protect creditors against opportunistic asset transfers. Last but not least, major debt contracts usually restrict a debtor's ability to sell off a substantial part of its assets.

To be sure, a contract might also require approval for a merger, and many important ones do. In general, as always, contractual arrangements, including charter arrangements, can add or efface distinctions between asset sales and mergers. What will usually remain, however, is the hassle of transferring assets individually in an asset sale.

The ease of mergers

The merger, on the other hand, is easy. It usually requires only an agreement between the two corporations, and approval by both boards and shareholder meetings, usually by simple majority vote. Unanimous approval is not required.

In addition, the merger agreement can freely determine just about anything in the organization of the joint entity: its charter, its ownership, and its management. For example, there is no requirement that the shareholders of both merging corporations remain shareholders in the joint entity.

A warning: Don't be misled by expressions such as "surviving entity." They are merely naming conventions. In particular, the shareholders, board, management, and charter of the "surviving entity" could all be eliminated in the merger (in the case of shareholders, for due compensation) and replaced by those of the other entity.

A side note: Because the merger is so easy and flexible, it is a versatile device with many uses outside of M&A. For example, it can be used for internal rearrangements inside a corporate group (cf. DGCL 253, 267), reincorporation from one state to another (by merging the corporation into a shell company incorporated in the destination state; this can also be achieved directly by "conversion" under DGCL 265, 266), and so on.

(b) Other steps in the acquisition process

To be sure, the merger is not the only step in many acquisitions. This is most obvious in a hostile takeover. A merger requires approval by the target board. By definition, the hostile takeover is a situation in which the target board is unwilling to approve a merger. So how can a merger happen in a hostile takeover?

The answer is that the merger will come last in a chain of hostile acquisition steps. In a standard hostile takeover, the acquirer would first acquire a majority of the target stock through a "tender offer" (i.e., an offer addressed to all target shareholders to purchase their stock) and then replace the resisting target board. The new board would then cause the target to enter into a merger agreement with the acquirer.

Friendly acquisitions can also involve more than just the merger step. In these cases, however, the merger agreement may act as a road map containing the earlier steps. The 3G / Burger King agreement below provides an example of such a structure.

3. Sources of law

M&A involves a complicated mix of statutes, rules, and precedents, from many areas of law, including corporate law, securities law, and antitrust.

(a) Securities laws

The securities laws and rules not only regulate disclosure, but also set important timing requirements. In particular, the Williams Act of 1968 requires an acquirer of 5% or more of a corporation's voting stock to disclose this fact within ten days of crossing the 5% threshold (Exchange Act §13(d)). This means that an acquirer cannot gain control of the target secretly and slowly.

The Williams Act also regulates tender offers (Exchange Act §14(d)/(e)). Among other things, the SEC rules require that any tender offer remain open for at least 20 business days (rule 14e-1). This prevents quick acquisitions by way of a tender offer. Moreover, while the offer remains open, shareholders who already tendered may reverse their decision and withdraw their shares (rule 14d-7(1)).

Other Williams Act rules of particular importance for deal structure are:

- "All holders, best price:" the tender offer must be open to all shareholders, and all must be paid the same consideration (rule 14d-10);
- Conversely, the tender offeror may not buy stock in side deals between public announcement and expiry of the offer (rule 14e-5: "Prohibiting purchases outside of a tender offer");
- Pro-rata allocation: if the tender offer is oversubscribed — the tender offer is for less than all of the corporation's outstanding stock, and more shares are tendered — the offeror must take up tendered shares pro rata (Exchange Act §14(d)(6), rule 14d-8).

(b) Stock exchange listing rules

The listing rules of the stock exchanges can play an important role as well. For example, rule 312.03 of the New York Stock Exchange's Listed Company Manual requires stockholder approval for certain stock issuances, including those of a certain size (≥20%) or leading to a change in control. Rule 402.04 requires active proxy solicitation for any stockholder meeting, triggering the SEC's proxy rules and associated delay.

(c) Corporate law

Within corporate law, the statutory provisions relating to mergers are of obvious importance for M&A (e.g., DGCL 251, 253, 262, 271). But as we have already seen (*Blasius*), many general and perhaps deceivingly innocuous provisions of the DGCL, such as those governing director removal and appointment (DGCL 141, 223), can also play an important role in M&A.

Fiduciary duties play a major role in M&A as well. In fact, most of the cases that we will read will deal with the shaping of fiduciary duties in the M&A context. Nevertheless, this should not lead you to think that the statute is unimportant. Fiduciary duties only become important to the extent that the statute has not preempted a particular question. In other words, the statute demarcates the field on which the game is played, and fiduciary duties regulate the behavior of the players on the field. Both are important to understand the game.

(d) Other law

Depending on the industry, various other areas of law may come into play. For example, banks require approval from the banking regulator for acquisitions.

One area of law that is always important in M&A is antitrust. It is covered in a separate course. Here you just need to know that the Hart-Scott-Rodino Act requires that certain antitrust filings be made fifteen or thirty days before the closing of an acquisition. This may be an additional source of delay — and, in the case of "hostile" acquisitions, an early warning to the corporation's management.

4. Delaware Merger ABC

The following paragraphs summarize the basic statutory rules for mergers of Delaware corporations: who needs to approve them, and who has appraisal rights. You should look up the cited statutory provisions and verify that this summary is correct.

(a) Approval requirements

Generally, both corporations' boards (DGCL 251(b)) and shareholders (DGCL 251(c)) need to approve the merger.
Exceptions:

- **cash-deal, small deal** (DGCL 251(f)): the approval by shareholders of a *surviving* corporation is not required if
  - the surviving corporation's charter is not amended through the merger, and
  - the surviving corporation issues less than 20% of new shares in the merger
- **"short-form merger"** (DGCL 253(a)): if one of the constituent corporations ("parent") already owns at least 90% of all classes of voting stock of the other ("subsidiary"):

- o   the approval of subsidiary's board and shareholders is never required;
  - o   the approval of parent's shareholders is not required if parent is the surviving corporation and its charter is not changed in the merger
- **"back-end squeeze-out"** (DGCL 251(h) – since 2013): the approval by remaining target shareholders is not required if
  - o   the target is a public corporation (listed or >2,000 shareholders),
  - o   the bidder acquires the otherwise requisite majority of shares in a tender offer for all of the target's stock pursuant to a merger agreement with the target, and
  - o   the merger consideration is the same as the tender offer consideration.

(b) Appraisal rights

NB: To perfect appraisal rights, the shareholder must not vote in favor of the merger, must deliver a written notice of objection before the vote, and must hold the shares through the effective date of the merger (DGCL 262(a)/(d)). Shareholders who demand appraisal do not receive the merger consideration; they only receive the value of their shares as appraised by the court (cf. DGCL 262(k)).

Appraisal rights are generally available for shareholders of both corporations (DGCL 262(b)).

Exceptions:

- **"short-form merger"**: the parent's shareholders do not have appraisal rights (DGCL 253(c)/(d), 262(b)(3))
- **"market-out"** (DGCL 262(b)(1)/(2)): Shareholders
  - o   of a public corporation (listed or >2,000 shareholders), or
  - o   whose approval vote was not required for the merger under DGCL 251(f)

  do not have appraisal rights if they receive as merger consideration shares of the surviving corporation or shares of another public corporation.

Questions

1.   Do the exceptions to the shareholder approval requirement make sense?

2.   Do the exceptions to the appraisal remedy make sense?

3.   What is the point of the appraisal remedy, if any?

B. Hariton v. Arco Electronics, Inc. (Del. 1963)

This case addresses the question whether an asset sale that achieves the same purpose as a merger should be subjected to the rules applicable to mergers as "*de facto merger.*"

Questions

1. Why did the defendant structure the deal as an asset sale rather than a merger?

2. What is the Delaware Supreme Court's position on the de facto merger theory? (NB: This position is still good law in Delaware.)

188 A.2d 123 (1963)

Martin HARITON, Appellant,

v.

ARCO ELECTRONICS, INC., a Delaware corporation, Appellee.

Supreme Court of Delaware.

January 24, 1963.

Irving Morris and J. A. Rosenthal, of Cohen & Morris, Wilmington, for appellant.

S. Samuel Arsht and Walter K. Stapleton, of Morris, Nichols, Arsht & Tunnell, Wilmington, for appellee.

SOUTHERLAND, Chief Justice, and WOLCOTT and TERRY, JJ., sitting. [124]

SOUTHERLAND, Chief Justice.

This case involves a sale of assets under § 271 of the corporation law, 8 Del.C. It presents for decision the question presented, but not decided, in Heilbrunn v. Sun Chemical Corporation, Del., 150 A.2d 755. It may be stated as follows:

A sale of assets is effected under § 271 in consideration of shares of stock of the purchasing corporation. The agreement of sale embodies also a plan to dissolve the selling corporation and distribute the shares so received to the stockholders of the seller, so as to accomplish the same result as would be accomplished by a merger of the seller into the purchaser. Is the sale legal?

The facts are these:

The defendant Arco and Loral Electronics Corporation, a New York corporation, are both engaged, in somewhat different forms, in the electronic equipment business. In the summer of 1961 they negotiated for an amalgamation of the companies. As of October 27, 1961, they entered into a "Reorganization Agreement and Plan." The provisions of this Plan pertinent here are in substance as follows:

> 1. Arco agrees to sell all its assets to Loral in consideration (inter alia) of the issuance to it of 283,000 shares of Loral.
> 2. Arco agrees to call a stockholders meeting for the purpose of approving the Plan and the voluntary dissolution.
> 3. Arco agrees to distribute to its stockholders all the Loral shares received by it as a part of the complete liquidation of Arco.

At the Arco meeting all the stockholders voting (about 80%) approved the Plan. It was thereafter consummated.

Plaintiff, a stockholder who did not vote at the meeting, sued to enjoin the comsummation of the Plan on the grounds (1) that it was illegal, and (2) that it was unfair. The second ground was abandoned. Affidavits and documentary evidence were filed, and defendant moved for summary judgment and dismissal of the complaint. The Vice Chancellor granted the motion and plaintiff appeals.

The question before us we have stated above. Plaintiff's argument that the sale is illegal runs as follows:

The several steps taken here accomplish the same result as a merger of Arco into Loral. In a "true" sale of assets, the stockholder of the seller retains the right to elect whether the selling company shall continue as a holding company. Moreover, the stockholder of the selling company is forced to accept an investment in a new enterprise without the right of appraisal granted under the merger statute. § 271 cannot therefore be legally combined with a dissolution proceeding under § 275 and a consequent distribution of the purchaser's stock. Such a proceeding is a misuse of the power granted under § 271, and a *de facto* merger results.

The foregoing is a brief summary of plaintiff's contention.

[125] Plaintiff's contention that this sale has achieved the same result as a merger is plainly correct. The same contention was made to us in Heilbrunn v. Sun Chemical Corporation, Del., 150 A.2d 755. Accepting it as correct, we noted that this result is made possible by the overlapping scope of the merger statute and section 271, mentioned in Sterling v. Mayflower Hotel Corporation, 33 Del.Ch. 293, 93 A.2d 107, 38 A. L.R.2d 425. We also adverted to the increased use, in connection with corporate reorganization

plans, of § 271 instead of the merger statute. Further, we observed that no Delaware case has held such procedure to be improper, and that two cases appear to assume its legality. Finch v. Warrior Cement Corporation, 16 Del.Ch. 44, 141 A. 54, and Argenbright v. Phoenix Finance Co., 21 Del.Ch. 288, 187 A. 124. But we were not required in the Heilbrunn case to decide the point.

We now hold that the reorganization here accomplished through § 271 and a mandatory plan of dissolution and distribution is legal. This is so because the sale-of-assets statute and the merger statute are independent of each other. They are, so to speak, of equal dignity, and the framers of a reorganization plan may resort to either type of corporate mechanics to achieve the desired end. This is not an anomalous result in our corporation law. As the Vice Chancellor pointed out, the elimination of accrued dividends, though forbidden under a charter amendment (Keller v. Wilson & Co., 21 Del.Ch. 391, 190 A. 115) may be accomplished by a merger. Federal United Corporation v. Havender, 24 Del.Ch. 318, 11 A.2d 331.

In Langfelder v. Universal Laboratories, D.C., 68 F.Supp. 209, Judge Leahy commented upon "the general theory of the Delaware Corporation Law that action taken pursuant to the authority of the various sections of that law constitute acts of independent legal significance and their validity is not dependent on other sections of the Act." 68 F.Supp. 211, footnote.

In support of his contentions of a *de facto* merger plaintiff cites Finch v. Warrior Cement Corporation, 16 Del.Ch. 44, 141 A. 54, and Drug Inc. v. Hunt, 5 W.W.Harr. 339, 35 Del. 339, 168 A. 87. They are patently inapplicable. Each involved a disregard of the statutory provisions governing sales of assets. Here it is admitted that the provisions of the statute were fully complied with.

Plaintiff concedes, as we read his brief, that if the several steps taken in this case had been taken separately they would have been legal. That is, he concedes that a sale of assets, followed by a separate proceeding to dissolve and distribute, would be legal, even though the same result would follow. This concession exposes the weakness of his contention. To attempt to make any such distinction between sales under § 271 would be to create uncertainty in the law and invite litigation.

We are in accord with the Vice Chancellor's ruling, and the judgment below is affirmed.

C. 3G / Burger King Merger Agreement (2010)

Most of the action in M&A is in the contracts. The following is an excerpt from the acquisition agreement whereby 3G Capital, a private equity fund, acquired Burger King. The full agreement is available on EDGAR.

Questions

Try to answer the following questions in reading the excerpts:

1. What is the sequence of events mapped out in this agreement?

2. What are the main economic terms?

3. What will happen to Burger King Holdings, Inc. (its shares, its board, etc.) in the merger?

AGREEMENT AND PLAN OF MERGER

This AGREEMENT AND PLAN OF MERGER (this "Agreement"), dated as of September 2, 2010, is entered into by and among Blue Acquisition Holding Corporation, a Delaware corporation ("Parent"), Blue Acquisition Sub, Inc., a Delaware corporation and a wholly owned Subsidiary of Parent ("Sub"), and Burger King Holdings, Inc., a Delaware corporation (the "Company"). Each of Parent, Sub and the Company are referred to herein as a "Party" and together as "Parties". Capitalized terms used and not otherwise defined herein have the meanings set forth in Article X.

RECITALS

WHEREAS, the respective boards of directors of each of Parent, Sub and the Company have unanimously (i) determined that this Agreement and the transactions contemplated hereby, including the Offer and the Merger, are advisable, fair to and in the best interests of their respective stockholders and (ii) approved this Agreement and the transactions contemplated hereby, including the Offer and the Merger, on the terms and subject to the conditions set forth in this Agreement;

WHEREAS, Parent proposes to cause Sub to commence a tender offer (as it may be amended from time to time as permitted under this Agreement, the "Offer") to purchase all the outstanding shares of common stock, par value $0.01 per share, of the Company (the "Company Common Stock") at a price per share of Company Common Stock of $24.00, without interest (such amount, or any other amount per share paid pursuant to the Offer and this Agreement, the "Offer Price"), net to the seller thereof in cash, on the terms and subject to the conditions set forth in this Agreement;

WHEREAS, concurrently with the execution and delivery of this Agreement, the Company has entered into a Sponsor Tender Agreement with certain investment funds affiliated with Bain Capital Investors, LLC, TPG Capital, L.P. and The Goldman Sachs Group, Inc. and their respective Affiliates set forth therein (collectively, the "Sponsor Tender Agreements"), pursuant to which, among other things, such investment funds have irrevocably agreed to tender shares of Company Common Stock beneficially owned by them in the Offer (the shares subject to such agreements constituting, in the aggregate, approximately 31% of the Company Common Stock as of the date hereof) and to take certain actions and exercise certain rights, and to refrain from taking other actions or exercising other rights, in each case, as set forth therein;

WHEREAS, regardless of whether the Offer Closing occurs, Sub will merge with and into the Company, with the Company continuing as the surviving corporation in the merger (the "Merger"), upon the terms and subject to the conditions set forth in this Agreement, whereby, except as expressly provided in Section 3.01, each issued and outstanding share of Company Common Stock immediately prior to the effective time of the Merger will be cancelled and converted into the right to receive the Offer Price; and

WHEREAS Parent, Sub and the Company desire to make certain representations, warranties, covenants and agreements in connection with the Offer and the Merger and also to prescribe various conditions to the Offer and the Merger.

NOW, THEREFORE, in consideration of the foregoing premises and the representations, warranties, covenants and agreements contained in this Agreement, and subject to the conditions set forth herein, as well as other good and valuable consideration, the receipt and sufficiency of which are hereby acknowledged, and intending to be legally bound hereby, the Parties agree as follows:

ARTICLE I
The Offer

Section 1.01 The Offer.

(a) Commencement of the Offer. As promptly as reasonably practicable (and, in any event, within 10 business days) after the date of this Agreement, Sub shall, and Parent shall cause Sub to, commence (within the meaning of Rule 14d-2 under the Securities Exchange Act of 1934, as amended (together with the rules and regulations promulgated thereunder, the "Exchange Act")) the Offer to purchase all of the outstanding shares of

Company Common Stock at a price per share equal to the Offer Price (as adjusted as provided in Section 1.01(c), if applicable).

(b) Terms and Conditions of the Offer. The obligations of Sub to, and of Parent to cause Sub to, accept for payment, and pay for, any shares of Company Common Stock tendered pursuant to the Offer are subject only to the conditions set forth in Annex I (the "Offer Conditions"). The Offer Conditions are for the sole benefit of Parent and Sub, and Parent and Sub may waive, in whole or in part, any Offer Condition at any time and from time to time, in their sole discretion, other than the Minimum Tender Condition, which may be waived by Parent and Sub only with the prior written consent of the Company. Parent and Sub expressly reserve the right to increase the Offer Price or to waive or make any other changes in the terms and conditions of the Offer; provided, however, that unless otherwise provided in this Agreement or previously approved by the Company in writing, Sub shall not, and Parent shall not permit Sub to, (i) reduce the number of shares of Company Common Stock sought to be purchased in the Offer, (ii) reduce the Offer Price, (iii) change the form of consideration payable in the Offer, (iv) amend, modify or waive the Minimum Tender Condition, (v) add to the Offer Conditions or amend, modify or supplement any Offer Condition, or (vi) extend the expiration date of the Offer in any manner other than in accordance with the terms of Section 1.01(d).

(c) Adjustments to Offer Price. The Offer Price shall be adjusted appropriately to reflect the effect of any stock split, reverse stock split, stock dividend (including any dividend or distribution of securities convertible into Company Common Stock), cash dividend (other than the First Quarter Dividend), reorganization, recapitalization, reclassification, combination, exchange of shares or other like change with respect to Company Common Stock occurring on or after the date hereof and prior to Sub's acceptance for payment of, and payment for, Company Common Stock tendered in the Offer.

(d) Expiration and Extension of the Offer. The Offer shall initially be scheduled to expire at midnight, New York City time, on the later of (x) the 20th business day following the commencement of the Offer (determined using Rule 14d-1(g)(3) under the Exchange Act) and (y) the second business day following the No-Shop Period Start Date (such later date being the "Initial Offer Expiration Date"), provided, however, if at the Initial Offer Expiration Date, any Offer Condition is not satisfied or waived, Sub shall, and Parent shall cause Sub to, extend the Offer for ten (10) business days; provided, further, that if the only Offer Condition not satisfied at such time is the Financing Proceeds Condition, then such Initial Offer Expiration Date may be extended, at Parent's option, for less than ten (10) business days. Thereafter, if at any then scheduled expiration of the Offer, any Offer Condition is not satisfied or waived, Sub shall, and Parent shall cause Sub to, extend the Offer on one or more occasions, in consecutive increments of up to five (5) business days (or such longer period as the Parties may agree) each; provided, however, if the Proxy

Statement Clearance Date has occurred on or prior to November 24, 2010, then no such extension shall be required after November 24, 2010; provided, further, however, if the Proxy Statement Clearance Date has not occurred on or prior to November 24, 2010, then either Parent or the Company may request, and upon such request, Sub shall extend the Offer in increments of up to five (5) business days (or such longer period as the Parties may agree) each until the Proxy Statement Clearance Date; it being understood that nothing contained herein shall limit or otherwise affect the Company's right to terminate this Agreement pursuant to Section 9.01(g) in accordance with the terms thereof. "Proxy Statement Clearance Date" means the date on which the SEC has, orally or in writing, confirmed that it has no further comments on the Proxy Statement, including the first date following the tenth calendar day following the filing of the preliminary Proxy Statement if the SEC has not informed the Company that it intends to review the Proxy Statement. In addition, Sub shall, and Parent shall cause Sub to, extend the Offer on one or more occasions for the minimum period required by any rule, regulation, interpretation or position of the Securities and Exchange Commission (the "SEC") or the staff thereof applicable to the Offer; provided, however, that Sub shall not be required to extend the Offer beyond the Outside Date and such extension shall be subject to the right to terminate the Offer in accordance with Section 1.01(f). The last date on which the Offer is required to be extended pursuant to this Section 1.01(d) is referred to as the "Offer End Date" (it being understood that under no circumstances shall the Offer End Date occur prior to November 24, 2010).

(e) Payment. On the terms and subject to the conditions of the Offer and this Agreement, Sub shall, and Parent shall cause Sub to, accept for payment, and pay for, all shares of Company Common Stock validly tendered and not withdrawn pursuant to the Offer promptly (and in any event within 3 business days) after the applicable expiration date of the Offer (as it may be extended in accordance with Section 1.01(d)) and in any event in compliance with Rule 14e-1(c) promulgated under the Exchange Act. The date of payment for shares of Company Common Stock accepted for payment pursuant to and subject to the conditions of the Offer is referred to in this Agreement as the "Offer Closing", and the date on which the Offer Closing occurs is referred to in this Agreement as the "Offer Closing Date".

[...]

(h) Funds. Subject to the other terms and conditions of this Agreement and the Offer Conditions, Parent shall provide or cause to be provided to Sub on a timely basis the funds necessary to purchase any shares of Company Common Stock that Sub becomes obligated to purchase pursuant to the Offer.

[...]

Section 1.03 Top-Up. ◆

(a) Top-Up. The Company hereby grants to Sub an irrevocable right (the ''Top-Up''), exercisable on the terms and conditions set forth in this Section 1.03, to purchase at a price per share equal to the Offer Price that number of newly issued, fully paid and nonassessable shares of Company Common Stock (the "Top-Up Shares") equal to the lowest number of shares of Company Common Stock that, when added to the number of shares of Company Common Stock directly or indirectly owned by Parent and Sub at the time of the Top-Up Closing (after giving effect to the Offer Closing), shall constitute one share more than 90% of the shares of the Company Common Stock outstanding immediately after the issuance of the Top-Up Shares; provided, however, that the Top-Up may not be exercised to purchase an amount of Top-Up Shares in excess of the number of shares of Company Common Stock authorized and unissued (treating shares owned by the Company as treasury stock as unissued) and not reserved for issuance at the time of exercise of the Top-Up. The Top-Up shall be exercisable only once, in whole but not in part.

(b) Exercise of Top-Up; Top-Up Closing. If there shall have not been validly tendered and not validly withdrawn that number of shares of Company Common Stock which, when added to the shares of Company Common Stock owned by Parent and its Affiliates, would represent at least 90% of the shares of the Company Common Stock outstanding on the Offer Closing Date, Sub shall be deemed to have exercised the Top-Up and on such date shall give the Company prior written notice specifying the number of shares of Company Common Stock directly or indirectly owned by Parent and its Subsidiaries at the time of such notice (giving effect to the Offer Closing). The Company shall, as soon as practicable following receipt of such notice (and in any event no later than the Offer Closing), deliver written notice to Sub specifying, based on the information provided by Sub in its notice, the number of Top-Up Shares. At the closing of the purchase of the Top-Up Shares (the "Top-Up Closing"), which shall take place at the location of the Merger Closing specified in Section 2.02, and shall take place simultaneously with the Offer Closing, the purchase price owed by Sub to the Company to purchase the Top-Up Shares shall be paid to the Company, at Sub's option, (i) in cash, by wire transfer of same-day funds, or (ii) by (x) paying in cash, by wire transfer of same-day funds, an amount equal to not less than the aggregate par value of the Top-Up Shares and (y) executing and delivering to the Company a promissory note having a principal amount equal to the aggregate purchase price pursuant to the Top-Up less the amount paid in cash pursuant to the preceding clause (x) (the "Promissory Note"). The Promissory Note (i) shall be due on the first anniversary of the Top-Up Closing, (ii) shall bear simple interest of 5% per annum, (iii) shall be full recourse to Parent and Sub, (iv) may be prepaid, in whole or in part, at any time without premium or penalty, and (v) shall have no other material terms. At the Top-Up Closing, the Company shall cause to be issued to Sub a certificate representing the Top-Up Shares.

[...]

ARTICLE II
The Merger

Section 2.01 The Merger. Upon the terms and subject to the conditions set forth in this Agreement, and in accordance with the General Corporation Law of the State of Delaware (the "DGCL"), Sub shall be merged with and into the Company at the Effective Time. Following the Effective Time, the separate corporate existence of Sub shall cease, and the Company shall continue as the surviving corporation in the Merger (the "Surviving Corporation").

Section 2.02 Closing. The closing of the Merger (the "Merger Closing") will take place at (a) if the Offer Closing shall have not occurred at or prior to the Merger Closing, 10:00 a.m., New York City time, on the second business day after satisfaction or (to the extent permitted by Law) waiver of the conditions set forth in Article VIII (other than those conditions that by their terms are to be satisfied at the Merger Closing, but subject to the satisfaction or (to the extent permitted by Law) waiver of those conditions), or (b) if the Offer Closing shall have occurred on or prior to the Merger Closing, on the date of, and immediately following the Offer Closing (or the Top-Up Closing if the Top-Up has been exercised), in either case at the offices of Kirkland & Ellis LLP, located at 601 Lexington Avenue, New York, New York 10022, unless another time, date or place is agreed to in writing by Parent and the Company. The date on which the Merger Closing occurs is referred to in this Agreement as the "Merger Closing Date".

Section 2.03 Effective Time. Subject to the provisions of this Agreement, as promptly as reasonably practicable on the Merger Closing Date, the Parties shall file a certificate of merger (the "Certificate of Merger") in such form as is required by, and executed and acknowledged in accordance with, the relevant provisions of the DGCL, and shall make all other filings and recordings required under the DGCL. The Merger shall become effective on such date and time as the Certificate of Merger is filed with the Secretary of State of the State of Delaware or at such other date and time as Parent and the Company shall agree and specify in the Certificate of Merger. The date and time at which the Merger becomes effective is referred to in this Agreement as the "Effective Time".

Section 2.04 Effects of the Merger. The Merger shall have the effects set forth in the applicable provisions of the DGCL. Without limiting the generality of the foregoing, from and after the Effective Time, the Surviving Corporation shall possess all properties, rights, privileges, powers and franchises of the Company and Sub, and all of the claims, obligations, liabilities, debts and duties of the Company and Sub shall become the claims, obligations, liabilities, debts and duties of the Surviving Corporation.

Section 2.05 Certificate of Incorporation and By-Laws.

(a) At the Effective Time, the certificate of incorporation of Sub as in effect immediately prior to the Effective Time (which shall not be amended by Sub from the date hereof until such time except as otherwise contemplated hereby) shall be the certificate of incorporation of the Surviving Corporation until thereafter changed or amended (subject to Section 7.06(a)) as provided therein or by applicable Law; provided, however, that at the Effective Time the certificate of incorporation of the Surviving Corporation shall be amended so that the name of the Surviving Corporation shall be "Burger King Holdings, Inc."

(b) The by-laws of Sub as in effect immediately prior to the Effective Time shall be the by-laws of the Surviving Corporation until thereafter changed or amended (subject to Section 7.06(a)) as provided therein or by applicable Law.

Section 2.06 Directors. The directors of Sub immediately prior to the Effective Time shall be the directors of the Surviving Corporation until the earlier of their resignation or removal or until their respective successors are duly elected and qualified, as the case may be.

Section 2.07 Officers. The officers of the Company immediately prior to the Effective Time shall be the officers of the Surviving Corporation, until the earlier of their resignation or removal or until their respective successors are duly elected and qualified, as the case may be.

Section 2.08 Taking of Necessary Action. If at any time after the Effective Time any further action is necessary or desirable to carry out the purposes of this Agreement and to vest the Surviving Corporation with full right, title and possession to all assets, property, rights, privileges, powers and franchises of the Company and Sub, the Surviving Corporation, the board of directors of the Surviving Corporation and officers of the Surviving Corporation shall take all such lawful and necessary action, consistent with this Agreement, on behalf of the Company, Sub and the Surviving Corporation.

ARTICLE III

Effect of the Merger on the Capital Stock of the Constituent Corporations

Section 3.01 Effect on Capital Stock. At the Effective Time, by virtue of the Merger and without any action on the part of the holder of any shares of Company Common Stock or any shares of capital stock of Parent or Sub:

(a) Capital Stock of Sub. Each share of capital stock of Sub issued and outstanding immediately prior to the Effective Time shall be converted into and become one validly issued, fully paid and nonassessable share of common stock, par value $0.01 per share, of the Surviving Corporation.

(b) Cancellation of Treasury Stock and Parent-Owned Stock. Each share of Company Common Stock issued and outstanding immediately prior to the Effective Time that is directly owned by the Company as treasury stock, or by Parent or Sub at such time, shall automatically be canceled and shall cease to exist, and no consideration shall be delivered in exchange therefor.

(c) Conversion of Company Common Stock. Each share of Company Common Stock issued and outstanding immediately prior to the Effective Time (excluding shares to be canceled in accordance with Section 3.01(b)and, except as provided in Section 3.01(d), the Appraisal Shares) shall be converted into the right to receive the Offer Price in cash, without interest (the "Merger Consideration"). At the Effective Time, all such shares of Company Common Stock shall no longer be outstanding and shall automatically be canceled and shall cease to exist, and each holder of a certificate (or evidence of shares in book-entry form) that immediately prior to the Effective Time represented any such shares of Company Common Stock (each, a "Certificate") shall cease to have any rights with respect thereto, except the right to receive the Merger Consideration and any dividends declared from and after the date hereof in accordance with Section 6.01(a) with a record date prior to the Effective Time that remain unpaid at the Effective Time and that are due to such holder.

(d) Appraisal Rights. Notwithstanding anything in this Agreement to the contrary, shares of Company Common Stock issued and outstanding immediately prior to the Effective Time that are held by any holder who is entitled to demand and properly demands appraisal of such shares pursuant to, and who complies in all respects with, the provisions of Section 262 of the DGCL (the "Appraisal Shares") shall not be converted into the right to receive the Merger Consideration as provided in Section 3.01(c), but instead such holder shall be entitled to payment of the fair value of such shares in accordance with the provisions of Section 262 of the DGCL. At the Effective Time, the Appraisal Shares shall no longer be outstanding and shall automatically be canceled and shall cease to exist, and each holder of Appraisal Shares shall cease to have any rights with respect thereto, except the right to receive the fair value of such Appraisal Shares in accordance with the provisions of Section 262 of the DGCL. Notwithstanding the foregoing, if any such holder shall fail to perfect or otherwise shall waive, withdraw or lose the right to appraisal under Section 262 of the DGCL or a court of competent jurisdiction shall determine that such holder is not entitled to the relief provided by Section 262 of the DGCL, then the right of such holder to be paid the fair value of such holder's Appraisal Shares under Section 262 of the DGCL shall cease and such Appraisal Shares shall be deemed to have been converted at the Effective Time into, and shall have become, the right to receive the

Merger Consideration as provided in Section 3.01(c), without any interest thereon. The Company shall give prompt notice to Parent of any demands for appraisal of any shares of Company Common Stock or written threats thereof, withdrawals of such demands and any other instruments served pursuant to the DGCL received by the Company, and Parent shall have the right to participate in and direct all negotiations and proceedings with respect to such demands. Prior to the Effective Time, the Company shall not, without the prior written consent of Parent (which consent shall not be unreasonably withheld or delayed), voluntarily make any payment with respect to, or settle or offer to settle, any such demands, or agree to do or commit to do any of the foregoing.

[...]

ARTICLE V
Representations and Warranties of Parent and Sub

Parent and Sub jointly and severally represent and warrant to the Company as follows:

[...]

Section 5.04 Financing. Parent has delivered to the Company true and complete copies of (i) the executed equity commitment letter, dated as of the date of this Agreement (the "Equity Financing Commitment"), pursuant to which 3G Special Situations Fund II L.P. ("Sponsor") has committed, upon the terms and subject to the conditions thereof, to invest in Parent the cash amount set forth therein (the "Equity Financing"), and (ii) the executed commitment letter, dated as of the date hereof, among Parent, J.P. Morgan Chase Bank, N.A., J.P. Morgan Securities LLC, and Barclays Bank PLC (the "Debt Commitment Letter"), pursuant to which the lenders party thereto have agreed, upon the terms and subject to the conditions thereof, to lend the amounts (which includes up to $900,000,000.00 in bridge financing (the "Bridge Financing") to be utilized in the event the placement of senior notes (the "High Yield Financing") is not consummated) set forth therein for the purposes of financing the transactions contemplated by this Agreement and related fees and expenses and the refinancing of any outstanding indebtedness of the Company (including under the Existing Credit Agreement) (the ''Debt Financing'' and, together with the Equity Financing, the "Financing"). The Debt Commitment Letter and the related Fee Letter and the Equity Financing Commitment are referred to collectively in this Agreement as the "Financing Agreements". None of the Financing Agreements has been amended or modified prior to the date of this Agreement, no such amendment or modification is contemplated and none of the respective commitments contained in the Financing Agreements have been withdrawn or rescinded in any respect. As of the date of this Agreement, the Financing Agreements are in full force and effect. Except for a fee letter and fee credit letter relating to fees with respect to the Debt Financing and an engagement letter (complete copies of which have been provided to the Company, with only the fee amounts and certain economic terms of the market flex (none of which would adversely effect the amount or availability of the Debt Financing) redacted), as of the date of this Agreement there are no side letters or other agreements, Contracts or arrangements related to the funding or investment, as applicable, of the Financing other than as expressly set forth in the Financing Agreements delivered to the Company prior to the date hereof. Parent has fully paid any and all commitment fees or other fees in connection with the Financing Agreements that are payable on or prior to the date hereof. The only conditions precedent or other contingencies related to the obligations of the Sponsor to fund the full amount of the Equity Financing and lenders to fund the full amount of Debt Financing are those expressly set forth in the Equity Financing Commitment and the Debt Commitment Letter, respectively. As of the date of this Agreement, no event has occurred which, with or without notice, lapse of time or both, would constitute a default or breach on the part of Parent, Sub or any direct investor in Parent under any term, or a failure of any condition, of the Financing Agreements or otherwise be reasonably likely to result in any portion of the Financing contemplated thereby to be unavailable. As of the date of this Agreement, neither Parent nor Sub has any reason to believe that it will be unable to satisfy on a timely basis any term or condition of the Financing Agreements required to be satisfied by it. Based on the terms and conditions of this Agreement, the proceeds from the Financing will be sufficient to provide Parent and Sub with the funds necessary to pay the aggregate Offer Price and Merger Consideration, the Equity Awards Amount, any repayment or refinancing of debt contemplated in this Agreement or the Financing Agreements (including repayment of indebtedness under the Existing Credit Agreement), the payment of all other amounts required to be paid in connection with the consummation of the transactions contemplated by this Agreement and to allow Parent and Sub to perform all of their obligations under this Agreement and pay all fees and expenses to be paid by Parent or Sub related to the transactions contemplated by this Agreement.

[...]

ARTICLE VII
Additional Agreements

Section 7.01 Preparation of the Proxy Statement; Stockholders' Meeting.

(a) Preparation of Proxy Statement. As soon as practicable after the date hereof (and in any event, but subject to Parent's timely performance of its obligations under Section 7.01(b), within 15 business days hereof), the Company shall prepare and shall cause to be filed with the SEC in preliminary form a proxy statement relating to the Stockholders' Meeting (together with any amendments thereof or supplements thereto, the "Proxy Statement"). Except as expressly contemplated by Section 6.02(f), the Proxy Statement shall include the Recommendation with respect to the Merger, the Fairness

Opinions and a copy of Section 262 of the DGCL. The Company will cause the Proxy Statement, at the time of the mailing of the Proxy Statement or any amendments or supplements thereto, and at the time of the Stockholders' Meeting, to not contain any untrue statement of a material fact or omit to state any material fact required to be stated therein or necessary in order to make the statements therein, in light of the circumstances under which they were made, not misleading;provided, however, that no representation or warranty is made by the Company with respect to information supplied by Parent or Sub for inclusion or incorporation by reference in the Proxy Statement. The Company shall cause the Proxy Statement to comply as to form in all material respects with the provisions of the Exchange Act and the rules and regulations promulgated thereunder and to satisfy all rules of the NYSE. The Company shall promptly notify Parent and Sub upon the receipt of any comments from the SEC or the staff of the SEC or any request from the SEC or the staff of the SEC for amendments or supplements to the Proxy Statement, and shall provide Parent and Sub with copies of all correspondence between the Company and its Representatives, on the one hand, and the SEC or the staff of the SEC, on the other hand. The Company shall use reasonable best efforts to respond as promptly as reasonably practicable to any comments of the SEC or the staff of the SEC with respect to the Proxy Statement, and the Company shall provide Parent and Sub and their respective counsel a reasonable opportunity to participate in the formulation of any written response to any such written comments of the SEC or its staff. Prior to the filing of the Proxy Statement or the dissemination thereof to the holders of Company Common Stock, or responding to any comments of the SEC or the staff of the SEC with respect thereto, the Company shall provide Parent and Sub a reasonable opportunity to review and to propose comments on such document or response.

[...]

(c) Mailing of Proxy Statement; Stockholders' Meeting. If the adoption of this Agreement by the Company's stockholders is required by applicable Law, then the Company shall have the right at any time after the Proxy Statement Clearance Date to (and Parent and Sub shall have the right, at any time after the later of the Proxy Statement Clearance Date and November 1, 2010, to request in writing that the Company, and upon receipt of such written request, the Company shall, as promptly as practicable and in any event within ten (10) business days), (x) establish a record date for and give notice of a meeting of its stockholders, for the purpose of voting upon the adoption of this Agreement (the "Stockholders' Meeting"), and (y) mail to the holders of Company Common Stock as of the record date established for the Stockholders' Meeting a Proxy Statement (the date the Company elects to take such action or is required to take such action, the "Proxy Date"). The Company shall duly call, convene and hold the Stockholders' Meeting as promptly as reasonably practicable after the Proxy Date; provided, however, that in no event shall such meeting be held later than 35 calendar days following the date the Proxy Statement is mailed to the Company's stockholders and any adjournments of such meetings shall require the prior written consent of the Parent other than in the case it is required to allow reasonable additional time for the filing and mailing of any supplemental or amended disclosure which the SEC or its staff has instructed the Company is necessary under applicable Law and for such supplemental or amended disclosure to be disseminated and reviewed by the Company's stockholders prior to the Stockholders' Meeting. Notwithstanding the foregoing, Parent may require the Company to adjourn or postpone the Stockholders' Meeting one (1) time (for a period of not more than 30 calendar days but not past 2 business days prior to the Outside Date), unless prior to such adjournment the Company shall have received an aggregate number of proxies voting for the adoption of this Agreement and the transactions contemplated hereby (including the Merger), which have not been withdrawn, such that the condition in Section 8.01(a) will be satisfied at such meeting. Once the Company has established a record date for the Stockholders' Meeting, the Company shall not change such record date or establish a different record date for the Stockholders' Meeting without the prior written consent of Parent, unless required to do so by applicable Law or the Company's By-Laws. Unless the Company Board shall have withdrawn, modified or qualified its recommendation thereof or otherwise effected an Adverse Recommendation Change, the Company shall use reasonable best efforts to solicit proxies in favor of the adoption of this Agreement and shall ensure that all proxies solicited in connection with the Stockholders' Meeting are solicited in compliance with all applicable Laws and all rules of the NYSE. Unless this Agreement is validly terminated in accordance with Section 9.01, the Company shall submit this Agreement to its stockholders at the Stockholders' Meeting even if the Company Board shall have effected an Adverse Recommendation Change or proposed or announced any intention to do so. The Company shall, upon the reasonable request of Parent, advise Parent at least on a daily basis on each of the last seven business days prior to the date of the Stockholders' Meeting as to the aggregate tally of proxies received by the Company with respect to the Stockholder Approval. Without the prior written consent of Parent, the adoption of this Agreement and the transactions contemplated hereby (including the Merger) shall be the only matter (other than procedure matters) which the Company shall propose to be acted on by the stockholders of the Company at the Stockholders' Meeting.

[…]

(e) Short Form Merger. Notwithstanding the foregoing, if, following the Offer Closing and the exercise, if any, of the Top-Up, Parent and its Affiliates shall own at least 90% of the outstanding shares of the Company Common Stock, the Parties shall take all necessary and appropriate action, including with respect to the transfer to Sub of any shares of Company Common Stock held by Parent or its Affiliates, to cause the Merger to become effective as soon as practicable after the Offer Closing without the Stockholders' Meeting in accordance with Section 253 of the DGCL.

[...]

Section 7.08 Financing.

(a) Each of Parent and Sub shall use, and cause its Affiliates to use, its reasonable best efforts (unless, with respect to any action, another standard for performance is expressly provided for herein) to take, or cause to be taken, all actions and to do, or cause to be done, all things necessary, proper or advisable to consummate and obtain the Financing on the terms and conditions (including the flex provisions) set forth in the Financing Agreements and any related Fee Letter (taking into account the anticipated timing of the Marketing Period), including using reasonable best efforts to seek to enforce (including through litigation) its rights under the Debt Commitment Letter in the event of a material breach thereof by the Financing sources thereunder, and shall not permit any amendment or modification to be made to, or consent to any waiver of any provision or remedy under, the Financing Agreements or any related Fee Letter, if such amendment, modification or waiver (i) reduces the aggregate amount of the Financing (including by changing the amount of fees to be paid or original issue discount) from that contemplated in the Financing Agreements, (ii) imposes new or additional conditions or otherwise expands, amends or modifies any of the conditions to the receipt of the Financing in a manner adverse to Parent or the Company, (iii) decreases the aggregate Equity Financing as set forth in the Equity Financing Commitment delivered on the date hereof, (iv) amends or modifies any other terms in a manner that would reasonably be expected to (x) delay or prevent the Offer Closing or the Merger Closing Date or (y) make the timely funding of the Financing or satisfaction of the conditions to obtaining the Financing less likely to occur or (v) adversely impact the ability of Parent or Sub to enforce its rights against the other parties to the Financing Agreements. For purposes of clarification, the foregoing shall not prohibit Parent from amending the Debt Commitment Letter and any related Fee Letter to add additional lender(s) (and Affiliates of such additional lender(s)) as a party thereto. Any reference in this Agreement to (A) "Financing" shall include the financing contemplated by the Financing Agreements as amended or modified in compliance with this Section 7.08(a), and (B) "Financing Agreements" or "Debt Commitment Letter" shall include such documents as amended or modified in compliance with this Section 7.08(a).

[...]

ARTICLE VIII
Conditions Precedent

Section 8.01 Conditions to Each Party's Obligation to Effect the Merger. The respective obligation of each party to effect the Merger is subject to the satisfaction or (to the extent permitted by Law) waiver at or prior to the Effective Time of the following conditions:

(a) Stockholder Approval. If required by applicable Law, the Stockholder Approval shall have been obtained.

(b) Regulatory Approvals. The waiting period applicable to the consummation of the Merger and, unless the Offer Termination shall have occurred, the Offer under the HSR Act (or any extension thereof) shall have expired or early termination thereof shall have been granted. In addition, the consummation of the Merger and, unless the Offer Termination shall have occurred, the Offer, is not unlawful under any Foreign Merger Control Law of any jurisdiction set forth in Section 8.01(b) of the Company Disclosure Letter.

(c) No Injunctions or Restraints. No temporary restraining order, preliminary or permanent injunction, Law or other Judgment issued by any court of competent jurisdiction (collectively, "Restraints") shall be in effect enjoining or otherwise preventing or prohibiting the consummation of the Merger.

(d) Purchase of Company Common Stock in the Offer. Unless the Offer Termination shall have occurred, Sub shall have accepted for payment all shares of Company Common Stock validly tendered and not validly withdrawn pursuant to the Offer.

Section 8.02 Conditions to Obligations of Parent and Sub to Effect the Merger. Solely if the Offer Termination shall have occurred or the Offer Closing shall not have occurred, the obligations of Parent and Sub to effect the Merger are further subject to the satisfaction or (to the extent permitted by Law) waiver at or prior to the Effective Time of the following conditions:

(a) Representations and Warranties. The representations and warranties of the Company (i) set forth in Section 4.03, Section 4.04, Section 4.26and Section 4.27 shall be true and correct in all material respects as of the date of this Agreement and as of the Merger Closing Date as though made on the Merger Closing Date, (ii) set forth in Section 4.07 shall be true and correct as of the date of this Agreement and as of the Merger Closing Date as though made on the Merger Closing Date without disregarding the "Material Adverse Effect" qualification set forth therein and (iii) set forth in this Agreement, other than those described in clauses (i) and (ii) above, shall be true and correct (disregarding all qualifications or limitations as to "materiality", "Material Adverse Effect" and words of similar import set forth therein) as of the date of this Agreement and as of the Merger Closing Date as though made on the Merger Closing Date, except, in the case of this clause (iii), where the failure of such representations and warranties to be so true and correct would not, individually or in the aggregate, reasonably be expected to have a Material Adverse Effect; provided in each case that representations and warranties made as of a specific date shall be required to be so true and correct (subject to such qualifications) as of such date only. Parent shall have received a certificate signed on behalf of the Company by the chief executive officer or chief financial officer thereof to such effect.

(b) Performance of Obligations of the Company. The Company shall have performed or complied in all material respects with its obligations required to be performed or complied with by it under this Agreement at or prior to the Merger Closing, and Parent shall have received a certificate signed on behalf of the Company by the chief executive officer or chief financial officer thereof to such effect.

(c) No Material Adverse Effect. Since the date of this Agreement, there shall not have occurred any change, event or occurrence that has had or would reasonably be expected to have a Material Adverse Effect, and Parent shall have received a certificate signed on behalf of the Company the chief executive officer or chief financial officer thereof to such effect.

(d) Pre-Closing Solvency. As of immediately prior to the Merger Closing Date (and, for the avoidance of doubt, before giving effect to the incurrence of the Debt Financing and the consummation of the transactions contemplated by this Agreement and such Debt Financing), the Company is Solvent, and Parent shall have received a certificate signed on behalf of the Company by the chief executive officer or chief financial officer thereof to such effect.

Section 8.03 Conditions to Obligation of the Company to Effect the Merger. Solely if the Offer Termination shall have occurred or the Offer Closing shall not have occurred, then the obligation of the Company to effect the Merger is further subject to the satisfaction or (to the extent permitted by Law) waiver at or prior to the Effective Time of the following conditions:

(a) Representations and Warranties. The representations and warranties of Parent and Sub set forth in this Agreement shall be true and correct (disregarding all qualifications or limitations as to "materiality", "Parent Material Adverse Effect" and words of similar import set forth therein) as of the date of this Agreement and as of the Merger Closing Date as though made on the Merger Closing Date (except to the extent such representations and warranties expressly relate to an earlier date, in which case as of such earlier date), except where the failure of such representations and warranties to be so true and correct would not, individually or in the aggregate, reasonably be expected to have a Parent Material Adverse Effect. The Company shall have received a certificate signed on behalf of Parent by an executive officer thereof to such effect.

(b) Performance of Obligations of Parent and Sub. Parent and Sub shall have performed or complied in all material respects with its obligations required to be performed or complied with by it under this Agreement at or prior to the Merger Closing, and the Company shall have received a certificate signed on behalf of Parent by an executive officer thereof to such effect.

Section 8.04 Frustration of Closing Conditions. Neither Parent nor Sub may rely on the failure of any condition set forth in Sections 8.01 or 8.02 to be satisfied if such failure was caused by the failure of Parent or Sub to perform any of its obligations under this Agreement. The Company may not rely on the failure of any condition set forth in Sections 8.01 or 8.03 to be satisfied if such failure was caused by its failure to perform any of its obligations under this Agreement.

[…]

ANNEX I
Conditions to the Offer

Notwithstanding any other term of the Offer or this Agreement, Sub shall not be required to, and Parent shall not be required to cause Sub to, accept for payment or, subject to any applicable rules and regulations of the SEC, including Rule 14e-1(c) under the Exchange Act (relating to Sub's obligation to pay for or return tendered shares of Company Common Stock promptly after the termination or withdrawal of the Offer), pay for any shares of Company Common Stock tendered pursuant to the Offer if: (a) there shall have not been validly tendered and not validly withdrawn prior to the expiration of the Offer that number of shares of Company Common Stock which, when added to the shares of Company Common Stock owned by Parent and its Affiliates, would represent at least 79.1% of the shares of the Company Common Stock outstanding as of the expiration of the Offer (the "Minimum Tender Condition"); (b) the waiting period applicable to the purchase of shares of Company Common Stock pursuant to the Offer and the consummation of the Merger under the HSR Act (or any extension thereof) shall have neither expired nor terminated; (c) Parent (either directly or through its Subsidiaries) shall not have received the proceeds of the Debt Financing (or any Alternative Debt Financing) and/or the lenders party to the Debt Financing Letter (or New Debt Commitment Letter for any Alternative Debt Financing) shall not have confirmed to Parent or Sub that the Debt Financing (or any Alternative Debt Financing) in an amount sufficient to consummate the Offer and the Merger will be available at the Offer Closing on the terms and conditions set forth in the Debt Financing Letter (or New Debt Commitment Letter for any Alternative Debt Financing) ("Financing Proceeds Condition"), or (d) any of the following conditions shall have occurred and be continuing as of the expiration of the Offer:

(i) there shall be any Restraint in effect enjoining or otherwise preventing or prohibiting the making of the Offer or the consummation of the Merger or the Offer;

(ii) the consummation of the Offer is unlawful under any Foreign Merger Control Law of any jurisdiction set forth in Section 8.01(b) of the Company Disclosure Letter;

(iii) any of the representations and warranties of the Company (A) set forth in Section 4.03, Section 4.04,Section 4.26 and Section 4.27 shall not be true and correct in all material respects, (B) set forth in Section 4.07shall not be true and correct without disregarding the "Material Adverse Effect" qualification set forth therein and (C) set forth in this Agreement, other than those described in clauses (A) and (B) above, shall not be true and correct (disregarding all qualifications or limitations as to "materiality", "Material Adverse Effect" and words of similar import set forth therein), except, in the case of this clause (C), where the failure of such representations and warranties to be so true and correct would not, individually or in the aggregate, reasonably be expected to have a Material Adverse Effect and except, in each case, to the extent such representations and warranties are made as of a specific date (in which case such representations and warranties shall not be true and correct (subject to such qualifications) as of such specific date only);

(iv) the Company shall have failed to perform or comply in all material respects with its obligations required to be performed or complied with by it under this Agreement;

(v) since the date of this Agreement, there shall have occurred any change, event or occurrence that has had or would reasonably be expected to have a Material Adverse Effect;

(vi) as of immediately prior to the Offer Closing Date (and, for the avoidance of doubt, before giving effect to the incurrence of the Debt Financing and the consummation of the transactions contemplated by this Agreement and such Debt Financing), the Company is not Solvent;

(vii) in the event that the exercise of the Top-Up is necessary to ensure that Parent or Sub owns at least 90% of the outstanding shares of Company Common Stock immediately after the Acceptance Time, there shall exist under applicable Law or other Restraint any restriction or legal impediment on Sub's ability and right to exercise the Top-Up, or the shares of Company Common Stock issuable upon exercise of the Top-Up together with the shares of Company Common Stock validly tendered in the Offer and not properly withdrawn are insufficient for Sub to owns at least 90% of the outstanding shares of Company Common Stock;

(viii) a Triggering Event shall have occurred; and

(ix) this Agreement shall have been terminated in accordance with its terms.

At the request of Parent, the Company shall deliver to Parent a certificate executed on behalf of the Company by the chief executive officer or the chief financial officer of the Company certifying that none of the conditions set forth in clauses (d)(iii), (d)(iv), (d)(v) and (d)(vi) above shall have occurred and be continuing as of the expiration of the Offer.

For purposes of determining whether the Minimum Tender Condition and the condition set forth in clause (d)(vii) have been satisfied, Parent and Sub shall have the right to include or exclude for purposes of its determination thereof shares tendered in the Offer pursuant to guaranteed delivery procedures. [Eds: These are shares that are promised to be delivered pursuant to some pre-agreed form but that are not available for delivery immediately. This is not the same as the shares committed to be tendered under the Sponsor Tender Agreements, which presumably are available for delivery.]

The foregoing conditions shall be in addition to, and not a limitation of, the rights and obligations of Parent and Sub to extend, terminate or modify the Offer pursuant to the terms and conditions of this Agreement.

The foregoing conditions are for the sole benefit of Parent and Sub and, subject to the terms and conditions of this Agreement and the applicable rules and regulations of the SEC, may be waived by Parent and Sub in whole or in part at any time and from time to time in their sole discretion (other than the Minimum Tender Condition). The failure by Parent or Sub at any time to exercise any of the foregoing rights shall not be deemed a waiver of any such right and each such right shall be deemed an ongoing right that may be asserted at any time and from time to time.

The capitalized terms used in this Annex I and not defined in this Annex I shall have the meanings set forth in the Agreement and Plan of Merger, dated as of September 2, 2010, by and among Blue Acquisition Holding Corporation, Blue Acquisition Sub, Inc. and Burger King Holdings, Inc.

Chapter 7. Controlling Shareholders in M&A

7.1 Squeeze-Outs / Going-Privates

Controlling shareholders deserve particular attention in M&A because they may have acute conflicts of interest.

To be sure, notwithstanding the presence of a controlling shareholder, every merger and most other steps in an M&A transaction still need to be reviewed by the full board, whose members may not have the same conflict of interest (in particular, the controlling shareholder may not be a member of the board). Technically, the board may recommend the transaction only if it is good for the corporation as a whole. But even if all directors are technically completely independent, the directors must also be aware that the controlling shareholder could replace them at any moment (under the default rules, DGCL 141(k), 228; but even a staggered board etc. would merely delay the replacement). There is thus always a suspicion that the board may be driven to be partial to the controlling shareholder's interests.

In a squeeze-out a/k/a cash-out merger, a controlling shareholder acquires complete ownership of the corporation's equity, squeezing/cashing out the minority. Technically, the transaction is structured as a merger between the controlled corporation and a corporation wholly-owned by the controlled corporation's controlling shareholder. The controlling shareholder retains all the equity of the surviving corporation, while the merger consideration for the outside shareholders is cash (or something else that is *not* stock in the surviving corporation). If the controlled corporation was previously publicly traded on a stock exchange, the transaction is also known as a going private merger because the surviving corporation will no longer be public, i.e., it will be delisted from the stock exchange.

There can be good economic reasons for a squeeze-out. It facilitates subsequent everyday business between the controller and the corporation, among other things because there are no more conflicts of interest to manage (cf. *Sinclair*). Private corporations do not need to make filings with the SEC and the stock exchange. Finally, the controlling shareholder may be more motivated to develop the corporation's business when owning 100% of it.

At the same time, squeeze-outs pose an enormous conflict of interest. Any dollar less paid to the minority is a dollar more to the controlling shareholder. For this reason, the SEC requires additional disclosure under rule 13e-3, and Delaware courts police squeezeouts under the duty of loyalty. In fact, controlling shareholders' duty of loyalty was developed principally in squeeze-out mergers, in particular the adaptation in *Kahn v. MFW* below.

Questions

1. Can you think of another, procedural reason why squeeze-outs generate most duty of loyalty cases against controlling shareholders in Delaware courts? Hint: Consider *Zuckerberg* and its scope of application.

A. Weinberger v. UOP, Inc. (Del. 1983)

This decision introduced the modern standard of review for conflicted transactions involving a controlling shareholder. We could have read it in Chapter 4: The Duty of Loyalty, but we wanted you to read it together with the next two cases.

Review questions

1. What is the default standard of review for conflicted transactions?

2. Can the controlling shareholder do anything to obtain a more favorable standard, or at least a more sympathetic application of the standard?

3. How does the judicial treatment of self-dealing by a controlling shareholder compare to that of self-dealing by simple officers and directors (as described in Chapter 4: The Duty of Loyalty)?

Case questions

1. Why did Signal do this deal? Do any of its reasons strike you as inconsistent with Signal's corporate purposes, or with Signal's fiduciary duties towards UOP?

2. What was unfair about Signal's dealing with UOP?

3. Why did UOP's stockholder vote not shift the burden of proof?

4. Why does Weinberger bother bringing a fiduciary duty action? Couldn't he have obtained the same relief through appraisal, without having to prove a violation of fiduciary duty?

Policy questions

1. Does it make sense to treat controlling shareholders more harshly than other fiduciaries?

2. Why allow squeeze-outs at all?

3. Is there a connection between the Delaware Supreme Court's abandonment of the business purpose test (part III) and its refinement of the standard of review, in particular a more flexible approach to valuation (part II.E)?

457 A.2d 701 (1983)

William B. WEINBERGER, Plaintiff Below, Appellant,

v.

UOP, INC., et al., Defendants Below, Appellees.

Supreme Court of Delaware.

Submitted: July 16, 1982.

Decided: February 1, 1983.

William Prickett (argued), John H. Small, and George H. Seitz, III, of Prickett, Jones, Elliott, Kristol & Schnee, Wilmington, for plaintiff.

A. Gilchrist Sparks, III, of Morris, Nichols, Arsht & Tunnell, Wilmington, for defendant UOP, Inc.

Robert K. Payson and Peter M. Sieglaff, of Potter, Anderson & Corroon, Wilmington, and Alan N. Halkett (argued) of Latham & Watkins, Los Angeles, Cal., for defendant The Signal Companies, Inc.

Before HERRMANN, C.J., McNEILLY, QUILLEN, HORSEY and MOORE, JJ., constituting the Court en Banc. [702]

MOORE, Justice:

This post-trial appeal was reheard en banc from a decision of the Court of Chancery.[1] [703] It was brought by the class action plaintiff below, a former shareholder of UOP, Inc., who challenged the elimination of UOP's minority shareholders by a cash-out merger

---

[1] Accordingly, this Court's February 9, 1982 opinion is withdrawn.

between UOP and its majority owner, The Signal Companies, Inc.[2] Originally, the defendants in this action were Signal, UOP, certain officers and directors of those companies, and UOP's investment banker, Lehman Brothers Kuhn Loeb, Inc.[3] The present Chancellor held that the terms of the merger were fair to the plaintiff and the other minority shareholders of UOP. Accordingly, he entered judgment in favor of the defendants.

Numerous points were raised by the parties, but we address only the following questions presented by the trial court's opinion:

> 1) The plaintiff's duty to plead sufficient facts demonstrating the unfairness of the challenged merger;

> 2) The burden of proof upon the parties where the merger has been approved by the purportedly informed vote of a majority of the minority shareholders;

> 3) The fairness of the merger in terms of adequacy of the defendants' disclosures to the minority shareholders;

> 4) The fairness of the merger in terms of adequacy of the price paid for the minority shares and the remedy appropriate to that issue; and

> 5) The continued force and effect of *Singer v. Magnavox Co.*, Del.Supr., 380 A.2d 969, 980 (1977), and its progeny.

In ruling for the defendants, the Chancellor re-stated his earlier conclusion that the plaintiff in a suit challenging a cash-out merger must allege specific acts of fraud, misrepresentation, or other items of misconduct to demonstrate the unfairness of the merger terms to the minority.[4] We approve this rule and affirm it.

The Chancellor also held that even though the ultimate burden of proof is on the majority shareholder to show by a preponderance of the evidence that the transaction is fair, it is first the burden of the plaintiff attacking the merger to demonstrate some basis for invoking the fairness obligation. We agree with that principle. However, where corporate action has been approved by an informed vote of a majority of the minority shareholders, we conclude that the burden entirely shifts to the plaintiff to show that the transaction was

---

[2] For the opinion of the trial court see *Weinberger v. UOP, Inc.*, Del.Ch., 426 A.2d 1333 (1981).

[3] Shortly before the last oral argument, the plaintiff dismissed Lehman Brothers from the action. Thus, we do not deal with the issues raised by the plaintiff's claims against this defendant.

[4] In a pre-trial ruling the Chancellor ordered the complaint dismissed for failure to state a cause of action. *See Weinberger v. UOP, Inc.*, Del.Ch., 409 A.2d 1262 (1979).

unfair to the minority. *See, e.g., Michelson v. Duncan*, Del.Supr., 407 A.2d 211, 224 (1979). But in all this, the burden clearly remains on those relying on the vote to show that they completely disclosed all material facts relevant to the transaction.

Here, the record does not support a conclusion that the minority stockholder vote was an informed one. Material information, necessary to acquaint those shareholders with the bargaining positions of Signal and UOP, was withheld under circumstances amounting to a breach of fiduciary duty. We therefore conclude that this merger does not meet the test of fairness, at least as we address that concept, and no burden thus shifted to the plaintiff by reason of the minority shareholder vote. Accordingly, we reverse and remand for further proceedings consistent herewith.

[...]

Our treatment of these matters has necessarily led us to a reconsideration of the business purpose rule announced in the trilogy of *Singer v. Magnavox Co., supra; Tanzer v. International General Industries, Inc.*, Del.Supr., 379 A.2d 1121 (1977); and *Roland International Corp. v. Najjar*, Del.Supr., 407 A.2d 1032 (1979). For the reasons hereafter set forth we consider that the business purpose requirement of these cases is no longer the law of Delaware.

I.

The facts found by the trial court, pertinent to the issues before us, are supported by the record, and we draw from them as set out in the Chancellor's opinion.[5]

Signal is a diversified, technically based company operating through various subsidiaries. Its stock is publicly traded on the New York, Philadelphia and Pacific Stock Exchanges. UOP, formerly known as Universal Oil Products Company, was a diversified industrial company engaged in various lines of business, including petroleum and petro-chemical services and related products, construction, fabricated metal products, transportation equipment products, chemicals and plastics, and other products and services including land development, lumber products and waste disposal. Its stock was publicly held and listed on the New York Stock Exchange.

In 1974 Signal sold one of its wholly-owned subsidiaries for $420,000,000 in cash. *See Gimbel v. Signal Companies, Inc.*, Del. Ch., 316 A.2d 599, *aff'd*, Del.Supr., 316 A.2d 619 (1974). While looking to invest this cash surplus, Signal became interested in UOP as a possible acquisition. Friendly negotiations ensued, and Signal proposed to acquire a

---

[5] *Weinberger v. UOP, Inc.*, Del.Ch., 426 A.2d 1333, 1335-40 (1981).

controlling interest in UOP at a price of $19 per share. UOP's representatives sought $25 per share. In the arm's length bargaining that followed, an understanding was reached whereby Signal agreed to purchase from UOP 1,500,000 shares of UOP's authorized but unissued stock at $21 per share.

This purchase was contingent upon Signal making a successful cash tender offer for 4,300,000 publicly held shares of UOP, also at a price of $21 per share. This combined method of acquisition permitted Signal to acquire 5,800,000 shares of stock, representing 50.5% of UOP's outstanding shares. The UOP board of directors advised the company's shareholders that it had no objection to Signal's tender offer at that price. Immediately before the announcement of the tender offer, UOP's common stock had been trading on the New York Stock Exchange at a fraction under $14 per share.

The negotiations between Signal and UOP occurred during April 1975, and the resulting tender offer was greatly oversubscribed. However, Signal limited its total purchase of the tendered shares so that, when coupled with the stock bought from UOP, it had achieved its goal of becoming a 50.5% shareholder of UOP.

Although UOP's board consisted of thirteen directors, Signal nominated and elected only six. Of these, five were either directors or employees of Signal. The sixth, a partner in the banking firm of Lazard Freres & Co., had been one of Signal's representatives in the negotiations and bargaining with UOP concerning the tender offer and purchase price of the UOP shares.

[705] However, the president and chief executive officer of UOP retired during 1975, and Signal caused him to be replaced by James V. Crawford, a long-time employee and senior executive vice president of one of Signal's wholly-owned subsidiaries. Crawford succeeded his predecessor on UOP's board of directors and also was made a director of Signal.

By the end of 1977 Signal basically was unsuccessful in finding other suitable investment candidates for its excess cash, and by February 1978 considered that it had no other realistic acquisitions available to it on a friendly basis. Once again its attention turned to UOP.

The trial court found that at the instigation of certain Signal management personnel, including William W. Walkup, its board chairman, and Forrest N. Shumway, its president, a feasibility study was made concerning the possible acquisition of the balance of UOP's outstanding shares. This study was performed by two Signal officers, Charles S. Arledge, vice president (director of planning), and Andrew J. Chitiea, senior vice president (chief financial officer). Messrs. Walkup, Shumway, Arledge and Chitiea were all directors of UOP in addition to their membership on the Signal board.

Arledge and Chitiea concluded that it would be a good investment for Signal to acquire the remaining 49.5% of UOP shares at any price up to $24 each. Their report was discussed between Walkup and Shumway who, along with Arledge, Chitiea and Brewster L. Arms, internal counsel for Signal, constituted Signal's senior management. In particular, they talked about the proper price to be paid if the acquisition was pursued, purportedly keeping in mind that as UOP's majority shareholder, Signal owed a fiduciary responsibility to both its own stockholders as well as to UOP's minority. It was ultimately agreed that a meeting of Signal's executive committee would be called to propose that Signal acquire the remaining outstanding stock of UOP through a cash-out merger in the range of $20 to $21 per share.

The executive committee meeting was set for February 28, 1978. As a courtesy, UOP's president, Crawford, was invited to attend, although he was not a member of Signal's executive committee. On his arrival, and prior to the meeting, Crawford was asked to meet privately with Walkup and Shumway. He was then told of Signal's plan to acquire full ownership of UOP and was asked for his reaction to the proposed price range of $20 to $21 per share. Crawford said he thought such a price would be "generous", and that it was certainly one which should be submitted to UOP's minority shareholders for their ultimate consideration. He stated, however, that Signal's 100% ownership could cause internal problems at UOP. He believed that employees would have to be given some assurance of their future place in a fully-owned Signal subsidiary. Otherwise, he feared the departure of essential personnel. Also, many of UOP's key employees had stock option incentive programs which would be wiped out by a merger. Crawford therefore urged that some adjustment would have to be made, such as providing a comparable incentive in Signal's shares, if after the merger he was to maintain his quality of personnel and efficiency at UOP.

Thus, Crawford voiced no objection to the $20 to $21 price range, nor did he suggest that Signal should consider paying more than $21 per share for the minority interests. Later, at the executive committee meeting the same factors were discussed, with Crawford repeating the position he earlier took with Walkup and Shumway. Also considered was the 1975 tender offer and the fact that it had been greatly oversubscribed at $21 per share. For many reasons, Signal's management concluded that the acquisition of UOP's minority shares provided the solution to a number of its business problems.

Thus, it was the consensus that a price of $20 to $21 per share would be fair to both Signal and the minority shareholders of UOP. Signal's executive committee authorized [706] its management "to negotiate" with UOP "for a cash acquisition of the minority ownership in UOP, Inc., with the intention of presenting a proposal to [Signal's] board of directors ... on March 6, 1978". Immediately after this February 28, 1978 meeting, Signal issued a press release stating:

> The Signal Companies, Inc. and UOP, Inc. are conducting negotiations for the acquisition for cash by Signal of the 49.5 per cent of UOP which it does not presently own, announced Forrest N. Shumway, president and chief executive officer of Signal, and James V. Crawford, UOP president.
>
> Price and other terms of the proposed transaction have not yet been finalized and would be subject to approval of the boards of directors of Signal and UOP, scheduled to meet early next week, the stockholders of UOP and certain federal agencies.

The announcement also referred to the fact that the closing price of UOP's common stock on that day was $14.50 per share.

Two days later, on March 2, 1978, Signal issued a second press release stating that its management would recommend a price in the range of $20 to $21 per share for UOP's 49.5% minority interest. This announcement referred to Signal's earlier statement that "negotiations" were being conducted for the acquisition of the minority shares.

Between Tuesday, February 28, 1978 and Monday, March 6, 1978, a total of four business days, Crawford spoke by telephone with all of UOP's non-Signal, i.e., outside, directors. Also during that period, Crawford retained Lehman Brothers to render a fairness opinion as to the price offered the minority for its stock. He gave two reasons for this choice. First, the time schedule between the announcement and the board meetings was short (by then only three business days) and since Lehman Brothers had been acting as UOP's investment banker for many years, Crawford felt that it would be in the best position to respond on such brief notice. Second, James W. Glanville, a long-time director of UOP and a partner in Lehman Brothers, had acted as a financial advisor to UOP for many years. Crawford believed that Glanville's familiarity with UOP, as a member of its board, would also be of assistance in enabling Lehman Brothers to render a fairness opinion within the existing time constraints.

Crawford telephoned Glanville, who gave his assurance that Lehman Brothers had no conflicts that would prevent it from accepting the task. Glanville's immediate personal reaction was that a price of $20 to $21 would certainly be fair, since it represented almost a 50% premium over UOP's market price. Glanville sought a $250,000 fee for Lehman Brothers' services, but Crawford thought this too much. After further discussions Glanville finally agreed that Lehman Brothers would render its fairness opinion for $150,000.

During this period Crawford also had several telephone contacts with Signal officials. In only one of them, however, was the price of the shares discussed. In a conversation with

Walkup, Crawford advised that as a result of his communications with UOP's non-Signal directors, it was his feeling that the price would have to be the top of the proposed range, or $21 per share, if the approval of UOP's outside directors was to be obtained. But again, he did not seek any price higher than $21.

Glanville assembled a three-man Lehman Brothers team to do the work on the fairness opinion. These persons examined relevant documents and information concerning UOP, including its annual reports and its Securities and Exchange Commission filings from 1973 through 1976, as well as its audited financial statements for 1977, its interim reports to shareholders, and its recent and historical market prices and trading volumes. In addition, on Friday, March 3, 1978, two members of the Lehman Brothers team flew to UOP's headquarters in Des Plaines, Illinois, to perform a "due diligence" visit, during the course of which they interviewed Crawford as well as UOP's general counsel, its chief financial officer, and other key executives and personnel.

[707] As a result, the Lehman Brothers team concluded that "the price of either $20 or $21 would be a fair price for the remaining shares of UOP". They telephoned this impression to Glanville, who was spending the weekend in Vermont.

On Monday morning, March 6, 1978, Glanville and the senior member of the Lehman Brothers team flew to Des Plaines to attend the scheduled UOP directors meeting. Glanville looked over the assembled information during the flight. The two had with them the draft of a "fairness opinion letter" in which the price had been left blank. Either during or immediately prior to the directors' meeting, the two-page "fairness opinion letter" was typed in final form and the price of $21 per share was inserted.

On March 6, 1978, both the Signal and UOP boards were convened to consider the proposed merger. Telephone communications were maintained between the two meetings. Walkup, Signal's board chairman, and also a UOP director, attended UOP's meeting with Crawford in order to present Signal's position and answer any questions that UOP's non-Signal directors might have. Arledge and Chitiea, along with Signal's other designees on UOP's board, participated by conference telephone. All of UOP's outside directors attended the meeting either in person or by conference telephone.

First, Signal's board unanimously adopted a resolution authorizing Signal to propose to UOP a cash merger of $21 per share as outlined in a certain merger agreement and other supporting documents. This proposal required that the merger be approved by a majority of UOP's outstanding minority shares voting at the stockholders meeting at which the merger would be considered, and that the minority shares voting in favor of the merger, when coupled with Signal's 50.5% interest would have to comprise at least two-thirds of all UOP shares. Otherwise the proposed merger would be deemed disapproved.

UOP's board then considered the proposal. Copies of the agreement were delivered to the directors in attendance, and other copies had been forwarded earlier to the directors participating by telephone. They also had before them UOP financial data for 1974-1977, UOP's most recent financial statements, market price information, and budget projections for 1978. In addition they had Lehman Brothers' hurriedly prepared fairness opinion letter finding the price of $21 to be fair. Glanville, the Lehman Brothers partner, and UOP director, commented on the information that had gone into preparation of the letter.

Signal also suggests that the Arledge-Chitiea feasibility study, indicating that a price of up to $24 per share would be a "good investment" for Signal, was discussed at the UOP directors' meeting. The Chancellor made no such finding, and our independent review of the record, detailed *infra,* satisfies us by a preponderance of the evidence that there was no discussion of this document at UOP's board meeting. Furthermore, it is clear beyond peradventure that nothing in that report was ever disclosed to UOP's minority shareholders prior to their approval of the merger.

After consideration of Signal's proposal, Walkup and Crawford left the meeting to permit a free and uninhibited exchange between UOP's non-Signal directors. Upon their return a resolution to accept Signal's offer was then proposed and adopted. While Signal's men on UOP's board participated in various aspects of the meeting, they abstained from voting. However, the minutes show that each of them "if voting would have voted yes".

On March 7, 1978, UOP sent a letter to its shareholders advising them of the action taken by UOP's board with respect to Signal's offer. This document pointed out, among other things, that on February 28, 1978 "both companies had announced negotiations were being conducted".

Despite the swift board action of the two companies, the merger was not submitted to UOP's shareholders until their annual [708] meeting on May 26, 1978. In the notice of that meeting and proxy statement sent to shareholders in May, UOP's management and board urged that the merger be approved. The proxy statement also advised:

> The price was determined after *discussions* between James V. Crawford, a director of Signal and Chief Executive Officer of UOP, and officers of Signal which took place during meetings on February 28, 1978, and in the course of several subsequent telephone conversations. (Emphasis added.)

In the original draft of the proxy statement the word "negotiations" had been used rather than "discussions". However, when the Securities and Exchange Commission sought details of the "negotiations" as part of its review of these materials, the term was deleted and the word "discussions" was substituted. The proxy statement indicated that the vote of UOP's board in approving the merger had been unanimous. It also advised the shareholders that Lehman Brothers had given its opinion that the merger price of $21 per share was fair to UOP's minority. However, it did not disclose the hurried method by which this conclusion was reached.

As of the record date of UOP's annual meeting, there were 11,488,302 shares of UOP common stock outstanding, 5,688,302 of which were owned by the minority. At the meeting only 56%, or 3,208,652, of the minority shares were voted. Of these, 2,953,812, or 51.9% of the total minority, voted for the merger, and 254,840 voted against it. When Signal's stock was added to the minority shares voting in favor, a total of 76.2% of UOP's outstanding shares approved the merger while only 2.2% opposed it.

By its terms the merger became effective on May 26, 1978, and each share of UOP's stock held by the minority was automatically converted into a right to receive $21 cash.

II.

A.

A primary issue mandating reversal is the preparation by two UOP directors, Arledge and Chitiea, of their feasibility study for the exclusive use and benefit of Signal. This document was of obvious significance to both Signal and UOP. Using UOP data, it described the advantages to Signal of ousting the minority at a price range of $21-$24 per share. Mr. Arledge, one of the authors, outlined the benefits to Signal:[6]

Purpose Of The Merger

> 1) Provides an outstanding investment opportunity for Signal — (Better than any recent acquisition we have seen.)

> 2) Increases Signal's earnings.

> 3) Facilitates the flow of resources between Signal and its subsidiaries — (Big factor — works both ways.)

> 4) Provides cost savings potential for Signal and UOP.

> 5) Improves the percentage of Signal's "operating earnings' as opposed to "holding company earnings'.

> 6) Simplifies the understanding of Signal.

---

[6] The parentheses indicate certain handwritten comments of Mr. Arledge.

7) Facilitates technological exchange among Signal's subsidiaries.

8) Eliminates potential conflicts of interest.

Having written those words, solely for the use of Signal, it is clear from the record that neither Arledge nor Chitiea shared this report with their fellow directors of UOP. We are satisfied that no one else did either. This conduct hardly meets the fiduciary standards applicable to such a transaction. While Mr. Walkup, Signal's chairman of the board and a UOP director, attended the March 6, 1978 UOP board meeting and testified at trial that he had discussed the Arledge-Chitiea report with the UOP directors at this meeting, the record does not support this assertion. Perhaps it is the result of some confusion on Mr. Walkup's [709] part. In any event Mr. Shumway, Signal's president, testified that he made sure the Signal outside directors had this report prior to the March 6, 1978 Signal board meeting, but he did not testify that the Arledge-Chitiea report was also sent to UOP's outside directors.

Mr. Crawford, UOP's president, could not recall that any documents, other than a draft of the merger agreement, were sent to UOP's directors before the March 6, 1978 UOP meeting. Mr. Chitiea, an author of the report, testified that it was made available to Signal's directors, but to his knowledge it was not circulated to the outside directors of UOP. He specifically testified that he "didn't share" that information with the outside directors of UOP with whom he served.

None of UOP's outside directors who testified stated that they had seen this document. The minutes of the UOP board meeting do not identify the Arledge-Chitiea report as having been delivered to UOP's outside directors. This is particularly significant since the minutes describe in considerable detail the materials that actually were distributed. While these minutes recite Mr. Walkup's presentation of the Signal offer, they do not mention the Arledge-Chitiea report or any disclosure that Signal considered a price of up to $24 to be a good investment. If Mr. Walkup had in fact provided such important information to UOP's outside directors, it is logical to assume that these carefully drafted minutes would disclose it. The post-trial briefs of Signal and UOP contain a thorough description of the documents purportedly available to their boards at the March 6, 1978, meetings. Although the Arledge-Chitiea report is specifically identified as being available to the Signal directors, there is no mention of it being among the documents submitted to the UOP board. Even when queried at a prior oral argument before this Court, counsel for Signal did not claim that the Arledge-Chitiea report had been disclosed to UOP's outside directors. Instead, he chose to belittle its contents. This was the same approach taken before us at the last oral argument.

Actually, it appears that a three-page summary of figures was given to all UOP directors. Its first page is identical to one page of the Arledge-Chitiea report, but this dealt with nothing more than a justification of the $21 price. Significantly, the contents of this three-page summary are what the minutes reflect Mr. Walkup told the UOP board. However, nothing contained in either the minutes or this three-page summary reflects Signal's study regarding the $24 price.

The Arledge-Chitiea report speaks for itself in supporting the Chancellor's finding that a price of up to $24 was a "good investment" for Signal. It shows that a return on the investment at $21 would be 15.7% versus 15.5% at $24 per share. This was a difference of only two-tenths of one percent, while it meant over $17,000,000 to the minority. Under such circumstances, paying UOP's minority shareholders $24 would have had relatively little long-term effect on Signal, and the Chancellor's findings concerning the benefit to Signal, even at a price of $24, were obviously correct. *Levitt v. Bouvier*, Del.Supr., 287 A.2d 671, 673 (1972).

Certainly, this was a matter of material significance to UOP and its shareholders. Since the study was prepared by two UOP directors, using UOP information for the exclusive benefit of Signal, and nothing whatever was done to disclose it to the outside UOP directors or the minority shareholders, a question of breach of fiduciary duty arises. This problem occurs because there were common Signal-UOP directors participating, at least to some extent, in the UOP board's decision-making processes without full disclosure of the conflicts they faced.[7] [710]

B.

In assessing this situation, the Court of Chancery was required to:

> examine what information defendants had and to measure it against what they gave to the minority stockholders, in a context in which "complete candor' is required. In other words, the limited function of the Court was to determine whether defendants had disclosed all information in their possession germane to the transaction in issue. And by "germane' we mean, for present purposes, information such as a

---

[7] Although perfection is not possible, or expected, the result here could have been entirely different if UOP had appointed an independent negotiating committee of its outside directors to deal with Signal at arm's length. *See, e.g., Harriman v. E.I. duPont de Nemours & Co.*, 411 F.Supp. 133 (D.Del.1975). Since fairness in this context can be equated to conduct by a theoretical, wholly independent, board of directors acting upon the matter before them, it is unfortunate that this course apparently was neither considered nor pursued. *Johnston v. Greene*, Del.Supr., 121 A.2d 919, 925 (1956). Particularly in a parent-subsidiary context, a showing that the action taken was as though each of the contending parties had in fact exerted its bargaining power against the other at arm's length is strong evidence that the transaction meets the test of fairness. *Getty Oil Co. v. Skelly Oil Co.*, Del.Supr., 267 A.2d 883, 886 (1970); *Puma v. Marriott*, Del.Ch., 283 A.2d 693, 696 (1971).

reasonable shareholder would consider important in deciding whether to sell or retain stock.

* * * * * *

... Completeness, not adequacy, is both the norm and the mandate under present circumstances.

Lynch v. Vickers Energy Corp., Del.Supr., 383 A.2d 278, 281 (1977) (*Lynch I*). This is merely stating in another way the long-existing principle of Delaware law that these Signal designated directors on UOP's board still owed UOP and its shareholders an uncompromising duty of loyalty. The classic language of *Guth v. Loft, Inc.*, Del.Supr., 5 A.2d 503, 510 (1939), requires no embellishment:

> A public policy, existing through the years, and derived from a profound knowledge of human characteristics and motives, has established a rule that demands of a corporate officer or director, peremptorily and inexorably, the most scrupulous observance of his duty, not only affirmatively to protect the interests of the corporation committed to his charge, but also to refrain from doing anything that would work injury to the corporation, or to deprive it of profit or advantage which his skill and ability might properly bring to it, or to enable it to make in the reasonable and lawful exercise of its powers. The rule that requires an undivided and unselfish loyalty to the corporation demands that there shall be no conflict between duty and self-interest.

Given the absence of any attempt to structure this transaction on an arm's length basis, Signal cannot escape the effects of the conflicts it faced, particularly when its designees on UOP's board did not totally abstain from participation in the matter. There is no "safe harbor" for such divided loyalties in Delaware. When directors of a Delaware corporation are on both sides of a transaction, they are required to demonstrate their utmost good faith and the most scrupulous inherent fairness of the bargain. *Gottlieb v. Heyden Chemical Corp.*, Del.Supr., 91 A.2d 57, 57-58 (1952). The requirement of fairness is unflinching in its demand that where one stands on both sides of a transaction, he has the burden of establishing its entire fairness, sufficient to pass the test of careful scrutiny by the courts. *Sterling v. Mayflower Hotel Corp.*, Del.Supr., 93 A.2d 107, 110 (1952); *Bastian v. Bourns, Inc.*, Del.Ch., 256 A.2d 680, 681 (1969), *aff'd*, Del.Supr., 278 A.2d 467 (1970); *David J. Greene & Co. v. Dunhill International Inc.*, Del.Ch., 249 A.2d 427, 431 (1968).

There is no dilution of this obligation where one holds dual or multiple directorships, as in a parent-subsidiary context. *Levien v. Sinclair Oil Corp.*, Del.Ch., 261 A.2d 911, 915 (1969). Thus, individuals who act in a dual capacity as directors of two corporations, one of whom is parent and the other subsidiary, owe the same duty of good management to both corporations, and in the absence of an independent negotiating [711] structure (see note 7, *supra*), or the directors' total abstention from any participation in the matter, this duty is to be exercised in light of what is best for both companies. *Warshaw v. Calhoun,* Del. Supr., 221 A.2d 487, 492 (1966). The record demonstrates that Signal has not met this obligation.

C.

The concept of fairness has two basic aspects: fair dealing and fair price. The former embraces questions of when the transaction was timed, how it was initiated, structured, negotiated, disclosed to the directors, and how the approvals of the directors and the stockholders were obtained. The latter aspect of fairness relates to the economic and financial considerations of the proposed merger, including all relevant factors: assets, market value, earnings, future prospects, and any other elements that affect the intrinsic or inherent value of a company's stock. Moore, *The "Interested" Director or Officer Transaction,* 4 Del.J. Corp.L. 674, 676 (1979); Nathan & Shapiro, *Legal Standard of Fairness of Merger Terms Under Delaware Law,* 2 Del.J. Corp.L. 44, 46-47 (1977). *See Tri-Continental Corp. v. Battye,* Del.Supr., 74 A.2d 71, 72 (1950); 8 *Del.C.* § 262(h). However, the test for fairness is not a bifurcated one as between fair dealing and price. All aspects of the issue must be examined as a whole since the question is one of entire fairness. However, in a non-fraudulent transaction we recognize that price may be the preponderant consideration outweighing other features of the merger. Here, we address the two basic aspects of fairness separately because we find reversible error as to both.

D.

Part of fair dealing is the obvious duty of candor required by *Lynch I, supra.* Moreover, one possessing superior knowledge may not mislead any stockholder by use of corporate information to which the latter is not privy. *Lank v. Steiner,* Del. Supr., 224 A.2d 242, 244 (1966). Delaware has long imposed this duty even upon persons who are not corporate officers or directors, but who nonetheless are privy to matters of interest or significance to their company. *Brophy v. Cities Service Co.,* Del. Ch., 70 A.2d 5, 7 (1949). With the well-established Delaware law on the subject, and the Court of Chancery's findings of fact here, it is inevitable that the obvious conflicts posed by Arledge and Chitiea's preparation of their "feasibility study", derived from UOP information, for the sole use and benefit of Signal, cannot pass muster.

The Arledge-Chitiea report is but one aspect of the element of fair dealing. How did this merger evolve? It is clear that it was entirely initiated by Signal. The serious time constraints under which the principals acted were all set by Signal. It had not found a suitable outlet for its excess cash and considered UOP a desirable investment, particularly since it was now in a position to acquire the whole company for itself. For whatever reasons, and they were only Signal's, the entire transaction was presented to and approved by UOP's board within four business days. Standing alone, this is not necessarily indicative of any lack of fairness by a majority shareholder. It was what occurred, or more properly, what did not occur, during this brief period that makes the time constraints imposed by Signal relevant to the issue of fairness.

The structure of the transaction, again, was Signal's doing. So far as negotiations were concerned, it is clear that they were modest at best. Crawford, Signal's man at UOP, never really talked price with Signal, except to accede to its management's statements on the subject, and to convey to Signal the UOP outside directors' view that as between the $20-$21 range under consideration, it would have to be $21. The latter is not a surprising outcome, but hardly arm's length negotiations. Only the protection of benefits for UOP's key employees and the issue of Lehman Brothers' fee approached any concept of bargaining.

[712] As we have noted, the matter of disclosure to the UOP directors was wholly flawed by the conflicts of interest raised by the Arledge-Chitiea report. All of those conflicts were resolved by Signal in its own favor without divulging any aspect of them to UOP.

This cannot but undermine a conclusion that this merger meets any reasonable test of fairness. The outside UOP directors lacked one material piece of information generated by two of their colleagues, but shared only with Signal. True, the UOP board had the Lehman Brothers' fairness opinion, but that firm has been blamed by the plaintiff for the hurried task it performed, when more properly the responsibility for this lies with Signal. There was no disclosure of the circumstances surrounding the rather cursory preparation of the Lehman Brothers' fairness opinion. Instead, the impression was given UOP's minority that a careful study had been made, when in fact speed was the hallmark, and Mr. Glanville, Lehman's partner in charge of the matter, and also a UOP director, having spent the weekend in Vermont, brought a draft of the "fairness opinion letter" to the UOP directors' meeting on March 6, 1978 with the price left blank. We can only conclude from the record that the rush imposed on Lehman Brothers by Signal's timetable contributed to the difficulties under which this investment banking firm attempted to perform its responsibilities. Yet, none of this was disclosed to UOP's minority.

Finally, the minority stockholders were denied the critical information that Signal considered a price of $24 to be a good investment. Since this would have meant over $17,000,000 more to the minority, we cannot conclude that the shareholder vote was an informed one. Under the circumstances, an approval by a majority of the minority was meaningless. *Lynch I*, 383 A.2d at 279, 281; *Cahall v. Lofland*, Del.Ch., 114 A. 224 (1921).

Given these particulars and the Delaware law on the subject, the record does not establish that this transaction satisfies any reasonable concept of fair dealing, and the Chancellor's findings in that regard must be reversed.

E.

Turning to the matter of price, plaintiff also challenges its fairness. His evidence was that on the date the merger was approved the stock was worth at least $26 per share. In support, he offered the testimony of a chartered investment analyst who used two basic approaches to valuation: a comparative analysis of the premium paid over market in ten other tender offer-merger combinations, and a discounted cash flow analysis.

In this breach of fiduciary duty case, the Chancellor perceived that the approach to valuation was the same as that in an appraisal proceeding. Consistent with precedent, he rejected plaintiff's method of proof and accepted defendants' evidence of value as being in accord with practice under prior case law. This means that the so-called "Delaware block" or weighted average method was employed wherein the elements of value, i.e., assets, market price, earnings, etc., were assigned a particular weight and the resulting amounts added to determine the value per share. This procedure has been in use for decades. See In re General Realty & Utilities Corp., Del.Ch., 52 A.2d 6, 14-15 (1947). However, to the extent it excludes other generally accepted techniques used in the financial community and the courts, it is now clearly outmoded. It is time we recognize this in appraisal and other stock valuation proceedings and bring our law current on the subject.

While the Chancellor rejected plaintiff's discounted cash flow method of valuing UOP's stock, as not corresponding with "either logic or the existing law" (426 A.2d at 1360), it is significant that this was essentially the focus, i.e., earnings potential of UOP, of Messrs. Arledge and Chitiea in their evaluation of the merger. Accordingly, the standard "Delaware block" or weighted average method of valuation, formerly [713] employed in appraisal and other stock valuation cases, shall no longer exclusively control such proceedings. We believe that a more liberal approach must include proof of value by any techniques or methods which are generally considered acceptable in the financial community and otherwise admissible in court[...]

Fair price obviously requires consideration of all relevant factors involving the value of a company. This has long been the law of Delaware as stated in Tri-Continental Corp., 74 A.2d at 72:

> The basic concept of value under the appraisal statute is that the stockholder is entitled to be paid for that which has been taken from him, viz., his proportionate interest in a going concern. By value of the

stockholder's proportionate interest in the corporate enterprise is meant the true or intrinsic value of his stock which has been taken by the merger. In determining what figure represents this true or intrinsic value, the appraiser and the courts must take into consideration all factors and elements which reasonably might enter into the fixing of value. Thus, market value, asset value, dividends, earning prospects, the nature of the enterprise and any other facts which were known or which could be ascertained as of the date of merger and which throw any light on *future prospects* of the merged corporation are not only pertinent to an inquiry as to the value of the dissenting stockholders' interest, but *must be considered* by the agency fixing the value. (Emphasis added.)

[...]

Although the Chancellor received the plaintiff's evidence, his opinion indicates that the use of it was precluded because of past Delaware practice. While we do not suggest a monetary result one way or the other, we do think the plaintiff's evidence should be part of the factual mix and weighed as such. Until the $21 price is measured on remand by the valuation standards mandated by Delaware law, there can be no finding at the present stage of these proceedings that the price is fair. Given the lack of any candid disclosure of the material facts surrounding establishment of the $21 price, the majority of the minority vote, approving the merger, is meaningless.

[...]

III.

Finally, we address the matter of business purpose. The defendants contend that the purpose of this merger was not a proper subject of inquiry by the trial court. The plaintiff says that no valid purpose existed — the entire transaction was a mere subterfuge designed to eliminate the minority. The Chancellor ruled otherwise, but in so doing he clearly circumscribed the thrust and effect of *Singer. Weinberger v. UOP*, 426 A.2d at 1342-43, 1348-50. This has led to the thoroughly sound observation that the business purpose test "may be ... virtually interpreted out of existence, as it was in *Weinberger*".[9]

The requirement of a business purpose is new to our law of mergers and was a departure from prior case law. *See Stauffer v. Standard Brands, Inc., supra; David J. Greene & Co. v. Schenley Industries, Inc., supra.*

---

[9] Weiss, *The Law of Take Out Mergers: A Historical Perspective,* 56 N.Y.U.L.Rev. 624, 671, n. 300 (1981).

In view of the fairness test which has long been applicable to parent-subsidiary mergers [...] and the broad discretion of the Chancellor to fashion such relief as the facts of a given case may dictate, we do not believe that any additional meaningful protection is afforded minority shareholders by the business purpose requirement of the trilogy of *Singer, Tanzer,*[10] *Najjar,*[11] and their progeny. Accordingly, such requirement shall no longer be of any force or effect.

The judgment of the Court of Chancery, finding both the circumstances of the merger and the price paid the minority shareholders to be fair, is reversed. The matter is remanded for further proceedings consistent herewith. Upon remand the plaintiff's post-trial motion to enlarge the class should be granted.

* * * * * *

REVERSED AND REMANDED.

B. Glassman v. Unocal Exploration Corp. (Del. 2001)

The most basic facts of this case are similar to those in *Weinberger*: parent attempts a cash-out merger, or squeeze out; minority stockholders of the subsidiary complain.

Questions

1. Why is the outcome in this case different from *Weinberger*?

2. What is the practical difference in this case and going forward – can't plaintiffs get the same remedy in an appraisal action?

3. If there is a practical difference, does it make sense from a policy perspective?

4. The Glassman court's reasoning puts much weight on the ostensible incompatibility of DGCL 253 and entire fairness review. Are they truly incompatible, or can you think of a different way to reconcile them?

---

[10] *Tanzer v. International General Industries, Inc.,* Del.Supr., 379 A.2d 1121, 1124-25 (1977).
[11] *Roland International Corp. v. Najjar,* Del. Supr., 407 A.2d 1032, 1036 (1979).

777 A.2d 242 (2001)

Morris I. GLASSMAN and William Steiner, Plaintiffs Below, Appellants,

v.

UNOCAL EXPLORATION CORPORATION, Unocal Corporation, John W. Amerman, Roger C. Beach, MacDonald G. Becket, Claude S. Brinegar, Malcolm R. Currie, Richard K. Eamer, Frank C. Herringer, John F. Imle, Jr., Donald P. Jacobs, Ann McLaughlin, Neal E. Schmale, Thomas B. Sleeman, Richard J. Stegemeier, and Charles R. Weaver, Defendants Below, Appellees.

In re Unocal Exploration Corporation Shareholders Litigation.

No. 390, 2000.

Supreme Court of Delaware.

Submitted: April 3, 2001.

Decided: July 25, 2001.

R. Bruce McNew, Esquire (argued), of Taylor & McNew, LLP, Greenville, Delaware, and Pamela S. Tikellis, Esquire, Robert J. Kriner, Jr., Esquire, and Timothy R. Dudderar, Esquire, of Chimicles & [243] Tikellis, LLP, Wilmington, Delaware, for Appellants.

Kenneth J. Nachbar, Esquire (argued) and Jon E. Abramczyk, Esquire, of Morris, Nichols, Arsht & Tunnell, Wilmington, Delaware, for Appellees Unocal Corporation, John W. Amerman, Roger C. Beach, Claude S. Brinegar, Malcolm R. Currie, Richard K. Eamer, Frank C. Herringer, John F. Imle, Jr., Donald P. Jacobs, Neal E. Schmale, Thomas B. Sleeman and Richard J. Stegemeier; and Brett D. Fallon, Esquire, of Morris, James, Hitchens & Williams, Wilmington, Delaware, for Appellees Unocal Exploration Corporation, MacDonald G. Becket, Ann McLaughlin and Charles R. Weaver.

Before VEASEY, Chief Justice, WALSH, HOLLAND, BERGER and STEELE, Justices, constituting the Court en Banc.

BERGER, Justice.

In this appeal, we consider the fiduciary duties owed by a parent corporation to the subsidiary's minority stockholders in the context of a "short-form" merger. Specifically, we take this opportunity to reconcile a fiduciary's seemingly absolute duty to establish the entire fairness of any self-dealing transaction with the less demanding requirements of the short-form merger statute. The statute authorizes the elimination of minority stockholders by a summary process that does not involve the "fair dealing" component of entire fairness. Indeed, the statute does not contemplate any "dealing" at all. Thus, a parent corporation cannot satisfy the entire fairness standard if it follows the terms of the short-form merger statute without more.

Unocal Corporation addressed this dilemma by establishing a special negotiating committee and engaging in a process that it believed would pass muster under traditional entire fairness review. We find that such steps were unnecessary. By enacting a statute that authorizes the elimination of the minority without notice, vote, or other traditional indicia of procedural fairness, the General Assembly effectively circumscribed the parent corporation's obligations to the minority in a short-form merger. The parent corporation does not have to establish entire fairness, and, absent fraud or illegality, the only recourse for a minority stockholder who is dissatisfied with the merger consideration is appraisal.

I. Factual and Procedural Background

Unocal Corporation is an earth resources company primarily engaged in the exploration for and production of crude oil and natural gas. At the time of the merger at issue, Unocal owned approximately 96% of the stock of Unocal Exploration Corporation ("UXC"), an oil and gas company operating in and around the Gulf of Mexico. In 1991, low natural gas prices caused a drop in both companies' revenues and earnings. Unocal investigated areas of possible cost savings and decided that, by eliminating the UXC minority, it would reduce taxes and overhead expenses.

In December 1991 the boards of Unocal and UXC appointed special committees to consider a possible merger. The UXC committee consisted of three directors who, although also directors of Unocal, were not officers or employees of the parent company. The UXC committee retained financial and legal advisors and met four times before agreeing to a merger exchange ratio of .54 shares of Unocal stock for each share of UXC. Unocal and UXC announced the merger on February 24, 1992, and it was effected, pursuant to 8 *Del.C.* § 253, on May 2, 1992. The Notice of Merger and Prospectus stated the terms of the merger and advised the former [244] UXC stockholders of their appraisal rights.

Plaintiffs filed this class action, on behalf of UXC's minority stockholders, on the day the merger was announced. They asserted, among other claims, that Unocal and its directors breached their fiduciary duties of entire fairness and full disclosure. The Court of Chancery conducted a two day trial and held that: (i) the Prospectus did not contain any material misstatements or omissions; (ii) the entire fairness standard does not control in a short-form merger; and (iii) plaintiffs' exclusive remedy in this case was appraisal. The decision of the Court of Chancery is affirmed.

II. Discussion

The short-form merger statute, as enacted in 1937, authorized a parent corporation to merge with its wholly-owned subsidiary by filing and recording a certificate evidencing the parent's ownership and its merger resolution. In 1957, the statute was expanded to include parent/subsidiary mergers where the parent company owns at least 90% of the stock of the subsidiary. The 1957 amendment also made it possible, for the first time and only in a short-form merger, to pay the minority cash for their shares, thereby eliminating their ownership interest in the company. In its current form, which has not changed significantly since 1957, 8 *Del.C.* § 253 provides in relevant part:

> (a) In any case in which at least 90 percent of the outstanding shares of each class of the stock of a corporation... is owned by another corporation..., the corporation having such stock ownership may ... merge the other corporation ... into itself... by executing, acknowledging and filing, in accordance with § 103 of this title, a certificate of such ownership and merger setting forth a copy of the resolution of its board of directors to so merge and the date of the adoption; provided, however, that in case the parent corporation shall not own all the outstanding stock of ... the subsidiary corporation[ ],... the resolution ... shall state the terms and conditions of the merger, including the securities, cash, property or rights to be issued, paid delivered or granted by the surviving corporation upon surrender of each share of the subsidiary corporation....
>
> * * *
>
> (d) In the event that all of the stock of a subsidiary Delaware corporation... is not owned by the parent corporation immediately prior to the merger, the stockholders of the subsidiary Delaware corporation party to the merger shall have appraisal rights as set forth in Section 262 of this Title.

This Court first reviewed § 253 in *Coyne v. Park & Tilford Distillers Corporation.*[1] There, minority stockholders of the merged-out subsidiary argued that the statute could not mean what it says because Delaware law "never has permitted, and does not now permit, the payment of cash for whole shares surrendered in a merger and the consequent expulsion of a stockholder from the enterprise in which he has invested." The *Coyne* court held that § 253 plainly does permit such a result and that the statute is constitutional.

---

[1] Del.Supr., 154 A.2d 893 (1959).

The next question presented to this Court was whether any equitable relief is available to minority stockholders who object to a short-form merger. In *Stauffer v. Standard Brands Incorporated,*[3] minority [245] stockholders sued to set aside the contested merger or, in the alternative, for damages. They alleged that the merger consideration was so grossly inadequate as to constitute constructive fraud and that Standard Brands breached its fiduciary duty to the minority by failing to set a fair price for their stock. The Court of Chancery held that appraisal was the stockholders' exclusive remedy, and dismissed the complaint. This Court affirmed, but explained that appraisal would not be the exclusive remedy in a short-form merger tainted by fraud or illegality:

> [T]he exception [eds: to appraisal's exclusivity] [...] refers generally to all mergers, and is nothing but a reaffirmation of the ever-present power of equity to deal with illegality or fraud. But it has no bearing here. No illegality or overreaching is shown. The dispute reduces to nothing but a difference of opinion as to value. Indeed it is difficult to imagine a case under the short merger statute in which there could be such actual fraud as would entitle a minority to set aside the merger. This is so because the very purpose of the statute is to provide the parent corporation with a means of eliminating the minority shareholder's interest in the enterprise. Thereafter the former stockholder has only a monetary claim.

The *Stauffer* doctrine's viability rose and fell over the next four decades. [...]

Mindful of this history, we must decide whether a minority stockholder may challenge a short-form merger by seeking equitable relief through an entire fairness claim. Under settled principles, a parent corporation and its directors undertaking a short-form merger are self-dealing fiduciaries who should be required to establish entire fairness, including fair dealing and fair price. The problem is that § 253 authorizes a summary procedure that is inconsistent with any reasonable notion of fair dealing. In a short-form merger, there is no agreement of merger negotiated by two companies; there is only a unilateral act — a decision by the parent company that its 90% owned subsidiary shall no longer exist as a separate entity. The minority stockholders receive no advance notice of the merger; their directors do not consider or approve it; and there is no vote. Those who object are given the right to obtain fair value for their shares through appraisal.

The equitable claim plainly conflicts with the statute. If a corporate fiduciary follows the truncated process authorized by § 253, it will not be able to establish the fair dealing prong of entire fairness. If, instead, the corporate fiduciary sets up negotiating committees, hires independent [248] financial and legal experts, etc., then it will have lost

---

[3] Del.Supr., 187 A.2d 78 (1962).

the very benefit provided by the statute — a simple, fast and inexpensive process for accomplishing a merger. We resolve this conflict by giving effect the intent of the General Assembly. In order to serve its purpose, § 253 must be construed to obviate the requirement to establish entire fairness.

Thus, we again return to *Stauffer,* and hold that, absent fraud or illegality, appraisal is the exclusive remedy available to a minority stockholder who objects to a short-form merger. In doing so, we also reaffirm *Weinberger's* statements about the scope of appraisal. The determination of fair value must be based on *all* relevant factors, including damages and elements of future value, where appropriate. So, for example, if the merger was timed to take advantage of a depressed market, or a low point in the company's cyclical earnings, or to precede an anticipated positive development, the appraised value may be adjusted to account for those factors. We recognize that these are the types of issues frequently raised in entire fairness claims, and we have held that claims for unfair dealing cannot be litigated in an appraisal. But our prior holdings simply explained that equitable claims may not be engrafted onto a statutory appraisal proceeding; stockholders may not receive rescissionary relief in an appraisal. Those decisions should not be read to restrict the elements of value that properly may be considered in an appraisal.

Although fiduciaries are not required to establish entire fairness in a short-form merger, the duty of full disclosure remains, in the context of this request for stockholder action. Where the only choice for the minority stockholders is whether to accept the merger consideration or seek appraisal, they must be given all the factual information that is material to that decision. The Court of Chancery carefully considered plaintiffs' disclosure claims and applied settled law in rejecting them. We affirm this aspect of the appeal on the basis of the trial court's decision.

III. Conclusion

Based on the foregoing, we affirm the Court of Chancery and hold that plaintiffs' only remedy in connection with the short-form merger of UXC into Unocal was appraisal.

C. Kahn v. MFW (Del. 2014)

This decision epitomizes the Delaware judiciary's approach to tricky conflict situations. Practitioners have figured out the court's approach and structure deals accordingly.

Questions

1. What standard of review does the court apply? Is it different from the cases we have seen thus far?

2. How does the court want to protect minority shareholders? Does it work? Does it work better than alternatives?

3. Why did this case proceed to summary judgment, whereas the complaint in *Dorsey* was dismissed even before discovery? Hint: what sort of action was *Dorsey*, and what is the present case?

88 A.3d 635 (2014)

Alan KAHN, Samuel Pill, Irwin Pill, Rachel Pill and Charlotte Martin,
Plaintiffs Below, Appellants,

v.

M & F WORLDWIDE CORP., Ronald O. Perelman, Barry F.
Schwartz, William C. Bevins, Bruce Slovin, Charles T. Dawson,
Stephen G. Taub, John M. Keane, Theo W. Folz, Philip E. Beekman,
Martha L. Byorum, Viet D. Dinh, Paul M. Meister, Carl B. Webb and
MacAndrews & Forbes Holdings, Inc., Defendants Below, Appellees.

No. 334, 2013.

Supreme Court of Delaware.

Submitted: December 18, 2013.
Decided: March 14, 2014.

[638] Carmella P. Keener, Esquire, Rosenthal, Monhait & Goddess, P.A., Wilmington, Delaware, Peter B. Andrews, Esquire, Nadeem Faruqi, Esquire, Beth A. Keller, Esquire, Faruqi & Faruqi, LLP, Wilmington, Delaware, Carl L. Stine, Esquire (argued) and Matthew Insley-Pruitt, Esquire, Wolf Popper LLP, New York, New York, and James S. Notis,

Esquire and Kira German, Esquire, Gardy & Notis, LLP, New York, New York, for appellants.

William M. Lafferty, Esquire, and D. McKinley Measley, Esquire, Morris, Nichols, Arsht & Tunnell LLP, Wilmington, Delaware, and Tariq Mundiya, Esquire (argued), Todd G. Cosenza, Esquire and Christopher J. Miritello, Esquire, Willkie Farr & Gallagher LLP, New York, New York, for appellees, Paul M. Meister, Martha L. Byorum, Viet D. Dinh and Carl B. Webb.

Thomas J. Allingham, II, Esquire (argued), Christopher M. Foulds, Esquire, Joseph O. Larkin, Esquire, and Jessica L. Raatz, Esquire, Skadden, Arps, Slate, Meagher & Flom LLP, Wilmington, Delaware, for appellees MacAndrews & Forbes Holdings, Inc., Ronald O. Perelman, Barry F. Schwartz, and William C. Bevins.

Stephen P. Lamb, Esquire and Meghan M. Dougherty, Esquire, Paul, Weiss, Rifkind, Wharton & Garrison LLP, Wilmington, Delaware, for appellees M & F Worldwide Corp., Bruce Slovin, Charles T. Dawson, Stephen G. Taub, John M. Keane, Theo W. Folz, and Philip E. Beekman.

Before HOLLAND, BERGER, JACOBS and RIDGELY, Justices and JURDEN, Judge,[1] constituting the Court en Banc.

HOLLAND, Justice:

This is an appeal from a final judgment entered by the Court of Chancery in a proceeding that arises from a 2011 acquisition by MacAndrews & Forbes Holdings, Inc. ("M & F" or "MacAndrews & Forbes") — a 43% stockholder in M & F Worldwide Corp. ("MFW") — of the remaining common stock of MFW (the "Merger"). From the outset, M & F's proposal to take MFW private was made contingent upon two stockholder-protective procedural conditions. First, M & F required the Merger to be negotiated and approved by a special committee of independent MFW directors (the "Special Committee"). Second, M & F required that the Merger be approved by a majority of stockholders unaffiliated with M & F. The Merger closed in December 2011, after it was approved by a vote of 65.4% of MFW's minority stockholders.

The Appellants initially sought to enjoin the transaction. They withdrew their request for injunctive relief after taking expedited discovery, including several depositions. The Appellants then sought post-closing relief against M & F, Ronald O. Perelman, and MFW's directors (including the members of the Special Committee) for breach of fiduciary duty. Again, the Appellants were provided with extensive discovery. The

---

[1] Sitting by designation pursuant to Del. Const. art. IV, § 12 and Supr. Ct. R. 2 and 4.

Defendants then moved for [639] summary judgment, which the Court of Chancery granted.

Court of Chancery Decision

The Court of Chancery found that the case presented a "novel question of law," specifically, "what standard of review should apply to a going private merger conditioned upfront by the controlling stockholder on approval by both a properly empowered, independent committee and an informed, uncoerced majority-of-the-minority vote." The Court of Chancery held that business judgment review, rather than entire fairness, should be applied to a very limited category of controller mergers. That category consisted of mergers where the controller voluntarily relinquishes its control — such that the negotiation and approval process replicate those that characterize a third-party merger.

The Court of Chancery held that, rather than entire fairness, the business judgment standard of review should apply "if, *but only if:* (i) the controller conditions the transaction on the approval of both a Special Committee and a majority of the minority stockholders; (ii) the Special Committee is independent; (iii) the Special Committee is empowered to freely select its own advisors and to say no definitively; (iv) the Special Committee acts with care; (v) the minority vote is informed; and (vi) there is no coercion of the minority."[2]

The Court of Chancery found that those prerequisites were satisfied and that the Appellants had failed to raise any genuine issue of material fact indicating the contrary. The court then reviewed the Merger under the business judgment standard and granted summary judgment for the Defendants.

Appellants' Arguments

The Appellants raise two main arguments on this appeal. First, they contend that the Court of Chancery erred in concluding that no material disputed facts existed regarding the conditions precedent to business judgment review. The Appellants submit that the record contains evidence showing that the Special Committee was not disinterested and independent, was not fully empowered, and was not effective. The Appellants also contend, as a legal matter, that the majority-of-the-minority provision did not afford MFW stockholders protection sufficient to displace entire fairness review.

Second, the Appellants submit that the Court of Chancery erred, as a matter of law, in holding that the business judgment standard applies to controller freeze-out mergers where the controller's proposal is conditioned on both Special Committee approval and a favorable majority-of-the-minority vote. Even if both procedural protections are adopted,

---

[2] Emphasis by the Court of Chancery.

the Appellants argue, entire fairness should be retained as the applicable standard of review.

Defendants' Arguments

The Defendants argue that the judicial standard of review should be the business judgment rule, because the Merger was conditioned *ab initio* on two procedural protections that together operated to replicate an arm's-length merger: the employment of an active, unconflicted negotiating agent free to turn down the transaction; and a requirement that any transaction negotiated by that agent be approved by a majority of the disinterested stockholders. The Defendants argue that using and *establishing* pretrial that both protective conditions were extant renders a going private transaction analogous to that of a third-party arm's-length merger under [640] Section 251 of the Delaware General Corporation Law. That is, the Defendants submit that a Special Committee approval in a going private transaction is a proxy for board approval in a third-party transaction, and that the approval of the unaffiliated, noncontrolling stockholders replicates the approval of all the (potentially) adversely affected stockholders.

FACTS

MFW and M & F

MFW is a holding company incorporated in Delaware. Before the Merger that is the subject of this dispute, MFW was 43.4% owned by MacAndrews & Forbes, which in turn is entirely owned by Ronald O. Perelman. MFW had four business segments. Three were owned through a holding company, Harland Clarke Holding Corporation ("HCHC"). They were the Harland Clarke Corporation ("Harland"), which printed bank checks; Harland Clarke Financial Solutions, which provided technology products and services to financial services companies; and Scantron Corporation, which manufactured scanning equipment used for educational and other purposes. The fourth segment, which was not part of HCHC, was Mafco Worldwide Corporation, a manufacturer of licorice flavorings.

The MFW board had thirteen members. They were: Ronald Perelman, Barry Schwartz, William Bevins, Bruce Slovin, Charles Dawson, Stephen Taub, John Keane, Theo Folz, Philip Beekman, Martha Byorum, Viet Dinh, Paul Meister, and Carl Webb. Perelman, Schwartz, and Bevins were officers of both MFW and MacAndrews & Forbes. Perelman was the Chairman of MFW and the Chairman and CEO of MacAndrews & Forbes; Schwartz was the President and CEO of MFW and the Vice Chairman and Chief Administrative Officer of MacAndrews & Forbes; and Bevins was a Vice President at MacAndrews & Forbes.

The Taking MFW Private Proposal

In May 2011, Perelman began to explore the possibility of taking MFW private. At that time, MFW's stock price traded in the $20 to $24 per share range. MacAndrews & Forbes engaged a bank, Moelis & Company, to advise it. After preparing valuations based on projections that had been supplied to lenders by MFW in April and May 2011, Moelis valued MFW at between $10 and $32 a share.

On June 10, 2011, MFW's shares closed on the New York Stock Exchange at $16.96. The next business day, June 13, 2011, Schwartz sent a letter proposal ("Proposal") to the MFW board to buy the remaining MFW shares for $24 in cash. The Proposal stated, in relevant part:

> The proposed transaction would be subject to the approval of the Board of Directors of the Company [*i.e.,* MFW] and the negotiation and execution of mutually acceptable definitive transaction documents. It is our expectation that the Board of Directors will appoint a special committee of independent directors to consider our proposal and make a recommendation to the Board of Directors. *We will not move forward with the transaction unless it is approved by such a special committee. In addition, the transaction will be subject to a non-waivable condition requiring the approval of a majority of the shares of the Company not owned by M & F or its affiliates* ....[3]

> ... In considering this proposal, you should know that in our capacity as a stockholder of the Company we are interested [641] only in acquiring the shares of the Company not already owned by us and that in such capacity we have no interest in selling any of the shares owned by us in the Company nor would we expect, in our capacity as a stockholder, to vote in favor of any alternative sale, merger or similar transaction involving the Company. If the special committee does not recommend or the public stockholders of the Company do not approve the proposed transaction, such determination would not adversely affect our future relationship with the Company and we would intend to remain as a long-term stockholder.

> ....

> In connection with this proposal, we have engaged Moelis & Company as our financial advisor and Skadden, Arps, Slate, Meagher & Flom LLP

---

[3] Emphasis added.

as our legal advisor, and we encourage the special committee to retain its own legal and financial advisors to assist it in its review.

MacAndrews & Forbes filed this letter with the U.S. Securities and Exchange Commission ("SEC") and issued a press release disclosing substantially the same information.

The Special Committee Is Formed

The MFW board met the following day to consider the Proposal. At the meeting, Schwartz presented the offer on behalf of MacAndrews & Forbes. Subsequently, Schwartz and Bevins, as the two directors present who were also directors of MacAndrews & Forbes, recused themselves from the meeting, as did Dawson, the CEO of HCHC, who had previously expressed support for the proposed offer.

The independent directors then invited counsel from Willkie Farr & Gallagher — a law firm that had recently represented a Special Committee of MFW's independent directors in a potential acquisition of a subsidiary of MacAndrews & Forbes — to join the meeting. The independent directors decided to form the Special Committee, and resolved further that:

> [T]he Special Committee is empowered to: (i) make such investigation of the Proposal as the Special Committee deems appropriate; (ii) evaluate the terms of the Proposal; (iii) negotiate with Holdings [*i.e.,* MacAndrews & Forbes] and its representatives any element of the Proposal; (iv) negotiate the terms of any definitive agreement with respect to the Proposal (it being understood that the execution thereof shall be subject to the approval of the Board); (v) report to the Board its recommendations and conclusions with respect to the Proposal, including a determination and *recommendation as to whether the Proposal is fair and in the best interests of the stockholders of the Company other than Holdings* and its affiliates and should be approved by the Board; and (vi) determine to elect not to pursue the Proposal....[4]

> ....

> ... [T]he Board shall not approve the Proposal without a prior favorable recommendation of the Special Committee....

> ... [T]he Special Committee [is] empowered to retain and employ legal counsel, a financial advisor, and such other agents as the Special

---

[4] Emphasis added.

Committee shall deem necessary or desirable in connection with these matters....

The Special Committee consisted of Byorum, Dinh, Meister (the chair), Slovin, and Webb. The following day, Slovin recused himself because, although the MFW [642] board had determined that he qualified as an independent director under the rules of the New York Stock Exchange, he had "some current relationships that could raise questions about his independence for purposes of serving on the Special Committee."

ANALYSIS

What Should Be The Review Standard?

Where a transaction involving self-dealing by a controlling stockholder is challenged, the applicable standard of judicial review is "entire fairness," with the defendants having the burden of persuasion.[5] In other words, the defendants bear the ultimate burden of proving that the transaction with the controlling stockholder was entirely fair to the minority stockholders. In *Kahn v. Lynch Communication Systems, Inc.,*[6] however, this Court held that in "entire fairness" cases, the defendants may shift the burden of persuasion to the plaintiff if either (1) they show that the transaction was approved by a well-functioning committee of independent directors; **or** (2) they show that the transaction was approved by an informed vote of a majority of the minority stockholders.

This appeal presents a question of first impression: what should be the standard of review for a merger between a controlling stockholder and its subsidiary, where the merger is conditioned *ab initio* upon the approval of **both** an independent, adequately-empowered Special Committee that fulfills its duty of care, and the uncoerced, informed vote of a majority of the minority stockholders. The question has never been put directly to this Court.

Almost two decades ago, in *Kahn v. Lynch,* we held that the approval by *either* a Special Committee *or* the majority of the noncontrolling stockholders of a merger with a buying controlling stockholder would shift the burden of proof under the entire fairness standard from the defendant to the plaintiff. *Lynch* did not involve a merger conditioned by the controlling stockholder on both procedural protections. The Appellants submit, nonetheless, that statements in *Lynch* and its progeny could be (and were) read to suggest that even if both procedural protections were used, the standard of review would remain entire fairness. However, in *Lynch* and the other cases that Appellants cited, *Southern*

---

[5] *Kahn v. Tremont Corp.,* 694 A.2d 422, 428 (Del. 1997); *Weinberger v. UOP, Inc.,* 457 A.2d 701, 710 (Del.1983); *see also Rosenblatt v. Getty Oil Co.,* 493 A.2d 929, 937 (Del. 1985).

[6] *Kahn v. Lynch Comc'n Sys., Inc.,* 638 A.2d 1110 (Del. 1994).

Peru and *Kahn v. Tremont,* the controller did not give up its voting power by agreeing to a non-waivable majority-of-the-minority condition. That is the vital distinction between those cases and this one. The question is what the legal consequence of that distinction should be in these circumstances.

The Court of Chancery held that the consequence should be that the business judgment standard of review will govern going private mergers with a controlling stockholder that are conditioned *ab initio* upon (1) the approval of an independent and fully-empowered Special Committee that fulfills its duty of care and (2) the uncoerced, informed vote of the majority of the minority stockholders.

[643] The Court of Chancery rested its holding upon the premise that the common law equitable rule that best protects minority investors is one that encourages controlling stockholders to accord the minority both procedural protections. A transactional structure subject to both conditions differs fundamentally from a merger having only one of those protections, in that:

> By giving controlling stockholders the opportunity to have a going private transaction reviewed under the business judgment rule, a strong incentive is created to give minority stockholders much broader access to the transactional structure that is most likely to effectively protect their interests.... That structure, it is important to note, is critically different than a structure that uses only *one* of the procedural protections. The "or" structure does not replicate the protections of a third-party merger under the DGCL approval process, because it only requires that one, and not both, of the statutory requirements of director and stockholder approval be accomplished by impartial decisionmakers. The "both" structure, by contrast, replicates the arm's-length merger steps of the DGCL by "requir[ing] two independent approvals, which it is fair to say serve independent integrity-enforcing functions."[10]

Before the Court of Chancery, the Appellants acknowledged that "this transactional structure is the optimal one for minority shareholders." Before us, however, they argue that neither procedural protection is adequate to protect minority stockholders, because "possible ineptitude and timidity of directors" may undermine the special committee protection, and because majority-of-the-minority votes may be unduly influenced by arbitrageurs that have an institutional bias to approve virtually any transaction that offers a market premium, however insubstantial it may be. Therefore, the Appellants claim,

---

[10] *In re MFW Shareholders Litigation,* 67 A.3d 496, 528 (Del.Ch.2013) (citing *In re Cox Commc'ns, Inc. S'holders Litig.,* 879 A.2d 604, 618 (Del.Ch.2005)).

these protections, even when combined, are not sufficient to justify "abandon[ing]" the entire fairness standard of review.

With regard to the Special Committee procedural protection, the Appellants' assertions regarding the MFW directors' inability to discharge their duties are not supported either by the record or by well-established principles of Delaware law. As the Court of Chancery correctly observed:

> Although it is possible that there are independent directors who have little regard for their duties or for being perceived by their company's stockholders (and the larger network of institutional investors) as being effective at protecting public stockholders, the court thinks they are likely to be exceptional, and certainly our Supreme Court's jurisprudence does not embrace such a skeptical view.

Regarding the majority-of-the-minority vote procedural protection, as the Court of Chancery noted, "plaintiffs themselves do not argue that minority stockholders will vote against a going private transaction because of fear of retribution." Instead, as the Court of Chancery summarized, the Appellants' argued as follows:

> [Plaintiffs] just believe that most investors like a premium and will tend to vote for a deal that delivers one and that many long-term investors will sell out when they can obtain most of the premium without waiting for the ultimate vote. But that argument is not one that suggests that the voting decision is not voluntary, it is simply an editorial about [644] the motives of investors and does not contradict the premise that a majority-of-the-minority condition gives minority investors a free and voluntary opportunity to decide what is fair for themselves.

Business Judgment Review Standard Adopted

We hold that business judgment is the standard of review that should govern mergers between a controlling stockholder and its corporate subsidiary, where the merger is conditioned *ab initio* upon both the approval of an independent, adequately-empowered Special Committee that fulfills its duty of care; and the uncoerced, informed vote of a majority of the minority stockholders. We so conclude for several reasons.

First, entire fairness is the highest standard of review in corporate law. It is applied in the controller merger context as a substitute for the dual statutory protections of disinterested board and stockholder approval, because both protections are potentially undermined by the influence of the controller. However, as this case establishes, that undermining influence does not exist in every controlled merger setting, regardless of the circumstances. The simultaneous deployment of the procedural protections employed here create a countervailing, offsetting influence of equal — if not greater — force. That is, where the controller irrevocably and publicly disables itself from using its control to dictate the outcome of the negotiations and the shareholder vote, the controlled merger then acquires the shareholder-protective characteristics of third-party, arm's-length mergers, which are reviewed under the business judgment standard.

Second, the dual procedural protection merger structure optimally protects the minority stockholders in controller buyouts. As the Court of Chancery explained:

> [W]hen these two protections are established up-front, a potent tool to extract good value for the minority is established. From inception, the controlling stockholder knows that it cannot bypass the special committee's ability to say no. And, the controlling stockholder knows it cannot dangle a majority-of-the-minority vote before the special committee late in the process as a deal-closer rather than having to make a price move.

Third, and as the Court of Chancery reasoned, applying the business judgment standard to the dual protection merger structure:

> ... is consistent with the central tradition of Delaware law, which defers to the informed decisions of impartial directors, especially when those decisions have been approved by the disinterested stockholders on full information and without coercion. Not only that, the adoption of this rule will be of benefit to minority stockholders because it will provide a strong incentive for controlling stockholders to accord minority investors the transactional structure that respected scholars believe will provide them the best protection, a structure where stockholders get the benefits of independent, empowered negotiating agents to **bargain for the best price and say no** if the agents believe the deal is not advisable for any proper reason, plus the critical ability to determine for themselves whether to accept any deal that their negotiating agents recommend to them. A transactional structure with both these protections is fundamentally different from one with only one protection.[11]

Fourth, the underlying purposes of the dual protection merger structure utilized [645] here and the entire fairness standard of review both converge and are fulfilled at the same critical point: **price**. Following *Weinberger v. UOP, Inc.*, this Court has consistently held that, although entire fairness review comprises the dual components of fair dealing and fair price, in a non-fraudulent transaction "price may be the preponderant consideration

---

[11] Emphasis added.

outweighing other features of the merger."[12] The dual protection merger structure requires two price-related pretrial determinations: first, that a fair price was achieved by an empowered, independent committee that acted with care;[13] and, second, that a fully-informed, uncoerced majority of the minority stockholders voted in favor of the price that was recommended by the independent committee.

The New Standard Summarized

To summarize our holding, in controller buyouts, the business judgment standard of review will be applied *if and only if:* (i) the controller conditions the procession of the transaction on the approval of both a Special Committee and a majority of the minority stockholders; (ii) the Special Committee is independent; (iii) the Special Committee is empowered to freely select its own advisors and to say no definitively; (iv) the Special Committee meets its duty of care in negotiating a fair price; (v) the vote of the minority is informed; and (vi) there is no coercion of the minority.[14]

If a plaintiff that can plead a reasonably conceivable set of facts showing that any or all of those enumerated conditions did not exist, that complaint would state a claim for relief that would entitle the plaintiff to proceed and conduct discovery.[15] If, after discovery, triable issues of fact remain about whether either or both of the dual procedural protections were [646] established, or if established were effective, the case will proceed to a trial in which the court will conduct an entire fairness review.

---

[12] *Weinberger v. UOP, Inc.*, 457 A.2d 701, 711 (Del. 1983).

[13] In *Americas Mining*, for example, it was not possible to make a pretrial determination that the independent committee had negotiated a fair price. After an entire fairness trial, the Court of Chancery held that the price was not fair. *See Ams. Mining. Corp. v. Theriault*, 51 A.3d 1213, 1241-44 (Del.2012).

[14] The Verified Consolidated Class Action Complaint would have survived a motion to dismiss under this new standard. First, the complaint alleged that Perelman's offer "value[d] the company at just four times" MFW's profits per share and "five times 2010 pre-tax cash flow," and that these ratios were "well below" those calculated for recent similar transactions. Second, the complaint alleged that the final Merger price was two dollars per share *lower* than the trading price only about two months earlier. Third, the complaint alleged particularized facts indicating that MWF's share price was depressed at the times of Perelman's offer and the Merger announcement due to short-term factors such as MFW's acquisition of other entities and Standard & Poor's downgrading of the United States' creditworthiness. Fourth, the complaint alleged that commentators viewed both Perelman's initial $24 per share offer and the final $25 per share Merger price as being surprisingly low. These allegations about the sufficiency of the price call into question the adequacy of the Special Committee's negotiations, thereby necessitating discovery on all of the new prerequisites to the application of the business judgment rule.

[15] [...] We have emphasized on several occasions that stockholder "[p]laintiffs may well have the 'tools at hand' to develop the necessary facts for pleading purposes," including the inspection of the corporation's books and records under Del. Code Ann. tit. 8, § 220. There is also a variety of public sources from which the details of corporate act actions may be discovered, including governmental agencies such as the U.S. Securities and Exchange Commission. []

This approach is consistent with *Weinberger, Lynch* and their progeny. A controller that employs and/or establishes only one of these dual procedural protections would continue to receive burden-shifting within the entire fairness standard of review framework. Stated differently, unless *both* procedural protections for the minority stockholders are established *prior to trial*, the ultimate judicial scrutiny of controller buyouts will continue to be the entire fairness standard of review.

Having articulated the circumstances that will enable a controlled merger to be reviewed under the business judgment standard, we next address whether those circumstances have been established as a matter of undisputed fact and law in this case.

Dual Protection Inquiry

To reiterate, in this case, the controlling stockholder conditioned its offer upon the MFW Board agreeing, *ab initio*, to both procedural protections, *i.e.*, approval by a Special Committee and by a majority of the minority stockholders. For the combination of an effective committee process and majority-of-the-minority vote to qualify (jointly) for business judgment review, each of these protections must be effective singly to warrant a burden shift.

We begin by reviewing the record relating to the independence, mandate, and process of the Special Committee. In *Kahn v. Tremont Corp.*, this Court held that "[t]o obtain the benefit of burden shifting, the controlling stockholder must do more than establish a perfunctory special committee of outside directors."

Rather, the special committee must "function in a manner which indicates that the controlling stockholder did not dictate the terms of the transaction and that the committee exercised real bargaining power "at an arms-length.'" As we have previously noted, deciding whether an independent committee was effective in negotiating a price is a process so fact-intensive and inextricably intertwined with the merits of an entire fairness review (fair dealing and fair price) that a pretrial determination of burden shifting is often impossible. Here, however, the Defendants have successfully established a record of independent committee effectiveness and process that warranted a grant of summary judgment entitling them to a burden shift prior to trial.

We next analyze the efficacy of the majority-of-the-minority vote, and we conclude that it was fully informed and not coerced. That is, the Defendants also established a pretrial majority-of-the-minority vote record that constitutes an independent [647] and alternative basis for shifting the burden of persuasion to the Plaintiffs.

The Special Committee Was Independent

The Appellants do not challenge the independence of the Special Committee's Chairman, Meister. They claim, however, that the three other Special Committee members — Webb, Dinh, and Byorum — were beholden to Perelman because of their prior business and/or social dealings with Perelman or Perelman-related entities.

The Appellants first challenge the independence of Webb. They urged that Webb and Perelman shared a "longstanding and lucrative business partnership" between 1983 and 2002 which included acquisitions of thrifts and financial institutions, and which led to a 2002 asset sale to Citibank in which Webb made "a significant amount of money." The Court of Chancery concluded, however, that the fact of Webb having engaged in business dealings with Perelman nine years earlier did not raise a triable fact issue regarding his ability to evaluate the Merger impartially.[21] We agree.

Second, the Appellants argued that there were triable issues of fact regarding Dinh's independence. The Appellants demonstrated that between 2009 and 2011, Dinh's law firm, Bancroft PLLC, advised M & F and Scientific Games (in which M & F owned a 37.6% stake), during which time the Bancroft firm earned $200,000 in fees. The record reflects that Bancroft's limited prior engagements, which were inactive by the time the Merger proposal was announced, were fully disclosed to the Special Committee soon after it was formed. The Court of Chancery found that the Appellants failed to proffer any evidence to show that compensation received by Dinh's law firm was material to Dinh, in the sense that it would have influenced his decisionmaking with respect to the M & F proposal.[22] The only evidence of record, the Court of Chancery concluded, was that these fees were *"de minimis"* and that the Appellants had offered no contrary evidence that would create a genuine issue of material fact.[23]

The Court of Chancery also found that the relationship between Dinh, a Georgetown University Law Center professor, and M & F's Barry Schwartz, who sits on the Georgetown Board of Visitors, did not create a triable issue of fact as to Dinh's independence. No record evidence suggested that Schwartz could exert influence on

---

[21] *Beam ex rel. Martha Stewart Living Omnimedia, Inc. v. Stewart*, 845 A.2d 1040, 1051 (Del.2004) ("Allegations that [the controller] and the other directors ... developed business relationships before joining the board... are insufficient, without more, to rebut the presumption of independence.").

[22] *See In re Gaylord Container Corp. S'holder Litig.*, 753 A.2d 462, 465 n. 3 (Del.Ch.2000) (no issue of fact concerning director's independence where director's law firm "has, over the years, done some work" for the company because plaintiffs did not provide evidence showing that the director "had a material financial interest" in the representation).

[23] *See* Ct. Ch. R. 56(e) ("An adverse party may not rest upon the mere allegations or denials in the adverse party's pleading, but the adverse party's response, by affidavits or otherwise provided in this rule, must set forth specific facts showing that there is a genuine issue for trial.").

Dinh's position at Georgetown based on his recommendation regarding the Merger. Indeed, Dinh had earned tenure as a professor at Georgetown before he ever knew Schwartz.

The Appellants also argue that Schwartz's later invitation to Dinh to join [648] the board of directors of Revlon, Inc. "illustrates the ongoing personal relationship between Schwartz and Dinh." There is no record evidence that Dinh expected to be asked to join Revlon's board at the time he served on the Special Committee. Moreover, the Court of Chancery noted, Schwartz's invitation for Dinh to join the Revlon board of directors occurred months after the Merger was approved and did not raise a triable fact issue concerning Dinh's independence from Perelman. We uphold the Court of Chancery's findings relating to Dinh.

Third, the Appellants urge that issues of material fact permeate Byorum's independence and, specifically, that Byorum "had a business relationship with Perelman from 1991 to 1996 through her executive position at Citibank." The Court of Chancery concluded, however, the Appellants presented no evidence of the nature of Byorum's interactions with Perelman while she was at Citibank. Nor was there evidence that after 1996 Byorum had an ongoing economic relationship with Perelman that was material to her in any way. Byorum testified that any interactions she had with Perelman while she was at Citibank resulted from her role as a senior executive, because Perelman was a client of the bank at the time. Byorum also testified that she had no business relationship with Perelman between 1996 and 2007, when she joined the MFW Board.

The Appellants also contend that Byorum performed advisory work for Scientific Games in 2007 and 2008 as a senior managing director of Stephens Cori Capital Advisors ("Stephens Cori"). The Court of Chancery found, however, that the Appellants had adduced no evidence tending to establish that the $100,000 fee Stephens Cori received for that work was material to either Stephens Cori or to Byorum personally.[24] Stephens Cori's engagement for Scientific Games, which occurred years before the Merger was announced and the Special Committee was convened, was fully disclosed to the Special Committee, which concluded that "it was not material, and it would not represent a conflict."[25] We uphold the Court of Chancery's findings relating to Byorum as well.

---

[24] The Court of Chancery observed that Stephens Cori's fee from the Scientific Games engagement was "only one tenth of the $1 million that Stephens Cori would have had to have received for Byorum not to be considered independent under NYSE rules."

[25] Although the Appellants note that Stephens Cori did some follow-up work for Scientific Games in 2011, it is undisputed that work was also fully disclosed to the Special Committee, and that Stephens Cori did not receive any additional compensation as a result.

To evaluate the parties' competing positions on the issue of director independence, the Court of Chancery applied well-established Delaware legal principles.[26] To show that a director is not independent, a plaintiff must demonstrate that the director is "beholden" to the controlling party [649] "or so under [the controller's] influence that [the director's] discretion would be sterilized."[27] Bare allegations that directors are friendly with, travel in the same social circles as, or have past business relationships with the proponent of a transaction or the person they are investigating are not enough to rebut the presumption of independence.

A plaintiff seeking to show that a director was not independent must satisfy a materiality standard. The court must conclude that the director in question had ties to the person whose proposal or actions he or she is evaluating that are sufficiently substantial that he or she could not objectively discharge his or her fiduciary duties. Consistent with that predicate materiality requirement, the existence of some financial ties between the interested party and the director, without more, is not disqualifying. The inquiry must be whether, applying a subjective standard, those ties were *material*, in the sense that the alleged ties could have affected the impartiality of the individual director.

The Appellants assert that the materiality of any economic relationships the Special Committee members may have had with Mr. Perelman "should not be decided on summary judgment." But Delaware courts have often decided director independence as a matter of law at the summary judgment stage. In this case, the Court of Chancery noted, that despite receiving extensive discovery, the Appellants did "nothing ... to compare the actual circumstances of the [challenged directors] to the ties [they] contend affect their impartiality" and "fail[ed] to proffer any real evidence of their economic circumstances."

The Appellants could have, but elected not to, submit any Rule 56 affidavits, either factual or expert, in response to the Defendants' summary judgment motion. The Appellants argue that they were entitled to wait until trial to proffer evidence compromising the Special Committee's independence. That argument misapprehends how Rule 56 operates. Court of Chancery Rule 56 states that "the adverse [non-moving] party's response, by affidavits or as otherwise provided in this rule, [650] must set forth specific facts showing that there is a genuine issue for trial."

The Court of Chancery found that to the extent the Appellants claimed the Special Committee members, Webb, Dinh, and Byorum, were beholden to Perelman based on

---

[26] [...] The Court of Chancery explicitly acknowledged that directors' compliance with NYSE independence standards "[...]"

[27] *Rales v. Blasband*, 634 A.2d 927, 936 (Del. 1993) (citing *Aronson v. Lewis*, 473 A.2d 805, 815 (Del.1984)).

prior economic relationships with him, the Appellants never developed or proffered evidence showing the materiality of those relationships:

> Despite receiving the chance for extensive discovery, the plaintiffs have done nothing ... to compare the actual economic circumstances of the directors they challenge to the ties the plaintiffs contend affect their impartiality. In other words, the plaintiffs have ignored a key teaching of our Supreme Court, requiring a showing that a specific director's independence is compromised by factors material to her. As to each of the specific directors the plaintiffs challenge, the plaintiffs fail to proffer any real evidence of their economic circumstances.

The record supports the Court of Chancery's holding that none of the Appellants' claims relating to Webb, Dinh or Byorum raised a triable issue of material fact concerning their individual independence or the Special Committee's collective independence.[34]

The Special Committee Was Empowered

It is undisputed that the Special Committee was empowered to hire its own legal and financial advisors, and it retained Willkie Farr & Gallagher LLP as its legal advisor. After interviewing four potential financial advisors, the Special Committee engaged Evercore Partners ("Evercore"). The qualifications and independence of Evercore and Willkie Farr & Gallagher LLP are not contested.

Among the powers given the Special Committee in the board resolution was the authority to "report to the Board its recommendations and conclusions with respect to the [Merger], including a determination and recommendation as to whether the Proposal is fair and in the best interests of the stockholders...." The Court of Chancery also found that it was "undisputed that the [S]pecial [C]ommittee was empowered not simply to "evaluate' the offer, like some special committees with weak mandates, but to negotiate with [M & F] over the terms of its offer to buy out the noncontrolling stockholders. This negotiating power was accompanied by the clear authority to say no definitively to [M & F]" and to "make that decision stick." MacAndrews & Forbes promised that it would not proceed with any going private proposal that did not have the support of the Special Committee. Therefore, the Court of Chancery concluded, "the MFW committee did not have to fear that if it bargained too hard, MacAndrews & Forbes could bypass the committee and make a tender offer directly to the minority stockholders."

---

[34] *See In re W. Nat'l Corp. S'holders Litig.*, 2000 WL 710192, at *6 (Del.Ch. May 22, 2000) (to survive summary judgment, nonmoving party "must affirmatively state facts — not guesses, innuendo, or unreasonable inferences....").

[651] The Court of Chancery acknowledged that even though the Special Committee had the authority to negotiate and "say no," it did not have the authority, as a practical matter, to sell MFW to other buyers. MacAndrews & Forbes stated in its announcement that it was not interested in selling its 43% stake. Moreover, under Delaware law, MacAndrews & Forbes had no duty to sell its block, which was large enough, again as a practical matter, to preclude any other buyer from succeeding unless MacAndrews & Forbes decided to become a seller. Absent such a decision, it was unlikely that any potentially interested party would incur the costs and risks of exploring a purchase of MFW.

Nevertheless, the Court of Chancery found, "this did not mean that the MFW Special Committee did not have the leeway to get advice from its financial advisor about the strategic options available to MFW, including the potential interest that other buyers might have *if MacAndrews & Forbes was willing to sell*."[36] The undisputed record shows that the Special Committee, with the help of its financial advisor, did consider whether there were other buyers who might be interested in purchasing MFW, and whether there were other strategic options, such as asset divestitures, that might generate more value for minority stockholders than a sale of their stock to MacAndrews & Forbes.

The Special Committee Exercised Due Care

The Special Committee insisted from the outset that MacAndrews (including any "dual" employees who worked for both MFW and MacAndrews) be screened off from the Special Committee's process, to ensure that the process replicated arm's-length negotiations with a third party. In order to carefully evaluate M & F's offer, the Special Committee held a total of eight meetings during the summer of 2011.

From the outset of their work, the Special Committee and Evercore had projections that had been prepared by MFW's business segments in April and May 2011. Early in the process, Evercore and the Special Committee asked MFW management to produce new projections that reflected management's most up-to-date, and presumably most accurate, thinking. Consistent with the Special Committee's determination to conduct its analysis free of any MacAndrews influence, MacAndrews — including "dual" MFW/MacAndrews executives who normally vetted MFW projections — were excluded from the process of preparing the updated financial projections. Mafco, the licorice business, advised Evercore that all of its projections would remain the same. Harland Clarke updated its projections. On July 22, 2011, Evercore received new projections from HCHC, which incorporated the updated projections from Harland Clarke. Evercore then constructed a valuation model based upon all of these updated projections.

---

[36] Emphasis added.

The updated projections, which formed the basis for Evercore's valuation analyses, reflected MFW's deteriorating results, especially in Harland's check-printing business. Those projections forecast EBITDA for MFW of $491 million in 2015, as opposed to $535 million under the original projections.

On August 10, Evercore produced a range of valuations for MFW, based on the updated projections, of $15 to $45 per share. Evercore valued MFW using a variety of accepted methods, including a discounted cash flow ("DCF") model. Those valuations generated a range of fair value of $22 to $38 per share, and a premiums [652] paid analysis resulted in a value range of $22 to $45. MacAndrews & Forbes's $24 offer fell within the range of values produced by each of Evercore's valuation techniques.

Although the $24 Proposal fell within the range of Evercore's fair values, the Special Committee directed Evercore to conduct additional analyses and explore strategic alternatives that might generate more value for MFW's stockholders than might a sale to MacAndrews. The Special Committee also investigated the possibility of other buyers, e.g., private equity buyers, that might be interested in purchasing MFW. In addition, the Special Committee considered whether other strategic options, such as asset divestitures, could achieve superior value for MFW's stockholders. Mr. Meister testified, "The Committee made it very clear to Evercore that we were interested in any and all possible avenues of increasing value to the stockholders, including meaningful expressions of interest for meaningful pieces of the business."

The Appellants insist that the Special Committee had "no right to solicit alternative bids, conduct any sort of market check, or even consider alternative transactions." But the Special Committee did just that, even though MacAndrews' stated unwillingness to sell its MFW stake meant that the Special Committee did not have the practical ability to market MFW to other buyers. The Court of Chancery properly concluded that despite the Special Committee's inability to solicit alternative bids, it *could* seek Evercore's advice about strategic alternatives, including *values that might be available if MacAndrews was willing to sell.*

Although the MFW Special Committee considered options besides the M & F Proposal, the Committee's analysis of those alternatives proved they were unlikely to achieve added value for MFW's stockholders. The Court of Chancery summarized the performance of the Special Committee as follows:

> [t]he special committee did consider, with the help of its financial advisor, whether there were other buyers who might be interested in purchasing MFW, and whether there were other strategic options, such as asset divestitures, that might generate more value for minority stockholders than a sale of their stock to MacAndrews & Forbes.

On August 18, 2011, the Special Committee rejected the $24 a share Proposal, and countered at $30 per share. The Special Committee characterized the $30 counteroffer as a negotiating position. The Special Committee recognized that $30 per share was a very aggressive counteroffer and, not surprisingly, was prepared to accept less.

On September 9, 2011, MacAndrews & Forbes rejected the $30 per share counteroffer. Its representative, Barry Schwartz, told the Special Committee Chair, Paul Meister, that the $24 per share Proposal was now far less favorable to MacAndrews & Forbes — but more attractive to the minority — than when it was first made, because of continued declines in MFW's businesses. Nonetheless, MacAndrews & Forbes would stand behind its $24 offer. Meister responded that he would not recommend the $24 per share Proposal to the Special Committee. Later, after having discussions with Perelman, Schwartz conveyed MacAndrews's "best and final" offer of $25 a share.

At a Special Committee meeting the next day, Evercore opined that the $25 per share *price was fair* based on generally accepted valuation methodologies, including DCF and comparable companies analyses. At its eighth and final meeting on [653] September 10, 2011, the Special Committee, although empowered to say "no," instead unanimously approved and agreed to recommend the Merger at a price of $25 per share.

Influencing the Special Committee's assessment and acceptance of M & F's $25 a share price were developments in both MFW's business and the broader United States economy during the summer of 2011. For example, during the negotiation process, the Special Committee learned of the underperformance of MFW's Global Scholar business unit. The Committee also considered macroeconomic events, including the downgrade of the United States' bond credit rating, and the ongoing turmoil in the financial markets, all of which created financing uncertainties.

In scrutinizing the Special Committee's execution of its broad mandate, the Court of Chancery determined there was no "evidence indicating that the independent members of the special committee did not meet their duty of care...." To the contrary, the Court of Chancery found, the Special Committee "met frequently and was presented with a rich body of financial information relevant to whether and at what *price* a going private transaction was advisable." The Court of Chancery ruled that "the plaintiffs d[id] not make any attempt to show that the MFW Special Committee failed to meet its duty of care...." Based on the undisputed record, the Court of Chancery held that, "there is no triable issue of fact regarding whether the [S]pecial [C]ommittee fulfilled its duty of care." In the context of a controlling stockholder merger, a pretrial determination that the *price* was negotiated by an empowered independent committee that acted with care would shift the burden of persuasion to the plaintiffs under the entire fairness standard of review.[37]

Majority of Minority Stockholder Vote

We now consider the second procedural protection invoked by M & F — the majority-of-the-minority stockholder vote.[38] Consistent with the second condition imposed by M & F at the outset, the Merger was then put before MFW's stockholders for a vote. On November 18, 2011, the stockholders were provided with a proxy statement, which contained the history of the Special Committee's work and recommended that they vote in favor of the transaction at a price of $25 per share.

The proxy statement disclosed, among other things, that the Special Committee had countered M & F's initial $24 per share offer at $30 per share, but only was able to achieve a final offer of $25 per share. The proxy statement disclosed that the MFW business divisions had discussed with Evercore whether the initial projections Evercore received reflected management's latest thinking. It also disclosed that the updated projections were lower. The proxy statement also included the five separate price ranges for the value of MFW's stock that Evercore had generated with its different valuation analyses.

Knowing the proxy statement's disclosures of the background of the Special Committee's work, of Evercore's valuation ranges, and of the analyses supporting [654] Evercore's *fairness opinion*, MFW's stockholders — representing more than 65% of the minority shares — approved the Merger. In the controlling stockholder merger context, it is settled Delaware law that an uncoerced, informed majority-of-the-minority vote, without any other procedural protection, is itself sufficient to shift the burden of persuasion to the plaintiff under the entire fairness standard of review.[39] The Court of Chancery found that "the plaintiffs themselves do not dispute that the majority-of-the-minority vote was fully informed and uncoerced, because they fail to allege any failure of disclosure or any act of coercion."

---

[37] *Kahn v. Lynch Commc'n Sys. (Lynch I)*, 638 A.2d 1110, 1117 (Del.1994).

[38] The MFW board discussed the Special Committee's recommendation to accept the $25 a share offer. The three directors affiliated with MacAndrews & Forbes, Perelman, Schwartz, and Bevins, and the CEOs of HCHC and Mafco, Dawson and Taub, recused themselves from the discussions. The remaining eight directors voted unanimously to recommend the $25 a share offer to the stockholders.

[39] *Rosenblatt v. Getty Oil Co.*, 493 A.2d 929, 937 (Del.1985).

Both Procedural Protections Established

Based on a highly extensive record,[40] the Court of Chancery concluded that the procedural protections upon which the Merger was conditioned — approval by an independent and empowered Special Committee and by a uncoerced informed majority of MFW's minority stockholders — had *both* been undisputedly established *prior to trial*. We agree and conclude the Defendants' motion for summary judgment was properly granted on all of those issues.

Business Judgment Review Properly Applied

We have determined that the business judgment rule standard of review applies to this controlling stockholder buyout. Under that standard, the claims against the Defendants must be dismissed unless no rational person could have believed that the merger was favorable to MFW's minority stockholders.[41] In this case, it cannot be credibly argued (let alone concluded) that no rational person would find the Merger favorable to MFW's minority stockholders.

Conclusion

For the above-stated reasons, the judgment of the Court of Chancery is affirmed.

---

[40] The Appellants received more than 100,000 pages of documents, and deposed all four Special Committee members, their financial advisors, and senior executives of MacAndrews and MFW. After eighteen months of discovery, the Court of Chancery found that the Appellants offered no evidence to create a triable issue of fact with regard to: (1) the Special Committee's independence; (2) the Special Committee's power to retain independent advisors and to say no definitively; (3) the Special Committee's due care in approving the Merger; (4) whether the majority-of-the-minority vote was fully informed; and (5) whether the minority vote was uncoerced.

[41] *E.g., In re Walt Disney Co. Deriv. Litig.,* 906 A.2d 27, 74 (Del.2006) ("[W]here business judgment presumptions are applicable, the board's decision will be upheld unless it cannot be "attributed to any rational business purpose.'" (quoting *Sinclair Oil Corp. v. Levien,* 280 A.2d 717, 720 (Del.1971))).

7.2 Sales of Control

When the controlling shareholder is not buying but selling, a different problem arises: The controlling shareholder may sell control to a buyer who makes the minority shareholders worse off.[6] Concretely, upon assuming control, the buyer might divert more value from the corporation than the seller did, be it through self-dealing transactions or by failing to develop the corporation's business (e.g., imagine the buyer is a competitor of the acquired corporation or of one of its major clients). Technically, such diversion would violate the buyer's duty of loyalty, but enforcement is always imperfect. In particular, the controlling shareholder may find a majority of nominally independent but servile directors to approve self-dealing transactions other than mergers.

Questions

1.   Why will this be enough to isolate the transactions from judicial review?

Such diversion might even be the business rationale for the sale: the buyer might be able to pay more than the controlling shareholder's valuation of the control block precisely because the buyer plans to divert more value. To guard against this possibility, many jurisdictions around the world, such as the UK, require the buyer of a control block to offer to buy out all minority shareholders at the same price. The U.S., however, does not have such a mandatory bid rule – control blocks in U.S. corporations can be bought and sold freely without having to deal with the minority stockholders at all, short of selling to a "known looter."[7]

One reason not to have a mandatory bid rule is that it creates problems of its own when the buyer is benign, i.e., when the buyer does not divert value, or at least not more than the seller. If the buyer has to offer the same price to everyone, it has to pay

---

[6] By definition, the controlling shareholder owns and can thus sell enough shares to convey full control to a buyer. Absent special rules, the controlling shareholder can therefore transfer control without the minority's consent.

[7] See *Harris v. Carter*, 582 A.2d 222, 235 (Del. Ch. 1990, per Allen Ch.): "while a person who transfers corporate control to another is surely not a surety for his buyer, when the circumstances would alert a reasonably prudent person to a risk that his buyer is dishonest or in some material respect not truthful, a duty devolves upon the seller to make such inquiry as a reasonably prudent person would make, and generally to exercise care so that others who will be affected by his actions should not be injured by wrongful conduct."

everyone as much as it pays the selling controlling shareholder. But the controlling shareholder owns more than the minority shareholder: it has control, which it may value either because it allows diversion of pecuniary benefits, and/or simply because it (or now we should say: he or she) enjoys being in charge. And the controlling shareholder will refuse to sell unless it/he/she is fully compensated for giving up control. So paying the same to the controlling shareholder and to the minority on a per share basis probably means overpaying the minority – and possibly means overpaying for the firm as a whole. Since buyers cannot be expected to overpay, the deal may simply fall through. As a result, insisting on equal treatment may end up hurting everyone, including the minority shareholders.

To illustrate, consider the following numerical example. Imagine a firm with 100 shares outstanding that is worth $125 in total under the current governance arrangements. It has a controlling shareholder who holds 10 shares (= 10% of the equity) but enough votes for control (e.g., through a dual class arrangement). The controlling shareholder diverts 20% of the firm's value ($25) to herself in private benefits.[8] In addition, the controlling shareholder gets 10% of the remaining value by virtue of her equity stake. Her total stake is thus worth $25 + 10% × ($125-$25) = $35 to her. Minority shareholders get the rest: $125 – $35 = $90, or $1 per share (there are 100 shares total, and the controlling shareholder owns 10 of them). Now imagine a sale under a mandatory bid rule. The controlling shareholder will accept an offer only if the per share price P gives her more for her 10 shares than what she gets without the deal: $10 \times P > \$35$, or $P > \$3.50$. At $P > \$3.50$, the minority shareholders will obviously accept the offer, since the status quo value of their shares is only $1. Consequently, all 100 shares will be tendered, and the acquirer will have to pay $100 \times P > 100 \times \$3.50 = \$350$ for the firm. This will only be worthwhile for the acquirer if the firm is worth more than $350 to the acquirer, i.e., more than 2.8 times the status quo value. Such buyers will be rare. By contrast, without the mandatory bid rule, any buyer to whom the firm is worth more than $125 could make an offer that makes *everyone* better off: for example, a buyer valuing the firm at $125.03 could pay $35.01 to the controller (= $3.501 per controller share), $90.01/90 for each minority share (= $1.0001 per minority share), and still make a $0.01 profit. In short, even the minority shareholders might be better off if the controlling shareholder is allowed to get a control premium.

---

[8] This could be $25 in cash through a transfer pricing scheme etc., or simply a psychic benefit of being in control that the controlling shareholder values at $25—that, too, is value. In the latter case, you should think of the firm as generating $100 in financial value plus $25 in psychic value.

Chapter 8. Takeover Defenses

A. Unocal v. Mesa Petroleum (Del. 1985)

In this famous decision, the Delaware Supreme Court ruled that the board has the power to defend against hostile takeovers, even with discriminatory measures, and laid down the judicial standard of review for scrutinizing such defenses.

The most important things to look for are therefore the following questions, which you should think about as you read the case.

Questions

1. What is the threat that the board is defending against?

2. Who is being protected?

3. What is the standard of review? How does it relate to our two old friends: the business judgment rule and entire fairness? If it is different, why?

493 A.2d 946 (1985)

UNOCAL CORPORATION, a Delaware corporation, Defendant Below, Appellant,

v.

MESA PETROLEUM CO., a Delaware corporation, Mesa Asset Co., a Delaware corporation, Mesa Eastern, Inc., a Delaware corporation and Mesa Partners II, a Texas partnership, Plaintiffs Below, Appellees.

Supreme Court of Delaware.

Submitted: May 16, 1985.

Oral Decision: May 17, 1985.

Written Decision: June 10, 1985.

A. Gilchrist Sparks, III (argued), and Kenneth J. Nachbar of Morris, Nichols, Arsht & Tunnell, Wilmington, James R. Martin and Mitchell A. Karlan of Gibson, Dunn & Crutcher and Paul, Hastings, Janofsky & Walker, Los Angeles, Cal., of counsel, for appellant.

Charles F. Richards, Jr. (argued), Samuel A. Nolen, and Gregory P. Williams of Richards, Layton & Finger, Wilmington, for appellees.

Before McNEILLY and MOORE, JJ., and TAYLOR, Judge (Sitting by designation pursuant to Del. Const., Art. 4, § 12.) [949]

MOORE, Justice.

We confront an issue of first impression in Delaware — the validity of a corporation's self-tender for its own shares which excludes from participation a stockholder making a hostile tender offer for the company's stock.

The Court of Chancery granted a preliminary injunction to the plaintiffs, Mesa Petroleum Co., Mesa Asset Co., Mesa Partners II, and Mesa Eastern, Inc. (collectively "Mesa")[1], enjoining an exchange offer of the defendant, Unocal Corporation (Unocal) for its own stock. The trial court concluded that a selective exchange offer, excluding Mesa, was legally impermissible. We cannot agree with such a blanket rule. The factual findings of the Vice Chancellor, fully supported by the record, establish that Unocal's board, consisting of a majority of independent directors, acted in good faith, and after reasonable investigation found that Mesa's tender offer was both inadequate and coercive. Under the circumstances the board had both the power and duty to oppose a bid it perceived to be harmful to the corporate enterprise. On this record we are satisfied that the device Unocal adopted is reasonable in relation to the threat posed, and that the board acted in the proper exercise of sound business judgment. We will not substitute our views for those of the board if the latter's decision can be "attributed to any rational business purpose." *Sinclair Oil Corp. v. Levien*, Del.Supr., 280 A.2d 717, 720 (1971). Accordingly, we reverse the decision of the Court of Chancery and order the preliminary injunction vacated.[2]

I.

The factual background of this matter bears a significant relationship to its ultimate outcome.

On April 8, 1985, Mesa, the owner of approximately 13% of Unocal's stock, commenced a two-tier "front loaded" cash tender offer for 64 million shares, or approximately 37%, of Unocal's outstanding stock at a price of $54 per share. The "back-end" was designed to eliminate the remaining publicly held shares by an exchange of securities purportedly

---

[1] T. Boone Pickens, Jr., is President and Chairman of the Board of Mesa Petroleum and President of Mesa Asset and controls the related Mesa entities.

[2] This appeal was heard on an expedited basis in light of the pending Mesa tender offer and Unocal exchange offer. We announced our decision to reverse in an oral ruling in open court on May 17, 1985 with the further statement that this opinion would follow shortly thereafter. *See infra* n. 5.

worth $54 per share. However, pursuant to an order entered by the United States District Court for the Central District of California on April 26, 1985, Mesa issued a supplemental proxy statement to Unocal's stockholders disclosing that the securities offered in the second-step merger would be highly subordinated, and that Unocal's capitalization would differ significantly from its present [950] structure. Unocal has rather aptly termed such securities "junk bonds".[3]

Unocal's board consists of eight independent outside directors and six insiders. It met on April 13, 1985, to consider the Mesa tender offer. Thirteen directors were present, and the meeting lasted nine and one-half hours. The directors were given no agenda or written materials prior to the session. However, detailed presentations were made by legal counsel regarding the board's obligations under both Delaware corporate law and the federal securities laws. The board then received a presentation from Peter Sachs on behalf of Goldman Sachs & Co. (Goldman Sachs) and Dillon, Read & Co. (Dillon Read) discussing the bases for their opinions that the Mesa proposal was wholly inadequate. Mr. Sachs opined that the minimum cash value that could be expected from a sale or orderly liquidation for 100% of Unocal's stock was in excess of $60 per share. In making his presentation, Mr. Sachs showed slides outlining the valuation techniques used by the financial advisors, and others, depicting recent business combinations in the oil and gas industry. The Court of Chancery found that the Sachs presentation was designed to apprise the directors of the scope of the analyses performed rather than the facts and numbers used in reaching the conclusion that Mesa's tender offer price was inadequate.

---

[3] Mesa's May 3, 1985 supplement to its proxy statement states:

> (i) following the Offer, the Purchasers would seek to effect a merger of Unocal and Mesa Eastern or an affiliate of Mesa Eastern (the "Merger") in which the remaining Shares would be acquired for a combination of subordinated debt securities and preferred stock; (ii) the securities to be received by Unocal shareholders in the Merger would be subordinated to $2,400 million of debt securities of Mesa Eastern, indebtedness incurred to refinance up to $1,000 million of bank debt which was incurred by affiliates of Mesa Partners II to purchase Shares and to pay related interest and expenses and all then-existing debt of Unocal; (iii) the corporation surviving the Merger would be responsible for the payment of all securities of Mesa Eastern (including any such securities issued pursuant to the Merger) and the indebtedness referred to in item (ii) above, and such securities and indebtedness would be repaid out of funds generated by the operations of Unocal; (iv) the indebtedness incurred in the Offer and the Merger would result in Unocal being much more highly leveraged, and the capitalization of the corporation surviving the Merger would differ significantly from that of Unocal at present; and (v) in their analyses of cash flows provided by operations of Unocal which would be available to service and repay securities and other obligations of the corporation surviving the Merger, the Purchasers assumed that the capital expenditures and expenditures for exploration of such corporation would be significantly reduced.

Mr. Sachs also presented various defensive strategies available to the board if it concluded that Mesa's two-step tender offer was inadequate and should be opposed. One of the devices outlined was a self-tender by Unocal for its own stock with a reasonable price range of $70 to $75 per share. The cost of such a proposal would cause the company to incur $6.1-6.5 billion of additional debt, and a presentation was made informing the board of Unocal's ability to handle it. The directors were told that the primary effect of this obligation would be to reduce exploratory drilling, but that the company would nonetheless remain a viable entity.

The eight outside directors, comprising a clear majority of the thirteen members present, then met separately with Unocal's financial advisors and attorneys. Thereafter, they unanimously agreed to advise the board that it should reject Mesa's tender offer as inadequate, and that Unocal should pursue a self-tender to provide the stockholders with a fairly priced alternative to the Mesa proposal. The board then reconvened and unanimously adopted a resolution rejecting as grossly inadequate Mesa's tender offer. Despite the nine and one-half hour length of the meeting, no formal decision was made on the proposed defensive self-tender.

On April 15, the board met again with four of the directors present by telephone [951] and one member still absent.[4] This session lasted two hours. Unocal's Vice President of Finance and its Assistant General Counsel made a detailed presentation of the proposed terms of the exchange offer. A price range between $70 and $80 per share was considered, and ultimately the directors agreed upon $72. The board was also advised about the debt securities that would be issued, and the necessity of placing restrictive covenants upon certain corporate activities until the obligations were paid. The board's decisions were made in reliance on the advice of its investment bankers, including the terms and conditions upon which the securities were to be issued. Based upon this advice, and the board's own deliberations, the directors unanimously approved the exchange offer. Their resolution provided that if Mesa acquired 64 million shares of Unocal stock through its own offer (the Mesa Purchase Condition), Unocal would buy the remaining 49% outstanding for an exchange of debt securities having an aggregate par value of $72

---

[4] Under Delaware law directors may participate in a board meeting by telephone. Thus, 8 *Del.C.*§ 141(i) provides:

> Unless otherwise restricted by the certificate of incorporation or by-laws, members of the board of directors of any corporation, or any committee designated by the board, may participate in a meeting of such board or committee by means of conference telephone or similar communications equipment by means of which all persons participating in the meeting can hear each other, and participation in a meeting pursuant to this subsection shall constitute presence in person at such meeting.

per share. The board resolution also stated that the offer would be subject to other conditions that had been described to the board at the meeting, or which were deemed necessary by Unocal's officers, including the exclusion of Mesa from the proposal (the Mesa exclusion). Any such conditions were required to be in accordance with the "purport and intent" of the offer.

Unocal's exchange offer was commenced on April 17, 1985, and Mesa promptly challenged it by filing this suit in the Court of Chancery. On April 22, the Unocal board met again and was advised by Goldman Sachs and Dillon Read to waive the Mesa Purchase Condition as to 50 million shares. This recommendation was in response to a perceived concern of the shareholders that, if shares were tendered to Unocal, no shares would be purchased by either offeror. The directors were also advised that they should tender their own Unocal stock into the exchange offer as a mark of their confidence in it.

Another focus of the board was the Mesa exclusion. Legal counsel advised that under Delaware law Mesa could only be excluded for what the directors reasonably believed to be a valid corporate purpose. The directors' discussion centered on the objective of adequately compensating shareholders at the "back-end" of Mesa's proposal, which the latter would finance with "junk bonds". To include Mesa would defeat that goal, because under the proration aspect of the exchange offer (49%) every Mesa share accepted by Unocal would displace one held by another stockholder. Further, if Mesa were permitted to tender to Unocal, the latter would in effect be financing Mesa's own inadequate proposal.

On April 24, 1985 Unocal issued a supplement to the exchange offer describing the partial waiver of the Mesa Purchase Condition. On May 1, 1985, in another supplement, Unocal extended the withdrawal, proration and expiration dates of its exchange offer to May 17, 1985.

Meanwhile, on April 22, 1985, Mesa amended its complaint in this action to challenge the Mesa exclusion. A preliminary injunction hearing was scheduled for May 8, 1985. However, on April 23, 1985, Mesa moved for a temporary restraining order in response to Unocal's announcement that it was partially waiving the Mesa Purchase Condition. After expedited briefing, the Court of Chancery heard Mesa's motion on April 26.

[952] On April 29, 1985, the Vice Chancellor temporarily restrained Unocal from proceeding with the exchange offer unless it included Mesa. The trial court recognized that directors could oppose, and attempt to defeat, a hostile takeover which they considered adverse to the best interests of the corporation. However, the Vice Chancellor decided that in a selective purchase of the company's stock, the corporation bears the

burden of showing: (1) a valid corporate purpose, and (2) that the transaction was fair to all of the stockholders, including those excluded.

Unocal immediately sought certification of an interlocutory appeal to this Court pursuant to Supreme Court Rule 42(b). On May 1, 1985, the Vice Chancellor declined to certify the appeal on the grounds that the decision granting a temporary restraining order did not decide a legal issue of first impression, and was not a matter to which the decisions of the Court of Chancery were in conflict.

However, in an Order dated May 2, 1985, this Court ruled that the Chancery decision was clearly determinative of substantive rights of the parties, and in fact decided the main question of law before the Vice Chancellor, which was indeed a question of first impression. We therefore concluded that the temporary restraining order was an appealable decision. However, because the Court of Chancery was scheduled to hold a preliminary injunction hearing on May 8 at which there would be an enlarged record on the various issues, action on the interlocutory appeal was deferred pending an outcome of those proceedings.

In deferring action on the interlocutory appeal, we noted that on the record before us we could not determine whether the parties had articulated certain issues which the Vice Chancellor should have an opportunity to consider in the first instance. These included the following:

> a) Does the directors' duty of care to the corporation extend to protecting the corporate enterprise in good faith from perceived depredations of others, including persons who may own stock in the company?

> b) Have one or more of the plaintiffs, their affiliates, or persons acting in concert with them, either in dealing with Unocal or others, demonstrated a pattern of conduct sufficient to justify a reasonable inference by defendants that a principle objective of the plaintiffs is to achieve selective treatment for themselves by the repurchase of their Unocal shares at a substantial premium?

> c) If so, may the directors of Unocal in the proper exercise of business judgment employ the exchange offer to protect the corporation and its shareholders from such tactics? *See Pogostin v. Rice*, Del. Supr., 480 A.2d 619 (1984).

> d) If it is determined that the purpose of the exchange offer was not illegal as a matter of law, have the directors of Unocal carried their burden of showing that they acted in good faith? *See Martin v.*

American Potash & Chemical Corp., 33 Del.Ch. 234, 92 A.2d 295 at 302.

After the May 8 hearing the Vice Chancellor issued an unreported opinion on May 13, 1985 granting Mesa a preliminary injunction. Specifically, the trial court noted that "[t]he parties basically agree that the directors' duty of care extends to protecting the corporation from perceived harm whether it be from third parties or shareholders." The trial court also concluded in response to the second inquiry in the Supreme Court's May 2 order, that "[a]lthough the facts, ... do not appear to be sufficient to prove that Mesa's principle objective is to be bought off at a substantial premium, they do justify a reasonable inference to the same effect."

As to the third and fourth questions posed by this Court, the Vice Chancellor stated that they "appear to raise the more fundamental issue of whether directors owe fiduciary duties to shareholders who they perceive to be acting contrary to the best interests of the corporation as a whole." While determining that the directors' decision to oppose Mesa's tender [953] offer was made in a good faith belief that the Mesa proposal was inadequate, the court stated that the business judgment rule does not apply to a selective exchange offer such as this.

On May 13, 1985 the Court of Chancery certified this interlocutory appeal to us as a question of first impression, and we accepted it on May 14. The entire matter was scheduled on an expedited basis.[5]

II.

The issues we address involve these fundamental questions: Did the Unocal board have the power and duty to oppose a takeover threat it reasonably perceived to be harmful to the corporate enterprise, and if so, is its action here entitled to the protection of the business judgment rule?

Mesa contends that the discriminatory exchange offer violates the fiduciary duties Unocal owes it. Mesa argues that because of the Mesa exclusion the business judgment rule is inapplicable, because the directors by tendering their own shares will derive a financial benefit that is not available to all Unocal stockholders. Thus, it is Mesa's ultimate contention that Unocal cannot establish that the exchange offer is fair to all shareholders,

---

[5] Such expedition was required by the fact that if Unocal's exchange offer was permitted to proceed, the proration date for the shares entitled to be exchanged was May 17, 1985, while Mesa's tender offer expired on May 23. After acceptance of this appeal on May 14, we received excellent briefs from the parties, heard argument on May 16 and announced our oral ruling in open court at 9:00 a.m. on May 17. See supra n. 2.

and argues that the Court of Chancery was correct in concluding that Unocal was unable to meet this burden.

Unocal answers that it does not owe a duty of "fairness" to Mesa, given the facts here. Specifically, Unocal contends that its board of directors reasonably and in good faith concluded that Mesa's $54 two-tier tender offer was coercive and inadequate, and that Mesa sought selective treatment for itself. Furthermore, Unocal argues that the board's approval of the exchange offer was made in good faith, on an informed basis, and in the exercise of due care. Under these circumstances, Unocal contends that its directors properly employed this device to protect the company and its stockholders from Mesa's harmful tactics.

III.

We begin with the basic issue of the power of a board of directors of a Delaware corporation to adopt a defensive measure of this type. Absent such authority, all other questions are moot. Neither issues of fairness nor business judgment are pertinent without the basic underpinning of a board's legal power to act.

The board has a large reservoir of authority upon which to draw. Its duties and responsibilities proceed from the inherent powers conferred by 8 *Del.C.* § 141(a), respecting management of the corporation's "business and affairs".[6] Additionally, the powers here being exercised derive from 8 *Del.C.* § 160(a), conferring broad authority upon a corporation to deal in its own stock.[7] From this it is now well established that in the acquisition of its shares a [954] Delaware corporation may deal selectively with its stockholders, provided the directors have not acted out of a sole or primary purpose to entrench themselves in office. *Cheff v. Mathes*, Del.Supr., 199 A.2d 548, 554 (1964); *Bennett v. Propp*, Del.Supr., 187 A.2d 405, 408 (1962); *Martin v. American Potash & Chemical Corporation*, Del.Supr., 92 A.2d 295, 302 (1952); *Kaplan v. Goldsamt*,

---

[6] The general grant of power to a board of directors is conferred by 8 *Del.C.* § 141(a), which provides:

> (a) The business *and affairs* of every corporation organized under this chapter shall be managed by or under the direction of a board of directors, except as may be otherwise provided in this chapter or in its certificate of incorporation. If any such provision is made in the certificate of incorporation, the powers and duties conferred or imposed upon the board of directors by this chapter shall be exercised or performed to such extent and by such person or persons as shall be provided in the certificate of incorporation. (Emphasis added)

[7] This power under 8 *Del.C.* § 160(a), with certain exceptions not pertinent here, is as follows:

> (a) Every corporation may purchase, redeem, receive, take or otherwise acquire, own and hold, sell, lend, exchange, transfer or otherwise dispose of, pledge, use and otherwise deal in and with its own shares; ...

Del.Ch., 380 A.2d 556, 568-569 (1977); *Kors v. Carey,* Del. Ch., 158 A.2d 136, 140-141 (1960).

Finally, the board's power to act derives from its fundamental duty and obligation to protect the corporate enterprise, which includes stockholders, from harm reasonably perceived, irrespective of its source. *See e.g. Panter v. Marshall Field & Co.,* 646 F.2d 271, 297 (7th Cir.1981); *Crouse-Hinds Co. v. Internorth, Inc.,* 634 F.2d 690, 704 (2d Cir.1980); *Heit v. Baird,* 567 F.2d 1157, 1161 (1st Cir.1977); *Cheff v. Mathes,* 199 A.2d at 556; *Martin v. American Potash & Chemical Corp.,* 92 A.2d at 302; *Kaplan v. Goldsamt,* 380 A.2d at 568-69; *Kors v. Carey,* 158 A.2d at 141; *Northwest Industries, Inc. v. B.F. Goodrich Co.,* 301 F.Supp. 706, 712 (M.D.Ill. 1969). Thus, we are satisfied that in the broad context of corporate governance, including issues of fundamental corporate change, a board of directors is not a passive instrumentality.[8]

Given the foregoing principles, we turn to the standards by which director action is to be measured. In *Pogostin v. Rice,* Del.Supr., 480 A.2d 619 (1984), we held that the business judgment rule, including the standards by which director conduct is judged, is applicable in the context of a takeover. *Id.* at 627. The business judgment rule is a "presumption that in making a business decision the directors of a corporation acted on an informed basis, in good faith and in the honest belief that the action taken was in the best interests of the company." *Aronson v. Lewis,* Del.Supr., 473 A.2d 805, 812 (1984) (citations omitted). A hallmark of the business judgment rule is that a court will not substitute its judgment for that of the board if the latter's decision can be "attributed to any rational business purpose." *Sinclair Oil Corp. v. Levien,* Del.Supr., 280 A.2d 717, 720 (1971).

When a board addresses a pending takeover bid it has an obligation to determine whether the offer is in the best interests of the corporation and its shareholders. In that respect a board's duty is no different from any other responsibility it shoulders, and its decisions should be no less entitled to the respect they otherwise would be accorded in the realm of business judgment.[9] *See also Johnson v. Trueblood,* 629 F.2d 287, 292-293 (3d Cir.1980). There are, however, certain caveats to a proper exercise of this function.

---

[8] Even in the traditional areas of fundamental corporate change, i.e., charter, amendments [8 *Del.C.* § 242(b)], mergers [8 *Del.C.* §§ 251(b), 252(c), 253(a), and 254(d)], sale of assets [8 *Del.C.* § 271(a)], and dissolution [8 *Del.C.* § 275(a)], director action is a prerequisite to the ultimate disposition of such matters. *See also, Smith v. Van Gorkom,* Del.Supr., 488 A.2d 858, 888 (1985).

[9] This is a subject of intense debate among practicing members of the bar and legal scholars. Excellent examples of these contending views are: Block & Miller, *The Responsibilities and Obligations of Corporate Directors in Takeover Contests,* 11 Sec.Reg. L.J. 44 (1983); Easterbrook & Fischel, *Takeover Bids, Defensive Tactics, and Shareholders' Welfare,* 36 Bus.Law. 1733 (1981); Easterbrook & Fischel, *The Proper Role of a Target's Management In Responding to a Tender Offer,* 94 Harv.L.Rev. 1161 (1981). Herzel, Schmidt & Davis, *Why Corporate Directors Have a Right To Resist Tender Offers,* 3 Corp.L.Rev. 107 (1980); Lipton, *Takeover Bids in the Target's Boardroom,* 35 Bus.Law. 101 (1979).

Because of the omnipresent specter that a board may be acting primarily in its own interests, rather than those of the corporation and its shareholders, there is an enhanced duty which calls for judicial examination at the threshold before the protections of the business judgment rule may be conferred.

This Court has long recognized that:

> [955] We must bear in mind the inherent danger in the purchase of shares with corporate funds to remove a threat to corporate policy when a threat to control is involved. The directors are of necessity confronted with a conflict of interest, and an objective decision is difficult.

Bennett v. Propp, Del.Supr., 187 A.2d 405, 409 (1962). In the face of this inherent conflict directors must show that they had reasonable grounds for believing that a danger to corporate policy and effectiveness existed because of another person's stock ownership. *Cheff v. Mathes*, 199 A.2d at 554-55. However, they satisfy that burden "by showing good faith and reasonable investigation...." *Id.* at 555. Furthermore, such proof is materially enhanced, as here, by the approval of a board comprised of a majority of outside independent directors who have acted in accordance with the foregoing standards. *See Aronson v. Lewis*, 473 A.2d at 812, 815; *Puma v. Marriott*, Del.Ch., 283 A.2d 693, 695 (1971); *Panter v. Marshall Field & Co.*, 646 F.2d 271, 295 (7th Cir.1981).

IV.

A.

In the board's exercise of corporate power to forestall a takeover bid our analysis begins with the basic principle that corporate directors have a fiduciary duty to act in the best interests of the corporation's stockholders. *Guth v. Loft, Inc.*, Del. Supr., 5 A.2d 503, 510 (1939). As we have noted, their duty of care extends to protecting the corporation and its owners from perceived harm whether a threat originates from third parties or other shareholders.[10] But such powers are not absolute. A corporation does not have unbridled discretion to defeat any perceived threat by any Draconian means available.

The restriction placed upon a selective stock repurchase is that the directors may not have acted solely or primarily out of a desire to perpetuate themselves in office. *See Cheff v. Mathes*, 199 A.2d at 556; *Kors v. Carey*, 158 A.2d at 140. Of course, to this is added the further caveat that inequitable action may not be taken under the guise of law. *Schnell*

---

[10] It has been suggested that a board's response to a takeover threat should be a passive one. Easterbrook & Fischel, *supra*, 36 Bus.Law. at 1750. However, that clearly is not the law of Delaware, and as the proponents of this rule of passivity readily concede, it has not been adopted either by courts or state legislatures. Easterbrook & Fischel, *supra*, 94 Harv.L.Rev. at 1194.

v. Chris-Craft Industries, Inc., Del.Supr., 285 A.2d 437, 439 (1971). The standard of proof established in *Cheff v. Mathes* and discussed *supra* at page 955, is designed to ensure that a defensive measure to thwart or impede a takeover is indeed motivated by a good faith concern for the welfare of the corporation and its stockholders, which in all circumstances must be free of any fraud or other misconduct. *Cheff v. Mathes*, 199 A.2d at 554-55. However, this does not end the inquiry.

B.

A further aspect is the element of balance. If a defensive measure is to come within the ambit of the business judgment rule, it must be reasonable in relation to the threat posed. This entails an analysis by the directors of the nature of the takeover bid and its effect on the corporate enterprise. Examples of such concerns may include: inadequacy of the price offered, nature and timing of the offer, questions of illegality, the impact on "constituencies" other than shareholders (i.e., creditors, customers, employees, and perhaps even the community generally), the risk of nonconsummation, and the quality of securities being offered in the exchange. *See* Lipton and Brownstein, *Takeover Responses and Directors' Responsibilities: An Update*, p. 7, ABA National Institute on the Dynamics of Corporate Control (December 8, 1983). While not a controlling factor, it also seems to us that a board may reasonably consider the basic stockholder [956] interests at stake, including those of short term speculators, whose actions may have fueled the coercive aspect of the offer at the expense of the long term investor.[11] Here, the threat posed was viewed by the Unocal board as a grossly inadequate two-tier coercive tender offer coupled with the threat of greenmail.

Specifically, the Unocal directors had concluded that the value of Unocal was substantially above the $54 per share offered in cash at the front end. Furthermore, they determined that the subordinated securities to be exchanged in Mesa's announced squeeze out of the remaining shareholders in the "back-end" merger were "junk bonds" worth far less than $54. It is now well recognized that such offers are a classic coercive measure designed to

---

[11] There has been much debate respecting such stockholder interests. One rather impressive study indicates that the stock of over 50 percent of target companies, who resisted hostile takeovers, later traded at higher market prices than the rejected offer price, or were acquired after the tender offer was defeated by another company at a price higher than the offer price. *See* Lipton, *supra* 35 Bus.Law. at 106-109, 132-133. Moreover, an update by Kidder Peabody & Company of this study, involving the stock prices of target companies that have defeated hostile tender offers during the period from 1973 to 1982 demonstrates that in a majority of cases the target's shareholders benefited from the defeat. The stock of 81% of the targets studied has, since the tender offer, sold at prices higher than the tender offer price. When adjusted for the time value of money, the figure is 64%. *See* Lipton & Brownstein, *supra* ABA Institute at 10. The thesis being that this strongly supports application of the business judgment rule in response to takeover threats. There is, however, a rather vehement contrary view. *See* Easterbrook & Fischel, *supra* 36 Bus.Law. at 1739-1745.

stampede shareholders into tendering at the first tier, even if the price is inadequate, out of fear of what they will receive at the back end of the transaction.[12] Wholly beyond the coercive aspect of an inadequate two-tier tender offer, the threat was posed by a corporate raider with a national reputation as a "greenmailer".[13]

In adopting the selective exchange offer, the board stated that its objective was either to defeat the inadequate Mesa offer or, should the offer still succeed, provide the 49% of its stockholders, who would otherwise be forced to accept "junk bonds", with $72 worth of senior debt. We find that both purposes are valid.

However, such efforts would have been thwarted by Mesa's participation in the exchange offer. First, if Mesa could tender its shares, Unocal would effectively be subsidizing the former's continuing effort to buy Unocal stock at $54 per share. Second, Mesa could not, by definition, fit within the class of shareholders being protected from its own coercive and inadequate tender offer.

Thus, we are satisfied that the selective exchange offer is reasonably related to the threats posed. It is consistent with the principle that "the minority stockholder shall receive the substantial equivalent in value of what he had before." *Sterling v. Mayflower Hotel Corp.,* Del.Supr., 93 A.2d 107, 114 (1952). *See also Rosenblatt v. Getty Oil Co.,* Del.Supr., 493 A.2d 929, 940 (1985). This concept of fairness, while stated in the merger context, is also relevant [957] in the area of tender offer law. Thus, the board's decision to offer what it determined to be the fair value of the corporation to the 49% of its shareholders, who would otherwise be forced to accept highly subordinated "junk bonds", is reasonable and consistent with the directors' duty to ensure that the minority stockholders receive equal value for their shares.

---

[12] For a discussion of the coercive nature of a two-tier tender offer see e.g., Brudney & Chirelstein, *Fair Shares in Corporate Mergers and Takeovers,* 88 Harv.L.Rev. 297, 337 (1974); Finkelstein, *Antitakeover Protection Against Two-Tier and Partial Tender Offers: The Validity of Fair Price, Mandatory Bid, and Flip-Over Provisions Under Delaware Law,* 11 Sec.Reg. L.J. 291, 293 (1984); Lipton, *supra,* 35 Bus.Law at 113-14; Note, *Protecting Shareholders Against Partial and Two-Tiered Takeovers: The Poison Pill Preferred,* 97 Harv.L.Rev. 1964, 1966 (1984).

[13] The term "greenmail" refers to the practice of buying out a takeover bidder's stock at a premium that is not available to other shareholders in order to prevent the takeover. The Chancery Court noted that "Mesa has made tremendous profits from its takeover activities although in the past few years it has not been successful in acquiring any of the target companies on an unfriendly basis." Moreover, the trial court specifically found that the actions of the Unocal board were taken in good faith to eliminate both the inadequacies of the tender offer and to forestall the payment of "greenmail".

V.

Mesa contends that it is unlawful, and the trial court agreed, for a corporation to discriminate in this fashion against one shareholder. It argues correctly that no case has ever sanctioned a device that precludes a raider from sharing in a benefit available to all other stockholders. However, as we have noted earlier, the principle of selective stock repurchases by a Delaware corporation is neither unknown nor unauthorized. *Cheff v. Mathes*, 199 A.2d at 554; *Bennett v. Propp*, 187 A.2d at 408; *Martin v. American Potash & Chemical Corporation*, 92 A.2d at 302; *Kaplan v. Goldsamt*, 380 A.2d at 568-569; *Kors v. Carey*, 158 A.2d at 140-141; 8 *Del. C.* § 160. The only difference is that heretofore the approved transaction was the payment of "greenmail" to a raider or dissident posing a threat to the corporate enterprise. All other stockholders were denied such favored treatment, and given Mesa's past history of greenmail, its claims here are rather ironic.

However, our corporate law is not static. It must grow and develop in response to, indeed in anticipation of, evolving concepts and needs. Merely because the General Corporation Law is silent as to a specific matter does not mean that it is prohibited. *See Providence and Worcester Co. v. Baker*, Del.Supr., 378 A.2d 121, 123-124 (1977). In the days when *Cheff, Bennett, Martin* and *Kors* were decided, the tender offer, while not an unknown device, was virtually unused, and little was known of such methods as two-tier "front-end" loaded offers with their coercive effects. Then, the favored attack of a raider was stock acquisition followed by a proxy contest. Various defensive tactics, which provided no benefit whatever to the raider, evolved. Thus, the use of corporate funds by management to counter a proxy battle was approved. *Hall v. Trans-Lux Daylight Picture Screen Corp.*, Del.Supr., 171 A. 226 (1934); *Hibbert v. Hollywood Park, Inc.*, Del.Supr., 457 A.2d 339 (1983). Litigation, supported by corporate funds, aimed at the raider has long been a popular device.

More recently, as the sophistication of both raiders and targets has developed, a host of other defensive measures to counter such ever mounting threats has evolved and received judicial sanction. These include defensive charter amendments and other devices bearing some rather exotic, but apt, names: Crown Jewel, White Knight, Pac Man, and Golden Parachute. Each has highly selective features, the object of which is to deter or defeat the raider.

Thus, while the exchange offer is a form of selective treatment, given the nature of the threat posed here the response is neither unlawful nor unreasonable. If the board of directors is disinterested, has acted in good faith and with due care, its decision in the absence of an abuse of discretion will be upheld as a proper exercise of business judgment.

To this Mesa responds that the board is not disinterested, because the directors are receiving a benefit from the tender of their own shares, which because of the Mesa exclusion, does not devolve upon *all* stockholders equally. *See Aronson v. Lewis*, Del.Supr., 473 A.2d 805, 812 (1984). However, Mesa concedes that if the exclusion is valid, then the directors and all other stockholders share the same benefit. The answer of course is that the exclusion is valid, and the directors' participation in the exchange offer does not rise to the level of a disqualifying interest. The excellent discussion in *Johnson v. Trueblood*, 629 F.2d at 292-293, of the use of the business judgment rule in takeover contests also seems pertinent here.

[958] Nor does this become an "interested" director transaction merely because certain board members are large stockholders. As this Court has previously noted, that fact alone does not create a disqualifying "personal pecuniary interest" to defeat the operation of the business judgment rule. *Cheff v. Mathes*, 199 A.2d at 554.

Mesa also argues that the exclusion permits the directors to abdicate the fiduciary duties they owe it. However, that is not so. The board continues to owe Mesa the duties of due care and loyalty. But in the face of the destructive threat Mesa's tender offer was perceived to pose, the board had a supervening duty to protect the corporate enterprise, which includes the other shareholders, from threatened harm.

Mesa contends that the basis of this action is punitive, and solely in response to the exercise of its rights of corporate democracy.[14] Nothing precludes Mesa, as a stockholder, from acting in its own self-interest. *See e.g., DuPont v. DuPont*, 251 Fed. 937 (D.Del.1918), *aff'd* 256 Fed. 129 (3d Cir.1918); *Ringling Bros.-Barnum & Bailey Combined Shows, Inc. v. Ringling*, Del.Supr., 53 A.2d 441, 447 (1947); *Heil v. Standard Gas & Electric Co.*, Del.Ch., 151 A. 303, 304 (1930). *But see, Allied Chemical & Dye Corp. v. Steel & Tube Co. of America*, Del.Ch., 120 A. 486, 491 (1923) (majority shareholder owes a fiduciary duty to the minority shareholders). However, Mesa, while pursuing its own interests, has acted in a manner which a board consisting of a majority of independent directors has reasonably determined to be contrary to the best interests of Unocal and its other shareholders. In this situation, there is no support in Delaware law for the proposition that, when responding to a perceived harm, a corporation must guarantee a benefit to a stockholder who is deliberately provoking the danger being addressed. There

---

[14] This seems to be the underlying basis of the trial court's principal reliance on the unreported Chancery decision of *Fisher v. Moltz*, Del.Ch. No. 6068 (1979), published in 5 Del.J.Corp.L. 530 (1980). However, the facts in *Fisher* are thoroughly distinguishable. There, a corporation offered to repurchase the shares of its former employees, except those of the plaintiffs, merely because the latter were then engaged in lawful competition with the company. No threat to the enterprise was posed, and at best it can be said that the exclusion was motivated by pique instead of a rational corporate purpose.

is no obligation of self-sacrifice by a corporation and its shareholders in the face of such a challenge.

Here, the Court of Chancery specifically found that the "directors' decision [to oppose the Mesa tender offer] was made in the good faith belief that the Mesa tender offer is inadequate." Given our standard of review under *Levitt v. Bouvier*, Del. Supr., 287 A.2d 671, 673 (1972), and *Application of Delaware Racing Association*, Del.Supr., 213 A.2d 203, 207 (1965), we are satisfied that Unocal's board has met its burden of proof. *Cheff v. Mathes*, 199 A.2d at 555.

VI.

In conclusion, there was directorial power to oppose the Mesa tender offer, and to undertake a selective stock exchange made in good faith and upon a reasonable investigation pursuant to a clear duty to protect the corporate enterprise. Further, the selective stock repurchase plan chosen by Unocal is reasonable in relation to the threat that the board rationally and reasonably believed was posed by Mesa's inadequate and coercive two-tier tender offer. Under those circumstances the board's action is entitled to be measured by the standards of the business judgment rule. Thus, unless it is shown by a preponderance of the evidence that the directors' decisions were primarily based on perpetuating themselves in office, or some other breach of fiduciary duty such as fraud, overreaching, lack of good faith, or being uninformed, a Court will not substitute its judgment for that of the board.

In this case that protection is not lost merely because Unocal's directors have [959] tendered their shares in the exchange offer. Given the validity of the Mesa exclusion, they are receiving a benefit shared generally by all other stockholders except Mesa. In this circumstance the test of *Aronson v. Lewis*, 473 A.2d at 812, is satisfied. *See also Cheff v. Mathes*, 199 A.2d at 554. If the stockholders are displeased with the action of their elected representatives, the powers of corporate democracy are at their disposal to turn the board out. *Aronson v. Lewis*, Del.Supr., 473 A.2d 805, 811 (1984). *See also 8 Del.C.* §§ 141(k) and 211(b).

With the Court of Chancery's findings that the exchange offer was based on the board's good faith belief that the Mesa offer was inadequate, that the board's action was informed and taken with due care, that Mesa's prior activities justify a reasonable inference that its principle objective was greenmail, and implicitly, that the substance of the offer itself was reasonable and fair to the corporation and its stockholders if Mesa were included, we cannot say that the Unocal directors have acted in such a manner as to have passed an "unintelligent and unadvised judgment". *Mitchell v. Highland-Western Glass Co.*, Del. Ch., 167 A. 831, 833 (1933). The decision of the Court of Chancery is therefore REVERSED, and the preliminary injunction is VACATED.

B. Moran v. Household International (Del. 1985)

This decision approved the "rights plan" a/k/a "poison pill" invented by Martin Lipton. "Rights plan" may sound innocuous. But it completely transformed US takeover law and practice.

The pill has only one goal: to deter the acquisition of a substantial block of shares by anyone not approved by the board. It does so by diluting, or rather threatening to dilute, the acquired block. If anyone "triggers" the pill by acquiring more than the threshold percentage of shares (usually 15%), the corporation issues additional shares to all *other* shareholders. The number of additional shares is generally chosen so as to reduce the acquirer's stake by about half. Needless to say, that would be painful – arguably prohibitively painful – to any would-be acquirer.

Questions

1. How does the pill compare to DGCL 203 – what are their respective trigger conditions, and what are their consequences for the acquirer if triggered? (We recommend that you consult the simplified version of section 203 on simplifiedcodes.com. Note that section 203 was completely overhauled in 1988; the Moran opinion quotes the old version.)

The pill ingeniously obscures this discriminatory mechanism in complicated warrants. The corporation declares a dividend of warrants to purchase additional stock or preferred stock. Initially, these warrants are neither tradeable nor exercisable. If anybody becomes an "acquiring person" by acquiring more than the threshold percentage, however, the warrants grant the right to buy corporate stock for prices below value. Of course, all shareholders will then rationally choose to exercise the warrant. So what is the point? The point is that by their terms, the *warrants held by the acquiring person* are automatically void.

(The description of the pill in *Moran* may read slightly differently. The reason is that the industry standard pill has evolved since *Moran*. You can find a contemporary example at https://perma.cc/89UT-G4QQ.)

The pill is extraordinarily powerful. In the 30 years since *Moran*, only one bidder has dared triggering the pill, and that was one with a particularly low trigger of 5% (chosen to preserve a tax advantage). The exercise of the rights not only diluted the acquirer but caused massive administrative problems (a lot of new stock had to be issued!), leading to a suspension of issuer stock from trading. The issuer, Selectica, also violated the listing rules. What this shows is that the pill really is designed purely as a deterrent – it is intended never to be triggered. It's MAD (Mutually Assured Destruction) intended to keep out the unwanted acquirer, nothing else.

The upshot is that nowadays no Delaware corporation can be acquired unless the board agrees to sell. The pill has stopped not only hostile two-tier bids, but all hostile bids. To be sure, a would-be acquirer could attempt to replace a reluctant board through a proxy fight. But one proxy fight may not be enough, if and because the corporation has a staggered board in its charter (cf. *Airgas* below). In any event, the point is that board acquiescence is ultimately indispensable. The acceptance of the pill was thus a fundamental power shift from shareholders to boards in dealing with "hostile" offers (read: offers that the *board* doesn't like).

Perhaps understandably, the *Moran* court did not fully understand these implications. Or perhaps it didn't want to? The SEC's amicus brief certainly predicted as much. As it were, the Court gives mainly technical, statutory reasons for approving the pill. But as you know, much of corporate law is not statutory, and perhaps the Court *could* have invoked equitable principles to reach a different result.

Questions

1. Do you agree with the Court that the pill is consistent with the statute's text?

2. What about the Court's treatment of the statute's purpose? Compare *Glassman*!

3. Why isn't the pill "inequitable"?

4. Or, if that's easier, why do you think the Court did not *want* to find the pill inequitable? Hint: What does the Court see as the pill's alternative?

500 A.2d 1346 (1985)

John A. MORAN and the Dyson-Kissner-Moran Corporation,
Plaintiffs Below-Appellants, and
Gretl Golter, individually and in a derivative capacity, Plaintiff
Intervenor Below-Appellant,

v.

HOUSEHOLD INTERNATIONAL, INC., a Delaware Corporation,
Donald C. Clark, Thomas D. Flynn, Mary Johnston Evans, William D.
Hendry, Joseph W. James, Mitchell P. Kartalia, Gordon P. Osler,
Arthur E. Rasmussen, George W. Rauch, James M. Tait, Miller
Upton, Bernard F. Brennan and Gary G. Dillon, Defendants Below-
Appellees.

Supreme Court of Delaware.
Submitted: May 21, 1985.
Decided: November 19, 1985.
As Amended: November 20, 1985.

Irving S. Shapiro (argued), Rodman Ward, Jr., Stuart L. Shapiro, Stephen P. Lamb,
Thomas J. Allingham II and Andrew J. Turezyn of Skadden, Arps, Slate, Meagher & Flom,
Wilmington, and Michael W. Mitchell, Jeffrey Glekel, Jeremy A. Berman and Joseph A.
Guglielmelli of Skadden, Arps, Slate, Meagher & Flom, New York City, for plaintiffs
below-appellants.

Joseph A. Rosenthal and Norman M. Monhait of Morris and Rosenthal, P.A., Wilmington,
and Marshall Patner of Orlikoff, Flamm and Patner, Chicago, Frederick Brace of Brace &
O'Donnell, and Geoffrey P. Miller (argued), Chicago, Ill., of counsel, for plaintiff
intervenor below-appellant.

[1348] Charles E. Richards, Jr. (argued), Donald A. Bussard, Jesse A. Finkelstein, and
Gregory P. Williams of Richards, Layton & Finger, Wilmington, and George A. Katz,
William C. Sterling, Jr., Michael W. Schwartz, Eric M. Roth, Warren R. Stern and Karen
B. Shaer of Wachtell, Lipton, Rosen & Katz, New York City, of counsel, for defendants
below-appellees.

Lawrence C. Ashby of Ashby, McKelvie & Geddes, Wilmington, Marc P. Cherno, Harvey
L. Pitt, Pamela Jarvis of Fried, Frank, Harris, Shriver & Jacobson, New York City, amicus

curiae, and Matthew P. Fink, Thomas D. Maher, Investment Co. Institute, Washington, D.C., of counsel, for Investment Co. Institute.

Robert J. Katzenstein and Clark W. Furlow of Lassen, Smith, Katzenstein & Furlow, Wilmington, and Kurt L. Schultz, Columbus R. Gangemi, Jr., Robert F. Wall, Jerome W. Pope of Winston & Strawn, Chicago, Ill., amicus curiae, for the United Food and Commercial Workers Intern. Union.

Joseph J. Farnan, Jr., U.S. Atty., Sue L. Robinson, Asst. U.S. Atty., Wilmington, Del., Daniel L. Goelzer, Jacob H. Stillman, Eric Summergrad, Gerard S. Citera, amicus curiae, and Paul Gonson, of counsel, for Securities and Exchange Com'n, Washington, D.C.

Before CHRISTIE, Chief Justice, and McNEILLY and MOORE, JJ. [1347]

McNEILLY, Justice:

This case presents to this Court for review the most recent defensive mechanism in the arsenal of corporate takeover weaponry— the Preferred Share Purchase Rights Plan ("Rights Plan" or "Plan"). The validity of this mechanism has attracted national attention. *Amici curiae* briefs have been filed in support of appellants by the Security and Exchange Commission ("SEC")[1] and the Investment Company Institute. An *amicus curiae* brief has been filed in support of appellees ("Household") by the United Food and Commercial Workers International Union.

In a detailed opinion, the Court of Chancery upheld the Rights Plan as a legitimate exercise of business judgment by Household. *Moran v. Household International, Inc.,* Del.Ch., 490 A.2d 1059 (1985). We agree, and therefore, affirm the judgment below.

I

The facts giving rise to this case have been carefully delineated in the Court of Chancery's opinion. *Id.* at 1064-69. A review of the basic facts is necessary for a complete understanding of the issues.

On August 14, 1984, the Board of Directors of Household International, Inc. adopted the Rights Plan by a fourteen to two vote.[2] The intricacies of the Rights Plan are contained in

---

[1] The SEC split 3-2 on whether to intervene in this case. The two dissenting Commissioners have publicly disagreed with the other three as to the merits of the Rights Plan. 17 Securities Regulation & Law Report 400; The Wall Street Journal, March 20, 1985, at 6.

[2] Household's Board has ten outside directors and six who are members of management. Messrs. Moran (appellant) and Whitehead voted against the Plan. The record reflects that Whitehead voted against the Plan not on its substance but because he thought it was novel and would bring unwanted publicity to Household.

a 48-page document entitled "Rights Agreement". Basically, the Plan provides that Household common stockholders are entitled to the issuance of one Right per common share under certain triggering conditions. There are two triggering events that can activate the Rights. The first is the announcement of a tender offer for 30 percent of Household's shares ("30% trigger") and the second is the acquisition of 20 percent of Household's shares by any single entity or group ("20% trigger").

[1349] If an announcement of a tender offer for 30 percent of Household's shares is made, the Rights are issued and are immediately exercisable to purchase 1/100 share of new preferred stock for $100 and are redeemable by the Board for $.50 per Right. If 20 percent of Household's shares are acquired by anyone, the Rights are issued and become non-redeemable and are exercisable to purchase 1/100 of a share of preferred. If a Right is not exercised for preferred, and thereafter, a merger or consolidation occurs, the Rights holder can exercise each Right to purchase $200 of the common stock of the tender offeror for $100. This "flip-over" provision of the Rights Plan is at the heart of this controversy.

Household is a diversified holding company with its principal subsidiaries engaged in financial services, transportation and merchandising. HFC, National Car Rental and Vons Grocery are three of its wholly-owned entities.

Household did not adopt its Rights Plan during a battle with a corporate raider, but as a preventive mechanism to ward off future advances. The Vice-Chancellor found that as early as February 1984, Household's management became concerned about the company's vulnerability as a takeover target and began considering amending its charter to render a takeover more difficult. After considering the matter, Household decided not to pursue a fair price amendment.[3]

In the meantime, appellant Moran, one of Household's own Directors and also Chairman of the Dyson-Kissner-Moran Corporation, ("D-K-M") which is the largest single stockholder of Household, began discussions concerning a possible leveraged buyout of Household by D-K-M. D-K-M's financial studies showed that Household's stock was significantly undervalued in relation to the company's break-up value. It is uncontradicted that Moran's suggestion of a leveraged buy-out never progressed beyond the discussion stage.

Concerned about Household's vulnerability to a raider in light of the current takeover climate, Household secured the services of Wachtell, Lipton, Rosen and Katz ("Wachtell,

---

[3] A fair price amendment to a corporate charter generally requires supermajority approval for certain business combinations and sets minimum price criteria for mergers. *Moran*, 490 A.2d at 1064, n. 1.

Lipton") and Goldman, Sachs & Co. ("Goldman, Sachs") to formulate a takeover policy for recommendation to the Household Board at its August 14 meeting. After a July 31 meeting with a Household Board member and a pre-meeting distribution of material on the potential takeover problem and the proposed Rights Plan, the Board met on August 14, 1984.

Representatives of Wachtell, Lipton and Goldman, Sachs attended the August 14 meeting. The minutes reflect that Mr. Lipton explained to the Board that his recommendation of the Plan was based on his understanding that the Board was concerned about the increasing frequency of "bust-up"[4] takeovers, the increasing takeover activity in the financial service industry, such as Leucadia's attempt to take over Arco, and the possible adverse effect this type of activity could have on employees and others concerned with and vital to the continuing successful operation of Household even in the absence of any actual bust-up takeover attempt. Against this factual background, the Plan was approved.

Thereafter, Moran and the company of which he is Chairman, D-K-M, filed this suit. On the eve of trial, Gretl Golter, the holder of 500 shares of Household, was permitted to intervene as an additional plaintiff. The trial was held, and the Court [1350] of Chancery ruled in favor of Household.[5] Appellants now appeal from that ruling to this Court.

II

The primary issue here is the applicability of the business judgment rule as the standard by which the adoption of the Rights Plan should be reviewed. Much of this issue has been decided by our recent decision in *Unocal Corp. v. Mesa Petroleum Co.*, Del.Supr., 493 A.2d 946 (1985). In *Unocal*, we applied the business judgment rule to analyze Unocal's discriminatory self-tender. We explained:

> When a board addresses a pending takeover bid it has an obligation to determine whether the offer is in the best interests of the corporation and its shareholders. In that respect a board's duty is no different from any other responsibility it shoulders, and its decisions should be no less entitled to the respect they otherwise would be accorded in the realm of business judgment.

Id. at 954 (citation and footnote omitted).

---

[4] "Bust-up" takeover generally refers to a situation in which one seeks to finance an acquisition by selling off pieces of the acquired company.

[5] The Vice-Chancellor did rule in favor of appellants on Household's counterclaim, but that ruling is not at issue in this appeal.

Other jurisdictions have also applied the business judgment rule to actions by which target companies have sought to forestall takeover activity they considered undesirable. *See Gearhart Industries, Inc. v. Smith International,* 5th Cir., 741 F.2d 707 (1984) (sale of discounted subordinate debentures containing springing warrants); *Treco, Inc. v. Land of Lincoln Savings and Loan,* 7th Cir., 749 F.2d 374 (1984) (amendment to by-laws); *Panter v. Marshall Field,* 7th Cir., 646 F.2d 271 (1981) (acquisitions to create antitrust problems); *Johnson v. Trueblood,* 3d Cir., 629 F.2d 287 (1980), *cert. denied,* 450 U.S. 999, 101 S.Ct. 1704, 68 L.Ed.2d 200 (1981) (refusal to tender); *Crouse-Hinds Co. v. InterNorth, Inc.,* 2d Cir., 634 F.2d 690 (1980) (sale of stock to favored party); *Treadway v. Cane Corp.,* 2d Cir., 638 F.2d 357 (1980) (sale to White Knight), *Enterra Corp. v. SGS Associates,* E.D.Pa., 600 F.Supp. 678 (1985) (standstill agreement); *Buffalo Forge Co. v. Ogden Corp.,* W.D.N.Y., 555 F.Supp. 892, *aff'd,* (2d Cir.) 717 F.2d 757, *cert. denied,* 464 U.S. 1018, 104 S.Ct. 550, 78 L.Ed.2d 724 (1983) (sale of treasury shares and grant of stock option to White Knight); *Whittaker Corp. v. Edgar,* N.D.Ill., 535 F.Supp. 933 (1982) (disposal of valuable assets); *Martin Marietta Corp. v. Bendix Corp.,* D.Md., 549 F.Supp. 623 (1982) (PacMan defense).[6]

This case is distinguishable from the ones cited, since here we have a defensive mechanism adopted to ward off possible future advances and not a mechanism adopted in reaction to a specific threat. This distinguishing factor does not result in the Directors losing the protection of the business judgment rule. To the contrary, pre-planning for the contingency of a hostile takeover might reduce the risk that, under the pressure of a takeover bid, management will fail to exercise reasonable judgment. Therefore, in reviewing a pre-planned defensive mechanism it seems even more appropriate to apply the business judgment rule. *See Warner Communications v. Murdoch,* D.Del., 581 F.Supp. 1482, 1491 (1984).

Of course, the business judgment rule can only sustain corporate decision making or transactions that are within the power or authority of the Board. Therefore, before the business judgment rule can be applied it must be determined whether the Directors were authorized to adopt the Rights Plan. [1351]

III

Appellants vehemently contend that the Board of Directors was unauthorized to adopt the Rights Plan. First, appellants contend that no provision of the Delaware General Corporation Law authorizes the issuance of such Rights. Secondly, appellants, along with

---

[6] The "Pac-Man" defense is generally a target company countering an unwanted tender offer by making its own tender offer for stock of the would-be acquirer. Block & Miller, *The Responsibilities and Obligations of Corporate Directors in Takeover Contests,* 11 Sec.Reg.L.J. 44, 64 (1983).

the SEC, contend that the Board is unauthorized to usurp stockholders' rights to receive hostile tender offers. Third, appellants and the SEC also contend that the Board is unauthorized to fundamentally restrict stockholders' rights to conduct a proxy contest. We address each of these contentions in turn.

A.

While appellants contend that no provision of the Delaware General Corporation Law authorizes the Rights Plan, Household contends that the Rights Plan was issued pursuant to 8 *Del.C.* §§ 151(g) and 157. It explains that the Rights are authorized by § 157[7] and the issue of preferred stock underlying the Rights is authorized by § 151.[8] Appellants respond by making several attacks upon the authority to issue the Rights pursuant to § 157.

Appellants begin by contending that § 157 cannot authorize the Rights Plan since § 157 has never served the purpose of authorizing a takeover defense. Appellants contend that § 157 is a corporate financing statute, and that nothing in its legislative history suggests a purpose that has anything to do with corporate control or a takeover defense. Appellants are unable to demonstrate that the legislature, in its adoption of § 157, meant to limit the applicability of § 157 to only the issuance of Rights for the purposes of corporate financing. Without such affirmative evidence, we decline to impose such a limitation upon the section that the legislature has not. *Compare Providence & Worchester Co. v. Baker,*

---

[7] The power to issue rights to purchase shares is conferred by 8 *Del.C.* § 157 which provides in relevant part:

> Subject to any provisions in the certificate of incorporation, every corporation may create and issue, whether or not in connection with the issue and sale of any shares of stock or other securities of the corporation, rights or options entitling the holders thereof to purchase from the corporation any shares of its capital stock of any class or classes, such rights or options to be evidenced by or in such instrument or instruments as shall be approved by the board of directors.

[8] 8 *Del.C.* § 151(g) provides in relevant part:

> When any corporation desires to issue any shares of stock of any class or of any series of any class of which the voting powers, designations, preferences and relative, participating, optional or other rights, if any, or the qualifications, limitations or restrictions thereof, if any, shall not have been set forth in the certificate of incorporation or in any amendment thereto but shall be provided for in a resolution or resolutions adopted by the board of directors pursuant to authority expressly vested in it by the provisions of the certificate of incorporation or any amendment thereto, a certificate setting forth a copy of such resolution or resolutions and the number of shares of stock of such class or series shall be executed, acknowledged, filed, recorded, and shall become effective, in accordance with § 103 of this title.

Del.Supr., 378 A.2d 121, 124 (1977) (refusal to read a bar to protective voting provisions into 8 *Del.C.* § 212(a)).

As we noted in *Unocal:*

> [O]ur corporate law is not static. It must grow and develop in response to, indeed in anticipation of, evolving concepts and needs. Merely because the General Corporation Law is silent as to a specific matter does not mean that it is prohibited.

493 A.2d at 957. *See also Cheff v. Mathes,* Del.Supr., 199 A.2d 548 (1964).

Secondly, appellants contend that § 157 does not authorize the issuance of sham rights such as the Rights Plan. They contend that the Rights were designed never to be exercised, and that the Plan has no economic value. In addition, they contend the preferred stock made subject to the Rights is also illusory, citing *Telvest, Inc.* [1352] *v. Olson,* Del.Ch., C.A. No. 5798, Brown, V.C. (March 8, 1979).

Appellants' sham contention fails in both regards. As to the Rights, they can and will be exercised upon the happening of a triggering mechanism, as we have observed during the current struggle of Sir James Goldsmith to take control of Crown Zellerbach. *See* Wall Street Journal, July 26, 1985, at 3, 12. As to the preferred shares, we agree with the Court of Chancery that they are distinguishable from sham securities invalidated in *Telvest, supra.* The Household preferred, issuable upon the happening of a triggering event, have superior dividend and liquidation rights.

Third, appellants contend that § 157 authorizes the issuance of Rights "entitling holders thereof to purchase from the corporation any shares of *its* capital stock of any class ..." (emphasis added). Therefore, their contention continues, the plain language of the statute does not authorize Household to issue rights to purchase another's capital stock upon a merger or consolidation.

Household contends, *inter alia,* that the Rights Plan is analogous to "anti-destruction" or "anti-dilution" provisions which are customary features of a wide variety of corporate securities. While appellants seem to concede that "anti-destruction" provisions are valid under Delaware corporate law, they seek to distinguish the Rights Plan as not being incidental, as are most "anti-destruction" provisions, to a corporation's statutory power to finance itself. We find no merit to such a distinction. We have already rejected appellants' similar contention that § 157 could only be used for financing purposes. We also reject that distinction here.

"Anti-destruction" clauses generally ensure holders of certain securities of the protection of their right of conversion in the event of a merger by giving them the right to convert their securities into whatever securities are to replace the stock of their company. *See Broad v. Rockwell International Corp.*, 5th Cir., 642 F.2d 929, 946, *cert. denied*, 454 U.S. 965, 102 S.Ct. 506, 70 L.Ed.2d 380 (1981); *Wood v. Coastal States Gas Corp.*, Del.Supr., 401 A.2d 932, 937-39 (1979); *B.S.F. Co. v. Philadelphia National Bank*, Del.Supr., 204 A.2d 746, 750-51 (1964). The fact that the rights here have as their purpose the prevention of coercive two-tier tender offers does not invalidate them.

[Eds: The opinion here refers to the old version of DGCL 203, which was completely overhauled in 1988.] Fourth, appellants contend that Household's reliance upon § 157 is contradictory to 8 Del.C. § 203.[9] Section 203 is a "notice" statute which generally requires that [1353] timely notice be given to a target of an offeror's intention to make a tender offer. Appellants contend that the lack of stronger regulation by the State indicates a legislative intent to reject anything which would impose an impediment to the tender offer process. Such a contention is a *non sequitur*. The desire to have little state regulation of tender offers cannot be said to also indicate a desire to also have little private

---

[9] 8 *Del.C.* § 203 provides in relevant part:
(a) No offeror shall make a tender offer unless:

> (1) Not less than 20 nor more than 60 days before the date the tender offer is to be made, the offeror shall deliver personally or by registered or certified mail to the corporation whose equity securities are to be subject to the tender offer, at its registered office in this State or at its principal place of business, a written statement of the offeror's intention to make the tender offer....

> (2) The tender offer shall remain open for a period of at least 20 days after it is first made to the holders of the equity securities, during which period any stockholder may withdraw any of the equity securities tendered to the offeror, and any revised or amended tender offer which changes the amount or type of consideration offered or the number of equity securities for which the offer is made shall remain open at least 10 days following the amendment; and

> (3) The offeror and any associate of the offeror will not purchase or pay for any tendered equity security for a period of at least 20 days after the tender offer is first made to the holders of the equity securities, and no such purchase or payment shall be made within 10 days after an amended or revised tender offer if the amendment or revision changes the amount or type of consideration offered or the number of equity securities for which the offer is made. If during the period the tender offer must remain open pursuant to this section, a greater number of equity securities is tendered than the offeror is bound or willing to purchase, the equity securities shall be purchased pro rata, as nearly as may be, according to the number of shares tendered during such period by each equity security holder.

regulation. Furthermore, as we explain *infra*, we do not view the Rights Plan as much of an impediment on the tender offer process.

Fifth, appellants contend that if § 157 authorizes the Rights Plan it would be unconstitutional pursuant to the Commerce Clause and Supremacy Clause of the United States Constitution. Household counters that appellants have failed to properly raise the issues in the Court of Chancery and are, therefore, precluded from raising them. Moreover, Household counters that appellants' contentions are without merit since the conduct complained of here is private conduct of corporate directors and not state regulation.

It is commonly known that issues not properly raised in the trial court will not be considered in the first instance by this Court. Supreme Court Rule 8. We cannot conclude here that appellants have failed to adequately raise their constitutional issues in the Court of Chancery. Appellants raised the Commerce Clause and Supremacy Clause contentions in their "pretrial memo of points and authorities" and in their opening argument at trial. The fact that they did not again raise the issues in their post-trial briefing will not preclude them from raising the issues before this Court.

Appellants contend that § 157 authorization for the Rights Plan violates the Commerce Clause and is void under the Supremacy Clause, since it is an obstacle to the accomplishment of the policies underlying the Williams Act. Appellants put heavy emphasis upon the case of *Edgar v. MITE Corp.*, 457 U.S. 624, 102 S.Ct. 2629, 73 L.Ed.2d 269 (1982), in which the United States Supreme Court held that the Illinois Business Takeover Act was unconstitutional, in that it unduly burdened interstate commerce in violation of the Commerce Clause.[10] We do not read the analysis in *Edgar* as applicable to the actions of private parties. The fact that directors of a corporation act pursuant to a state statute provides an insufficient nexus to the state for there to be state action which may violate the Commerce Clause or Supremacy Clause. *See Data Probe Acquisition Corp. v. Datatab, Inc.*, 2d Cir., 722 F.2d 1, 5 (1983).

Having concluded that sufficient authority for the Rights Plan exists in 8 *Del.C.* § 157, we note the inherent powers of the Board conferred by 8 *Del.C.* § 141(a),[11] concerning the

---

[10] Justice White, joined by Chief Justice Burger and Justice Blackman also concluded that the Illinois Business Takeover Act was pre-empted by the Williams Act. *Edgar*, 457 U.S. at 630, 102 S.Ct. at 2634.

[11] 8 *Del.C.* § 141(a) provides:

> (a) The business and affairs of every corporation organized under this chapter shall be managed by or under the direction of a board of directors, except as may be otherwise provided in this chapter or in its certificate of incorporation. If any such provision is made in the certificate of incorporation, the powers and duties conferred or imposed upon the board of directors by this chapter shall be exercised or

management of the corporation's "business and *affairs*" (emphasis added), also provides the Board additional authority upon which to enact the Rights Plan. *Unocal*, 493 A.2d at 953.

B.

Appellants contend that the Board is unauthorized to usurp stockholders' [1354] rights to receive tender offers by changing Household's fundamental structure. We conclude that the Rights Plan does not prevent stockholders from receiving tender offers, and that the change of Household's structure was less than that which results from the implementation of other defensive mechanisms upheld by various courts.

Appellants' contention that stockholders will lose their right to receive and accept tender offers seems to be premised upon an understanding of the Rights Plan which is illustrated by the SEC *amicus* brief which states: "The Chancery Court's decision seriously understates the impact of this plan. In fact, as we discuss below, the Rights Plan will deter not only two-tier offers, but virtually all hostile tender offers."

The fallacy of that contention is apparent when we look at the recent takeover of Crown Zellerbach, which has a similar Rights Plan, by Sir James Goldsmith.♦ Wall Street Journal, July 26, 1985, at 3, 12. The evidence at trial also evidenced many methods around the Plan ranging from tendering with a condition that the Board redeem the Rights, tendering with a high minimum condition of shares and Rights, tendering and soliciting consents to remove the Board and redeem the Rights, to acquiring 50% of the shares and causing Household to self-tender for the Rights. One could also form a group of up to 19.9% and solicit proxies for consents to remove the Board and redeem the Rights. These are but a few of the methods by which Household can still be acquired by a hostile tender offer.

♦ The rights issued under Crown Zellerbach's pill became exercisable only in the event of a merger or the acquisition of 100% of Crown's shares. Goldsmith acquired only 51%, replaced the board, and did not pursue a merger, thus avoiding dilution. See https://goo.gl/smg425.

In addition, the Rights Plan is not absolute. When the Household Board of Directors is faced with a tender offer and a request to redeem the Rights, they will not be able to arbitrarily reject the offer. They will be held to the same fiduciary standards any other board of directors would be held to in deciding to adopt a defensive mechanism, the same standard as they were held to in originally approving the Rights Plan. *See Unocol*, 493 A.2d at 954-55, 958.

---

performed to such extent and by such person or persons as shall be provided in the certificate of incorporation.

In addition, appellants contend that the deterence of tender offers will be accomplished by what they label "a fundamental transfer of power from the stockholders to the directors." They contend that this transfer of power, in itself, is unauthorized.

The Rights Plan will result in no more of a structural change than any other defensive mechanism adopted by a board of directors. The Rights Plan does not destroy the assets of the corporation. The implementation of the Plan neither results in any outflow of money from the corporation nor impairs its financial flexibility. It does not dilute earnings per share and does not have any adverse tax consequences for the corporation or its stockholders. The Plan has not adversely affected the market price of Household's stock.

Comparing the Rights Plan with other defensive mechanisms, it does less harm to the value structure of the corporation than do the other mechanisms. Other mechanisms result in increased debt of the corporation. *See Whittaker Corp. v. Edgar, supra* (sale of "prize asset"), *Cheff v. Mathes, supra,* (paying greenmail to eliminate a threat), *Unocal Corp. v. Mesa Petroleum Co., supra,* (discriminatory self-tender).

There is little change in the governance structure as a result of the adoption of the Rights Plan. The Board does not now have unfettered discretion in refusing to redeem the Rights. The Board has no more discretion in refusing to redeem the Rights than it does in enacting any defensive mechanism.

The contention that the Rights Plan alters the structure more than do other defensive mechanisms because it is so effective as to make the corporation completely safe from hostile tender offers is likewise without merit. As explained above, there [1355] are numerous methods to successfully launch a hostile tender offer.

C.

Appellants' third contention is that the Board was unauthorized to fundamentally restrict stockholders' rights to conduct a proxy contest. Appellants contend that the "20% trigger" effectively prevents any stockholder from first acquiring 20% or more shares before conducting a proxy contest and further, it prevents stockholders from banding together into a group to solicit proxies if, collectively, they own 20% or more of the stock.[12] In addition, at trial, appellants contended that read literally, the Rights Agreement triggers the Rights upon the mere acquisition of the right to vote 20% or more of the

---

[12] Appellants explain that the acquisition of 20% of the shares trigger the Rights, making them non-redeemable, and thereby would prevent even a future friendly offer for the ten-year life of the Rights.

shares through a proxy solicitation, and thereby precludes any proxy contest from being waged.[13]

Appellants seem to have conceded this last contention in light of Household's response that the receipt of a proxy does not make the recipient the "beneficial owner" of the shares involved which would trigger the Rights. In essence, the Rights Agreement provides that the Rights are triggered when someone becomes the "beneficial owner" of 20% or more of Household stock. Although a literal reading of the Rights Agreement definition of "beneficial owner" would seem to include those shares which one has the right to vote, it has long been recognized that the relationship between grantor and recipient of a proxy is one of agency, and the agency is revocable by the grantor at any time. Henn, *Corporations* § 196, at 518. Therefore, the holder of a proxy is not the "beneficial owner" of the stock. As a result, the mere acquisition of the right to vote 20% of the shares does not trigger the Rights.

The issue, then, is whether the restriction upon individuals or groups from first acquiring 20% of shares before waging a proxy contest fundamentally restricts stockholders' right to conduct a proxy contest. Regarding this issue the Court of Chancery found:

> Thus, while the Rights Plan does deter the formation of proxy efforts of a certain magnitude, it does not limit the voting power of individual shares. On the evidence presented it is highly conjectural to assume that a particular effort to assert shareholder views in the election of directors or revisions of corporate policy will be frustrated by the proxy feature of the Plan. Household's witnesses, Troubh and Higgins described recent corporate takeover battles in which insurgents holding less than 10% stock ownership were able to secure corporate control through a proxy contest or the threat of one.

Moran, 490 A.2d at 1080.

We conclude that there was sufficient evidence at trial to support the Vice-Chancellor's finding that the effect upon proxy contests will be minimal. Evidence at trial established that many proxy contests are won with an insurgent ownership of less than 20%, and that very large holdings are no guarantee of success. There was also testimony that the key variable in proxy contest success is the merit of an insurgent's issues, not the size of his holdings.

---

[13] The SEC still contends that the mere acquisition of the right to vote 20% of the shares through a proxy solicitation triggers the rights. We do not interpret the Rights Agreement in that manner.

IV

Having concluded that the adoption of the Rights Plan was within the authority of the Directors, we now look to whether the Directors have met their burden under the business judgment rule.

[1356] The business judgment rule is a "presumption that in making a business decision the directors of a corporation acted on an informed basis, in good faith and in the honest belief that the action taken was in the best interests of the company." *Aronson v. Lewis,* Del.Supr., 473 A.2d 805, 812 (1984) (citations omitted). Notwithstanding, in *Unocal* we held that when the business judgment rule applies to adoption of a defensive mechanism, the initial burden will lie with the directors. The "directors must show that they had reasonable grounds for believing that a danger to corporate policy and effectiveness existed.... [T]hey satisfy that burden "by showing good faith and reasonable investigation...."" *Unocal,* 493 A.2d at 955 (citing *Cheff v. Mathes,* 199 A.2d at 554-55). In addition, the directors must show that the defensive mechanism was "reasonable in relation to the threat posed." *Unocal,* 493 A.2d at 955. Moreover, that proof is materially enhanced, as we noted in *Unocal,* where, as here, a majority of the board favoring the proposal consisted of outside independent directors who have acted in accordance with the foregoing standards. *Unocal,* 493 A.2d at 955; *Aronson,* 473 A.2d at 815. Then, the burden shifts back to the plaintiffs who have the ultimate burden of persuasion to show a breach of the directors' fiduciary duties. *Unocal,* 493 A.2d at 958.

There are no allegations here of any bad faith on the part of the Directors' action in the adoption of the Rights Plan. There is no allegation that the Directors' action was taken for entrenchment purposes. Household has adequately demonstrated, as explained above, that the adoption of the Rights Plan was in reaction to what it perceived to be the threat in the market place of coercive two-tier tender offers. Appellants do contend, however, that the Board did not exercise informed business judgment in its adoption of the Plan.

Appellants contend that the Household Board was uninformed since they were, *inter alia,* told the Plan would not inhibit a proxy contest, were not told the plan would preclude all hostile acquisitions of Household, and were told that Delaware counsel opined that the plan was within the business judgment of the Board.

As to the first two contentions, as we explained above, the Rights Plan will not have a severe impact upon proxy contests and it will not preclude all hostile acquisitions of Household. Therefore, the Directors were not misinformed or uninformed on these facts.

Appellants contend the Delaware counsel did not express an opinion on the flip-over provision of the Rights, rather only that the Rights would constitute validly issued and outstanding rights to subscribe to the preferred stock of the company.

To determine whether a business judgment reached by a board of directors was an informed one, we determine whether the directors were grossly negligent. *Smith v. Van Gorkom*, Del.Supr., 488 A.2d 858, 873 (1985). Upon a review of this record, we conclude the Directors were not grossly negligent. The information supplied to the Board on August 14 provided the essentials of the Plan. The Directors were given beforehand a notebook which included a three-page summary of the Plan along with articles on the current takeover environment. The extended discussion between the Board and representatives of Wachtell, Lipton and Goldman, Sachs before approval of the Plan reflected a full and candid evaluation of the Plan. Moran's expression of his views at the meeting served to place before the Board a knowledgeable critique of the Plan. The factual happenings here are clearly distinguishable from the actions of the directors of Trans Union Corporation who displayed gross negligence in approving a cash-out merger. *Id.*

In addition, to meet their burden, the Directors must show that the defensive [1357] mechanism was "reasonable in relation to the threat posed". The record reflects a concern on the part of the Directors over the increasing frequency in the financial services industry of "boot-strap" and "bust-up" takeovers. The Directors were also concerned that such takeovers may take the form of two-tier offers.[14] In addition, on August 14, the Household Board was aware of Moran's overture on behalf of D-K-M. In sum, the Directors reasonably believed Household was vulnerable to coercive acquisition techniques and adopted a reasonable defensive mechanism to protect itself.

V

In conclusion, the Household Directors receive the benefit of the business judgment rule in their adoption of the Rights Plan.

The Directors adopted the Plan pursuant to statutory authority in 8 *Del.C.* §§ 141, 151, 157. We reject appellants' contentions that the Rights Plan strips stockholders of their rights to receive tender offers, and that the Rights Plan fundamentally restricts proxy contests.

The Directors adopted the Plan in the good faith belief that it was necessary to protect Household from coercive acquisition techniques. The Board was informed as to the details of the Plan. In addition, Household has demonstrated that the Plan is reasonable in relation to the threat posed. Appellants, on the other hand, have failed to convince us that the Directors breached any fiduciary duty in their adoption of the Rights Plan.

---

[14] We have discussed the coercive nature of two-tier tender offers in *Unocal*, 493 A.2d at 956, n. 12. We explained in *Unocal* that a discriminatory self-tender was reasonably related to the threat of two-tier tender offers and possible greenmail.

While we conclude for present purposes that the Household Directors are protected by the business judgment rule, that does not end the matter. The ultimate response to an actual takeover bid must be judged by the Directors' actions at that time, and nothing we say here relieves them of their basic fundamental duties to the corporation and its stockholders. *Unocal*, 493 A.2d at 954-55, 958; *Smith v. Van Gorkom*, 488 A.2d at 872-73; *Aronson*, 473 A.2d at 812-13; *Pogostin v. Rice*, Del.Supr., 480 A.2d 619, 627 (1984). Their use of the Plan will be evaluated when and if the issue arises.

* * *

AFFIRMED.

C. Revlon v. MacAndrews & Forbes (Del. 1986)

As you have just read, in 1985, *Unocal* and *Moran* approved boards' use of powerful, discriminatory defensive tactics. You will now read *Revlon*, the 1986 decision that drew the line at playing favorites: *if* the board decides to sell or break up the company, then it can no longer defend selectively against some bidders but not others.

Questions

1. Does this distinction make sense?

2. Where would you draw the line?

506 A.2d 173 (1986)

REVLON, INC., a Delaware corporation, Michel C. Bergerac, Simon Aldewereld, Sander P. Alexander, Jay I. Bennett, Irving J. Bottner, Jacob Burns, Lewis L. Glucksman, John Loudon, Aileen Mehle, Samuel L. Simmons, Ian R. Wilson, Paul P. Woolard, Ezra K. Zilkha, Forstmann Little & Co., a New York limited partnership, and Forstmann Little & Co. Subordinated Debt and Equity Management Buyout Partnership-II, a New York limited partnership, Defendants Below, Appellants,

v.

MacANDREWS & FORBES HOLDINGS, INC., a Delaware corporation, Plaintiff Below, Appellee.

Supreme Court of Delaware.
Submitted: October 31, 1985.
Oral Decision: November 1, 1985.
Written Opinion: March 13, 1986.

A. Gilchrist Sparks, III (argued), Lawrence A. Hamermesh, and Kenneth Nachbar, of Morris, Nichols, Arsht & Tunnell, Wilmington, and Herbert M. Wachtell, Douglas S. Liebhafsky, Kenneth B. Forrest, and Theodore N. Mirvis, of Wachtell, Lipton, Rosen & Katz, New York City, of counsel, for appellant Revlon.

Michael D. Goldman, James F. Burnett, Donald J. Wolfe, Jr., Richard L. Horwitz, of Potter, Anderson & Corroon, Wilmington, and Leon Silverman (argued), and Marc P. Cherno, of Fried, Frank, Harris, Shriver & Jacobson, New York City, of counsel, for appellant Forstmann Little.

Bruce M. Stargatt (argued), Edward B. Maxwell, 2nd, David C. McBride, Josy W. Ingersoll, of Young, Conaway, Stargatt & Taylor, Wilmington, and Stuart L. Shapiro (argued), Stephen P. Lamb, Andrew J. Turezyn, and Thomas P. White, of Skadden, Arps, Slate, Meagher & Flom, Wilmington, and Michael W. Mitchell (New York City) and Marc B. Tucker, Washington, D.C., of Skadden, Arps, Slate, Meagher & Flom, for appellee.

Before McNEILLY and MOORE, JJ., and BALICK, Judge (Sitting by designation pursuant to Del. Const., Art. IV, § 12.). [175]

MOORE, Justice:

In this battle for corporate control of Revlon, Inc. (Revlon), the Court of Chancery enjoined certain transactions designed to thwart the efforts of Pantry Pride, Inc. (Pantry

Pride) to acquire Revlon.[1] The defendants are Revlon, its board of directors, and Forstmann Little & Co. and the latter's affiliated limited partnership (collectively, Forstmann). The injunction barred consummation of an option granted Forstmann to purchase certain Revlon assets (the lockup option), a promise by Revlon to deal exclusively with Forstmann in the face of a takeover (the no-shop provision), and the payment of a $25 million cancellation fee to Forstmann if the transaction was aborted. The Court of Chancery found that the Revlon directors had breached their duty of care by entering into the foregoing transactions [176] and effectively ending an active auction for the company. The trial court ruled that such arrangements are not illegal *per se* under Delaware law, but that their use under the circumstances here was impermissible. We agree. *See MacAndrews & Forbes Holdings, Inc. v. Revlon, Inc.*, Del. Ch., 501 A.2d 1239 (1985). Thus, we granted this expedited interlocutory appeal to consider for the first time the validity of such defensive measures in the face of an active bidding contest for corporate control.[2] Additionally, we address for the first time the extent to which a corporation may consider the impact of a takeover threat on constituencies other than shareholders. *See Unocal Corp. v. Mesa Petroleum Co.*, Del.Supr., 493 A.2d 946, 955 (1985).

In our view, lock-ups and related agreements are permitted under Delaware law where their adoption is untainted by director interest or other breaches of fiduciary duty. The actions taken by the Revlon directors, however, did not meet this standard. Moreover, while concern for various corporate constituencies is proper when addressing a takeover threat, that principle is limited by the requirement that there be some rationally related benefit accruing to the stockholders. We find no such benefit here.

Thus, under all the circumstances we must agree with the Court of Chancery that the enjoined Revlon defensive measures were inconsistent with the directors' duties to the stockholders. Accordingly, we affirm.

I.

The somewhat complex maneuvers of the parties necessitate a rather detailed examination of the facts. The prelude to this controversy began in June 1985, when Ronald O. Perelman, chairman of the board and chief executive officer of Pantry Pride,

---

[1] The nominal plaintiff, MacAndrews & Forbes Holdings, Inc., is the controlling stockholder of Pantry Pride. For all practical purposes their interests in this litigation are virtually identical, and we hereafter will refer to Pantry Pride as the plaintiff.

[2] This appeal was heard on an expedited basis in light of the pending Pantry Pride offer and the Revlon-Forstmann transactions. We accepted the appeal on Friday, October 25, 1985, received the parties' opening briefs on October 28, their reply briefs on October 29, and heard argument on Thursday, October 31. We announced our decision to affirm in an oral ruling in open court at 9:00 a.m. on Friday, November 1, with the proviso that this more detailed written opinion would follow in due course.

met with his counterpart at Revlon, Michel C. Bergerac, to discuss a friendly acquisition of Revlon by Pantry Pride. Perelman suggested a price in the range of $40-50 per share, but the meeting ended with Bergerac dismissing those figures as considerably below Revlon's intrinsic value. All subsequent Pantry Pride overtures were rebuffed, perhaps in part based on Mr. Bergerac's strong personal antipathy to Mr. Perelman.

Thus, on August 14, Pantry Pride's board authorized Perelman to acquire Revlon, either through negotiation in the $42-$43 per share range, or by making a hostile tender offer at $45. Perelman then met with Bergerac and outlined Pantry Pride's alternate approaches. Bergerac remained adamantly opposed to such schemes and conditioned any further discussions of the matter on Pantry Pride executing a standstill agreement prohibiting it from acquiring Revlon without the latter's prior approval.

On August 19, the Revlon board met specially to consider the impending threat of a hostile bid by Pantry Pride.[3] At the meeting, Lazard Freres, Revlon's investment [177] banker, advised the directors that $45 per share was a grossly inadequate price for the company. Felix Rohatyn and William Loomis of Lazard Freres explained to the board that Pantry Pride's financial strategy for acquiring Revlon would be through "junk bond" financing followed by a break-up of Revlon and the disposition of its assets. With proper timing, according to the experts, such transactions could produce a return to Pantry Pride of $60 to $70 per share, while a sale of the company as a whole would be in the "mid 50" dollar range. Martin Lipton, special counsel for Revlon, recommended two defensive measures: first, that the company repurchase up to 5 million of its nearly 30 million outstanding shares; and second, that it adopt a Note Purchase Rights Plan. Under this plan, each Revlon shareholder would receive as a dividend one Note Purchase Right (the Rights) for each share of common stock, with the Rights entitling the holder to exchange one common share for a $65 principal Revlon note at 12% interest with a one-year maturity. The Rights would become effective whenever anyone acquired beneficial ownership of 20% or more of Revlon's shares, unless the purchaser acquired all the company's stock for cash at $65 or more per share. In addition, the Rights would not be available to the acquiror, and prior

---

[3] There were 14 directors on the Revlon board. Six of them held senior management positions with the company, and two others held significant blocks of its stock. Four of the remaining six directors were associated at some point with entities that had various business relationships with Revlon. On the basis of this limited record, however, we cannot conclude that this board is entitled to certain presumptions that generally attach to the decisions of a board whose majority consists of truly outside independent directors. See *Polk v. Good & Texaco*, Del.Supr., ___ A.2d ___, ___ (1986); *Moran v. Household International, Inc.*, Del.Supr., 500 A.2d 1346, 1356 (1985); *Unocal Corp. v. Mesa Petroleum Co.*, Del.Supr., 493 A.2d 946, 955 (1985); *Aronson v. Lewis*, Del.Supr., 473 A.2d 805, 812, 815 (1984); *Puma v. Marriott*, Del. Ch., 283 A.2d 693, 695 (1971).

to the 20% triggering event the Revlon board could redeem the rights for 10 cents each. Both proposals were unanimously adopted.

Pantry Pride made its first hostile move on August 23 with a cash tender offer for any and all shares of Revlon at $47.50 per common share and $26.67 per preferred share, subject to (1) Pantry Pride's obtaining financing for the purchase, and (2) the Rights being redeemed, rescinded or voided.

The Revlon board met again on August 26. The directors advised the stockholders to reject the offer. Further defensive measures also were planned. On August 29, Revlon commenced its own offer for up to 10 million shares, exchanging for each share of common stock tendered one Senior Subordinated Note (the Notes) of $47.50 principal at 11.75% interest, due 1995, and one-tenth of a share of $9.00 Cumulative Convertible Exchangeable Preferred Stock valued at $100 per share. Lazard Freres opined that the notes would trade at their face value on a fully distributed basis.[4] Revlon stockholders tendered 87 percent of the outstanding shares (approximately 33 million), and the company accepted the full 10 million shares on a pro rata basis. The new Notes contained covenants which limited Revlon's ability to incur additional debt, sell assets, or pay dividends unless otherwise approved by the "independent" (nonmanagement) members of the board.

At this point, both the Rights and the Note covenants stymied Pantry Pride's attempted takeover. The next move came on September 16, when Pantry Pride announced a new tender offer at $42 per share, conditioned upon receiving at least 90% of the outstanding stock. Pantry Pride also indicated that it would consider buying less than 90%, and at an increased price, if Revlon removed the impeding Rights. While this offer was lower on its face than the earlier $47.50 proposal, Revlon's investment banker, Lazard Freres, described the two bids as essentially equal in view of the completed exchange offer.

The Revlon board held a regularly scheduled meeting on September 24. The directors rejected the latest Pantry Pride offer and authorized management to negotiate with other parties interested in acquiring Revlon. Pantry Pride remained determined in its efforts and continued to make cash bids for the company, offering $50 per share on September 27, and raising its bid to $53 on October 1, and then to $56.25 on October 7.

---

[4] Like bonds, the Notes actually were issued in denominations of $1,000 and integral multiples thereof. A separate certificate was issued in a total principal amount equal to the remaining sum to which a stockholder was entitled. Likewise, in the esoteric parlance of bond dealers, a Note trading at par ($1,000) would be quoted on the market at 100.

[178] In the meantime, Revlon's negotiations with Forstmann and the investment group Adler & Shaykin had produced results. The Revlon directors met on October 3 to consider Pantry Pride's $53 bid and to examine possible alternatives to the offer. Both Forstmann and Adler & Shaykin made certain proposals to the board. As a result, the directors unanimously agreed to a leveraged buyout by Forstmann. The terms of this accord were as follows: each stockholder would get $56 cash per share; management would purchase stock in the new company by the exercise of their Revlon "golden parachutes";[5] Forstmann would assume Revlon's $475 million debt incurred by the issuance of the Notes; and Revlon would redeem the Rights and waive the Notes covenants for Forstmann or in connection with any other offer superior to Forstmann's. The board did not actually remove the covenants at the October 3 meeting, because Forstmann then lacked a firm commitment on its financing, but accepted the Forstmann capital structure, and indicated that the outside directors would waive the covenants in due course. Part of Forstmann's plan was to sell Revlon's Norcliff Thayer and Reheis divisions to American Home Products for $335 million. Before the merger, Revlon was to sell its cosmetics and fragrance division to Adler & Shaykin for $905 million. These transactions would facilitate the purchase by Forstmann or any other acquiror of Revlon.

When the merger, and thus the waiver of the Notes covenants, was announced, the market value of these securities began to fall. The Notes, which originally traded near par, around 100, dropped to 87.50 by October 8. One director later reported (at the October 12 meeting) a "deluge" of telephone calls from irate noteholders, and on October 10 the Wall Street Journal reported threats of litigation by these creditors.

Pantry Pride countered with a new proposal on October 7, raising its $53 offer to $56.25, subject to nullification of the Rights, a waiver of the Notes covenants, and the election of three Pantry Pride directors to the Revlon board. On October 9, representatives of Pantry Pride, Forstmann and Revlon conferred in an attempt to negotiate the fate of Revlon, but could not reach agreement. At this meeting Pantry Pride announced that it would engage in fractional bidding and top any Forstmann offer by a slightly higher one. It is also significant that Forstmann, to Pantry Pride's exclusion, had been made privy to certain Revlon financial data. Thus, the parties were not negotiating on equal terms.

Again privately armed with Revlon data, Forstmann met on October 11 with Revlon's special counsel and investment banker. On October 12, Forstmann made a new $57.25

---

[5] In the takeover context "golden parachutes" generally are understood to be termination agreements providing substantial bonuses and other benefits for managers and certain directors upon a change in control of a company.

per share offer, based on several conditions.[6] The principal demand was a lock-up option to purchase Revlon's Vision Care and National Health Laboratories divisions for $525 million, some $100-$175 million below the value ascribed to them by Lazard Freres, if another acquiror got 40% of Revlon's shares. Revlon also was required to accept a no-shop provision. The Rights and Notes covenants had to be removed as in the October 3 agreement. There would be a $25 million cancellation fee to be placed in escrow, and released to Forstmann if the new agreement terminated or if another acquiror got more than 19.9% of Revlon's stock. Finally, there would be no participation by Revlon management in the merger. In return, Forstmann agreed to support the par value [179] of the Notes, which had faltered in the market, by an exchange of new notes. Forstmann also demanded immediate acceptance of its offer, or it would be withdrawn. The board unanimously approved Forstmann's proposal because: (1) it was for a higher price than the Pantry Pride bid, (2) it protected the noteholders, and (3) Forstmann's financing was firmly in place.[7] The board further agreed to redeem the rights and waive the covenants on the preferred stock in response to any offer above $57 cash per share. The covenants were waived, contingent upon receipt of an investment banking opinion that the Notes would trade near par value once the offer was consummated.

Pantry Pride, which had initially sought injunctive relief from the Rights plan on August 22, filed an amended complaint on October 14 challenging the lock-up, the cancellation fee, and the exercise of the Rights and the Notes covenants. Pantry Pride also sought a temporary restraining order to prevent Revlon from placing any assets in escrow or transferring them to Forstmann. Moreover, on October 22, Pantry Pride again raised its bid, with a cash offer of $58 per share conditioned upon nullification of the Rights, waiver of the covenants, and an injunction of the Forstmann lock-up.

On October 15, the Court of Chancery prohibited the further transfer of assets, and eight days later enjoined the lock-up, no-shop, and cancellation fee provisions of the agreement. The trial court concluded that the Revlon directors had breached their duty of loyalty by making concessions to Forstmann, out of concern for their liability to the noteholders,

---

[6] Forstmann's $57.25 offer ostensibly is worth $1 more than Pantry Pride's $56.25 bid. However, the Pantry Pride offer was immediate, while the Forstmann proposal must be discounted for the time value of money because of the delay in approving the merger and consummating the transaction. The exact difference between the two bids was an unsettled point of contention even at oral argument.

[7] Actually, at this time about $400 million of Forstmann's funding was still subject to two investment banks using their "best efforts" to organize a syndicate to provide the balance. Pantry Pride's entire financing was not firmly committed at this point either, although Pantry Pride represented in an October 11 letter to Lazard Freres that its investment banker, Drexel Burnham Lambert, was highly confident of its ability to raise the balance of $350 million. Drexel Burnham had a firm commitment for this sum by October 18.

rather than maximizing the sale price of the company for the stockholders' benefit. *MacAndrews & Forbes Holdings, Inc. v. Revlon, Inc.,* 501 A.2d at 1249-50.

II.

To obtain a preliminary injunction, a plaintiff must demonstrate both a reasonable probability of success on the merits and some irreparable harm which will occur absent the injunction. *Gimbel v. Signal Companies,* Del.Ch., 316 A.2d 599, 602 (1974), *aff'd,* Del.Supr., 316 A.2d 619 (1974). Additionally, the Court shall balance the conveniences of and possible injuries to the parties. *Id.*

A.

We turn first to Pantry Pride's probability of success on the merits. The ultimate responsibility for managing the business and affairs of a corporation falls on its board of directors. 8 *Del.C.* § 141(a).[8] In discharging this function the directors owe fiduciary duties of care and loyalty to the corporation and its shareholders. *Guth v. Loft, Inc.,* 23 Del.Supr. 255, 5 A.2d 503, 510 (1939); *Aronson v. Lewis,* Del.Supr., 473 A.2d 805, 811 (1984). These principles apply with equal force when a board approves a corporate merger pursuant to 8 *Del.C.* § 251(b);[9] *Smith v. Van Gorkom,* Del.Supr., 488 A.2d 858, 873 (1985); and of course they are the bedrock of our law regarding corporate takeover issues. *Pogostin v. Rice,* Del.Supr., 480 A.2d 619, 624 (1984); *Unocal Corp. v. Mesa* [180] *Petroleum Co.,* Del.Supr., 493 A.2d 946, 953, 955 (1985); *Moran v. Household International, Inc.,* Del.Supr., 500 A.2d 1346, 1350 (1985). While the business judgment rule may be applicable to the actions of corporate directors responding to takeover threats, the principles upon which it is founded — care, loyalty and independence — must first be satisfied.[10] *Aronson v. Lewis,* 473 A.2d at 812.

---

[8] The pertinent provision of the statute is:

> (a) The business and affairs of every corporation organized under this chapter shall be managed by or under the direction of a board of directors, except as may be otherwise provided in this chapter or in its certificate of incorporation. 8 *Del.C.* § 141(a).

[9] The statute provides in pertinent part:

> (b) The board of directors of each corporation which desires to merge or consolidate shall adopt a resolution approving an agreement of merger or consolidation. 8 *Del.C.* § 251(b).

[10] One eminent corporate commentator has drawn a distinction between the business judgment rule, which insulates directors and management from personal liability for their business decisions, and the business judgment doctrine, which protects the decision itself from attack. The principles upon which the rule and doctrine operate are identical, while the objects of their protection are different. *See* Hinsey, *Business Judgment and the American Law Institute's Corporate Governance Project: The Rule, the*

If the business judgment rule applies, there is a "presumption that in making a business decision the directors of a corporation acted on an informed basis, in good faith and in the honest belief that the action taken was in the best interests of the company." *Aronson v. Lewis*, 473 A.2d at 812. However, when a board implements anti-takeover measures there arises "the omnipresent specter that a board may be acting primarily in its own interests, rather than those of the corporation and its shareholders ..." *Unocal Corp. v. Mesa Petroleum Co.*, 493 A.2d at 954. This potential for conflict places upon the directors the burden of proving that they had reasonable grounds for believing there was a danger to corporate policy and effectiveness, a burden satisfied by a showing of good faith and reasonable investigation. *Id.* at 955. In addition, the directors must analyze the nature of the takeover and its effect on the corporation in order to ensure balance — that the responsive action taken is reasonable in relation to the threat posed. *Id.*

B.

The first relevant defensive measure adopted by the Revlon board was the Rights Plan, which would be considered a "poison pill" in the current language of corporate takeovers — a plan by which shareholders receive the right to be bought out by the corporation at a substantial premium on the occurrence of a stated triggering event. *See generally Moran v. Household International, Inc.*, Del.Supr., 500 A.2d 1346 (1985). By 8 *Del.C.* §§ 141 and 122(13),[11] the board clearly had the power to adopt the measure. *See Moran v. Household International, Inc.*, 500 A.2d at 1351. Thus, the focus becomes one of reasonableness and purpose.

The Revlon board approved the Rights Plan in the face of an impending hostile takeover bid by Pantry Pride at $45 per share, a price which Revlon reasonably concluded was

---

Doctrine and the Reality, 52 Geo. Wash. L.Rev. 609, 611-13 (1984). In the transactional justification cases, where the doctrine is said to apply, our decisions have not observed the distinction in such terminology. *See Polk v. Good & Texaco*, Del.Supr., ___ A.2d ___, ___ (1986); *Moran v. Household International, Inc.*, Del. Supr., 500 A.2d 1346, 1356 (1985); *Unocal Corp. v. Mesa Petroleum Co.*, Del.Supr., 493 A.2d 946, 953-55 (1985); *Rosenblatt v. Getty Oil Co.*, Del. Supr., 493 A.2d 929, 943 (1985). Under the circumstances we do not alter our earlier practice of referring only to the business judgment rule, although in transactional justification matters such reference may be understood to embrace the concept of the doctrine.

[11] The relevant provision of Section 122 is:

Every corporation created under this chapter shall have power to:

(13) Make contracts, including contracts of guaranty and suretyship, incur liabilities, borrow money at such rates of interest as the corporation may determine, issue its notes, bonds and other obligations, and secure any of its obligations by mortgage, pledge or other encumbrance of all or any of its property, franchises and income, ...". 8 *Del.C.* § 122(13).

See Section 141(a) in n. 8, *supra*. See also Section 160(a), n. 13, *infra*.

grossly inadequate. Lazard Freres had so advised the directors, and had also informed them that Pantry Pride was a small, highly leveraged company bent on a "bust-up" takeover by using "junk bond" financing to buy Revlon cheaply, sell the acquired assets to pay the [181] debts incurred, and retain the profit for itself.[12] In adopting the Plan, the board protected the shareholders from a hostile takeover at a price below the company's intrinsic value, while retaining sufficient flexibility to address any proposal deemed to be in the stockholders' best interests.

To that extent the board acted in good faith and upon reasonable investigation. Under the circumstances it cannot be said that the Rights Plan as employed was unreasonable, considering the threat posed. Indeed, the Plan was a factor in causing Pantry Pride to raise its bids from a low of $42 to an eventual high of $58. At the time of its adoption the Rights Plan afforded a measure of protection consistent with the directors' fiduciary duty in facing a takeover threat perceived as detrimental to corporate interests. *Unocal*, 493 A.2d at 954-55. Far from being a "show-stopper," as the plaintiffs had contended in *Moran*, the measure spurred the bidding to new heights, a proper result of its implementation. *See Moran*, 500 A.2d at 1354, 1356-67.

Although we consider adoption of the Plan to have been valid under the circumstances, its continued usefulness was rendered moot by the directors' actions on October 3 and October 12. At the October 3 meeting the board redeemed the Rights conditioned upon consummation of a merger with Forstmann, but further acknowledged that they would also be redeemed to facilitate any more favorable offer. On October 12, the board unanimously passed a resolution redeeming the Rights in connection with any cash proposal of $57.25 or more per share. Because all the pertinent offers eventually equalled or surpassed that amount, the Rights clearly were no longer any impediment in the contest for Revlon. This mooted any question of their propriety under *Moran* or *Unocal*.

C.

The second defensive measure adopted by Revlon to thwart a Pantry Pride takeover was the company's own exchange offer for 10 million of its shares. The directors' general broad powers to manage the business and affairs of the corporation are augmented by the specific authority conferred under 8 *Del.C.* § 160(a), permitting the company to deal in its own stock.[13] *Unocal*, 493 A.2d at 953-54; *Cheff v. Mathes*, 41 Del.Supr. 494, 199

---

[12] As we noted in *Moran*, a "bust-up" takeover generally refers to a situation in which one seeks to finance an acquisition by selling off pieces of the acquired company, presumably at a substantial profit. *See Moran*, 500 A.2d at 1349, n. 4.

[13] The pertinent provision of this statute is:

A.2d 548, 554 (1964); *Kors v. Carey*, 39 Del.Ch. 47, 158 A.2d 136, 140 (1960). However, when exercising that power in an effort to forestall a hostile takeover, the board's actions are strictly held to the fiduciary standards outlined in *Unocal*. These standards require the directors to determine the best interests of the corporation and its stockholders, and impose an enhanced duty to abjure any action that is motivated by considerations other than a good faith concern for such interests. *Unocal*, 493 A.2d at 954-55; *see Bennett v. Propp*, 41 Del.Supr. 14, 187 A.2d 405, 409 (1962).

The Revlon directors concluded that Pantry Pride's $47.50 offer was grossly inadequate. In that regard the board acted in good faith, and on an informed basis, with reasonable grounds to believe that there existed a harmful threat to the corporate enterprise. The adoption of a defensive measure, reasonable in relation to the threat posed, was proper and fully accorded with the powers, duties, and responsibilities conferred upon directors under our law. *Unocal*, 493 A.2d at 954; *Pogostin v. Rice*, 480 A.2d at 627. [182]

D.

However, when Pantry Pride increased its offer to $50 per share, and then to $53, it became apparent to all that the break-up of the company was inevitable. The Revlon board's authorization permitting management to negotiate a merger or buyout with a third party was a recognition that the company was for sale. The duty of the board had thus changed from the preservation of Revlon as a corporate entity to the maximization of the company's value at a sale for the stockholders' benefit. This significantly altered the board's responsibilities under the *Unocal* standards. It no longer faced threats to corporate policy and effectiveness, or to the stockholders' interests, from a grossly inadequate bid. The whole question of defensive measures became moot. The directors' role changed from defenders of the corporate bastion to auctioneers charged with getting the best price for the stockholders at a sale of the company.

III.

This brings us to the lock-up with Forstmann and its emphasis on shoring up the sagging market value of the Notes in the face of threatened litigation by their holders. Such a focus was inconsistent with the changed concept of the directors' responsibilities at this stage of the developments. The impending waiver of the Notes covenants had caused the value of the Notes to fall, and the board was aware of the noteholders' ire as well as their subsequent threats of suit. The directors thus made support of the Notes an integral part

---

(a) Every corporation may purchase, redeem, receive, take or otherwise acquire, own and hold, sell, lend, exchange, transfer or otherwise dispose of, pledge, use and otherwise deal in and with its own shares. 8 *Del.C.* § 160(a).

of the company's dealings with Forstmann, even though their primary responsibility at this stage was to the equity owners.

The original threat posed by Pantry Pride — the break-up of the company — had become a reality which even the directors embraced. Selective dealing to fend off a hostile but determined bidder was no longer a proper objective. Instead, obtaining the highest price for the benefit of the stockholders should have been the central theme guiding director action. Thus, the Revlon board could not make the requisite showing of good faith by preferring the noteholders and ignoring its duty of loyalty to the shareholders. The rights of the former already were fixed by contract. *Wolfensohn v. Madison Fund, Inc.,* Del.Supr., 253 A.2d 72, 75 (1969); *Harff v. Kerkorian,* Del.Ch., 324 A.2d 215 (1974). The noteholders required no further protection, and when the Revlon board entered into an auction-ending lock-up agreement with Forstmann on the basis of impermissible considerations at the expense of the shareholders, the directors breached their primary duty of loyalty.

The Revlon board argued that it acted in good faith in protecting the noteholders because *Unocal* permits consideration of other corporate constituencies. Although such considerations may be permissible, there are fundamental limitations upon that prerogative. A board may have regard for various constituencies in discharging its responsibilities, provided there are rationally related benefits accruing to the stockholders. *Unocal,* 493 A.2d at 955. However, such concern for non-stockholder interests is inappropriate when an auction among active bidders is in progress, and the object no longer is to protect or maintain the corporate enterprise but to sell it to the highest bidder.

Revlon also contended that by *Gilbert v. El Paso Co.,* Del. Ch., 490 A.2d 1050, 1054-55 (1984), it had contractual and good faith obligations to consider the noteholders. However, any such duties are limited to the principle that one may not interfere with contractual relationships by improper actions. Here, the rights of the noteholders were fixed by agreement, and there is nothing of substance to suggest that any of those terms were violated. The Notes covenants specifically contemplated a waiver to permit sale of the company at a fair price. The Notes were accepted by the holders on that basis, including the risk of an adverse market effect stemming from a waiver. Thus, nothing remained for Revlon [183] to legitimately protect, and no rationally related benefit thereby accrued to the stockholders. Under such circumstances we must conclude that the merger agreement with Forstmann was unreasonable in relation to the threat posed.

A lock-up is not *per se* illegal under Delaware law. Its use has been approved in an earlier case. *Thompson v. Enstar Corp.,* Del. Ch., ____ A.2d ____ (1984). Such options can entice other bidders to enter a contest for control of the corporation, creating an auction for the company and maximizing shareholder profit. Current economic conditions in the takeover market are such that a "white knight" like Forstmann might only enter the bidding for the target company if it receives some form of compensation to cover the risks and costs involved. Note, *Corporations-Mergers — "Lock-up" Enjoined Under Section 14(e) of Securities Exchange Act — Mobil Corp. v. Marathon Oil Co., 669 F.2d 366 (6th Cir.1981),* 12 Seton Hall L.Rev. 881, 892 (1982). However, while those lock-ups which draw bidders into the battle benefit shareholders, similar measures which end an active auction and foreclose further bidding operate to the shareholders' detriment. Note, *Lock-up Options: Toward a State Law Standard,* 96 Harv. L. Rev. 1068, 1081 (1983).[14]

Recently, the United States Court of Appeals for the Second Circuit invalidated a lock-up on fiduciary duty grounds similar to those here.[15] *Hanson Trust PLC, et al. v. ML SCM Acquisition Inc., et al.,* 781 F.2d 264 (2nd Cir.1986). Citing *Thompson v. Enstar Corp., supra,* with approval, the court stated:

> In this regard, we are especially mindful that some lock-up options may be beneficial to the shareholders, such as those that induce a bidder to compete for control of a corporation, while others may be harmful, such as those that effectively preclude bidders from competing with the optionee bidder. 781 F.2d at 274.

In *Hanson Trust,* the bidder, Hanson, sought control of SCM by a hostile cash tender offer. SCM management joined with Merrill Lynch to propose a leveraged buy-out of the company at a higher price, and Hanson in turn increased its offer. Then, despite very little improvement in its subsequent bid, the management group sought a lock-up option to purchase SCM's two main assets at a substantial discount. The SCM directors granted the lock-up without adequate information as to the size of the discount or the effect the transaction would have on the company. Their action effectively ended a competitive bidding situation. The Hanson Court invalidated the lock-up because the directors failed to fully inform themselves about the value of a transaction in which management had a strong self-interest. "In short, the Board appears to have failed to ensure that negotiations

---

[14] For further discussion of the benefits and detriments of lock-up options, also see: Nelson, *Mobil Corp. v. Marathon Oil Co. — The Decision and Its Implications for Future Tender Offers,* 7 Corp. L.Rev. 233, 265-68 (1984); Note, *Swallowing the Key to Lock-up Options: Mobil Corp. v. Marathon Oil Co.,* 14 U.Tol.L.Rev. 1055, 1081-83 (1983).

[15] The federal courts generally have declined to enjoin lock-up options despite arguments that lock-ups constitute impermissible "manipulative" conduct forbidden by Section 14(e) of the Williams Act [15 U.S.C. § 78n(e)]. *See Buffalo Forge Co. v. Ogden Corp.,* 717 F.2d 757 (2nd Cir.1983), *cert. denied,* 464 U.S. 1018, 104 S.Ct. 550, 78 L.Ed.2d 724 (1983); *Data Probe Acquisition Corp. v. Datatab, Inc.,* 722 F.2d 1 (2nd Cir.1983); *cert. denied* 465 U.S. 1052, 104 S.Ct. 1326, 79 L.Ed.2d 722 (1984); *but see Mobil Corp. v. Marathon Oil Co.,* 669 F.2d 366 (6th Cir.1981). The cases are all federal in nature and were not decided on state law grounds.

for alternative bids were conducted by those whose only loyalty was to the shareholders." *Id.* at 277.

The Forstmann option had a similar destructive effect on the auction process. Forstmann had already been drawn into the contest on a preferred basis, so the result of the lock-up was not to foster bidding, but to destroy it. The board's stated reasons for approving the transactions were: (1) better financing, (2) noteholder [184] protection, and (3) higher price. As the Court of Chancery found, and we agree, any distinctions between the rival bidders' methods of financing the proposal were nominal at best, and such a consideration has little or no significance in a cash offer for any and all shares. The principal object, contrary to the board's duty of care, appears to have been protection of the noteholders over the shareholders' interests.

While Forstmann's $57.25 offer was objectively higher than Pantry Pride's $56.25 bid, the margin of superiority is less when the Forstmann price is adjusted for the time value of money. In reality, the Revlon board ended the auction in return for very little actual improvement in the final bid. The principal benefit went to the directors, who avoided personal liability to a class of creditors to whom the board owed no further duty under the circumstances. Thus, when a board ends an intense bidding contest on an insubstantial basis, and where a significant by-product of that action is to protect the directors against a perceived threat of personal liability for consequences stemming from the adoption of previous defensive measures, the action cannot withstand the enhanced scrutiny which *Unocal* requires of director conduct. *See Unocal,* 493 A.2d at 954-55.

In addition to the lock-up option, the Court of Chancery enjoined the no-shop provision as part of the attempt to foreclose further bidding by Pantry Pride. *MacAndrews & Forbes Holdings, Inc. v. Revlon, Inc.,* 501 A.2d at 1251. The no-shop provision, like the lock-up option, while not *per se* illegal, is impermissible under the *Unocal* standards when a board's primary duty becomes that of an auctioneer responsible for selling the company to the highest bidder. The agreement to negotiate only with Forstmann ended rather than intensified the board's involvement in the bidding contest.

It is ironic that the parties even considered a no-shop agreement when Revlon had dealt preferentially, and almost exclusively, with Forstmann throughout the contest. After the directors authorized management to negotiate with other parties, Forstmann was given every negotiating advantage that Pantry Pride had been denied: cooperation from management, access to financial data, and the exclusive opportunity to present merger proposals directly to the board of directors. Favoritism for a white knight to the total exclusion of a hostile bidder might be justifiable when the latter's offer adversely affects shareholder interests, but when bidders make relatively similar offers, or dissolution of the company becomes inevitable, the directors cannot fulfill their enhanced *Unocal* duties by playing favorites with the contending factions. Market forces must be allowed to operate freely to bring the target's shareholders the best price available for their equity.[16] Thus, as the trial court ruled, the shareholders' interests necessitated that the board remain free to negotiate in the fulfillment of that duty.

The court below similarly enjoined the payment of the cancellation fee, pending a resolution of the merits, because the fee was part of the overall plan to thwart Pantry Pride's efforts. We find no abuse of discretion in that ruling.

IV.

Having concluded that Pantry Pride has shown a reasonable probability of success on the merits, we address the issue of irreparable harm. The Court of Chancery ruled that unless the lock-up and other aspects of the agreement were enjoined, Pantry Pride's opportunity to bid for Revlon was lost. The court also held that the need for both bidders to compete [185] in the marketplace outweighed any injury to Forstmann. Given the complexity of the proposed transaction between Revlon and Forstmann, the obstacles to Pantry Pride obtaining a meaningful legal remedy are immense. We are satisfied that the plaintiff has shown the need for an injunction to protect it from irreparable harm, which need outweighs any harm to the defendants.

V.

In conclusion, the Revlon board was confronted with a situation not uncommon in the current wave of corporate takeovers. A hostile and determined bidder sought the company at a price the board was convinced was inadequate. The initial defensive tactics worked to the benefit of the shareholders, and thus the board was able to sustain its *Unocal* burdens in justifying those measures. However, in granting an asset option lock-up to Forstmann, we must conclude that under all the circumstances the directors allowed considerations other than the maximization of shareholder profit to affect their judgment, and followed a course that ended the auction for Revlon, absent court intervention, to the ultimate detriment of its shareholders. No such defensive measure can be sustained when it represents a breach of the directors' fundamental duty of care. *See Smith v. Van Gorkom*, Del.Supr., 488 A.2d 858, 874 (1985). In that context the board's action is not entitled to the deference accorded it by the business judgment rule. The measures were properly enjoined. The decision of the Court of Chancery, therefore, is AFFIRMED.

---

[16] By this we do not embrace the "passivity" thesis rejected in *Unocal. See* 493 A.2d at 954-55, nn. 8-10. The directors' role remains an active one, changed only in the respect that they are charged with the duty of selling the company at the highest price attainable for the stockholders' benefit.

D. Beyond the Trilogy

1. The Delaware Takeover Trilogy: *Unocal*, *Moran*, and *Revlon*

Unocal established the principle that "the board ha[s] both the power and duty to oppose a bid it perceive[s] to be harmful to the corporate enterprise." In recognition of the possibility of board entrenchment, however, the Delaware Supreme Court formulated an "intermediate scrutiny" standard of review for defensive actions:

> Because of the *omnipresent specter* that a board [defending against a takeover] may be acting primarily in its own interests [of keeping its job], rather than those of the corporation and its shareholders, there is an *enhanced duty* which calls for judicial examination at the threshold before the protections of the business judgment rule may be conferred. ... If a defensive measure is to come within the ambit of the business judgment rule, it must be *reasonable in relation to the threat posed*.
>
> — *Unocal Corp. v. Mesa Petroleum Co.*, 493 A.2d 946, 954-5 (Del. 1985) (emphasis added)

Unocal explicitly blessed discriminatory defensive measures — measures that treat the bidder differently from other shareholders. The SEC subsequently prohibited the particular defense used by Unocal Corp. against Mesa, a discriminatory self-tender (cf. SEC rule 13e-4(f)(8)(i)). But this prohibition turned out to be without consequence for hostile bids because *Moran* approved the one discriminatory defense that made all others unnecessary: the "rights plan," a/k/a the "poison pill."

Revlon announced the main limit to these defenses. If the board is set to sell, it must simply get the highest price for shareholders; it cannot use defenses to play favorites between bidders or to protect some non-shareholder constituency. In the words of the Court:

> [W]hen [...] it became apparent to all that the *break-up* of the company was inevitable [and] that *the company was for sale* [...] [t]he duty of the board [...] changed from the preservation of [the] corporate entity to the *maximization of the company's value at a sale for the stockholders' benefit*. This significantly altered the board's responsibilities under the Unocal standards. It no longer faced threats to corporate policy and effectiveness, or to the stockholders' interests, from a grossly inadequate bid. The whole question of defensive

> measures became moot. *The directors' role changed from defenders of the corporate bastion to auctioneers charged with getting the best price for the stockholders at a sale of the company.*
>
> — *Revlon, Inc. v. MacAndrews & Forbes Holdings*, 506 A.2d 173, 182 (Del. 1986) (emphasis added)

In particular, the Court explicitly held that the board breached its duty of loyalty to shareholders when it favored one bidder over another out of concern for certain non-shareholder constituents — the note-holders. "Instead, obtaining the highest price for the benefit of the stockholders should have been the central theme guiding director action."

2. A Brief Critical Intermission

The Delaware trilogy is now firmly established law, and fundamental change is highly unlikely. Nevertheless, it is worth pausing for a brief moment to note some irony in the Delaware Supreme Court's reasoning.

Both *Unocal* and *Moran* argue that defenses are necessary to protect shareholders from the coercive nature of front-loaded two-tiered bids. But the defenses that the Court endorses are themselves coercive. In *Unocal* and in *Revlon*, the Court approved partial self-tenders that any individual shareholder will rationally tender into (because the price offered is higher than the share value) even if that shareholder believes the self-tender is a bad idea for the shareholders collectively. Similarly, the poison pill approved in *Moran* relies on the fact that all shareholders will rationally exercise their rights once they become exercisable, regardless of the collective effect of such exercise. Additionally, the board adopts the pill unilaterally without approval from the shareholders.

Moreover, the Delaware Supreme Court could have easily shut down coercive two-tiered bids. All it had to do was remind shareholders and deal-makers that the demanding "entire fairness" standard also applied to the consideration offered in the second tier squeeze-out merger. Recall that "coercion" emanates from the lower consideration expected in the second tier squeeze-out: shareholders tender in the first tier because they fear they will otherwise only receive low value in the second tier squeeze-out. But the merger consideration in the squeeze-out is subject to fiduciary duty review. In fact, it is subject to the exacting "entire fairness" standard because the bidder will be a controlling stockholder at the time of the squeeze-out. It seems quite straightforward to argue that any second tier (merger) consideration less than the first tier (tender) consideration is presumptively unfair.

Finally, coercive two-tiered bids entirely disappeared after the 1980s. As we will see in the next section, however, the Court's attitude towards defenses became, if anything, more permissive. As a result, Delaware boards are now allowed to deploy unilateral, coercive defenses against even non-coercive bids.

Rather than allowing coercive defenses against coercive bids, the Court *could have* attempted to suppress all coercive devices, no matter who deploys them. It could have attempted to facilitate uncoerced shareholder choice to decide the merits of a takeover bid. UK law (surveyed later in the course) employs such an approach. However, that is not Delaware law and presumably never will be.

3. Refinements of the Trilogy

Countless decisions have interpreted the Delaware trilogy, driven by deal-makers probing its limits.

(a) The Power of the Pill

The poison pill is now all but ubiquitous and defines the playing field for any takeover contest. It is not necessary for a corporation to formally adopt a "rights plan" because such a plan can be adopted on very short notice in the face of a threat. Thus, all Delaware corporations have a "shadow pill," and a bidder must plan accordingly.

While some technical details have changed over time, the basic design and idea of the pill has remained the same, and it is as deadly as ever. In the 30 years since *Moran*, only one bidder has dared to trigger the pill. Thus, practically speaking, the only way to take over a Delaware corporation is by replacing the board. The so-called "dead-hand pill" attempted to eliminate even this possibility. It provided that only the *existing* board could redeem the poison pill "rights." That is, if a bidder succeeded in electing a new board, the "rights" would cease to be redeemable. In *Quickturn Design Systems v. Mentor Graphics* (1998), the Delaware Supreme Court ruled that this "scorched earth" strategy violated DGCL 141(a), as it deprived the new board of its power to "manage" the "business and affairs" of the corporation.

(b) Unocal – Anything Left?

Unocal could have placed important limits on the use of the pill. But subsequent decisions interpreted both cognizable "threats" and "reasonable" defensive measures extremely broadly.

In *Paramount v. Time* (1989, a/k/a *"Time-Warner"*) and even more clearly in *Unitrin v. American General* (1995), the Delaware Supreme Court confirmed that inadequacy of price was a sufficient threat, at least in conjunction with the risk that "shareholders might elect to tender into [the] offer in ignorance or a mistaken belief" about the alternative. Such threats have been labeled "substantive coercion."

As to the "reasonableness" of the defense, the *Time-Warner* decision blessed the restructuring of a deal for the sole purpose of avoiding a shareholder vote–something we will see later that Delaware courts usually do not condone.

Cynics have argued that this has provided Delaware boards with the power to "just say no" to any takeover bid. In response, Delaware courts have pointed out that the board still has to lay out an argument for *why* it thinks the offer is inadequate. The excerpt from *Airgas* below references this debate.

(c) Revlon Duties

"Revlon Land"

With *Unocal* review weak at best, the boundary to "Revlon land" assumes great importance. When does the board's duty shift to maximization of the sale price?

Revlon duties are clearly triggered in a break-up or sale for cash. But what about "stock-for-stock deals," i.e., deals in which the shareholders of both merging corporations become shareholders of the surviving corporation? In these situations, it may not even be obvious who is "the buyer" and who is "the seller."

In the aforementioned *Time-Warner* (1989) and in *Paramount v. QVC* (1994), the Delaware Supreme Court ruled that a stock deal triggered *Revlon* duties only if there was a change of control. In particular, *Time-Warner* held that *Revlon* duties were not triggered if the corporation is not broken up and was widely held both before and after the merger. By contrast, the Court found a change of control in *Paramount v. QVC* because the other constituent corporation had a controlling stockholder who would also control the surviving corporation. Control of the corporation would thus pass from the "fluid aggregation of unaffiliated stockholders" to the controlling stockholder of the merger partner.

Deal protections

Even in "Revlon land," however, some defensive measures are permissible. The reason is that some protections granted to certain buyers at certain times may actually increase price. Clearly, the target has to be able to commit to a deal at *some* point, or else buyers would never be willing to engage in the transaction in the first place. Perhaps most obviously, if the board runs a genuine auction, it must be able to promise the winner a deal without further "bid jumping" (based on later information, etc.). Otherwise, bidders would rationally not bid top dollar.

More generally, a board may need to give some "deal protections" to friendly bidders to entice them to come forward. For example, an early bidder risks being a "stalking horse"— an initial bidder who attracts superior bids by others —and may agree to accept this risk only if it receives in exchange a promise of a termination fee if another bidder later tops the first bidder's price. Consequently, courts and deal-makers have been engaging in a subtle balancing act of enticing (initial) bidders without stifling possible bidding competition (or, as far as deal-makers are concerned, drawing the ire of the courts). For example, there has been a debate about the maximum percentage of deal price that could be promised as a termination fee. Section 6.02 of the 3G / Burger King agreement below is an example of deal-makers handling this issue. The details belong to a specialized M&A course.

(d) Liability

Finally and importantly, *Unocal* and *Revlon* are not generally available to support a claim for monetary damages. Under *Corwin*, excerpts of which are included below, "when a transaction not subject to the entire fairness standard is approved by a fully informed, uncoerced vote of the disinterested stockholders, the business judgment rule applies."

The following three excerpts—*Airgas*, the 3G/Burger King "go shop", and *Corwin*—illustrate the state of play in practice.

E. Air Products v. Airgas (Del. Ch. 2011)

16 A.3d 48 (2011)

AIR PRODUCTS AND CHEMICALS, INC., Plaintiff,

v.

AIRGAS, INC., Peter McCausland, James W. Hovey, Paula A. Sneed, David M. Stout, Ellen C. Wolf, Lee M. Thomas and John C. van Roden, Jr., Defendants.

In re Airgas Inc. Shareholder Litigation.

[...]

OPINION

CHANDLER, Chancellor.

This case poses the following fundamental question: Can a board of directors, acting in good faith and with a reasonable factual basis for its decision, when faced with a structurally non-coercive [eds.: i.e., with equal front-end and back-end consideration, unlike Mesa's bid for Unocal], all-cash, fully financed tender offer directed to the stockholders of the corporation, keep a poison pill in place so as to prevent the stockholders from making their own decision about whether they want to tender their shares—even after the incumbent board has lost one election contest, [eds: but there is a staggered board, so 2/3 of the incumbent directors are still on the board] a full year has gone by since the offer was first made public, and the stockholders are fully informed as to the target board's views on the inadequacy of the offer? If so, does that effectively mean that a board can "just say never" to a hostile tender offer?

The answer to the latter question is "no." A board cannot *"just* say no" to a tender offer. Under Delaware law, it must first pass through two prongs of exacting judicial scrutiny by a judge who will evaluate the actions taken by, and the motives of, the board. Only a board of directors found to be acting in good faith, after reasonable investigation and reliance on the advice of outside advisors, which articulates and convinces the Court that a hostile tender offer poses a legitimate threat to the corporate enterprise, may address that perceived threat by blocking the tender offer and forcing the bidder to elect a board majority that supports its bid.

In essence, this case brings to the fore one of the most basic questions animating all of corporate law, which relates to the allocation of power between directors and stockholders. That is, "when, if ever, will a board's duty to `the corporation and its shareholders' require [the board] to abandon concerns for `long term' values (and other constituencies) and enter a current share value maximizing mode?" More to the point, in the context of a hostile tender offer, who gets to decide when and if the corporation is for sale?

[55] Since the Shareholder Rights Plan (more commonly known as the "poison pill") was first conceived and throughout the development of Delaware corporate takeover jurisprudence during the twenty-five-plus years that followed, the debate over who ultimately decides whether a tender offer is adequate and should be accepted—the shareholders of the corporation or its board of directors—has raged on. Starting with *Moran v. Household International, Inc.* in 1985, when the Delaware Supreme Court first upheld the adoption of the poison pill as a valid takeover defense, through the hostile takeover years of the 1980s, and in several recent decisions of the Court of Chancery and the Delaware Supreme Court, this fundamental question has engaged practitioners, academics, and members of the judiciary, but it has yet to be confronted head on.

For the reasons much more fully described in the remainder of this Opinion, I conclude that, as Delaware law currently stands, the answer must be that the power to defeat an inadequate hostile tender offer ultimately lies with the board of directors. As such, I find that the Airgas board has met its burden under *Unocal* to articulate a legally cognizable threat (the allegedly inadequate price of Air Products' offer, coupled with the fact that a majority of Airgas's stockholders would likely tender into that inadequate offer) and has taken defensive measures that fall within a range of reasonable responses proportionate to that threat. I thus rule in favor of defendants. Air Products' and the Shareholder Plaintiffs' requests for relief are denied, and all claims asserted against defendants are dismissed with prejudice.

INTRODUCTION

This is the Court's decision after trial, extensive post-trial briefing, and a supplemental evidentiary hearing in this long-running takeover battle between Air Products & Chemicals, Inc. ("Air Products") and Airgas, Inc. ("Airgas"). The now very public saga began quietly in mid-October 2009 when John McGlade, President and CEO of Air Products, privately approached Peter McCausland, founder and CEO of Airgas, about a potential acquisition or combination. After McGlade's private advances were rebuffed, Air Products went hostile in February 2010, launching a public tender offer for all outstanding Airgas shares.

Now, over a year since Air Products first announced its all-shares, all-cash tender offer, the terms of that offer (other than price) remain essentially unchanged. After several price bumps and extensions, the offer currently stands at $70 per share and is set to expire today, February 15, 2011—Air Products' stated "best and final" offer. The Airgas board unanimously rejected that offer as being "clearly inadequate." The Airgas board has repeatedly [56] expressed the view that Airgas is worth at least $78 per share in a sale transaction—and at any rate, far more than the $70 per share Air Products is offering.

So, we are at a crossroads. Air Products has made its "best and final" offer—apparently its offer to acquire Airgas has reached an end stage. Meanwhile, the Airgas board believes the offer is clearly inadequate and its value in a sale transaction is at least $78 per share. At this stage, it appears, neither side will budge. Airgas continues to maintain its defenses, blocking the bid and effectively denying shareholders the choice whether to tender their shares. Air Products and Shareholder Plaintiffs now ask this Court to order Airgas to redeem its poison pill and other defenses that are stopping Air Products from moving forward with its hostile offer, and to allow Airgas's stockholders to decide for themselves whether they want to tender into Air Products' (inadequate or not) $70 "best and final" offer.

A week-long trial in this case was held from October 4, 2010 through October 8, 2010. Hundreds of pages of post-trial memoranda were submitted by the parties. After trial, several legal, factual, and evidentiary questions remained to be answered. In ruling on certain outstanding evidentiary issues, I sent counsel a Letter Order on December 2, 2010 asking for answers to a number of questions to be addressed in supplemental post-trial briefing. On the eve of the parties' submissions to the Court in response to that Letter Order, Air Products raised its offer to the $70 "best and final" number. At that point, defendants vigorously opposed a ruling based on the October trial record, suggesting that the entire trial (indeed, the entire case) was moot because the October trial predominantly focused on the Airgas board's response to Air Products' then-$65.50 offer and the board's decision to keep its defenses in place with respect to that offer. Defendants further suggested that any ruling with respect to the $70 offer was not ripe because the board had not yet met to consider that offer.

I rejected both the mootness and ripeness arguments. As for mootness, Air Products had previously raised its bid several times throughout the litigation but the core question before me—whether Air Products' offer continues to pose a threat justifying Airgas's continued maintenance of its poison pill—remained, and remains, the same. And as for ripeness, by the time of the December 23 Letter Order the Airgas board had met and rejected Air Products' revised $70 offer. I did, however, allow the parties to take supplemental discovery relating to the $70 offer. A supplemental evidentiary hearing was held from January 25 through January 27, 2011, in order to complete the record on the $70 offer. Counsel presented closing arguments on February 8, 2011.

Now, having thoroughly read, reviewed, and reflected upon all of the evidence presented to me, and having carefully considered the arguments made by counsel, I conclude that the Airgas board, in proceeding as it has since October 2009, has not breached its fiduciary duties owed to the Airgas stockholders. I find that the board has acted in good faith and in the honest belief that the Air Products offer, at $70 per share, is inadequate.

Although I have a hard time believing that inadequate price alone (according to the target's board) in the context of a nondiscriminatory, all-cash, all-shares, fully financed offer poses any "threat"—particularly given the wealth of information available to Airgas's stockholders at this point [57] in time—under existing Delaware law, it apparently does. Inadequate price has become a form of "substantive coercion" as that concept has been developed by the Delaware Supreme Court in its takeover jurisprudence. That is, the idea that Airgas's stockholders will disbelieve the board's views on value (or in the case of merger arbitrageurs who may have short-term profit goals in mind, they may simply ignore the board's recommendations), and so they may mistakenly tender into an inadequately priced offer. Substantive coercion has been clearly recognized by our Supreme Court as a valid threat.

Trial judges are not free to ignore or rewrite appellate court decisions. Thus, for reasons explained in detail below, I am constrained by Delaware Supreme Court precedent to conclude that defendants have met their burden under *Unocal* to articulate a sufficient threat that justifies the continued maintenance of Airgas's poison pill. That is, assuming defendants have met their burden to articulate a legally cognizable threat (prong 1), Airgas's defenses have been recognized by Delaware law as reasonable responses to the threat posed by an inadequate offer—even an all-shares, all-cash offer (prong 2).

In my personal view, Airgas's poison pill has served its legitimate purpose. Although the "best and final" $70 offer has been on the table for just over two months (since December 9, 2010), Air Products' advances have been ongoing for over sixteen months, and Airgas's use of its poison pill—particularly in combination with its staggered board—has given the Airgas board over a full year to inform its stockholders about its view of Airgas's intrinsic value and Airgas's value in a sale transaction. It has also given the Airgas board a full year to express its views to its stockholders on the purported opportunistic timing of Air Products' repeated advances and to educate its stockholders on the inadequacy of Air Products' offer. It has given Airgas *more time than any litigated poison pill in Delaware history*—enough time to show stockholders four quarters of improving financial results, demonstrating that Airgas is on track to meet its projected goals. And it has helped the Airgas board push Air Products to raise its bid by $10 per share from when it was first publicly announced to what Air Products has now represented is its highest offer. The record at both the October trial and the January supplemental evidentiary hearing confirm that Airgas's stockholder base is sophisticated and well-informed, and that essentially all the information they would need to make an informed decision is available to them. In short, there seems to be no threat here—the stockholders know what they need to know (about both the offer and the Airgas board's opinion of the offer) to make an informed decision.

That being said, however, as I understand binding Delaware precedent, I may not substitute my business judgment for that of the Airgas board. The Delaware Supreme Court has recognized inadequate price as a valid threat to corporate policy and effectiveness. The Delaware Supreme Court has also made clear that the [58] "selection of a time frame for achievement of corporate goals ... may not be delegated to the stockholders." Furthermore, in powerful dictum, the Supreme Court has stated that "[d]irectors are not obliged to abandon a deliberately conceived corporate plan for a short-term shareholder profit unless there is clearly no basis to sustain the corporate strategy." Although I do not read that dictum as eliminating the applicability of heightened *Unocal* scrutiny to a board's decision to block a non-coercive bid as underpriced, I do read it, along with the actual holding in *Unitrin*, as indicating that a board that has a good faith, reasonable basis to believe a bid is inadequate may block that bid using a poison pill, irrespective of stockholders' desire to accept it.

Here, even using heightened scrutiny, the Airgas board has demonstrated that it has a reasonable basis for sustaining its long term corporate strategy—the Airgas board is independent, and has relied on the advice of three different outside independent financial advisors in concluding that Air Products' offer is inadequate. Air Products' *own three nominees* who were elected to the Airgas board in September 2010 have joined wholeheartedly in the Airgas board's determination, and when the Airgas board met to consider the $70 "best and final" offer in December 2010, it was one of those Air Products Nominees who said, "We have to protect the pill." Indeed, one of Air Products' *own directors* conceded at trial that the Airgas board members had acted within their fiduciary duties in their desire to "hold out for the proper price," and that "if an offer was made for Air Products that [he] considered to be unfair to the stockholders of Air Products ... [he would likewise] use every legal mechanism available" to hold out for the proper price as well. Under Delaware law, the Airgas directors have complied with their fiduciary duties. Thus, as noted above, and for the reasons more fully described in the remainder of this Opinion, I am constrained to deny Air Products' and the Shareholder Plaintiffs' requests for relief.

[...]

F. 3G / Burger King Merger Agreement: "Go Shop"

To discharge target boards' *Revlon* duties, so-called "go shop" provisions have become standard features in merger agreements. The details of these clauses—length of the "go shop" period, topping rights of the original bidder, etc.—can be heavily negotiated, and Delaware courts have frequently been called to police them. The details belong to an M&A course. Here we focus on the basics:

Questions

1. Do you think buyers like these provisions?

2. What about sellers? (Hint: it may matter at what point in time you ask them.)

Section 6.02 *Solicitation; Takeover Proposals; Change of Recommendation.*

(a) *Solicitation.* Notwithstanding any other provision of this Agreement to the contrary, during the period beginning on the date of this Agreement and continuing until 11:59 p.m, New York City time, on October 12, 2010 (the "No-Shop Period Start Date"), the Company may, directly or through its Representatives: (i) solicit, initiate or encourage, whether publicly or otherwise, any Takeover Proposals, including by way of providing access to non-public information; provided, however, that the Company shall only permit such non-public information related to the Company to be provided pursuant to an Acceptable Confidentiality Agreement, and provided further that (A) the Company shall promptly provide to Parent any non-public information concerning the Company or its Subsidiaries to which any person is provided such access and which was not previously provided to Parent, and (B) the Company shall withhold such portions of documents or information, or provide pursuant to customary "clean-room" or other appropriate procedures, to the extent relating to any pricing or other matters that are highly sensitive or competitive in nature if the exchange of such information (or portions thereof) could reasonably be likely to be harmful to the operation of the Company in any material respect; and (ii) engage in and maintain discussions or negotiations with respect to any inquiry, proposal or offer that constitutes or may reasonably be expected to lead to any Takeover Proposal or otherwise cooperate with or assist or participate in, or facilitate any such inquiries, proposals, offers, discussions or negotiations or the making of any Takeover Proposal.

The term "Takeover Proposal" means any inquiry, proposal or offer from any person or group providing for (a) any direct or indirect acquisition or purchase, in a single transaction or a series of related transactions, of (1) 20% or more (based on the fair market value, as determined in good faith by the Company Board) of assets (including capital stock of the Subsidiaries of the Company) of the Company and its Subsidiaries, taken as a whole, or (2)(A) shares of Company Common Stock, which together with any other shares of Company Common Stock beneficially owned by such person or group, would equal to 20% or more of the outstanding shares of Company Common Stock, or

(B) any other equity securities of the Company or any of its Subsidiaries, (b) any tender offer or exchange offer that, if consummated, would result in any person or group owning, directly or indirectly, 20% or more of the outstanding shares of Company Common Stock or any other equity securities of the Company or any of its Subsidiaries, (c) any merger, consolidation, business combination, binding share exchange or similar transaction involving the Company or any of its Subsidiaries pursuant to which any person or group (or the shareholders of any person) would own, directly or indirectly, 20% or more of the aggregate voting power of the Company or of the surviving entity in a merger or the resulting direct or indirect parent of the Company or such surviving entity, or (d) any recapitalization, liquidation, dissolution or any other similar transaction involving the Company or any of its material operating Subsidiaries, other than, in each case, the transactions contemplated by this Agreement.

Wherever the term "group" is used in this Section 6.02, it is used as defined in Rule 13d-3 under the Exchange Act.

(b) *No Solicitation.* From the No-Shop Period Start Date until the Effective Time, or, if earlier, the termination of this Agreement in accordance with Section 9.01, the Company shall not, nor shall it permit any Representative of the Company to, directly or indirectly, (i) solicit, initiate or knowingly encourage (including by way of providing information) the submission or announcement of any inquiries, proposals or offers that constitute or would reasonably be expected to lead to any Takeover Proposal, (ii) provide any non-public information concerning the Company or any of its Subsidiaries related to, or to any person or group who would reasonably be expected to make, any Takeover Proposal, (iii) engage in any discussions or negotiations with respect thereto, (iv) approve, support, adopt, endorse or recommend any Takeover Proposal, or (v) otherwise cooperate with or assist or participate in, or knowingly facilitate any such inquiries, proposals, offers, discussions or negotiations. Subject to Section 6.02(c), at the No-Shop Period Start Date, the Company shall immediately cease and cause to be terminated any solicitation, encouragement, discussion or negotiation with any person or groups (other than a Qualified Go-Shop Bidder) conducted theretofore by the Company, its Subsidiaries or any of their respective Representatives with respect to any Takeover Proposal and shall use reasonable best efforts to require any other parties (other than a Qualified Go-Shop Bidder) who have made or have indicated an intention to make a Takeover Proposal to promptly return or destroy any confidential information previously furnished by the Company, any of its Subsidiaries or any of their respective Representatives.

The term "Qualified Go-Shop Bidder" means any person or group from whom the Company or any of its Representatives has received a Takeover Proposal after the execution of this Agreement and prior to the No-Shop Period Start Date that the Company Board determines, prior to or as of the No-Shop Period Start Date, in good faith, after consultation with its financial advisor and outside legal counsel, constitutes or could reasonably be expected to result in a Superior Proposal.

The term "Superior Proposal" means any *bona fide*, written Takeover Proposal that if consummated would result in a person or group (or the shareholders of any person) owning, directly or indirectly, (a) 75% or more of the outstanding shares of Company Common Stock or (b) 75% or more of the assets of the Company and its Subsidiaries, taken as a whole, in either case which the Company Board determines in good faith (after consultation with its financial advisor and outside legal counsel) (x) is reasonably likely to be consummated in accordance with its terms, and (y) if consummated, would be more favorable to the stockholders of the Company from a financial point of view than the Offer and the Merger, in each case taking into account all financial, legal, financing, regulatory and other aspects of such Takeover Proposal (including the person or group making the Takeover Proposal) and of this Agreement (including any changes to the terms of this Agreement proposed by Parent pursuant to Section 6.02(f)).

(c) *Response to Takeover Proposals.* Notwithstanding anything to the contrary contained in Section 6.02(b) or any other provisions of this Agreement, if at any time following the No-Shop Period Start Date and prior to the earlier to occur of the Offer Closing and obtaining the Stockholder Approval, (i) the Company has received a *bona fide*, written Takeover Proposal from a third party that did not result from a breach of this Section 6.02, and (ii) the Company Board determines in good faith, after consultation with its financial advisor and outside legal counsel, that such Takeover Proposal constitutes or could reasonably be expected to result in a Superior Proposal, then the Company may (A) furnish information with respect to the Company and its Subsidiaries to the person making such Takeover Proposal pursuant to an Acceptable Confidentiality Agreement and the other restrictions imposed by clause (A) and (B) of Section 6.02(a) related to the sharing of information, or (B) engage in discussions or negotiations with the person making such Takeover Proposal regarding such Takeover Proposal. The Company shall be permitted prior to the earlier to occur of the Offer Closing and obtaining the Stockholder Approval to take the actions described in clauses (A) and (B) above with respect to any Qualified Go-Shop Bidder.

(d) *Notice to Parent of Takeover Proposals.* The Company shall promptly (and, in any event, within one (1) business day) notify Parent in the event that the Company or any of its Representatives receives any Takeover Proposal, or any initial request for non-public information concerning the Company or any of its Subsidiaries related to, or from any person or group who would reasonably be expected to make any Takeover Proposal, or any initial request for discussions or negotiations related to any Takeover Proposal (including any material changes related to the foregoing), and in connection with such notice, provide the identity of the person or group making such Takeover Proposal or request and the material terms and conditions thereof (including, if applicable, copies of any written requests, proposals or offers, including proposed agreements), and thereafter the Company shall keep Parent reasonably informed of any material changes to the terms thereof.

(e) *Prohibited Activities.* Neither the Company Board nor any committee thereof shall (i) withdraw or rescind (or modify in a manner adverse to Parent), or publicly propose to withdraw (or modify in a manner adverse to Parent), the Recommendation or the findings or conclusions of the Company Board referred to in Section 4.04(b), (ii) approve or recommend the adoption of, or publicly propose to approve, declare the advisability of or recommend the adoption of, any Takeover Proposal, (iii) or cause or permit the Company or any of its Subsidiaries to execute or enter into, any letter of intent, memorandum of understanding, agreement in principle, merger agreement, acquisition agreement or other similar agreement related to any Takeover Proposal, other than any Acceptable Confidentiality Agreement referred to in Section 6.02(a) or 6.02(c) (an "Acquisition Agreement"), or (iv) publicly proposed or announced an intention to take any of the foregoing actions (any action described in clauses (i), (ii), (iii) or (iv) being referred to as an "Adverse Recommendation Change").

(f) *Change of Recommendation.* Notwithstanding any provision of Section 6.02(e), at any time prior to the earlier to occur of the Offer Closing and obtaining the Stockholder Approval, the Company Board may effect an Adverse Recommendation Change only if the Company Board determines in good faith (after consultation with its outside legal counsel) that the failure to take such action would be inconsistent with its fiduciary duties under applicable Law. [...]

G. Corwin v. KKR Fin. Holdings LLC (Del. 2015)

Questions

1. After *Corwin*, what mechanisms can shareholders employ to hold directors accountable for a perceived breach of their duties under *Unocal* or *Revlon*?

2. What is the policy rationale behind this decision? Do you agree with it?

125 A.3d 304 (2015)

ROBERT A. CORWIN, MARGARET DEMAURO, ERIC GREENE,
PIPEFITTERS LOCAL UNION NO. 120 PENSION FUND, and
POMPANO BEACH POLICE & FIREFIGHTERS' RETIREMENT
SYSTEM, Plaintiffs Below-Appellants,

v.

KKR FINANCIAL HOLDINGS LLC, TRACY COLLINS, ROBERT L.
EDWARDS, CRAIG J. FARR, VINCENT PAUL FINIGAN, JR.,
PAUL M. HAZEN, R. GLENN HUBBARD, ROSS J. KARI, ELY L.
LICHT, DEBORAH H. MCANENY, SCOTT C. NUTTALL, SCOTT
RYLES, WILLY STROTHOTTE, KKR & CO. L.P., KKR FUND
HOLDINGS L.P., and COPAL MERGER SUB LLC, Defendants
Below-Appellees.

[...]

OPINION

STRINE, Chief Justice:

In a well-reasoned opinion, the Court of Chancery held that the business judgment rule is invoked as the appropriate standard of review for a post-closing damages action when a merger that is not subject to the entire fairness standard of review has been approved by a fully informed, uncoerced majority of the disinterested stockholders. For that and other reasons, the Court of Chancery dismissed the plaintiffs' complaint. In this decision, we find that the Chancellor was correct in finding that the voluntary judgment of the disinterested stockholders to approve the merger invoked the business judgment rule standard of review and that the plaintiffs' complaint should be dismissed. For sound policy reasons, Delaware corporate law has long been reluctant to second-guess the judgment of a disinterested stockholder majority that determines that a transaction with a party other than a controlling stockholder is in their best interests.

I. The Court Of Chancery Properly Held That The Complaint Did Not Plead Facts Supporting An Inference That KKR Was A Controlling Stockholder of Financial Holdings

The plaintiffs filed a challenge in the Court of Chancery to a stock-for-stock merger between KKR & Co. L.P. ("KKR") and KKR Financial Holdings LLC ("Financial Holdings") in which KKR acquired each share of Financial Holdings's stock for 0.51 of a share of KKR stock, a 35% premium to the unaffected market price. Below, the plaintiffs' primary argument was that the transaction was presumptively subject to the entire fairness standard of review because Financial Holdings's primary business was financing KKR's leveraged buyout activities, and instead of having employees manage the company's day-to-day operations, Financial Holdings was managed by KKR Financial Advisors, an affiliate of KKR, under a contractual management agreement that could only be terminated by Financial Holdings if it paid a termination fee. As a result, the plaintiffs alleged that KKR was a controlling stockholder of Financial Holdings, which was an LLC, not a corporation.[3]

The defendants filed a motion to dismiss, taking issue with that argument. In a thoughtful and thorough decision, the Chancellor found that the defendants were correct that the plaintiffs' complaint did not plead facts supporting an inference that KKR was Financial Holdings's controlling stockholder. Among other things, the Chancellor noted that KKR owned less than 1% of Financial Holdings's stock, had no right to appoint any directors, and had no contractual right to veto any board action. Although the Chancellor acknowledged the unusual existential circumstances the plaintiffs cited, he noted that those were known at all relevant times by investors, and that Financial Holdings had real assets its independent board controlled and had the option of pursuing any path its directors chose.

In addressing whether KKR was a controlling stockholder, the Chancellor was focused on the reality that in cases where a party that did not have majority control of the entity's voting stock was found to be a controlling stockholder, the Court of Chancery, consistent with the instructions of this Court, looked for a combination of potent voting power and management control such that the stockholder could be deemed to have effective control of the board without actually owning a majority of stock. Not finding that combination here, the Chancellor noted:

> Plaintiffs' real grievance, as I see it, is that [Financial Holdings] was structured from its inception in a way that limited its value-maximizing options. According to plaintiffs, [Financial Holdings] serves as little more than a public vehicle for financing KKR-sponsored transactions and the terms of the Management Agreement make [Financial Holdings] unattractive as an acquisition target to anyone other than KKR because of [Financial Holdings]'s operational dependence on KKR

---

[3] We wish to make a point. We are keenly aware that this case involves a merger between a limited partnership and a limited liability company, albeit both ones whose ownership interests trade on public exchanges. But, it appears that both before the Chancellor, and now before us on appeal, the parties have acted as if this case was no different from one between two corporations whose internal affairs are governed by the Delaware General Corporation Law and related case law. We have respected the parties' approach to arguing this complex case, but felt obliged to note that we recognize that this case involved alternative entities, and that in cases involving those entities, distinctive arguments often arise due to the greater contractual flexibility given to those entities under our statutory law.

and because of the significant cost that would be incurred to terminate the Management Agreement. I assume all that is true. But, every contractual obligation of a corporation constrains the corporation's freedom to operate to some degree and, in this particular case, the stockholders cannot claim to be surprised. Every stockholder of [Financial Holdings] knew about the limitations the Management Agreement imposed on [Financial Holdings]'s business when he, she or it acquired shares in [Financial Holdings]. They also knew that the business and affairs of [Financial Holdings] would be managed by a board of directors that would be subject to annual stockholder elections.

At bottom, plaintiffs ask the Court to impose fiduciary obligations on a relatively nominal stockholder, not because of any coercive power that stockholder could wield over the board's ability to independently decide whether or not to approve the merger, but because of pre-existing contractual obligations with that stockholder that constrain the business or strategic options available to the corporation. Plaintiffs have cited no legal authority for that novel proposition, and I decline to create such a rule.

After carefully analyzing the pled facts and the relevant precedent, the Chancellor held:

> [T]here are no well-pled facts from which it is reasonable to infer that KKR could prevent the [Financial Holdings] board from freely exercising its independent judgment in considering the proposed merger or, put differently, that KKR had the power to exact retribution by removing the [Financial Holdings] directors from their offices if they did not bend to KKR's will in their consideration of the proposed merger.

Although the plaintiffs reiterate their position on appeal, the Chancellor correctly applied the law and we see no reason to repeat his lucid analysis of this question.

II. The Court of Chancery Correctly Held That The Fully Informed, Uncoerced Vote Of The Disinterested Stockholders Invoked The Business Judgment Rule Standard Of Review

On appeal, the plaintiffs further contend that, even if the Chancellor was correct in determining that KKR was not a controlling stockholder, he was wrong to dismiss the complaint because they contend that if the entire fairness standard did not apply, *Revlon* did [...]

But we need not delve into whether the Court of Chancery's determination that *Revlon* did not apply to the merger [eds: the Chancery Court's rejected Revlon's applicability on the basis that there was no change of control] is correct for a single reason: it does not matter. Because the Chancellor was correct in determining that the entire fairness standard did not apply to the merger, the Chancellor's analysis of the effect of the uncoerced, informed stockholder vote is outcome-determinative, even if *Revlon* applied to the merger.

As to this point, the Court of Chancery noted, and the defendants point out on appeal, that the plaintiffs did not contest the defendants' argument below that if the merger was not subject to the entire fairness standard, the business judgment standard of review was invoked because the merger was approved by a disinterested stockholder majority. The Chancellor agreed with that argument below, and adhered to precedent supporting the proposition that when a transaction not subject to the entire fairness standard is approved by a fully informed, uncoerced vote of the disinterested stockholders, the business judgment rule applies. [...]

[A]lthough the plaintiffs argue that adhering to the proposition that a fully informed, uncoerced stockholder vote invokes the business judgment rule would impair the operation of *Unocal* and *Revlon,* or expose stockholders to unfair action by directors without protection, the plaintiffs ignore several factors. First, *Unocal* and *Revlon* are primarily designed to give stockholders and the Court of Chancery the tool of injunctive relief to address important M & A decisions in real time, before closing. They were not tools designed with post-closing money damages claims in mind, the standards they articulate do not match the gross negligence standard for director due care liability under *Van Gorkom,* and with the prevalence of exculpatory charter provisions, due care liability is rarely even available.

Second and most important, the doctrine applies only to fully informed, uncoerced stockholder votes, and if troubling facts regarding director behavior were not disclosed that would have been material to a voting stockholder, then the business judgment rule is not invoked. Here, however, all of the objective facts regarding the board's interests, KKR's interests, and the negotiation process, were fully disclosed.

Finally, when a transaction is not subject to the entire fairness standard, the long-standing policy of our law has been to avoid the uncertainties and costs of judicial second-guessing when the disinterested stockholders have had the free and informed chance to decide on the economic merits of a transaction for themselves. There are sound reasons for this policy. When the real parties in interest—the disinterested equity owners—can easily protect themselves at the ballot box by simply voting no, the utility of a litigation-intrusive standard of review promises more costs to stockholders in the form of litigation rents and inhibitions on risk-taking than it promises in terms of benefits to them. The reason for that is tied to the core rationale of the business judgment rule, which is that judges are poorly positioned to evaluate the wisdom of business decisions and there is little utility to having them second-guess the determination of impartial decision-makers with more information (in the case of directors) or an actual economic stake in the outcome (in the case of informed, disinterested stockholders). In circumstances, therefore, where the stockholders have had the voluntary choice to accept or reject a transaction, the business judgment rule standard of review is the presumptively correct one and best facilitates wealth creation through the corporate form.

For these reasons, therefore, we affirm the Court of Chancery's judgment on the basis of its well-reasoned decision.

H. Current US Debate

So where are we now?

The *Airgas* excerpt summarized the current state of Delaware fiduciary law for takeover defenses. A board can maintain a poison pill for as long as it likes and for the mere reason that it believes the offer price to be inadequate. This means that the only way to overcome determined resistance by an incumbent board is to replace it in a proxy fight.

Until recently, most large corporations' charters did not permit replacing a majority of the board in a single annual meeting. Their boards were staggered, i.e., only a third of the directors were up for reelection each year (re-read DGCL 141(d), (k)(1)!). Consequently, an acquirer had to win proxy fights at two successive annual meetings to replace the majority of an intransigent board. This takes at a minimum one year and a couple months, and the acquirer would have had to keep the tender offer open (and capital tied up etc.) during that entire time. Hardly any challenger was willing to attempt this. *Airgas* was about one of the very few exceptions.

In recent years, however, the incidence of staggered boards has declined precipitously among the largest U.S. corporations. By 2012, only a fourth of the corporations in the S&P 500 index had staggered boards. Between 2012 and 2014, most of these hold-outs "destaggered" as well. The impetus came from a law school clinic, the Shareholder Rights Project (SRP) based at Harvard Law School. Acting on behalf of several institutional shareholders, the SRP submitted precatory destaggering proposals (why not binding proposals?) for the corporations' annual meetings. Under rule 14a-8, the targeted corporations had to include these proposals on their proxies. Other shareholders generally supported these proposals, and most recipient corporations soon agreed to destagger. At the same time, staggered boards remain the norm in IPO charters — the charters of corporations selling their stock to the public for the first time.

Questions

1. Most observers believe that staggered boards have important consequences for corporate governance and thus ultimately the value of these very large firms. In other words, hundreds of billions are at stake. Other shareholders generally supported destaggering. Why did it take a law school clinic to bring about this change?

2. Why do institutional investors vote against staggered boards in established corporations but continue buying staggered IPO firms? Put differently, why do IPO charters still include staggered boards?

Opinions are sharply divided about the desirability of takeover defenses in general, and of staggered boards in particular. Managers and their advisors argue that defenses allow boards to focus on long-term value creation rather than on catering to short-term pressures from the stock market. Opponents claim that defenses shield slack and prevent efficient reallocations of productive assets.

3. The accountability argument for takeovers is easy to understand. What about the short-termism counterargument? Why would stock markets exert short-termist pressures on boards?

4. Many are concerned that the rules on poison pills, as policed by Delaware courts, allow management and boards to entrench themselves against shareholder interest, but also believe that the pill can be a valuable tool in the hands of a well-motivated management and board. Distinguishing good and bad uses of the pill in a charter or bylaw provision is probably impossible. What other governance device might align use of the poison pill with shareholder interest?

I. The UK Approach

In global perspective, Delaware's heavy reliance on fiduciary duties and judicial case-by-case scrutiny is an outlier. Some countries are more takeover friendly, others less. Almost all, however, are more rule-centric than Delaware.

As a counterpoint to Delaware, the UK is particularly interesting. Like the U.S., the UK is a common law country with very developed financial markets and dispersed ownership of most large corporations. You might, therefore, expect UK takeover law to resemble Delaware's. You would be quite wrong.

Please read the following excerpts of the Takeover Code, the Companies Act 2006, and the FCA Disclosure Rules and Transparency Rules. Do these rules have analogues in Delaware law or U.S. federal securities law?

In particular, consider the following questions.

Questions

1. Would the poison pill be legal in the UK?

2. Would other takeover defenses that we have encountered (think of the board actions in *Unocal* and *Revlon*) be legal in the UK?

3. If not, what other rules, if any, protect UK shareholders?

4. Who makes the rules?

5. What is the role of the courts?

1. The City Code on Takeovers and Mergers (UK)

Section A: Introduction

§ 1: Overview

The Panel on Takeovers and Mergers (the "Panel") is an independent body, established in 1968, whose main functions are to issue and administer the City Code on Takeovers and Mergers (the "Code") and to supervise and regulate takeovers and other matters to which the Code applies in accordance with the rules set out in the Code. [Its] statutory functions are set out in and under Chapter 1 of Part 28 of the Companies Act 2006 [...] (the "Act") [...]

§ 2: The Code

[...]

(a) Nature and purpose of the Code

The Code is designed principally to ensure that shareholders in an offeree company are treated fairly and are not denied an opportunity to decide on the merits of a takeover and that shareholders in the offeree company of the same class are afforded equivalent treatment by an offeror. The Code also provides an orderly framework within which takeovers are conducted. In addition, it is designed to promote, in conjunction with other regulatory regimes, the integrity of the financial markets.

The Code is not concerned with the financial or commercial advantages or disadvantages of a takeover. These are matters for the offeree company and its shareholders. In addition, it is not the purpose of the Code either to facilitate or to impede takeovers. Nor is the Code concerned with those issues, such as competition policy, which are the responsibility of government and other bodies.

The Code has been developed since 1968 to reflect the collective opinion of those professionally involved in the field of takeovers as to appropriate business standards and as to how fairness to offeree company shareholders and an orderly framework for takeovers can be achieved. The rules set out in the Code have a statutory basis in relation to the United Kingdom and comply with the relevant requirements of the Act.

[...]

(b) General Principles and Rules

The Code is based upon a number of General Principles, which are essentially statements of standards of commercial behaviour. These General Principles are the same as the general principles set out in Part 1 of Schedule 1C to the Act. They apply to takeovers and other matters to which the Code applies. They are expressed in broad general terms and the Code does not define the precise extent of, or the limitations on, their application. They are applied in accordance with their spirit in order to achieve their underlying purpose.

In addition to the General Principles, the Code contains a series of rules. Although most of the rules are expressed in less general terms than the General Principles, they are not framed in technical language and, like the General Principles, are to be interpreted to achieve their underlying purpose. Therefore, their spirit must be observed as well as their letter.

(c) Derogations and Waivers

The Panel may derogate or grant a waiver to a person from the application of a rule (providedthat the General Principles are respected) either:

(i) in the circumstances set out in the rule; or

(ii) in other circumstances where the Panel considers that the particular rule would operate unduly harshly or in an unnecessarily restrictive or burdensome or otherwise inappropriate manner (in which case a reasoned decision will be given).

[...]

§ 4: The Panel and its Committees

[...]

(a) The Panel

The Panel assumes overall responsibility for the policy, financing and administration of the Panel's functions and for the functioning and operation of the Code. The Panel operates through a number of Committees and is directly responsible for those matters which are not dealt with through one of its Committees.

The Panel comprises up to 35 members:

(i) the Chair, who is appointed by the Panel;

(ii) up to three Deputy Chairs, who are appointed by the Panel;

(iii) up to twenty other members, who are appointed by the Panel; and

(iv) individuals appointed by each of the following bodies:

The Association for Financial Markets in Europe

The Association of British Insurers

The Association of Investment Companies

The Confederation of British Industry

The Institute of Chartered Accountants in England and Wales

The Investment Association

The Pensions and Lifetime Savings Association

The Personal Investment Management and Financial Advice Association

The Quoted Companies Alliance

UK Finance (with a separate appointee also for its Corporate Finance Committee).

[...]

§ 5: The Executive

[...]

The day-to-day work of takeover supervision and regulation is carried out by the Executive. In carrying out these functions, the Executive operates independently of the Panel. This includes, either on its own initiative or at the instigation of third parties, the conduct of investigations, the monitoring of relevant dealings in connection with the Code and the giving of rulings on the interpretation, application or effect of the Code. The Executive is available both for consultation and also the giving of rulings on the interpretation, application or effect of the Code before, during and, where appropriate, after takeovers or other relevant transactions.

The Executive is staffed by a mixture of employees and secondees from law firms, accountancy firms, corporate brokers, investment banks and other organisations. It is headed by the Director General, usually an investment banker on secondment, who is an officer of the Panel [...]

§ 6: Interpreting the Code

[...]

(a) Interpreting the Code — guidance

The Executive may be approached for general guidance on the interpretation or effect of the Code and how it is usually applied in practice. It may also be approached for guidance in relation to a specific issue on a "no names" basis, where the person seeking the guidance does not disclose to the Executive the names of the companies concerned. In either case, the guidance given by the Executive is not binding [...]

(b) Interpreting the Code — rulings of the Executive and the requirement for consultation

When a person or its advisers are in any doubt whatsoever as to whether a proposed course of conduct is in accordance with the General Principles or the rules, or whenever a waiver or derogation from the application of the provisions of the Code is sought, that person or its advisers must consult the Executive in advance. In this way, they can obtain a ruling as to the basis on which they can properly proceed and thus minimise the risk of taking action which might, in the event, be a breach of the Code. To take legal or other professional advice on the interpretation, application or effect of the Code is not an appropriate alternative to obtaining a ruling from the Executive [...]

§ 10: Enforcing the Code

[...]

(b) Compliance rulings

If the Panel is satisfied that:

(i) there is a reasonable likelihood that a person will contravene a requirement imposed by or under rules; or

(ii) a person has contravened a requirement imposed by or under rules,

the Panel may give any direction that appears to it to be necessary in order:

(A) to restrain a person from acting (or continuing to act) in breach of rules; or

(B) to restrain a person from doing (or continuing to do) a particular thing, pending determination of whether that or any other conduct of the person is or would be a breach of rules; or

(C) otherwise to secure compliance with rules.

(c) Compensation rulings

Where a person has breached the requirements of any of Rule 6, Rule 9, Rule 11, Rule 14, Rule 15, Rule 16.1 or Rule 35.3 of the Code, the Panel may make a ruling requiring the person concerned to pay, within such period as is specified, to the holders, or former holders, of securities of the offeree company such amount as it thinks just and reasonable so as to ensure that such holders receive what they would have been entitled to receive if the relevant Rule had been complied with. ...

§ 11: Disciplinary Powers

[...]

(a) Disciplinary action

The Executive may itself deal with a disciplinary matter where the person who is to be subject to the disciplinary action agrees the facts and the action proposed by the Executive. In any other case, where it considers that there has been a breach of the Code or of a ruling of the Executive, the Hearings Committee and/or the Board, the Executive may commence disciplinary proceedings before the Hearings Committee. [...]

(b) Sanctions or other remedies for breach of the Code

If the Hearings Committee finds a breach of the Code or of a ruling of the Executive, the Hearings Committee and/or the Board, it may:

(i) issue a private statement of censure; or

(ii) issue a public statement of censure; or(iii) suspend or withdraw any exemption, approval or other special status which the Panel has granted to a person, or impose conditions on the continuing enjoyment of such exemption, approval or special status, in respect of all or part of the activities to which such exemption, approval or special status relates; or

[...]

(iv) report the offender's conduct to a United Kingdom or overseas regulatory authority or professional body ... so that that authority or body can consider whether to take disciplinary or enforcement action [...] or

(v) publish a Panel Statement indicating that the offender is someone who, in the Hearings Committee's opinion, is not likely to comply with the Code. The Panel Statement will normally indicate that this sanction will remain effective for only a specified period. [...]

Section B: General Principles

1. (1) All holders of the securities of an offeree company of the same class must be afforded equivalent treatment.

(2) If a person acquires control of a company, the other holders of securities must be protected.

2. (1) The holders of the securities of an offeree company must have sufficient time and information to enable them to reach a properly informed decision on the bid.

(2) Where it advises the holders of securities, the board of the offeree company must give its views on the effects of implementation of the bid on:

(a) employment;

(b) conditions of employment; and

(c) the locations of the company's places of business.

3. The board of an offeree company must act in the interests of the company as a whole and must not deny the holders of securities the opportunity to decide on the merits of the takeover bid.

4. False markets must not be created in the securities of:

(a) the offeree company;

(b) if the offeror is a company, that company; or

(c) any other company concerned by the takeover bid

in such a way that the rise or fall of the prices of the securities becomes artificial and the normal functioning of the markets is distorted.

5. An offeror must announce a bid only after:

(a) ensuring that offeror can fulfil in full any cash consideration, if such is offered; and

(b) taking all reasonable measures to secure the implementation of any other type of consideration.

6. An offeree company must not be hindered in the conduct of its affairs for longer than is reasonable by a takeover bid for its securities.

Section C: Definitions

[...]

Offer period

[...] An offer period will commence when the first announcement is made of an offer or possible offer for a company, or when certain other announcements are made, such as an announcement that a purchaser is being sought for an interest in shares carrying 30% or more of the voting rights of the company or that the board of the company is seeking potential offerors.

[...] [A]n offer period will end when an announcement is made that an offer has become or has been declared unconditional [...] that all announced offers have been withdrawn or have lapsed or following certain other announcements having been made ...

Section D: The Approach, Announcements, and Independent Advice

Rule 1: The Approach

(a) An offeror (or its advisers) must notify a firm intention to make an offer in the first instance to the board of the offeree company (or its advisers).

[...]

Rule 2: Secrecy Before Announcements; The Timing and Contents of Announcements

2.1: Secrecy

(a) Prior to the announcement of an offer or possible offer, all persons privy to confidential information, and particularly price-sensitive information, concerning the offer or possible offer must treat that information as secret and may only pass it to another person if it is necessary to do so and if that person is made aware of the need for secrecy. All such persons must conduct themselves so as to minimise the chances of any leak of information. [...]

2.2: When an Announcement is Required

An announcement is required:

(a) when a firm intention to make an offer is notified to the board of the offeree company by or on behalf of an offeror, irrespective of the attitude of the board to the offer;

(b) immediately upon an acquisition of any interest in shares which gives rise to an obligation to make an offer under Rule 9.1. [...]

(c) when, following an approach by or on behalf of a potential offeror to the board of the offeree company, the offeree company is the subject of rumour and speculation or there is an untoward movement in its share price;

(d) when, after a potential offeror first actively considers an offer but before an approach has been made to the board of the offeree company, the offeree company is the subject of rumour and speculation or there is an untoward movement in its share price and there are reasonable grounds for concluding that it is the potential offeror's actions (whether through inadequate security or otherwise) which have led to the situation;

(e) when negotiations or discussions relating to a possible offer are about to be extended to include more than a very restricted number of people (outside those who need to know in the parties concerned and their immediate advisers); or

(f) when a purchaser is being sought for an interest, or interests, in shares carrying in aggregate 30% or more of the voting rights of a company or when the board of a company is seeking one or more potential offerors, and:

(i) the company is the subject of rumour and speculation or there is an untoward movement in its share price; or

(ii) the number of potential purchasers or offerors approached is about to be increased to include more than a very restricted number of people. [...]

2.6: Timing Following a Possible Offer Announcement

(a) Subject to Rule 2.6(b), by not later than 5.00 pm on the 28th day following the date of the announcement in which it is first identified, or by not later than any extended deadline, a potential offeror must either:

(i) announce a firm intention to make an offer [...] or

(ii) announce that it does not intend to make an offer [...]

unless the Panel has consented to an extension of the deadline.

(b) Rule 2.6(a) will not apply [...] to a potential offeror if another offeror has already announced, or subsequently announces [...] a firm intention to make an offer for the offeree company. [...]

(c) The Panel will normally consent to an extension of a deadline [...] at the request of the board of the offeree company and after taking into account all relevant factors, including:

(i) the status of negotiations between the offeree company and the potential offeror; and

(ii) the anticipated timetable for their completion. [...]

2.7 The Announcement of a Firm Intention to Make an Offer

[...]

(b) Following an announcement of a firm intention to make an offer, the offeror must proceed to make the offer unless, in accordance with the provisions of Rule 13, it is permitted to invoke a pre-condition to the making of the offer or would be permitted to invoke a condition to the offer if the offer were made. [...]

Section E: Restrictions on Dealings

[...]

Rule 6: Acquisitions Resulting in an Obligation to Offer a Minimum Level of Consideration

6.1: Acquisitions Before a Firm Offer Announcement

(a) Except with the consent of the Panel in cases falling under (i) or (ii), when an offeror or any person acting in concert with it has acquired an interest in shares in the offeree company:

(i) within the three month period prior to the commencement of the offer period; or

(ii) during the period, if any, between the commencement of the offer period and an announcement made by the offeror [...] or

(iii) prior to the three month period referred to in (a), if in the view of the Panel there are circumstances which render such a course necessary in order to give effect to General Principle 1,

the offer to the holders of shares of the same class shall not be on less favourable terms. [...]

6.2: Acquisitions after a Firm Offer Announcement

(a) If, after an announcement made [...] and before the offer closes for acceptance, an offeror or any person acting in concert with it acquires any interest in shares at above the offer price (being the then current value of the offer), it shall increase its offer to not less than the highest price paid for the interest in shares so acquired. [...]

Section F: The Mandatory Offer and Its Terms

Rule 9

9.1: When a Mandatory Offer is Required and Who is Primarily Responsible for Making It

Except with the consent of the Panel, when:

(a) any person acquiresan interest in shares which (taken together with shares in which the person or persons acting in concert with that person are interested) carry 30% or more of the voting rights of a company; or

(b) any person, together with persons acting in concert with that person, is interested in shares which in the aggregate carry not less than 30% of the voting rights of a company but does not hold shares carrying more than 50% of such voting rights and such person, or any person acting in concert with that person, acquires an interest in any other shares which increases the percentage of shares carrying voting rights in which that person is interested,

such person shall extend offers, on the basis set out in Rules 9.3, 9.4 and 9.5, to the holders of any class of equity share capital [...]

An offer will not be required under this Rule where control of the offeree company is acquired as a result of a voluntary offer made in accordance with the Code to all the holders of voting equity share capital [...]

9.3: Conditions and Consents

[...]

Except with the consent of the Panel...an offer made under Rule 9 must be conditional only upon the offeror having received acceptances in respect of shares which, together with shares acquired or agreed to be acquired before or during the offer, will result in the offeror and any person acting in concert with it holding shares carrying more than 50% of the voting rights; [...]

9.5: Consideration to be Offered

(a) An offer made under Rule 9 must, in respect of each class of share capital involved, be in cash or be accompanied by a cash alternative at not less than the highest price paid by the offeror or any person acting in concert with it for any interest in shares of that class during the 12 months prior to the announcement of that offer. ...

Section G: The Voluntary Offer and Its Terms

[...]

Rule 11: Nature of Consideration to be Offered

11.1: When a Cash Offer is Required

Except with the consent of the Panel in cases falling under (a) or (b), a cash offer is required where:

(a) the shares of any class under offer in the offeree company in which interests are acquired for cash (but see Note 5) by an offeror and any person acting in concert with it during the offer period and within 12 months prior to its commencement represent 10% or more of the shares of that class in issue, in which case the offer for that class shall be in cash or accompanied by a cash alternative at not less than the highest price paid by the offeror or any person acting in concert with it for any interest in shares of that class acquired during the offer period and within 12 months prior to its commencement; or

(b) subject to paragraph (a) above, any interest in shares of any class under offer in the offeree company is acquired for cash [...] by an offeror or any person acting in concert with it during the offer period, in which case the offer for that class shall be in cash or accompanied by a cash alternative at not less than the highest price paid by the offeror or any person acting in concert with it for any interest in shares of that class acquired during the offer period; or

(c) in the view of the Panel there are circumstances which render such a course necessary in order to give effect to General Principle 1. [...]

11.2: When a Securities Offer is Required

(a) Where interests in shares of any class of the offeree company representing 10% or more of the shares of that class in issue have been acquired by an offeror and any person acting in concert with it in exchange for securities in the three months prior to the commencement of and during the offer period, such securities will normally be required to be offered to all other holders of shares of that class. [...]

Rule 13: Pre-conditions in Firm Offer Announcements and Offer Conditions

13.1: Subjectivity

An offer must not normally be subject to conditions or pre-conditions which depend solely on subjective judgements by the offeror or the offeree company (as the case may be) or, in either case, its directors or the fulfilment of which is in their hands. The Panel may be prepared to accept an element of subjectivity in certain circumstances where it is not practicable to specify all the factors on which satisfaction of a particular condition or pre-condition may depend, especially in cases involving official authorisations or regulatory clearances, the granting of which may be subject to additional material obligations for the offeror or the offeree company (as the case may be). [...]

13.4: Financing Conditions and Pre-conditions

(a) [...] an offer must not be made subject to a condition or pre-condition relating to financing.

[...]

Section I: Conduct During the Offer

[...]

Rule 21: Restrictions on Frustrating Action

21.1: When Shareholders' Consent is Required

(a) During the course of an offer, or even before the date of the offer if the board of the offeree company has reason to believe that a bona fide offer might be imminent, the board must not, without the approval of the shareholders in general meeting: take any action which may result in any offer or bona fide possible offer being frustrated or in shareholders being denied the opportunity to decide on its merits; or

(i) issue any shares or transfer or sell, or agree to transfer or sell, any shares out of treasury or effect any redemption or purchase by the company of its own shares;

(ii) issue or grant options in respect of any unissued shares;

(iii) create or issue, or permit the creation or issue of, any securities carrying rights of conversion into or subscription for shares;

(iv) sell, dispose of or acquire, or agree to sell, dispose of or acquire, assets of a material amount; or

(v) enter into contracts otherwise than in the ordinary course of business.

(b) The Panel must be consulted in advance if there is any doubt as to whether any proposed action may fall within Rule 21.1(a).

(c) The Panel will normally agree to disapply Rule 21.1(a) if:

(i) the taking of the proposed action is conditional on the offer being withdrawn or lapsing (see also Rule 21.1(e));

(ii) the offeror consents to the action proposed to be taken by the board of the offeree company;

(iii) holders of shares carrying more than 50% of the voting rights of the offeree company state in writing that they approve the proposed action and would vote in favour of any resolution to that effect proposed at a general meeting;

(iv) the proposed action is in pursuance of a contract entered into before the beginning of the period referred to in Rule 21.1(a) or another pre-existing obligation; or

(v) a decision to take the proposed action had been taken before the beginning of the period referred to in Rule 21.1(a) which:

(A) has been partly or fully implemented before the beginning of that period; or

(B) has not been partly or fully implemented before the beginning of that period but is in the ordinary course of business.

(d) Where shareholder approval is to be sought in general meeting for a proposed action in accordance with Rule 21.1(a):

(i) the board of the offeree company must obtain competent independent advice as to whether the financial terms of the proposed action are fair and reasonable;

[...]

21.2 Offer-Related Arrangements

(a) Except with the consent of the Panel, neither the offeree company nor any person acting in concert with it may enter into any offer-related arrangement with either the offeror or any person acting in concert with it during an offer period or when an offer is reasonably in contemplation.

(b) An offer-related arrangement means any agreement, arrangement or commitment in connection with an offer, including any inducement fee arrangement or other arrangement having a similar or comparable financial or economic effect [...]

Notes on Rule 21.2

1. Competing offerors

Where an offeror has announced a firm intention to make an offer which was not recommended by the board of the offeree company at the time of that announcement and remains not recommended, the Panel will normally consent to the offeree company entering into an inducement fee arrangement with a competing offeror at the time of the announcement of its firm intention to make a competing offer, provided that:

(a) the aggregate value of the inducement fee or fees that may be payable by the offeree company is de minimis, i.e. normally no more than 1% of the value of the offeree company [...]

2. Formal sale process

Where, prior to an offeror having announced a firm intention to make an offer, the board of the offeree company announces that it is seeking one or more potential offerors by means of a formal sale process, the Panel will normally grant a dispensation from the prohibition in Rule 21.2, such that the offeree company would be permitted, subject to the same provisos as set out in Note 1(a) and (b) above, to enter into an inducement fee arrangement with one offeror (who had participated in that process) at the time of the announcement of its firm intention to make an offer. [...]

Section P: Partial Offers

Rule 36

36.1: Panel's Consent Required

The Panel's consent is required for any partial offer. In the case of an offer which could not result in the offeror and persons acting in concert with it being interested in shares carrying 30% or more of the voting rights of a company, consent will normally be granted. [...]

36.3: Acquisitions During and After the Offer

The offeror and persons acting in concert with it may not acquire any interest in shares in the offeree company during the offer period. [...]

2. Companies Act 2006 ss. 979(2), 983(2) (UK)

Section 979. Right of offeror to buy out minority shareholder ["Squeeze-Out"]

(2) If the offeror has, by virtue of acceptances of the offer, acquired or unconditionally contracted to acquire—

(a) not less than 90% in value of the shares to which the offer relates, and

(b) in a case where the shares to which the offer relates are voting shares, not less than 90% of the voting rights carried by those shares,

he may give notice to the holder of any shares to which the offer relates which the offeror has not acquired or unconditionally contracted to acquire that he desires to acquire those shares.

Section 983. Right of minority shareholder to be bought out by offeror ["Sell-Out"]

(2) The holder of any voting shares to which the offer relates who has not accepted the offer may require the offeror to acquire those shares if, at any time before the end of the period within which the offer can be accepted—

(a) the offeror has by virtue of acceptances of the offer acquired or unconditionally contracted to acquire some (but not all) of the shares to which the offer relates, and

(b) those shares, with or without any other shares in the company which he has acquired or contracted to acquire (whether unconditionally or subject to conditions being met)—

(i) amount to not less than 90% in value of all the voting shares in the company (or would do so but for section 990(1)), and

(ii) carry not less than 90% of the voting rights in the company (or would do so but for section 990(1)).

3. FCA Disclosure & Transparency Rule 5 (UK)

[Eds: Italicized words in the rule are terms that are defined in the glossary of the handbook.]

DTR 5.1.2. [...] a *person* must notify the *issuer* of the percentage of its voting rights he holds as *shareholder* or holds or is deemed to hold through his direct or indirect holding of *financial instruments* falling within DTR 5.3.1R (1) [...] (or a combination of such holdings) if the percentage of those voting rights: (1) reaches, exceeds or falls below 3%, 4%, 5%, 6%, 7%, 8%, 9%, 10% and each 1% threshold thereafter up to 100% [...] as a result of an acquisition or disposal of *shares* or *financial instruments* falling within DTR 5.3.1 R2; [...]

DTR 5.8.3. The notification to the *issuer* shall be effected as soon as possible, but not later than four *trading days* in the case of a non-UK issuer and two *trading days* in all other cases, after the date on which the relevant *person*:(1) learns of the acquisition or disposal or of the possibility of exercising voting rights, or on which, having regard to the circumstances, should have learned of it, regardless of the date on which the acquisition, disposal or possibility of exercising voting rights takes effect [...]

DTR 5.9. (1) A *person* making a notification to an *issuer* to which this chapter applies must, if the notification relates to *shares* admitted to trading on a *regulated market*, at the same time file a copy of such notification with the *FCA*. [...]

Part IV: Shareholder Voting

Chapter 9. The Problem of Incumbent Control

We will now dive deeper into critical aspects of shareholder voting. We begin with incumbents' control of the voting process, specifically its potential for abuse.

A. Schnell v. Chris-Craft Industries, Inc. (Del. 1971)

Questions

1. What is the basis for the Supreme Court's decision?
2. Does this basis constrain or at least guide the Supreme Court? Or can the Court do whatever it wants?

285 A.2d 437 (1971)

Andrew H. SCHNELL, Jr. and Jack Safer, Plaintiffs Below,
Appellants,
v.
CHRIS-CRAFT INDUSTRIES, INC., a Delaware corporation,
Defendant Below, Appellee.

Supreme Court of Delaware.
November 29, 1971.

H. Albert Young and Edward B. Maxwell, 2nd, of Young, Conaway, Stargatt & Taylor, Wilmington, and Carl F. Goodman, New York City, and Jay L. Westbrook, of Surrey, Karasik & Greene, Washington, D. C., for plaintiffs below, appellants.

David F. Anderson and Charles S. Crompton, Jr., of Potter, Anderson & Corroon, Wilmington, and Arthur L. Liman and Daniel P. Levitt, of Paul, Weiss, Rifkind, Wharton & Garrison, New York City, and Washington, D. C., for defendant below, appellee.

Before WOLCOTT, C.J., and CAREY and HERRMANN, Associate Justices: [438]

HERRMANN, Justice (for the majority of the Court):

This is an appeal from the denial by the Court of Chancery of the petition of dissident stockholders for injunctive relief to prevent management* from advancing the date of the annual stockholders' meeting from January 11, 1972, as previously set by the by-laws, to December 8, 1971.

The opinion below is reported at 285 A.2d 430. This opinion is confined to the frame of reference of the opinion below for the sake of brevity and because of the strictures of time imposed by the circumstances of the case.

[Eds—The Chancellor had stated the most pertinent facts as follows:

> Plaintiffs, who are stockholders of the defendant, seek a preliminary injunction against the carrying out by such corporation of a change in the date of its annual meeting of stockholders which was ostensibly accomplished by an amendment to its by-laws adopted at a directors' meeting held on October 18, 1971. As a result of such change in by-law and the fixing of a new date by the directors, such annual meeting is now scheduled to be held on December 8, 1971 instead of on the date fixed in the by-law in question before its amendment, namely the second Tuesday in January, 1972. Plaintiffs ... are dissatisfied with defendant's recent business performance ... Accordingly, they have embarked on a proxy contest against present management with the purpose in mind of electing new directors and installing new management at Chris-Craft. ... Plaintiffs contend that by advancing the date of defendant's annual meeting by over a month and by the selection of an allegedly isolated town in up-state New York as the place for such meeting, defendant's board has deliberately sought to handicap the efforts of plaintiffs and other stockholders sympathetic to plaintiffs' views adequately to place their case before their fellow stockholders for decision because of the exigencies of time.]

It will be seen that the Chancery Court considered all of the reasons stated by management as business reasons for changing the date of the meeting; but that those reasons were rejected by the Court below in making the following findings:

---

* We use this word as meaning "managing directors".

"I am satisfied, however, in a situation in which present management has disingenuously resisted the production of a list of its stockholders to plaintiffs or their confederates and has otherwise turned a deaf ear to plaintiffs' demands about a change in management designed to lift defendant from its present business [439] doldrums, management has seized on a relatively new section of the Delaware Corporation Law for the purpose of cutting down on the amount of time which would otherwise have been available to plaintiffs and others for the waging of a proxy battle. Management thus enlarged the scope of its scheduled October 18 directors' meeting to include the by-law amendment in controversy after the stockholders committee had filed with the S.E.C. its intention to wage a proxy fight on October 16.

"Thus plaintiffs reasonably contend that because of the tactics employed by management (which involve the hiring of two established proxy solicitors as well as a refusal to produce a list of its stockholders, coupled with its use of an amendment to the Delaware Corporation Law to limit the time for contest), they are given little chance, because of the exigencies of time, including that required to clear material at the S.E.C., to wage a successful proxy fight between now and December 8. * * *."

In our view, those conclusions amount to a finding that management has attempted to utilize the corporate machinery and the Delaware Law for the purpose of perpetuating itself in office; and, to that end, for the purpose of obstructing the legitimate efforts of dissident stockholders in the exercise of their rights to undertake a proxy contest against management. These are inequitable purposes, contrary to established principles of corporate democracy. The advancement by directors of the by-law date of a stockholders' meeting, for such purposes, may not be permitted to stand. Compare Condec Corporation v. Lunkenheimer Company, Del.Ch., 230 A.2d 769 (1967).

When the by-laws of a corporation designate the date of the annual meeting of stockholders, it is to be expected that those who intend to contest the reelection of incumbent management will gear their campaign to the by-law date. It is not to be expected that management will attempt to advance that date in order to obtain an inequitable advantage in the contest.

Management contends that it has complied strictly with the provisions of the new Delaware Corporation Law in changing the by-law date. The answer to that contention, of course, is that inequitable action does not become permissible simply because it is legally possible.

Management relies upon American Hardware Corp. v. Savage Arms Corp., 37 Del.Ch. 10, 135 A.2d 725, aff'd 37 Del.Ch. 59, 136 A.2d 690 (1957). That case is inapposite for two reasons: it involved an effort by stockholders, engaged in a proxy contest, to have the stockholders' meeting adjourned and the period for the proxy contest enlarged; and there was no finding there of inequitable action on the part of management. We agree with the rule of American Hardware that, in the absence of fraud or inequitable conduct, the date for a stockholders' meeting and notice thereof, duly established under the by-laws, will not be enlarged by judicial interference at the request of dissident stockholders solely because of the circumstance of a proxy contest. That, of course, is not the case before us.

We are unable to agree with the conclusion of the Chancery Court that the stockholders' application for injunctive relief here was tardy and came too late. The stockholders learned of the action of management unofficially on Wednesday, October 27, 1971; they filed this action on Monday, November 1, 1971. Until management changed the date of the meeting, the stockholders had no need of judicial assistance in that connection. There is no indication of any prior warning of management's intent to take such action; indeed, it appears that an attempt was made by management to conceal its action as long as possible. Moreover, stockholders may not be charged with the duty of anticipating inequitable action by management, and of seeking anticipatory injunctive relief to foreclose such action, simply because the [440] new Delaware Corporation Law makes such inequitable action legally possible.

Accordingly, the judgment below must be reversed and the cause remanded, with instructions to nullify the December 8 date as a meeting date for stockholders; to reinstate January 11, 1972 as the sole date of the next annual meeting of the stockholders of the corporation; and to take such other proceedings and action as may be consistent herewith regarding the stock record closing date and any other related matters.

WOLCOTT, Chief Justice (dissenting):

I do not agree with the majority of the Court in its disposition of this appeal. The plaintiff stockholders concerned in this litigation have, for a considerable period of time, sought to obtain control of the defendant corporation. These attempts took various forms.

In view of the length of time leading up to the immediate events which caused the filing of this action, I agree with the Vice Chancellor that the application for injunctive relief came too late.

I would affirm the judgment below on the basis of the Vice Chancellor's opinion.

B. Blasius Industries, Inc. v. Atlas Corp. (Del. Ch. 1988)

Questions

1. In what way does *Blasius* not only apply but expand on *Schnell*?
2. Is the vote at issue a normal vote taken at a meeting?
3. What did the Atlas board do to frustrate the vote, and why would that work?
4. What exactly does Chancellor Allen have to say about corporate voting—what is it about voting that is important?
5. Does Allen's discussion of voting, its importance, and its judicial treatment matter for the ultimate outcome of the case here?
6. If not, why would he have bothered?

564 A.2d 651 (1988)

BLASIUS INDUSTRIES, INC., [...]

v.

ATLAS CORPORATION, [...]

Court of Chancery of Delaware, New Castle County.

Submitted: June 6, 1988.

Decided: July 25, 1988.

[...]

OPINION

ALLEN, Chancellor.

Two cases pitting the directors of Atlas Corporation against that company's largest (9.1%) shareholder, Blasius Industries, have been consolidated and tried together. Together, these cases ultimately require the court to determine who is entitled to sit on Atlas' board of directors. Each, however, presents discrete and important legal issues.

The first of the cases was filed on December 30, 1987. As amended, it challenges the validity of board action taken at a telephone meeting of December 31, 1987 that added two new members to Atlas' seven member board. That action was taken as an immediate response to the delivery to Atlas by Blasius the previous day of a form of stockholder consent that, if joined in by holders of a majority of Atlas' stock, would have increased the board of Atlas from seven to fifteen members and would have elected eight new members nominated by Blasius.

As I find the facts of this first case, they present the question whether a board acts consistently with its fiduciary duty when it acts, in good faith and with appropriate care, for the primary purpose of preventing or impeding an unaffiliated majority of shareholders from expanding the board and electing a new majority. For the reasons that follow, I conclude that, even though defendants here acted on their view of the corporation's interest and not selfishly, their December 31 action constituted an offense to the relationship between corporate directors and shareholders that has traditionally been protected in courts of equity. As a consequence, I conclude that the board action taken on December 31 was invalid and must be voided. [...]

The second filed action was commenced on March 9, 1988. It arises out of the consent solicitation itself (or an amended [653] version of it) and requires the court to determine the outcome of Blasius' consent solicitation, which was warmly and actively contested on both sides. The vote was, on either view of the facts and law, extremely close. For the reasons set forth at pages 663-670 below, I conclude that the judges of election properly confined their count to the written "ballots" (so to speak) before them; that on that basis, they made several errors, but that correction of those errors does not reverse the result they announced. I therefore conclude that plaintiffs' consent solicitation failed to garner the support of a majority of Atlas shares.

The facts set forth below represent findings based upon a preponderance of the admissible evidence, as I evaluate it.

I.

Blasius Acquires a 9% Stake in Atlas.

Blasius is a new stockholder of Atlas. It began to accumulate Atlas shares for the first time in July, 1987. On October 29, it filed a Schedule 13D with the Securities Exchange Commission disclosing that, with affiliates, it then owed 9.1% of Atlas' common stock.[♦] It stated in that filing that it intended to encourage management of Atlas to consider a restructuring of the Company or other transaction to enhance shareholder values. It also disclosed that Blasius was exploring the feasibility of obtaining control of Atlas, including instituting a tender offer or seeking "appropriate" representation on the Atlas board of directors.

♦ Under section 13(d) of the Securities Exchange Act, anyone acquiring 5% of (any class of) a corporation's voting stock must within ten days file a Schedule 13D disclosing this and any subsequent acquisitions.

Blasius has recently come under the control of two individuals, Michael Lubin and Warren Delano [...]. Since then, [Lubin and Delano] have made several attempts to effect leveraged buyouts,[♦♦] but without success.

In May, 1987, [...] Lubin and Delano caused Blasius to raise $60 million[and] acquire a 9% position in Atlas. [...] The prospect of Messrs. Lubin and Delano involving themselves in Atlas' affairs, was not a development welcomed by Atlas' management. Atlas had a new CEO, defendant Weaver, who [...] wrote in his diary on October 30, 1987:

> 13D by Delano & Lubin came in today. Had long conversation w/MAH & Mark Golden [of Goldman, Sachs] on issue. All agree we must dilute these people down by the acquisition of another Co. w/stock, or merger or something else.

♦♦ Leveraged buyout (LBO) = a purchase financed largely with debt. The debt is usually secured by the purchased corporation's assets. LBOs became frequent and spectacularly large in the 1980s. For the LBO to succeed post-acquisition, the target corporation must produce high and steady cash flows to service the high levels of debt incurred. Otherwise, the target will end up in bankruptcy.

The Blasius Proposal of A Leverage Recapitalization Or Sale.

Immediately after filing its 13D on October 29, Blasius' representatives sought a meeting with the Atlas management. Atlas dragged its feet. A meeting was arranged for December 2, 1987 following the regular meeting of the Atlas board. Attending that meeting were Messrs. Lubin and Delano for Blasius, and, for Atlas, Messrs. Weaver, Devaney (Atlas' CFO), Masinter (legal counsel and director) and Czajkowski (a representative of Atlas' investment banker, Goldman Sachs).

[654] At that meeting, Messrs. Lubin and Delano suggested that Atlas engage in a leveraged restructuring and distribute cash to shareholders. In such a transaction, which is by this date a commonplace form of transaction, a corporation typically raises cash by sale of assets and significant borrowings and makes a large one time cash distribution to shareholders. The shareholders are typically left with cash and an equity interest in a smaller, more highly leveraged enterprise. Lubin and Delano gave the outline of a leveraged recapitalization for Atlas as they saw it.

Immediately following the meeting, the Atlas representatives expressed among themselves an initial reaction that the proposal was infeasible. On December 7, Mr. Lubin sent a letter detailing the proposal. [...]

Atlas Asks Its Investment Banker to Study the Proposal.

This written proposal was distributed to the Atlas board on December 9 and Goldman Sachs was directed to review and analyze it.

[...]

Blasius attempted on December 14 and December 22 to arrange a further meeting with the Atlas management without success. During this period, Atlas provided Goldman Sachs with projections for the Company. Lubin was told that a further meeting would await completion of Goldman's analysis. A meeting after the first of the year was proposed.

The Delivery of Blasius' Consent Statement.

On December 30, 1987, Blasius caused Cede & Co. (the registered owner of its Atlas stock) to deliver to Atlas a signed written consent (1) adopting a precatory resolution recommending that the board develop and implement a restructuring proposal, (2) amending the Atlas bylaws to, among other things, expand the size of the board from seven to fifteen members — the maximum number under Atlas' charter, and (3) electing eight named persons to fill the new directorships. Blasius also filed suit that day in this court seeking a declaration that certain bylaws adopted by the board on September 1, 1987 acted as an unlawful restraint on the shareholders' right, created by Section 228 of our corporation statute, to act through consent without undergoing a meeting.

The reaction was immediate. Mr. Weaver conferred with Mr. Masinter, the Company's outside counsel and a director, who viewed the consent as an attempt to take control of the Company. They decided to call an emergency meeting of the board, even though a regularly scheduled meeting was to occur only one week hence, on January [655] 6, 1988. The point of the emergency meeting was to act on their conclusion (or to seek to have the board act on their conclusion) "that we should add at least one and probably two directors to the board ..." A quorum of directors, however, could not be arranged for a telephone meeting that day. A telephone meeting was held the next day. At that meeting, the board voted to amend the bylaws to increase the size of the board from seven to nine and appointed John M. Devaney and Harry J. Winters, Jr. to fill those newly created positions. Atlas' Certificate of Incorporation creates staggered terms for directors; the terms to which Messrs. Devaney and Winters were appointed would expire in 1988 and 1990, respectively.

The Motivation of the Incumbent Board In Expanding the Board and Appointing New Members.

In increasing the size of Atlas' board by two and filling the newly created positions, the members of the board realized that they were thereby precluding the holders of a majority of the Company's shares from placing a majority of new directors on the board through Blasius' consent solicitation, should they want to do so. Indeed the evidence establishes that that was the principal motivation in so acting.

The conclusion that, in creating two new board positions on December 31 and electing Messrs. Devaney and Winters to fill those positions the board was principally motivated to prevent or delay the shareholders from possibly placing a majority of new members on the board, is critical to my analysis of the central issue posed by the first filed of the two pending cases. If the board in fact was not so motivated, but rather had taken action completely independently of the consent solicitation, which merely had an incidental impact upon the possible effectuation of any action authorized by the shareholders, it is very unlikely that such action would be subject to judicial nullification. [...] The board, as a general matter, is under no fiduciary obligation to suspend its active management of the firm while the consent solicitation process goes forward.

There is testimony in the record to support the proposition that, in acting on December 31, the board was principally motivated simply to implement a plan to expand the Atlas board that preexisted the September, 1987 emergence of Blasius as an active shareholder. [Eds: The court bases this finding on the timing of the events and on testimony indicating that the board members were aware that their actions would frustrate Blasius's attempt to gain control of the board.]

The January 6 Rejection of the Blasius Proposal.

On January 6, the board convened for its scheduled meeting. At that time, it heard a full report from its financial advisor concerning the feasibility of the Blasius restructuring proposal. [...]

The board then voted to reject the Blasius proposal. Blasius was informed of that action. The next day, Blasius caused a second, modified consent to be delivered to Atlas. A contest then ensued between the Company and Blasius for the votes of Atlas' shareholders. The facts relating to that contest, and a determination of its outcome, form the subject of the second filed lawsuit to be now decided. That matter, however, will be deferred for the moment as the facts set forth above are sufficient to frame and decide the principal remaining issue raised by the first filed action: whether the December 31 board action, in increasing the board by two and appointing members to fill those new positions, constituted, in the circumstances, an inequitable interference with the exercise of shareholder rights.

II.

Plaintiff attacks the December 31 board action as a selfishly motivated effort to protect the incumbent board from a perceived threat to its control of Atlas. Their conduct is said to constitute a violation of the principle, applied in such cases as *Schnell v. Chris Craft Industries,* Del. Supr., 285 A.2d 437 (1971), that directors hold legal powers subjected to a supervening duty to exercise such powers in good faith pursuit of what they reasonably believe to be in the corporation's interest. The December 31 action is also said to have been taken in a grossly negligent manner, since it was designed to preclude the recapitalization from being pursued, and the board had no basis at that time to make a prudent determination about the wisdom of that proposal, nor was there any emergency that required it to act in any respect regarding that proposal before putting itself in a position to do so advisedly.

Defendants, of course, contest every aspect of plaintiffs' claims. They claim the formidable protections of the business judgment rule. [...]

They say that, in creating two new board positions and filling them on December 31, they acted without a conflicting interest [658] (since the Blasius proposal did not, in any event, challenge *their* places on the board), they acted with due care (since they well knew the persons they put on the board and did not thereby preclude later consideration of the recapitalization), and they acted in good faith (since they were motivated, they say, to protect the shareholders from the threat of having an impractical, indeed a dangerous, recapitalization program foisted upon them). Accordingly, defendants assert there is no basis to conclude that their December 31 action constituted any violation of the duty of the fidelity that a director owes by reason of his office to the corporation and its shareholders.

[...]

III.

One of the principal thrusts of plaintiffs' argument is that, in acting to appoint two additional persons of their own selection, including an officer of the Company, to the board, defendants were motivated not by any view that Atlas' interest (or those of its shareholders) required that action, but rather they were motivated improperly, by selfish concern to maintain their collective control over the Company. That is, plaintiffs say that the evidence shows there was no policy dispute or issue that really motivated this action, but that asserted policy differences were pretexts for entrenchment for selfish reasons. If this were found to be factually true, one would not need to inquire further. The action taken would constitute a breach of duty. *Schnell v. Chris Craft Industries*, Del.Supr., 285 A.2d 437 (1971); *Guiricich v. Emtrol Corp.*, Del.Supr., 449 A.2d 232 (1982).

In support of this view, plaintiffs point to the early diary entry of Mr. Weaver (p. 653, *supra*), to the lack of any consideration at all of the Blasius recapitalization proposal at the December 31 meeting, the lack of any substantial basis for the outside directors to have had any considered view on the subject by that time — not having had any view from Goldman Sachs nor seen the financial data that it regarded as necessary to evaluate the proposal — and upon what it urges is the grievously flawed, slanted analysis that Goldman Sachs finally did present.

While I am satisfied that the evidence is powerful, indeed compelling, that the board was chiefly motivated on December 31 to forestall or preclude the possibility that a majority of shareholders might place on the Atlas board eight new members sympathetic to the Blasius proposal, it is less clear with respect to the more subtle motivational question: whether the existing members of the board did so because they held a good faith belief that such shareholder action would be self-injurious and shareholders needed to be protected from their own judgment.

On balance, I cannot conclude that the board was acting out of a self-interested motive in any important respect on December 31. I conclude rather that the board saw the "threat" of the Blasius recapitalization proposal as posing vital policy differences between itself and Blasius. It acted, I conclude, in a good faith effort to protect its incumbency, not selfishly, but in order to thwart implementation of the recapitalization that it feared, reasonably, would cause great injury to the Company.

The real question the case presents, to my mind, is whether, in these circumstances, the board, even if it *is* acting with subjective good faith (which will typically, if not always, be a contestable or debatable judicial conclusion), may validly act for the principal purpose of preventing the shareholders from electing a majority of new directors. The question thus posed is not one of intentional wrong (or even negligence), but one of authority *as between the fiduciary and the beneficiary* (not simply [659] legal authority, *i.e.*, as between the fiduciary and the world at large).

IV.

[...]

1. Why the deferential business judgment rule does not apply to board acts taken for the primary purpose of interfering with a stockholder's vote, even if taken advisedly and in good faith.

A. The question of legitimacy.

The shareholder franchise is the ideological underpinning upon which the legitimacy of directorial power rests. Generally, shareholders have only two protections against perceived inadequate business performance. They may sell their stock (which, if done in sufficient numbers, may so affect security prices as to create an incentive for altered managerial performance), or they may vote to replace incumbent board members.

It has, for a long time, been conventional to dismiss the stockholder vote as a vestige or ritual of little practical importance.[...] It may be that we are now witnessing the emergence of new institutional voices and arrangements that will make the stockholder vote a less predictable affair than it has been. Be that as it may, however, whether the vote is seen functionally as an unimportant formalism, or as an important tool of discipline, it is clear that it is critical to the theory that legitimates the exercise of power by some (directors and officers) over vast aggregations of property that they do not own. Thus, when viewed from a broad, institutional perspective, it can be seen that matters involving the integrity of the shareholder voting process involve consideration not present in any other context in which directors exercise delegated power.

B. Questions of this type raise issues of the allocation of authority as between the board and the shareholders.

The distinctive nature of the shareholder franchise context also appears when the matter is viewed from a less generalized, doctrinal point of view. From this point of view, as well, it appears that the ordinary considerations to which the business judgment rule originally responded are simply not present in the shareholder voting context.[2] That is, a decision by the [660] board to act for the primary purpose of preventing the effectiveness of a shareholder vote inevitably involves the question who, as between the principal and the agent, has authority with respect to a matter of internal corporate governance. That, of course, is true in a very specific way in this case which deals with the question who should constitute the board of directors of the corporation, but it will be true in every instance in which an incumbent board seeks to thwart a shareholder majority. A board's decision to act to prevent the shareholders from creating a majority of new board positions and filling them does not involve the exercise of *the corporation's power* over its property, or with respect to *its* rights or obligations; rather, it involves allocation, between shareholders as a class and the board, of effective power with respect to governance of the corporation. This need not be the case with respect to other forms of corporate action that may have an entrenchment effect [...] Action designed principally to interfere with the effectiveness of a vote inevitably involves a conflict between the board and a shareholder majority. Judicial review of such action involves a determination of the legal and equitable

---

[2] A similar concern, for credible corporate democracy, underlies those cases that strike down board action that sets or moves an annual meeting date upon a finding that such action was intended to thwart a shareholder group from effectively mounting an election campaign. *See, e.g., Schnell v. Chris Craft,* [...]

The cases invalidating stock issued for the primary purpose of diluting the voting power of a control block also reflect the law's concern that a credible form of corporate democracy be maintained. [...]

Similarly, a concern for corporate democracy is reflected (1) in our statutory requirement of annual meetings (8 *Del.C.* § 211), and in the cases that aggressively and summarily enforce that right [...,] and (2) in our consent statute (8 *Del.C.* § 228) and the interpretation it has been accorded.

obligations of an agent towards his principal. This is not, in my opinion, a question that a court may leave to the agent finally to decide so long as he does so honestly and competently; that is, it may not be left to the agent's business judgment. [...]

2. What rule does apply: per se invalidity of corporate acts intended primarily to thwart effective exercise of the franchise or is there an intermediate standard?

Plaintiff argues for a rule of *per se* invalidity once a plaintiff has established that a board has acted for the primary purpose of thwarting the exercise of a shareholder vote. [...]

A *per se* rule that would strike down, in equity, any board action taken for the primary purpose of interfering with the effectiveness of a corporate vote would have the advantage of relative clarity and predictability. It also has the advantage of most vigorously enforcing the concept of corporate democracy. The disadvantage it brings along is, of course, the disadvantage a *per se* rule always has: it may sweep too broadly.

In two recent cases dealing with shareholder votes, this court struck down board acts done for the primary purpose of impeding the exercise of stockholder voting power. In doing so, a per se rule was not applied. Rather, it was said that, in such a case, the board bears the heavy burden of demonstrating a compelling justification for such action. [...]

In my view, our inability to foresee now all of the future settings in which a board might, in good faith, paternalistically seek to thwart a shareholder vote, counsels against the adoption of a *per se* rule invalidating, in equity, every board action taken for the sole or primary purpose of thwarting a shareholder vote, even though I recognize the transcending significance of the franchise to the claims to legitimacy of our scheme of corporate governance. It may be that some set of facts would justify such extreme action. [...] This, however, is not such a case.

3. Defendants have demonstrated no sufficient justification for the action of December 31 which was intended to prevent an unaffiliated majority of shareholders from effectively exercising their right to elect eight new directors.

The board was not faced with a coercive action taken by a powerful shareholder against the interests of a distinct shareholder constituency (such as a public minority). It was presented with a consent [663] solicitation by a 9% shareholder. Moreover, here it had time (and understood that it had time) to inform the shareholders of its views on the merits of the proposal subject to stockholder vote. The only justification that can, in such a situation, be offered for the action taken is that the board knows better than do the shareholders what is in the corporation's best interest. While that premise is no doubt true for any number of matters, it is irrelevant (except insofar as the shareholders wish to be guided by the board's recommendation) when the question is who should comprise the board of directors. The theory of our corporation law confers power upon directors as the agents of the shareholders; it does not create Platonic masters. It may be that the Blasius restructuring proposal was or is unrealistic and would lead to injury to the corporation and its shareholders if pursued. Having heard the evidence, I am inclined to think it was not a sound proposal. The board certainly viewed it that way, and that view, held in good faith, entitled the board to take certain steps to evade the risk it perceived. It could, for example, expend corporate funds to inform shareholders and seek to bring them to a similar point of view. [...]But there is a vast difference between expending corporate funds to inform the electorate and exercising power for the primary purpose of foreclosing effective shareholder action. A majority of the shareholders, who were not dominated in any respect, could view the matter differently than did the board. If they do, or did, they are entitled to employ the mechanisms provided by the corporation law and the Atlas certificate of incorporation to advance that view. They are also entitled, in my opinion, to restrain their agents, the board, from acting for the principal purpose of thwarting that action.

I therefore conclude that, even finding the action taken was taken in good faith, it constituted an unintended violation of the duty of loyalty that the board owed to the shareholders. I note parenthetically that the concept of an unintended breach of the duty of loyalty is unusual but not novel. [...] That action will, therefore, be set aside by order of this court.

V.

I turn now to a discussion of the second case which is a Section 225 case designed to determine whether the nominees of Blasius were elected to an expanded Atlas board pursuant to the consent procedure. [...]

On March 6, 1988, after several rounds of mailings by each side, Blasius presented consents to the corporation purporting to adopt its five proposals. The corporation appointed an independent fiduciary (Manufacturers Hanover Trust Company) to act as judge of the stockholder vote. It reported a final tally report on March 17 and issued a Certificate of the Stockholder Vote on March 22. That certificate stated that the vote had been exceedingly close and that, as calculated by Manufacturer's Hanover, none of Blasius' proposals had succeeded. In order to be adopted by a majority of shares entitled to vote, each proposition needed to garner 1,486,293 consents. Each was about 45,000 shares short (about 1.5% of the total outstanding stock). [...]

VI.

The multilevel system of beneficial ownership of stock and the interposition of other institutional players between investors and corporations (*e.g.*, [...] brokers whose customers hold stock beneficially) renders the process of corporate voting complex. This case demonstrates that the currently employed process by which consents are solicited and counted is even more prone to problems than is the process of proxy counting. [...]

There were mistakes made by the judges [...] and by record owners and their agents; there appears to have been unauthorized and perhaps even wrongful behavior (*e.g.*, B.C. Christopher & Co.). Much of the problem arises from the perhaps thoughtless utilization of proxy contest procedures for a consent solicitation contest. But the mistakes of the judges, on balance, tend to cut against plaintiff. [...]

We cannot know, in these circumstances, what the outcome of this close contest would have been if the true wishes of all beneficial owners had been accurately measured. The parties must, in my opinion, be content with the result announced by the judges. Those mistakes that were made by the judges do not alter the outcome.

Judgment will be entered in favor of defendants. [...]

C. Coster v. UIP II (Del. 2023)

Famous though they are, *Schnell* and *Blasius* proved difficult to apply and rarely provided the decisive argument in subsequent cases. *Coster* positions *Schnell* and *Blasius* in relation to other standards of review. We expect *Coster* to become the standard framework going forward.

Please also pay attention to the facts that gave rise to *Coster*. This is one of two cases in this book (the other being *eBay*) that demonstrate conflicts that can (and frequently do) arise in closely held corporations.

Questions

1. Could the dispute have been avoided? Hint: Think back to the moment Schwat and Wout became the sole shareholders in UIP.
2. What action by the board triggered enhanced scrutiny in this case, and why?
3. Why did the court consider the board's actions preferable to the statutory rules for resolving deadlock under DGCL 226(1)(a)? Under what circumstances and conditions can boards circumvent the appointment of a guardian by means of a maneuver similar to the one used in this case?
4. The Supreme Court applies a version of the *Unocal* test to the board actions. Might a different standard of review have led to a different outcome?

5. Reflecting on the outcome of the first appeal as described in the facts of the case, can you imagine situations where a defendant's action would pass entire fairness review, but the plaintiff might still prevail under another standard of review?

MARION COSTER, Plaintiff Below, Appellant,

v.

UIP COMPANIES, INC., STEVEN SCHWAT, and SCHWAT REALTY, LLC, Defendants Below, Appellees.

Submitted: March 29, 2023

Decided: June 28, 2023

[...]

SEITZ, Chief Justice:

This appeal returns to the Supreme Court following remand. As the Court of Chancery recognized in its latest opinion, "[m]any aspects of the facts of this case were vexingly complicated or unique" and "the case gave rise to many close calls on which reasonable minds could differ." We agree with the court's assessment and appreciate its work to address the issues remanded for reconsideration. [...]

As described in our first opinion and in the Court of Chancery opinions, Marion Coster and Steven Schwat – the two UIP stockholders who each owned fifty percent of the company – deadlocked after attempting several times to elect directors. In response to the director election deadlock, Marion Coster filed a petition for appointment of a custodian for UIP. The UIP board responded by issuing stock to a long-time employee representing a one-third interest in UIP. The stock issuance diluted Coster's ownership interest, broke the deadlock, and mooted the custodian action. Coster countered by requesting that the Court of Chancery cancel the stock issuance.

After trial, the Court of Chancery found that the stock sale met the most exacting standard of judicial review under Delaware law – entire fairness. As a result, according to the court, review under any other standard was unnecessary. On appeal, we concluded that the court erred by evaluating the stock sale solely under the entire fairness standard of review. We reasoned that, even though the stock sale price might have been entirely fair, issuing stock while a contested board election was taking place interfered with Coster's voting rights as a half owner of UIP. Therefore, the court needed to conduct a further review to assess whether the board approved the stock issuance for inequitable reasons. If not, the court still had to decide whether the board, even if it acted in good faith, approved the stock sale to thwart Coster's leverage to vote against the board's director nominees and to moot the custodian action. To uphold the stock issuance under those circumstances, the board had to demonstrate a compelling justification to interfere with Coster's voting rights.

On remand, the Court of Chancery found that the UIP board had not acted for inequitable purposes and had compelling justifications for the dilutive stock issuance. Among the justifications for the stock sale was the threat that a custodian would pose to UIP due to termination provisions in many of its key contracts. It also cemented UIP's relationship with an employee critical to the success of the business.

In this second appeal after remand, Coster makes two primary arguments – first, the Court of Chancery misinterpreted *Schnell* when it restricted its review for inequitable conduct to "the limited scenario wherein the directors have no good faith basis" for board action; and second, the court erred when it found that the board had a compelling justification for the stock issuance. As explained below, the Court of Chancery did not err as a legal matter, and its factual findings are not clearly wrong. Thus, we affirm the Court of Chancery's remand decision.

I.

To recap the events leading to this appeal, UIP Companies, Inc. is a real estate services company founded in 2007 by Steven Schwat, Cornelius Bruggen, and Wout Coster ("Wout"). The company operates through various subsidiaries that provide a range of services to investment properties in the Washington, D.C. area. Many of these properties are held in special purpose entities ("SPEs") that UIP owns alongside third-party investors.

Each of the three founders initially controlled a third of UIP's shares. In 2011, Bruggen left UIP and tendered his shares to the Company at no cost. This left Schwat and Wout as half owners of UIP.

In 2013, Wout notified Schwat and Peter Bonnell, a senior UIP executive, that he had been diagnosed with leukemia. Shortly after, the group began negotiations for a buyout in which Bonnell and Heath Wilkinson, another UIP executive, would purchase Wout's shares in the company. Bonnell had previously been promised equity in UIP on multiple occasions. As the prospect for promotion had stalled, Bonnell and Wilkinson had both considered leaving UIP. Therefore, beyond providing Wout with an exit, the buyout was also useful in incentivizing Bonnell and Wilkinson to stay.

Unfortunately, negotiations were unsuccessful. While the parties agreed on a non-binding term sheet in April 2014 in which Wout would receive $2,125,000 for his half of UIP shares, the parties continued to go back and forth over the deal terms. Wout did not feel comfortable with the terms so "[n]o deal was ever finalized." Wout passed away on April 8, 2015, and his widow, Marion Coster ("Coster"), inherited his UIP interests.

Immediately after Wout's death, Schwat and Bonnell continued exploring buyout options with Coster. Discussions continued throughout 2015 with no resolution. During this time, Coster became "very distressed about her financial situation" as she had not received income distributions or the benefits she had expected. By May 2016, "Coster appeared primarily interested in a lump sum buyout or arrangement that would provide her with a consistent stream of income."

A July 2016 email reveals three "divorce" options that Bonnell had identified for Coster. These included a lump sum buyout, an installment buyout, and a distribution scheme. Seeking more information on these options and the status of any current outstanding distributions, Mike Pace, a friend of Wout and one of Coster's lawyers, reached out to Bonnell regarding the profitability of the UIP operating companies. Bonnell responded that the "companies operate close to even" and that Schwat also "ha[d] not taken any distributions . . . after Wout's passing" since "there [had not] been much positive revenue generated." As the Court of Chancery noted, "Pace did not believe that Bonnell was forthcoming about the operating companies' true profitability." Negotiations between the parties continued throughout 2016 and into 2017 as Coster sought an independent valuation of UIP.

A.

In August 2017, Coster provided UIP with a $7.3 million valuation and demanded to inspect UIP books and records. Coster followed up with a second inspection demand in October 2017. Then, "[a]fter much back and forth about the adequacy of the documents provided, on April 4, 2018, Coster called for a UIP stockholders special meeting to elect new board members." At this time, UIP had a five-member board composed of Schwat, Bonnell, and Stephen Cox, UIP's Chief Financial Officer. Two seats were vacant due to Wout's passing and Cornelius Bruggen's departure in 2011.

The stockholder meeting took place on May 22, 2018. Coster, represented by counsel, raised multiple motions affecting the size and composition of the board. Predictably, each of Coster's motions failed due to Schwat's opposition. Later that day, the UIP board reduced the number of board seats to three through unanimous written consent.

A second stockholder meeting followed on June 4, 2018. The meeting also ended in deadlock as Schwat and Coster each opposed the other's respective motions. With the deadlock, Schwat, Bonnell, and Cox remained UIP's directors.

B.

Coster filed a complaint in the Court of Chancery seeking appointment of a custodian under 8 Del. C. § 226(a)(1) (the "Custodian Action"). Coster's "complaint mainly sought to impose a neutral tie-breaker to facilitate director elections, but it also lodged allegations against Schwat" about the lack of distributions and transparency into the company's affairs. Coster "sought the appointment of a custodian with broad oversight and managerial powers."

Coster's request for a "broadly empowered" custodian rather than one specifically tailored to target the stockholder deadlock "posed new risks to the Company." As the Court of Chancery would later find, "[t]he appointment of a custodian with these powers would have given rise to broad termination rights in SPE contracts and threatened UIP's revenue stream, as UIP's business model is dependent on the continued viability of those contracts." "Facing this threat to the Company," the UIP board decided to "issue the equity that they had long promised to Bonnell." Having conducted its own valuation that "valued a 100-percent, noncontrolling equity interest in UIP at $123,869," the UIP board offered, and Bonnell purchased, a one-third interest in the company for $41,289.67 (the "Stock Sale").

The Stock Sale diluted Coster's ownership interest from one half to one third and negated her ability to block stockholder action as a half owner of the company. The Stock Sale also mooted the Custodian Action. Coster responded by filing suit and sought to cancel the Stock Sale.

C.

In its opinion following trial, the Court of Chancery upheld the Stock Sale under the entire fairness standard of review. According to the court, once the Stock Sale "satisfie[d] Delaware's most onerous standard of review," no further review was required. The deadlock broken, the court did not need to consider appointing a custodian and dismissed the action.

D.

In the first appeal, this Court did not disturb the Court of Chancery's entire fairness decision but remanded with instructions to review the Stock Sale under *Schnell* and *Blasius*. As explained in our first decision, while entire fairness is "Delaware's most onerous standard of review," it is "not [a] substitute for further equitable review" under *Schnell* or *Blasius* when the board interferes with director elections:

> In a vacuum, it might be that the price at which the board agreed to sell
> the one-third UIP equity interest to Bonnell was entirely fair, as was the

process to set the price for the stock. But "inequitable action does not become permissible simply because it is legally possible." If the board approved the Stock Sale for inequitable reasons, the Court of Chancery should have cancelled the Stock Sale. And if the board, acting in good faith, approved the Stock Sale for the "primary purpose of thwarting" Coster's vote to elect directors or reduce her leverage as an equal stockholder, it must "demonstrat[e] a compelling justification for such action" to withstand judicial scrutiny.

[...]

In the first appellate decision, we recounted the "undisputed facts or facts found by the court" that could "support the conclusion, under *Schnell*, that the UIP board approved the Stock Sale for inequitable reasons." Those facts included that "[t]he Stock Sale occurred while buyout negotiations stalled between UIP's two equal stockholders," that "[t]he Stock Sale entrenched the existing board in control of UIP," and the Court of Chancery's finding that "Defendants obviously desired to eliminate Plaintiff's ability to block stockholder action, including the election of directors, and the leverage that accompanied those rights." We recognized, however, "that the [Court of Chancery] made other findings inconsistent with this conclusion," and therefore gave the Court of Chancery the "opportunity to review all of its factual findings in any manner it sees fit in light of its new focus on *Schnell/Blasius* review."

E.

On remand, the Court of Chancery found that the UIP board had not acted for inequitable purposes under *Schnell* and had compelling justifications for the Stock Sale under *Blasius*. For Coster's *Schnell* claim, the court held that "the UIP board had multiple reasons for approving the Stock Sale" and that "the UIP board's decision did not totally lack a good faith basis." The court also found that the UIP board was primarily motivated by "retaining and rewarding Bonnell, mooting the Custodian Action, and undermining [Coster's] leverage."

Turning to *Blasius* review, the court concluded that "[i]n the exceptionally unique circumstances of this case, Defendants have met the onerous burden of demonstrating a compelling justification." The court's compelling justification analysis largely borrowed from *Unocal*'s reasonableness and proportionality test for defensive measures adopted by a board in response to a takeover threat. As the court explained:

> To satisfy the compelling justification standard, "the directors must show that their actions were reasonable in relation to their legitimate objective, and did not preclude the stockholders from exercising their right to vote or coerce them into voting a particular way." "In this

context, the shift from 'reasonable' to 'compelling' requires that the directors establish a closer fit between means and ends."

The court found that the threat posed by the Custodian Action was "an existential crisis" that justified the UIP board's actions and "that the Stock Sale was appropriately tailored to achieve the goal of mooting the Custodian Action while also achieving other important goals, such as implementing the succession plan that Wout favored and rewarding Bonnell."

II.

In her second appeal, Coster has challenged the Court of Chancery's ruling on both remand questions. This Court reviews the Court of Chancery's legal conclusions de novo but defers to the Court of Chancery's factual findings supported by the record. We will set aside a trial court's factual findings only if "they are clearly wrong and the doing of justice requires their overturn." "When there are two permissible views of the evidence, the factfinder's choice between them cannot be clearly erroneous."

A.

In her lead argument on appeal, Coster argues that the Court of Chancery erred when it limited its *Schnell* review to board action totally lacking a good faith basis. To frame our analysis, it is helpful to review again the circumstances of *Schnell* and *Blasius*. [...]

B.

In the years since the Supreme Court and the Court of Chancery decided these iconic cases, the courts deployed *Schnell* to police board action that, although technically legal, was motivated for selfish reasons to interfere with corporate elections and stockholder voting. It was reserved, however, for "those instances that threaten the fabric of the law, or which by an improper manipulation of the law, would deprive a person of a clear right." In other words, "[a]lmost all of the post-*Schnell* decisions involved situations where boards of directors deliberately employed various legal strategies either to frustrate or completely disenfranchise a shareholder vote." While the Supreme Court was a bit hyperbolic to say that only claims that tear the fabric of our law come within *Schnell*, the Chancellor was correct in this case to cabin *Schnell* and its equitable review to those cases where the board acts within its legal power, but is motivated for selfish reasons to interfere with the stockholder franchise.

C.

The Court of Chancery in this case also interpreted *Blasius* with a sensitivity to how, in practice, the Supreme Court and the Court of Chancery have effectively folded *Blasius* into *Unocal* review. [...]

Blasius [...] requir[ed] a board, even if acting in good faith, to demonstrate a "compelling justification" for interfering with the stockholder franchise. But another standard of review could also apply when the board interferes with the stockholder vote during a contest for control. In *Unocal Corporation v. Mesa Petroleum Company*, this Court noted the "omnipresent specter" that incumbent directors might take action to further their own interests or those of incumbent management "rather than those of the corporation and its shareholders." When stockholders challenge a board's use of anti-takeover measures, the board must show (i) that "they had reasonable grounds for believing that a danger to corporate policy and effectiveness existed," and (ii) that the response was "reasonable in relation to the threat posed." A defensive measure is an unreasonable response in relation to the threat if it is either draconian – coercive or preclusive – or falls outside a range of reasonable responses.

In *Stroud v. Grace*, our Court first recognized how both *Blasius* and *Unocal* review were called for in a proxy fight involving a tender offer [...]

In *MM Companies v. Liquid Audio, Inc.*, the Supreme Court took the formal step to incorporate *Blasius* "within *Unocal*." [...]

Even though the Supreme Court in Liquid Audio combined *Blasius* and *Unocal* review, it did not solve the practical problem of how to turn *Unocal*'s reasonableness review and *Blasius*' "primary purpose" and "compelling justification" elements into a useful standard of review. The *Blasius* "compelling justification" standard of review turned out to be unworkable in practice. Once the court required a compelling justification to justify the board's action, the outcome was, for the most part, preordained. The Court of Chancery also skirted *Blasius* review by limiting the "primary purpose" requirement and redefining what it meant to be compelling.

In *Mercier v. Inter-Tel* (Del.), the Court of Chancery reflected on these practical problems with Blasius review and took a different approach to the standard of review. The minority stockholders in *Mercier* claimed that a special committee of independent directors breached its fiduciary duties by rescheduling stockholder special meeting to consider a proposed merger. The committee also set a new record date. Instead of applying *Schnell* and *Blasius* "within *Unocal*," the Court of Chancery turned to *Unocal* and its "reasonableness" review but applied it with greater sensitivity to the interests at stake because the "director action . . . could have the effect of influencing the outcome of corporate director elections or other stockholder votes having consequences for corporate control." [...]

[Eds: The court summarizes two additional cases, indicating that the Chancery court consistently applied the Unocal standard in situations where the board interfered with shareholder voting. In these cases, the court required a compelling justification and/or applied the test with 'special sensitivity.]

D.

In *Unocal*, the Supreme Court remarked that "our corporate law is not static." Experience has shown that *Schnell* and *Blasius* review, as a matter of precedent and practice, have been and can be folded into *Unocal* review to accomplish the same ends – enhanced judicial scrutiny of board action that interferes with a corporate election or a stockholder's voting rights in contests for control. When *Unocal* is applied in this context, it can "subsume[] the question of loyalty that pervades all fiduciary duty cases, which is whether the directors have acted for proper reasons" and "thus address[] issues of good faith such as were at stake in *Schnell*." *Unocal* can also be applied with the sensitivity *Blasius* review brings to protect the fundamental interests at stake – the free exercise of the stockholder vote as an essential element of corporate democracy.

As we explained in our earlier decision in this case, the court's review is situationally specific and is independent of other standards of review. When a stockholder challenges board action that interferes with the election of directors or a stockholder vote in a contest for corporate control, the board bears the burden of proof. First, the court should review whether the board faced a threat "to an important corporate interest or to the achievement of a significant corporate benefit." The threat must be real and not pretextual, and the board's motivations must be proper and not selfish or disloyal. As Chancellor Allen stated long ago, the threat cannot be justified on the grounds that the board knows what is in the best interests of the stockholders.

Second, the court should review whether the board's response to the threat was reasonable in relation to the threat posed and was not preclusive or coercive to the stockholder franchise. To guard against unwarranted interference with corporate elections or stockholder votes in contests for corporate control, a board that is properly motivated and has identified a legitimate threat must tailor its response to only what is necessary to counter the threat. The board's response to the threat cannot deprive the stockholders of a vote or coerce the stockholders to vote a particular way.

Applying *Unocal* review in this case with sensitivity to the stockholder franchise is no stretch for our law. […]

E.

In our first decision, we highlighted facts in the Court of Chancery's first decision that might have led to the conclusion that the board acted for selfish reasons. But we recognized that the court had made findings inconsistent with this result and remanded to allow the Court of Chancery to reconsider its decision in light of our first opinion. On remand the court did as requested. The court found that there was "more to the story" than contained in its first opinion. It supplemented the earlier factual findings with the following:

- "Without making any meaningful effort to negotiate board composition, Plaintiff filed a complaint in this Court seeking the appointment of a custodian;"

- "Plaintiff's request for custodial relief was extremely broad. Plaintiff did not present a tailored request for relief that targeted the stockholder deadlock. Rather, she asked the court to empower a custodian to 'exercise full authority and control over the Company, its operations, and management;'"

- "The threat of a court-appointed custodian so broadly empowered posed new risks to the Company. The appointment of a custodian with these powers would have given rise to broad termination rights in SPE contracts and threatened UIP's revenue stream, as UIP's business model is dependent on the continued viability of those contracts;"

- "Facing this threat to the Company," the UIP board "identified a solution" to issue equity "long promised to Bonnell" that "implent[ed] a succession plan" proposed "on a clear day;"

- The Stock Sale would "moot the Custodian Action and eliminate the risks the appointment of a custodian posed to UIP" and would "eliminate the stockholder leverage that Plaintiff was using to try to force a buyout at a price detrimental to the Company;"

- The UIP board's motives were not "pretexts for entrenchment for selfish reasons" or "post-hoc justifications;" and

- "[T]hese were genuine motivations for their actions that stood alongside the more problematic purposes that [*Coster I*] identified and the Appellate Decision collected."

After its additional fact findings, the Court of Chancery gathered the many strands of precedent and conducted a careful review of the UIP board's actions. The Chancellor found that the UIP board faced a threat – which the court described as an "existential crisis" – to UIP's existence through a deadlocked stockholder vote and the risk of a custodian appointment. Although the court thought that some of the board's reasons for approving the Stock Sale were problematic, on balance the court held that the board was properly motivated in responding to the threat. According to the court, the UIP board acted in good faith "to advance the best interests of UIP" by "reward[ing] and retain[ing] an essential employee," "implement[ing] a succession plan that Wout had favored," and "moot[ing] the Custodian Action to avoid risk of default under key contracts." The court also relied on its earlier finding that the UIP board issued UIP stock to Bonnell at an entirely fair price.

The Court of Chancery also found that the UIP board responded reasonably and proportionately to the threat posed when it approved the Stock Sale and mooted the Custodian Action. As it held, "in the exceptionally unique circumstances of this case," without the Stock Sale, the possibility that a custodian appointed with broad powers would jeopardize key contracts caused an existential crisis at UIP. The Stock Sale, the court held, "was appropriately tailored to achieve the goal of mooting the Custodian Action" while implementing the succession plan and retaining Bonnell. And the court noted that there were more aggressive options that could have been, but were not, pursued to break the deadlock.

Finally, the board's response to the existential threat posed by the stockholder deadlock and custodian action was not preclusive or coercive. Although the Stock Sale effectively foreclosed Coster from perpetuating the deadlock facing UIP, the new three-way ownership of the company presented a potentially more effective way for her to exercise actual control. As the Court of Chancery noted, Schwat and Bonnell are not bound to vote together, meaning Coster could cast a swing vote at stockholder meetings. As an equal one third owner with the two other stockholders, Coster can join forces with either one of UIP's other owners "at some point in the future." A realistic path to control of UIP negates the preclusive impact of the Stock Sale.

F.

Coster's remaining arguments on appeal pick at the court's factual findings without success. As noted above, Coster has a steep hill to climb because we review those findings to see whether they are "clearly wrong." First, the main thread running through several of her arguments is that, instead of diluting her equity, the UIP board could have made the same arguments about an existential crisis when it opposed the appointment of a custodian. If the court declined to appoint a custodian, the argument goes, the Stock Sale would have been unnecessary to defeat the custodian action. Coster also claims that "there was nothing exigent about allowing Bonnell to buy equity in UIP" as there was no "evidence that Bonnell threatened to leave UIP if he did not receive equity."

But the Chancellor found, under the unusual facts of this case, that it was the pendency of the Custodian Action itself that caused the existential crisis at UIP. The Board was not required to risk court appointment of a custodian with broad powers that would trigger defaults under UIP's SPE contracts. The court also found that the Stock Sale fulfilled a prior equity commitment to Bonnell, which encouraged him, as a key employee, to remain with UIP. According to the court, Bonnell was "essential to the Company's survival."

Coster also contests the relevance of the "broad termination rights" in UIP's various contracts. At trial, Bonnell testified that a "primary investor" in each SPE holds termination authority. Coster contends that "many, if not most, of the thirdparty contracts relied upon by Defendants are contracts between UIP and SPEs owned and controlled by Schwat and Bonnell," who supposedly control the termination decision.

The record contains only excerpts of the UIP contracts. While these excerpts reveal superficial links between UIP and the SPEs, as would be expected of affiliated companies, the excerpts do not have provisions clearly placing termination rights in Schwat or Bonnell's control. The record, therefore, does not unequivocally support Coster's contention. Bonnell also testified at trial that an independent primary investor in each SPE has the authority to terminate the contracts. UIP also confirmed at oral argument that UIP representatives did not control the termination rights.

Finally, Coster takes issue with two other aspects of the Court of Chancery's decision. [Eds: But the Supreme Court finds that these additional aspects did not have much impact on the decision's outcome.]

III.

The judgment of the Court of Chancery is affirmed.

Chapter 10. The Shareholder Collective Action Problem

The second critical aspect of shareholder voting that deserves greater attention even in an introductory course is shareholders' collective action problem, and the controversial solutions that have emerged to deal with it. Since the collective action problem is most acute when a corporation has many shareholders, the topics in this chapter are mostly only relevant for public corporations.

A. Proxy Advisors

In large corporations with dispersed ownership, an individual small shareholder has practically no influence on the outcome. It is rational for the shareholder not to spend time and resources learning about the complex issues at stake ("**rational apathy**"), and unlike in political elections, there is typically no emotional or moral impetus propelling voters (shareholders) to vote. It is thus unsurprising that the majority of such "retail shareholders" tend not to vote.

Today, **institutional investors** such as mutual funds or pension funds own approximately 70% of all publicly traded shares in the U.S. These investors are certainly better positioned to vote than retail shareholders. Nonetheless, even they find the task arduous. They tend to hold shares in a vast number of corporations, making it an enormous task to accumulate and analyze the comprehensive information necessary to make well-informed decisions in shareholder votes. And large as they may be, these investors still only own a small fraction of each stock (the largest fund managers control funds owning on the order of 5% of each stock).⁺ Some might prefer not to vote. But many are legally required to, most notably those regulated under the Employee Retirement Income Security Act of 1974 (ERISA).

So-called proxy advisory firms, also known as proxy advisors, have **emerged to help institutional investors overcome the considerable costs of gathering the information** necessary to make well-informed decisions in shareholder votes. The market leaders are Institutional Shareholder Services (ISS) and Glass Lewis. These

⁺ Moreover, the fund manager who controls the vote captures only a tiny fraction—the management fee percentage—of any benefit the vote might create for the fund and, ultimately, its investors. You might think that a fund manager benefits indirectly from voting well by attracting new customers if the fund generates a higher return for its existing customers. This is true for some idiosyncratic funds. But many funds, particularly index funds—which are the largest funds by far—invest in the same assets as their competitors and are evaluated relative to one another. The only way such funds can distinguish themselves from their competitors is through lower costs. For these funds, spending resources on voting *hurts* their competitive position relative to passive competitors even if the voting does lead to higher asset values.

firms provide institutional investors with analyses and recommendations on all matters put to a shareholder vote, including board elections, executive remuneration, and corporate transactions.

Proxy advisors arguably **wield considerable powers** as intermediaries between shareholders and boards of directors. This is true at the level of individual decisions, where the voting recommendation of the most important proxy advisors will oftentimes be a decisive factor for the outcome of a shareholder vote. This is also true at the level of corporate governance more generally. Proxy advisors like ISS have established voting guidelines that seek to identify good corporate governance practices and formulate voting recommendations depending on whether corporations adhere to these practices or not. For example, ISS's current voting guidelines (https://www.issgovernance.com/file/policy/active/americas/US-Voting-Guidelines.pdf?v=1) contain the following rule for recommendations concerning votes on non-independent directors:

> Vote against or withhold from non-independent directors (Executive Directors and Non-Independent Non-Executive Directors per ISS' Classification of Directors) when:
>
> - Independent directors comprise 50 percent or less of the board;
> - The non-independent director serves on the audit, compensation, or nominating committee;
> - The company lacks an audit, compensation, or nominating committee so that the full board functions as that committee; or
> - The company lacks a formal nominating committee, even if the board attests that the independent directors fulfill the functions of such a committee.
>
> —ISS United States Proxy Voting Guidelines, p. 9 (footnotes omitted).

In order to ensure that their proposals will succeed at shareholder meetings, boards often feel compelled to comply with the (de-facto) standards set by these organizations.

In recent years, the power wielded by proxy advisory firms like ISS has sparked **debates about the need for regulation and oversight**, and the SEC has taken several stabs at regulating them. One of the most important criticisms levied against proxy advisors pertains to a potential conflict of interest: These firms often run corporate governance consulting businesses on the side, and there is a perception that corporations might be able to increase their chances of receiving favorable voting recommendations by engaging the services of these advisors.

B. Proxy Access

The collective action problem in voting has a parallel in **initiating** a vote, in particular when it comes to launching a proxy fight. The shareholder who initiates the fight incurs all the associated costs, while receiving only a fraction of any benefit created. When compared to voting, the benefits of initiating proxy fights can be larger, but the costs are definitely larger as well.

To reduce these costs, the SEC adopted **rule 14a-8**, which deals with shareholder proposals. Under this rule, any shareholder holding a sufficient number of shares for a sufficient period of time can force the corporation to include on its proxy statement and proxy card a proposal submitted by the shareholder. Rule 14a-8(i)(8)(iv) is very explicit, however, that the rule does *not* apply "[i]f the proposal ... [s]eeks to include a specific individual in the company's proxy materials for election to the board of directors."

With rule 14a-8 unavailable, by default the only means for a dissident shareholder to propose alternative board candidates is to file a separate proxy statement, i.e., to initiate a full-on **proxy fight**. This is expensive. Note that the "universal proxy" rule 14a-19, adopted in 2021, does not change this equation because it is only triggered if the dissident files a proxy statement and commits to soliciting shareholders holding at least 67% of the voting power.

The ability to get dissident candidates onto the corporation's proxy *without* the need for a separate dissident proxy solicitation is called **proxy access**. As our discussion of rules 14a-8 and 14a-19 demonstrates, proxy access is *not* provided by SEC rules (nor is it mandatory under state law). The issue of whether this policy should be changed has been one of the most hotly debated issues in corporate governance for decades.

In this millennium, the **SEC** first proposed formal rules dealing with proxy access in 2003 and 2007. In 2009, the SEC again proposed to require proxy access in a new rule 14a-11. In response, it received about 700 comments. The comments were sharply divided on the merits of the proposed rule. Major corporations and their law firms opposed it, whereas institutional investors supported it. Congress weighed in with Section 971 of the Dodd-Frank Act of 2010, which amended section 14 of the Securities Exchange Act to give the SEC explicit authority to require proxy access. The SEC ultimately adopted a modified rule 14a-11 in 2010. In *Business*

Roundtable v. SEC (2011), however, the D.C. Circuit struck down this new rule as "arbitrary and capricious" under the Administrative Procedure Act. Judge Ginsburg's opinion is noticeable for its hostility towards the SEC and its strict demands of cost-benefit analysis. The SEC long seemed intent on trying it again but did not muster the resources to do so.

1. Why might proxy access matter?: The shareholder collective action problem

To understand its magnitude, let us look more closely at the collective action problem in unseating an incompetent board.

A critical piece of legal background is that dissident shareholders have **no right to reimbursement for the costs** of running their own proxy campaign (hundreds of thousands or even millions of dollars). The board *may* legally reimburse a dissident's cost if the contest was about corporate policy rather than mere personnel issues. But realistically, no incumbent board will do so. The only practical way for a dissident to be reimbursed is to win control of the board.

Let's look at the resulting incentives in a simple **numerical example**. Imagine better management could increase the value of a corporation's shares by $100m (say, from $1 billion to $1.1 billion). You own 1% of those shares. Your individual benefit from better management would hence be $1m. Let's say a proxy contest would cost $2m.

If you win and replace the board, your candidates will vote to reimburse you. You will hence make a $1m gain because your shares are worth more with better management. But if you lose, you won't be reimbursed, your shares' value does not appreciate, and you are stuck with the $2m costs.

Imagine the chances of winning the proxy contest are 50-50 (in practice, that's high — people tend to be suspicious of dissidents). In expectation, you would lose $500,000 (50% × $1m – 50% × $2m = -$500,000). Thus, you won't do it. And this happens even though in this example (1) you own $10m worth of shares of this one corporation — a big stake for most investors, and (2) the expected collective benefit to all shareholders combined is $48m (50% × $100m - $2m = $48m).

2. Variations in the bylaws or the charter

As usual, these default rules **can be changed in the charter** (cf. DGCL 102(b)(1)) or in the bylaws (cf. DGCL 109). Details of permissible bylaws were disputed, prompting the adoption of DGCL 112 and 113 in 2009 (read!).

Shareholders can use bylaw amendments to obtain the right to proxy access and/or to proxy expense reimbursement even against the opposition of the board (why can shareholders not use charter amendments for this purpose?). And SEC rule 14a-8 allows them to collect "votes" for such amendments using the corporation's proxy. Rule 14a-8(i)(8) excludes director nominations from 14a-8, but it does not exclude bylaw proposals relating to such nominations in subsequent meetings. In 2014/15, activist shareholders — in particular, New York City's Comptroller, responsible for the City's pension funds— used this route at dozens of US corporations, and many of these proxy access proposals passed. By 2020, more than 75% of the S&P 500 corporations, and more than 600 U.S. corporations in total, had adopted proxy access bylaws under investor pressure.

3. A skeptical note: Why are proxy campaigns so costly?

Until now, however, **proxy access has been used only once**, and even then the challenger ultimately withdrew its candidate. Why? As explained above, the idea is that proxy access will make it much cheaper for an activist to propose a candidate, and hence alleviate the collective action problem. But let's take a closer look at the costs, and whether proxy access really reduces them.

Traditionally, an important expense in running proxy campaigns was mailing costs. These seem relatively minor now that challengers can make their materials available electronically (cf. rule 14a-16(l)) or solicit only a small number of large institutional investors, who now hold a large fraction of most corporations' shares. But challengers still need to buy a lot of lawyer time to comply with SEC requirements and to avoid fraud lawsuits under rule 14a-9. A successful campaign also tends to require lots of canvassing by proxy solicitors and campaigning with the help of public relations firms. After all, the insurgent must compete with the board, who buys the same services (including litigation) with the corporation's coffers. Costs for legal and other advice are rather independent of proxy access.

4. The Ideology of Proxy Access

If proxy access does not indeed reduce costs for "insurgent" shareholders, why is it such a hotly contested topic? The answer is suggested by the following comment from Ted Mirvis of Wachtell, Lipton, Rosen, & Katz in response to the 2007 proposals:

> Wars have many fronts. The battle lines in the fight between the director-centric and the shareholder-centric models of the world now once again include the SEC, as it considers whether to allow

shareholders to use a company's proxy statement for director nominations.

C. Shareholder Activism

While most shareholders tend to be rationally apathetic, engaging minimally with the corporations in which they are invested, some adopt a more proactive stance. These so-called activist investors, often institutional investors or hedge funds, utilize the mechanisms of corporate governance as levers to influence a company's decision-making processes and overall governance. One of their most important weapons is the proxy fight.

Shareholder activism can be driven by **financial and/or social goals**. Socially motivated activism seeks to address environmental, social, or governance (ESG) issues within a company. An example of a recent high-profile activist campaign with social objectives is Engine No. 1's campaign against ExxonMobil's board in 2021. Engine No. 1, a small hedge fund, successfully pressed for changes in the company's approach to climate change and its board composition. We focus on the more common and more controversial financially motivated activism, in which activist investors—primarily hedge funds—make it their business model to invest in companies with the intention to conduct activist campaigns.

The **business model of financial activists** must overcome the shareholder collective action problem—the challenge that shareholders bear the full costs of their engagement with a corporation, while reaping only a fraction of the resulting benefits. Hedge funds often resolve this by acquiring sizable stakes in a target company, often up to (and sometimes even exceeding) 5% prior to initiating their activist campaigns. If their activism is successful and leads to an increase in the company's share price, these large holdings enable activists to claim a significant portion of the overall rise in company value—ideally, enough to (more than) offset their expenses.

Section 13(d) of the Securities Exchange Act plays a significant role here. It requires anyone acquiring 5% of a corporation's voting stock with the intent to influence corporate control to disclose their acquisition to the SEC and the public on **Schedule 13D** within 10 days. This alerts the target and the market. To the extent the activist is expected to increase the value of the shares, this will now be reflected in the stock price, meaning that, from the filing onwards, the activist will not be able to profit from further acquisitions even if the activist's intervention is indeed beneficial for the stock's value.

The rise in financially motivated "hedge fund activism" has sparked heated **policy debates** that partially mirror the earlier debates about hostile takeovers. Like critics of hostile takeovers, critics of hedge fund activism—often the same people!—argue that these activists tend to prioritize short-term gains over the company's long-term interests. In support, they point to the fact that activists often encourage actions such as stock buybacks or special dividends that transfer cash from the corporation to shareholders, which might come at the expense of longer-term corporate investments in research, development, or infrastructure. Proponents of activism counter that cash transfers from corporations to shareholders may be anything but short-termist: shareholders may have better use for the cash than the target corporation, in particular investing it in other corporations with better long-term projects.

In deciding which view is right, a key institution is the stock market: to the extent **stock prices** accurately reflect a corporation's prospects, short-termist actions will be counterproductive for the activists. In particular, if correctly incorporated into the stock price, inefficient cash payouts will reduce the stock price by more than the cash being paid out, thus harming, not helping, the activist who owns the stock while lobbying for the payouts. Inefficient corporate actions could generate value for the activist only if the market not only fails to recognize the inefficiency but mistakes it for a beneficial action. In that case, the activist could walk away with a profit while leaving the other shareholders holding the bag. On the flip side, insofar as activism does generate value at the target company, passive shareholders also benefit.

The mere *potential* of an activist campaign might also **influence management behavior,** even if such a campaign is not currently active. However, it can be challenging to predict the nature and implications of management's preemptive actions. The threat of activism might discourage inefficient practices that could invite activist attention, thereby benefiting shareholders. But it could also encourage wasteful conduct as managers attempt to present their companies as unattractive targets for activism. Managers, after all, know things about their company that outsiders, including activists, do not, so managers can engage in costly window-dressing, at least for a while. Managers can also waste resources on "activism defense." The overall effects of activism can therefore be hard to discern. Yet, insofar as activists' presence profits shareholders, it might provide a counterweight to passive investors' rational apathy.

Like hostile takeovers, activist campaigns usually encounter **resistance from boards of directors**. Boards have actively sought to hinder activist shareholders from launching proxy fights and influencing corporate decision-making. One important defensive measure are advance notice bylaws, which impose long lead times and extensive disclosure requirements on shareholders seeking to nominate alternative director slates. Another important defense is the anti-activist poison pill, which threatens to dilute the stakes of activist shareholders, particularly when they attempt to coordinate their campaigns with others.

In a departure from their approach to defensive devices in the takeover context, the **Delaware courts** have generally been hesitant to endorse defensive devices against activist campaigns. An instantly famous example of this approach is the Delaware Chancery Court's recent *Williams Companies Stockholder Litigation* decision invalidating an anti-activist poison pill.

D. Williams Cos. S'holder Litig. (Del. Ch. 2021)

Questions

1. Instead of applying *Unocal*, could the Chancery Court have reviewed the pill under other standards of review? Would the application of these alternative standards have altered the outcome of the case?

2. One of the Williams board's main motivations for the adoption of the pill was directors' concern over activists engaging in "'short-term' agendas." Do you find this concern compelling? How does Vice Chancellor McCormick respond to it?

3. Recall that *Moran* approved the use of a clear-day anti-takeover pill. By contrast, VC McCormick invalidates the Williams pill in part because Williams did not face a tangible threat of shareholder activism. What, if anything, justifies this disparate treatment of anti-takeover and anti-activist pills?

4. Under what circumstances, if any, would it be permissible for a board to deploy a pill similar to the one adopted by Williams?

The WILLIAMS COMPANIES STOCKHOLDER LITIGATION

Consolidated C.A. No. 2020-0707-KSJM

Date Submitted: February 5, 2021
Date Decided: February 26, 2021

Gregory V. Varallo, BERNSTEIN LITOWITZ BERGER & GROSSMANN LLP, Wilmington, DE; Michael J. Barry, Christine M. Mackintosh, Kelly L. Tucker, GRANT & EISENHOFER P.A., Wilmington, DE; Mark Lebovitch, Thomas G. James, BERNSTEIN LITOWITZ BERGER & GROSSMANN LLP, New York, NY; Jeremy S. Friedman, David F.E. Tejtel, FRIEDMAN OSTER & TEJTEL PLLC, Bedford Hills, NY; Counsel for Plaintiffs.

William M. Lafferty, Kevin M. Coen, Lauren K. Neal, Sabrina M. Hendershot, MORRIS, NICHOLS, ARSHT & TUNNELL LLP, Wilmington, DE; Andrew Ditchfield, Brian M. Burnovski, Mari Byrne, DAVIS POLK & WARDWELL LLP, New York, NY; Counsel for Defendants The Williams Companies, Inc., Alan S. Armstrong, Stephen W. Bergstrom, Nancy K. Buese, Stephen I. Chazen, Charles I. Cogut, Michael A. Creel, Vicki L. Fuller, Peter A. Ragauss, Scott D. Sheffield, Murray D. Smith, and William H. Spence.

Patricia R. Urban, Michael A. Weidinger, Megan Ix Brison, PINCKNEY, WEIDINGER, URBAN & JOYCE LLC, Wilmington, DE; Counsel for Defendant Computershare Trust Company, N.A.

MEMORANDUM OPINION

McCORMICK, V.C.

This litigation concerns the validity of a stockholder rights plan, or so-called "poison pill," a device that came to popularity in the 1980s as a response to front-end loaded, two-tiered tender offers. Coercive tender offers of the 1980s were "to takeovers what the forward pass was to Notre Dame football in the days of Knute Rockne," and a powerful offense required a powerful defense. Of all the defenses developed to fend off hostile takeovers, the poison pill was among the most muscular. These bulwarks gained judicial imprimatur in 1985 when the Delaware Supreme Court upheld a poison pill as an antitakeover device in *Moran v. Household International, Inc. Moran* also established intermediate scrutiny under *Unocal* as the legal framework for reviewing stockholder challenges to poison pills.

Poison pills metamorphosed post-*Moran*. The flip-over feature of the *Moran* pill was augmented by a flip-in feature. After the adoption of state anti-takeover statutes, trigger thresholds crept down from the 20% threshold of *Moran* to 15% and then to 10% in some instances. The pill's initial success engendered mission creep. Originally conceived as anti-takeover armaments, poison pills were redirected to address other corporate purposes such as protecting net operating loss assets.[8] Recently, pills have been deployed to defend against stockholder activism.

The plaintiffs in this litigation challenge an anti-activist pill adopted by the board of directors of The Williams Companies, Inc. ("Williams" or the "Company") at the outset of the COVID-19 pandemic and amid a global oil price war. The Williams pill is unprecedented in that it contains a more extreme combination of features than any pill previously evaluated by this court—a 5% trigger threshold, an expansive definition of "acting in concert," and a narrow definition of "passive investor."

Unocal calls for a two-part inquiry, asking first whether the board had reasonable grounds for identifying a threat to the corporate enterprise and second whether the response was reasonable in relation to the threat posed. The defendants identify three supposed threats: first, the desire to prevent stockholder activism during a time of market uncertainty and a low stock price, although the Williams board was not aware of any specific activist plays afoot; second, the apprehension that hypothetical activists might pursue "short-term" agendas or distract management from guiding Williams through uncertain times; and third, the concern that activists might stealthily and rapidly accumulate over 5% of Williams stock.

Of these three threats, the first two run contrary the tenet of Delaware law that directors cannot justify their actions by arguing that, without board intervention, the stockholders would vote erroneously out of ignorance or mistaken belief. This decision assumes for the sake of analysis that the third threat presents a legitimate corporate objective but concludes that the Company's response was not proportional and enjoins the Williams pill.

I. FACTUAL BACKGROUND

Trial took place over three days. The record comprises 206 trial exhibits, live testimony from four fact and three expert witnesses, deposition testimony from eight fact and three expert witnesses, and one-hundred stipulations of fact. These are the facts as the court finds them after trial.

A. Williams and Its Board

Williams is a publicly traded Delaware corporation with its headquarters in Tulsa, Oklahoma. It owns and operates natural gas infrastructure assets, including over 30,000

---

[8] *See, e.g., Versata Enters., Inc. v. Selectica, Inc.,* 5 A.3d 586, 607 (Del. 2010) ("*Selectica II*") (validating an NOL pill).

miles of pipelines and 28 processing facilities, and handles approximately 30% of the nation's natural gas volumes.

[...]

As of March 2020, the Board comprised twelve members—CEO Alan Armstrong and eleven outside directors. The complaint names as defendants Armstrong and ten of the outside directors—Stephen W. Bergstrom, Nancy K. Buese, Stephen I. Chazen, Charles I. Cogut, Michael A. Creel, Vicki L. Fuller, Peter A. Ragauss, Scott D. Sheffield, Murray D. Smith, and William H. Spence (collectively, the "Director Defendants").

B. Williams' Prior Experience with Stockholder Activism

In late 2011, Soroban Capital Partners LLC (led by Eric Mandelblatt) ("Soroban") and Corvex Management LP (led by Keith Meister) ("Corvex") each acquired slightly less than 5% of Williams stock. Through a February 2014 agreement with Williams, Mandelblatt and Meister joined the Board.

During their tenure, Mandelblatt and Meister were instrumental in pressing for a merger with Energy Transfer Equity LP. After the merger was terminated, six of the Board's thirteen members—including Mandelblatt and Meister—attempted to remove and replace Armstrong as CEO. When this effort failed, those six directors resigned. Meister then threatened a proxy fight to replace the entire Board, but he agreed to stand down when Williams named three new independent directors—Bergstrom, Sheffield, and Spence. Bergstrom became Chair.

Management also underwent significant change. Armstrong remained as CEO, but the Company hired several new executives, including CFO John D. Chandler and General Counsel T. Lane Wilson.

Armstrong and Smith are the only two Director Defendants who served on the Board during the Soroban and Corvex era; the others joined the Board in either 2016 or 2018. [...]

C. Williams Stock Price Plummets

Before 2020, Williams stock price traded at a high of $24.04 and had been relatively stable over the preceding months. In early 2020, however, the COVID-19 pandemic and the ensuing oil price war between Saudi Arabia and Russia shocked the oil market and sent stock prices plummeting.

The COVID-19 pandemic hit first. [...] Williams stock price fell to $18.90 by the end of February 2020. During this period, trading volume in Williams stock was high and fluctuated dramatically from day to day, indicating "a lot of unusual and short-term-type trading."

The Board met on March 2, 2020, to discuss solutions for the declining stock price. Management and representatives from Morgan Stanley explained that the stock was approaching lows similar to those in 2010 and 2016, despite the fact that earnings were 25% higher and the Company was carrying significantly less debt. The Board discussed a share repurchase program but opted to preserve liquidity and continue to de-leverage instead.

Then came the oil price war. [...] By March 19, Williams stock price had fallen to approximately $11, which was close to a 55% decline since January 2020.

D. Cogut's Plan

Around early March 2020, outside director Cogut conceived of an alternative to the repurchase program—a stockholder rights plan (the "Plan"). Cogut, a retired lawyer who had led the M&A and private equity practices of a prominent New York law firm, had joined the Board in 2016. Cogut had helped clients adopt rights plans roughly a dozen times beginning in the 1980s.

Cogut witnessed the evolution of poison pills throughout his career and described them at trial as "the nuclear weapon of corporate governance." He explained his understanding that the poison pill was historically designed to protect companies from hostile takeovers and that they originated in response to front-end loaded, two-tier tender offers. Cogut knew that acceptable trigger thresholds had declined from 20% to 15%, with the occasional 10% trigger. As trigger levels shrank, the pills' uses expanded. Cogut observed that companies began using pills to protect their net operating losses ("NOLs") and not just as a takeover deterrent.

Like many Delaware corporations, Williams had an "on-the-shelf" pill (the "Shelf Pill")— a rights plan that the Company could quickly adopt in the event a threat arose. The Board considered a "refreshment" of the Shelf Pill every so often; the last such refreshment took place in October 2019. The Shelf Pill was geared towards a traditional change of control situation. None of the Company representatives could testify as to details of the Shelf Pill other than its existence, though Cogut testified that it likely had a trigger of 15% and certainly greater than 5%.

Cogut was not concerned with a potential takeover or with NOLs. He felt that the "circumstances that existed because of the pandemic" warranted "a different type of pill." The "uncertainty" in the market required a solution that could "insulat[e]" management from activists "who were trying to influence the control of the company."

Cogut suggested a rights plan to Wilson around March 2 when management was considering its share repurchase proposal. Cogut's proposal "was not meant to deal with the same issues as the stock buyback" and was not fully developed—he simply recommended that "the concept [of a pill] should be considered" by management. The goal was to prevent "[a]ny activism that would influence control over the company at an aggregate level above 5 percent."

[...]

E. Williams Management Proposes the Plan to the Board

After Cogut proposed the Plan, Wilson consulted with Davis Polk & Wardwell LLP ("Davis Polk"), the Company's outside counsel. Davis Polk then revised the Shelf Pill and sent a draft to Wilson on March 11, 2020.

After receiving the draft from Davis Polk, Wilson socialized the Plan among senior management including Armstrong. Cogut expected Armstrong to support the idea because he had "barely survived" Soroban and Corvex's "attempt to get him fired."

Management liked the pill. [...]

On March 17, Wilson forwarded a draft pill to Cogut, along with Davis Polk's "explanation of changes." Wilson noted that he, Armstrong, and Chandler were "all supportive of moving forward proactively."

Wilson also asked Cogut to discuss the Plan with Bergstrom, who lacked any experience with poison pills. [...] Bergstrom agreed to discuss the Plan with Cogut the following morning.

In the meantime, Armstrong, Bergstrom, and Wilson scheduled an emergency Board meeting to further evaluate Cogut's Plan. Wilson had also advised that holding two meetings would look better; he recommended scheduling a "second board meeting to approve, at least a day later, to show appropriate consideration by the Board."

[...]

F. The Board Calls an Urgent Meeting

The Board scheduled its first meeting for the evening of March 18. [...]

Although the Board had not yet seen a draft of the Plan, by the end of the March 18 meeting, the Board had decided to adopt it. [...] The only open issues were logistical questions and a formal vote.

As recommended by Wilson, the Board scheduled a second meeting for the following day, the evening of March 19. [...]

G. The Board Adopts the Plan.

[...]

The March 19 Board meeting began at 6 p.m. with the full Board and representatives from Morgan Stanley and Davis Polk in attendance. The Morgan Stanley team opened the meeting, beginning its presentation with an executive summary of the Plan before turning to "Considerations Regarding a 5% Trigger." [...]

The executive summary stated that "campaigns from well-known activists are expected to continue at a reasonable pace in the current market." In connection with this prediction, the presentation stated that:

> The rights plan would deter an activist from taking advantage of the current market dislocation and challenges in monitoring unusual trading patterns that results in a rapid accumulation of a >5% stake.

The presentation displayed a chart signaling an upward trend in stockholder activism and predicting that such activism would not decline as significantly as it did in response to the market downturn of 2008.

As to the trigger, the presentation informed the Board that: (a) only 2% of rights plans had triggers below 10%; (b) 76% of rights plans "set the trigger" between 15% and 20%; and (c) "[n]o precedents exist below 5%." The presentation did not cover any other provisions of the Plan.

[...]

Following discussion, the Board unanimously resolved to adopt a stockholder rights plan "in substantially the form presented at the meeting." [...]

The Board elected not to subject the Plan to a stockholder vote. [...]

H. The Plan's Features

The Plan will expire at the end of one year and has four key features: (i) a 5% trigger; (ii) a definition of "acquiring person" that captures beneficial ownership as well as ownership of certain derivative interests, such as warrants and options; (iii) an "acting in concert" provision that extends to parallel conduct and includes a "daisy chain" concept (the "AIC Provision"); and (iv) a limited "passive investor" exemption.

While the Plan's features were a focal point of trial, they received little attention during the March 18 and March 19 Board meetings. The Director Defendants confirmed that Board discussions focused almost exclusively on the 5% trigger. [...] Most directors admitted that they had not even read the key features of the Plan before this litigation began.

The Plan operates in conjunction with regulatory requirements established by federal and state law. Understanding the Plan's features requires a quick refresher of certain of those requirements.

- Section 13(d) of the Securities Exchange Act (the "Exchange Act") requires that non-passive investors report "beneficial ownership" of more than 5% of a class of stock but gives investors a ten-day window to report ownership levels using a Schedule 13D form. During that window, the investor is permitted to continue accumulating stock.

- Section 13(d) does not include derivative securities in the definition of "beneficial ownership."

- Section 13(d) aggregates the beneficial ownership of investors who are acting in concert, which under the Exchange Act occurs where "two or more persons agree to act together for the purpose of acquiring, holding, voting or disposing of equity securities of an issuer." Section 13(d)'s definition of "acting in concert" does not capture "parallel conduct" (discussed below) nor a "daisy chain" concept (discussed below).

- Section 13(d) excludes "passive investors," defined as persons who acquired "securities in the ordinary course of [their] business and not with the purpose nor with the effect of changing or influence the control of the issuer."

1. The 5% Trigger

The Plan established a trigger threshold of "5% or more." The Plan is triggered, and the rights distributed, on "the close of business on the tenth Business Day after" a "Person" (defined as an individual, firm, or entity) acquires "beneficial ownership" of 5% or more of Williams stock or commences "a tender or exchange offer" that would result in their ownership reaching that threshold. Given Williams' market capitalization in March 2020, triggering the 5% threshold at the time the Plan was adopted would have required an economic investment (sometimes referred to as a "toehold") of approximately $650 million.

2. Beneficial Ownership Definition

The Plan's definition of "beneficial ownership" starts with the definition found in Rule 13d–3 of the Exchange Act, then extends more broadly to include "[c]ertain synthetic interests in securities created by derivative positions," such as warrants and options.

3. The AIC Provision

The AIC Provision deems a Person to be "Acting in Concert" with another Person if:

> such Person knowingly acts (whether or not pursuant to an express agreement, arrangement or understanding) at any time after the first public announcement of the adoption of this Right Agreement, in concert or in parallel with such other Person, or towards a common goal with such other Person, relating to changing or influencing the control of the Company or in connection with or as a participant in any transaction having that purpose or effect, where (i) each Person is conscious of the other Person's conduct and this awareness is an element in their respective decision-making processes and (ii) at least one additional factor supports a determination by the Board that such Persons intended to act in concert or in parallel, which additional factors may include exchanging information, attending meetings, conducting discussions, or making or soliciting invitations to act in concert or in parallel.

Breaking it down, the AIC Provision deems a Person to be "Acting in Concert" with another where the Person: (1) "knowingly acts ... in concert or in parallel ... or towards a common goal" with another; (2) if the goal "relat[es] to changing or influencing the control of the Company or [is] in connection with or as a participant in any transaction having that purpose or effect;" (3) where each Person is "conscious of the other Person's conduct" and "this awareness is an element in their respective decision-making processes;" and (4) there is the presence of at least one additional factor to be determined by the Board, "which additional factors may include exchanging information, attending meetings, conducting discussions, or making or soliciting invitations to act in concert or in parallel." The fourth factor of this definition gives the Board "a great amount of latitude" for making the "Acting in Concert" determination.

The "parallel-conduct" dimension of the "acting in concert" provision (sometimes referred to as a "wolfpack" provision) is a feature of modern pills [...]

The AIC Provision includes a "daisy chain" concept, providing that "[a] Person who is Acting in Concert with another Person shall be deemed to be Acting in Concert with any third party who is also Acting in Concert with such other Person." Put differently, stockholders act in concert with one another by separately and independently "Acting in Concert" with the same third party.

The AIC Provision does not apply to a public proxy solicitation or tender offer. Persons are not deemed to be "Acting in Concert" solely as a result of soliciting proxies in connection with a "public proxy or consent solicitation made to more than 10 holders of shares of a class of stock" or when soliciting tenders pursuant to a "public tender or exchange offer." While this provision allows stockholders to initiate a proxy contest and solicit proxies without triggering the Plan, it does not exempt routine communications among stockholder before the launch of a proxy contest or tender offer.

The AIC Provision is also asymmetrical. It excludes "actions by an officer or director of the Company acting in such capacities," such that incumbents can act in concert without suffering the consequences of the Plan.

4. The Passive Investor Definition

The Plan carves out "Passive Investors" from the definition of "Acquiring Persons." The Plan defines "Passive Investor" to mean:

> [A] Person who (i) is the Beneficial Owner of Common Shares of the Company and either (a) has a Schedule 13G on file with the Securities and Exchange Commission pursuant to the requirements of Rule 13d-1(b) or (c) under the Exchange Act with respect to such holdings (and does not subsequently convert such filing to a Schedule 13D) or (b) has a Schedule 13D on file with the Securities and Exchange Commission and either has stated in its filing that it has no plan or proposal that relates to or would result in any of the actions or events set forth in Item 4 of Schedule 13D or otherwise has no intent to seek control of the Company or has certified to the Company that it has no such plan, proposal or intent (other than by voting the shares of the Common Shares of the Company over which such Person has voting power), (ii) acquires Beneficial Ownership of Common Shares of the Company pursuant to trading activities undertaken in the ordinary course of such Person's business and not with the purpose nor the effect, either alone or in concert with any Person, of exercising the power to direct or cause the direction of the management and policies of the Company or of otherwise changing or influencing the control of the Company, nor in connection with or as a participant in any transaction having such purpose or effect, including any transaction subject to Rule 13d-3(b) of the Exchange Act, and (iii) in the case of clause (i)(b) only, does not amend either its Schedule 13D on file or its certification to the Company in a manner inconsistent with its representation that it has no plan or proposal that relates to or would result in any of the actions or events

set forth in Item 4 of Schedule 13D or otherwise has no intent to seek control of the Company (other than by voting the Common Shares of the Company over which such Person has voting power).

This carve-out was intended to ensure that truly passive investors would be exempt from the definition of Acquiring Person under the Plan. Director Defendants testified as to their belief that the definition excludes Schedule 13G filers, defined under the Exchange Act as an investor that "acquired such securities in the ordinary course of his business and not with the purpose nor with *the effect of changing or influencing the control of the issuer."*

As drafted, however, the carve-out is far more exclusive. The definition uses "and" before romanette (iii), which makes the three requirements of the provision conjunctive. Thus, a stockholder must meet all three conditions to qualify as an exempt "Passive Investor." [...]

As most of the defense witnesses testified, this conjunctive language appears to have been a mistake. [...] Yet, the Board never discussed nor corrected this error.

Even a disjunctive reading of the Rights Plan's Passive Investor Definition is quite narrow. At the time the Board adopted the Plan, Williams had only three 13G filers in its stock: BlackRock, Vanguard, and State Street. Read disjunctively, the Passive Investor Definition would include at most those three investors.

I. Public Reaction to the Plan

The Board correctly anticipated that the market and stockholders would react negatively to the Plan. Two of Williams' largest stockholders reached out regarding the Plan shortly after its announcement, and ISS recommended in an April 8 report that stockholders vote against Bergstrom's re-election at the Company's annual meeting.

[...]

At the April 28, 2020 annual meeting, the stockholders re-elected Bergstrom to the Board, but by a slim margin [...]

J. The Board Fails to Redeem the Plan.

The Board has the authority to redeem or amend the Plan, but it remains in place.

[...]

Meanwhile, Williams stock price has substantially recovered. By June 8, 2020, Williams stock price had returned to $21.58 [...]

II. LEGAL ANALYSIS

Plaintiffs claim that the Director Defendants breached their fiduciary duties when adopting and maintaining the Plan. This decision agrees and issues a mandatory injunction requiring redemption.

A. Direct Versus Derivative

The parties dispute whether Plaintiffs' claim is derivative or direct. Plaintiffs argue that their claim is direct. Defendants argue that Plaintiffs' claim is derivative and thus subject to Court of Chancery Rule 23.1, which requires Plaintiffs to either make a pre-suit demand on the Board or to demonstrate that demand would have been futile. Plaintiffs did not make a pre-suit demand [...]

[The court applies *Tooley* and finds that by combining a parsimonious trigger of 5% with the AIC Provision and a limited passive ownership exception], the Plan limits the act of communicating itself, whether with other stockholders or management. It also restricts the stockholder's ability to nominate directors. It thus infringes on the stockholders' ability to communicate freely in connection with the stockholder franchise, much of which occurs outside the context of proxy contests. This articulation of the harm flows to stockholders and not the Company. In this way, enjoining the Plan is a remedy that affects stockholders alone and not the Company. Thus, Plaintiffs' claim is direct under *Tooley*.

B. The Standard of Review

The parties also dispute the applicable standard of review. Plaintiffs contend that *Unocal* governs the court's analysis. Defendants argue that the more deferential business judgment standard applies.

Since the Delaware Supreme Court's decision in *Moran*, this court "and the Supreme Court have used *Unocal* exclusively as the lens through which the validity of a contested rights plan is analyzed."

Defendants nevertheless argue that the Board's adoption and maintenance of the Plan should be subject to business judgment review. Defendants say that the sole justification for *Unocal's* enhanced standard is "the omnipresent specter that a board may be acting primarily in its own interests, rather than those of the corporation and its shareholders." Defendants argue that this specter is not present where a poison pill is designed to address stockholder activism as opposed to hostile takeover attempts.

There are many possible responses to Defendants' attempt to parse finely the concept of entrenchment, but it suffices for present purposes to say that Defendants' contention runs contrary to the Delaware Supreme Court's decision in *Selectica II*. There, the poison pill was adopted for the purpose of preserving NOL assets and not warding off hostile takeover attempts. The court held that the *Unocal* standard nevertheless applied because all poisons pills, "by ... nature," have a potentially entrenching "effect." It is therefore settled law that the Board's compliance with their fiduciary duties in adopting and then failing to redeem the Plan must be assessed under *Unocal*.

C. The *Unocal* Analysis

Having addressed the two threshold issues, this decision now turns to the merits of the enhanced scrutiny analysis. *Unocal* calls for a two-part inquiry. "The first part of *Unocal* review requires a board to show that it had reasonable grounds for concluding that a threat to the corporate enterprise existed." Framed more broadly, directors must demonstrate that they acted in good faith to achieve a "legitimate corporate objective."

To satisfy the first part of *Unocal*, Defendants must demonstrate that the Board conducted a "good faith and reasonable investigation." The reasonableness of the investigation is "materially enhanced" where the corporate decision is approved by a board comprising a majority of outside, nonemployee directors "coupled with a showing of reliance on advice by legal and financial advisors."

To meet their burden under the first part of *Unocal*, however, Defendants must do more than show good faith and reasonable investigation. "[T]he first part of *Unocal* review requires more than that; it requires the board to show that its good faith and reasonable investigation *ultimately gave the board 'grounds for concluding that a threat to the corporate enterprise existed.'* " In other words, after conducting a reasonable investigation and acting in good faith, the board must show that it sought to serve a legitimate corporate objective by responding to a legitimate threat. If the threat is not legitimate, then a reasonable investigation into the illegitimate threat, or a good faith belief that the threat warranted a response, will not be enough to save the board.

The second part of *Unocal* requires a board to show that the defensive measures were "reasonable in relation to the threat posed." This element of the *Unocal* test recognizes that a board's powers to act "are not absolute" and that a board "does not have unbridled discretion to defeat any perceived threat by any Draconian means available." When applying the reasonableness standard, the court does not substitute its judgment for that of the board. The court instead determines whether the measure falls within "the range of reasonableness."

When conducting the proportionality analysis, the court also examines the relationship between the defensive action that the directors took and the problem they sought to address. The court thus examines "the reasonableness of the end that the directors chose to pursue, the path that they took to get there, and the fit between the means and the end." It is the specific nature of the threat that "sets the parameters for the range of permissible defensive tactics" and a "reasonableness analysis requires an evaluation of the importance of the corporate objective threatened; alternative methods for protecting that objective; impacts of the defensive action and other relevant factors."

1. The Director Defendants' Reasons for Acting

The Director Defendants' actual and articulated reason for taking action figures prominently in the *Unocal* analysis. In the traditional language of *Unocal*, the directors must have identified and responded to a legitimate corporate threat. They cannot justify their conduct based on threats that they never identified or beliefs they did not hold. Before turning to the question of whether the threat is legitimate, the court must determine why the Director Defendants acted. This decision therefore starts by making factual findings concerning the threat or corporate objective to which the Board was responding when adopting the Plan.

a. The Actual Threats That the Board Identified

It is often difficult to distill a unified purpose behind a decision made by a group of people; often, members of the group have different reasons for supporting a decision. It is particularly difficult to discern such a purpose in the context of litigation, where there is always the risk that fact witnesses will recall events that occurred prior to litigation through the lens of newly crafted litigation positions.

This challenging task is further complicated here because the lawyer-drafted documents to which one would typically look for a statement of a board's purpose—e.g., board resolutions, board minutes, company disclosures—do not reflect the Board's actual intent. The materials from the March 19 Board meeting, including the resolution, the March 20 Press Release, and the March 30 Proxy Supplement, all state that the Plan was intended in part to serve as a takeover deterrent. But the Plan was not designed for that purpose, and some of the directors did not have that in mind when adopting the Plan. The Plan was not adopted with the objective of deterring takeover attempts.

In fact, the Plan was not adopted to protect against any *specific* threat at all. The Board was not concerned about any specific activist threat. Nor was the Board acting to preserve any specific asset like an NOL. Instead, the Board was acting pre-emptively to interdict hypothetical future threats.

The Plan was also not adopted in light of the Company's prior experience with activism, although Defendants took that position throughout this litigation. It is true that Williams management cited prior activism as a justification for the Plan when communicating with stockholders in advance of the annual meeting. It is also true that Smith's prior experience appears to have contributed to his support of the Plan. But there is no evidence that it was a motivating factor of the Board as a whole. The Board simply did not discuss the Company's prior experience with activism during the March 18 or March 19 meetings. This justification appears to have emerged at the Board level after the Plan had been adopted. [...]

The record is clear that the Company's declining stock price was the initial catalyst for the Board's decision. [...]

When asked during trial and at their respective depositions about the reasons for adopting the Plan, Cogut, Smith, Buese, Bergstrom, and Fuller testified generally that the intent of the Plan was to deter stockholder activism, although they all added their own gloss when articulating this purpose.

[...]

A few themes emerge from the Director Defendants' testimony. First, they all expressed the sentiment that the Plan was intended to deter stockholder activism. Second, they desired to insulate the board from activists pursuing "short-term" agendas and from distraction and disruption generally. Third, they were concerned that a stockholder might stealthily and rapidly accumulate large amounts of stock.

b. The Legitimacy of the Actual Threats

The first prong of *Unocal* requires evaluating whether the Board has demonstrated that it conducted a good faith reasonable investigation and had "grounds for concluding that a threat to the corporate enterprise existed." Defendants have demonstrated that the Board conducted a good faith, reasonable investigation when adopting the Plan. The Director Defendants are nearly all independent, outside directors. They considered the Plan over the course of two meetings. Although aspects of the record create the impression that the second Board meeting was window dressing, it is clear that there was genuine deliberation concerning the Plan. Defendants were advised by outside legal and financial advisors who were available to answer questions. Certainly, aspects of the process were less than perfect. Still, nothing about the process jumps out as unreasonable.

The real problem is not the process that Defendants followed, but the threats they identified. The first threat was quite general—the desire to prevent stockholder activism during a time of market uncertainty and a low stock price. The second threat was only slightly more specific—the concern that activists might pursue "short-term" agendas or distract management. The third threat was just a hair more particularized—the concern that activists might rapidly accumulate over 5% of the stock and the possibility that the Plan could serve as an early detection device to plug the gaps in the federal disclosure regime. Each of the three threats were purely hypothetical; the Board was not aware of any specific activist plays afoot. The question presented is whether these hypothetical threats present legitimate corporate objectives under Delaware law.

i. Stockholder Activism

"Stockholder activism" is a broad concept that refers to a range of stockholder activities intended to change or influence a corporation's direction. Activists may pressure a corporation to make management changes, implement operational improvements, or pursue a sale transaction. They may seek to catalyze or halt a merger or acquisition. More recently, "ESG activism" has come to the fore, and stockholders have begun pressuring corporations to adopt or modify policies to accomplish environmental, social, and governance goals. Many forms of stockholder activism can be beneficial to a corporation, as Defendants themselves recognize.

Under Delaware law, the board of directors manages the business and affairs of the corporation. Thus, stockholder activism is directed to the board. And activists' ability to replace directors through the stockholder franchise is the reason why boards listen to activists. Most activists hold far less than a hard majority of a corporation's stock, making the main lever at an activist's disposal a proxy fight. In this way, stockholder activism is intertwined with the stockholder franchise.

Under Delaware law, directors cannot justify their actions by arguing that "without their intervention, the stockholders would vote erroneously out of ignorance or mistaken belief" in an uncoerced, fully informed election. "The notion that directors know better than the stockholders about who should be on the board is no justification at all."

Viewing all stockholder activism as a threat is an extreme manifestation of the proscribed we-know-better justification for interfering with the franchise. That is, categorically concluding that *all* stockholder efforts to change or influence corporate direction constitute a threat to the corporation runs directly contrary to the ideological underpinnings of Delaware law. The broad category of conduct referred to as stockholder activism, therefore, cannot constitute a cognizable threat under the first prong of *Unocal*.

To be sure, Delaware law does not categorically foreclose the possibility that certain conduct by activist stockholders might give rise to a cognizable threat. Defendants cite to four cases where a Delaware court upheld defensive actions taken in response to types of stockholder activism. All involved different scenarios and more specific threats.

[...]

ii. Short-Termism and Distraction

The Board's second concern was that activists might pursue short-term agendas or disrupt or distract management. The "short-termism" justification refers to the concern that "a particular activist seeks short-term profit without regard to the impact on the company's long-term prospects." The "disruption" justification typically refers to the concern that the actions of the activists might cause operational disruption, as in *Cheff*. Here, the Director Defendants instead frame this concern as a desire to insulate the management team from distraction.

No case has evaluated under *Unocal* whether these types of particularized activist concerns constitute cognizable threats. The threats validated in Defendants' four cases discussed above involved threats that differed materially from the factual context here.

Each of Defendants' cases, unlike this case, involved takeover threats. [...] None of the cases involved a response to activism *per se*. Moreover, each of Defendants' cases, unlike this case, involved defensive measures adopted in response to a specific activist or group of activists. The threat was not hypothetical.

Reasonable minds can dispute whether short-termism or distraction could be deemed cognizable threats under Delaware law. These sorts of justifications, particularly short-termism, are conspicuous in the policy debate, but they become nebulous when viewed through a doctrinal lens. The central criticism of short-termism is that "shareholders who favor short-termism ... are hurting themselves as much as they are hurting their fellow shareholders." This is a valid policy argument, but as one group of scholars have commented, the "'short-termism' argument just particularizes the concern that shareholders will cast votes in a mistaken assessment of their own best interests." That is, short-termism and distraction concerns boil down to the sort of we-know-better justification that Delaware law eschews in the voting context.

Although there is room to disagree as to whether short-termism or distraction could be deemed cognizable threats under Delaware law, this decision does not resolve that issue. Even if justifications of short-termism or disruption could rise to the level of a cognizable threat, hypothetical versions of these justifications cannot. The concerns in this case are raised in the abstract—there is no "specific, immediate" activist play seeking short-term profit or threatening disruption. When used in the hypothetical sense untethered to any concrete event, the phrases "short-termism" and "disruption" amount to mere euphemisms for stereotypes of stockholder activism generally and thus are not cognizable threats.

iii. Rapid Accumulation of Stock

The third justification for the Plan is the concern that activists might rapidly accumulate over 5% of the stock and the belief that the Plan could serve as an early-detection devise to plug the gaps in the federal disclosure regime.

[...] Rapid, undetected accumulation of stock in a short period of time [...] go undetected under the federal disclosure regime, which requires stockholders to disclose their ownership position after crossing the 5% threshold but gives stockholders ten days to do so. The federal disclosure regime does not prohibit stockholders from continuing to acquire stock during that ten-day period and does not capture "wolf pack" activity.

[...]

This decision need not address whether a true gap-filling pill [eds: a poison pill that forces investors to disclose acquisitions crossing the 5%-threshold earlier than the ten-day deadline] would be permissible. As discussed below, the features of the Plan are more extreme [...]

2. The Proportionality of the Response

Because Plaintiffs do not claim that the Plan is coercive or preclusive, the second prong of the *Unocal* inquiry requires the court to evaluate whether Defendants proved that adopting the Plan fell within a range of reasonable responses to the lightning-strike threat posed.

The thirty-thousand-foot view looks bad for Defendants. As Morgan Stanley advised the Board at the March 19 Meeting, the 5% trigger alone distinguished the Plan; only 2% of all plans identified by Morgan Stanley had a trigger lower than 10%. Even among pills with 5% triggers, the Plan ranked as one of only nine pills to ever utilize a 5% trigger outside the NOL context. Among Delaware corporations, it was one of only two. The other Delaware corporation to adopt a 5% trigger for a non-NOL pill did so in distinguishable circumstances—in the face of a campaign launched by an activist who held 7% of the company's outstanding shares at the time the pill was adopted. Of the twenty-one pills adopted between March 13 and April 6, 2020, only the Plan had a 5% triggering threshold. Of the twenty-one companies that adopted pills during that time, thirteen faced ongoing activist campaigns when adopting their pill.

The Plan's other key features are also extreme. The Plan's "beneficial ownership" definition goes beyond the default federal definitions to capture synthetic equity, such as options. The Plan's definition of "acting in concert" goes beyond the express-agreement default of federal law to capture "parallel conduct" and add the daisy-chain concept. The

Plan's "passive investor" definition goes beyond the influence-control default of federal law to exclude persons who seek to direct corporate policies. In sum, the Plan increases the range of Williams' nuclear missile range by a considerable distance beyond the ordinary poison pill.

The fact that the Plan's features depart from the default federal disclosure regulations is consistent with a gap-filling purpose, but [... h]ad the Board desired to close some of the gaps in the federal disclosure regime, the Board might have considered one of the less extreme options aimed at detection and designed to compel stockholder disclosure. Instead, the Board selected a Plan with features that went beyond those of gap-filling pills. Regardless of whether the Board intended to gap fill federal disclosure regulations—and whether that intent is permissible—the Plan's combination of features created a response that was disproportionate to its stated hypothetical threat.

The Plan's features also raise concerns when evaluated independently and divorced from comparisons. As Plaintiffs' proxy solicitor testified at trial, the Plan's combination of features are likely to chill a wide range of anodyne stockholder communications. Although the 5% trigger is a marked departure from market norms, it is not the most problematic aspect of the Plan, because a 5% ownership limit still permits an activist to buy a larger dollar value toehold in Williams than the vast majority of other poison pills with higher triggers. The primary offender is the AIC Provision, whose broad language sweeps up potentially benign stockholder communications "relating to changing *or influencing* the control of the Company." The definition gives the Board discretion to determine whether "plus" factors as innocuous as "exchanging information, attending meetings, [or] conducting discussions" can trigger the Plan. This language encompasses routine activities such as attending investor conferences and advocating for the same corporate action. It gloms on to this broad scope the daisy-chain concept that operates to aggregate stockholders even if members of the group have no idea that the other stockholders exist.

[...]

Defendants have a few responses to these criticisms of the AIC Provision. First, they say that the Plan does not preclude any stockholder from launching a proxy contest, and that "[a]ny purported impact the Plan might have on routine activism, short of a proxy contest, is irrelevant under *Unocal*." That argument misunderstands the proportionality inquiry of *Unocal*, which is not limited to the analysis conducted in *Moran*; rather, the proportionality analysis is tied to a pill's purpose, and with new purposes come new considerations. Moreover, as Plaintiffs' expert [Mills] opined, activity leading up to a proxy contest can impede a stockholder's ability to launch a proxy contest by cutting off private communications in advance of proxy contests. Mills explained that stockholders frequently "take the temperature" of other stockholders in advance of launching a proxy contest in light of the risk of financial and reputational damage resulting from a failed contest.

Second, Defendants observe that the AIC Provision is limited to actions that "relating to changing or influencing control" of Williams. Defendants contend that most routine forms of stockholder activism do not involve changing or influencing control of a company. Defendants argue that the AIC Provision contains several other "guardrails" limiting its applicability even when stockholders' do act in ways "relating to changing or influencing control" of the Company. [...] [H]owever, terms like "relating to" and "influencing," along with the other broad guardrails, are nebulous and broad. [...]

Third, Defendants argue that the Board would never trigger the Plan in response to [certain activities.] They [...] say that the court should not presume that the Board would misuse its power under the Plan. But this line of logic would excuse nearly any combination of poison pill terms and does not support a finding that the Plan's terms were reasonable in relation to the threat posed. It also provides cold comfort to [stockholders whose activities nominally trigger the Plan], who cannot rely on the Board's benevolence and must regulate their behavior based on what the Board could do.

The Passive Investor Definition sets another easily activated tripwire. Mills cites to a concrete example of this concern. On the day the Plan was announced, a representative of BlackRock, which holds over 5% of Williams' outstanding common stock [and a 13G filer], criticized Williams for failing to be fully transparent concerning the adoption of the Plan, stating "[t]his doesn't look good from an ESG perspective." This email reflects BlackRock "exercising the power to direct or cause the direction of the management and policies of the Company" and thus excludes BlackRock from the Passive Investor Definition. While it is probably true that the Board would exempt Blackrock and not risk angering a major stockholder player, other stockholders may not be so fortunate.

In the end, Defendants "bear the burden to show their actions were reasonable." They have failed to show that this extreme, unprecedented collection of features bears a reasonable relationship to their stated corporate objective. Because Defendants failed to prove that the Plan falls within the range of reasonable responses, the Plan is invalid.

III. CONCLUSION

For the foregoing reasons, judgment is entered in favor of the certified class declaring the Plan unenforceable and permanently enjoining the continued operation of the Plan. [...]

Part V: Securities Trading

The stock and other securities of large corporations tend to be traded on securities markets. In particular, listed securities such as Apple or IBM stock trade on securities exchanges like the New York Stock Exchange. (These days, exchanges are essentially computer systems matching buy and sell orders received through brokers.) Such trading between investors is also referred to as the secondary market. The primary market denotes sales by the corporation of its own securities to investors—in other words, the primary market is the market where the corporation actually raises capital. By contrast, secondary market trades between investors do not *directly* impact the finances of the corporation.

Nevertheless, the secondary market is very important for the issuing corporation, and indirectly affects its primary market. Most importantly, the secondary market provides liquidity to its investors, i.e., the ability to turn their investment into cash when desired (by selling to another investor). Investors pay more in the primary market for securities that have a liquid secondary market. In fact, once the secondary market is up and running, the corporation can anonymously sell additional stock directly into the secondary market, or buy it back for that matter (provided it has publicly announced its intention to do this in special SEC filings). Similarly, the liquidity afforded by the secondary market facilitates the acceptance of the corporation's securities as a means of payment. In particular, public corporations tend to pay their executives mostly in (restricted) stock, and often pay for acquisitions with stock as well ("stock deals"). Illiquid securities without a secondary market are sometimes accepted as payment as well, but less often and only at a discount. Finally, a liquid secondary market supports the accumulation of large minority blocks by activist shareholders without much of a price impact. As a blockholder, the activist will reap a sizeable reward from share price appreciation if the activist's intervention (engagement with the board, proxy fight, etc.) increases the value of the corporation (see price efficiency below), making the activist's intervention worthwhile. In this way, liquidity helps overcome the shareholder collective action problem.

Information asymmetry reduces liquidity. The higher the chance that your (anonymous) trading counterparty knows more than you do and trades only because you are getting a bad deal, the less willing you are to trade. To reduce information asymmetry, and to facilitate the exercise of voting and other rights covered in this course, the Exchange Act requires extensive periodic and ad hoc disclosures from

* Actually, the utility of information by itself does not quite explain why disclosure needs to be *mandated by statute*, rather than provided voluntarily or, more to the point, under an obligation self-imposed in the corporate charter. We get to these questions in the last part of the course.

issuers of publicly traded securities (see the Securities Law Primer in the introductory part of the course).*

Even with ample disclosure, you might worry that you will lose out against a savvy trader who is quicker at collecting or better at processing the information. Fortunately, savvy traders compete with one another for good deals, pushing the security's price close to the savvy traders' best estimate of the security's value. In fact, the efficient capital market hypothesis (ECMH) holds that, in a liquid market, the price will always be exactly equal to the best estimate of the security's fundamental value given publicly available information. There are two problems with the ECMH, which had its heyday in the 1970s and early 1980s and features prominently in *Basic* below. First, the ECMH cannot be completely true: if the price were always equal to the best estimate of fundamental value, then nobody could gain from informed trading, and hence nobody would have an incentive to learn and analyze the information required to bring prices in line in the first place. Second, in a world of uncertainty, "fundamental value" is in the eye of the beholder, and savvy traders may just try to predict the misperceptions of others with whom they hope to trade the security tomorrow.

In the memorable words of John Maynard Keynes's General Theory of Employment, Interest, and Money (1935):

> [P]rofessional investment may be likened to those newspaper competitions in which the competitors have to pick out the six prettiest faces from a hundred photographs, the prize being awarded to the competitor whose choice most nearly corresponds to the average preferences of the competitors as a whole; so that each competitor has to pick, not those faces which he himself finds prettiest, but those which he thinks likeliest to catch the fancy of the other competitors, all of whom are looking at the problem from the same point of view. It is not a case of choosing those which, to the best of one's judgment, are really the prettiest, nor even those which average opinion genuinely thinks the prettiest. We have reached the third degree where we devote our intelligences to anticipating what average opinion expects the average opinion to be. And there are some, I believe, who practise the fourth, fifth and higher degrees.

Much empirical work has shown that the truth is somewhere between that cynical view and the ECMH, and mostly closer to the ECMH: security prices are not completely efficient (i.e., equal to fundamental value), but they are usually a very good approximation. (In either case, most people who think they can outguess everyone else are fools.)

If security prices are a good approximation of fundamental value, it means they summarize information that can be used to evaluate performance. This is the idea behind stock and options as performance pay for executives: the value of their stock and options will track the price of the stock, which is an indicator, albeit a noisy one, of the executives' performance. By the same logic, price efficiency ensures that an activist shareholder will increase the stock price and hence gain from an intervention only if the activist's intervention actually improves the corporation. In the case of the executives (but not of the activist!), an important caveat is that even a fully efficient price only reflects *public* information.[9] Top executives can use their discretion under the accounting and disclosure rules to manage the information flow and hence the stock price to increase the value of their performance pay, or simply to avoid being fired. Similarly, corporate insiders (executives, engineers, etc.) can profitably—but not legally, see below—trade their corporation's securities even in fully efficient markets because they frequently possess "material nonpublic information" (mineral discoveries, engineering breakthroughs, regulatory matters, etc.).

Securities trading and securities regulation are thus inextricably intertwined with corporate governance and corporate law. In this course, we cannot cover the details of the disclosure and trading rules under the securities acts. We must, however, spend at least a little time discussing the enforcement of the disclosure rules that we have encountered in this class (e.g., 8-Ks, 10-Ks, 13-Ds, proxy statements, etc.), and more generally of truthfulness of the corporation's communications to its shareholders. Much of the enforcement burden falls on the SEC, which again belongs in a specialized course. But some of the enforcement is through private securities litigation, often brought by the same law firms that prosecute shareholder actions in Delaware courts. Indeed, these plaintiff law firms used to substitute federal securities lawsuits for Delaware litigation when Delaware courts were less receptive to shareholder lawsuits, and may try to do so again after *Trulia*. Specifically, we will study private securities fraud litigation under the Securities Exchange Act (Exchange Act) rule 10b-5, which is

---

[9] Technically, this is known as the semi-strong form of market efficiency. The strong form holds that the price includes all information, even private information. The strong form is quite clearly false, even though some private information does seep into the stock price, in part through legal and illegal insider trading (covered below).

the most general and hence most important and most controversial basis for such litigation.

The other aspect of securities law we will study is the prohibition and prevention of insider trading. The reason to do so is twofold. First, it is another area that might have fallen under state corporate law if doctrine had developed differently, and to a limited extent still does. Second, insider trading turns out to involve an important corporate governance issue: If insider trading were legal, executives might manage the corporation to maximize trading opportunities rather than corporate value. Besides, insider trading is a crime that most young lawyers will have opportunity and temptation to commit, so it is in your self-interest to learn what not to do. We will study insider trading liability under rules 10b-5 and 14e-3 and §16(b) of the Exchange Act.

Rule 10b-5

Before delving into the details, let us take a look at rule 10b-5, which is the formal basis of most securities litigation and most insider trading enforcement.

Rule 10b-5 is only one of many anti-fraud rules in securities law (cf., e.g., Exchange Act §14(e) for statements in connection with tender offers). Rule 10b-5 is just the most general, "catch-all" provision—among other things, it applies to any security, not just registered securities. It implements Exchange Act §10(b), which is not self-executing. §10(b) reads in its most relevant substantive part:

> It shall be unlawful for any person [...] [t]o use or employ, in connection with the purchase or sale of any security [...] any manipulative or deceptive device or contrivance in contravention of such rules and regulations as the Commission may prescribe [...]

Rule 10b-5 was adopted in 1942 without, it appears, much thought or any anticipation of the role it would come to play in the hands of the SEC and the courts later on. SEC staffers wanted to go after an instance of clear common law fraud. To obtain jurisdiction over the case, however, they needed the Commission to adopt a rule under §10(b) first. So the staffers copied §17 of the Securities Act and submitted it to the Commissioners. The Commissioners approved the rule without discussion.[10]

The rule reads:

---

[10] See Louis Loss & Joel Seligman, Fundamentals of Securities Regulation 937-8 (4th ed. 2004).

It shall be unlawful for any person, directly or indirectly, by the use of any means or instrumentality of interstate commerce, or of the mails or of any facility of any national securities exchange,

a. To employ any device, scheme, or artifice to defraud,

b. To make any untrue statement of a material fact or to omit to state a material fact necessary in order to make the statements made, in the light of the circumstances under which they were made, not misleading, or

c. To engage in any act, practice, or course of business which operates or would operate as a fraud or deceit upon any person,

in connection with the purchase or sale of any security.

The rule mentions neither a private right of action nor insider trading. But the courts soon implied a private right of action, and the SEC, with approval of the courts, brought insider trading cases under the rule. Ironically, these judicial creations are now recognized in the statute itself. For example, a later amendment of Exchange Act §10 explicitly references "insider trading" rules adopted by the SEC and by judicial precedent, extending such rules to "security-based swap agreements" (i.e., derivatives).

Plaintiffs attempted to bring even more corporate disputes under 10b-5, including cases unrelated to disclosure. In fact, in the early 1970s, most corporate law litigation was brought in the federal district courts under rule 10b-5, rather than in Delaware state courts under state law. Delaware was, at that time, unreceptive to shareholder suits involving fiduciary duty claims. By contrast, the Second Circuit read rule 10b-5 very expansively. The Supreme Court put an end to this in *Santa Fe Industries v. Green* (U.S. 1977). In that case, the Second Circuit had ruled that an unfair cash-out merger could be actionable "fraud" under rule 10b-5 even if defendants had fully disclosed all price-relevant information. The Supreme Court insisted, however, that 10b-5 required "deception, misrepresentation, or nondisclosure." In general, the Supreme Court has become much more hostile to private securities litigation over time. Thus, you should not expect a judicial expansion beyond what you will read below.

To avoid confusion, it is important to understand that insider trading cases and securities fraud actions involve and emphasize very different aspects of rule 10b-5. Usually, securities fraud cases turn on whether the information was misleading and material, whereas insider trading cases turn on whether the defendant had access to the information and, if so, whether the defendant improperly obtained or traded on it.

The main policy question in securities fraud is the availability of the class action (Do class attorneys force defendants into settlements by the threat of enormous litigation costs, irrespective of the merits [strike suits]? And even if suits are meritorious, who is deterred if the corporation pays the damages?), whereas the insider trading debate revolves around the definition of inside information and hence the boundaries of legitimate trading. Procedurally, securities fraud is typically litigated in a private class action, while insider trading is typically prosecuted by the S.E.C. or even the U.S. Attorney's Office. As a result, the legal questions are quite different, even though they formally arise under the same rule 10b-5.

Chapter 11. Securities Litigation

You know that listed corporations have extensive affirmative disclosure obligations under the securities acts (see the Securities Law Primer in Chapter 1). But what happens if the corporation does not disclose truthfully? One possibility is that the SEC will bring an enforcement action. Another possibility that we will look at here is that a specialized plaintiff law firm will file a "securities fraud" class action against the corporation (!). If the corporate disclosure was misleadingly positive, then the suit will attempt to recover damages for shareholders who bought at an inflated price — inflated because it was based on erroneously positive information. Inversely, sellers will sue if the disclosure was misleadingly negative and thus the price was deflated. Notice that those on the other side of these trades—sellers who sell at an inflated price, or buyers who buy at a deflated price—benefitted from the erroneous corporate disclosure, but they are not party to the litigation.

Most of the time, any individual trader's losses from the fraud are too small to make an individual lawsuit worthwhile. The big question in securities litigation is therefore the availability of the class action. That is the main question addressed in *Basic*, besides defining the standard of materiality for securities fraud. By endorsing the fraud-on-the-market theory, *Basic* paved the way for an entire industry of specialized class action law firms. Congress and recently the Supreme Court have tried to reign in some of this litigation, which remains controversial. In 1995, Congress passed the Private Securities Litigation Reform Act, which, among other things, introduced very strict pleading requirements via Exchange Act §21D.

Doctrinally, the fraud-on-the-market theory is an interpretation of the reliance element of the private right of action under rule 10b-5. Notwithstanding the convoluted text of the rule, the elements of a 10b-5 claim appear to be exactly the same as those of common law fraud: (1) a **false or misleading statement** (2) of a **material fact** (3) made with **scienter** that (4) the plaintiff reasonably **relied** on, (5) **causing injury** to the plaintiff. As the *Basic* decision shows, however, these similarities are deceptive. These elements have a special meaning in the context of 10b-5.

A. Basic Inc. v. Levinson (U.S. 1988)

Questions

1. How does the fraud-on-the-market theory relate to reliance? Why is this important for class certification?

2. According to the fraud-on-the-market theory, who relies on what? Why do they trade?

3. What social good, if any, do private securities fraud class actions generate? In other words, what is the policy justification, if any, for allowing this costly litigation to proceed?

4. In particular, how does the measure of damages relate to the social harm (as opposed to the private harm suffered by a subset of traders)?

485 U.S. 224 (1988)

BASIC INC. ET AL.

v.

LEVINSON ET AL.

[...]

JUSTICE BLACKMUN delivered the opinion of the Court.

This case requires us to apply the materiality requirement of § 10(b) of the Securities Exchange Act of 1934 (1934 Act), 48 Stat. 881, as amended, 15 U. S. C. § 78a *et seq.*, and the Securities and Exchange Commission's Rule 10b-5, 17 CFR § 240.10b-5 (1987), promulgated thereunder, in the context of preliminary corporate merger discussions. We must also determine whether a person who traded a corporation's shares on a securities exchange after the issuance of a materially misleading statement by the corporation may invoke a rebuttable presumption that, in trading, he relied on the integrity of the price set by the market.

I

Prior to December 20, 1978, Basic Incorporated was a publicly traded company primarily engaged in the business of manufacturing chemical refractories for the steel industry. As early as 1965 or 1966, Combustion Engineering, Inc., a company producing mostly alumina-based refractories, expressed some interest in acquiring Basic, but was deterred from pursuing this inclination seriously because of antitrust concerns it then entertained. See App. 81-83. In 1976, however, regulatory action opened the way to a renewal of [227] Combustion's interest. The "Strategic Plan," dated October 25, 1976, for Combustion's Industrial Products Group included the objective: "Acquire Basic Inc. $30 million." App. 337.

Beginning in September 1976, Combustion representatives had meetings and telephone conversations with Basic officers and directors, including petitioners here, concerning the possibility of a merger. During 1977 and 1978, Basic made three public statements denying that it was engaged in merger negotiations. On December 18, 1978, Basic asked [228] the New York Stock Exchange to suspend trading in its shares and issued a release stating that it had been "approached" by another company concerning a merger. *Id.*, at 413. On December 19, Basic's board endorsed Combustion's offer of $46 per share for its common stock, *id.*, at 335, 414-416, and on the following day publicly announced its approval of Combustion's tender offer for all outstanding shares.

Respondents are former Basic shareholders who sold their stock after Basic's first public statement of October 21, 1977, and before the suspension of trading in December 1978. Respondents brought a class action against Basic and its directors, asserting that the defendants issued three false or misleading public statements and thereby were in violation of § 10(b) of the 1934 Act and of Rule 10b-5. Respondents alleged that they were injured by selling Basic shares at artificially depressed prices in a market affected by petitioners' misleading statements and in reliance thereon.

The District Court adopted a presumption of reliance by members of the plaintiff class upon petitioners' public statements that enabled the court to conclude that common questions of fact or law predominated over particular questions pertaining to individual plaintiffs. See Fed. Rule Civ. Proc. 23(b)(3). The District Court therefore certified respondents' class. On the merits, however, the District Court granted [229] summary judgment for the defendants. It held that, as a matter of law, any misstatements were immaterial: there were no negotiations ongoing at the time of the first statement, and although negotiations were taking place when the second and third statements were issued, those negotiations were not "destined, with reasonable certainty, to become a merger agreement in principle." App. to Pet. for Cert. 103a.

The United States Court of Appeals for the Sixth Circuit affirmed the class certification, but reversed the District Court's summary judgment, and remanded the case. 786 F. 2d 741 (1986). The court reasoned that while petitioners were under no general duty to disclose their discussions with Combustion, any statement the company voluntarily released could not be " "so incomplete as to mislead.' " *Id.*, at 746, quoting *SEC* v. *Texas Gulf Sulphur Co.*, 401 F. 2d 833, 862 (CA2 1968) (en banc), cert. denied *sub nom.*

Coates v. SEC, 394 U. S. 976 (1969). In the Court of Appeals' view, Basic's statements that no negotiations were taking place, and that it knew of no corporate developments to account for the heavy trading activity, were misleading. With respect to materiality, the court rejected the argument that preliminary merger discussions are immaterial as a matter of law, and held that "once a statement is made denying the existence of any discussions, even discussions that might not have been material in absence of the denial are material because they make the statement made untrue." 786 F. 2d, at 749.

The Court of Appeals joined a number of other Circuits in accepting the "fraud-on-the-market theory" to create a rebuttable presumption that respondents relied on petitioners' material [230] misrepresentations, noting that without the presumption it would be impractical to certify a class under Federal Rule of Civil Procedure 23(b)(3). See 786 F. 2d, at 750-751.

We granted certiorari, 479 U. S. 1083 (1987), to resolve the split, see Part III, *infra*, among the Courts of Appeals as to the standard of materiality applicable to preliminary merger discussions, and to determine whether the courts below properly applied a presumption of reliance in certifying the class, rather than requiring each class member to show direct reliance on Basic's statements.

II

The 1934 Act was designed to protect investors against manipulation of stock prices. See S. Rep. No. 792, 73d Cong., 2d Sess., 1-5 (1934). Underlying the adoption of extensive disclosure requirements was a legislative philosophy: "There cannot be honest markets without honest publicity. Manipulation and dishonest practices of the market place thrive upon mystery and secrecy." H. R. Rep. No. 1383, 73d Cong., 2d Sess., 11 (1934). This Court "repeatedly has described the "fundamental purpose' of the Act as implementing a "philosophy of full disclosure.' " Santa Fe Industries, Inc. v. Green, 430 U. S. 462, 477-478 (1977), quoting SEC v. Capital Gains Research Bureau, Inc., 375 U. S. 180, 186 (1963).

Pursuant to its authority under § 10(b) of the 1934 Act, 15 U. S. C. § 78j, the Securities and Exchange Commission promulgated Rule 10b-5. Judicial interpretation and application, [231] legislative acquiescence, and the passage of time have removed any doubt that a private cause of action exists for a violation of § 10(b) and Rule 10b-5, and constitutes an essential tool for enforcement of the 1934 Act's requirements. [...]

The Court also explicitly has defined a standard of materiality under the securities laws, see TSC Industries, Inc. v. Northway, Inc., 426 U. S. 438 (1976), concluding in the proxy-solicitation context that "[a]n omitted fact is material if there is a substantial likelihood that a reasonable shareholder would consider it important in deciding how to vote." Id., at 449. Acknowledging that certain information concerning corporate developments could well be of "dubious significance," *id.*, at 448, the Court was careful not to set too low a standard of materiality; it was concerned that a minimal standard might bring an overabundance of information within its reach, and lead management "simply to bury the shareholders in an avalanche of trivial information — a result that is hardly conducive to informed decisionmaking." *Id.*, at 448-449. It further explained that to fulfill the materiality requirement "there must be a substantial likelihood that the disclosure of the omitted fact would have been viewed by the [232] reasonable investor as having significantly altered the "total mix' of information made available." *Id.*, at 449. We now expressly adopt the *TSC Industries* standard of materiality for the § 10(b) and Rule 10b-5 context.

III

The application of this materiality standard to preliminary merger discussions is not self-evident. Where the impact of the corporate development on the target's fortune is certain and clear, the *TSC Industries* materiality definition admits straightforward application. Where, on the other hand, the event is contingent or speculative in nature, it is difficult to ascertain whether the "reasonable investor" would have considered the omitted information significant at the time. Merger negotiations, because of the ever-present possibility that the contemplated transaction will not be effectuated, fall into the latter category.

A

Petitioners urge upon us a Third Circuit test for resolving this difficulty. [...] Under this [233] approach, preliminary merger discussions do not become material until "agreement-in-principle" as to the price and structure of the transaction has been reached between the would-be merger partners. [...]

Three rationales have been offered in support of the "agreement-in-principle" test. The first derives from the concern expressed in *TSC Industries* that an investor not be overwhelmed by excessively detailed and trivial information, and focuses on the substantial risk that preliminary merger discussions may collapse: because such discussions are inherently tentative, disclosure of their existence itself could mislead investors and foster false optimism. [...] The other two justifications for the agreement-in-principle standard are based on management concerns: because the requirement of "agreement-in-principle" limits the scope of disclosure obligations, it helps preserve the confidentiality of merger discussions where earlier disclosure might prejudice the negotiations; and the test also provides a usable, bright-line rule for determining when disclosure must be made. [...]

The first rationale, [...] assumes that investors are nitwits, unable to appreciate — even when told — that mergers are risky propositions up until the closing." *Flamm* v. *Eberstadt*, 814 F. 2d, at 1175. Disclosure, and not paternalistic withholding of accurate information, is the policy chosen and expressed by Congress. We have recognized time and again, a "fundamental purpose" of the various Securities Acts, "was to substitute a philosophy of full disclosure for the philosophy of *caveat emptor* and thus to achieve a high standard of business ethics in the securities industry." [...] The role of the materiality requirement is not to "attribute to investors a child-like simplicity, and inability to grasp the probabilistic significance of negotiations," *Flamm* v. *Eberstadt*, 814 F. 2d, at 1175, but to filter out essentially useless information that a reasonable investor would not consider significant, even as part of a larger "mix" of factors to consider in making his investment decision. *TSC Industries, Inc.* v. *Northway, Inc.*, 426 U. S., at 448-449.

The second rationale, the importance of secrecy during the early stages of merger discussions, also seems irrelevant to an assessment whether their existence is significant to the trading decision of a reasonable investor. [...]

Arguments based on the premise that some disclosure would be "premature" in a sense are more properly considered under the rubric of an issuer's duty to disclose. The "secrecy" rationale is simply inapposite to the definition of materiality.

[236] The final justification offered in support of the agreement-in-principle test seems to be directed solely at the comfort of corporate managers. A bright-line rule indeed is easier to follow than a standard that requires the exercise of judgment in the light of all the circumstances. But ease of application alone is not an excuse for ignoring the purposes of the Securities Acts and Congress' policy decisions. Any approach that designates a single fact or occurrence as always determinative of an inherently fact-specific finding such as materiality, must necessarily be overinclusive or underinclusive. In *TSC Industries* this Court explained: "The determination [of materiality] requires delicate assessments of the inferences a "reasonable shareholder' would draw from a given set of facts and the significance of those inferences to him ... ." 426 U. S., at 450. After much study, the Advisory Committee on Corporate Disclosure cautioned the SEC against administratively confining materiality to a rigid formula. Courts also would do well to heed this advice.

We therefore find no valid justification for artificially excluding from the definition of materiality information concerning merger discussions, which would otherwise be considered significant to the trading decision of a reasonable investor, merely because agreement-in-principle as to price and structure has not yet been reached by the parties or their representatives.

B

[237] The Sixth Circuit explicitly rejected the agreement-in-principle test, as we do today, but in its place adopted a rule that, if taken literally, would be equally insensitive, in our view, to the distinction between materiality and the other elements of an action under Rule 10b-5:

> "When a company whose stock is publicly traded makes a statement, as Basic did, that "no negotiations' are underway, and that the corporation knows of "no reason for the stock's activity,' and that "management is unaware of any present or pending corporate development that would result in the abnormally heavy trading activity,' information concerning ongoing acquisition discussions becomes material *by virtue of the statement denying their existence...* .

> ...

> "... In analyzing whether information regarding merger discussions is material such that it must be affirmatively disclosed to avoid a violation of Rule 10b-5, the discussions and their progress are the primary considerations. However, once a statement is made denying the existence of any discussions, even discussions that might not have been material in absence of the denial are material because they make the statement made untrue." 786 F. 2d, at 748-749 (emphasis in original).

[238] This approach, however, fails to recognize that, in order to prevail on a Rule 10b-5 claim, a plaintiff must show that the statements were *misleading* as to a *material* fact. It is not enough that a statement is false or incomplete, if the misrepresented fact is otherwise insignificant.

C

Even before this Court's decision in *TSC Industries*, the Second Circuit had explained the role of the materiality requirement of Rule 10b-5, with respect to contingent or speculative information or events, in a manner that gave that term meaning that is independent of the other provisions of the Rule. Under such circumstances, materiality "will depend at any given time upon a balancing of both the indicated probability that the event will occur and the anticipated magnitude of the event in light of the totality of the company activity." *SEC* v. *Texas Gulf Sulphur Co.*, 401 F. 2d, at 849. [...]

In a subsequent decision, the late Judge Friendly, writing for a Second Circuit panel, applied the *Texas Gulf Sulphur* probability/magnitude approach in the specific context of preliminary merger negotiations. After acknowledging that materiality is something to be determined on the basis of the particular facts of each case, he stated:

"Since a merger in which it is bought out is the most important event that can occur in a small corporation's life, to wit, its death, we think that inside information, as regards a merger of this sort, can become material at an earlier stage than would be the case as regards lesser transactions — and this even though the mortality rate of mergers in such formative stages is doubtless high." *SEC* v. *Geon Industries, Inc.,* 531 F. 2d 39, 47-48 (1976).

[239] We agree with that analysis.

Whether merger discussions in any particular case are material therefore depends on the facts. Generally, in order to assess the probability that the event will occur, a factfinder will need to look to indicia of interest in the transaction at the highest corporate levels. Without attempting to catalog all such possible factors, we note by way of example that board resolutions, instructions to investment bankers, and actual negotiations between principals or their intermediaries may serve as indicia of interest. To assess the magnitude of the transaction to the issuer of the securities allegedly manipulated, a factfinder will need to consider such facts as the size of the two corporate entities and of the potential premiums over market value. No particular event or factor short of closing the transaction need be either necessary or sufficient by itself to render merger discussions material. [...]

IV

A

We turn to the question of reliance and the fraud-on-the-market theory. Succinctly put:

> "The fraud on the market theory is based on the hypothesis that, in an open and developed securities market, the price of a company's stock is determined by the available material information regarding the company and its business.... Misleading statements will therefore [242] defraud purchasers of stock even if the purchasers do not directly rely on the misstatements.... The causal connection between the defendants' fraud and the plaintiffs' purchase of stock in such a case is no less significant than in a case of direct reliance on misrepresentations." *Peil* v. *Speiser,* 806 F. 2d 1154, 1160-1161 (CA3 1986).

Our task, of course, is not to assess the general validity of the theory, but to consider whether it was proper for the courts below to apply a rebuttable presumption of reliance, supported in part by the fraud-on-the-market theory. Cf. the comments of the dissent, *post,* at 252-255.

This case required resolution of several common questions of law and fact concerning the falsity or misleading nature of the three public statements made by Basic, the presence or absence of scienter, and the materiality of the misrepresentations, if any. In their amended complaint, the named plaintiffs alleged that in reliance on Basic's statements they sold their shares of Basic stock in the depressed market created by petitioners. [...] Requiring proof of individualized reliance from each member of the proposed plaintiff class effectively would have prevented respondents from proceeding with a class action, since individual issues then would have overwhelmed the common ones. The District Court found that the presumption of reliance created by the fraud-on-the-market theory provided "a practical resolution to the problem of balancing the substantive requirement of proof of reliance in securities cases against the procedural requisites of [Federal Rule of Civil Procedure] 23." The District Court thus concluded that with reference to each public statement and its impact upon the open market for Basic shares, common questions predominated over individual questions, as required by Federal Rules of Civil Procedure 23(a)(2) and (b)(3).

[243] Petitioners and their *amici* complain that the fraud-on-the-market theory effectively eliminates the requirement that a plaintiff asserting a claim under Rule 10b-5 prove reliance. They note that reliance is and long has been an element of common-law fraud, [...] and argue that because the analogous express right of action includes a reliance requirement, see, *e. g.*, § 18(a) of the 1934 Act, as amended, 15 U. S. C. § 78r(a), so too must an action implied under § 10(b).

We agree that reliance is an element of a Rule 10b-5 cause of action. See *Ernst & Ernst* v. *Hochfelder*, 425 U. S., at 206 (quoting Senate Report). Reliance provides the requisite causal connection between a defendant's misrepresentation and a plaintiff's injury. [...] There is, however, more than one way to demonstrate the causal connection. [...]

The modern securities markets, literally involving millions of shares changing hands daily, differ from the face-to-face [244] transactions contemplated by early fraud cases, and our understanding of Rule 10b-5's reliance requirement must encompass these differences.

> "In face-to-face transactions, the inquiry into an investor's reliance upon information is into the subjective pricing of that information by that investor. With the presence of a market, the market is interposed between seller and buyer and, ideally, transmits information to the investor in the processed form of a market price. Thus the market is performing a substantial part of the valuation process performed by the investor in a face-to-face transaction. The market is acting as the unpaid agent of the investor, informing him that given all the information

available to it, the value of the stock is worth the market price." *In re LTV Securities Litigation*, 88 F. R. D. 134, 143 (ND Tex. 1980).

[...]

B

Presumptions typically serve to assist courts in managing circumstances in which direct proof, for one reason or another, is rendered difficult. See, *e. g.*, 1 D. Louisell & C. Mueller, Federal Evidence 541-542 (1977). The courts below accepted a presumption, created by the fraud-on-the-market theory and subject to rebuttal by petitioners, that persons who had traded Basic shares had done so in reliance on the integrity of the price set by the market, but because of petitioners' material misrepresentations that price had been fraudulently depressed. Requiring a plaintiff to show a speculative state of facts, *i. e.*, how he would have acted if omitted material information had been disclosed, see *Affiliated Ute Citizens* v. *United States*, 406 U. S., at 153-154, or if the misrepresentation had not been made, see *Sharp* v. *Coopers & Lybrand*, 649 F. 2d 175, 188 (CA3 1981), cert. denied, 455 U. S. 938 (1982), would place an unnecessarily unrealistic evidentiary burden on the Rule 10b-5 plaintiff who has traded on an impersonal market. Cf. *Mills* v. *Electric Auto-Lite Co.*, 396 U. S., at 385.

Arising out of considerations of fairness, public policy, and probability, as well as judicial economy, presumptions are also useful devices for allocating the burdens of proof between parties. See E. Cleary, McCormick on Evidence 968-969 (3d ed. 1984); see also Fed. Rule Evid. 301 and Advisory Committee Notes, 28 U. S. C. App., p. 685. The presumption of reliance employed in this case is consistent with, and, by facilitating Rule 10b-5 litigation, supports, the congressional policy embodied in the 1934 Act. In drafting that Act, [246] Congress expressly relied on the premise that securities markets are affected by information, and enacted legislation to facilitate an investor's reliance on the integrity of those markets:

> "No investor, no speculator, can safely buy and sell securities upon the exchanges without having an intelligent basis for forming his judgment as to the value of the securities he buys or sells. The idea of a free and open public market is built upon the theory that competing judgments of buyers and sellers as to the fair price of a security brings [*sic*] about a situation where the market price reflects as nearly as possible a just price. Just as artificial manipulation tends to upset the true function of an open market, so the hiding and secreting of important information obstructs the operation of the markets as indices of real value." H. R. Rep. No. 1383, at 11.

[...]

The presumption is also supported by common sense and probability. Recent empirical studies have tended to confirm Congress' premise that the market price of shares traded on well-developed markets reflects all publicly available information, and, hence, any material misrepresentations. It has been noted that "it is hard to imagine that [247] there ever is a buyer or seller who does not rely on market integrity. Who would knowingly roll the dice in a crooked crap game?" [...]

C

[...]

Any showing that severs the link between the alleged misrepresentation and either the price received (or paid) by the plaintiff, or his decision to trade at a fair market price, will be sufficient to rebut the presumption of reliance. For example, if petitioners could show that the "market makers" were privy to the truth about the merger discussions here with Combustion, and thus that the market price would not have been affected by their misrepresentation, the causal connection could be broken: the basis for finding that the fraud had been transmitted through market price would be gone. Similarly, if, despite petitioners' allegedly fraudulent attempt [249] to manipulate market price, news of the merger discussions credibly entered the market and dissipated the effects of the misstatements, those who traded Basic shares after the corrective statements would have no direct or indirect connection with the fraud. Petitioners also could rebut the presumption of reliance as to plaintiffs who would have divested themselves of their Basic shares without relying on the integrity of the market. For example, a plaintiff who believed that Basic's statements were false and that Basic was indeed engaged in merger discussions, and who consequently believed that Basic stock was artificially underpriced, but sold his shares nevertheless because of other unrelated concerns, e. g., potential antitrust problems, or political pressures to divest from shares of certain businesses, could not be said to have relied on the integrity of a price he knew had been manipulated.

V

In summary:

1. We specifically adopt, for the § 10(b) and Rule 10b-5 context, the standard of materiality set forth in *TSC Industries, Inc.* v. *Northway, Inc.*, 426 U. S., at 449.

2. We reject "agreement-in-principle as to price and structure" as the bright-line rule for materiality.

3. We also reject the proposition that "information becomes material by virtue of a public statement denying it." [250]

4. Materiality in the merger context depends on the probability that the transaction will be consummated, and its significance to the issuer of the securities. Materiality depends on the facts and thus is to be determined on a case-by-case basis.

5. It is not inappropriate to apply a presumption of reliance supported by the fraud-on-the-market theory.

6. That presumption, however, is rebuttable.

7. The District Court's certification of the class here was appropriate when made but is subject on remand to such adjustment, if any, as developing circumstances demand.

The judgment of the Court of Appeals is vacated, and the case is remanded to that court for further proceedings consistent with this opinion.

It is so ordered.

THE CHIEF JUSTICE, JUSTICE SCALIA, and JUSTICE KENNEDY took no part in the consideration or decision of this case.

JUSTICE WHITE, with whom JUSTICE O'CONNOR joins, concurring in part and dissenting in part.

I join Parts I-III of the Court's opinion, [...] But I dissent from the remainder of the Court's holding because I do not agree that the "fraud-on-the-market" theory should be applied in this case.

I

[...]

A

At the outset, I note that there are portions of the Court's fraud-on-the-market holding with which I am in agreement. [...] I agree with the Court that if Rule 10b-5's reliance requirement is to be left with any content at all, the fraud-on-the-market presumption must be capable of being rebutted by a showing that a plaintiff did not "rely" on the market price. [...]

A nonrebuttable presumption of reliance [...] would effectively convert Rule 10b-5 into "a scheme of investor's insurance." [...]

B

But even as the Court attempts to limit the fraud-on-the-market theory it endorses today, the pitfalls in its approach are revealed by previous uses by the lower courts of the broader versions of the theory. [...]

The "wrong turns" in those Court of Appeals and District Court fraud-on-the-market decisions which the Court implicitly rejects as going too far should be ample illustration of the dangers when economic theories replace legal rules as the basis for recovery. Yet the Court today ventures into this area beyond its expertise, beyond — by its own admission — the confines of our previous fraud cases. See *ante*, at 243-244. Even if I agreed with the Court that "modern securities [254] markets ... involving millions of shares changing hands daily" require that the "understanding of Rule 10b-5's reliance requirement" be changed, *ibid.*, I prefer that such changes come from Congress in amending § 10(b). [...]

C

At the bottom of the Court's conclusion that the fraud-on-the-market theory sustains a presumption of reliance is the assumption that individuals rely "on the integrity of the market price" when buying or selling stock in "impersonal, well-developed market[s] for securities." *Ante*, at 247. Even if I was prepared to accept (as a matter of common sense or general understanding) the assumption that most persons buying or selling stock do so in response to the market price, the fraud-on-the-market theory goes further. For in adopting a "presumption of reliance," the Court *also* assumes that buyers and sellers rely — not just on the market price — but on the *"integrity"* of that price. It is this aspect of the fraud-on-the-market hypothesis which most mystifies me.

To define the term "integrity of the market price," the majority quotes approvingly from cases which suggest that investors are entitled to " 'rely on the price of a stock as a reflection of its value.' " *Ante*, at 244 (quoting *Peil v. Speiser*, 806 F. 2d 1154, 1161 (CA3 1986)). But the meaning of this phrase eludes me, for it implicitly suggests that stocks have some "true value" that is measurable by a standard other than their market price. While the scholastics of medieval times professed a means to make such a valuation of a commodity's "worth," I doubt that the federal courts of our day are similarly equipped.

[256] Even if securities had some "value" — knowable and distinct from the market price of a stock — investors do not always share the Court's presumption that a stock's price is a "reflection of [this] value." Indeed, "many investors purchase or sell stock because they believe the price *inaccurately* reflects the corporation's worth." See Black, Fraud on the Market: A Criticism of Dispensing with Reliance Requirements in Certain Open Market Transactions, 62 N. C. L. Rev. 435, 455 (1984) (emphasis added). If investors really

believed that stock prices reflected a stock's "value," many sellers would never sell, and many buyers never buy (given the time and cost associated with executing a stock transaction). [...]

III

Finally, the particular facts of this case make it an exceedingly poor candidate for the Court's fraud-on-the-market theory, [260] and illustrate the illogic achieved by that theory's application in many cases.

Respondents here are a class of sellers who sold Basic stock between October 1977 and December 1978, a 14-month period. At the time the class period began, Basic's stock was trading at $20 a share (at the time, an all-time high); the last members of the class to sell their Basic stock got a price of just over $30 a share. App. 363, 423. It is indisputable that virtually every member of the class made money from his or her sale of Basic stock.

The oddities of applying the fraud-on-the-market theory in this case are manifest. First, there are the facts that the plaintiffs are sellers and the class period is so lengthy — both are virtually without precedent in prior fraud-on-the-market cases. For reasons I discuss in the margin, I think these two facts render this case less apt to application of the fraud-on-the-market hypothesis.

Second, there is the fact that in this case, there is no evidence that petitioner Basic's officials made the troublesome misstatements for the purpose of manipulating stock prices, or with any intent to engage in underhanded trading of Basic stock. Indeed, during the class period, petitioners do not [261] appear to have purchased or sold *any* Basic stock whatsoever. App. to Pet. for Cert. 27a. I agree with *amicus* who argues that "[i]mposition of damages liability under Rule 10b-5 makes little sense ... where a defendant is neither a purchaser nor a seller of securities." See Brief for American Corporate Counsel Association as *Amicus Curiae* 13. In fact, in previous cases, we had recognized that Rule 10b-5 is concerned primarily with cases where the fraud is committed by one trading the security at issue. See, *e. g., Blue Chip Stamps* v. *Manor Drug Stores,* 421 U. S. 723, 736, n. 8 (1975). And it is difficult to square liability in this case with § 10(b)'s express provision that it prohibits fraud "*in connection with* the purchase or sale of any security." See 15 U. S. C. § 78j(b) (emphasis added).

Third, there are the peculiarities of what kinds of investors will be able to recover in this case. As I read the District Court's class certification order, App. to Pet. for Cert. 123a-126a; *ante,* at 228-229, n. 5, there are potentially many persons who did not purchase Basic stock until *after* the first false statement (October 1977), but who nonetheless *will* be able to recover under the Court's fraud-on-the-market theory. Thus, it is possible that a person who heard the first corporate misstatement and *disbelieved* it — *i. e.,* someone who purchased Basic stock thinking that petitioners' statement was false — may still be included in the plaintiff-class on remand. How a person who undertook such a speculative stock-investing strategy — and made $10 a share doing so (if he bought on October 22, 1977, and sold on December 15, 1978) — can say that he was "defrauded" by virtue of his reliance on the "integrity" of the market price is beyond me. [262] And such speculators may not be uncommon, at least in this case. See App. to Pet. for Cert. 125a.

Indeed, the facts of this case lead a casual observer to the almost inescapable conclusion that many of those who bought or sold Basic stock during the period in question flatly disbelieved the statements which are alleged to have been "materially misleading." Despite three statements denying that merger negotiations were underway, Basic stock hit record-high after record-high during the 14-month class period. It seems quite possible that, like Casca's knowing disbelief of Caesar's "thrice refusal" of the Crown, clever investors were skeptical of petitioners' three denials that merger talks were going on. Yet such investors, the saviest of the savvy, will be able to recover under the Court's opinion, as long as they now claim that they believed in the "integrity of the market price" when they sold their stock (between September and December 1978). Thus, persons who bought after hearing and relying on the *falsity* of petitioners' statements may be able to prevail and recover money damages on remand.

And who will pay the judgments won in such actions? I suspect that all too often the majority's rule will "lead to large judgments, payable in the last analysis by innocent investors, for the benefit of speculators and their lawyers." [...]

It has been suggested that given current market practices, a "no comment" statement is tantamount to an admission that merger discussions are underway. See *Flamm* v. *Eberstadt,* 814 F. 2d, at 1178. That may well hold true to the extent that issuers adopt a policy of truthfully denying merger rumors when no discussions are underway, and of issuing "no comment" statements when they are in the midst of negotiations. There are, of course, other statement policies firms could adopt; we need not now advise issuers as to what kind of practice to follow, within the range permitted by law. Perhaps more importantly, we think that creating an exception to a regulatory scheme founded on a prodisclosure legislative philosophy, because complying with the regulation might be "bad for business," is a role for Congress, not this Court. [...]

Chapter 12. Insider Trading

A. Overview

We now turn to insider trading. As mentioned above, the main rule is again 10b-5, but the questions are rather different than those in standard securities fraud cases. Doctrinally, the main question is how to fit the idea of insider trading (use of inside information) under an anti-fraud rule (answer: by inventing a duty to disclose, such that insiders commit fraud by omission if they don't disclose). The main policy question is how far insider trading liability should reach. There must be some informed trading if prices are supposed to be "efficient," i.e., correct. The three cases we will read are about that.

Practically speaking, the biggest issue of insider trading law is enforcement. In the words of Judge Rakoff at the sentencing of Rajat Gupta (the retired chief executive of McKinsey and board member of Goldman Sachs who passed confidential information from Goldman's board meeting to a hedge fund as soon as he left the meeting):

> Insider trading is an easy crime to commit but a difficult crime to catch. Others similarly situated to the defendant must therefore be made to understand that when you get caught, you will go to jail.

These enforcement difficulties are one reason why insider trading is policed primarily through criminal and administrative enforcement, not private litigation. Many insider trading cases come to light only through criminal law enforcement tools such as wire-tapping. The exchanges also have monitoring systems and report unusual trading activity to the SEC.

Another reason why private litigation plays a minor role is the lack of incentives for plaintiff law firms. The courts and Exchange Act §20A(b)(1), adopted in 1988, have capped insider trading damages at the gain derived by the defendant. In any event, the individual defendants are usually judgment proof beyond some comparatively small amount of personal wealth (compared, that is, to the hundreds of millions the plaintiff law firms can win from corporations).

1. Law

(a) Exchange Act §16

Perhaps in recognition of these enforcement difficulties, §16 of the Exchange Act provides two rules that do not directly target insider trading but may catch or expose most of it.

Subsection (a) provides that corporate directors, officers, and principal stockholders must within two business days disclose each and every transaction in the corporation's equity securities, including derivatives written on those securities. The Act defines principal stockholders as those who own at least 10% of the corporation's stock. The SEC provides further definitions of the subsection's terms in rules 16a-1 and 16a-2. Rule 16a-3(a) stipulates that filings are to be made on the so-called "form 4."

Naturally, not all trades by corporate insiders disclosed on form 4 are illegal. If the insider does not possess any material non-public information at the time of trade, the trade is permissible. But once disclosed on form 4, the insiders' trades can be scrutinized by private and public investigators.

Subsection (b) of §16 grants the corporation a right of action to recover any so-called short swing trading profits from its officers, directors, and principal stockholders. (The provision explicitly contemplates a shareholder derivative action if the corporation does not bring suit within 60 days of a request.) The provision is explicitly targeting insider trading in a prophylactic manner. It reads, in its core part:

> For the purpose of preventing the unfair use of information which may
> have been obtained by such beneficial owner, director, or officer by
> reason of his relationship to the issuer, any profit realized by him from
> any purchase and sale, or any sale and purchase, of any equity security
> of such issuer … within any period of less than six months … shall inure
> to and be recoverable by the issuer.

Clearly, not all trades occurring within six months of one another use insider information. Nor are all trades that do use insider information unwound within six months. The provision is thus both over- and under-inclusive as a weapon against insider trading. It is, however, very easy to administer, especially given the information provided on forms 4.

(b) 10b-5

The main rule that directly targets the impermissible use of insider information is 10b-5.

As already mentioned, the issues arising under 10b-5 in insider trading cases are quite different from the main issues in standard securities fraud litigation. Many of the issues occupying private securities fraud litigators are simply irrelevant in criminal insider trading cases. Criminal liability requires only a misrepresentation of a material fact committed with scienter. The other, victim-centric elements of private fraud claims, namely reliance, injury, and loss causation, are irrelevant. Moreover, prosecutors tend to shy away from cases where materiality is not self-evident.

The main doctrinal question in insider trading cases is whether there was a misrepresentation. To cast the mere use of inside information in impersonal security markets as a misrepresentation towards an anonymous counterparty required considerable doctrinal work by the courts. Before rule 10b-5, most courts had refused to subsume insider trading under common law fraud. The SEC, the federal courts, and ultimately the Supreme Court brought insider trading under the 10b-5 anti-fraud rule by stipulating a "duty to abstain [from trading] or disclose." In reading the cases, you might wonder where exactly that duty comes from. In any event, Congress explicitly endorsed this jurisprudence *post hoc*.

In comparative perspective, the Supreme Court's wrestling with the notion of a "duty to disclose or abstain" is an anomaly. Other jurisdictions, such as the UK, have insider trading rules distinct from general anti-fraud rules. The doctrinal issue of a "duty to disclose" does not arise there. Of course, all jurisdictions have to grapple with the legal and policy question of what exactly does and should constitute illegal insider trading.

(c) Other federal rules

There are other, more specialized insider trading rules. In particular, after losing *Chiarella* below, the SEC adopted rule 14e-3 against insider trading in the context of tender offers. As discussed in *O'Hagan* below, this rule is not directly based on the fraud concept and therefore broader.

Many other SEC rules deal with details of insider trading, in particular under rule 10b-5. Again, the irony is that the SEC never passed an explicit rule against insider trading under Exchange Act §10, even though it did pass rules interpreting the court decisions interpreting rule 10b-5 with respect to insider trading.

For example, the SEC adopted a safe harbor provision for "trading plans" under which executives pre-commit to buy or sell their corporation's securities at certain future points in time (rule 10b5-1). This rule is important because a large part of executive compensation is stock or options. Executives could hardly ever monetize these awards before retirement if they did not have this safe harbor.

Rule 10b5-2 purports to define the "duty of trust" whose breach can give rise to insider trading liability under the misappropriation theory (see *O'Hagan* below). Of note, paragraph (b)(3) of the rule presumes such a duty between family members.

(d) State law

Insider trading may also raise a claim under state law. The Delaware Supreme Court reaffirmed this rule in *Kahn v. Kolberg Kravis Roberts* (2011). Relying on *Guth*, the Court held that such a "*Brophy*" claim (after a 1949 decision) is not limited to damages sustained by the corporation or even to the loss of a corporate opportunity (to trade). Instead, the Court predicated insider-trading liability on "unjust enrichment based on the misuse of confidential corporate information." Again, however, such private claims are rarely brought, presumably because of the enforcement difficulties outlined above.

2. Policy

While insider trading is criminal today, it used to be considered a normal executive perk in the not too distant past. Moreover, serious policy analysts have argued that insider trading ought to be permissible. Their main argument is that insider trades reveal information to the market. To wit, if insiders buy, the market can infer good news, and the stock price will go up. Inversely, if insiders sell, the market can infer bad news, and the stock price will go down. In either case, the insider trades move the prices closer to the "fundamental value" of the stock. Insider trading thus makes the price more "informationally efficient," i.e., correct.

The standard objection is that like any trading gain, the inside trader's gain is another trader's loss. Insider trading thus systematically shifts value from outside investors and speculators to insiders. As a result, such outside investment and speculation may be deterred.

The standard objection is seriously incomplete because losing against a better informed trader is a normal part of trading. For an uninformed trader, it is irrelevant if he or she loses to an insider or to hedge funds who compiled the information from public sources. A more subtle objection is that hedge funds might not enter the market if they had to compete against better informed insiders. The net effect of insider trading could thus be *less* information in stock prices. As long as the information content is at least not less, however, having the insiders do the trading is actually preferable: it saves the resources (personnel, computing power, spy satellites, etc.) that the hedge funds would have directed at figuring out information that the insiders already possess.

There is a much bigger problem with the contrarian view favoring insider trading. It assumes that all other insider behavior would be unchanged if insider trading were allowed. Realistically, insiders would probably be much more reluctant to disclose information if keeping it secret increased their trading profits. Thus, allowing insider trading might reduce, rather than increase, the information available to the public and ultimately the informational efficiency of stock prices. Worse, insiders might intentionally increase the riskiness of the corporation's business if they could use inside information about risk realizations for profitable trading. That is, the ability to trade would divert insiders' attention and warp their incentives in choosing projects. They could attempt to profit from, and expend resources on, trading (a social zero-sum game), rather than focusing on producing good products, etc. (a social welfare improvement). Prohibiting insider trading thus helps align insiders' incentives with social welfare.

B. Chiarella v. United States (U.S. 1980)

This decision rejects the so-called "equal access theory" of insider trading, according to which anyone trading while in possession of material nonpublic information violates rule 10b-5.

Questions

1. According to the majority, why is the equal access theory inconsistent with rule 10b-5? In other words, what else is required for a 10b-5 violation, besides trading while in possession of material nonpublic information?

2. As Burger's dissent points out, Chiarella did not simply trade while in possession of material nonpublic information: Chiarella misappropriated that information from his employer. Why is such misappropriation not sufficient to subject his trades to 10b-5 liability? Or is it? Cf. part IV of the majority opinion and *O'Hagan*, infra.

3. Do you think the equal access theory would be good policy? What interests would it protect, if any? What desirable activities might it hamper?

445 U.S. 222 (1980)

CHIARELLA

v.

UNITED STATES.

[...]

MR. JUSTICE POWELL delivered the opinion of the Court.

The question in this case is whether a person who learns from the confidential documents of one corporation that it is planning an attempt to secure control of a second corporation violates § 10 (b) of the Securities Exchange Act of 1934 if he fails to disclose the impending takeover before trading in the target company's securities.

I

Petitioner is a printer by trade. In 1975 and 1976, he worked as a "markup man" in the New York composing room of Pandick Press, a financial printer. Among documents that petitioner handled were five announcements of corporate takeover bids. When these documents were delivered to the printer, the identities of the acquiring and target corporations were concealed by blank spaces or false names. The true names were sent to the printer on the night of the final printing.

The petitioner, however, was able to deduce the names of the target companies before the final printing from other information contained in the documents. Without disclosing his knowledge, petitioner purchased stock in the target companies and sold the shares immediately after the takeover attempts were made public. By this method, petitioner realized a gain of slightly more than $30,000 in the course of 14 months. Subsequently, the Securities and Exchange Commission (Commission or SEC) began an investigation of his trading activities. In May 1977, petitioner entered into a consent decree with the Commission in which he agreed to return his profits to the sellers of the shares. On the same day, he was discharged by Pandick Press.

[225] In January 1978, petitioner was indicted on 17 counts of violating § 10 (b) of the Securities Exchange Act of 1934 (1934 Act) and SEC Rule 10b-5. After petitioner unsuccessfully moved to dismiss the indictment, he was brought to trial and convicted on all counts.

The Court of Appeals for the Second Circuit affirmed petitioner's conviction. 588 F. 2d 1358 (1978). We granted certiorari, 441 U. S. 942 (1979), and we now reverse.

II

[...]

This case concerns the legal effect of the petitioner's silence. The District Court's charge permitted the jury to convict the petitioner if it found that he willfully failed to inform sellers of target company securities that he knew of a forthcoming takeover bid that would make their shares more valuable. [...]

§ 10 (b) does not state whether silence may constitute a manipulative or deceptive device. Section 10 (b) was designed as a catchall clause to prevent fraudulent practices. 425 U. S., at 202, 206. But neither the legislative history nor the statute itself affords specific guidance for the resolution of this case. When Rule 10b-5 was promulgated in 1942, the SEC did not discuss the possibility that failure to provide information might run afoul of § 10 (b). [...]

At common law, misrepresentation made for the purpose of inducing reliance [228] upon the false statement is fraudulent. But one who fails to disclose material information prior to the consummation of a transaction commits fraud only when he is under a duty to do so. And the duty to disclose arises when one party has information "that the other [party] is entitled to know because of a fiduciary or other similar relation of trust and confidence between them." In its *Cady, Roberts* decision, the Commission recognized a relationship of trust and confidence between the shareholders of a corporation and those insiders who have obtained confidential information by reason of their position with that corporation. This relationship gives rise to a duty to disclose because of the "necessity of preventing a corporate insider from ... tak[ing] unfair advantage of the [229] uninformed minority stockholders." *Speed* v. *Transamerica Corp.*, 99 F. Supp. 808, 829 (Del. 1951).

The federal courts have found violations of § 10 (b) where corporate insiders used undisclosed information for their own benefit. *E. g., SEC* v. *Texas Gulf Sulphur Co.*, 401 F. 2d 833 (CA2 1968), cert. denied, 404 U. S. 1005 (1971). [...] Accordingly, a purchaser of stock who has no duty to a prospective seller because he is neither an insider nor a fiduciary has been held to have no obligation to reveal material facts. See *General Time Corp.* v. *Talley Industries, Inc.*, 403 F. 2d 159, 164 (CA2 1968), cert. denied, 393 U. S. 1026 (1969).

This Court followed the same approach in *Affiliated Ute Citizens* v. *United States*, 406 U. S. 128 (1972). [...]

Thus, administrative and judicial interpretations have established that silence in connection with the purchase or sale of securities may operate as a fraud actionable under § 10 (b) despite the absence of statutory language or legislative history specifically addressing the legality of nondisclosure. But such liability is premised upon a duty to disclose arising from a relationship of trust and confidence between parties to a transaction. Application of a duty to disclose prior to trading guarantees that corporate insiders, who have an obligation to place the shareholder's welfare before their own, will not benefit personally through fraudulent use of material, nonpublic information. [231]

III

In this case, the petitioner was convicted of violating § 10 (b) although he was not a corporate insider and he received no confidential information from the target company. Moreover, the "market information" upon which he relied did not concern the earning power or operations of the target company, but only the plans of the acquiring company. Petitioner's use of that information was not a fraud under § 10 (b) unless he was subject to an affirmative duty to disclose it before trading. In this case, the jury instructions failed to specify any such duty. In effect, the trial court instructed the jury that petitioner owed a duty to everyone; to all sellers, indeed, to the market as a whole. The jury simply was told to decide whether petitioner used material, nonpublic information at a time when "he knew other people trading in the securities market did not have access to the same information." Record 677.

The Court of Appeals affirmed the conviction by holding that "[a]nyone—corporate insider or not—who regularly receives material nonpublic information may not use that information to trade in securities without incurring an affirmative duty to disclose." 588 F. 2d, at 1365 (emphasis in original). [...] The use by anyone of material information not generally available is fraudulent, this theory suggests, because such information gives certain buyers or sellers an unfair advantage over less informed buyers and sellers.

This reasoning suffers from two defects. First, not every instance of financial unfairness constitutes fraudulent activity under § 10 (b). See *Santa Fe Industries, Inc. v. Green*, 430 U. S. 462, 474-477 (1977). Second, the element required to make silence fraudulent—a duty to disclose—is absent in this case. No duty could arise from petitioner's relationship with the sellers of the target company's securities, for petitioner had no prior dealings with them. He was not their agent, he was not a fiduciary, he was not a person in whom the sellers had placed their trust and confidence. He was, in fact, a complete [233] stranger who dealt with the sellers only through impersonal market transactions.

We cannot affirm petitioner's conviction without recognizing a general duty between all participants in market transactions to forgo actions based on material, nonpublic information. Formulation of such a broad duty, which departs radically from the established doctrine that duty arises from a specific relationship between two parties, see n. 9, *supra*, should not be undertaken absent some explicit evidence of congressional intent.

As we have seen, no such evidence emerges from the language or legislative history of § 10 (b). Moreover, neither the Congress nor the Commission ever has adopted a parity-of-information rule. [...]

IV

In its brief to this Court, the United States offers an alternative theory to support petitioner's conviction. It argues that petitioner breached a duty to the acquiring corporation when he acted upon information that he obtained by virtue of his position as an employee of a printer employed by the corporation. The breach of this duty is said to support a [236] conviction under § 10 (b) for fraud perpetrated upon both the acquiring corporation and the sellers.

We need not decide whether this theory has merit for it was not submitted to the jury. [...]

MR. CHIEF JUSTICE BURGER, dissenting.

I believe that the jury instructions in this case properly charged a violation of § 10 (b) and Rule 10b-5, and I would affirm the conviction.

I

As a general rule, neither party to an arm's-length business transaction has an obligation to disclose information to the [240] other unless the parties stand in some confidential or fiduciary relation. See W. Prosser, Law of Torts § 106 (2d ed. 1955). This rule permits a businessman to capitalize on his experience and skill in securing and evaluating relevant information; it provides incentive for hard work, careful analysis, and astute forecasting. But the policies that underlie the rule also should limit its scope. In particular, the rule should give way when an informational advantage is obtained, not by superior experience, foresight, or industry, but by some unlawful means. One commentator has written:

> "[T]he way in which the buyer acquires the information which he conceals from the vendor should be a material circumstance. The information might have been acquired as the result of his bringing to bear a superior knowledge, intelligence, skill or technical judgment; it might have been acquired by mere chance; or it might have been acquired by means of some tortious action on his part... . *Any time information is acquired by an illegal act it would seem that there should be a duty to disclose that information.*" Keeton, Fraud—Concealment and Non-Disclosure, 15 Texas L. Rev. 1, 25-26 (1936) (emphasis added).

I would read § 10 (b) and Rule 10b-5 to encompass and build on this principle: to mean that a person who has misappropriated nonpublic information has an absolute duty to disclose that information or to refrain from trading.

The language of § 10 (b) and of Rule 10b-5 plainly supports such a reading. By their terms, these provisions reach *any* person engaged in *any* fraudulent scheme. [...]

The history of the statute and of the Rule also supports this reading. The antifraud provisions were designed in large measure "to assure that dealing in securities is fair and without undue preferences or advantages among investors." H. R. Conf. Rep. No. 94-229, p. 91 (1975). These provisions prohibit "those manipulative and deceptive practices which have been demonstrated to fulfill no useful function." S. Rep. No. 792, 73d Cong., 2d Sess., 6 (1934). An investor who purchases securities on the basis of misappropriated nonpublic information possesses just such an "undue" trading advantage; his conduct quite clearly serves no useful function except his own enrichment at the expense of others.

This interpretation of § 10 (b) and Rule 10b-5 is in no sense novel. It follows naturally from legal principles enunciated by the Securities and Exchange Commission in its seminal *Cady, Roberts* decision. 40 S. E. C. 907 (1961). There, the Commission relied upon two factors to impose a duty to disclose on corporate insiders: (1) "… access … to information intended to be available only for a corporate purpose *and not for the personal benefit of anyone*" (emphasis added); and (2) the unfairness inherent in trading on such information when it is inaccessible to those with whom one is dealing. Both of these factors are present whenever a party gains an [242] informational advantage by unlawful means. [...]

MR. JUSTICE BLACKMUN, with whom MR. JUSTICE MARSHALL joins, dissenting.

Although I agree with much of what is said in Part I of the dissenting opinion of THE CHIEF JUSTICE, *ante,* p. 239, I write separately because, in my view, it is unnecessary to rest petitioner's conviction on a "misappropriation" theory. The fact that petitioner Chiarella purloined, or, to use THE CHIEF [246] JUSTICE's word, *ante,* at 245, "stole," information concerning pending tender offers certainly is the most dramatic evidence that petitioner was guilty of fraud. He has conceded that he knew it was wrong, and he and his co-workers in the printshop were specifically warned by their employer that actions of this kind were improper and forbidden. But I also would find petitioner's conduct fraudulent within the meaning of § 10 (b) of the Securities Exchange Act of 1934, 15 U. S. C. § 78j (b), and the Securities and Exchange Commission's Rule 10b-5, 17 CFR § 240.10b-5 (1979), even if he had obtained the blessing of his employer's principals before embarking on his profiteering scheme. Indeed, I think petitioner's brand of manipulative trading, with or without such approval, lies close to the heart of what the securities laws are intended to prohibit.

The Court continues to pursue a course, charted in certain recent decisions, designed to transform § 10 (b) from an intentionally elastic "catchall" provision to one that catches relatively little of the misbehavior that all too often makes investment in securities a needlessly risky business for the uninitiated investor. [...]

C. Dirks v. SEC (US 1983)

Dirks is the leading case on "tippee" liability under rule 10b-5. A "tippee" is a corporate outsider who trades after receiving material nonpublic information from an insider or another tippee.

Questions

1. According to the majority, when are tippees liable under rule 10b-5?

2. Why did the majority exonerate Dirks?

3. As a policy matter, should Dirks have been obliged to report to the SEC before telling his clients?

463 U.S. 646 (1983)

DIRKS

v.

SECURITIES AND EXCHANGE COMMISSION

[...]

JUSTICE POWELL delivered the opinion of the Court.

Petitioner Raymond Dirks received material nonpublic information from "insiders" of a corporation with which he had no connection. He disclosed this information to investors who relied on it in trading in the shares of the corporation. The question is whether Dirks violated the antifraud provisions of the federal securities laws by this disclosure.

I

In 1973, Dirks was an officer of a New York broker-dealer firm who specialized in providing investment analysis of insurance company securities to institutional investors. On [649] March 6, Dirks received information from Ronald Secrist, a former officer of Equity Funding of America. Secrist alleged that the assets of Equity Funding, a diversified corporation primarily engaged in selling life insurance and mutual funds, were vastly overstated as the result of fraudulent corporate practices. Secrist also stated that various regulatory agencies had failed to act on similar charges made by Equity Funding employees. He urged Dirks to verify the fraud and disclose it publicly.

Dirks decided to investigate the allegations. He visited Equity Funding's headquarters in Los Angeles and interviewed several officers and employees of the corporation. The senior management denied any wrongdoing, but certain corporation employees corroborated the charges of fraud. Neither Dirks nor his firm owned or traded any Equity Funding stock, but throughout his investigation he openly discussed the information he had obtained with a number of clients and investors. Some of these persons sold their holdings of Equity Funding securities, including five investment advisers who liquidated holdings of more than $16 million.

While Dirks was in Los Angeles, he was in touch regularly with William Blundell, the Wall Street Journal's Los Angeles bureau chief. Dirks urged Blundell to write a story on the fraud allegations. Blundell did not believe, however, that such a massive fraud could go undetected and declined to [650] write the story. He feared that publishing such damaging hearsay might be libelous.

During the 2-week period in which Dirks pursued his investigation and spread word of Secrist's charges, the price of Equity Funding stock fell from $26 per share to less than $15 per share. This led the New York Stock Exchange to halt trading on March 27. Shortly thereafter California insurance authorities impounded Equity Funding's records and uncovered evidence of the fraud. Only then did the Securities and Exchange Commission (SEC) file a complaint against Equity Funding[3] and only then, on April 2, did the Wall Street Journal publish a front-page story based largely on information assembled by Dirks. Equity Funding immediately went into receivership.

The SEC began an investigation into Dirks' role in the exposure of the fraud. After a hearing by an Administrative Law Judge, the SEC found that Dirks had aided and abetted violations of § 17(a) of the Securities Act of 1933, 48 Stat. 84, as amended, 15 U. S. C. § 77q(a), § 10(b) of the Securities [651] Exchange Act of 1934, 48 Stat. 891, 15 U. S. C. § 78j(b), and SEC Rule 10b-5, 17 CFR § 240.10b-5 (1983), by repeating the allegations of fraud to members of the investment community who later sold their Equity Funding stock. The SEC concluded: "Where "tippees' — regardless of their motivation or occupation — come into possession of material "corporate information that they know is confidential and know or should know came from a corporate insider,' they must either publicly disclose that information or refrain from trading." 21 S. E. C. Docket 1401, 1407 (1981) (footnote omitted) (quoting *Chiarella* v. *United States*, 445 U. S. 222, 230, n. 12 (1980)). Recognizing, however, that Dirks "played an important role in bringing [Equity

---

[3] As early as 1971, the SEC had received allegations of fraudulent accounting practices at Equity Funding. Moreover, on March 9, 1973, an official of the California Insurance Department informed the SEC's regional office in Los Angeles of Secrist's charges of fraud. Dirks himself voluntarily presented his information at the SEC's regional office beginning on March 27.

Funding's] massive fraud [652] to light," 21 S. E. C. Docket, at 1412, the SEC only censured him.

Dirks sought review in the Court of Appeals for the District of Columbia Circuit. The court entered judgment against Dirks "for the reasons stated by the Commission in its opinion." [...]

In view of the importance to the SEC and to the securities industry of the question presented by this case, we granted a writ of certiorari. 459 U. S. 1014 (1982). We now reverse. [653]

II

In the seminal case of *In re Cady, Roberts & Co.*, 40 S. E. C. 907 (1961), the SEC recognized that the common law in some jurisdictions imposes on "corporate "insiders,' particularly officers, directors, or controlling stockholders" an "affirmative duty of disclosure ... when dealing in securities." [...]

III

We were explicit in *Chiarella* in saying that there can be no duty to disclose where the person who has traded on inside information "was not [the corporation's] agent, ... was not a fiduciary, [or] was not a person in whom the sellers [of the securities] had placed their trust and confidence." [...]This requirement of a specific relationship between the shareholders and the individual trading on inside information has created analytical difficulties for the SEC and courts in policing tippees who trade on inside information. Unlike insiders who have independent fiduciary duties to both the corporation and its shareholders, the typical tippee has no such relationships. In view of this absence, it has been unclear how a tippee acquires the *Cady, Roberts* duty to refrain from trading on inside information.

A

The SEC's position, as stated in its opinion in this case, is that a tippee "inherits" the *Cady, Roberts* obligation to shareholders whenever he receives inside information from an insider:

[...]

In effect, the SEC's theory of tippee liability in both cases appears rooted in the idea that the antifraud provisions require equal information among all traders. This conflicts with the principle set forth in *Chiarella* that only some persons, under some circumstances, will be barred from trading while in possession of material nonpublic information.[...]

Imposing a duty to disclose or abstain solely because a person knowingly receives material nonpublic information from an insider and trades on it could have an inhibiting influence on the role of market analysts, which the SEC itself recognizes is necessary to the preservation of a healthy market. It is commonplace for analysts to "ferret out and analyze information," 21 S. E. C. Docket, at 1406, and this often is done by meeting with and questioning corporate officers and others who are insiders.♦ And information that the analysts [659] obtain normally may be the basis for judgments as to the market worth of a corporation's securities. The analyst's judgment in this respect is made available in market letters or otherwise to clients of the firm. It is the nature of this type of information, and indeed of the markets themselves, that such information cannot be made simultaneously available to all of the corporation's stockholders or the public generally.

♦ This description is outdated. In 2000, the SEC adopted Regulation FD. It requires the corporation to make *simultaneous* public disclosure of any information it discloses to analysts and certain others in private meetings. In practice, this is done by having meetings only via publicly accessible telephone conference.

B

The conclusion that recipients of inside information do not invariably acquire a duty to disclose or abstain does not mean that such tippees always are free to trade on the information. The need for a ban on some tippee trading is clear. Not only are insiders forbidden by their fiduciary relationship from personally using undisclosed corporate information to their advantage, but they also may not give such information to an outsider for the same improper purpose of exploiting the information for their personal gain. [...] Similarly, the transactions of those who knowingly participate with the fiduciary in such a breach are "as forbidden" as transactions "on behalf of the trustee himself." [...]

Thus, some tippees must assume an insider's duty to the shareholders not because they receive inside information, but rather because it has been made available to them *improperly*. And for Rule 10b-5 purposes, the insider's disclosure is improper only where it would violate his *Cady, Roberts* duty. Thus, a tippee assumes a fiduciary duty to the shareholders of a corporation not to trade on material nonpublic information only when the insider has breached his fiduciary duty to the shareholders by disclosing the information to the tippee and the tippee knows or should know that there has been a breach. [...] Tipping thus properly is viewed only as a means of indirectly violating the *Cady, Roberts* disclose-or-abstain rule.

C

In determining whether a tippee is under an obligation to disclose or abstain, it thus is necessary to determine whether the insider's "tip" constituted a breach of the insider's fiduciary duty. All disclosures of confidential corporate information [662] are not inconsistent with the duty insiders owe to shareholders. [...] Whether disclosure is a breach of duty therefore depends in large part on the purpose of the disclosure. [...] the test is whether the insider personally will benefit, directly or indirectly, from his disclosure. Absent some personal gain, there has been no breach of duty to stockholders. And absent a breach by the insider, there is no derivative breach. [...]

The SEC argues that, if inside-trading liability does not exist when the information is transmitted for a proper purpose but is used for trading, it would be a rare situation when the parties could not fabricate some ostensibly legitimate business justification for transmitting the information. We think the SEC is unduly concerned. In determining whether the insider's purpose in making a particular disclosure is fraudulent, the SEC and the courts are not required to read the parties' minds. Scienter in some cases is relevant in determining whether the tipper has violated his *Cady, Roberts* duty. But to determine whether the disclosure itself "deceive[s], manipulate[s], or defraud[s]" shareholders, *Aaron v. SEC*, 446 U. S. 680, 686 (1980), the initial inquiry is whether there has been a breach of duty by the insider. This requires courts to focus on objective criteria, *i.e.*, whether the insider receives a direct or indirect personal benefit from the disclosure, such as a pecuniary gain or a reputational benefit that will translate into future earnings. [...] There are objective facts and circumstances that often justify such an inference. For example, there may be a relationship between the insider and the recipient that suggests a *quid pro quo* from the latter, or an intention to benefit the particular recipient. The elements of fiduciary duty and exploitation of nonpublic information also exist when an insider makes a gift of confidential information to a trading relative or friend. The tip and trade resemble trading by the insider himself followed by a gift of the profits to the recipient.

Determining whether an insider personally benefits from a particular disclosure, a question of fact, will not always be easy for courts. But it is essential, we think, to have a guiding principle for those whose daily activities must be limited and instructed by the SEC's inside-trading rules, and we believe that there must be a breach of the insider's fiduciary duty before the tippee inherits the duty to disclose or abstain. In contrast, the rule adopted by the SEC in this case would have no limiting principle. [665]

IV

Under the inside-trading and tipping rules set forth above, we find that there was no actionable violation by Dirks. It is undisputed that Dirks himself was a stranger to Equity Funding, with no pre-existing fiduciary duty to its shareholders. He took no action, directly or indirectly, that induced the shareholders or officers of Equity Funding to repose trust or confidence in him. There was no expectation by Dirks' sources that he would keep their information in confidence. Nor did Dirks misappropriate or illegally obtain the information about Equity Funding. Unless the insiders breached their *Cady, Roberts* duty to shareholders in disclosing the nonpublic information to Dirks, he breached no duty when he passed it on to investors as well as to the Wall Street Journal.

[666] It is clear that neither Secrist nor the other Equity Funding employees violated their *Cady, Roberts* duty to the corporation's shareholders by providing information to Dirks. [667] The tippers received no monetary or personal benefit for revealing Equity Funding's secrets, nor was their purpose to make a gift of valuable information to Dirks. As the facts of this case clearly indicate, the tippers were motivated by a desire to expose the fraud. See *supra*, at 648-649. In the absence of a breach of duty to shareholders by the insiders, there was no derivative breach by Dirks. See n. 20, *supra*. Dirks therefore could not have been "a participant after the fact in [an] insider's breach of a fiduciary duty." [...]

JUSTICE BLACKMUN, with whom JUSTICE BRENNAN and JUSTICE MARSHALL join, dissenting.

The Court today takes still another step to limit the protections provided investors by § 10(b) of the Securities Exchange [668] Act of 1934. See *Chiarella* v. *United States*, 445 U. S. 222, 246 (1980) (dissenting opinion). The device employed in this case engrafts a special motivational requirement on the fiduciary duty doctrine. This innovation excuses a knowing and intentional violation of an insider's duty to shareholders if the insider does not act from a motive of personal gain. Even on the extraordinary facts of this case, such an innovation is not justified.

I

As the Court recognizes, *ante*, at 658, n. 18, the facts here are unusual. After a meeting with Ronald Secrist, a former Equity Funding employee, on March 7, 1973, App. 226, petitioner Raymond Dirks found himself in possession of material nonpublic information of massive fraud within the company. In the Court's words, "[h]e uncovered ... startling information that required no analysis or exercise of judgment as to [669] its market relevance." *Ibid*. In disclosing that information to Dirks, Secrist intended that Dirks would disseminate the information to his clients, those clients would unload their Equity Funding securities on the market, and the price would fall precipitously, thereby triggering a reaction from the authorities. App. 16, 25, 27.

Dirks complied with his informant's wishes. Instead of reporting that information to the Securities and Exchange Commission (SEC or Commission) or to other regulatory agencies, Dirks began to disseminate the information to his clients and undertook his own investigation. One of his first steps was to direct his associates at Delafield Childs to draw up a list of Delafield clients holding Equity Funding securities. On March 12, eight days before Dirks flew to Los Angeles to investigate Secrist's story, he reported the full allegations to Boston Company Institutional Investors, Inc., which on March 15 and 16 sold approximately $1.2 million of Equity securities. See *id.*, at 199. As he gathered more [670] information, he selectively disclosed it to his clients. To those holding Equity Funding securities he gave the "hard" story — all the allegations; others received the "soft" story — a recitation of vague factors that might reflect adversely on Equity Funding's management. See *id.*, at 211, n. 24.

Dirks' attempts to disseminate the information to nonclients were feeble, at best. On March 12, he left a message for Herbert Lawson, the San Francisco bureau chief of The Wall Street Journal. Not until March 19 and 20 did he call Lawson again, and outline the situation. William Blundell, a Journal investigative reporter based in Los Angeles, got in touch with Dirks about his March 20 telephone call. On March 21, Dirks met with Blundell in Los Angeles. Blundell began his own investigation, relying in part on Dirks' contacts, and on March 23 telephoned Stanley Sporkin, the SEC's Deputy Director of Enforcement. On March 26, the next business day, Sporkin and his staff interviewed Blundell and asked to see Dirks the following morning. Trading was halted by the New York Stock Exchange at about the same time Dirks was talking to Los Angeles SEC personnel. The next day, March 28, the SEC suspended trading in Equity Funding securities. By that time, Dirks' clients had unloaded close to $15 million of Equity Funding stock and the price had plummeted from $26 to $15. The effect of Dirks' selective dissemination of Secrist's information was that Dirks' clients were able to shift the losses that were inevitable due to the Equity Funding fraud from themselves to uninformed market participants.

II

A

No one questions that Secrist himself could not trade on his inside information to the disadvantage of uninformed shareholders and purchasers of Equity Funding securities. See Brief for United States as *Amicus Curiae* 19, n. 12. Unlike the printer in *Chiarella*, Secrist stood in a fiduciary relationship [671] with these shareholders. [...]

The Court also acknowledges that Secrist could not do by proxy what he was prohibited from doing personally. [...]

B

The Court holds, however, that Dirks is not liable because Secrist did not violate his duty; according to the Court, this is so because Secrist did not have the improper purpose of personal gain. *Ante*, at 662-663, 666-667. In so doing, the Court imposes a new, subjective limitation on the scope of the duty owed by insiders to shareholders. The novelty of this limitation is reflected in the Court's lack of support for it.

[...]

C

The fact that the insider himself does not benefit from the breach does not eradicate the shareholder's injury. Cf. Restatement (Second) of Trusts § 205, Comments *c* and *d* (1959) (trustee liable for acts causing diminution of value of trust); 3 [674] A. Scott, Law of Trusts § 205, p. 1665 (3d ed. 1967) (trustee liable for any losses to trust caused by his breach). [...]

III

The improper-purpose requirement not only has no basis in law, but it also rests implicitly on a policy that I cannot accept. The Court justifies Secrist's and Dirks' action because the general benefit derived from the violation of Secrist's duty to shareholders outweighed the harm caused to those [677] shareholders, see Heller, *Chiarella,* SEC Rule 14e-3 and *Dirks:* "Fairness" versus Economic Theory, 37 Bus. Lawyer 517, 550 (1982); Easterbrook, Insider Trading, Secret Agents, Evidentiary Privileges, and the Production of Information, 1981 S. Ct. Rev. 309, 338 — in other words, because the end justified the means. Under this view, the benefit conferred on society by Secrist's and Dirks' activities may be paid for with the losses caused to shareholders trading with Dirks' clients.

[...]

Dirks and Secrist were under a duty to disclose the information or to refrain from trading on it. I agree that disclosure in this case would have been difficult. *Ibid.* I also recognize that the SEC seemingly has been less than helpful in its view of the nature of disclosure necessary to satisfy the disclose-or-refrain duty. The Commission tells persons with inside information that they cannot trade on that information unless they disclose; it refuses, however, to tell them how to disclose. See *In re Faberge, Inc.,* 45 S. E. C. 249, 256 (1973) (disclosure requires public release through public media designed to reach investing public generally). This seems to be a less than sensible policy, which it is incumbent on the Commission to correct. The Court, however, has no authority to remedy the problem by opening a hole in the congressionally mandated prohibition on insider trading, thus rewarding such trading.

[...]

D. U.S. v. O'Hagan (U.S. 1997)

In *O'Hagan*, the Supreme Court endorsed the so-called "misappropriation theory" of insider trading liability under rule 10b-5, and upheld rule 14e-3.

Questions

1. The misappropriation theory rests 10b-5 liability on deceiving the source of the information. What exactly is the deception, and does it occur "in connection with the purchase or sale of any security" (see Exchange Act §10(b) and rule 10b-5)?

2. Does rule 14e-3 expand liability beyond rule 10b-5? If so, what is the statutory basis for the expansion?

3. Did *O'Hagan* overrule *Chiarella* and *Dirks*?

4. Could the defendant in *Chiarella* have been convicted under *O'Hagan*'s theory of rule 10b-5? If so, why wasn't he? Hint: re-read part IV of *Chiarella*.

5. Could the defendant in *Chiarella* have been convicted under rule 14e-3? If so, why wasn't he?

6. Does *O'Hagan*'s misappropriation theory of 10b-5 insider trading liability replace the "classical theory" as endorsed and applied by *Chiarella* and *Dirks*—liability premised on a duty to the shareholders of the corporation whose shares are being traded? Or are the two theories complementary? What behavior would violate rule 10b-5 under the classical theory but not under the misappropriation theory?

521 U.S. 642 (1997)

UNITED STATES

v.

O'HAGAN

[...]

Ginsburg, J., delivered the opinion of the Court, in which Stevens, O'Connor, Kennedy, Souter, and Breyer, JJ., joined, and in which Scalia, J., joined as to Parts I, III, and IV. Scalia, J., filed an opinion concurring in part and dissenting in part, *post*, p. 679. Thomas, J., filed an opinion concurring in the judgment in part and dissenting in part, in which Rehnquist, C. J., joined, *post*, p. 680. [...]

I

Respondent James Herman O'Hagan was a partner in the law firm of Dorsey & Whitney in Minneapolis, Minnesota. In July 1988, Grand Metropolitan PLC (Grand Met), a company based in London, England, retained Dorsey & Whitney as local counsel to represent Grand Met regarding a potential tender offer for the common stock of the Pillsbury Company, headquartered in Minneapolis. Both Grand Met and Dorsey & Whitney took precautions to protect the confidentiality of Grand Met's tender offer plans. O'Hagan did no work on the Grand Met representation. Dorsey & Whitney withdrew from representing Grand Met on September 9, 1988. Less than a month later, on October 4, 1988, Grand Met publicly announced its tender offer for Pillsbury stock.

On August 18, 1988, while Dorsey & Whitney was still representing Grand Met, O'Hagan began purchasing call options for Pillsbury stock. Each option gave him the right to purchase 100 shares of Pillsbury stock by a specified date in September 1988. Later in August and in September, O'Hagan made additional purchases of Pillsbury call options. By the end of September, he owned 2,500 unexpired Pillsbury options, apparently more than any other individual investor. [648] See App. 85, 148. O'Hagan also purchased, in September 1988, some 5,000 shares of Pillsbury common stock, at a price just under $39 per share. When Grand Met announced its tender offer in October, the price of Pillsbury stock rose to nearly $60 per share. O'Hagan then sold his Pillsbury call options and common stock, making a profit of more than $4.3 million.

The Securities and Exchange Commission (SEC or Commission) initiated an investigation into O'Hagan's transactions, culminating in a 57-count indictment. The indictment alleged that O'Hagan defrauded his law firm and its client, Grand Met, by using for his own trading purposes material, nonpublic information regarding Grand Met's planned tender offer. *Id.*, at 8. According to the indictment, O'Hagan used the profits he gained through this trading to conceal his previous embezzlement and conversion of unrelated client trust funds. *Id.*, at 10. O'Hagan was charged with 20 counts of mail fraud, in violation of 18 U. S. C. § 1341; 17 counts of securities fraud, in violation of § 10(b) of the Securities Exchange Act of 1934 (Exchange Act), 48 Stat. 891, 15 U. S. C. § 78j(b), and SEC Rule 10b—5, 17 CFR § 240.10b—5 [649] (1996); 17 counts of fraudulent trading in connection with a tender offer, in violation of § 14(e) of the Exchange Act, 15 U. S. C. § 78n(e), and SEC Rule 14e—3(a), 17 CFR § 240.14e— 3(a) (1996); and 3 counts of violating federal money laundering statutes, 18 U. S. C. §§ 1956(a)(1)(B)(i), 1957. See App. 13-24. A jury convicted O'Hagan on all 57 counts, and he was sentenced to a 41-month term of imprisonment.

A divided panel of the Court of Appeals for the Eighth Circuit reversed all of O'Hagan's convictions. 92 F. 3d 612 (1996). Liability under § 10(b) and Rule 10b-5, the Eighth Circuit held, may not be grounded on the "misappropriation theory" of securities fraud on which the prosecution relied. *Id.*, at 622. The Court of Appeals also held that Rule 14e-3(a)—which prohibits trading while in possession of material, nonpublic information relating to a tender offer—exceeds the SEC's § 14(e) rulemaking authority because the Rule contains no breach of fiduciary duty requirement. *Id.*, at 627. The Eighth Circuit further concluded that O'Hagan's mail fraud and money laundering convictions rested on violations of the securities laws, and therefore could not stand once the securities fraud convictions were reversed. [...]

II

We address first the Court of Appeals' reversal of O'Hagan's convictions under § 10(b) and Rule 10b-5. [...]

A

[...] Liability under Rule 10b-5, our precedent indicates, does not extend beyond conduct encompassed by § 10(b)'s prohibition. [...]

Under the "traditional" or "classical theory" of insider trading liability, § 10(b) and Rule 10b-5 are violated when a corporate insider trades in the securities of his corporation [652] on the basis of material, nonpublic information. Trading on such information qualifies as a "deceptive device" under § 10(b), we have affirmed, because "a relationship of trust and confidence [exists] between the shareholders of a corporation and those insiders who have obtained confidential information by reason of their position with that corporation." *Chiarella* v. *United States*, 445 U. S. 222, 228 (1980). That relationship, we recognized, "gives rise to a duty to disclose [or to abstain from trading] because of the "necessity of preventing a corporate insider from ... tak[ing] unfair advantage of ... uninformed ... stockholders.' " *Id.*, at 228-229 (citation omitted). The classical theory applies not only to officers, directors, and other permanent insiders of a corporation, but also to attorneys, accountants, consultants, and others who temporarily become fiduciaries of a corporation. See *Dirks* v. *SEC*, 463 U. S. 646, 655, n. 14 (1983).

The "misappropriation theory" holds that a person commits fraud "in connection with" a securities transaction, and thereby violates § 10(b) and Rule 10b-5, when he misappropriates confidential information for securities trading purposes, in breach of a duty owed to the source of the information. See Brief for United States 14. Under this theory, a fiduciary's undisclosed, self-serving use of a principal's information to purchase or sell securities, in breach of a duty of loyalty and confidentiality, defrauds the principal of the exclusive use of that information. In lieu of premising liability on a fiduciary relationship between company insider and purchaser or seller of the company's stock, the misappropriation theory premises liability on a fiduciary-turned-trader's deception of those who entrusted him with access to confidential information.

The two theories are complementary, each addressing efforts to capitalize on nonpublic information through the purchase or sale of securities. The classical theory targets a corporate insider's breach of duty to shareholders with whom the insider transacts; the misappropriation theory outlaws [653] trading on the basis of nonpublic information by a corporate "outsider" in breach of a duty owed not to a trading party, but to the source of the information. The misappropriation theory is thus designed to "protec[t] the integrity of the securities markets against abuses by "outsiders' to a corporation who have access to confidential information that will affect th[e] corporation's security price when revealed, but who owe no fiduciary or other duty to that corporation's shareholders." *Ibid.*

In this case, the indictment alleged that O'Hagan, in breach of a duty of trust and confidence he owed to his law firm, Dorsey & Whitney, and to its client, Grand Met, traded on the basis of nonpublic information regarding Grand Met's planned tender offer for Pillsbury common stock. App. 16. This conduct, the Government charged, constituted a fraudulent device in connection with the purchase and sale of securities.

B

We agree with the Government that misappropriation, as just defined, satisfies § 10(b)'s requirement that chargeable conduct involve a "deceptive device or contrivance" used "in connection with" the purchase or sale of securities. We observe, first, that misappropriators, as the Government describes them, deal in deception. A fiduciary who "[pretends] loyalty to the principal while secretly converting the principal's information for personal gain," Brief for United States [654] 17, "dupes" or defrauds the principal. [...]

The misappropriation theory advanced by the Government is consistent with *Santa Fe Industries, Inc.* v. *Green*, 430 U. S. 462 (1977), a decision underscoring that § 10(b) is not an all-purpose breach of fiduciary duty ban; rather, it trains on conduct involving manipulation or deception. See *id.*, at 473-476. In contrast to the Government's allegations in this case, in *Santa Fe Industries*, all pertinent facts were disclosed by the persons charged with violating § 10(b) and Rule 10b-5, see *id.*, at 474; therefore, there was no deception through nondisclosure to which liability under those provisions could attach, see *id.*, at 476. Similarly, full disclosure forecloses liability under the misappropriation theory: Because the deception essential to the misappropriation theory involves feigning fidelity to the source of information, if the fiduciary discloses to the source that he plans to trade on the nonpublic information, there is no "deceptive device" and thus no § 10(b) violation—although the fiduciary-turnedtrader may remain liable under state law for breach of a duty of loyalty.

We turn next to the § 10(b) requirement that the misappropriator's deceptive use of information be "in connection with [656] the purchase or sale of [a] security." This element is satisfied because the fiduciary's fraud is consummated, not when the fiduciary gains the confidential information, but when, without disclosure to his principal, he uses the information to purchase or sell securities. The securities transaction and the breach of duty thus coincide. This is so even though the person or entity defrauded is not the other party to the trade, but is, instead, the source of the nonpublic information. [...]

The misappropriation theory comports with § 10(b)'s language, which requires deception "in connection with the purchase or sale of any security," not deception of an identifiable purchaser or seller. The theory is also well tuned to an animating purpose of the Exchange Act: to insure honest securities markets and thereby promote investor confidence. See 45 Fed. Reg. 60412 (1980) (trading on misappropriated information "undermines the integrity of, and investor confidence in, the securities markets"). Although informational disparity is inevitable in the securities markets, investors likely would hesitate to venture their capital in a market where trading based on misappropriated nonpublic information is unchecked by law. [...]

III

We consider next the ground on which the Court of Appeals reversed O'Hagan's convictions for fraudulent trading in connection with a tender offer, in violation of § 14(e) of the Exchange Act and SEC Rule 14e-3(a). A sole question is before us as to these convictions: Did the Commission, as the Court of Appeals held, exceed its rulemaking authority under § 14(e) when it adopted Rule 14e-3(a) without requiring a showing that the trading at issue entailed a breach of [667] fiduciary duty? We hold that the Commission, in this regard and to the extent relevant to this case, did not exceed its authority.

The governing statutory provision, § 14(e) of the Exchange Act, reads in relevant part:

> "It shall be unlawful for any person ... to engage in any fraudulent, deceptive, or manipulative acts or practices, in connection with any tender offer .... The [SEC] shall, for the purposes of this subsection, by rules and regulations define, and prescribe means reasonably designed to prevent, such acts and practices as are fraudulent, deceptive, or manipulative." [...]

Relying on § 14(e)'s rulemaking authorization, the Commission, in 1980, promulgated Rule 14e—3(a). That measure provides:

> "(a) If any person has taken a substantial step or steps to commence, or has commenced, a tender offer (the 'offering person'), it shall constitute a fraudulent, deceptive or manipulative act or practice within the meaning of section 14(e) of the [Exchange] Act for any other person who is in possession of material information relating to such tender offer which information he knows or has reason to know is nonpublic and which he knows or has reason to know has been acquired directly or indirectly from:

> "(1) The offering person,

> "(2) The issuer of the securities sought or to be sought by such tender offer, or

> "(3) Any officer, director, partner or employee or any other person acting on behalf of the offering person or such issuer, to purchase or sell or cause to be purchased or sold any of such securities or any securities convertible into or exchangeable for any such securities or any option or right to obtain or to dispose of any of the foregoing securities, unless within a reasonable time prior to any purchase or sale such information and its source [669] are publicly disclosed by press release or otherwise." 17 CFR § 240.14e-3(a) (1996).

As characterized by the Commission, Rule 14e-3(a) is a "disclose or abstain from trading" requirement. [...]

We need not resolve in this case whether the Commission's authority under § 14(e) to "define ... such acts and practices as are fraudulent" is broader than the Commission's fraud-defining authority under § 10(b), for we agree with the United States that Rule 14e-3(a), as applied to cases of this genre, qualifies under § 14(e) as a "means reasonably designed to prevent" fraudulent trading on material, nonpublic information in the tender offer context. A prophylactic [673] measure, because its mission is to prevent, typically encompasses more than the core activity prohibited. [...]

Because Congress has authorized the Commission, in § 14(e), to prescribe legislative rules, we owe the Commission's judgment "more than mere deference or weight." *Batterton* v. *Francis,* 432 U. S. 416, 424-426 (1977). Therefore, in determining whether Rule 14e-3(a)'s "disclose or abstain from trading" requirement is reasonably designed to prevent fraudulent acts, we must accord the Commission's assessment "controlling weight unless [it is] arbitrary, capricious, or manifestly contrary to the statute." *Chevron U. S. A. Inc.* v. *Natural Resources Defense Council, Inc.* , 467 U. S. 837, 844 (1984). In this case, we conclude, the Commission's assessment is none of these.

[674] In adopting the "disclose or abstain" rule, the SEC explained:

> "The Commission has previously expressed and continues to have serious concerns about trading by persons in possession of material, nonpublic information relating to a tender offer. This practice results in unfair disparities in market information and market disruption. Security holders who purchase from or sell to such persons are effectively denied the benefits of disclosure and the substantive protections of the Williams Act. If furnished with the information, these security holders would be able to make an informed investment decision, which could involve deferring the purchase or sale of the securities until the material information had been disseminated or until the tender offer had been commenced or terminated." 45 Fed. Reg. 60412 (1980) (footnotes omitted).

The Commission thus justified Rule 14e-3(a) as a means necessary and proper to assure the efficacy of Williams Act protections.

The United States emphasizes that Rule 14e-3(a) reaches trading in which "a breach of duty is likely but difficult to prove." Reply Brief 16. "Particularly in the context of a tender offer," as the Tenth Circuit recognized, "there is a fairly wide circle of people with confidential information," *Peters,* 978 F. 2d, at 1167, notably, the attorneys, investment [675] bankers, and accountants involved in structuring the transaction. The availability of that information may lead to abuse, for "even a hint of an upcoming tender offer may send the price of the target company's stock soaring." *SEC* v. *Materia,* 745 F. 2d 197, 199 (CA2 1984). Individuals entrusted with nonpublic information, particularly if they have no long-term loyalty to the issuer, may find the temptation to trade on that information hard to resist in view of "the very large short-term profits potentially available [to them]." *Peters,* 978 F. 2d, at 1167.

"[I]t may be possible to prove circumstantially that a person [traded on the basis of material, nonpublic information], but almost impossible to prove that the trader obtained such information in breach of a fiduciary duty owed either by the trader or by the ultimate insider source of the information." *Ibid.* The example of a "tippee" who trades on information received from an insider illustrates the problem. Under Rule 10b-5, "a tippee assumes a fiduciary duty to the shareholders of a corporation not to trade on material nonpublic information only when the insider has breached his fiduciary duty to the shareholders by disclosing the information to the tippee and the tippee knows or should know that there has been a breach." *Dirks*, 463 U. S., at 660. To show that a tippee who traded on nonpublic information about a tender offer had breached a fiduciary duty would require proof not only that the insider source breached a fiduciary duty, but that the tippee knew or should have known of that breach. "Yet, in most cases, the only parties to the [information transfer] will be the insider and the alleged tippee." *Peters*, 978 F. 2d, at 1167.

[676] In sum, it is a fair assumption that trading on the basis of material, nonpublic information will often involve a breach of a duty of confidentiality to the bidder or target company or their representatives. The SEC, cognizant of the proof problem that could enable sophisticated traders to escape responsibility, placed in Rule 14e-3(a) a "disclose or abstain from trading" command that does not require specific proof of a breach of fiduciary duty. That prescription, we are satisfied, applied to this case, is a "means reasonably designed to prevent" fraudulent trading on material, nonpublic information in the tender offer context. See *Chestman*, 947 F. 2d, at 560 ("While dispensing with the subtle problems of proof associated with demonstrating fiduciary breach in the problematic area of tender offer insider trading, [Rule 14e-3(a)] retains a close nexus between the prohibited conduct and the statutory aims."); accord, *Maio*, 51 F. 3d, at 635, and n. 14; *Peters*, 978 F. 2d, at 1167. Therefore, insofar as it serves to prevent the type of misappropriation charged against O'Hagan, Rule 14e-3(a) is a proper exercise of the Commission's prophylactic power under § 14(e).[...]

Justice Scalia, concurring in part and dissenting in part.

[...] While the Court's explanation of the scope of § 10(b) and Rule 10b-5 would be entirely reasonable in some other context, it does not seem to accord with the principle of lenity we apply to criminal statutes (which cannot be mitigated here by the Rule, which is no less ambiguous than the statute). [...] In light of that principle, it seems to me that the unelaborated statutory language: "[t]o use or employ, in connection with the purchase or sale of any security ... any manipulative or deceptive device or contrivance," § 10(b), must be construed to require the manipulation or deception of a party to a securities transaction.

[...]

Part VI: Creditors and Other Non-Shareholder Constituencies

So far, we have been discussing the relationships between boards (managers) and shareholders, and between majority (controlling) shareholders and minority shareholders. We now broaden our horizon and consider other constituencies, such as creditors, workers, and consumers.

1. The Corporation as a Nexus of Contracts

You might think that non-shareholder constituencies are fundamentally different because they are "outsiders" to the corporation, while shareholders (and boards) are "insiders." But this is misleading, at least in large publicly held corporations. Most investors in these corporations are "outsiders" no matter how they invest, be it through debt or equity. In fact, from most investors' and the controller's (founder's) point of view, debt and equity are largely interchangeable as investment vehicles, and the choice between them hinges on details of cash flow and control rights, rather than on any notion of inside/outside.

One frequently hears that shareholders are the corporation's "owners," while other constituencies are "merely" contracting partners. This may contain some truth for small businesses, but it is clearly not true for large businesses. In the technical legal sense of the term, shareholders only own their shares, not the corporation. In the functional sense, shareholders lack the control rights that one generally associates with ownership. Obviously, individual shareholders cannot deal with corporate property as they please. And at least in Delaware, shareholders cannot even make decisions about corporate property collectively, since business decisions are the prerogative of the board (cf. DGCL 141(a)). As to replacing the board, this is difficult for dispersed shareholders in practice, as we have seen. In fact, shareholders may not even have the legal right to replace the board, or any other meaningful control rights. For example, the dual class share structure in Google and Facebook gives the founders full control of their corporations even though they have sold off most of the equity.

The better, modern view is that the corporation is simply a nexus of contracts (and other obligations). In this view, many different constituents transact with one another through the corporate form. In addition to managers and shareholders, these constituents include creditors, workers, customers, suppliers, and others. Corporate law's goal is to facilitate their transactions, not to defend ostensible ownership rights. In this view, shareholders are not special — at least in principle.

2. Shareholder Primacy?

This is not to say that the law should not, or does not, treat shareholders differently for pragmatic reasons. In fact, as you have probably already guessed and we will now confirm, *corporate law* is almost exclusively concerned with the relationships between shareholders and boards, and between shareholders themselves.

(a) Corporate Law vs. The Laws Governing Corporations

To be sure, for the most part, this is mere nomenclature. Many legal rules govern relationships between corporations and other constituencies. It's just that we group these rules under different headings: "labor and employment law," "consumer law," "antitrust," "contract law," etc. In this perspective, corporate law is merely the name we give to those legal rules that specifically deal with "internal governance" — the misleading term (see above) for relationships between shareholders and boards, and between shareholders themselves. By definition then, this "area of law" does not deal with other constituencies. But this is without substantive content.

(b) Fiduciary Duties

The substantive question is the content of corporate fiduciary duties. Corporate directors and officers obviously have to comply with all the laws protecting other constituencies (cf. DGCL 102(b)(7)(ii)). In exercising their remaining discretion, however, can or must they take into account the interests of all affected? Or must they act solely for shareholders' benefit?

Delaware law: fiduciary duties to whom?

As we have already glimpsed in *Revlon* and will now see very clearly in *Gheewalla* and *eBay*, directors and officers of Delaware corporations owe fiduciary duties only to common stockholders. To be sure, Delaware courts continue to assert that corporate fiduciaries owe their duties "to the corporation and its shareholders." But when the rubber hits the road, recent Delaware decisions have opted for shareholders. This is often dubbed "shareholder primacy" — the idea that, within the boundaries of contracts and regulations, corporations are to be run for the benefit of shareholders alone.

The competing *"stakeholder model"* suggests that boards should and do manage corporations for the benefit of all their stakeholders. As a matter of positive law, proponents interpret the words *"to the corporation* and its shareholders" (emphasis added) as shorthand for their broader view of fiduciary duties. This interpretation sounds sensible, for what else would the words "to the corporation" mean? Then again, the Delaware courts don't see it that way (see previous paragraph).

In 2013, the Delaware General Assembly dealt a further blow to the stakeholder model by amending the DGCL to add a new "Subchapter XV. Public Benefit Corporations." The new DGCL 362(a) explicitly provides:

> A 'public benefit corporation' is a for-profit corporation organized under and subject to the requirements of this chapter that is intended to produce a public benefit or public benefits and to operate in a responsible and sustainable manner. To that end, a public benefit corporation shall be managed in a manner that balances the stockholders' pecuniary interests, the best interests of those materially affected by the corporation's conduct, and the public benefit or public benefits identified in its certificate of incorporation. In the certificate of incorporation, a public benefit corporation shall: (1) Identify ... one or more specific public benefits to be promoted ...; and (2) State within its heading that it is a public benefit corporation.

Thus, corporations organized for a public benefit are clearly distinct from standard Delaware corporations under the DGCL. This strongly suggests that standard Delaware corporations are *not* to be managed for the public benefit.

(c) Practical relevance?

In normal times, these debates are almost entirely irrelevant from a purely legal point of view. The reason is the lenient standard of review for normal board decisions (i.e., the duty of care). As you already know, the business judgment rule gives boards almost unfettered discretion. This discretion insulates the board's actions, whatever their nominal duty.

Consider first the current legal landscape where shareholders are the sole beneficiaries of fiduciary duties. If the board of directors nonetheless favors other stakeholders, the business judgment rule will typically shield such decisions from judicial review. As an example, consider *Shlensky v. Wrigley* (Ill. App. 1968). A shareholder brought a lawsuit against Philip K. Wrigley, the majority owner of the company that owned and operated the Chicago Cubs, and his fellow directors. Plaintiff argued that the company incurred substantial losses by not scheduling night games at Wrigley Field, the team's home stadium. Plaintiff claimed that this scheduling was influenced, at least in part, by Wrigley's concern that night baseball games "will have a deteriorating effect upon the surrounding neighborhood." The court did not find fault with this motivation:

> [W]e are not satisfied that the motives assigned to Philip K. Wrigley, and through him to the other directors, are contrary to the best interests of the corporation and the stockholders. For example, it appears to us that the effect on the surrounding neighborhood might well be considered by a director who was considering the patrons who would or would not attend the games if the park were in a poor neighborhood. Furthermore, the long run interest of the corporation in its property value at Wrigley Field might demand all efforts to keep the neighborhood from deteriorating. By these thoughts we do not mean to say that we have decided that the decision of the directors was a correct one. That is beyond our jurisdiction and ability. We are merely saying that the decision is one properly before directors and the motives alleged in the amended complaint showed no fraud, illegality or conflict of interest in their making of that decision.

—95 Ill.App.2d 173, 180.

Now consider the contrary scenario where the law recognizes fiduciary duties towards stakeholders other than shareholders. Analogously to the previous scenario, the business judgment rule would now protect a board that prioritizes the interests of shareholders over those of other stakeholders, as long as the board acknowledged, or at least paid lip service to, the interests of other stakeholders.

Consequently, for a very long time, there was only one reported case where "shareholder primacy" mattered, and of course, everyone cited this one case. The case is *Dodge v. Ford Motor Co.* (Mich. 1919). Henry Ford took the stand and argued that the Ford Motor Company did not pay dividends because it needed the money to benefit its workers and customers. In truth, Ford probably just wanted to avoid paying out money to his minority stockholders the Dodge brothers, who had by then become his competitors. In any event, the court held against Ford, on the grounds that "[a] business corporation is organized and carried on primarily for the profit of the stockholders." But Ford almost certainly would have won if he had argued that the company needed the cash for future investment or some other business purpose (cf. *Shlensky v. Wrigley*).

There are, however, two ways in which the debate does matter. First, the legal rule probably matters directly in the sale of the company. This is because in this "end game" situation, conflicts between constituencies become very visible. The board can no longer hide behind "long-term shareholder interest" to justify some action that directly benefits a non-shareholder constituency. Cf. the passage on non-shareholder constituencies in *Revlon*, and watch out for the kind of very nasty things corporate managers are allowed to do to creditors in *MetLife v. RJR Nabisco*.

Second, the legal rule may matter inasmuch as it guides the behavior of honest, faithful fiduciaries — to the extent it influences "board room culture," if you will. A director may genuinely care about whether she is legally bound to benefit only shareholders or stakeholders as a whole. Thus, she may vote differently depending on what her legal advisors tell her about the content of fiduciary duties. That these fiduciary duties are not enforceable in court *may* be irrelevant.

3. Normative considerations

(a) The right goal vs. an achievable goal

To the extent that the content of fiduciary duties does matter and works literally as intended, it is clearly bad. By definition, maximizing the interests of one group only (common shareholders) generates less social welfare than maximizing the interests of all groups combined. *Ex ante*, this harms even the favored group, because it will have to make concessions on other points to obtain the collaboration of the other constituencies. Since the pie is smaller (because the law doesn't maximize it), there will be less for everyone to share.

For example, taken at face value, *In re Trados Inc. Shareholder Litigation (Del. Ch. 2013)* would force boards of insolvent corporations to bet the corporation's last cash at the casino (or embark on some similarly risky, negative net present value project). For without the gamble, common stockholders get nothing. With the gamble, there is a chance that the board will win and shareholders get something. To be sure, the gamble is bad *for all stakeholders combined*, i.e., once creditors and preferred stockholders are included: on average, casino gamblers lose. But *Trados* claims that boards should work only for common stockholders. *Ex ante*, this rule is bad even for the common stockholders: to obtain investments from creditors etc., they will have to make other promises that compensate creditors for their anticipated losses from gambling.

Shareholder primacy advocates do not deny the conceptual validity of the preceding argument. They merely question its practical relevance on two complementary grounds. Firstly, they point out that various legal rules and in particular contracts restrict the ability of boards to favor shareholders at the expense of other constituencies. Secondly, they question if there could be any legal oversight over boards if boards were charged with maximizing the interests of all stakeholders. What are those "interests," and what actions maximize them? It's hard enough to figure out, e.g., what action maximizes the share price (under *Revlon*'s deceptively simple maxim of getting the highest price). Shareholder primacy advocates fear that stakeholder interests are so diffuse that they will always provide a pretext for managers to favor themselves. In this view, being accountable to everyone in theory means being accountable to no one in practice.

(b) Framing corporate law: two perspectives

Importantly, no *serious* commentator argues that shareholders are the only people who matter in the grand scheme of things, workers etc. be damned. Rather, the disagreement is about the method of getting the best collective outcome. The debate between shareholder primacy and stakeholder models is thus closely related to the framing of the main conflict surrounding corporations. Which is the worse problem: (1) unfaithful managers wasting (mostly) shareholders' money, or (2) shareholders and their faithful managers exploiting other constituencies?

In favor of shareholder primacy, commentators argue that shareholders have no legal means beyond fiduciary duties to get any of their money back. They have no right to dividends, or to withdraw their principal investment. By contrast, creditors (including, e.g., workers as wage claimants) have contractually specified payment rights, and the corporation must file for bankruptcy if it does not fulfill these obligations. Moreover, many other constituencies can withdraw or withhold their contribution if the corporation does not keep to its bargain: workers can move to a different job, customers can buy from different providers, etc. By contrast, shareholders part with their equity investment up front and do not get it back unless the board in its discretion decides to make a distribution. Importantly, this feature is arguably essential to equity as the most flexible form of financing.

Against this, proponents of the stakeholder model argue that shareholders in fact already have strong protection, namely their right to elect the board. No board would completely disregard shareholder wishes, or else it would be fired. There is, therefore, a tendency for boards to favor shareholders at the expense of everybody else, or so the argument goes, and fiduciary duties should at least not exacerbate this tendency. Moreover, the argument that laws other than corporate law sufficiently protect other constituencies is circular and defective to the extent that corporations in fact *shape* those other laws through lobbying. (To this latter argument, shareholder primacy proponents reply that this is a much broader problem of deficient rules on political spending and lobbying. You should keep this connection in mind when reading *Citizens United* later in the course.)

4. The big (comparative) picture

In this connection, it is worth pointing out that some countries push the stakeholder model considerably further in large corporations. They *mandate* that workers elect part of the board (so-called *co-determination* in Germany and many other Northern and Central European countries), or that the board be self-perpetuating (Netherlands). In this comparative perspective, U.S. corporate law heavily leans towards shareholder primacy, both normatively and factually, because only common shareholders elect the board in U.S. corporations.

To be sure, shareholder governance is merely the U.S. default. The charter *may* give board seats to other constituencies. (For example, *preferred* stockholders nominated the majority of the board of Trados Inc. in the aforementioned *Trados* case.) That so few large corporations adopt such alternative arrangements may provide some clues about their desirability. But this is an even deeper question that we must postpone until we have encountered some more concrete scenarios.

Chapter 13. Creditors

We begin with creditors because (1) creditors are the only constituency that still has some remnants of protections in corporate law, and (2) most other claims ultimately resolve into damages or other financial claims, transforming all constituencies into creditors at the end of the day.

Gheewalla sets forth the principle that creditors cannot invoke the protections of fiduciary duties against corporate directors (although they may occasionally have standing to enforce a derivative claim on behalf of the corporation). *MetLife v. RJR Nabisco* declines to protect the plaintiff-creditor under a contractual implied duty of good faith and fair dealing. The bottom line is that creditors have to rely on contractual protections. The *MetLife* decision reviews many customary protective clauses.

Do you find the courts' reasonings convincing?

A. NACEPF v. Gheewalla (Del. 2007)

Questions

The decision addresses, and you should look out for, two related but separate questions:

1. Who has standing to assert a fiduciary duty claim?

2. To whom is the fiduciary duty owed, i.e., whose interests does it protect?

3. How might the answer to the second question have made a difference in this case? Whose interests were conflicting, and how, if at all, could the courts have adjudicated this conflict?

930 A.2d 92 (2007)

NORTH AMERICAN CATHOLIC EDUCATIONAL
PROGRAMMING FOUNDATION, INC., Plaintiff Below, Appellant
v.
Rob GHEEWALLA, Gerry Cardinale and Jack Daly, Defendants
Below, Appellees.

[...]

HOLLAND, Justice:

This is the appeal of the plaintiff-appellant, North American Catholic Educational Programming Foundation, Inc. ("NACEPF") from a final judgment of the Court of Chancery that dismissed NACEPF's Complaint for failure to state a claim. NACEPF holds certain radio wave spectrum licenses regulated by the Federal Communications Commission ("FCC"). In March 2001, NACEPF, together with other similar spectrum license-holders, entered into the Master Use and Royalty Agreement (the "Master Agreement") with Clearwire Holdings, Inc. ("Clearwire"), a Delaware corporation. Under the Master Agreement, Clearwire could obtain rights to those licenses as then-existing leases expired and the then-current lessees failed to exercise rights of first refusal.

The defendant-appellees are Rob Gheewalla, Gerry Cardinale, and Jack Daly (collectively, the "Defendants"), who served as directors of Clearwire at the behest of Goldman Sachs & Co. ("Goldman Sachs"). NACEPF's Complaint alleges that the Defendants, even though they comprised less than a majority of the board, were able to control Clearwire because its only source of funding was Goldman Sachs. According to NACEPF, they used that power to favor Goldman Sachs' agenda in derogation of their fiduciary duties as directors of Clearwire. [...]

NACEPF is not a shareholder of Clearwire. Instead, NACEPF filed its Complaint in the Court of Chancery as a putative [94] *creditor* of Clearwire. The Complaint alleges *direct,* not derivative, fiduciary duty claims against the Defendants, who served as directors of Clearwire while it was either insolvent or in the "zone of insolvency."

[...]

In this opinion, we hold that the creditors of a Delaware corporation that is either insolvent or in the zone of insolvency have no right, as a matter of law, to assert direct claims for breach of fiduciary duty against the corporation's directors. Accordingly, we have concluded that the judgments of the Court of Chancery must be affirmed.

Facts

[...]

NACEPF is an independent lay organization incorporated under the laws of Rhode Island. In 2000, NACEPF joined with Hispanic Information and Telecommunications Network, Inc. ("HITN"), Instructional Telecommunications Foundation, Inc. ("ITF"), and various affiliates of ITF to form the ITFS Spectrum Development Alliance, Inc. (the "Alliance"). Collectively, the Alliance owned a significant percentage of FCC-approved licenses for microwave signal transmissions ("spectrum") used for educational programs that were known as "Instruction Television Fixed Service" spectrum ("ITFS") licenses.

The Defendants were directors of Clearwire. The Defendants were also all employed by Goldman Sachs and served on the Clearwire Board of Directors at the behest of Goldman Sachs. NACEPF alleges that the Defendants effectively controlled Clearwire through the financial and other influence that Goldman Sachs had over Clearwire.

According to the Complaint, the Defendants represented to NACEPF and the other Alliance members that Clearwire's stated business purpose was to create a national system of wireless connections to the internet. Between 2000 and March 2001, Clearwire negotiated a Master Agreement with the Alliance, which Clearwire and the Alliance members entered into in March 2001. NACEPF asserts [95] that it negotiated the terms of the Master Agreement with several individuals, including the Defendants. NACEPF submits that all of the Defendants purported to be acting on the behalf of Goldman Sachs and the entity that became Clearwire.

Under the terms of the Master Agreement, Clearwire was to acquire the Alliance members' ITFS spectrum licenses when those licenses became available. To do so, Clearwire was obligated to pay NACEPF and other Alliance members more than $24.3 million. The Complaint alleges that the Defendants knew but did not tell NACEPF that Goldman Sachs did not intend to carry out the business plan that was the stated rationale for asking NACEPF to enter into the Master Agreement, i.e., by funding Clearwire.

In June 2002, the market for wireless spectrum collapsed when WorldCom announced its accounting problems. It appeared that there was or soon would be a surplus of spectrum available from WorldCom. Thereafter, Clearwire began negotiations with the members of the Alliance to end Clearwire's obligations to the members. Eventually, Clearwire paid over $2 million to HITN and ITF to settle their claims and; according to NACEPF, was only able to limit its payments to that amount by otherwise threatening to file for bankruptcy protection. These settlements left the NACEPF as the sole remaining member of the Alliance. The Complaint alleges that, by October 2003, Clearwire "had been unable to obtain any further financing and effectively went out of business."

NACEPF's Complaint

In its Complaint, NACEPF asserts three claims against the Defendants. [...] In Count II, NACEPF alleges that because, at all relevant times, Clearwire was either insolvent or in the "zone of insolvency," the Defendants owed fiduciary duties to NACEPF "as a substantial creditor of Clearwire," and that the Defendants breached those duties by:

> (1) not preserving the assets of Clearwire for its benefit and that of its creditors when it became apparent that Clearwire would not be able to continue as a going concern and would need to be liquidated and (2) holding on to NACEPF's ITFS license rights when Clearwire would not use them, solely to keep Goldman Sachs's investment "in play."

[...]

In the Court of Chancery and in this appeal, NACEPF waived any basis it may have had for pursuit of its claim derivatively. Instead, NACEPF seeks to assert only a *direct claim* for breach of fiduciary duties. It contends that such direct claims by creditors should be recognized in the context of both insolvency and the zone of insolvency. Accordingly, in ruling on the 12(b)(6) motion to dismiss Count II of the Complaint, the Court of Chancery was confronted with two legal questions: whether, as a matter of law, a corporation's *creditors* may assert *direct* claims against directors for breach of fiduciary duties when the corporation is either: first, insolvent or second, in the zone of insolvency.

Allegations of Insolvency and Zone of Insolvency

In support of its claim that Clearwire was either insolvent or in the zone of insolvency during the relevant periods, NACEPF alleged that Clearwire needed "substantially more financial support than it had obtained in March 2001." The Complaint alleges Goldman Sachs had invested $47 million in Clearwire, which "represent[ed] 84% of the total sums invested in Clearwire in March 2001, when Clearwire was otherwise virtually out of funds."

> *After March 2001*, Clearwire had financial obligations related to its agreement with NACEPF and others that *potentially* exceeded $134 million, did not have the ability to raise sufficient cash from operations to pay its debts as they became due and was dependent on Goldman [98] Sachs to make additional investments to fund Clearwire's operations for the foreseeable future.[14]

---

[14] [...] (emphasis added) [...].

The Complaint also alleges:

> For example, upon the closing of the Master Agreement, Clearwire had approximately $29.2 million in cash and of that $24.3 million would be needed for future payments for spectrum to the Alliance members. Clearwire's "burn" rate was $2.1 million per month and it had then no significant revenues. The process of acquiring spectrum upon expiration of existing licenses was both time consuming and expensive, particularly if existing licenseholders contested the validity of any Clearwire offer that those license holders were required to match under their rights of first refusal.

Additionally, in the Complaint, NACEPF alleges that, "[b]y October 2003, Clearwire had been unable to obtain any further financing and effectively went out of business. Except for money advanced to it as a stopgap measure by Goldman Sachs in late 2001, Clearwire was never able to raise any significant money." [...]

Corporations in the Zone of Insolvency Direct Claims for Breach of Fiduciary Duty May Not Be Asserted by Creditors

In order to withstand the Defendant's Rule 12(b)(6) motion to dismiss, the Plaintiff [99] was required to demonstrate that the breach of fiduciary duty claims [...] are cognizable under Delaware law. This procedural requirement requires us to address a substantive question of first impression that is raised by the present appeal: as a matter of Delaware law, can the *creditor* of a corporation that is operating within the *zone of insolvency* bring a *direct action* against its directors for an alleged *breach of fiduciary* duty?

It is well established that the directors owe their fiduciary obligations to the corporation and its shareholders. While shareholders rely on directors acting as fiduciaries to protect their interests, creditors are afforded protection through contractual agreements, fraud and fraudulent conveyance law, implied covenants of good faith and fair dealing, bankruptcy law, general commercial law and other sources of creditor rights. Delaware courts have traditionally been reluctant to expand existing fiduciary duties. Accordingly, "the general rule is that directors do not owe creditors duties beyond the relevant contractual terms."

In this case, NACEPF argues that when a corporation is in the zone of insolvency, this Court should recognize a new direct right for creditors to challenge directors' exercise of business judgments as breaches of the fiduciary duties owed to them. This Court has never directly addressed the zone of insolvency issue involving directors' purported fiduciary duties to creditors that is presented by NACEPF in this appeal. That subject has been discussed, however, in several judicial opinions and many scholarly articles.

[100] In *Production Resources,* the Court of Chancery remarked that recognition of fiduciary duties to creditors in the "zone of insolvency" context may involve:

> using the law of fiduciary duty to fill gaps that do not exist. Creditors are often protected by strong covenants, liens on assets, and other negotiated contractual protections. The implied covenant of good faith and fair dealing also protects creditors. So does the law of fraudulent conveyance. With these protections, when creditors are unable to prove that a corporation or its directors breached any of the specific legal duties owed to them, one would think that the conceptual room for concluding that the creditors were somehow, nevertheless, injured by inequitable conduct would be extremely small, *if extant.* Having complied with all legal obligations owed to the firm's creditors, the board would, in that scenario, ordinarily be free to take economic risk for the benefit of the firm's equity owners, so long as the directors comply with their fiduciary duties to the firm by selecting and pursuing with fidelity and prudence a plausible strategy to maximize the firm's value.

In this case, the Court of Chancery noted that creditors' existing protections — among which are the protections afforded by their negotiated agreements, their security instruments, the implied covenant of good faith and fair dealing, fraudulent conveyance law, and bankruptcy law — render the imposition of an additional, unique layer of protection through direct claims for breach of fiduciary duty unnecessary. It also noted that "any benefit to be derived by the recognition of such additional direct claims appears minimal, at best, and significantly outweighed by the costs to economic efficiency." The Court of Chancery reasoned that "an otherwise solvent corporation operating in the zone of insolvency is one in most need of effective and proactive leadership — as well as the ability to negotiate in good faith with its creditors — [101] goals which would likely be significantly undermined by the prospect of individual liability arising from the pursuit of direct claims by creditors." We agree.

Delaware corporate law provides for a separation of control and ownership. The directors of Delaware corporations have "the legal responsibility to manage the business of a corporation for the benefit of its shareholders owners." Accordingly, fiduciary duties are imposed upon the directors to regulate their conduct when they perform *that* function. Although the fiduciary duties of the directors of a Delaware corporation are unremitting:

> the exact cause of conduct that must be charted to properly discharge that responsibility will change in the specific context of the action the director is taking with regard to either the corporation or its shareholders. This Court has endeavored to provide the directors with clear signal beacons and brightly lined channel markers as they navigate

with due care, good faith, a loyalty on behalf of a Delaware corporation and its shareholders. This Court has also endeavored to mark the safe harbors clearly.

In this case, the need for providing directors with definitive guidance compels us to hold that no direct claim for breach of fiduciary duties may be asserted by the creditors of a solvent corporation that is operating in the zone of insolvency. When a solvent corporation is navigating in the zone of insolvency, the focus for Delaware directors does not change: directors must continue to discharge their fiduciary duties to the corporation and its shareholders by exercising their business judgment in the best interests of the corporation for the benefit of its shareholder owners. Therefore, we hold the Court of Chancery properly concluded that Count II of the NACEPF Complaint fails to state a claim, as a matter of Delaware law, to the extent that it attempts to assert a direct claim for breach of fiduciary duty to a creditor while Clearwire was operating in the zone of insolvency.

Insolvent Corporations Direct Claims For Breach of Fiduciary Duty May Not Be Asserted by Creditors

It is well settled that directors owe fiduciary duties to the corporation.[36] When a corporation is *solvent*, those duties may be enforced by its shareholders, who have standing to bring *derivative* actions on behalf of the corporation because they are the ultimate beneficiaries of the corporation's growth and increased value.[37] When a corporation is *insolvent*, however, its creditors take the place of the shareholders as the residual beneficiaries of any increase in value.

Consequently, the creditors of an *insolvent* corporation have standing to maintain derivative claims against directors on behalf of the corporation for breaches of fiduciary duties.[38] The corporation's [102] insolvency "makes the creditors the principal constituency injured by any fiduciary breaches that diminish the firm's value." Therefore, equitable considerations give creditors standing to pursue derivative claims against the directors of an insolvent corporation. Individual creditors of an insolvent corporation have the same incentive to pursue valid derivative claims on its behalf that shareholders have when the corporation is solvent.

---

[36] *See, e.g., Guth v. Loft, Inc.,* 5 A.2d 503, 510 (Del.1939).

[37] *See, e.g., Aronson v. Lewis,* 473 A.2d 805, 811 (Del.1984) *partially overruled on other grounds by Brehm v. Eisner,* 746 A.2d 244 (Del.2000).

[38] *Agostino v. Hicks,* 845 A.2d 1110, 1117 (Del.Ch.2004); *see also Tooley v. Donaldson, Lufkin & Jenrette, Inc.,* 845 A.2d at 1036 ("The derivative suit has been generally described as "one of the most interesting and ingenious of accountability mechanisms for large formal organizations."') (quoting *Kramer v. W. Pac. Indus., Inc.,* 546 A.2d 348, 351 (Del.1988)); *Guttman v. Huang,* 823 A.2d 492, 500 (Del.Ch.2003) (noting the "deterrence effects of meritorious derivative suits on faithless conduct.").

In *Production Resources,* the Court of Chancery recognized that — in most, if not all instances — creditors of insolvent corporations could bring derivative claims against directors of an insolvent corporation for breach of fiduciary duty. In that case, in response to the creditor plaintiff's contention that derivative claims for breach of fiduciary duty were transformed into *direct* claims upon insolvency, the Court of Chancery stated:

> The fact that the corporation has become insolvent does not turn [derivative] claims into direct creditor claims, it simply provides creditors with standing to assert those claims. At all times, claims of this kind belong to the corporation itself because even if the improper acts occur when the firm is insolvent, they operate to injure the firm in the first instance by reducing its value, injuring creditors only indirectly by diminishing the value of the firm and therefore the assets from which the creditors may satisfy their claims.

Nevertheless, in *Production Resources,* the Court of Chancery stated that it was "not prepared to rule out" the *possibility* that the creditor plaintiff had alleged conduct that "might support" a *limited* direct claim. Since the complaint in *Production Resources* sufficiently alleged a derivative claim, however, it was unnecessary to decide if creditors had a legal right to bring direct fiduciary claims against directors in the insolvency context.

In this case, NACEPF did not attempt to allege a derivative claim in Count II of its Complaint. It only asserted a *direct* claim against the director Defendants for alleged breaches of fiduciary duty when Clearwire was insolvent. The Court of Chancery did not decide that issue. Instead, the Court of Chancery *assumed arguendo* that a direct claim for a breach of fiduciary duty to a creditor is legally cognizable in the context of actual insolvency. It then held that Count II of NACEPF's Complaint failed to state such a direct creditor claim because it did not satisfy the pleading requirements described by the decisions in *Production Resources*[43] and [103] *Big Lots Stores, Inc. v. Bain Capital Fund VII, LLC.*[44]

---

[43] In *Production Resources,* the Court of Chancery expressed in *dicta* a "conservative assumption that there might, possibly exist circumstances in which the directors [of an actually insolvent corporation] display such a marked degree of animus towards a particular creditor with a proven entitlement to payment that they expose themselves to a direct fiduciary duty claim by that creditor." *Production Resources Group, L.L.C. v. NCT Group, Inc.,* 863 A.2d at 798. We think not. While there may well be a basis for a direct claim arising out of contract or tort, our holding today precludes a direct claim arising out of a purported breach of a fiduciary duty owed to that creditor by the directors of an insolvent corporation.

[44] *Big Lots Stores, Inc. v. Bain Capital Fund VII, LLC,* 922 A.2d 1169 (Del.Ch.2006). In *Big Lots,* the Court of Chancery reiterated, also in *dicta,* that any potentially cognizable direct claims asserted by creditors in actual insolvency should be confined to the limited circumstances in *Production Resources,* namely, instances in which invidious conduct toward a particular "creditor" with a "proven entitlement

To date, the Court of Chancery has never recognized that a creditor has the right to assert a *direct* claim for breach of fiduciary duty against the directors of an *insolvent* corporation. However, prior to this opinion, that possibility remained an open question because of the "arguendo assumption" in this case and the *dicta* in *Production Resources* and *Big Lots Stores*. In this opinion, we recognize "the pragmatic conduct-regulating legal realms ... calls for more precise conceptual line drawing."[45]

Recognizing that directors of an insolvent corporation owe direct fiduciary duties to creditors, would create uncertainty for directors who have a fiduciary duty to exercise their business judgment in the best interest of the insolvent corporation. To recognize a new right for creditors to bring direct fiduciary claims against those directors would create a conflict between those directors' duty to maximize the value of the insolvent corporation for the benefit of all those having an interest in it, and the newly recognized direct fiduciary duty to individual creditors. Directors of insolvent corporations must retain the freedom to engage in vigorous, good faith negotiations with individual creditors for the benefit of the corporation. Accordingly, we hold that individual *creditors* of an *insolvent* corporation have *no right to assert direct* claims for breach of fiduciary duty against corporate directors. Creditors may nonetheless protect their interest by bringing derivative claims on behalf of the insolvent corporation or any *other* direct nonfiduciary claim, as discussed earlier in this opinion, that may be available for individual creditors.

Conclusion

The creditors of a Delaware corporation that is either insolvent or in the zone of insolvency have no right, as a matter of law, to assert direct claims for breach of fiduciary duty against its directors. Therefore, Count II of NACEPF's Complaint failed to state a claim upon which relief could be granted. Consequently, the final judgment of the Court of Chancery is affirmed.

---

to payment" has been alleged. *Id.* The suggestion in that *dicta* is also inconsistent with and precluded by our holding in this opinion.

[45] *In Re Walt Disney Co. Derivative Litigation,* 906 A.2d 27, 65 (Del.2006).

B. Metropolitan Life Ins. Co. v. RJR Nabisco Inc. (SDNY 1989)

Questions

1. MetLife, a very sophisticated creditor of RJR, claimed that the leveraged buyout of RJR by KKR was an entirely unanticipated event that violated RJR's implied duty of good faith and fair dealing towards its creditors. The court doesn't buy it. Do you?

2. Regardless, notice the striking contrast between the treatment of creditors and shareholders in this and other 1980s takeover cases. In *MetLife*, the court blesses a takeover that clearly reduced creditor value by billions of dollars without the deal-specific approval of creditors. At about the same time, Delaware cases empowered and even required boards to defeat takeovers in the name of "inadequate value" to shareholders even when the latter would have approved the deal. Does this make sense?

NB: The book *Barbarians at the Gate* tells the tale of the "bidding war" referred to in Judge Walker's introduction — it is a fun read.

716 F.Supp. 1504 (1989)

METROPOLITAN LIFE INSURANCE COMPANY and Jefferson-Pilot Life Insurance Company, Plaintiffs,

v.

RJR NABISCO, INC. and F. Ross Johnson, Defendants.

No. 88 Civ. 8266 (JMW).

United States District Court, S.D. New York.

[...]

OPINION AND ORDER

WALKER, District Judge:

I. INTRODUCTION

The corporate parties to this action are among the country's most sophisticated financial institutions, as familiar with the Wall Street investment community and the securities market as American consumers are with the Oreo cookies and Winston cigarettes made by defendant RJR Nabisco, Inc. (sometimes "the company" or "RJR Nabisco"). The present action traces its origins to October 20, 1988, when F. Ross Johnson, then the Chief Executive Officer of RJR Nabisco, proposed a $17 billion leveraged buy-out ("LBO") of the company's shareholders, at $75 per share.[1] Within a few days, a bidding war developed among the investment group led by Johnson and the investment firm of Kohlberg Kravis Roberts & Co. ("KKR"), and others. On December 1, 1988, a special committee of RJR Nabisco directors, established by the company specifically to consider the competing proposals, recommended that the company accept the KKR proposal, a $24 billion LBO that called for the purchase of the company's outstanding stock at roughly $109 per share.

[...T]he merger was ultimately completed during the week of April 24, 1989.

Plaintiffs now allege, in short, that RJR Nabisco's actions have drastically impaired the value of bonds previously issued to plaintiffs by, in effect, misappropriating the value of those bonds to help finance the LBO and to distribute an enormous windfall to the company's shareholders. As a result, plaintiffs argue, they have unfairly suffered a multimillion dollar loss in the value of their bonds.[4] [...]

Although the numbers involved in this case are large, and the financing necessary to complete the LBO unprecedented,[8] the legal principles nonetheless remain discrete and familiar. Yet while the instant motions thus primarily require the Court to evaluate and apply traditional rules of equity and contract interpretation, plaintiffs do raise issues of

---

[1] A leveraged buy-out occurs when a group of investors, usually including members of a company's management team, buy the company under financial arrangements that include little equity and significant new debt. The necessary debt financing typically includes mortgages or high risk/high yield bonds, popularly known as "junk bonds." Additionally, a portion of this debt is generally secured by the company's assets. Some of the acquired company's assets are usually sold after the transaction is completed in order to reduce the debt incurred in the acquisition.

[4] Agencies like Standard & Poor's and Moody's generally rate bonds in two broad categories: investment grade and speculative grade. Standard & Poor's rates investment grade bonds from "AAA" to "BBB." Moody's rates those bonds from "AAA" to "Baa3." Speculative grade bonds are rated either "BB" and lower, or "Ba1" and lower, by Standard & Poor's and Moody's, respectively. See, e.g., Standard and Poor's Debt Rating Criteria at 10-11. No one disputes that, subsequent to the announcement of the LBO, the RJR Nabisco bonds lost their "A" ratings.

[8] On February 9, 1989, KKR completed its tender offer for roughly 74 percent of RJR Nabisco's common stock (of which approximately 97% of the outstanding shares were tendered) and all of its Series B Cumulative Preferred Stock (of which approximately 95% of the outstanding shares were tendered). Approximately $18 billion in cash was paid out to these stockholders. KKR acquired the remaining stock in the late April merger through the issuance of roughly $4.1 billion of pay-in-kind exchangeable preferred stock and roughly $1.8 billion in face amount of convertible debentures. See Bradley Reply Aff. ¶ 2.

first impression in the context of an LBO. At the heart of the present motions lies plaintiffs' claim that RJR Nabisco violated a restrictive covenant — not an explicit covenant found within the four corners of the relevant bond indentures, but rather an *implied* covenant of good faith and fair dealing — not to incur the debt necessary to facilitate the LBO and thereby betray what plaintiffs claim was the fundamental basis of their bargain with the company. The company, plaintiffs assert, consistently reassured its bondholders that it had a "mandate" from its Board of Directors to maintain RJR Nabisco's preferred credit rating. Plaintiffs ask this Court first to imply a covenant of good faith and fair dealing that would prevent the recent transaction, then to hold that this covenant has been breached, and finally [1508] to require RJR Nabisco to redeem their bonds.

RJR Nabisco defends the LBO by pointing to express provisions in the bond indentures that, *inter alia*, permit mergers and the assumption of additional debt. These provisions, as well as others that could have been included but were not, were known to the market and to plaintiffs, sophisticated investors who freely bought the bonds and were equally free to sell them at any time. Any attempt by this Court to create contractual terms *post hoc*, defendants contend, not only finds no basis in the controlling law and undisputed facts of this case, but also would constitute an impermissible invasion into the free and open operation of the marketplace.

For the reasons set forth below, this Court agrees with defendants. There being no express covenant between the parties that would restrict the incurrence of new debt, and no perceived direction to that end from covenants that are express, this Court will not imply a covenant to prevent the recent LBO and thereby create an indenture term that, while bargained for in other contexts, was not bargained for here and was not even within the mutual contemplation of the parties.

II. BACKGROUND

[...]

A. The Parties:

Metropolitan Life Insurance Co. ("MetLife"), incorporated in New York, is a life insurance company that provides pension benefits for 42 million individuals. According to its most recent annual report, MetLife's assets exceed $88 billion and its debt securities holdings exceed $49 billion. Bradley Aff. ¶ 11. MetLife is a mutual company and therefore has no stockholders and is instead operated for the benefit of its policyholders. Am.Comp. ¶ 5. MetLife alleges that it owns $340,542,000 in principal amount of six separate RJR Nabisco debt issues, bonds allegedly purchased between July 1975 and July 1988. Some bonds become due as early as this year; others will not become due until 2017. The bonds bear interest rates of anywhere from 8 to 10.25 percent. MetLife also owned 186,000 shares of RJR Nabisco common stock at the time this suit was filed. Am. Comp. ¶ 12.

Jefferson-Pilot Life Insurance Co. ("Jefferson-Pilot") is a North Carolina company that has more than $3 billion in total assets, $1.5 billion of which are invested in debt securities. Bradley Aff. ¶ 12. Jefferson-Pilot alleges that it owns $9.34 million in principal amount of three separate RJR Nabisco debt issues, allegedly purchased between June 1978 and June 1988. Those bonds, bearing interest rates of anywhere from 8.45 to 10.75 percent, become due in 1993 and 1998. Am.Comp. ¶ 13.

[1509] RJR Nabisco, a Delaware corporation, is a consumer products holding company that owns some of the country's best known product lines, including LifeSavers candy, Oreo cookies, and Winston cigarettes. The company was formed in 1985, when R.J. Reynolds Industries, Inc. ("R.J. Reynolds") merged with Nabisco Brands, Inc. ("Nabisco Brands"). In 1979, and thus before the R.J. Reynolds-Nabisco Brands merger, R.J. Reynolds acquired the Del Monte Corporation ("Del Monte"), which distributes canned fruits and vegetables. From January 1987 until February 1989, co-defendant Johnson served as the company's CEO. KKR, a private investment firm, organizes funds through which investors provide pools of equity to finance LBOs. Bradley Aff. ¶¶ 12-15.

B. The Indentures:

The bonds implicated by this suit are governed by long, detailed indentures, which in turn are governed by New York contract law.[10] No one disputes that the holders of public bond issues, like plaintiffs here, often enter the market after the indentures have been negotiated and memorialized. Thus, those indentures are often not the product of face-to-face negotiations between the ultimate holders and the issuing company. What remains equally true, however, is that underwriters ordinarily negotiate the terms of the indentures with the issuers. Since the underwriters must then sell or place the bonds, they necessarily negotiate in part with the interests of the buyers in mind. Moreover, these indentures were not secret agreements foisted upon unwitting participants in the bond market. No successive holder is required to accept or to continue to hold the bonds, governed by their accompanying indentures; indeed, plaintiffs readily admit that they could have sold their bonds right up until the announcement of the LBO. Tr. at 15. Instead, sophisticated

---

[10] Both sides agree that New York law controls this Court's interpretation of the indentures, which contain explicit designations to that effect. *See, e.g.,* P.Mem. at 26; D. Mem at 15 n. 23. The indentures themselves provide that they "shall be deemed to be a contract under the laws of the State of New York, and for all purposes shall be construed in accordance with the laws of said State, except as may otherwise be required by mandatory provisions of law." Bradley Aff., Exh. L, § 12.8.

investors like plaintiffs are well aware of the indenture terms and, presumably, review them carefully before lending hundreds of millions of dollars to any company.

Indeed, the prospectuses for the indentures contain a statement relevant to this action:

> The Indenture contains no restrictions on the creation of unsecured short-term debt by [RJR Nabisco] or its subsidiaries, no restriction on the creation of unsecured Funded Debt by [RJR Nabisco] or its subsidiaries which are not Restricted Subsidiaries, and no restriction on the payment of dividends by [RJR Nabisco].

Bradley Resp.Aff., Exh. L at 24. Further, as plaintiffs themselves note, the contracts at issue "[do] not impose debt limits, since debt is assumed to be used for productive purposes." P. Reply at 34.

1. The relevant Articles:

A typical RJR Nabisco indenture contains thirteen Articles. At least four of them are relevant to the present motions and thus merit a brief review.

Article Three delineates the covenants of the issuer. Most important, it first provides for payment of principal and interest. It then addresses various mechanical provisions regarding such matters as payment [1510] terms and trustee vacancies. The Article also contains "negative pledge" and related provisions, which restrict mortgages or other liens on the assets of RJR Nabisco or its subsidiaries and seek to protect the bond-holders from being subordinated to other debt.

Article Five describes various procedures to remedy defaults and the responsibilities of the Trustee. This Article includes the distinction in the indentures noted above, *see supra* n. 11. In seven of the nine securities at issue, a provision in Article Five prohibits bondholders from suing for any remedy based on rights in the indentures unless 25 percent of the holders have requested in writing that the indenture trustee seek such relief, and, after 60 days, the trustee has not sued. *See, e.g.,* Bradley Aff.Exh. L, §§ 5.6, 5.7. Defendants argue that this provision precludes plaintiffs from suing on these seven securities. *See* D.Mem. at 22-25. Given its holdings today, *see infra,* the Court need not address this issue.

Article Nine governs the adoption of supplemental indentures. It provides, *inter alia,* that the Issuer and the Trustee can

> add to the covenants of the Issuer such further covenants, restrictions, conditions or provisions as its Board of Directors by Board Resolution and the Trustee shall consider to be for the protection of the holders of

Securities, and to make the occurrence, or the occurrence and continuance, of a default in any such additional covenants, restrictions, conditions or provisions an Event of Default permitting the enforcement of all or any of the several remedies provided in this Indenture as herein set forth ...

Bradley Aff.Exh. L, § 9.1(c).

Article Ten addresses a potential "Consolidation, Merger, Sale or Conveyance," and explicitly sets forth the conditions under which the company can consolidate or merge into or with any other corporation. It provides explicitly that RJR Nabisco "may consolidate with, or sell or convey, all or substantially all of its assets to, or merge into or with any other corporation," so long as the new entity is a United States corporation, and so long as it assumes RJR Nabisco's debt. The Article also requires that any such transaction not result in the company's default under any indenture provision.

2. The elimination of restrictive covenants:

In its Amended Complaint, MetLife lists the six debt issues on which it bases its claims. Indentures for two of those issues — the 10.25 percent Notes due in 1990, of which MetLife continues to hold $10 million, and the 8.9 percent Debentures due in 1996, of which MetLife continues to hold $50 million — once contained express covenants that, among other things, restricted the company's ability to incur precisely the sort of debt involved in the recent LBO. In order to eliminate those restrictions, the parties to this action renegotiated the terms of those indentures, first in 1983 and then again in 1985.

MetLife acquired $50 million principal amount of 10.25 percent Notes from Del Monte in July of 1975. To cover the $50 million, MetLife and Del Monte entered into a loan agreement. That agreement restricted Del Monte's ability, among other things, to incur the sort of indebtedness involved in the RJR Nabisco LBO. *See* promissory note §§ 2.6-2.15, attached as Exhibit A to Bradley Aff.Exh. E. In 1979, R.J. Reynolds — the corporate predecessor to RJR Nabisco — purchased Del Monte and [1511] assumed its indebtedness. Then, in December of 1983, R.J. Reynolds requested MetLife to agree to deletions of those restrictive covenants in exchange for various guarantees from R.J. Reynolds. *See* Bradley Aff. ¶ 17. A few months later, MetLife and R.J. Reynolds entered into a guarantee and amendment agreement reflecting those terms. *See* Bradley Aff. ¶ 17, Exh. G. Pursuant to that agreement, and in the words of Robert E. Chappell, Jr., MetLife's Executive Vice President, MetLife thus "gave up the restrictive covenants applicable to the Del Monte debt ... in return for [the parent company's] guarantee and public covenants." Chappell Dep. at 196.

MetLife acquired the 8.9 percent Debentures from R.J. Reynolds in October of 1976 in a private placement. A promissory note evidenced MetLife's $100 million loan. That note, like the Del Monte agreement, contained covenants that restricted R.J. Reynolds' ability to incur new debt. *See* Bradley Aff., Exh. H, §§ 2.5-2.9. In June of 1985, R.J. Reynolds announced its plans to acquire Nabisco Brands in a $3.6 billion transaction that involved the incurrence of a significant amount of new debt. R.J. Reynolds requested MetLife to waive compliance with these restrictive covenants in light of the Nabisco acquisition. *See* D.Mem. at 45; Bradley Aff. ¶ 18.

In exchange for certain benefits, MetLife agreed to exchange its 8.9 percent debentures — which *did* contain explicit debt limitations — for debentures issued under a public indenture — which contain no explicit limits on new debt. An internal MetLife memorandum explained the parties' understanding:

> [MetLife's $100 million financing of the Nabisco Brands purchase] had its origins in discussions with RJR regarding potential covenant violations in the 8.90% Notes. More specifically, *in its acquisition of Nabisco Brands, RJR was slated to incur significant new long-term debt, which would have caused a violation in the funded indebtedness incurrence tests in the 8.90% Notes.* In the discussions regarding [MetLife's] willingness to consent to the additional indebtedness, *it was determined that a mutually beneficial approach to the problem* was to 1) agree on a new financing having a rate and a maturity desirable for [MetLife] and 2) modify the 8.90% Notes. The former was accomplished with agreement on the proposed financing, while the latter was accomplished by [MetLife] agreeing to substitute RJR's public indenture covenants for the covenants in the 8.90% Notes. In addition to the covenant substitution, RJR has agreed to "debenturize" the 8.90% Notes upon [MetLife's] request. This will permit [MetLife] to sell the 8.90% Notes to the public.

MetLife Southern Office Memorandum, dated July 11, 1985 [...] (emphasis added).

3. The recognition and effect of the LBO trend:

Other internal MetLife documents help frame the background to this action, for they accurately describe the changing securities markets and the responses those changes engendered from sophisticated market participants, such as MetLife and Jefferson-Pilot. At least as early as 1982, MetLife recognized an LBO's effect on bond values.[14] In the

---

[14] MetLife itself began investing in LBOs as early as 1980. *See* MetLife Special Projects Memorandum, dated June 17, 1989, attached as Bradley Aff.Exh. V, at 1 ("[MetLife's] history of investing in leveraged buyout transactions dates back to 1980; and through 1984, [MetLife] reviewed a large number of LBO

spring of that year, MetLife participated in the financing of an LBO of a company called Reeves Brothers ("Reeves"). At the time of that LBO, MetLife also held bonds in that company. Subsequent to the LBO, as a MetLife memorandum explained, the "Debentures of Reeves were downgraded by Standard & Poor's from BBB to B and by Moody's from Baa1 to Ba3, thereby lowering the value of the Notes and Debentures held by [1512] [MetLife]." MetLife Memorandum, dated August 20, 1982, [...]

A more comprehensive memorandum, prepared in late 1985, evaluated and explained several aspects of the corporate world's increasing use of mergers, takeovers and other debt-financed transactions. That memorandum first reviewed the available protection for lenders such as MetLife:

> Covenants are incorporated into loan documents to ensure that after a lender makes a loan, the creditworthiness of the borrower and the lender's ability to reach the borrower's assets do not deteriorate substantially. *Restrictions on the incurrence of debt,* sale of assets, mergers, dividends, restricted payments and loans and advances to affiliates *are some of the traditional negative covenants that can help protect lenders in the event their obligors become involved in undesirable merger/takeover situations.*

[...] Indeed, MetLife does not dispute that, as a member of a bondholders' association, it [1513] received and discussed a proposed model indenture, which included a "comprehensive covenant" entitled "Limitations on Shareholders' Payments." As becomes clear from reading the proposed — but never adopted — provision, it was "intend[ed] to provide protection against all of the types of situations in which shareholders profit at the expense of bondholders." *Id.* The provision dictated that the "[c]orporation will not, and will not permit any [s]ubsidiary to, directly or indirectly, make any [s]hareholder [p]ayment unless ... (1) the aggregate amount of all [s]hareholder payments during the period [at issue] ... shall not exceed [figure left blank]." Bradley Resp.Aff.Exh. H, at 9. The term "shareholder payments" is defined to include "restructuring distributions, stock repurchases, debt incurred or guaranteed to finance merger payments to shareholders, etc." *Id.* at i.

Apparently, that provision — or provisions with similar intentions — never went beyond the discussion stage at MetLife. That fact is easily understood; indeed, MetLife's own documents articulate several reasonable, undisputed explanations:

---

investment opportunities presented to us by various investment banking firms and LBO specialists. Over this five-year period, [MetLife] invested, on a direct basis, approximately $430 million to purchase debt and equity securities in 10 such transactions ...").

While it would be possible to broaden the change in ownership covenant to cover any acquisition-oriented transaction, *we might well encounter significant resistance in implementation with larger public companies* [...]

III. DISCUSSION

[...] In interpreting these contracts, this Court must be concerned with what the parties intended, but only to the extent that what they intended is evidenced by what is written in the indentures. [...]

The indentures at issue clearly address the eventuality of a merger. They impose certain related restrictions not at issue in this suit, but no restriction that would prevent the recent RJR Nabisco merger transaction. *See supra* at 1510 (discussion of Article 10). The indentures also explicitly set forth provisions for the adoption of new covenants, if such a course is deemed appropriate. *See supra* at 1510 (discussion of Article 9). While it may be true that no explicit provision either permits or prohibits an LBO, such contractual silence itself cannot create ambiguity to avoid the dictates of the parol evidence rule, particularly where the indentures impose no debt limitations.

Under certain circumstances, however, courts will, as plaintiffs note, consider extrinsic evidence to evaluate the scope of an implied covenant of good faith. [...] However, the Second Circuit has established a different rule for customary, or boilerplate, provisions of detailed indentures used and relied upon throughout the securities market, such as those at issue. Thus, in *Sharon Steel Corporation v. Chase Manhattan Bank, N.A.*, 691 F.2d 1039 (2d Cir.1982), Judge Winter concluded that

> [b]oilerplate provisions are ... not the consequences of the relationship of particular borrowers and lenders and do not depend upon particularized intentions of the parties to an indenture. There are no adjudicative facts relating to the parties to the litigation for a jury to find and the meaning of boilerplate provisions is, therefore, a matter of law rather than fact. Moreover, uniformity in interpretation is important to the efficiency of capital markets ... Whereas participants in the capital market can adjust their affairs according to a uniform interpretation, whether it be correct or not as an initial proposition, the creation of enduring uncertainties as to the meaning of boilerplate provisions would decrease the value of all debenture issues and greatly impair the efficient working of capital markets ... Just such uncertainties would be created if interpretation of boilerplate provisions were submitted to juries sitting in every judicial district in the nation.

[...] Ignoring these principles, plaintiffs would have this Court vary what they themselves have admitted is "indenture boilerplate," P. Reply at 2, of "standard" agreements, P.

Mem. at 14, to comport with collateral representations and their subjective understandings.[20]

[... P]laintiffs assert that

> [d]efendant RJR Nabisco owes a continuing duty of good faith and fair dealing in connection with the contract [i.e., the indentures] through which it borrowed money from MetLife, Jefferson-Pilot and other holders of its debt, including a duty not to frustrate the purpose of the contracts to the debtholders or to deprive the debtholders of the intended object of the contracts — purchase of investment-grade securities.

> In the "buy-out," the [c]ompany breaches the duty [or implied covenant] of good faith and fair dealing by, *inter alia*, destroying the investment grade quality of the debt and transferring that value to the "buy-out" proponents and to the shareholders.

Am.Comp. ¶¶ 34, 35. In effect, plaintiffs contend that express covenants were not necessary because an *implied* covenant would prevent what defendants have now done.

A plaintiff always can allege a violation of an express covenant. If there has been such a violation, of course, the court need not reach the question of whether or not an *implied* covenant has been violated. [1517] That inquiry surfaces where, while the express terms may not have been technically breached, one party has nonetheless effectively deprived the other of those express, explicitly bargained-for benefits. In such a case, a court will read an implied covenant of good faith and fair dealing into a contract to ensure that neither party deprives the other of "the fruits of the agreement." [...]

---

[20] To a certain extent, this discussion is academic. Even if the Court did consider the extrinsic evidence offered by plaintiffs, its ultimate decision would be no different. Based on that extrinsic evidence, plaintiffs attempt to establish that an implied covenant of good faith is necessary to protect the benefits of their agreements. That inquiry necessarily asks the Court to determine whether the existing contractual terms should be construed to preclude defendants from engaging in an LBO along the lines of the recently completed transaction. However, even evaluating *all* facts—such as the public statements made by company executives—in the light most favorable to plaintiffs, these plaintiffs fail as a matter of law to establish that the purported "fundamental basis" of their bargain with defendants created a contractual obligation on the part of the defendants not to engage in an LBO. It is first worth noting that plaintiffs have quoted selectively from certain speeches and remarks made by RJR Nabisco executives; in some respects, those public statements are more equivocal than plaintiffs would have this Court believe. [...] Therefore, even if the parole evidence rule did not block plaintiffs' path, their course would not be followed. [...]

[1520] Plaintiffs argue in the most general terms that the fundamental basis of all these indentures was that an LBO along the lines of the recent RJR Nabisco transaction would never be undertaken, that indeed *no* action would be taken, intentionally or not, that would significantly deplete the company's assets. Accepting plaintiffs' theory, their fundamental bargain with defendants dictated that nothing would be done to jeopardize the extremely high probability that the company would remain able to make interest payments and repay principal over the 20 to 30 year indenture term — and perhaps by logical extension even included the right to ask a court "to make sure that plaintiffs had made a good investment." *Gardner*, 589 F.Supp. at 674. But as Judge Knapp aptly concluded in *Gardner*, "Defendants ... were under a duty to carry out the terms of the contract, but not to make sure that plaintiffs had made a good investment. The former they have done; the latter we have no jurisdiction over." *Id.* Plaintiffs' submissions and MetLife's previous undisputed internal memoranda remind the Court that a "fundamental basis" or a "fruit of an agreement" is often in the eye of the beholder, whose vision may well change along with the market, and who may, with hindsight, imagine a different bargain than the one he actually and initially accepted with open eyes. [...]

Ultimately, plaintiffs cannot escape the inherent illogic of their argument. On the one hand, it is undisputed that investors like plaintiffs recognized that companies like RJR Nabisco strenuously opposed additional restrictive covenants that might limit the incurrence of new debt or the company's ability to engage in a merger. Furthermore, plaintiffs argue that they had no choice other than to accept the indentures as written, without additional restrictive covenants, or to "abandon" the market. Tr. at 14-15.

Yet on the other hand, plaintiffs ask this Court to imply a covenant that would have just that restrictive effect because, they contend, it reflects precisely the fundamental assumption of the market and the fundamental basis of their bargain with defendants. If that truly were the case here, it is difficult to imagine why an insistence on that term would have forced the plaintiffs to abandon the market. The Second Circuit has offered a better explanation: "[a] promise by the defendant should be implied only if the court may rightfully assume that the parties would have included it in their written agreement had their attention been called to it ... *Any such assumption in this case would be completely unwarranted." Neuman v. Pike*, 591 F.2d 191, 195 (2d Cir.1979) (emphasis added [...]).

In the final analysis, plaintiffs offer no objective or reasonable standard for a court to use in its effort to define the sort of actions their "implied covenant" would permit a corporation to take, and those it would not.[28] Plaintiffs say only that investors like

---

[28] Under plaintiffs' theory, bondholders might ask a court to prohibit a company like RJR Nabisco not only from engaging in an LBO, but also from entering a new line of business — with the attendant costs

themselves rely upon the "skill" and "good faith" of a company's board and management, *see, e.g.,* P.Mem. at 35, and that their covenant would prevent the company [1522] from "destroy[ing] ... the legitimate expectations of its long-term bondholders." *Id.* at 54. As is clear from the preceding discussion, however, plaintiffs have failed to convince the Court that by upholding the explicit, bargained-for terms of the indenture, RJR Nabisco has either exhibited bad faith or destroyed plaintiffs' *legitimate,* protected expectations.

[...] Those burdens cannot be avoided by resorting to an overbroad, superficially appealing, but legally insufficient, implied covenant of good faith and fair dealing. [...]

III. CONCLUSION

For the reasons set forth above, the Court grants defendants summary judgment.

SO ORDERED.

---

of building new physical plants and hiring new workers — or from acquiring new businesses such as RJR Nabisco did when it acquired Del Monte.

C. Statutory Rules and Equitable Principles

As *Gheewalla* and *MetLife* show, creditors must mostly rely on explicit contractual provisions for protection. This note explains the little protection that is offered by statutory rules and equitable principles.

Questions

1. How might these have helped bondholders in *MetLife v. RJR Nabisco* (or a tobacco tort claimant of RJR)?

2. Should they have?

1. Minimum Legal Capital

In the old days, founding shareholders needed to provide some statutorily determined minimum amount of capital to a corporation. In some jurisdictions, that is still the case. In particular, Art. 6(1) of the Recast (2nd EU Company Law) Directive 2012/30/EU requires a minimum capital of €25,000 for European public limited liability companies. The Directive also prescribes elaborate provisions "for maintaining the capital, which constitutes the creditors' security, in particular by prohibiting any reduction thereof by distribution to shareholders where the latter are not entitled to it and by imposing limits on the company's right to acquire its own shares."

Such minimum legal capital rules are fundamentally flawed. They consume much of corporate lawyers' time and attention without affording creditors genuine protection. The basic problem is that the minimum is not calibrated to the proposed business of the corporation. For example, €25,000 is laughable for a large corporation like JPMorgan or Alcoa, but possibly prohibitive for a small grocery store. And even if the initial minimum capital were adequate, it would very quickly become outdated as the business of the corporation grows, shrinks, or changes. Nor do shareholders need to replenish capital once it is depleted – after all, that is the nature of limited liability. Even a small start-up corporation, however, might spend €25,000 on wages in the first month of its existence, leaving nothing of the minimum capital. As a result, minimum legal capital provides no guarantee whatsoever to a creditor that the corporation is adequately capitalized (whatever that means).

To be sure, capital regulation need not be as blunt as the European directive. Certain industries, notably banking, are subject to more finely calibrated capital requirements. In particular, these requirements tend to use ratios (e.g., debt to equity) rather than absolute amounts. Moreover, they are adapted to the risks of that particular industry, and perhaps even to the specific risks of individual companies — for example, bank capital requirements depend on the assets held by each bank. Last not least, they apply not only at the creation of the company but throughout its life. Similarly, debt *contracts* often contain finely calibrated covenants regarding financial ratios, permissible investments, and the like. General minimum capital rules, however, lack such finesse.

In recognition of these flaws, U.S. jurisdictions have fully abandoned minimum legal capital requirements.

2. Distribution Constraints

Under the DGCL, the only remaining role for legal capital is in determining the permissible amount of distributions to shareholders, i.e., dividends and share repurchases. The enforcement of the limits is quite strict: Directors are jointly and severally liable for negligent violations (DGCL 174). However, the limits are rarely binding outside of insolvency because legal capital can be, and usually is, reduced to a minimal amount.

DGCL 173 and 170 provide that dividends can be paid out of "surplus" (or, if there is no surplus, out of net profits for the last two years). DGCL 154 defines surplus as net assets minus capital, and net assets as total assets minus total liabilities (i.e., equity). In other words, Delaware corporations can declare dividends up to the value of their equity minus capital.

So, what is "capital"? It is what the board resolves it to be, provided it is at least aggregate "par value" (DGCL 154, 1st sentence). Par value is another number determined by the charter or, if authorized by the charter, the board (DGCL 151(a)). Par value's only other role is that the corporation cannot issue shares for consideration less than par value (DGCL 153(a)). In practice, Delaware corporations tend to issue stock with no par value or very low par value (e.g., 0.00001 cent per share), and set capital near zero. The bottom line is that the DGCL permits corporations to pay out almost their entire equity as dividends.

DGCL 160(a)(1) contains an equivalent restriction on share repurchases — practically none short of insolvency. Again, the limit is capital: repurchases may not impair capital. The only difference here is that the repurchase of par value shares reduces the aggregate par value of outstanding shares. This allows for a reduction in stated capital, if aggregate par value was previously a binding constraint (cf. DGCL 244(a)(2)).

By the way, it makes sense that the limits on dividends and repurchases are the same. Dividends and repurchases are largely equivalent as means for payouts to shareholders. Consider a corporation with equity worth $100 and 10 shares outstanding (such that the value of each share is $10). Imagine that the corporation wants to distribute $10 to shareholders. One option is to pay a $1 dividend on each share. Another option is to buy back one share for $10. The amount of cash returned to shareholders collectively will be the same. In the dividend option, 10 shares will remain outstanding, with a value of $9 per share. In the repurchase option, 9 shares will remain outstanding, with a value of $10 per share. The aggregate value of shares outstanding, or "market capitalization," will be the same under either option: $90. The choice between the two methods is mostly relevant for tax purposes. In particular, many shareholders would prefer not to receive dividends (taxed at personal income tax rates) and instead sell some of their shares to the corporation or a third party buyer (taxed at the lower capital gains tax rate).

3. Fraudulent Transfer

Of more practical relevance are restrictions on so-called fraudulent transfers (a/k/a fraudulent conveyances). The animating purpose behind fraudulent transfer rules is that creditors should be able to claim back an asset from a transferee who obtained the asset from the debtor without paying adequate consideration. A paradigmatic case is the heavily indebted wife who transfers her assets to her husband to shield them from her creditors. But the rules are considerably more general. Their main advantage over the aforementioned corporate distribution constraints is that they also catch transactions in which the recipients paid some, but insufficient, consideration.

Both state law and federal bankruptcy law contain fraudulent transfer rules. Please read both!

(a) Bankruptcy Code §548

(a)(1) The trustee may avoid any transfer (including any transfer to or for the benefit of an insider under an employment contract) of an interest of the debtor in property, or any obligation (including any obligation to or for the benefit of an insider under an employment contract) incurred by the debtor, that was made or incurred on or within 2 years before the date of the filing of the petition, if the debtor voluntarily or involuntarily

—

(A) made such transfer or incurred such obligation with actual intent to hinder, delay, or defraud any entity to which the debtor was or became, on or after the date that such transfer was made or such obligation was incurred, indebted; or

(B)   (i)   received less than a reasonably equivalent value in exchange for such transfer or obligation; and

          (ii)   (I) was insolvent on the date that such transfer was made or such obligation was incurred, or became insolvent as a result of such transfer or obligation;

                    (II) was engaged in business or a transaction, or was about to engage in business or a transaction, for which any property remaining with the debtor was an unreasonably small capital;

                    (III) intended to incur, or believed that the debtor would incur, debts that would be beyond the debtor's ability to pay as such debts matured; or

                    (IV) made such transfer to or for the benefit of an insider, or incurred such obligation to or for the benefit of an insider, under an employment contract and not in the ordinary course of business.

[...]

(C) Except to the extent that a transfer or obligation voidable under this section is voidable under section 544, 545, or 547 of this title, a transferee or obligee of such a transfer or obligation that takes for value and in good faith has a lien on or may retain any interest transferred or may enforce any obligation incurred, as the case may be, to the extent that such transferee or obligee gave value to the debtor in exchange for such transfer or obligation.

(b) Uniform Fraudulent Transfer Act

§ 2. Insolvency.

(a) A debtor is insolvent if the sum of the debtor's debts is greater than all of the debtor's assets at a fair valuation.

(b) A debtor who is generally not paying his [or her] debts as they become due is presumed to be insolvent.

(c) ...

§ 4. Transfers Fraudulent as to Present and Future Creditors.

(a) A transfer made or obligation incurred by a debtor is fraudulent as to a creditor, whether the creditor's claim arose before or after the transfer was made or the obligation was incurred, if the debtor made the transfer or incurred the obligation:

> (1) with actual intent to hinder, delay, or defraud any creditor of the debtor; or

> (2) without receiving a reasonably equivalent value in exchange for the transfer or obligation, and the debtor:
>> (i) was engaged or was about to engage in a business or a transaction for which the remaining assets of the debtor were unreasonably small in relation to the business or transaction; or
>> (ii) intended to incur, or believed or reasonably should have believed that he [or she] would incur, debts beyond his [or her] ability to pay as they became due.

(b) In determining actual intent under subsection (a)(1), consideration may be given, among other factors, to whether: (1) the transfer or obligation was to an insider; ...

§ 5. Transfers Fraudulent as to Present Creditors.

(a) A transfer made or obligation incurred by a debtor is fraudulent as to a creditor whose claim arose before the transfer was made or the obligation was incurred if the debtor made the transfer or incurred the obligation without receiving a reasonably equivalent value in exchange for the transfer or obligation and the debtor was insolvent at that time or the debtor became insolvent as a result of the transfer or obligation.

(b) A transfer made by a debtor is fraudulent as to a creditor whose claim arose before the transfer was made if the transfer was made to an insider for an antecedent debt, the debtor was insolvent at that time, and the insider had reasonable cause to believe that the debtor was insolvent.

§ 7. Remedies of Creditors.

(a) In an action for relief against a transfer or obligation under this [Act], a creditor, subject to the limitations in Section 8, may obtain: (1) avoidance of the transfer or obligation to the extent necessary to satisfy the creditor's claim; ...

§ 8. Defenses, Liability, and Protection of Transferee.

(a) A transfer or obligation is not voidable under Section 4(a)(1) against a person who took in good faith and for a reasonably equivalent value or against any subsequent transferee or obligee. ...

4. Equitable Subordination

In bankruptcy, courts may subordinate some creditors on equitable grounds. In particular, they may treat loans from shareholders to the corporation as corporate equity, i.e., rank these loans after all other creditor claims. Cf. Bankr. Code §510(c)(1).

Mere undercapitalization is generally not sufficient grounds for equitable subordination. But the exchange of capital (equity) for debt at a critical moment probably would be.

5. Piercing the Corporate Veil

Most radically, courts can hold shareholders directly liable for corporate debt under a doctrine called "piercing the corporate veil."

The conditions for this radical step are not well defined, to put it mildly. Generally, courts require at a minimum a "unity of interest and ownership" between shareholders and the corporation. They tend to find such "unity" if there has been (a) a disregard of corporate formalities (meetings, minutes, etc.), (b) a commingling of funds, and/or (c) undercapitalization. That is, mere control of the corporation by the shareholders, even in a single-owner corporation, is not sufficient for veil piercing.

From a practitioner's point of view, the lesson here is to respect corporate formalities. From a policy point of view, this makes some sense because enforcing any claim against anyone becomes difficult when ownership of assets cannot be established because formalities were not followed and funds were commingled.

Practically speaking, piercing hardly ever occurs in large corporations (perhaps because they follow formalities). Courts mostly (but still rarely) pierce the veil of small, single-owner corporations. And they mostly do so for the benefit of involuntary creditors such as tort creditors who did not choose their debtor. See *Peter Oh, Veil-Piercing*, 89 TEX. L. REV. 81 (2010).

In addition to the general principle of veil piercing, special statutory rules impose direct liability on (controlling) shareholders for particular types of obligations. For example, the Employee Retirement Income Security Act of 1974 (ERISA), as amended, holds controlling shareholders liable for the corporation's pro rata share of vested but unfunded pension benefits when withdrawing from a multi-employer plan.

Chapter 14. Other Stakeholders

A. eBay v. Newmark (Del. Ch. 2010)

This case pits eBay against Craig Newmark and Jim Buckmaster in a battle for control of craigslist. Craig and Jim are craigslist's founder and CEO, respectively.

craigslist is a close corporation — a corporation with only few shareholders and no public market for its shares. craigslist's only shareholders at the time were Craig, Jim, and eBay. Close corporations tend to generate two problems not seen in public corporations. First, personal relationships loom much larger. By the time close corporations show up in court, these relationships have generally soured. Second, exit for a shareholder is difficult in the absence of a public market for the shares. This is related to the first point, as it makes it harder to dissolve sour relationships. Moreover, it means that shareholders cannot obtain liquidity (i.e., cash for some, or all, of their stake) by selling, which leads to disputes over payout policy when some shareholders need liquidity and others don't (or they do but they are in control and pay themselves generous salaries). In fact, controlling shareholders may abuse a minority's liquidity need to force the minority to sell out at a low price. When no individual shareholder has control, disputes can easily lead to deadlock. Court intervention may be necessary to resolve the deadlock. Cf. DGCL 226 (read!; also skim DGCL 341, 342, and 350-353).

Both of these problems are at play in the present case, but with a twist. The twist is that the shareholders do not just disagree about payouts. They disagree about the more basic question of whether the corporation should be generating profits in the first place. eBay thinks so, but Craig and Jim do not. This is our main focus here.

We assign a long excerpt because (1) the context is crucial to understand the outcome, as always, and (2) the opinion is an excellent review of almost everything we have done so far: fiduciary duties, shareholder voting, shareholder litigation, and takeover defenses.

Questions

1. What is the purpose of a Delaware corporation, according to the court?

2. Can shareholders enforce that purpose in court? Hint: Beyond the confines of this particular lawsuit, what did eBay ultimately want, and do you think eBay could have successfully sued for it (eBay never did)?

16 A.3d 1 (2010)

EBAY DOMESTIC HOLDINGS, INC., Plaintiff,

v.

Craig NEWMARK and James Buckmaster, Defendants, and
craigslist, Inc., Nominal Defendant.

[...]

OPINION

CHANDLER, Chancellor

On June 29, 2007, eBay launched the online classifieds site www.Kijiji.com in the United States. eBay designed Kijiji to compete with www.craigslist.org, the most widely used online classifieds site in the United States, which is owned and operated by craigslist, Inc. ("craigslist" or "the Company"). At the time of Kijiji's launch, eBay owned 28.4% of craigslist and was one of only three craigslist stockholders. The other two stockholders were Craig Newmark ("Craig") and James Buckmaster ("Jim"), who together own a majority of craigslist's shares and dominate the craigslist board. eBay purchased its stake in craigslist in August 2004 pursuant to the terms of a stockholders' agreement between Jim, Craig, craigslist, and eBay that expressly permits eBay to compete with craigslist in the online classifieds arena. Under the stockholders' agreement, when eBay chose to compete with craigslist by launching Kijiji, eBay lost certain contractual consent rights that gave eBay the right to approve or disapprove of a variety of corporate actions at craigslist. Another consequence of eBay's choice to compete with craigslist, however, was that the craigslist shares eBay owns were freed of the right of first refusal Jim and Craig had held over the shares, and the shares became freely transferable.

Notwithstanding eBay's express right to compete, Jim and Craig were not enthusiastic about eBay's foray into online classifieds. Accordingly, they asked eBay to sell its stake in craigslist, indicating a preference that eBay either sell its craigslist shares back to the Company or to a third party who would be compatible with Jim, Craig, and craigslist's unique corporate culture. When eBay refused to sell, Jim and Craig deliberated with outside counsel for six months about how to respond. Finally, on January 1, 2008, Jim and Craig, acting in their capacity as directors, responded by (1) adopting a rights plan that restricted eBay from purchasing additional craigslist shares and hampered eBay's ability to freely sell the craigslist shares it owned to third parties, (2) implementing a staggered board that made it impossible for eBay to unilaterally elect a director to the craigslist board, and (3) seeking to obtain a right of first refusal in craigslist's favor over the craigslist shares eBay owns by offering to issue one new share of craigslist stock in exchange for every five shares over which any craigslist stockholder granted a right of first refusal in craigslist's favor. As to the third measure, Jim and Craig accepted the right of first refusal offer in their capacity as craigslist stockholders and received new shares; eBay, however, declined the offer, did not receive new shares, and had its ownership in craigslist diluted from 28.4% to 24.9%.

eBay filed this action challenging all three measures on April 22, 2008. eBay asserts that, in approving and implementing each measure, Jim and Craig, as directors and controlling stockholders, breached the fiduciary duties they owe to eBay as a minority stockholder of the corporation. After lengthy discovery and pre-trial motion practice, the Court held an extensive nine-day trial from December 7, 2009 to December 17, 2009. During trial, the parties examined nine live witnesses, offered seven witnesses by deposition, and presented over one thousand exhibits. The parties completed post-trial briefing on May 14, 2010. I conclude that Jim and Craig breached the fiduciary duties they owe to eBay by adopting the rights plan and by making the right of first refusal offer. I order rescission of these two measures. I also conclude that Jim and Craig did not breach the fiduciary duties they owe to eBay by implementing a staggered board. Accordingly, I leave that measure undisturbed, and craigslist may continue to operate with a staggered board.

I. FACTS

Since the time the parties completed their post-trial briefing, I have examined carefully the briefs, exhibits, deposition testimony and trial transcript. I have also reflected at length on my observations of witness testimony during trial, including my impressions regarding the credibility and demeanor of each witness. The following are my findings of the relevant facts in this dispute, based on evidence introduced at trial and my post-trial review.

A. Oil and Water

In 1995, two individuals in northern California began to develop modest ideas that would take hold in cyberspace and grow to become household names. Craig Newmark, founder of craigslist, started an email list for San Francisco events that in time has morphed into the most-used classifieds site in the United States. Pierre Omidyar, founder of eBay, Inc., started an online auction system that has grown to become one of the largest auction and shopping websites in the United States. As they grew, both companies expanded overseas and established a presence in international markets.

Now, even though both companies enjoy household-name status, craigslist and eBay are, to put it mildly, different animals. […] The dissimilarities between these two companies drive this dispute, so I will spend a moment discussing them. I will begin with craigslist. Though a for-profit concern, craigslist largely operates its business as a community service. Nearly all classified advertisements are placed on craigslist free of charge.

Moreover, craigslist does not sell advertising space on its website to third parties. Nor does craigslist advertise or otherwise market its services, craigslist's revenue stream consists solely of fees for online job postings in certain cities and apartment listings in New York City.

Despite ubiquitous name recognition, craigslist operates as a small business. [...] It is privately held and has never been owned by more than three stockholders at a time. It is not subject to the reporting requirements of federal securities laws, and its financial statements are not in the public domain. [...]

Almost since its inception, the craigslist website has maintained the same consistent look and simple functionality. [...] craigslist's management team—consisting principally of defendants Jim, CEO and President of craigslist, and Craig, Chairman and Secretary of the craigslist board—is committed to this community-service approach to doing business. They believe this approach is the heart of craigslist's business. For most of its history, craigslist has not focused on "monetizing" its site. The relatively small amount of monetization craigslist has pursued (for select job postings and apartment listings) does not approach what many craigslist competitors would consider an optimal or even minimally acceptable level. Nevertheless, craigslist's unique business strategy continues to be successful, even if it does run counter to the strategies used by the titans of online commerce. Thus far, no competing site has been able to dislodge craigslist from its perch atop the pile of most-used online classifieds sites in the United States, craigslist's lead position is made more enigmatic by the fact that it maintains its dominant market position with small-scale physical and human capital. Perhaps the most mysterious thing about craigslist's continued success is the fact that craigslist does not expend any great effort seeking to maximize its profits or to monitor its competition or its market share.

Now to eBay. Initially a venture with humble beginnings, eBay has grown to be a global enterprise. eBay is a for-profit concern that operates its business with an eye to maximizing revenues, profits, and market share. [...]

B. The Knowlton Crisis

[Eds: The Chancellor describes the events that led to the "curious" outcome that craigslist and eBay "ever formed a business relationship." Briefly, craigslist had a third shareholder and director, Knowlton, that wanted craigslist to monetize and threatened, inter alia, to sell his shares to a competitor. eBay wanted to acquire Knowlton's shares and more, which Jim and Craig refused. Eventually, Jim, Craig, and Meg Whitman—eBay's CEO—agreed that eBay would become a minority investor in craigslist by purchasing Knowlton's shares.]

C. The eBay Investment

After three months of negotiations, eBay ultimately agreed to pay $32 million for Knowlton's shares. Knowlton received $16 million of that amount, and Jim and Craig each received $8 million. eBay completed the purchase of Knowlton's shares on August 10, 2004. Since then, craigslist has been owned by Craig, Jim, and eBay. After eBay's investment, Craig owned 42.6% of craigslist, Jim owned 29% of craigslist, and eBay owned 28.4% of craigslist. The terms of eBay's investment in craigslist were set out in a stock purchase agreement (the "SPA") and a stockholders' agreement (the "Shareholders' Agreement"), both dated August 9, 2004. Jim and Craig also executed a voting agreement (the "Jim-Craig Voting Agreement") the same day. [...]

The SPA required [...] changing [craigslist]'s corporate domicile from California to Delaware [and adopting] a new charter for craigslist. craigslist's new charter provided for a three-person board of directors to be elected under a cumulative voting regime. The mechanics of cumulative voting ensured that eBay could use its 28.4% stake in craigslist to unilaterally elect one of the three members to the craigslist board.

The Shareholders' Agreement sets forth (1) eBay's confidentiality obligations as a craigslist stockholder; (2) eBay's right to consent to certain Company transactions; (3) numerous transfer restrictions on the craigslist shares owned by Craig, Jim, and eBay; (4) eBay's right to compete with craigslist subject to certain consequences; and, most importantly, (5) the consequences (i.e., changes in the rights and obligations of the parties) that will ensue should eBay decide to compete with craigslist. Each of these provisions deserves a little unpacking.

Section 4.3 of the Shareholders' Agreement requires eBay to treat confidential craigslist information with the same degree of care eBay affords its own confidential information. Section 4.3 also limits how eBay may use craigslist's confidential information. Specifically, eBay Holdings (the shell entity that acquired craigslist's shares) is permitted to share confidential information with its subsidiaries, outside advisors, or eBay, Inc. "for the purpose of evaluating [eBay Holdings'] investment in [craigslist]." Before sharing confidential information, eBay Holdings must obtain a written agreement from any subsidiary, advisor, or eBay, Inc., that they will abide by the confidentiality obligations in § 4.3.

Section 4.6(a) of the Shareholders' Agreement gives eBay the right to consent to certain transactions craigslist might enter into. The important consent rights provided eBay by § 4.6(a) include the right to consent to (1) any amendment to the craigslist charter "that adversely affects [eBay]," (2) any increase or decrease in the authorized number of shares of craigslist stock, (3) the adoption of any agreement between craigslist and its officers or directors providing for the issuance of stock, and (4) declarations of dividends. Effectively, Section 4.6(a) gives eBay a veto over a host of possible transactions even though its minority interest would not otherwise have permitted eBay to prevent actions that required a stockholder vote (e.g., a proposed amendment to the craigslist charter) or to influence actions typically left to the discretion of the board (e.g., dividend declarations).

Section 2.1 of the Shareholders' Agreement requires eBay, Jim, and Craig to comply with certain transfer restrictions in the Shareholders' Agreement when transferring their craigslist shares. The transfer restrictions are found in § 5.1 (preemptive rights) and in §§ 6.2 and 7.2 (rights of first refusal) of the Shareholders' Agreement. The preemptive rights give eBay, Jim, and Craig the right to purchase enough shares in a new issuance of craigslist stock to maintain their respective ownership percentages. The rights of first refusal give eBay, Jim, and Craig first dibs on the purchase of each other's shares should any one of them wish to sell to a third party, provided they match the purchase price and other terms offered by the third party.

In negotiations, eBay strove to maintain full leeway to compete with craigslist in online classifieds even after acquiring a minority interest. [...] Ultimately, eBay did not obtain an entirely unfettered ability to compete; the Shareholders' Agreement does expressly and unequivocally permit eBay to compete but guarantees certain consequences should eBay do so. [...] Section 8.3(e) provides that if eBay launches an online job posting site in the United States, craigslist may issue a notice to eBay that eBay has engaged in Competitive Activity. If eBay fails to cure within ninety days, eBay loses (1) its consent rights, (2) its preemptive rights over the issuance of new shares, and (3) its rights of first refusal over Jim and Craig's shares. Concomitantly, however, eBay is freed of the rights of first refusal Jim and Craig hold over eBay's shares in craigslist, making those shares freely transferable. eBay's confidentiality obligations remain firmly in place. [...]

Finally, I discuss the Jim-Craig Voting Agreement. The Jim-Craig Voting Agreement is an agreement between Jim and Craig, in their capacities as stockholders, that spells out how Jim and Craig will vote their shares in director elections. Specifically, the Jim-Craig Voting Agreement requires Jim and Craig to vote their shares "so as to elect one [ ] representative designated by Jim ... and one [ ] representative designated by Craig, as members of [craigslist's] Board of Directors[.]"Given that craigslist was to have a three-director board after eBay's investment, the Jim-Craig Voting Agreement ensured that two out of the three director positions would be filled by Jim's and Craig's designees, who have always been Jim and Craig. The third position would be filled by eBay—not by contractual right, but by the laws of mathematics under a cumulative voting system with a non-staggered board.[28]

D. eBay as a craigslist Stockholder

[... T]he eBay-craigslist relationship was marred by inconsistent expectations from the beginning. eBay wanted to acquire craigslist, and many eBay executives believed an acquisition was inevitable. Along the path to control, eBay hoped to combine the resources of the two companies to capitalize on international classifieds opportunities. During the first year of eBay's investment, eBay proposed at least three separate international joint ventures to craigslist, none of which materialized. eBay had also determined that if craigslist would not accompany it into the international classifieds arena, eBay was willing to delve into an international online classifieds business alone, hopefully using the "secret sauce" it learned from craigslist. Hence, even while eBay was proposing international partnerships to craigslist, eBay was independently building its own international portfolio of online classifieds sites.

Because Jim and Craig's expectations of the eBay-craigslist relationship diverged so sharply from eBay's, eBay's efforts to influence the direction of craigslist and to increase its craigslist holdings bore little fruit. Jim and Craig were typically slow to respond (or were entirely unresponsive) to eBay's suggestions. They did not implement most of eBay's ideas domestically and ultimately declined to partner with eBay on an international venture.

[...]

E. Kijiji and craigslist's Nonpublic Information

While eBay was attempting to form an international venture with craigslist, it was also forging ahead in foreign territories on its own. eBay had already begun acquiring international classifieds sites. In March 2005 eBay deployed [...] Kijiji. Although it is different in appearance than craigslist's site, Kijiji offered a similar free classifieds service with a broad selection of categories. Following Kijiji's unveiling, eBay expanded Kijiji to service countries throughout Europe and Asia and even launched a site in Canada.

[...]

---

[28] That is, eBay's 28.4% ownership stake was a sufficiently large enough interest to ensure eBay would be able to unilaterally elect one of the three craigslist directors.

Evidence introduced at trial suggests that the development of [...] Kijiji [...] was aided by nonpublic craigslist information that eBay had access to by virtue of eBay's minority investment and board seat. Evidence also suggests that, after launching Kijiji, eBay used craigslist's nonpublic information to expand Kijiji's reach and that eBay passed craigslist's nonpublic information around internally in a liberal fashion. [...]

Apart from the use of nonpublic craigslist information, evidence introduced at trial also suggests that eBay employed a practice known as "scraping" to obtain data from craigslist's website. "Scraping" in the Internet context refers to the (typically automated) process of remotely extracting data from a third-party website. On several occasions before and after eBay purchased Knowlton's shares, eBay used a third-party service to scrape craigslist's site. Jim and Craig were not aware this had occurred until they conducted discovery in this trial.

F. The United States Launch of Kijiji and the Notice of Competitive Activity

On June 19, 2007, Silverman 's lead executive for Kijiji, who also sat on craigslist's board for eBay called Jim and informed him that eBay planned to launch Kijiji in the United States on June 29, 2007. Silverman worked from a script on the call. [...] Three days later, on June 22, 2007, [eBay's in-house counsel] emailed a term sheet to craigslist's outside counsel proposing modifications to terms in the Shareholders' Agreement. Among other things, eBay sought to modify § 4.6 so that, although eBay would still lose its consent rights, craigslist would be required to give eBay "15 calendar days advance notice" before taking any § 4.6 actions, including an "adverse charter amendment" or "issuance of [craigslist] ... stock." [...] No one at craigslist responded to [eBay's] invitation to renegotiate the Shareholders' Agreement.

On June 29, 2007, Kijiji went live in two-hundred and twenty cities in all fifty states. The same day, craigslist sent eBay a notice of Competitive Activity per § 8.3(e) of the Shareholders' Agreement. The notice gave eBay ninety days to cure before eBay would lose (1) its consent rights, (2) its preemptive rights over the issuance of new shares, and (3) its rights of first refusal over Jim and Craig's shares. All was not dreary for eBay if it failed or declined to cure, however, because the craigslist shares eBay owned would become freely transferable. On July 6, 2007, Silverman resigned from the craigslist board, and Levey informed craigslist that eBay employee Tom Jeon would replace Silverman. Levey asked craigslist to send copies of the board resolutions appointing Jeon as a director. On the same day, craigslist's outside counsel asked Jeon for an introductory biography, which Jeon provided, but nobody communicated with Jeon thereafter. craigslist never seated Jeon; nor did it send confirmation to Levey that Jeon would be seated.

G. "Our Thoughts"

On July 12, 2007, Jim sent an email to Whitman captioned "Our Thoughts," informing Whitman that craigslist wished to "gracefully unwind the relationship" between the two companies because craigslist was no longer comfortable with eBay's shareholding and board seat. [...] When [craigslist's outside counsel] asked [eBay's in-house counsel] how Whitman felt about Jim's proposal that eBay divest its shares, Levey responded with his own question: How would Jim and Craig react if Whitman told them to go "pound sand?"

[...]

Whitman finally responded to Jim's "Our Thoughts" email on July 23, 2007 with the following:

> [W]e are so happy with our relationship with craigslist, that we could [not] imagine ... parting with our shareholding in craigslist, Inc. under any foreseeable circumstances. Quite to the contrary, we would welcome the opportunity to acquire the remainder of craigslist, Inc. we do not already own whenever you and Craig feel it would be appropriate.
>
> ... Given the foregoing long held and oft communicated sentiment, we are quite surprised that you would suggest any course of action to the contrary, especially given your recent comments to the Times:
>
> "Many companies offer classifieds, but since we don't concern ourselves with considerations such as market share or revenue maximization, we don't think of them as competition."
>
> "Our focus is providing what users want. If other companies are better positioned, then [users] should migrate over to that."
>
> In keeping with the emphasis [eBay] places on integrity, we have already taken even further steps to completely firewall off the operations relating to our Kijiji offering in the U.S. from the corporate management of our investment in craigslist Inc. Hence, more than ever, we feel we should, as we have unfortunately been unable to do to date, together leverage the myriad assets in the global eBay Inc. family to provide the craigslist community with the best possible user experience.

Jim and Craig interpreted this as Whitman's way of telling them to go "pound sand." They also began to suspect, based on Whitman's reference to an internal firewall, that nonpublic craigslist data had been used to develop and expand Kijiji. From that point, Jim and Craig were determined to take measures to keep eBay out of the craigslist boardroom and to limit eBay's ability to purchase additional craigslist shares.

H. Jim and Craig Develop the 2008 Board Actions

For the next six months, Jim and Craig consulted with outside counsel on ways to accomplish their objectives. This process ultimately resulted in the execution of three transactions that gave rise to this dispute: (1) implementation of a staggered board through amendments to the craigslist charter and bylaws (the "Staggered Board Amendments"); (2) approval of a stockholder rights plan (the "Rights Plan"); and (3) an offer to issue one new share of craigslist stock in exchange for every five shares on which a craigslist stockholder granted a right of first refusal in favor of craigslist (the "ROFR/Dilutive Issuance") (collectively these three transactions are referred to as the "2008 Board Actions" or "Actions").

[...]

By the end of December 2007, Jim and Craig had reached a final decision on the particulars of the 2008 Board Actions. Jim, Craig, and their counsel designed a sequence for approving and implementing the Actions at the beginning of 2008, planning to notify eBay after the Actions were a fait accompli. In accordance with this plan, on January 1, 2008, Jim and Craig executed a unanimous written consent as craigslist directors and a written consent as majority stockholders to approve the Actions. On January 2, they implemented the Actions. On January 3, they informed eBay.

I. The Practical Effect of the 2008 Board Actions

Jim and Craig implemented three separate Actions on January 2:(1) the Staggered Board Amendments, (2) the Rights Plan, and (3) the ROFR/Dilutive Issuance. I will explore the substance of each Action to illustrate the effect the 2008 Board Actions had on eBay as a minority stockholder and to illustrate how the Actions altered the eBay-craigslist relationship. I begin with the Staggered Board Amendments.

1. The Staggered Board Amendments

On January 2, 2008, Jim and Craig restated the craigslist charter and bylaws in their entirety. For present purposes, the important changes in these documents were the addition of provisions implementing a staggered board. The Staggered Board Amendments created three classes of directors, one director per class, with each class serving three-year terms. Each year one director is up for election. The restated charter appointed Craig as the Class I director and Jim as the Class II director, and left Class III open, to be filled at a later date. Craig was to serve until the 2008 stockholders' meeting, and Jim was to serve until the 2009 stockholders' meeting. Whoever was appointed to the Class III director position would serve until the 2010 stockholders' meeting. To date, the Class III director position has not been filled.

The Staggered Board Amendments did not eliminate cumulative voting. Article IX of the restated charter specifically provides for cumulative voting. Practically speaking, however, the cumulative voting provisions are not meaningful if only one director position is up for election in any given year. There must be at least two board seats in play in order for a stockholder to cumulate votes and direct those votes towards a single director candidate. Because eBay's ability to unilaterally elect a director depended on a cumulative voting regime where all three positions were up for grabs in a given year, the staggered board cut off eBay's unilateral ability to place a director on the craigslist board.

2. The Rights Plan

The Rights Plan implemented on January 2, 2008 contains some standard terms frequently seen in rights plans and some not-so-standard terms. The Rights Plan pays a dividend to craigslist stockholders of one right per share of craigslist stock. Each right allows its holder to purchase two shares of craigslist stock at $0.00005 per share if the rights are triggered. There are two triggers. The first trigger involves acquisitions by Jim, Craig, or eBay. If any of these three becomes the "Beneficial Owner" of 0.01% of additional craigslist stock, the rights are triggered. The second trigger involves anyone other than Jim, Craig, or eBay. Should any such person become the "Beneficial Owner" of 15% or more of craigslist's outstanding shares, the rights are triggered.

[...]

3. The ROFR/Dilutive Issuance

Under the ROFR/Dilutive Issuance, Jim, Craig, and craigslist executed a right of first refusal agreement that provided that Jim and Craig would receive one newly issued craigslist share for every five shares over which they granted a right of first refusal in craigslist's favor. By signing the right of first refusal agreement, Jim and Craig gave craigslist a right of first refusal over their shares in the event a third party wished to purchase their shares. Jim and Craig approved the right of first refusal agreement in their capacity as directors, and Jim signed the agreement on craigslist's behalf in his capacity as CEO. Jim and Craig then signed the right of first refusal agreement in their personal capacities as stockholders. The right of first refusal agreement gives eBay three years to execute a joinder to the right of first refusal agreement. If eBay does this, eBay will receive the same deal as Jim and Craig, namely a newly issued craigslist share for every five shares eBay encumbers with a right of first refusal in craigslist's favor.

Under the right of first refusal agreement, if craigslist receives the opportunity to exercise its right of first refusal and decides not to, the third-party purchaser of the shares, as a condition of the sale, must execute a joinder agreement leaving craigslist's right of first refusal in place.

[...]

Importantly, when the right of first refusal agreement was executed, eBay's shares were freely transferable. Jim and Craig's shares, on the other hand, already were encumbered by the right of first refusal each held over the other's shares under § 7.2 of the Shareholders' Agreement. Thus, in granting craigslist a right of first refusal, Jim and Craig were placing an encumbrance on shares that were already encumbered. If eBay were to grant a right of first refusal, however, it would be encumbering freely tradeable shares.

Because eBay chose not to grant a right of first refusal in craigslist's favor, eBay did not receive additional craigslist shares. The effect of the ROFR/Dilutive Issuance was to dilute eBay's ownership in craigslist from 28.4% to 24.9%. Concomitantly, Jim's ownership increased from 29% to 30.4%, and Craig's ownership increased from 42.6% to 44.7%. I will discuss the economic effects of this dilution in my analysis of the legitimacy of the ROFR/Dilutive Issuance below.

The ROFR/Dilutive Issuance was another nail in the coffin of eBay's ability unilaterally to elect a director to the craigslist board. Under a cumulative voting regime with no staggered board and three board seats up for election, the laws of mathematics require a minority stockholder to own at least 25% of the company for the minority stockholder's cumulated votes to be sufficient to elect one of the three directors. The ROFR/Dilutive Issuance diluted eBay to 24.9%, which made it impossible for eBay to unilaterally elect a director even if Jim and Craig had not approved the Staggered Board Amendments to implement a staggered board. Evidence introduced at trial suggests that Jim and Craig chose the five-to-one ratio to ensure that, if eBay did not grant a right of first refusal, it would be diluted to an ownership percentage just below 25%.

J. "David" and "Goliath" in the Courtroom

When David first confronted Goliath, the giant was chagrined.[69] Similarly, perhaps, eBay was chagrined when craigslist confronted it with the 2008 Board Actions on January 3, 2008. eBay responded by filing suit against craigslist on April 22, 2008, alleging that the Actions were a breach of fiduciary duty by Jim and Craig in their capacities as directors

---

[69] See 1 Samuel 17:43 (Goliath expressing annoyance when David first confronts him with staff, sling, and stone: "Am I a dog, that thou comest to me with staves?").

and as controlling stockholders. eBay also alleged that the ROFR/Dilutive Issuance violates 8 Del. C. §§ 152 and 202(b). craigslist responded by filing suit against eBay in California state court on May 13, 2008, alleging that eBay engaged in unfair competition, misappropriation of trade secrets, false advertising, trademark infringement, and other wrongs. In the California action, craigslist seeks, among other things, to have eBay restore the craigslist shares it owns to craigslist.

II. ANALYSIS

Jim and Craig owe fiduciary duties to eBay because they are directors [26] and controlling stockholders of craigslist, and eBay is a minority stockholder of craigslist. Even though neither Jim nor Craig individually owns a majority of craigslist's shares, the law treats them as craigslist's controlling stockholders because they form a control group, bound together by the Jim-Craig Voting Agreement, with the power to elect the majority of the craigslist board.

[...]

eBay's complaint asserts that Jim and Craig breached the fiduciary duties they owed to eBay by implementing the 2008 Board Actions. [...] Any time a stockholder challenges an action taken by the board of directors, the Court must first determine the appropriate standard of review to use in analyzing the challenged action. Identifying the appropriate standard of review ensures that the Court applies the proper level of judicial scrutiny to the board's decision-making process.

Although Jim and Craig implemented all the 2008 Board Actions on the same date, I analyze each Action individually. [...] The 2008 Board Actions are not an "inextricably related" set of responses to a takeover threat. In fact, I do not view the Staggered Board Amendments, in the unique circumstances of this case, as a defensive measure at all. Accordingly, I do not apply the heightened standard from *Unocal* and its progeny to the Staggered Board Amendments, and I apply a deferential business judgment standard for reasons outlined below. The Rights Plan, on the other hand, implicates *Unocal* concerns in my view because rights plans (known as "poison pills" in takeover parlance) fundamentally are defensive devices that, if used correctly, can enhance stockholder value but, if used incorrectly, can entrench management and deter value-maximizing bidders at the stockholders' expense. I therefore subject the Rights Plan to the *Unocal* standard of review. Finally, I subject the ROFR/Dilutive Issuance to entire fairness review because Jim and Craig stand on both sides of that Action in the classic sense. I begin my analysis with the Rights Plan.

A. The Rights Plan

I will review Jim and Craig's adoption of the Rights Plan using the intermediate standard of enhanced scrutiny, typically referred to as the *Unocal* test. Framed generally, enhanced scrutiny "requires directors to bear the burden to show their actions were reasonable." The directors must "(1) identify the proper corporate objectives served by their actions; and (2) justify their actions as reasonable in relationship to those objectives."

Enhanced scrutiny has been applied universally when stockholders challenge a board's use of a rights plan as a defensive device. In the typical scenario, the decision to deploy a rights plan will fall within the range of reasonableness if the directors use the plan in a good faith effort to promote stockholder value. For example, the Delaware Supreme Court originally validated the use of a rights plan so that boards could protect target stockholders from two-tiered, front-end loaded, structurally coercive offers. Subsequent case law has established that a board can use the protection of a rights plan to respond to an underpriced bid, counter the tender offeror's timing and informational advantages, and force the hostile acquirer to negotiate with the board. . .

Like any strong medicine, however, a pill can be misused. The Delaware Supreme Court understood from the outset that a rights plan can be deployed inappropriately to benefit incumbent managers and directors at the stockholders' expense. Therefore when deploying a rights plan, "directors must at minimum convince the court that they have not acted for an inequitable purpose." And more than mere subjective good faith is required. Human judgment can be clouded by subtle influences like the prestige and perquisites of board membership, personal relationships with management, or animosity towards a bidder. Because of the omnipresent specter that directors could use a rights plan improperly, even when acting subjectively in good faith, *Unocal* and its progeny require that this Court also review the use of a rights plan objectively. Like other defensive measures, a rights plan cannot be used preclusively or coercively; nor can its use fall outside the "range of reasonableness."

This case involves a unique set of facts heretofore not seen in the context of a challenge to a rights plan. To my knowledge, no decision under Delaware law has addressed a challenge to a rights plan adopted by a privately held company with so few stockholders. The ample case law addressing rights plans almost invariably involves publicly traded corporations with a widely dispersed, potentially disempowered, and arguably vulnerable stockholder base. In cases involving rights plans to date, Delaware courts have typically and understandably approved the use of rights plans to remedy the collective action problems that stockholders face, including but not limited to the classically coercive prisoner's dilemma imposed by a two-tiered offer. At the same time, Delaware courts have guarded against the overt risk of entrenchment and the less visible, yet more pernicious risk that incumbents acting in subjective good faith might nevertheless deprive stockholders of value-maximizing opportunities.

In this unique case, I do not face those same concerns. Jim and Craig are not dispersed, disempowered, or vulnerable stockholders. They are the majority. Jim and Craig are not using the Rights Plan improperly to preclude craigslist stockholders from considering and opting for a value-maximizing transaction. As the majority, Jim and Craig can consider and opt-for a value-maximizing transaction whenever they want.

Nor are Jim and Craig using the Rights Plan to protect their board seats. Together Jim and Craig own an overwhelming majority of craigslist's voting power, and they have entered into the Jim-Craig Voting Agreement which ensures that each votes the other onto the board. [...]

These unique factors do not, however, eliminate *Unocal*'s usefulness. *Unocal* has correctly been described as "the most innovative and promising" case in our corporation law and one whose insights "will [] continue to resonate with judges." The intermediate standard of review is not limited to the historic and now classic paradigm. Fiduciary duties apply regardless of whether a corporation is "registered and publicly traded, dark and delisted, or closely held." It is entirely possible that the board of a closely held company such as craigslist could deploy a rights plan improperly. The *Unocal* standard of review is best equipped to address this concern.

Thus, the two main issues I confront are: First, did Jim and Craig properly and reasonably perceive a threat to craigslist's corporate policy and effectiveness? Second, if they did, is the Rights Plan a proportional response to that threat?

As discussed above, there are several recognized and accepted corporate purposes for adopting a rights plan. Nevertheless, there is no formal exhaustive list of valid reasons for doing so. [... T]he Court of Chancery is mindful of changing conditions in the corporate world that may warrant the Court's recognition of a new, valid corporate purpose for adopting a rights plan. In that spirit, I have carefully considered Jim and Craig's contentions in this case and the evidence they presented in support of those contentions. I conclude, based on all of the evidence, that Jim and Craig in fact did not adopt the Rights Plan in response to a reasonably perceived threat or for a proper corporate purpose.

Jim and Craig contend that they identified a threat to craigslist and its corporate policies that will materialize after they both die and their craigslist shares are distributed to their heirs. At that point, they say, "eBay's acquisition of control [via the anticipated acquisition of Jim or Craig's shares from some combination of their heirs] would fundamentally alter craigslist's values, culture and business model, including departing from [craigslist's] public-service mission in favor of increased monetization of craigslist." To prevent this unwanted potential future reality, Jim and Craig have adopted the Rights Plan now so that their vision of craigslist's culture can bind future fiduciaries and stockholders from beyond the grave. Having given new meaning to the concept of a "dead-hand pill," Jim and Craig ask this Court to validate their attempt to use a pill to shape the future of the space-time continuum.

It is true that on the unique facts of a particular case—*Paramount Communications, Inc. v. Time Inc.*—this Court and the Delaware Supreme Court accepted defensive action by the directors of a Delaware corporation as a good faith effort to protect a specific corporate culture. It was a muted embrace. Chancellor Allen wrote only that he was "not persuaded that there may not be instances in which the law might recognize as valid a perceived threat to a `corporate culture' that is shown to be palpable (for lack of a better word), distinctive and advantageous." This conditional, limited, and double-negative-laden comment was offered in a case that involved the journalistic independence of an iconic American institution. Even in that fact-specific context, the acceptance of the amorphous purpose of "cultural protection" as a justification for defensive action did not escape criticism.

More importantly, *Time* did not hold that corporate culture, standing alone, is worthy of protection as an end in itself. Promoting, protecting, or pursuing non-stockholder considerations must lead at some point to value for stockholders. When director decisions are reviewed under the business judgment rule, this Court will not question rational judgments about how promoting non-stockholder interests—be it through making a charitable contribution, paying employees higher salaries and benefits, or more general norms like promoting a particular corporate culture—ultimately promote stockholder value. Under the *Unocal* standard, however, the directors must act within the range of reasonableness.

Ultimately, defendants failed to prove that craigslist possesses a palpable, distinctive, and advantageous culture that sufficiently promotes stockholder value to support the indefinite implementation of a poison pill. Jim and Craig did not make any serious attempt to prove that the craigslist culture, which rejects any attempt to further monetize its services, translates into increased profitability for stockholders. . .

Giving away services to attract business is a sales tactic, [...] not a corporate culture. [...] Having heard the evidence and judged witness credibility at trial, I find that there is nothing about craigslist's corporate culture that *Time* or *Unocal* protects. The existence of a distinctive craigslist "culture" was not proven at trial. It is a fiction, invoked almost talismanically for purposes of this trial in order to find deference under *Time's* dicta.

Jim and Craig did prove that they personally believe craigslist should not be about the business of stockholder wealth maximization, now or in the future. As an abstract matter, there is nothing inappropriate about an organization seeking to aid local, national, and global communities by providing a website for online classifieds that is largely devoid of monetized elements. Indeed, I personally appreciate and admire Jim's and Craig's desire to be of service to communities. The corporate form in which craigslist operates, however, is not an appropriate vehicle for purely philanthropic ends, at least not when there are other stockholders interested in realizing a return on their investment. Jim and Craig opted to form craigslist, Inc. as a for-profit Delaware corporation and voluntarily accepted millions of dollars from eBay as part of a transaction whereby eBay became a stockholder. Having chosen a for-profit corporate form, the craigslist directors are bound by the fiduciary duties and standards that accompany that form. Those standards include acting to promote the value of the corporation for the benefit of its stockholders. The "Inc." after the company name has to mean at least that. Thus, I cannot accept as valid for the purposes of implementing the Rights Plan a corporate policy that specifically, clearly, and admittedly seeks not to maximize the economic value of a for-profit Delaware corporation for the benefit of its stockholders—no matter whether those stockholders are individuals of modest means or a corporate titan of online commerce. If Jim and Craig were the only stockholders affected by their decisions, then there would be no one to object. eBay, however, holds a significant stake in craigslist, and Jim and Craig's actions affect others besides themselves.

Jim and Craig's defense of the Rights Plan thus fails the first prong of *Unocal* both factually and legally. I find that defendants failed to prove, as a factual matter, the existence of a distinctly protectable craigslist culture and further failed to prove, both factually and legally, that they actually decided to deploy the Rights Plan because of a craigslist culture. I find, instead, that Jim and Craig acted to punish eBay for competing with craigslist. Directors of a for-profit Delaware corporation cannot deploy a rights plan to defend a business strategy that openly eschews stockholder wealth maximization—at least not consistently with the directors' fiduciary duties under Delaware law.

Up to this point, I have evaluated the Rights Plan primarily through the lens of the first prong of *Unocal*. To the extent I assume for purposes of analysis that a craigslist culture was something that Jim and Craig reasonably could seek to protect, the Rights Plan nonetheless does not fall within the range of reasonable responses. [...] The avowed purpose of the Rights Plan is to protect the craigslist "culture" at some point in the future unrelated to when eBay sells some or all of its shares. As long as Jim and Craig have control, however, they can maintain the craigslist "culture" regardless of whether eBay sells some or all of its shares. The Rights Plan neither affects when eBay can sell its shares nor affects when the craigslist culture can change. It therefore does not have a reasonable connection to Jim and Craig's professed goal. [...] On the factual record presented at trial, therefore, the defendants also failed to meet their burden of proof under the second prong of *Unocal*.

Because defendants failed to prove that they acted to protect or defend a legitimate corporate interest and because they failed to prove that the rights plan was a reasonable response to a perceived threat to corporate policy or effectiveness, I rescind the Rights Plan in its entirety.

B. The Staggered Board Amendments

Before determining whether I should subject the Staggered Board Amendments to business judgment review or entire fairness review, I will first explain more fully why I conclude that the Staggered Board Amendments are not subject to *Unocal* review. Unlike the Rights Plan, the Staggered Board Amendments do not function as a defensive device under the unique facts of this case. Even if craigslist did not have a staggered board, Jim and Craig would control a majority of the board. The Jim-Craig Voting Agreement ensures that Jim's designee and Craig's designee will always fill two of the three director positions. At best, eBay places one director on the board; at worst, eBay places no directors on the board. So long as the Jim-Craig Voting Agreement remains in effect and there are only three authorized director positions, eBay will never have an opportunity to control the board. The number of authorized director positions will not change unless Jim and Craig, as the majority of the board, vote to change the number of director positions. Thus, the Staggered Board Amendments make it impossible for eBay to unilaterally place one of three directors on the board, but did not affect Jim and Craig's ability to control the board by filling two of the three director positions currently authorized by the craigslist bylaws. It would be inappropriate to apply *Unocal* to the Staggered Board Amendments because they do not implicate the concerns that drive *Unocal*; there is no "omnipresent specter" that the Staggered Board Amendments are being used for entrenchment purposes. I will now analyze whether the Staggered Board Amendments should be subject to the business judgment or the entire fairness standard of review.

Under the business judgment rule, when a party challenges the decisions of a board of directors, the Court begins with the "presumption that in making a business decision the directors of a corporation acted on an informed basis, in good faith and in the honest belief that the action taken was in the best interests of the company." [...]

To avoid application of the deferential business judgment standard, the plaintiff must produce evidence that rebuts the business judgment presumption. There are a number of ways the plaintiff can rebut the business judgment presumption, including by showing that the majority of directors who approved the action (1) had a personal interest in the subject matter of the action, (2) were not fully informed in approving the action, or (3) did not act in good faith in approving the action. If the plaintiff rebuts the business judgment presumption, the Court applies the entire fairness standard of review to the challenged action and places the burden on the directors to prove that the action was entirely fair.

eBay contends that the Staggered Board Amendments must pass muster under the entire fairness standard on two grounds: (1) Jim and Craig, as controlling stockholders and directors, were personally interested in the Staggered Board Amendments because implementing a staggered board redounded to their benefit but harmed eBay as the minority stockholder, and (2) Jim and Craig approved the Staggered Board Amendments in bad faith, with the intent to harm eBay. I will consider each argument in turn.

First, eBay contends that Jim and Craig are personally interested in the Staggered Board Amendments—even though they do not literally stand on both sides of that Action— because the Staggered Board Amendments treat eBay, the minority stockholder, differently than Jim and Craig, the majority stockholders and directors, by eliminating eBay's ability to unilaterally elect a director to the craigslist board but having no effect on Jim and Craig's abilities to elect craigslist directors. After they implemented the Staggered Board Amendments, Jim and Craig still were able to elect their director nominees to the craigslist board. In the years that the Class I and II director positions are up for election, the Jim-Craig Voting Agreement requires Jim and Craig to vote their shares together, thereby ensuring that their nominees will be elected. eBay, however, lost its ability to unilaterally elect an eBay nominee to the craigslist board. The Staggered Board Amendments leave eBay with only the mere possibility of having an eBay nominee elected in the year the Class III director position is voted upon. In that year, eBay has no guarantee that its nominee will be elected because eBay's minority ownership interest is insufficient to unilaterally elect a director if only one director position is up for election, even under a cumulative voting regime. Thus, eBay contends, the Staggered Board Amendments affect Jim and Craig differently than they affect eBay, and this disparate treatment between fiduciaries, on the one hand, and a minority stockholder, on the other hand, requires application of the entire fairness standard of review. [...]

I am not persuaded that entire fairness review applies to the Staggered Board Amendments on the ground that eBay was affected differently than Jim and Craig by the implementation of a staggered board. The cases eBay relies on do not support a rule of law that would invoke entire fairness review any time a corporate action affects directors or controlling stockholders differently than minority stockholders.[122] Entire fairness review ordinarily applies in cases where a fiduciary either literally stands on both sides of

---

[122] Disparate treatment of stockholders is not a *per se* violation of Delaware law. *See Nixon v. Blackwell*, 626 A.2d 1366 (Del. 1993) (concluding that defendants had established entire fairness of a policy that treated employee stockholders and non-employee stockholders differently).

the challenged transaction or where the fiduciary "expects to derive personal financial benefit from the [challenged] transaction in the sense of self-dealing, as opposed to a benefit which devolves upon the corporation or all stockholders generally." The three cases eBay relies on [...] involved situations where a fiduciary allegedly derived a personal financial benefit from the challenged transaction at the expense of the minority stockholders. [...] The transactions challenged in those three cases are quite dissimilar from the Staggered Board Amendments. First, Jim and Craig did not realize a financial benefit by approving the Staggered Board Amendments so there was no self-dealing on the basis of financial considerations. Second, and more importantly, Delaware law does not require that minority stockholders such as eBay have board representation. Delaware corporations do not have to adopt cumulative voting for the benefit of minority stockholders, and Delaware corporations have the express power to implement staggered boards. If a corporation implements a staggered board, and this renders the corporation's cumulative voting system ineffective, minority stockholders have not been deprived of anything they are entitled to under the common law or the DGCL, because minority stockholders are not entitled to a cumulative voting system in the first instance. It is true that by approving the Staggered Board Amendments, Jim and Craig implemented a corporate governance structure that had a disparate and, from eBay's point of view, unfavorable impact on eBay. This is not the sort of disparate treatment, however, that can be classified as self-dealing because the law expressly allows majority stockholders to elect the entire board. Thus, the Staggered Board Amendments cannot be subjected to entire fairness review on the grounds that eliminating eBay's ability to elect a director was a form of self-dealing.

Of course, even where fiduciaries are legally permitted to take a particular action, the action will not be countenanced if it works an inequity. But the Staggered Board Amendments do not work an inequity. eBay's ability to unilaterally elect a director to the craigslist board was solely based on a cumulative voting system combined with a non-staggered board. Before eBay engaged in Competitive Activity, eBay was able to ensure this voting system and board structure remained in place because it had the contractual right under § 4.6(a)(iii) of the Shareholders' Agreement to consent to any charter amendment that would "adversely affect[] [eBay]." This consent right, however, was not indefeasible. Section 8.3 of the Shareholders' Agreement provides that "all of the rights and obligations of [eBay] set forth in Section[] . . . [39] 4.6 . . . shall terminate" if eBay engages in Competitive Activity. Thus, eBay lost its consent rights over charter amendments by engaging in Competitive Activity. Throughout this dispute, eBay has protested that the 2008 Board Actions, including the Staggered Board Amendments, secured for Jim and Craig benefits that they were not able to obtain when negotiating the Shareholders' Agreement. The right to amend the craigslist charter, however, without eBay's consent if eBay chose to compete with craigslist was a benefit Jim and Craig negotiated for and secured in the Shareholders' Agreement. Section 8.3 plainly articulates that benefit. Thus, the Staggered Board Amendments cannot be inequitable because they were exactly the sort of consequence eBay accepted would occur if eBay decided to compete with craigslist.

By challenging the Staggered Board Amendments in this litigation, eBay, not Jim and Craig, seeks to obtain a benefit it was not able to obtain under the Shareholders' Agreement. In trying to undo the staggered board, and thereby protect its mathematical ability to fill a board seat, eBay is doing exactly what it accuses Jim and Craig of doing. eBay negotiated for and secured a fettered right to engage in Competitive Activity; the "fetter" being that eBay would lose its minority investor consent rights, including its right to block charter amendments, if eBay decided to compete with craigslist in online job postings in the United States. eBay engaged in Competitive Activity by launching Kijiji in the United States. eBay then chose not to cease its Competitive Activity (by either shutting down Kijiji or removing Kijiji's job listings) within the ninety-day cure period provided by § 8.3(e) after craigslist sent the Notice of Competitive Activity. The negotiated consequence of these decisions, as expressly provided for in the Shareholders' Agreement, is that eBay lost the ability to block charter amendments such as the Staggered Board Amendments. [...]

Because eBay failed to rebut the business judgment presumption in its challenge to the Staggered Board Amendments, I review the Staggered Board Amendments under the business judgment standard of review. When the business judgment rule applies, the board's business decisions "will not be disturbed if they can be attributed to any rational business purpose. A court under such circumstances will not substitute its own notions of what is or is not sound business judgment" for the board's notions. Accordingly, I will analyze the Staggered Board Amendments to see if they further any rational business purpose.

Throughout this dispute, Jim and Craig have argued that they designed the Staggered Board Amendments to keep eBay, a business competitor, from unilaterally being able to place a director on craigslist's board. Jim and Craig assert that competitively sensitive information is discussed in board meetings, and, even though craigslist does not typically concern itself with beating the competition, this competitively sensitive information could nevertheless be used by eBay to harm craigslist. [...] Preventing a competitor that is also a minority stockholder from unilaterally placing a director on the board so that confidential corporate information will not be freely shared with that competitor is a legitimate and rational business purpose. It was rational for Jim and Craig to want to ensure that they could trust any director nominated by eBay not to use his or her board seat to access confidential information and then surreptitiously pass it on to eBay. Implementing a staggered board was one way to accomplish this. It does not matter that there were (and are) other alternatives available to Jim and Craig because the Staggered Board

Amendments were sufficiently rational to satisfy business judgment review. Accordingly, I conclude that Jim and Craig did not breach their fiduciary duties by approving the Staggered Board Amendments, and I decline eBay's request that I rescind the Staggered Board Amendments.

C. The ROFR/Dilutive Issuance

The business judgment rule's protections only apply to transactions in which a majority of directors are disinterested and independent. A director is "interested" if he or she stands on both sides of a transaction or expects to derive a material personal financial benefit from the transaction that does not devolve on all stockholders generally. When the business judgment rule's protections do not apply, the burden is placed on the defendant directors to prove the challenged transaction is entirely fair. "When directors of a Delaware corporation are on both sides of a transaction, they are required to demonstrate their utmost good faith and the most scrupulous inherent fairness of the [transaction]." If directors structure a transaction that is unfair, they breach their duty of loyalty, and the Court may provide equitable relief to remedy the injury.

To prove a transaction was entirely fair, directors must demonstrate that the transaction was (1) effectuated at a fair price and (2) the product of fair dealing. The fair price element relates to the economics of the transaction; it focuses on whether the transaction was economically fair to the plaintiff. The analysis of price can draw on any valuation methods or techniques generally accepted in the financial community. Fair dealing focuses on the conduct of the fiduciaries involved in the transaction. In analyzing fair dealing the Court may inquire into how the transaction was timed, initiated, negotiated, and structured, as well as how approvals of the directors and stockholders were obtained. The entire fairness test is not bifurcated; the Court must consider allegations of unfair dealing and unfair price. Price, however, is the paramount consideration because procedural aspects of the deal are circumstantial evidence of whether the price is fair.

I conclude that the ROFR/Dilutive Issuance is subject to entire fairness review. Jim and Craig stood on both sides of that Action. The parties to the right of first refusal agreement underlying the ROFR/Dilutive Issuance are craigslist on the one side and Jim and Craig on the other. Jim and Craig approved the ROFR/Dilutive Issuance in their capacity as craigslist directors, and Jim, in his capacity as CEO, signed the right of first refusal agreement for craigslist. Jim and Craig then each counter-signed the right of first refusal agreement in their individual capacities as stockholders. The consideration in the right of first refusal agreement flows from craigslist to Jim and Craig (craigslist issuing shares to Jim and Craig) and vice-versa (Jim and Craig granting a right of first refusal to craigslist). In transactions such as this, where fiduciaries deal directly with the corporation, entire fairness is ordinarily the applicable standard of review.

Under the terms of the ROFR/Dilutive Issuance, Jim and Craig received an additional share of craigslist stock for every five shares over which they granted craigslist a right of first refusal. Jim and Craig likely had the contractual ability to implement the ROFR/Dilutive Issuance. Jim and Craig probably did not violate a technical provision of the Shareholders' Agreement when they approved the ROFR/Dilutive Issuance.

But the question before me is whether Jim and Craig breached their fiduciary duty of loyalty by approving the ROFR/Dilutive Issuance. Even if eBay lost its contractual ability to prevent the ROFR/Dilutive Issuance, eBay was entitled to the fiduciary duties Jim and Craig owed it as a minority stockholder. As fiduciaries, Jim and Craig were bound not to approve an interested transaction unless that transaction was entirely fair to craigslist and to eBay.

To determine whether the ROFR/Dilutive Issuance was entirely fair, I will first analyze whether that Action was effectuated at a fair price. The "price" of receiving an additional craigslist share under the ROFR/Dilutive Issuance was the granting of a right of first refusal over five shares. This same deal (a 5:1 ratio) was offered to each craigslist stockholder. Jim and Craig argue that the ROFR/Dilutive Issuance was fair to craigslist stockholders because all stockholders were offered the same deal. Superficially, this appears to be true. Deeper reflection, however, reveals that it actually costs eBay more to grant a right of first refusal over five of its craigslist shares than it costs Jim or Craig to do the same. When eBay engaged in Competitive Activity by launching Kijiji, Jim and Craig had to decide whether to issue a Notice of Competitive Activity. If they chose to do so and if eBay failed to cure within ninety days, eBay would lose its contractual consent rights. But there was an upside for eBay if it failed to cure: the rights of first refusal Jim and Craig held over eBay's craigslist shares under § 7.2 of the Shareholders' Agreement would terminate, and eBay's shares would become freely transferable. The rights of first refusal Jim and Craig held over each other's shares under § 7.2 of the Shareholders' Agreement, however, would remain intact. eBay failed to cure within ninety days after receiving the Notice of Competitive Activity, and the craigslist shares it owns became freely transferable. Jim and Craig's craigslist shares remained encumbered. Thus, the price Jim and Craig had to pay for a new share under the ROFR/Dilutive Issuance was their granting a right of refusal to craigslist on five already-encumbered shares. The price eBay had to pay for a new share under the ROFR/Dilutive Issuance was its granting a right of first refusal to craigslist on five freely transferable shares. Although each craigslist stockholder had to grant a right of first refusal over the same number of shares to obtain a newly issued share, eBay had to surrender full transferability of its shares to craigslist, but Jim and Craig only had to substitute craigslist for themselves as the party holding a right of first refusal on their shares. Thus, the price of the ROFR/Dilutive Issuance is not fair because it requires eBay, the minority stockholder, to give up more value per share than either Jim or Craig, the majority stockholders and directors. This disproportionate "price" is sufficient, standing alone, to render the ROFR/Dilutive Issuance void.

There is at least one other reason that the ROFR/Dilutive Issuance does not satisfy the fair price element of entire fairness. The ROFR/Dilutive Issuance put eBay in a position where it had to make one of two choices, and either choice would harm eBay economically while benefitting Jim and Craig. [...]

By choosing not to join the right of first refusal agreement, eBay's ownership interest was diluted from 28.4% to 24.9%. Jim and Craig's ownership interests were concomitantly increased from 29% to [45] 30.4% and 42.6% to 44.7%, respectively. The economic effect of this choice was to transfer wealth from eBay to Jim and Craig by virtue of increasing Jim and Craig's ownership of craigslist at eBay's expense.

Jim and Craig would [also] benefit if eBay [made the opposite decision and] decided to grant craigslist a right of first refusal. I find, as a matter of fact, that Jim and Craig implemented the ROFR/Dilutive Issuance because they wanted to control whom eBay sold its craigslist shares to. Jim and Craig knew that eBay's shares had become freely [46] transferable. This caused Jim and Craig to be concerned that another "Knowlton problem" was on the horizon; that is, they feared that eBay would sell its shares to a stockholder who did not fit with the craigslist culture. If Jim and Craig could coax eBay into giving craigslist a right of first refusal, then Jim and Craig could vote as directors to preempt eBay's sale to any unsuitable purchaser by simply having craigslist purchase eBay's shares. I find, as a matter of fact, that Jim and Craig desired a right of first refusal in craigslist's favor to protect their personal, sentimental interests in controlling the culture of craigslist, including the composition of its stockholders. Controlling the composition of stockholders or the respective ownership stakes of stockholders through a right of first refusal in the corporation's favor may be permitted, provided the right of first refusal bears some reasonably necessary relation to the corporation's best interests. Put another way, the right of first refusal must advance a valid corporate purpose. Moreover, when directors vote to issue new shares to themselves in exchange for giving the corporation a right of first refusal, and thus stand on both sides of the transaction, the right of first refusal arrangement must be entirely fair to the corporation and to its stockholders. The ROFR/Dilutive Issuance is invalid under Delaware law because Jim and Craig have sought to control craigslist's stockholder composition for their personal and sentimental benefit at eBay's expense.[160] Thus, it fails the price element of the entire fairness test and does not advance a proper corporate purpose.

Jim and Craig breached their fiduciary duty of loyalty by using their power as directors and controlling stockholders to implement an interested transaction that was not entirely fair to eBay, the minority stockholder. All parties agree that the most appropriate remedy for a breach of fiduciary duty in this case is rescission. I concur with that assessment. Accordingly, I rescind the ROFR/Dilutive Issuance.

D. The DGCL

eBay contends in Counts IV and V of the complaint that the ROFR/Dilutive Issuance violates 8 Del. C. §§ 152 and 202(b). Having concluded that the ROFR/Dilutive Issuance must be rescinded because it was not entirely fair to eBay, I need not address whether the ROFR/Dilutive Issuance violated the DGCL.

E. Attorneys' Fees

eBay asks the Court to order Jim and Craig to reimburse craigslist for all of the legal fees incurred in this action and for the legal fees relating to the 2008 Board Actions. eBay also asks the Court to award eBay the legal fees it has incurred in this action. I decline to order any shifting of fees.

[…] Under Delaware law, parties are ordinarily responsible for paying their own attorneys' fees. Equity may make an exception and shift fees to a party that has acted in bad faith in connection with the prosecution or defense of the litigation. […]

Neither Jim nor Craig engaged in behavior that could be characterized as bad faith for purposes of fee shifting. Their conduct during litigation was typical of litigants before this Court; they vigorously defended their legal position without making frivolous arguments. Moreover, the 2008 Board Actions cannot be described as "glaring[ly] egregious" pre-litigation conduct. As should be evident by this point in the narrative, this is a unique case with distinct facts and difficult legal issues. I find, as a matter of fact, after evaluating the credibility and demeanor of Jim and Craig, that both men subjectively believed the 2008 Board Actions, despite their uniqueness, were legally permissible under Delaware law. Their judgment was wrong, in my view, with respect to the Rights Plan and the ROFR/Dilutive Issuance. But that does not mean that Jim and Craig implemented the

---

[160] eBay alleges that the ROFR/Dilutive Issuance was also the product of unfair dealing. I need not explore those allegations because I have concluded that the ROFR/Dilutive Issuance does not satisfy the fair price element of the entire fairness test.

Rights Plan and the ROFR/Dilutive Issuance in bad faith. Neither Jim nor Craig acted with the sort of vexatious, wanton, or frivolous conduct consistent with bad faith. Rather, they deliberated with counsel over a period of six months regarding the 2008 Board Actions, considered the possibility of a legal challenge to the Actions, and decided to move forward after concluding, albeit incorrectly, that the Actions were consistent with law.

[...]

III. CONCLUSION

Based on the foregoing findings of fact and conclusions of law, I rescind the Rights Plan and the ROFR/Dilutive Issuance because Jim and Craig breached their fiduciary duties when they implemented those Actions. I do not rescind the Staggered Board Amendments because Jim and Craig did not breach their fiduciary duties when they implemented that Action. Further, I decline to order Jim and Craig to reimburse craigslist or eBay for attorneys' fees.

An Order has been entered consistent with this Opinion.

Chapter 15. Enforcement of Regulations against Corporations

As previously mentioned, corporations are subject to extensive regulations protecting non-shareholder constituencies. Regulatory enforcement is a major practice area, and virtually all corporations now employ dedicated regulatory compliance departments. Examples of such regulations include antitrust, banking regulation, and environmental protection law. While these laws all have their specialized courses, their enforcement presents some common issues that deserve mention even in an introductory corporate law course.

1. Civil Enforcement

Civil enforcement against corporations is easy, at least conceptually speaking, because it is similar to any other civil litigation. (In practice, corporate civil litigation employs armies of lawyers.) By and large, in civil proceedings, it does not matter whether the defendant is an individual or a corporation. In particular, under the law of agency, acts of individual employees are imputed to the corporation as they would be to an individual employer. Thus, the only question particular to corporate suits is whether the same corporate agent or group of agents — for example, the CEO or the board — had all relevant knowledge or intent where such is required, or whether "collective knowledge" is sufficient. On this question, courts have given divergent answers.

2. Criminal Enforcement

Unlike civil enforcement, criminal enforcement raises a host of issues particular to corporate defendants. This is because first, a corporation does not have a mind and hence cannot have a "guilty mind" —*mens rea*—, and second, it does not have a body and hence cannot be incarcerated.

(a) History

At common law, corporations could not be criminally liable. In the 19th century, however, criminal statutes regulating economic behavior through fines proliferated. Some of those statutes explicitly extended criminal liability to corporations. In 1909, the Supreme Court assessed the constitutionality of one such statute in *New York Central & Hudson River Railroad Co. v. U.S.*, holding that

Applying the principle [of *respondeat superior*] governing civil liability, we go only a step farther in holding that the act of the agent, while exercising the authority delegated to him ..., may be controlled, in the interest of public policy, by imputing his act to his employer and imposing penalties upon the corporation for which he is acting ....

"It is true that there are some crimes, which in their nature cannot be committed by corporations. But there is a large class of offenses ... wherein the crime consists in purposely doing the things prohibited by statute. In that class of crimes we see no good reason why corporations may not be held responsible for and charged with the knowledge and purposes of their agents, acting within the authority conferred upon them. ... If it were not so, many offenses might go unpunished and acts be committed in violation of law, where, as in the present case, the statute requires all persons, corporate or private, to refrain from certain practices forbidden in the interest of public policy.

— 212 U.S. 481, 494–95 (1909).

Nowadays, federal criminal statutes targeting a "person" — almost all statutes — presumptively apply to corporations (cf. 1 U.S.C. §1), as long as the agent acted within the scope of her employment and sought, at least in part, to benefit the corporation.

(b) Policy

Is this extension of criminal liability a good idea? Or is civil liability sufficient?

Basics: Deterrence and Incapacitation

Moral blame and retribution, important though they may be for individual criminal liability, make little sense for an abstraction, the corporation. Hence corporate criminal liability must justified by, and calibrated with respect to, its contribution to deterrence and incapacitation.

For individuals, the threat of (criminal) imprisonment can improve deterrence beyond (civil) monetary liability, which is limited by an individual's wealth. Corporations, however, cannot be imprisoned. They can only pay monetary fines. Thus, as far as penalties go, criminal liability does not improve deterrence for corporations beyond what civil liability could do. But criminal law does offer procedural enhancements that matter for corporate deterrence. First, certain aggressive enforcement tools, such as wiretaps, are only available in criminal prosecutions. These tools increase deterrence by increasing the probability that a violation will be discovered. Second, in criminal proceedings the government can act as a central enforcer on behalf of a dispersed class of injured parties, none of whom might have individual incentives to pursue a civil claim (but note that class actions would achieve the same purpose). For example, these two procedural enhancements are crucial for the government's enforcement of insider trading rules (but note that the majority of insider trading enforcement actions are brought by the S.E.C. in civil or administrative proceedings) and of antitrust rules against price fixing.

The second argument for individual criminal liability is incapacitation. Some individuals cannot be deterred, and society may be better off keeping them in prison. Similarly, if an organization is prone to illegal behavior despite the threat of civil liability, society may be better off shutting down that organization or at least excluding it from certain activities or businesses. In particular, some corporations may have more "aggressive" corporate cultures — the ingrained norms of behavior inside the organization — than others.

Overdeterrence?

Some commentators worry that corporations can offend with impunity because their well-financed legal defense teams overwhelm prosecutors' resources and resolve.

However, other commentators have the opposite concern — corporate criminal liability may overdeter. The optimal amount of certain crimes, such as the bribing of foreign officials, may well be zero. But shareholders, or even boards, do not have direct control over such crimes, which may be committed by lower-level employees. Therefore, shareholders and boards can prevent such crimes only through costly compliance programs. In other words, what is an intentional crime at the level of the acting individual (and, in the eyes of the law, for the corporation as a whole) is essentially a strict liability tort at the level of the overseeing board and shareholders.

If the criminal penalty equals the societal harm caused by the crime, then strict liability incentivizes corporations to spend the socially optimal amount on compliance programs, no more no less. However, if the penalty is higher than the social harm, then compliance spending may be socially excessive. A similar problem arises when it is unclear what constitutes lawful behavior, which is frequent in heavily regulated areas. For example, a bank might violate anti-money-laundering rules by not disclosing some transactions to its regulator, and violate privacy rules by disclosing too much. The net social benefit of disclosure is likely to vary little as the bank discloses a little bit more or less. But the bank itself is affected drastically if there is any small variation which leads to illegal disclosure or non-disclosure, since such violations can carry heavy sanctions. Again, the bank would be incentivized to spend more than the socially optimal amount on ensuring compliance.

A. Federal Sentencing Guidelines: Introductory Commentary to Chapter 8 - Sentencing of Organizations

Questions

1. How do the Federal Sentencing Guidelines address the concerns described in our introductory note on enforcement?

2. Do they profess to aim at optimal deterrence or optimal incapacitation?

3. Do they achieve either?

4. If not, what else do they aim to do, and does that make sense?

Introductory Commentary

The guidelines and policy statements in this chapter apply when the convicted defendant is an organization. Organizations can act only through agents and, under federal criminal law, generally are vicariously liable for offenses committed by their agents. At the same time, individual agents are responsible for their own criminal conduct. Federal prosecutions of organizations therefore frequently involve individual and organizational co-defendants. Convicted individual agents of organizations are sentenced in accordance with the guidelines and policy statements in the preceding chapters. This chapter is designed so that the sanctions imposed upon organizations and their agents, taken together, will provide just punishment, adequate deterrence, and incentives for organizations to maintain internal mechanisms for preventing, detecting, and reporting criminal conduct.

This chapter reflects the following general principles:

First, the court must, whenever practicable, order the organization to remedy any harm caused by the offense. The resources expended to remedy the harm should not be viewed as punishment, but rather as a means of making victims whole for the harm caused.

Second, if the organization operated primarily for a criminal purpose or primarily by criminal means, the fine should be set sufficiently high to divest the organization of all its assets.

Third, the fine range for any other organization should be based on the seriousness of the offense and the culpability of the organization. The seriousness of the offense generally will be reflected by the greatest of the pecuniary gain, the pecuniary loss, or the amount in a guideline offense level fine table. Culpability generally will be determined by six factors that the sentencing court must consider. The four factors that increase the ultimate punishment of an organization are: (i) the involvement in or tolerance of criminal activity; (ii) the prior history of the organization; (iii) the violation of an order; and (iv) the obstruction of justice. The two factors that mitigate the ultimate punishment of an organization are: (i) the existence of an effective compliance and ethics program; and (ii) self-reporting, cooperation, or acceptance of responsibility.

Fourth, probation is an appropriate sentence for an organizational defendant when needed to ensure that another sanction will be fully implemented, or to ensure that steps will be taken within the organization to reduce the likelihood of future criminal conduct.

These guidelines offer incentives to organizations to reduce and ultimately eliminate criminal conduct by providing a structural foundation from which an organization may self-police its own conduct through an effective compliance and ethics program. The prevention and detection of criminal conduct, as facilitated by an effective compliance and ethics program, will assist an organization in encouraging ethical conduct and in complying fully with all applicable laws.

B. The Yates Memo: Corporate vs. Individual Criminal Liability

In 2015, U.S. Deputy Attorney General Sally Yates sent an instantly famous memo on "Individual Accountability for Corporate Wrongdoing" to all U.S. Attorneys and Assistant Attorney Generals. The memo explained:

> One of the most effective ways to combat corporate misconduct is by seeking accountability from the individuals who perpetrated the wrongdoing. Such accountability is important for several reasons: it deters future illegal activity, it incentivizes changes in corporate behavior, it ensures that the proper parties are held responsible for their actions, and it promotes the public's confidence in our justice system.

> There are, however, many substantial challenges unique to pursuing individuals for corporate misdeeds. In large corporations, where responsibility can be diffuse and decisions are made at various levels, it can be difficult to determine if someone possessed the knowledge and criminal intent necessary to establish their guilt beyond a reasonable doubt.

> This is particularly true when determining the culpability of high-level executives, who may be insulated from the day-to-day activity in which the misconduct occurs. As a result, investigators often must reconstruct what happened based on a painstaking review of corporate documents, which can number in the millions, and which may be difficult to collect due to legal restrictions.

> These challenges make it all the more important that the Department fully leverage its resources to identify culpable individuals at all levels in corporate cases.

Concretely, Yates ordered:

> 1. in order to qualify for any cooperation credit, corporations must provide to the Department all relevant facts relating to the individuals responsible for the misconduct;

> 2. criminal and civil corporate investigations should focus on individuals from the inception of the investigation;

> 3. criminal and civil attorneys handling corporate investigations should be in routine communication with one another;

4. absent extraordinary circumstances or approved departmental policy, the Department will not release culpable individuals from civil or criminal liability when resolving a matter with a corporation;

5. Department attorneys should not resolve matters with a corporation without a clear plan to resolve related individual cases, and should memorialize any declinations as to individuals in such cases; and

6. civil attorneys should consistently focus on individuals as well as the company and evaluate whether to bring suit

Questions

1. Is corporate liability useful or counterproductive if individuals are the ultimate targets?

2. Could individual liability be good from the corporation's (better: shareholders') point of view?

3. Could there be too much individual liability from the corporation's (better: shareholders') perspective? How would you feel if you were a corporate employee, and what would you do?

C. Deferred Prosecution Agreement with General Motors (U.S. Attorney S.D.N.Y., 2015)

The complaint below memorializes the outcome of the federal government's investigation into General Motor's ignition switch scandal. Judge Nathan of the S.D.N.Y. entered the forfeiture order sought in December 2015.

Questions

1. What exactly did the government prosecute General Motors for?

2. Was GM's prosecution necessary for deterrence? For incapacitation?

UNITED STATES OF AMERICA,

Plaintiff,

-v.-

$900,000,000 in United States Currency,
Defendant *in rem*.

Verified Complaint

15 Civ. _____

Plaintiff United States of America, by its attorney, PREET BHARARA, United States Attorney for the Southern District of New York, for its Verified Complaint (the "Complaint") alleges, upon information and belief, as follows:

I. JURISDICTION AND VENUE

1. This action is brought by the United States of America pursuant to 18 U.S.C. § 981(a) (1) (C), seeking the forfeiture of $900,000,000 in United States Currency (the "Defendant Funds" or the "defendant-in-rem").

[...]

4. The Defendant Funds represent property constituting and derived from proceeds of wire fraud in violation of Title 18, United States Code, Sections 1343, and property traceable to such property and are thus subject to forfeiture to the United States pursuant to Title 18, United States Code, Section 981(a) (1) (C).

II. PROBABLE CAUSE FOR FORFEITURE

5. General Motors Company ("GM"), an automotive company headquartered in Detroit, Michigan, entered into a Deferred Prosecution Agreement with the United States, wherein, inter alia, GM agreed to forfeit a total of $900,000,000, i.e., the Defendant Funds, to the United States. GM agrees that the Defendant Funds are substitute res for the proceeds of GM's wire fraud offense. The Deferred Prosecution Agreement, with the accompanying Statement of Facts and Information, is attached as Exhibit A and incorporated herein.

III. CLAIM FOR FORFEITURE

[...]

WHEREFORE, plaintiff United States of America prays that process issue to enforce the forfeiture of the defendant-in-rem and that all persons having an interest in the defendant-in-rem be cited to appear and show cause why the forfeiture should not be decreed, and that this Court decree forfeiture of the defendant-in-rem to the United States of America for disposition according to law, and that this Court grant plaintiff such further relief as this Court may deem just and proper, together with the costs and disbursements of this action.

> Dated: New York, New York, September 16, 2015

> PREET BHARARA, United States Attorney for Plaintiff United States of America

[...]

Exhibit A

US Department of Justice; US Attorney, Southern District of NY

September 16, 2015

Anton R. Valukas, Esq., Reid J. Schar, Esq., Anthony S. Barkow, Esq.
Jenner & Block LLP, 919 Third Avenue New York, NY 10022

Re: General Motors Company- Deferred Prosecution Agreement

Dear Messrs. Valukas, Schar, and Barkow:

Pursuant to the understandings specified below, the Office of the United States Attorney for the Southern District of New York (the "Office") and the defendant General Motors

Company ("GM"), [...] under authority granted by its Board of Directors in the form of the written authorization attached as Exhibit A, hereby enter into this Deferred Prosecution Agreement (the "Agreement").

The Criminal Information

1. GM consents to the filing of a two-count Information (the "Information") in the United States District Court for the Southern District of New York (the "Court"), charging GM with engaging in a scheme to conceal a deadly safety defect from its U.S. regulator, in violation of Title 18, United States Code, Section 1001, and committing wire fraud, in violation of Title 18, United States Code, Section 1343. A copy of the Information is attached as Exhibit B. This Agreement shall take effect upon its execution by both parties.

Acceptance of Responsibility

2. GM admits and stipulates that the facts set forth in the Statement of Facts attached as Exhibit C and incorporated herein are true and accurate. In sum, GM admits that it failed to disclose to its U.S. regulator and the public a potentially lethal safety defect that caused airbag non-deployment in certain GM model cars, and that GM further affirmatively misled consumers about the safety of GM cars afflicted by the defect.

Forfeiture

3. As a result of the conduct described in the Information and the Statement of Facts, GM agrees to pay to the United States $900 million (the "Stipulated Forfeiture Amount") representing the proceeds resulting from such conduct. GM agrees that the allegations contained in the Information and the facts set forth in the Statement of Facts are sufficient to establish that the Stipulated Forfeiture Amount is subject to civil forfeiture to the United States [...]

Obligation to Cooperate

5. GM has cooperated with this Office's criminal investigation and agrees to cooperate fully and actively with the Office, the Federal Bureau of Investigation ("FBI"), the Department of Transportation ("DOT"), the Office of the Special Inspector General for the Troubled Asset Relief Program ("SIGTARP"), the National Highway Traffic Safety Administration ("NHTSA"), and any other agency of the government designated by the Office regarding any matter relating to the Office's investigation about which GM has knowledge or information.

6. It is understood that GM shall (a) truthfully and completely disclose all information with respect to the activities of itself and its subsidiaries, as well as with respect to the activities of officers, agents, and employees of GM and its subsidiaries, concerning all matters about

which the Office inquires of it, which information can be used for any purpose; (b) cooperate fully with the Office, FBI, DOT, SIGTARP, NHTSA, and any other law enforcement agency designated by the Office; [...]

7. GM agrees that its obligations pursuant to this Agreement, which shall commence upon the signing of this Agreement, will continue for three years from the date of the Court's acceptance of this Agreement, unless otherwise extended pursuant to paragraph 12 below. GM's obligation to cooperate is not intended to apply in the event that a prosecution against GM by this Office is pursued and not deferred.

Deferral of Prosecution

8. In consideration of GM's entry into this Agreement, the actions it has taken to date to demonstrate acceptance and acknowledgement of responsibility for its conduct (including, among other things, conducting a swift and robust internal investigation, furnishing this Office with a continuous flow of unvarnished facts gathered during the course of that internal investigation, voluntarily providing, without prompting, certain documents and information otherwise protected by the attorney-client privilege, providing timely and meaningful cooperation more generally in the investigation conducted by this Office, terminating wrongdoers, and establishing a full and independent victim compensation program that has to date paid out hundreds of millions of dollars in awards), and its commitment to: (a) continue to accept and acknowledge responsibility for its conduct; (b) continue to cooperate with the Office, FBI, DOT, SIGTARP, NHTSA, and any other law enforcement agency designated by this Office; (c) make the payments specified in this Agreement; (d) comply with Federal criminal laws; and (e) otherwise comply with all of the terms of this Agreement, the Office shall recommend to the Court that prosecution of GM on the Information be deferred for three years from the date of the signing of this Agreement. [...]

Independent Monitor

15. GM agrees to retain a Monitor upon selection by the Office and approval by the Office of the Deputy Attorney General, whose powers, rights and responsibilities shall be as set forth below.

(a) Jurisdiction, Powers, and Oversight Authority. To address issues related to the Statement of Facts and Information, the Monitor shall have the authorities and duties defined below. [...]

(1) Review and assess the efficacy of GM's current policies, practices, and procedures in ensuring that GM corrects prior statements and assurances concerning motor vehicle

(2) Review and assess the effectiveness of GM's current policies, practices, or procedures for sharing allegations and engineering analyses associated with lawsuits and not-in-suit matters with those responsible for recall decisions;

(3) Review and assess GM's current compliance with its stated recall processes; and

(4) Review and assess the adequacy of GM's current procedures for addressing known defects in certified pre-owned vehicles.

[...] GM shall adopt all recommendations submitted by the Monitor unless GM objects to any recommendation and the Office agrees that adoption of such recommendation should not be required.

(b) Access to Information. The Monitor shall have the authority to take such reasonable steps, in the Monitor's view, as necessary to be fully informed about those operations of GM within or relating to his or her jurisdiction. To that end, the Monitor shall have:

(1) Access to, and the right to make copies of, any and all non- privileged books, records, accounts, correspondence, files, and any and all other documents or electronic records, including e-mails, of GM and its subsidiaries, and of officers, agents, and employees of GM and its subsidiaries, within or relating to his or her jurisdiction that are located in the United States; and

(2) The right to interview any officer, employee, agent, or consultant of GM conducting business in or present in the United States and to participate in any meeting in the United States concerning any matter within or relating to the Monitor's jurisdiction.

To the extent that the Monitor seeks access to information contained within privileged documents or materials, GM shall use its best efforts to provide the Monitor with the information without compromising the asserted privilege.

(c) Confidentiality.

(1) The Monitor shall maintain the confidentiality of any non-public information entrusted or made available to the Monitor. [...]

(d) Hiring Authority. The Monitor shall have the authority to employ legal counsel, consultants, investigators, experts, and any other personnel necessary to assist in the proper discharge of the Monitor's duties.

(e) Implementing Authority. The Monitor shall have the authority to take any other actions in the United States that are necessary to effectuate the Monitor's oversight and monitoring responsibilities.

(f) Miscellaneous Provisions.

(1) Term. The Monitor's authority set forth herein shall extend for a period of three years from the commencement of the Monitor's duties, except that (a) in the event the Office determines during the period of the Monitorship (or any extensions thereof) that GM has violated any provision of this Agreement, an extension of the period of the Monitorship may be imposed in the sole discretion of the Office, up to an additional one-year extension, but in no event shall the total term of the Monitorship exceed the term of the Agreement [...]

(2) Selection of the Monitor. The Office shall consult with GM, including soliciting nominations from GM, using its best efforts to select and appoint a mutually acceptable Monitor (and any replacement Monitors, if required) as promptly as possible. In the event that the Office is unable to select a Monitor acceptable to GM, the Office shall have the sole right to select a monitor (and any replacement Monitors, if required). [...]

(3) Notice regarding the Monitor; Monitor's Authority to Act on Information received from Employees; No Penalty for Reporting. GM shall establish an independent, toll-free answering service to facilitate communication anonymously or otherwise with the Monitor [and] shall inform employees that they may communicate with the Monitor anonymously or otherwise, and that no agent, consultant, or employee of GM shall be penalized in any way for providing information to the Monitor. [...]

(5) Cooperation with the Monitor. GM and all of its officers, directors, employees, agents, and consultants, and all of the officers, directors, employees, agents, and consultants of GM's subsidiaries shall have an affirmative duty to cooperate with and assist the Monitor in the execution of his or her duties provided in this Agreement and shall inform the Monitor of any non-privileged information that may relate to the Monitor's duties or lead to information that relates to his or her duties. Failure of any GM officer, director, employee, or agent to cooperate with the Monitor may, in the sole discretion of the Monitor, serve as a basis for the Monitor to recommend dismissal or other disciplinary action.

(6) Compensation and Expenses. Although the Monitor shall operate under the supervision of the Office, the compensation and expenses of the Monitor, and of the persons hired under his or her authority, shall be paid by GM. [...]

By: PREET BHARARA, United States Attorney, Southern District of New York [...]

Accepted and agreed to:

Craig Glidden, Esq., General Counsel and Chief Legal Officer, GM Co.

Anton R Valukas, Esq., Reid J Schar, Esq., Anthony S Barkow, Esq., Attorneys for GM

Exhibit A to the Deferred Prosecution Agreement

GM CO. RESOLUTIONS OF THE BOARD OF DIRECTORS

[...]

Exhibit B to the Deferred Prosecution Agreement

U.S. DISTRICT COURT, S.D.N.Y.

U.S. V GENERAL MOTORS COMPANY, 15 Cr. ____

COUNT ONE (Scheme to Conceal Material Facts from a Government Regulator)

The United States Attorney charges:

1. GENERAL MOTORS COMPANY ("GM" or the "Company"), the defendant, is an automotive company headquartered in Detroit, Michigan. In 2012, GM was the largest automotive company in the world.

2. At all times relevant to this Information, GM designed, manufactured, assembled, and sold Chevrolet brand vehicles. From the earliest date relevant to this Information until in or about 2010, GM designed, manufactured, assembled, and sold Pontiac brand vehicles. From the earliest date relevant to this Information until in or about 2009, GM designed, manufactured, assembled, and sold Saturn brand vehicles. And from the earliest date relevant to this information until in or about the spring of 2013, GM promoted sales of "pre-owned" (i.e., used) Chevrolet, Pontiac, and Saturn brand vehicles by GM dealerships nationwide.

3. At all times relevant to this Information, GM was required to disclose to its U.S. regulator, the National Highway Traffic Safety Administration ("NHTSA"), any defect in its cars "related to motor vehicle safety" within five business days of identifying said defect. See 49 U.S.C. § 30118 (c) & 49 C.F.R. § 573.6.

4. From in or about the spring of 2012 through in or about February 2014, GM, through its agents and employees, concealed a potentially deadly safety defect from NHTSA and the public. The defect related to an ignition switch that had been designed and manufactured with too-low torque (the "Defective Switch"). As GM knew by no later than 2005, the Defective Switch was prone to too-easy movement from the "Run" to the "Accessory" or "Off" position. And as GM personnel well knew no later than the spring of 2012, when that movement occurred, the driver would lose not only the assistance of power steering and power brakes but also the protection afforded by the vehicle's frontal airbags in the event of a crash.

5. Rather than remedy the Defective Switch when its torque deficiencies and attendant stalling consequences became clear no later than in or about 2005, GM continued to sell and manufacture new cars equipped with the Defective Switch. Moreover, although the public was made aware, through media reports, of the Defective Switch's existence, GM affirmatively assured consumers in or about June 2005 that the Defective Switch presented no "safety" problem.

6. In or about April 2006, a GM engineer directed that the Defective Switch no longer be used in new cars, and that it be replaced with another non-defective switch that would bear the same part number as the Defective Switch. Nothing was done at this time to remedy the cars equipped with the Defective Switch that were already on the road.

7. When the fact that the Defective Switch could cause airbag non-deployment—and therefore undeniably presented a safety defect—became plain no later than in or about the spring of 2012, GM did not correct its earlier assurance that the Defective Switch posed no "safety" concern. Nor did it recall the affected vehicles. Instead, it concealed the defect from NHTSA and the public, taking the matter "offline" outside the normal recall process, so that the Company could buy time to package, present, explain, and manage the issue. Fearing an adverse impact on the Company's business, GM engineers and executives wanted to have answers to all questions that NHTSA, the media, and consumers might pose about the defect before alerting the regulator and the public to it.

8. GM did not recall the vehicles equipped with the Defective Switch until February 2014. In the meantime, in or about October 2012 and again in or about November 2013, GM personnel gave presentations to NHTSA in which they touted the robustness of GM's internal recall process and gave the misleading impression that GM worked promptly and efficiently to resolve known safety defects, including, specifically, defects related to non-deployment.

Statutory Allegations

9. From in or about the spring of 2012 through in or about February 2014, GM, the defendant, in a matter within the jurisdiction of the executive branch of the Government of the United States, willfully and knowingly did falsify, conceal, and cover up by trick, scheme, and device material facts, and made materially false, fictitious, and fraudulent statements and representations, to wit, GM engaged in a scheme to conceal from its federal U.S. regulator, NHTSA, a potentially deadly safety defect that GM was required to disclose within five business days of discovery thereof.

(Title 18, United States Code, Sections 1001 and 2.)

COUNT TWO (Wire Fraud)

The United States Attorney further charges:

10. The allegations contained in Paragraphs 1 through 8 are repeated and realleged as though fully set forth herein.

11. From in or about the spring of 2012 through in or about the spring of 2013, GM dealerships continued to sell GM- certified pre-owned Chevrolet, Pontiac, and Saturn brand vehicles equipped with the Defective Switch. To promote these sales and give customers assurance about the safety of the cars subject to its certified pre-owned program, GM made representations by means of interstate wires—that is, over the Internet—falsely assuring customers of the safety of the used cars they were purchasing. In particular, GM certified that used vehicles sold pursuant to this program had been checked for safety of their ignition systems and keys. In truth and in fact, and as GM well knew, cars equipped with the Defective Switch posed a potentially deadly safety threat related to the cars' ignition switches and keys.

12. In addition to making these false representations as part of its certified pre-owned program, GM, more generally, failed to disclose a material fact that it had a duty to disclose—namely, that cars equipped with the Defective Switch presented a safety defect. GM's duty to disclose this fact derived from two sources: (a) its false June 2005 representation that the Defective Switch presented no safety concern; and (b) its obligation under applicable regulations to inform NHTSA of any known safety defect within five business days of discovery thereof.

Statutory Allegation

13. From in or about the spring of 2012 through in or about February 2014, in the Southern District of New York and elsewhere, GM, the defendant, willfully and knowingly, having devised and intending, to devise a scheme and artifice to defraud, and for obtaining money and property by means of false and fraudulent pretenses, representations, and promises, did transmit and cause to be transmitted and aid and abet the transmission, by means of wire, radio, and television communication in interstate and foreign commerce, writings, signs, signals, pictures, and sounds for the purpose of executing such scheme and artifice, to wit, GM defrauded U.S. consumers into purchasing its products by concealing information and making misleading statements about the safety of vehicles equipped with the Defective Switch.

(Title 18, United States Code, Sections 1343 and 2.)

FORFEITURE ALLEGATION

14. As a result of committing the wire fraud offense alleged in Count Two of this Information, GM, the defendant, shall forfeit to the United States, pursuant to Title 18, United States Code, Section 981(a) (1) (C) and Title 28, United States Code, Section 2461, any property, real or personal, which constitutes or is derived from proceeds traceable to such offense. [...]

SIGNED, Preet Bharara, United States Attorney

Exhibit C to the Deferred Prosecution Agreement

STATEMENT OF FACTS

Overview

[...]

4. The defect at issue is a low-torque ignition switch installed in many of the vehicles identified below, which, under certain circumstances, may move out of the "Run" position (the "Defective Switch"). If this movement occurs, the driver loses the assistance of power steering and power brakes. And if a collision occurs while the switch is in the Accessory or Off position, the vehicle's safety airbags may fail to deploy-increasing the risk of death and serious injury in certain types of crashes in which the airbag was otherwise designed to deploy. The model year cars which may have been equipped with the Defective Switch are the 2005, 2006, and 2007 Chevrolet Cobalt; the 2005, 2006, and 2007 Pontiac G5; the 2003, 2004, 2005, 2006, and 2007 Saturn Ion; the 2006 and 2007 Chevrolet HHR; the 2007 Saturn Sky; and the 2006 and 2007 Pontiac Solstice. To date, GM has acknowledged a total of 15 deaths, as well as a number of serious injuries, that occurred in crashes in which the Defective Switch may have caused or contributed to frontal airbag non-deployment.

[...]

Regulatory Framework and GM's Formal Recall Process

12. Under regulations applicable to GM at all relevant times, the Company was required to disclose to NHTSA any "defect ... related to motor vehicle safety." "Motor vehicle safety" was defined as "performance of a motor vehicle ... in a way that protects the public against unreasonable risk of accidents ... and against unreasonable risk of death or injury in an accident." 49 U.S. C.§§ 30118(c)(l); 30102(a)(8). Such disclosure had to be "submitted not more than 5 working days after a defect in a vehicle or item of equipment

ha[d] been determined to be safety related." See 49 U.S.C.§ 30118(c) and 49 C.P.R.§ 573.6. [2]

[...]

GM Equips Cars with a Defective Switch

[...]

20. Development of the switch that would end up first in the Ion and then in the Cobalt and other models began in the late 1990s. By March 2001, the GM design release engineer then in charge of the Ion's switch (the "Switch DRE") had finalized the applicable design specifications and communicated them to the supplier in charge of testing and manufacturing the component (the "Switch Supplier"). Among the specifications communicated to the Switch Supplier was that the torque necessary to move the switch from Run to Accessory must be no less than 15 Newton centimeters ("N-cm") (the "Torque Specification"). Mechanically, this torque performance was to be maintained by a detent plunger and spring within the switch.

21. Testing conducted by the Switch Supplier in 2001 and early 2002 revealed that an early version of the pre-production Defective Switch was not meeting the Torque Specification; it repeatedly scored "Not OK." A July 2001 pre-production report for the Ion within GM made the same observation: the switch had "low detent plunger force."

22. In email correspondence between the Switch DRE and the Switch Supplier in early 2002, the Switch Supplier confirmed that an early version of the Defective Switch was not meeting the Torque Specification and outlined the problems that might arise if the part were brought into compliance-including pressure on other switch components, delay, and increased costs. Saying that he was "tired of the switch from hell" and did not want to either compromise the electrical performance of the switch or slow the production schedule, the Switch DRE directed the Switch Supplier to "maintain present course" notwithstanding that there was "still too soft of a detent." Accordingly, the Defective Switch was put into production and installed into the first model year of the Ion (model year 2003), which was first sold to the public in 2002.

---

[2] Congress has adopted no criminal penalty for violating this regulatory disclosure requirement. Instead, in order for a company to be held criminally liable under federal law for even an egregious failure to report a known safety defect, its conduct must have independently violated some other federal law to which criminal penalties do attach.

23. By email dated March 28, 2002, the Switch DRE recommended that the Defective Switch also be used in the Cobalt, which was to launch the next year. GM followed that recommendation.

24. Almost immediately, customers began to report problems with cars equipped with the Defective Switch. Meanwhile, GM employees tasked with driving early production versions of the Ion and then the Cobalt were reporting stalls while driving, and some of them were able to attribute the problem to the easy rotation of the key within the Defective Switch.

25. Members of the press covering the Cobalt's launch *also* experienced the unexpected shutoff problem. Alerted by one of the press reports, two executives in charge of   safety at GM determined to experience for themselves the complained-of phenomenon.[3] In June 2005, they test drove a Cobalt and found that, as reported, the Cobalt could be easily keyed off by contact with the driver's knee.

26. Shortly afterward, GM issued a press statement acknowledging the problem as it pertained to the Cobalt, which had the greatest number of consumer complaints: "In rare cases when a combination of factors is present, a Chevrolet Cobalt driver can cut power to the engine by inadvertently bumping the ignition key to the accessory or off position while the car is running." The press release further recommended that drivers remove "nonessential material from their key rings." Before its public release, this statement was reviewed and approved by the PI Senior Manager and by the senior GM attorney who advised engineers about safety- and recall-related issues (the "GM Safety Attorney"). In a response to further media inquiry, GM stated that it did not believe this condition presented a safety concern.

27. A June 2005 *Cleveland Plain Dealer* article reporting on the ignition switch problem marveled at GM's public statement, commenting "you have to admit it is pretty funny to hear somebody pretend that turning off the engine by mistake isn't a safety issue."

28. Just days before this article was published, GM engineers working on the Pontiac Solstice, another new car equipped with the Defective Switch, learned of a complaint about a Solstice that had experienced the same inadvertent shutoff problem as had been reported in the Ion and the Cobalt.

---

[3] The two executives were GM's then-Director of Vehicle Safety & Crashworthiness and the Senior Manager of the PI group (the "PI Senior Manager").

GM Considers a Fix

29. In November 2004, the Company opened the first of six engineering inquiries that would be initiated in the ensuing five years to consider ameliorative engineering changes for new cars being rolled off the production line. This first inquiry was closed "with no action" in March 2005. Fixes such as improving the torque performance of the Defective Switch itself and changing the head of the associated key to reduce the likelihood of inadvertent movement from Run to Accessory were rejected as not representing "an acceptable business case." Having decided that the switch did not pose a safety concern, GM engineers concluded that each proposed solution would take too long to implement, would cost too much, and would not fully fix "the possibility of the key being turned (ignition turn off) during driving."

30. Accordingly, GM decided to keep producing and selling new Cobalts, Ions, Solstices, Skys, G5s, and HHRs equipped with the Defective Switch.

31. Not all involved in the November 2004 engineering inquiry agreed with this outcome at the time. The Vehicle Performance Manager for the Cobalt believed that the Defective Switch presented a potential safety because it could cause sudden loss of power steering and power brakes. (This engineer did not have in mind at the time the loss of power to the airbag system.) He therefore thought a remedy should have been implemented without regard to cost concerns. His views did not prevail.

32. Meanwhile, in February 2005, while the November 2004 engineering inquiry was still open, the Company released a "Preliminary Information" to its dealers aimed at helping them diagnose and address the Defective Switch problem if a customer experienced it in a 2005 Cobalt or 2005 Pontiac Pursuit.[4] This publication explained that the Defective Switch's too-low "key ignition cylinder torque/effort" could cause "Engine Stalls" and "Loss of Electric Systems." It advised dealers to tell customers to remove non-essential items from their key chains. It offered no other fixes.

33. In May 2005, just two months after the November 2004 engineering inquiry into the Defective Switch was dosed without action, a GM brand quality manager opened a second inquiry to consider fixing the problem for new cars. This manager cited a customer complaint that the "vehicle ignition will turn off while driving," and noted that GM was having to buy back Cobalts as a result of the Defective Switch.

34. Still not believing this was a safety issue, GM engineers closed this inquiry too, without issuing a recall. Although GM engineers involved in the inquiry initially resolved to

---

[4] The Ion was not covered by this Preliminary Information.

ameliorate the low torque problem for newly produced 2007 Cobalts by changing the design of the key head so that the key ring would sit in a "hole" rather than a "slot" (thus reducing the lever arm and attendant potential torque), they ultimately rejected this solution.

35. GM continued producing and selling new cars equipped with the Defective Switch and accompanying slot-head key.

36. Meanwhile, GM's PI [eds: Product Investigations] group, which was responsible for addressing problems with cars already on the road, began in the summer of 2005 to study the low torque issue. Like the engineering inquiries targeted at yet-to-be-manufactured cars, this investigation essentially went nowhere. Although PI engineers presented the matter to the ISR [eds: Investigation Status Review] (the first stage of the potential recall process) in the summer of 2005, decision-makers who attended that ISR decided that the problem did not present a safety concern and thus did not warrant further consideration for recall. At the time, neither PI nor any member of the ISR seems to have appreciated that one of the electronic systems shut off by an inadvertent movement of the Defective Switch out of the Run position was the airbag system.

37. Having determined that the problem did not pose a safety concern and thus need not be considered further for recall, GM simply replaced the February 2005 Preliminary Information with a more formal "Service Bulletin" to its dealers (the "2005 Service Bulletin"), alerting them to an "inadvertent turning off' problem and instructing them to provide any complaining customers with inserts for their key heads that would transform the slot into a hole and thus reduce the lever arm. Unlike the Preliminary Information, which accurately described the condition caused by the Defective Switch as (among other things) a "stall," the 2005 Service Bulletin omitted that word. Thus, a dealer responding to a customer inquiry or complaint would not locate the bulletin if he or she only used the word "stall" in the search.

38. The omission of the word "stall" from the 2005 Service Bulletin was deliberate. The PI Senior Manager, who oversaw and could control the wording of GM service bulletins, directed that the word be kept out of this bulletin even though he knew customers would naturally describe the problem as "stalling." The reason for the omission was to avoid attracting the attention of GM's regulator, NHTSA. As it had happened, in the interim between the February 2005 Preliminary Information and the 2005 Service Bulletin, some within GM had been meeting with representatives of NHTSA to try to persuade them that defects causing vehicles to stall were not necessarily safety defects warranting recall action. NHTSA agreed that stalls were not necessarily safety issues, but certain GM personnel were also aware of the regulator's sensitivity to stalling problems throughout this period.

39. Although the bulletin referenced not just the Cobalt but also the ffi1R, the Ion, the Solstice, and the Pursuit, and although it was updated in October 2006 to cover the model year 2007 versions of these cars and the 2007 Saturn Sky, the customers who would ultimately receive the bulletin's recommended key-head inserts between 2005 and 2014 numbered only about 430.

The Changes to the Switch and the Key

40. As of the spring of 2006, the 2005 Service Bulletin was the lone measure in place to address the Defective Switch. There were no systematic efforts to provide key modifications for all owners of affected cars--or even all owners who came into dealerships for service. And every day more and more new cars with the Defective Switch were being manufactured and sold to unwary customers.

41. In April 2006, that changed. The Switch DRE, who had received numerous complaints about the Defective Switch from other GM employees, authorized replacement of the Defective Switch in new cars with a different one that had a longer detent plunger and therefore significantly greater torque. The Switch DRE further directed, in of accepted GM practice, that this change be implemented without a corresponding part number change. As a result, no one looking at the switch would be able, without taking it apart, to tell the difference between the old, Defective Switch and the new, non-defective one.

42. Although it was effectuated without a part number change, the switch change that the Switch DRE approved was documented internally, and other engineers were aware of it at the time and afterward. For example, a March 2007 note logged in connection with an engineering inquiry into another matter related to the Ion specifically observed that "[t]he detent plunger torque force was increased" by the Switch DRE in April 2006.

43. Another relevant change to the Cobalt was made in 2009. Having previously rejected the slot-to-hole alteration to the key head design, GM finally decided to implement that change. An engineer involved in the decision wrote at the time: "This issue has been around since man first lumbered out of [the] sea and stood on two feet." The long-overdue change went into effect for the model year 2010 Cobalt.

The Defective Switch's Deadly Consequences[5]

44. As noted, the too-easy movement of the Defective Switch from the Run to the Accessory or Off position resulted in an unexpected shutoff of the engine and-as both the

---

[5] GM has acknowledged 15 deaths occurring in crashes in which the Defective Switch may have caused or contributed to airbag non-deployment, not all of which are described herein. Many other deaths have been alleged to have been associated with the Defective Switch.

February 2005 Preliminary Information and the 2005 Service Bulletin properly described-a "loss of electrical system[s]." These electrical systems included power steering and power brakes. They also included the sensing diagnostic module or "SDM," which controlled airbag deployment. Internal GM documents reflect that although the impact of an engine shutoff on the SDM was not on GM engineers' minds, certain employees within GM understood no later than 2001 the natural connection between a loss of electrical systems and non-deployment of airbags: if the ignition switch turned to Off or Accessory, the SDM would "drop," and the airbags would therefore be disabled. If a crash then ensued, neither the driver nor any passengers could have the protection of an airbag.

45. And, indeed, the deadly effects of the Defective Switch on airbag non-deployment began manifesting themselves early on, in crashes about which GM was made aware contemporaneously. In July 2004, the 37 year-old driver of a 2004 Ion, a mother of three children and two step-children, died in a crash after her airbags failed to deploy. A few months later, in November 2004, the passenger of a 2004 Ion died in another crash where the airbags failed to deploy. The driver was charged with, and ultimately pled guilty to, negligent homicide. Then, in June 2005, a 40-year-old man suffered serious injuries after his 2005 Ion crashed and the airbags failed to deploy.

46. For each of these Ion crashes in which the subject vehicles evidently lost power before impact, the SDM data recovered from the crashed vehicles was unilluminating. Unlike the SDM installed in the Cobalt, the Ion's SDM was incapable of recording data-including power mode status-after the vehicle had lost power.

47. The Cobalt SDM data, by contrast, reflected a number of non-deployments accompanied by a power mode status recording of Accessory or Off.

48. In July 2005, just months after GM closed its first engineering inquiry into the Defective Switch, a 16-year-old driver died in Maryland when the airbags in her 2005 Cobalt failed to deploy. The power mode status recorded for that vehicle at the time of the crash was Accessory.

49. In October 2006, two more teenagers died, also in a 2005 Cobalt, in Wisconsin. The airbags in the vehicle failed to deploy when they should have, and the police officer who examined the crashed vehicle noted in a February 2007 report on the incident that the ignition switch "appeared to have been in the accessory position ... preventing the airbags from deploying." An 2007 report about the same crash by Indiana University likewise posited that the airbags had failed to deploy because the key was in the Accessory position. This report even specifically referenced the October 2006 version of the 2005 Service Bulletin, which described the Defective Switch.

50. In the spring of 2007, NHTSA approached certain GM personnel to express concern about a high number of airbag non-deployment complaints in Cobalts and Ions, and to ask questions about the July 2005 Cobalt crash resulting in the death of the 16-year-old girl. Around this same time, and as a result of NHTSA's inquiries, a GM field performance assessment engineer with expertise in airbags who worked principally with GM lawyers (the "Airbag FPA Engineer") began, at the request of his supervisors, to track reports of crashes in Cobalts where the airbags failed to deploy. And, in May 2007, the PI group even placed the issue of Cobalt airbag non-deployment into the first stage of GM's recall process, the ISR. But the PI group, under the supervision of the PI Senior Manager, conducted no follow-up at the time.

51. In September 2008, another crash, this one involving a 2006 Cobalt, killed two people. The airbags failed to deploy when they should have. GM sent the crashed car's SDM to the Company's SDM supplier for examination. In May 2009, the SDM supplier reported that the power mode status was at one point during the crash recorded as Off, and that this was one of two possible explanations for the failure of the airbags to deploy. This report was provided in writing, but also in person, at a meeting attended by several GM employees-including a member of the PI group, in-house counsel, and the Airbag FPA Engineer who had been tracking the Cobalt non-deploy incidents.

52. In April 2009, a 73-year-old grandmother and her 13-year-old granddaughter were killed in rural Pennsylvania in a crash when the ignition switch in the grandmother's 2005 Cobalt slipped into the Accessory position, thereby disabling the frontal airbags and preventing their deployment. The grandmother and her 13-year-old granddaughter, who was in the front passenger seat, both died at the scene. A 12-month-old great grandson, the sole survivor, was paralyzed from the waist down. He was hospitalized for 33 days following the crash.

53. In December 2009, a 35-year-old Virginia woman crashed her 2005 Cobalt, sustaining serious head injuries and rib fractures (hereinafter, the "Virginia Crash"). The airbags failed to deploy, and, as the Airbag FPA Engineer noted, the power mode at the time of the crash was recorded as Accessory.

54. Two weeks later, a 25-year-old nursing student died in Tennessee following a head-on collision in her 2006 Cobalt (hereinafter, the "Tennessee Crash"). Again, the airbags failed to deploy when they should have, and the power mode status was recorded as Off at the time of the crash.

55. In March 2010, a 29 year-old woman was killed in Georgia after her 2005 Cobalt crashed (hereinafter, the "Georgia Crash"). Although there was no allegation that the frontal airbag should have deployed, there was an allegation that loss of power steering

caused the crash. The SDM from the vehicle showed that the power mode status was recorded as Accessory at the time of the crash.

56. Notably, just nine days before the Georgia Crash, GM had conducted a safety recall for a power steering problem in the Cobalt unrelated to the Defective Switch, in which it acknowledged that loss of power steering, standing alone, constituted a "defect ... relate[d] to motor vehicle safety" and thus warranted recall action. The Defective Switch, of course, caused more than just loss of power steering; it also caused loss of other electrical systems. This was known by many within GM by no later than 2004-even if they did not appreciate precisely what electrical system components were affected (*e.g.*, the airbag SDM). Yet at no time before February 2014 did GM announce a recall for cars associated with the Defective Switch.

GM Identifies the Connection Between the Ignition Switch and Airbag Non-Deployment and Initiates a Formal Investigation

57. Many of the deaths and serious injuries associated with airbag non-deployment discussed in the foregoing paragraphs became the subject of legal claims—formal. and informal—against GM. Certain GM lawyers, aided by the Airbag FPA Engineer and others like him who assisted in evaluating causes of crashes; realized by no later than early 2011 that a number of these non-deployment cases involved some sort of "anomaly" in the ignition switch. Specifically, in connection with the Tennessee Crash, discussed above, a GM engineer explained to legal staff that when the ignition switch power mode status is in Off (as it was in that case), the SDM "powers down," and the airbags fail to deploy. The engineer further opined that the "a crash sensing system 'anomaly'" resulting in a power mode status of Off had indeed caused non- deployment in the Tennessee Crash case.

58. This crash sensing "anomaly" risked the prospect of punitive damages. Three months later, GM settled the Tennessee Crash case.

59. Just days before that settlement, a 15-year-old girl in South Carolina crashed her mother's 2007 Cobalt and suffered significant injuries when the airbag did not deploy. The power mode status was recorded as Accessory at the time of the crash. GM engineers evaluating the crash theorized that, as in the case of the Tennessee Crash, the non-deployment here may have been caused by a crash sensing "anomaly" related to the ignition switch.

60. Meanwhile, the GM attorney principally responsible for airbag non-deployment claims (the "GM Airbag Attorney"), who had become familiar with a number of Cobalt non- deployment incidents, grew concerned that the "anomaly" identified in these cases was getting insufficient attention from the PI group, which was supposed to investigate

and work toward remedying safety problems with cars on the road. At the time, no one within GM had yet sourced the "anomaly" to the Defective Switch's torque.

61. Certain members of the legal department took the unusual step of arranging a meeting with PI. The meeting, which took place on July 27, 2011, was attended not just by the PI Senior Manager, who ran the PI group on a day-to-day basis, but also by his boss, the GM Director of Product Investigations (the "GM Safety Director"). Also present were the Airbag FPA Engineer, the GM Airbag Attorney, and the GM Safety Attorney. In advance of the meeting, the PI Senior Manager wrote to a colleague that the Cobalt airbag non-deployment problem was "ugly" and would make for "a difficult investigation."

62. A t the July 27, 2011 meeting, the Airbag FPA Engineer showed photographs of three of the most serious non-deployment crashes be had seen involving Cobalts, including photographs of the Tennessee Crash, and specifically highlighted his observations that many of these Cobalt non-deployment crashes had occurred while the power mode was in Accessory or Off.

63. After the meeting, the PI Senior Manager assigned an investigator (the "PI Investigator") to examine the matter.

GM Identifies the Defective Switch as the Likely Cause of Airbag Non-Deployment in 2005-2007 Model Year Cobalts

64. One of the first steps the PI Investigator took, in or about August 2011, was to gather learning and materials from the Airbag FPA Engineer who had been tracking non-deployment incidents in Cobalts since 2007, and who had been involved in evaluating a number of crashes that were the subject of Cobalt non-deployment claims. The Airbag FPA Engineer explained to the PI Investigator that he had observed that in some of these cases the power mode was recorded as either Accessory or Off at the time of the subject crashes. The Airbag FPA Engineer further noted that the non-deployment problem appeared to be limited to 2005-2007 model years of the Cobalt and appeared not to affect model years 2008 and later.

65. By March 2012, more than six months after he had been assigned to the matter, the PI Investigator had done little to advance the investigation. The GM Airbag Attorney called another meeting with PI for March 15, 2012. Attendees at this meeting included the GM Safety Attorney, the GM Airbag Attorney, the GM Safety Director, the PI Investigator, the PI Senior Manager, and the Airbag FPA Engineer. During the meeting, the PI Investigator complained that he needed more support from GM's electrical engineeling group to investigate a potential electrical (as opposed to mechanical) explanation for the Accessory and Off power mode recordings in many of the subject crashes.

66. Two weeks later, the Airbag FPA Engineer, members of GM's electrical engineering group, and others travelled to an auto salvage yard to examine potential electric problems related to the ignition switch-to see whether, as the PI Investigator and others had posited, the Accessory and Off power mode status recordings within the SDMs of the subject vehicles were attributable to an electrical "bounce" in the ignition switch.

67. At the yard, one of the engineers noticed that the effort needed to turn the ignition switch of the 2006 Cobalt they were examining was low. The group immediately dispatched one of their members to retrieve fish scales from a local bait and tackle shop to measure the rotational force in this and other salvage yard Cobalts. A GM electrical engineer involved in the exercise (the "GM Electrical Engineer") recorded the findings, noted the unusually low force needed to move the examined switches out of Run, searched and found records of customer complaints about the low torque issue, and located the 2005 Service Bulletin addressing the issue.

68. The next day, the GM Electrical Engineer reported to his own boss these findings and his view that a probable root cause of the non-deployment problem was the Defective Switch moving out of Run to Accessory or Off. And that same day, the boss reported all of this to the PI Senior Manager and to the GM Safety Attorney.

69. At around the same time, the plaintiffs in a lawsuit stemming from the Virginia Crash, referenced above, located the 2005 Service Bulletin and identified the Defective Switch described therein as the cause of non-deployment in the vehicle at issue in that case. The GM Airbag Attorney identified the 2005 Service Bulletin as potentially related to the Virginia Crash.

70. In an April 23, 2012 email responding to a query about an ignition switch turning too easily from Run to Off, the PI Senior Manager wrote to colleagues claiming–inexplicably– that he had "not heard of' complaints about low torque in the "Cobalt or other models" since 2005, when the first PI examination was conducted and closed with the issuance of the 2005 Service Bulletin. The PI Investigator, meanwhile, pressed electrical engineers to continue to look into other possible causes of non-deployment, beyond the low torque problem.

71. No one from PI ushered the matter into the first stage of the formal recall process, the ISR, at this time. This approach represented a stark contrast even to the way in which the Defective Switch itself had been handled in 2005. Back then, *before* the dangerous connection to airbag non-deployment had been drawn, PI had promptly introduced the matter into the ISR.

72. In May 2012, the GM Safety Attorney asked a GM Vice President to act as an "Executive Champion" in order to propel the matter forward. During the first meeting

chaired by this Executive Champion, on May 15, 2012, the GM Electrical Engineer presented his view that the Defective Switch was the cause of non-deployment in the affected Cobalt models. Those in attendance included the GM Safety Attorney, the GM Safety Director, the PI Senior Manager, the PI Investigator, and others. The Executive Champion encouraged confirmation of this hypothesis through more scientific study.

73. Days later, on May 22, 2012, such confirmation was obtained. The GM Electrical Engineer, the PI Investigator, and others traveled once more to an auto salvage yard and, using equipment much more sophisticated than fish scales, conducted a thorough study of torque in the ignition switches of several model years of Cobalt, Ion, and other cars. The results confirmed that the majority of vehicles from model years 2003 through 2007 exhibited torque performance below the Torque Specification that GM had adopted in 2001. They also showed that starting somewhere in model year 2007 (that is, for vehicles produced at some point in 2006), the torque values were higher and within specification.

74. The observed discrepancy was, of course, due to the ignition switch part change that the Switch DRE had ordered in April 2006. But neither anyone from PI nor others working on the airbag non-deployment investigation in the spring of 2012 knew yet about that change; the part number was the same for the Defective Switch and the new one. Indeed, when the PI Investigator asked the Switch DRE in early 2012 to detail any changes that might account for the discrepancy observed at the salvage yard, the Switch DRE denied any of relevance. This was baffling to the PI Investigator and others.

75. Still, the engineers involved knew that studied cars built before a certain point in 2006 were equipped with low-torque ignition switches, and that low torque in an ignition switch could result in airbag non-deployment. At this no further engineering tests were conducted to explore any other purported root cause of the observed non-deployment pattern or to compare the 2005 through 2007 model year Cobalt ignition switches with those of later model years.

76. On June 12, 2012, three weeks after the May 2012 salvage yard expedition, an expert retained by the Virginia Crash plaintiffs issued a report. Noting both the 2005 Service Bulletin and the Indiana University study from 2007 that had identified a connection between the Defective Switch and non-deployment of an airbag in a fatal Cobalt crash, the expert opined that the Defective Switch was indeed responsible for non-deployment in the Virginia Crash. In early July, outside counsel for GM forwarded the Virginia Crash expert's report to the GM Airbag Attorney. In late July, the GM Airbag Attorney forwarded the Indiana University study to the PI Senior Manager, the GM Safety Attorney, and the Airbag FPA Engineer.

77. At a meeting among GM lawyers in late July 2012 in which the Virginia Crash expert's report was discussed, a newly hired GM attorney asked the group why the Cobalt had not been recalled for the Defective Switch. Those present explained that the engineers had yet to devise a solution to the problem but that engineering was looking into it. The new attorney took from this that the GM legal department had done all it could do.

78. The PI Investigator, the PI Senior Manager, the GM Safety Attorney, the GM Safety Director, and others met at lengthy intervals through the summer and fall of 2012 and early 2013 to consider potential solutions and further explore why the defect condition appeared to be limited to earlier model years. As one of the several Executive Champions who would be tasked with overseeing these meetings from early 2012 through 2013 has explained, the purpose of the meetings was *not* to identify the root cause of the problem, which had by approximately the spring of 2012 been traced to the Defective Switch, but rather to develop the optimal remedy for the defect condition and set with precision the scope of the anticipated recall. Certain GM personnel wanted to be sure that the fix adopted for the problem would be affordable and yet appeal to consumers; that GM would have sufficient parts on hand to address the recall; and that GM representatives would be able to fully articulate to NHTSA and the public a "complete root cause" accounting for the discrepancy between the earlier and later vehicle populations.

GM's Representations to NHTSA About Its Recall Process

79. At the same time, the manner in which the responsible GM personnel were approaching the Defective Switch and its deadly consequences in 2012 contrasted with the picture the Company was presenting to NHTSA about its recall process.

80. On October 22, 2012, certain GM personnel, including the GM Safety Director, met with NHTSA officials in Washington, D.C., and gave a description of the Company's recall process intended to assure the regulator that safety issues were routinely addressed in a methodical and efficient fashion. The presentation, which touted a "common global process" with "standard work templates," explained that the first step toward potential recall involved investigation by PI of the suspected safety problem. Then, according to the presentation, the matter would be placed promptly into the FPE [eds: Field Performance Evaluation] process, which was controlled not by engineers but by personnel in charge of Quality. At this stage, GM further explained, the FPET [eds: FPE Team] would consider the logistics of implementing the proposed recall or other contemplated action; the FPERC [eds: FPE Review Committee] would recommend the particular field action to be taken (recall or, for example, a customer advisory); and, in short order thereafter, the EFADC [eds: Executive Field Action Decision Committee] would either make the final decision concerning that recommended field action or order "further study." According to individuals who attended this meeting and others in 2012 and 2013, GM gave the impression that its recall process was linear, robust, uniform, and prompt.

81. To the extent this presentation may have accurately described GM's general recall process and handling of other defects, it did not accurately describe GM's handling of the Defective Switch (about which NHTSA would remain unaware until 2014). By approximately five months prior to this presentation, certain GM personnel had identified what they knew to be a dangerous safety defect and had not started it into the first phase of the recall process.[6]

GM Delays Recall After Learning of the 2006 Switch Change

82. By early 2013, the Defective Switch *still* had not been introduced into the FPE process. GM was exploring optimal remedies and trying to understand why the defect appeared to affect only a limited population. Those involved remained unaware of the part change that the Switch DRE had made back in April 2006-the change that explained why cars built after around late 2006 seemed not to be affected.

83. Meanwhile, during this same period, GM lawyers were engaged in heavy litigation related to the Georgia Crash, referenced above. The Georgia Crash plaintiffs' attorney had learned about the 2005 Service Bulletin, and had developed a theory that the Defective Switch caused the driver to lose control of her vehicle. The attorney was seeking discovery related to the bulletin and the Defective Switch more generally. He was also asking about any design changes that had been made to the switch.

84. GM denied that any such design changes had been made that would affect the amount of torque it takes to move the key from Run to Accessory.

85. Then, on April 29, 2013, the Georgia Crash plaintiffs' attorney took the deposition of the Switch DRE. During that deposition, the plaintiffs' attorney showed x-ray photographs of the ignition switch from the subject vehicle (the Defective Switch) and another switch from a later model year Cobalt (one installed after implementation of the Switch DRE's April 2006 part change directive). The photographs showed that the detent plunger in the Georgia Crash car was much shorter-and therefore would have had much lower torque performance-than the one in the later model year Cobalt. The Switch DRE, confronted with these photographs, continued to deny knowledge of any change to the switch that would have accounted for this difference.

86. But, as the Switch DRE has acknowledged, he knew almost immediately following his deposition that there had been a design change to the switch following production of the

---

[6] As NHTSA and GM understood, GM's regulatory obligation to disclose safety defects within five days of their discovery was an obligation of the Company and not of any individual employee. Indeed, as NHTSA further understood, neither the GM Safety Director nor any other GM employee was authorized to disclose a safety defect to NHTSA without a decision from the EFADC that such a defect existed.

model year 2005 Cobalt, and that he must have been the engineer responsible for that design change. He knew as much because, the day after the April 29, 2013 deposition, he personally collected and took apart switches from a 2005 Cobalt and a later model year Cobalt and observed the difference in lengths of their respective detent plungers.

87. The Switch DRE has said that he recalls communicating these observations to his boss and to another supervisor and being advised to let the legal department handle the matter.

88. The GM Safety Attorney learned what transpired during the Switch DRE's deposition. Having previously received a request from the PI group for retention of an outside expert (the "Switch Expert") to help determine why the Defective Switch seemed to affect only a limited vehicle population, the GM Safety Attorney, on or about May 2, 2013, authorized retention of the Switch Expert in connection with the Georgia Crash case. The PI Investigator and the PI Senior Manager did not participate in meetings with the Switch Expert until the Switch Expert presented his conclusions following the settlement of the Georgia Crash case. The PI Investigator understood that he was to put his own investigation on hold pending the Switch Expert's evaluation.

89. Of course, by the time the Switch Expert had been retained, certain GM personnel had already learned from the Georgia Crash plaintiffs' attorney about the design change to the Defective Switch, and the Switch DRE had already confirmed that the change had in fact occurred. GM thus had an explanation for why the defect condition did not appear to affect cars built after the middle of 2006. And, indeed, some within GM had known for approximately a year that a confirmed population of GM's compact cars was equipped with the Defective Switch. Yet still there was no recall; indeed, *still* there was no move to even place the matter into the FPE process. Instead, GM personnel awaited the study and conclusions of the Switch Expert.

90. Meanwhile, on June 22, 2013, a 23-year-old man was killed in a crash on a highway near Roxton Pond, Quebec after his 2007 Cobalt left the road and ran into some trees. The driver-side airbag in the Cobalt failed to deploy. The power mode status was recorded as Accessory.

GM Receives Documentary Evidence of the Part Change and Finally Begins the Recall Process

91. By July 2013, the Switch Expert had confirmed what the Georgia Crash plaintiffs' expert and the Switch DRE had known since no later than April 2013: Cobalts from model years 2008 through 2010 had longer detent plungers and springs than those from model years 2005 and 2006. GM's outside counsel in the Georgia Crash case urged GM in-house lawyers to settle it: "[T]here is little doubt that a jury here will find that the ignition switch used on [the Georgia Crash car] was defective and unreasonably dangerous, and

that it did not meet GM's own torque specifications. In addition, the [engineering inquiry documents about the Defective Switch from 2004 and 2005] and the on-going FPE investigation have enabled plaintiffs' counsel to develop a record from which he can compellingly argue that GM has known about this safety defect from the time the first 2005 Cobalts rolled off the assembly line and essentially has done nothing to correct the problem for the last nine years."

92. GM followed its outside counsel's advice and settled the Georgia Crash case at the end of August 2013, agreeing to pay $5 million.

93. Then, in late October 2013, GM received documentary confirmation from the Switch Supplier that the Switch DRE had in fact directed a part change to fix the Defective Switch in April 2006. This evidence further showed that the part was changed without a corresponding change to the part number.

94. Only at this point did GM finally place the Defective Switch matter into the formal FPE process. An ISR was scheduled for November 5, 2013. Meanwhile, on October 30, the PI Investigator, who was by now back working on the matter and helping to lay the practical groundwork for a recall, asked an employee in charge of ordering vehicle parts what the costs of new ignition switch components would be for the 2005 through 2007 Cobalts.

GM Makes Further Statements to NHTSA About Its Recall Process

95. On July 23, 2013, one day after GM's outside counsel had advised GM to settle the Georgia Crash case and noted that plaintiffs' counsel could make a "compelling" argument that GM "essentially has done nothing to correct" the Defective Switch "for the last nine years," the GM Safety Director received an email from NHTSA's Director of Defects Investigation accusing GM of being "slow to communicate" and "slow to act" in the face of safety defects- including defects unrelated to the Defective Switch (about which NHTSA remained unaware) but related to non-deployment of airbags.

96. Two days later, certain GM personnel, including the GM Safety Director, met with NHTSA to try to quell the agency's concerns. According to notes taken by the GM Safety Director at that meeting, NHTSA agreed with GM that the Company appeared to have a "robust and rigorous process" for evaluating and addressing safety issues, but worried that it "tend[ed] to focus on proving the issue [wa]s not a safety defect."

97. On November 7, 2013, two days after the ISR concerning the Defective Switch, certain GM personnel met again with NHTSA, this time to give a more in-depth presentation targeted at assuring the regulator that GM was "responsive" and "customer focused" when it came to safety concerns. Although the presentation did not specifically

address the Defective Switch-related airbag non-deployment problem-which, having just entered the recall process within GM, remained unknown to NHTSA-it did address concerns related to airbag non- deployment more generally.

98. First, certain GM personnel showed NHTSA slides that touted the increasing swiftness with which GM had addressed safety defects from 2008 through 2012. One graph reflected that the time taken from identification of the issue through to execution of the recall was 160 days in 2008 and 84 days in 2012. It further showed that the average time an issue remained in the "pre-FPE" stage was 105 days in 2008 and 33 days in 2012. And the average number of days between entry into the FPE process and recall decision was 15 days in 2008 and 13 days in 2012.

99. Other portions of GM's presentation suggested that any airbag defect that presented with a failure to warn the driver and/or certain other aggravating factors would be recalled swiftly.

GM Delays Recall for Three More Months

100. Although the Defective Switch matter entered the ISR on November 5, 2013, after approximately *804 days* of formal investigation, and although GM had at the November 7 meeting with NHTSA touted an average lag of just 13 days between entry into the FPE process and recall approval by the EFADC, GM would not ultimately decide to conduct a recall for the Defective Switch until January 31, 2014. The recall was announced to NHTSA seven days later, on February 7, 2014.

101. The individual principally responsible for shepherding the matter through the FPE process was GM's FPE Director, who worked closely with the GM Safety Director, the GM Safety Attorney, and a member of the EFADC responsible for deciding whether to recall.

102. As a general matter, EFADCs were scheduled weekly. The Defective Switch matter was initially contemplated for inclusion on the agenda of an EFADC scheduled for November 18. Citing the issue's "complex[ity]," however, an assistant to the FPE Director recommended-and the FPE Director agreed-that the matter be put off until an EFADC scheduled for December 3.

103. The matter did not go to the EFADC on December 3, however. Instead, it was pushed to December 17. On December 2, the FPE Director met with the GM Safety Director, the PI Investigator, the GM Safety Attorney, and a few others in yet another "offline" meeting to discuss the matter. Then, on December 16, the issue was the subject of an FPERC meeting that had been scheduled to occur right before the December 17 EFADC meeting.

104. After that meeting, the FPE Director expressed concern about "execution details" of the recall. She explained to one of the three EFADC decision-makers that "[t]he absolute last thing we need to do from a customer perspective is to rush a decision, post it on the NHTSA website that [sic] we have a safety decision but we cannot fix the customer vehicles for some period of time." The FPE Director informed this decision-maker that "we aren't ready for a decision" because there were "[t]oo many items on how we know how the fix will perform and the competitive solutions." The decision-maker pledged to "push [to] do additional follow up on this prior to a decision."

105. The EFADC meeting on December 17, 2013 yielded no decision, and further "study" was directed.

106. By this time, all involved understood-and some had for a period of time understood-that a Cobalt recall was inevitable.

107. Some within GM-including the GM Safety Director and the GM Safety Attorney-openly expressed concern about how the "timeline" of GM's response to the Defective Switch would look to NHTSA. As noted, a manufacturer must, under applicable regulations, report a known safety defect to NHTSA within five business days of its discovery. Here, certain GM personnel knew by approximately the spring of 2012 that the Defective Switch posed a serious safety issue because it disabled airbags in situations when they should have deployed. Yet more than a year and a half after that discovery, GM still had not conducted a recall.

Recall

108. On January 31, the voting members agreed that a recall of the affected model year Cobalts, G5s, and Pursuits was warranted. On February 7, 2014, GM announced the recall to the public and NHTSA.

109. Although other models-the Ion, most notably-were likewise equipped with the Defective Switch, these were not recalled on February 7. The stated reasons for not including these other models varied. Some believed there were differences in electronic architecture and physical switch placement between the unrecalled cars and the recalled cars, such that the risk of switch movement and/or airbag non-deployment was reduced. Others cited an error by the PI Investigator in collecting incident data about the Ion, which they said gave the erroneous impression that there was no comparable problem with the Ion.

110. In any event, following intense criticism from the press about the limited scope of the February 7 recall, GM held another EFADC meeting on February 24, 2014 to consider the affected model years of the Ion, Sky, HHR, and Solstice. Voting members agreed that

the February 7 recall should be expanded to encompass these other models. The next day, GM announced that decision.

GM's Certifications for Pre-Owned Vehicles

111. All of the cars subject to the February and March_ 2014 airbag non-deployment recalls were relatively old. GM stopped manufacturing the Ion in 2006; stopped manufacturing the Cobalt, the G5, the Sky, and the Solstice in 2009; and stopped manufacturing the HHR in 2010.

112. From in or about the spring of 2012, when certain GM personnel knew that the Defective Switch could cause airbag non-deployment, through at least in or about May of 2013, GM dealerships (which GM had not made aware of the issue) continued to sell "certified pre- owned" cars equipped with the Defective Switch. GM, which profited indirectly from these sales, certified the safety of the vehicles to the public, explaining that the certification process involved testing of over a hundred components, including, specifically, the ignition system.

113. But the safety certification was made despite there being no change or alteration to either the ignition switch itself or the accompanying key in these cars. The Defective Switch was left intact and unremedied.

114. Approximately 800 consumers purchased certified pre-owned vehicles equipped with the Defective Switch. The GM dealer certifications thus may have caused consumers who relied on the certifications to buy vehicles that they may incorrectly have believed to be safe.

Conclusion

115. As detailed above, starting no later than 2003, GM knowingly manufactured and sold several models of vehicles equipped with the Defective Switch. By approximately the spring of 2012, certain GM personnel knew that the Defective Switch could cause frontal airbag non- deployment in at least some model years of the Cobalt, and were aware of several fatal incidents and serious injuries that occurred as a result of accidents in which the Defective Switch may have caused or contributed to airbag non-deployment. This knowledge extended well above the ranks of investigating engineers to certain supervisors and attorneys at the Company-including GM's Safety Director and the GM Safety Attorney. Yet, GM overshot the five-day regulatory reporting requirement for safety defects by approximately 20 months. And throughout this 20-month period, GM failed to correct its 2005 statement that the Defective Switch posed no "safety" problem.

[...]

Part VII: 42

We have seen that U.S. corporate law focuses on protecting only shareholders, rather than all stakeholders — with some very limited protections for creditors. In fact, U.S. corporate law, at least the Delaware variety, contains few rules, period. Further, even those few rules can mostly be abrogated or circumvented in a corporation's charter. This lack of strict rules is why this course mainly focuses on fiduciary duties and the occasional shareholder approval requirement.

In sum, Delaware corporate law does little more than **enable** charter contracting by supplying default terms, gap-filling (?) fiduciary duties, and, importantly, an able judiciary to enforce these terms and duties. By contrast, corporate law outside the U.S. tends to be much more rule based. We have seen one example in UK takeover law. This raises questions: Why is U.S. corporate law as liberal as it is? Is this liberality a good thing?

U.S. corporate law's liberality and lack of concern for non-shareholder constituencies are intimately related to the rise of Delaware as the foremost state of incorporation. Delaware attracts so many corporate charters mainly because "foreign corporations" — corporations with few or even no operations in Delaware — can opt to be governed by Delaware law as long as they incorporate in Delaware. That is, Delaware's prominence is predicated on a choice of law rule. Under the "internal affairs doctrine" the applicable corporate law is the law of the state of incorporation. This doctrine undergirds Delaware's business of "competing for corporate charters." Such competition would not be possible if the applicable corporate law were, for example, the law of the state of the corporation's headquarters, as it is in many non-U.S. jurisdictions.

Charter competition treats corporate law as a product. That is, corporate law appears not as regulation, but as a service to contracting parties organizing a business. The "contract" consists of the charter terms and the applicable corporate law. The contracting parties, in a narrow sense, are those involved in drafting the charter. In a broader sense, the contracting parties include all those who *voluntarily* interact with the corporation, such as shareholders. To be sure, their agreement to the charter terms is not literally required. But they have the option not to interact, to charge higher prices, to invest less money, and so on, if the charter terms displease them. In anticipation of these options, the drafters of the charter have strong incentives to take these other parties' concerns into account. Or so the argument goes.

Such reliance on private contracting has indeed been the hallmark of U.S. state corporate law (but not federal securities law) for many decades. It complements the internal affairs doctrine in two ways. First, confidence in private contracting provides a normative underpinning for free choice of corporate law. Second, any restrictions on private contracting imposed by an individual state could be easily circumvented by (re-)incorporating in another state. Do you think this deference to private contracting is appropriate?

Chapter 16. Choice of Law: The Internal Affairs Doctrine

The "internal affairs doctrine" is a choice of law rule that applies the law of the state of incorporation to the corporation's "internal affairs."

While many in the U.S. treat the internal affairs doctrine as self-evident, other countries frequently insist on applying their corporate law to all corporations that have their headquarters in that country, or some other substantial connection to that country. Such insistence on a substantial connection is no stranger to U.S. choice of law. In fact, for most contracts, U.S. courts generally refuse to apply "[t]he law of the state chosen by the parties to govern their contractual rights and duties" if "the chosen state has no substantial relationship to the parties or the transaction and there is no other reasonable basis for the parties choice," *see* Restatement of the Law (2nd) Conflict of Laws § 187(2)(a). U.S. courts will, however, enforce any chosen state's corporate law under the internal affairs doctrine.

The internal affairs doctrine allowed corporations to migrate away from states that imposed restrictions. Again, "migration" is a mere figure of speech — no people or assets need to move out of state to avoid that state's corporate law. Mere reincorporation in another state is sufficient.

Nowadays this issue is mostly discussed in connection with shareholder rights. In recent decades, commentators have been intensely debating whether Delaware's enabling approach to shareholder rights is the result of a "race to the top" or a "race to the bottom" from the perspective of the *shareholder/manager* relationship. But Delaware actually became a major corporate domicile only because other states *tried* to protect *non-shareholder* constituencies through corporate law. In particular, in an attempt to combat "trusts," a/k/a cartels, first New York and then other industrialized states in the late 19th and early 20th century prohibited holding companies — that is, it prohibited its corporations from owning stock in other corporations. In response, corporations migrated to more permissive states, eventually coming to rest in Delaware. They have stayed there ever since. The issue of "trusts" was left to federal antitrust law.

In general, regulatory competition may work for the contracting parties writ large. As previously indicated, this group includes all those who voluntarily interact with the corporation. But regulatory competition clearly does not address the concerns of third parties, such as tort creditors or the general public. To the extent that these groups are affected by corporate law, regulatory competition is apt to generate negative externalities. Such externalities would then require federal intervention, such as the federal antitrust and securities laws.

Are negative externalities a real problem in corporate law, or a negligible quibble? The answer depends on two related issues: First, the scope of the internal affairs doctrine. The fewer rules the doctrine covers, the less potential for externalities. As its name implies, the internal affairs doctrine covers internal organizational rules, but the details can be tricky, as *Lidow* illustrates.

Second, do third parties really need the protection of rules covered by the internal affairs doctrine? After all, tort victims are already protected by tort law, the environment is protected by environmental statutes and so on. Nevertheless, additional protection through organizational law may be required. The reason is that this other law is imperfect, owing to the limits of both the political process and of law's capacity to regulate human affairs. Hence societies must rely on non-legal norms to regulate most human interaction. However, the corporate context may interfere with the operation of non-legal norms, be it by diffusing responsibility, by suppressing internalized norms, or by some other mechanism. Do we need to insist on some mandatory internal corporate structure to avoid "sociopathic" corporate behavior? Or to take a more positive view, does organizational law provide opportunities for "mandatory betterment" that would be infeasible or unethical for individuals?

Questions

1. For example, should we impose co-determination or affirmative action for boards? Until recently, this happened only in Europe. In 2018, however, California adopted a bill that requires all publicly traded corporations headquartered in California to have between one quarter and one half female directors, depending on board size, beginning in 2020.

If one concludes that externalities from corporate law are a real problem, then one should wonder why states accept the internal affairs doctrine. It is often said, especially in Delaware, that the U.S. Constitution enshrines the internal affairs doctrine; *CTS* is usually cited as support. *See, e.g., VantagePoint* below. Read *CTS* and judge for yourself.

A. CTS v. Dynamics (U.S. 1987)

This decision upheld Indiana's version of DGCL 203 against constitutional challenge. In the 1980s, most states passed some form of an anti-takeover statute. They were hotly politically contested, as you might infer from the heated debate between the Justices and the various amici.

In *Edgar v. MITE* (1982), a plurality of the Supreme Court struck down an Illinois law that purported to apply to any tender offer for shares of a "corporation or other issuer of securities of which shareholders located in Illinois own 10% of the class of equity securities subject to the offer, or for which any two of the following three conditions are met: the corporation (1) has its principal executive office in Illinois, (2) is organized under the laws of Illinois, or (3) has at least 10% of its stated capital and paid-in surplus represented within the State," 457 U.S. 624, 627 (1982).

The Indiana statute at issue here in *CTS* is different as it applies only to corporations chartered in Indiana. Does this fact or anything else in the decision imply that the internal affairs doctrine is enshrined in the U.S. Constitution?

481 U.S. 69 (1987)

CTS CORP.

v.

DYNAMICS CORPORATION OF AMERICA

[...]

JUSTICE POWELL delivered the opinion of the Court.

These cases present the questions whether the Control Share Acquisitions Chapter of the Indiana Business Corporation Law, Ind. Code § 23-1-42-1 *et seq.* (Supp. 1986), is preempted by the Williams Act, 82 Stat. 454, as amended, 15 U. S. C. §§ 78m(d)-(e) and 78n(d)-(f) (1982 ed. and Supp. III), [eds: i.e., sections 13(d)-(e) and 14(d)-(f) of the Securities Exchange Act of 1934, as amended in 1968] or violates the Commerce Clause of the Federal Constitution, Art. I, § 8, cl. 3.

I

A

On March 4, 1986, the Governor of Indiana signed a revised Indiana Business Corporation Law, Ind. Code § 23-1-17-1 *et seq.* (Supp. 1986). That law included the Control Share Acquisitions Chapter (Indiana Act or Act). Beginning on August 1, 1987, the Act will apply to any corporation incorporated in Indiana, § 23-1-17-3(a), unless the corporation amends its articles of incorporation or bylaws to opt out of the Act, § 23-1-42-5. Before that date, any Indiana corporation can opt into the Act by resolution of its board of directors. § 23-1-17-3(b). The Act applies only to "issuing [73] public corporations." The term "corporation" includes only businesses incorporated in Indiana. See § 23-1-20-5. An "issuing public corporation" is defined as:

> "a corporation that has:
>
> "(1) one hundred (100) or more shareholders;
>
> "(2) its principal place of business, its principal office, or substantial assets within Indiana; and
>
> "(3) either:
>
> "(A) more than ten percent (10%) of its shareholders resident in Indiana;
>
> "(B) more than ten percent (10%) of its shares owned by Indiana residents; or
>
> "(C) ten thousand (10,000) shareholders resident in Indiana." § 23-1-42-4(a).

The Act focuses on the acquisition of "control shares" in an issuing public corporation. Under the Act, an entity acquires "control shares" whenever it acquires shares that, but for the operation of the Act, would bring its voting power in the corporation to or above any of three thresholds: 20%, 33 1/3%, or 50%. § 23-1-42-1. An entity that acquires control shares does not necessarily acquire voting rights. Rather, it gains those rights only "to the extent granted by resolution approved by the shareholders of the issuing public corporation." § 23-1-42-9(a). Section 23-1-42-9(b) requires a majority vote of all disinterested shareholders holding each [74] class of stock for passage of such a resolution. The practical effect of this requirement is to condition acquisition of control of a corporation on approval of a majority of the pre-existing disinterested shareholders.

The shareholders decide whether to confer rights on the control shares at the next regularly scheduled meeting of the shareholders, or at a specially scheduled meeting. The [75] acquiror can require management of the corporation to hold such a special meeting within 50 days if it files an "acquiring person statement," requests the meeting, and agrees to pay the expenses of the meeting. See § 23-1-42-7. If the shareholders do not vote to restore voting rights to the shares, the corporation may redeem the control shares from the acquiror at fair market value, but it is not required to do so. § 23-1-42-10(b).

Similarly, if the acquiror does not file an acquiring person statement with the corporation, the corporation may, if its bylaws or articles of incorporation so provide, redeem the shares at any time after 60 days after the acquiror's last acquisition. § 23-1-42-10(a).

[...]

II

The first question in these cases is whether the Williams Act pre-empts the Indiana Act. As we have stated frequently, absent an explicit indication by Congress of an intent to pre-empt state law, a state statute is pre-empted only [79]

> "'where compliance with both federal and state regulations is a physical impossibility ... ,' *Florida Lime & Avocado Growers, Inc.* v. *Paul,* 373 U. S. 132, 142-143 (1963), or where the state "law stands as an obstacle to the accomplishment and execution of the full purposes and objectives of Congress.' *Hines* v. *Davidowitz,* 312 U. S. 52, 67 (1941) ... ." *Ray* v. *Atlantic Richfield Co.,* 435 U. S. 151, 158 (1978).

Because it is entirely possible for entities to comply with both the Williams Act and the Indiana Act, the state statute can be pre-empted only if it frustrates the purposes of the federal law. [...]

Our discussion begins with a brief summary of the structure and purposes of the Williams Act. Congress passed the Williams Act in 1968 in response to the increasing number of hostile tender offers. Before its passage, these transactions were not covered by the disclosure requirements of the federal securities laws. See *Piper* v. *Chris-Craft Industries, Inc.,* 430 U. S. 1, 22 (1977). The Williams Act, backed by regulations of the SEC, imposes requirements in two basic areas. First, it requires the offeror to file a statement disclosing information about the offer, including: the offeror's background and identity; the source and amount of the funds to be used in making the purchase; the purpose of the purchase, including any plans to liquidate the company or make major changes in its corporate structure; and the extent of the offeror's holdings in the target company. See 15 U. S. C. § 78n(d)(1) (incorporating § 78m(d)(1) by reference); 17 CFR §§ 240.13d-1, 240.14d-3 (1986).

Second, the Williams Act, and the regulations that accompany it, establish procedural rules to govern tender offers. For example, stockholders who tender their shares may withdraw them while the offer remains open, and, if the offeror has not purchased their shares, any time after 60 days from commencement of the offer. 15 U. S. C. § 78n(d)(5); 17 [80] CFR § 240.14d-7(a)(1) (1986), as amended, 51 Fed. Reg. 25873 (1986). The offer must remain open for at least 20 business days. 17 CFR § 240.14e-1(a) (1986). If more shares are tendered than the offeror sought to purchase, purchases must be made on a pro rata basis from each tendering shareholder. 15 U. S. C. § 78n(d)(6); 17 CFR § 240.14(8) (1986). Finally, the offeror must pay the same price for all purchases; if the offering price is increased before the end of the offer, those who already have tendered must receive the benefit of the increased price. § 78n(d)(7). [...]

[T]he statute now before the Court protects the independent shareholder against the contending parties. Thus, the Act furthers a basic purpose of the Williams Act, " "plac[ing] investors on an equal footing with the takeover bidder,' [...]

The Court of Appeals based its finding of pre-emption on its view that the practical effect of the Indiana Act is to delay consummation of tender offers until 50 days after the commencement of the offer. [...] This, it argues, conflicts with the shorter 20-business-day period established by the SEC as the minimum period for which a tender offer may be held open. 17 CFR § 240.14e-1 (1986). We find the alleged conflict illusory.

The Act does not impose an absolute 50-day delay on tender offers, nor does it preclude an offeror from purchasing shares as soon as federal law permits. If the offeror fears an adverse shareholder vote under the Act, it can make a conditional tender offer, offering to accept shares on the condition that the shares receive voting rights within a certain period of time. [...]

Finally, we note that the Williams Act would pre-empt a variety of state corporate laws of hitherto unquestioned validity if it were construed to pre-empt any state statute that may limit or delay the free exercise of power after a successful tender offer. State corporate laws commonly permit corporations to stagger the terms of their directors. [...]

In our view, the possibility that the Indiana Act will delay some tender offers is insufficient to require a conclusion that the Williams Act pre-empts the Act. The longstanding prevalence of state regulation in this area suggests that, if Congress had intended to pre-empt all state laws that delay the acquisition of voting control following a tender offer, it would have said so explicitly. The regulatory conditions that the Act places on tender offers are consistent with the text and the purposes of the Williams Act. Accordingly, we [87] hold that the Williams Act does not pre-empt the Indiana Act.

III

As an alternative basis for its decision, the Court of Appeals held that the Act violates the Commerce Clause of the Federal Constitution. We now address this holding. On its face, the Commerce Clause is nothing more than a grant to Congress of the power "[t]o regulate Commerce ... among the several States ... ," Art. I, § 8, cl. 3. But it has been settled for more than a century that the Clause prohibits States from taking certain actions respecting interstate commerce even absent congressional action. See, *e. g., Cooley* v.

Board of Wardens, 12 How. 299 (1852). The Court's interpretation of "these great silences of the Constitution," *H. P. Hood & Sons, Inc.* v. *Du Mond,* 336 U. S. 525, 535 (1949), has not always been easy to follow. Rather, as the volume and complexity of commerce and regulation have grown in this country, the Court has articulated a variety of tests in an attempt to describe the difference between those regulations that the Commerce Clause permits and those regulations that it prohibits. See, *e. g., Raymond Motor Transportation, Inc.* v. *Rice,* 434 U. S. 429, 441, n. 15 (1978).

A

The principal objects of dormant Commerce Clause scrutiny are statutes that discriminate against interstate commerce. [...] The Indiana Act is not such a statute. It has the same effects on tender offers whether or not the offeror is a domiciliary or resident of Indiana. Thus, it "visits its effects equally upon both interstate and local business," [...]

B

This Court's recent Commerce Clause cases also have invalidated statutes that may adversely affect interstate commerce by subjecting activities to inconsistent regulations. *E. g., Brown-Forman Distillers Corp.* v. *New York State Liquor Authority,* 476 U. S. 573, 583-584 (1986); *Edgar* v. *MITE Corp.,* 457 U. S., at 642 (plurality opinion of WHITE, J.); *Kassel* v. *Consolidated Freightways Corp.,* 450 U. S. 662, 671 (1981) (plurality opinion of POWELL, J.). See *Southern Pacific Co.* v. *Arizona,* 325 U. S. 761, 774 (1945) (noting the "confusion and difficulty" that would attend the "unsatisfied need for uniformity" in setting maximum limits on train lengths); *Cooley* v. *Board of Wardens, supra,* at 319 (stating that the Commerce Clause prohibits States from regulating [89] subjects that "are in their nature national, or admit only of one uniform system, or plan of regulation"). The Indiana Act poses no such problem. So long as each State regulates voting rights only in the corporations it has created, each corporation will be subject to the law of only one State. No principle of corporation law and practice is more firmly established than a State's authority to regulate domestic corporations, including the authority to define the voting rights of shareholders. See Restatement (Second) of Conflict of Laws § 304 (1971) (concluding that the law of the incorporating State generally should "determine the right of a shareholder to participate in the administration of the affairs of the corporation"). Accordingly, we conclude that the Indiana Act does not create an impermissible risk of inconsistent regulation by different States.

C

The Court of Appeals did not find the Act unconstitutional for either of these threshold reasons. Rather, its decision rested on its view of the Act's potential to hinder tender offers. We think the Court of Appeals failed to appreciate the significance for Commerce Clause analysis of the fact that state regulation of corporate governance is regulation of entities whose very existence and attributes are a product of state law. As Chief Justice Marshall explained:

> "A corporation is an artificial being, invisible, intangible, and existing only in contemplation of law. Being the mere creature of law, it possesses only those properties which the charter of its creation confers upon it, either expressly, or as incidental to its very existence. These are such as are supposed best calculated to effect the object for which it was created." *Trustees of Dartmouth College* v. *Woodward*, 4 Wheat. 518, 636 (1819).

See *First National Bank of Boston* v. *Bellotti*, 435 U. S. 765, 822-824 (1978) (REHNQUIST, J., dissenting). Every State in this country has enacted laws regulating corporate governance. [90] By prohibiting certain transactions, and regulating others, such laws necessarily affect certain aspects of interstate commerce. [...]

[91] It thus is an accepted part of the business landscape in this country for States to create corporations, to prescribe their powers, and to define the rights that are acquired by purchasing their shares. A State has an interest in promoting stable relationships among parties involved in the corporations it charters, as well as in ensuring that investors in such corporations have an effective voice in corporate affairs.

There can be no doubt that the Act reflects these concerns. The primary purpose of the Act is to protect the shareholders of Indiana corporations. It does this by affording shareholders, when a takeover offer is made, an opportunity to decide collectively whether the resulting change in voting control of the corporation, as they perceive it, would be desirable. A change of management may have important effects on the shareholders' interests; it is well within the State's role as overseer of corporate governance to offer this opportunity. The autonomy provided by allowing shareholders collectively to determine whether the takeover is advantageous to their [92] interests may be especially beneficial where a hostile tender offer may coerce shareholders into tendering their shares. [...]

[93] Dynamics argues in any event that the State has " 'no legitimate interest in protecting the nonresident shareholders.' " Brief for Appellee 21 (quoting *Edgar* v. *MITE Corp.*, 457 U. S., at 644). Dynamics relies heavily on the statement by the *MITE* Court that "[i]nsofar as the ... law burdens out-of-state transactions, there is nothing to be weighed in the balance to sustain the law." 457 U. S., at 644. But that comment was made in reference to an Illinois law that applied as well to out-of-state corporations as to in-state corporations. We agree that Indiana has no interest in protecting nonresident shareholders *of nonresident corporations*. But this Act applies only to corporations incorporated in Indiana. We reject the contention that Indiana has no interest in providing for the shareholders of its corporations the voting autonomy granted by the Act. Indiana has a

substantial interest in preventing the corporate form from becoming a shield for unfair business dealing. Moreover, unlike the Illinois statute invalidated in *MITE,* the Indiana Act applies only to corporations that have a substantial number of shareholders in Indiana. See Ind. Code § 23-1-42-4(a)(3) (Supp. 1986). Thus, every application of the Indiana Act will affect a substantial number of Indiana residents, whom Indiana indisputably has an interest in protecting.

D

Dynamics' argument that the Act is unconstitutional ultimately rests on its contention that the Act will limit the number of successful tender offers. There is little evidence that this will occur. But even if true, this result would not substantially affect our Commerce Clause analysis. We reiterate that this Act does not prohibit any entity — resident or nonresident — from offering to purchase, or from purchasing, shares in Indiana corporations, or from attempting thereby to gain control. It only provides regulatory procedures designed for the better protection of the corporations' shareholders. We have rejected the "notion that the Commerce [94] Clause protects the particular structure or methods of operation in a … market." *Exxon Corp.* v. *Governor of Maryland,* 437 U. S., at 127. The very commodity that is traded in the securities market is one whose characteristics are defined by state law. Similarly, the very commodity that is traded in the "market for corporate control" — the corporation — is one that owes its existence and attributes to state law. Indiana need not define these commodities as other States do; it need only provide that residents and nonresidents have equal access to them. This Indiana has done. Accordingly, even if the Act should decrease the number of successful tender offers for Indiana corporations, this would not offend the Commerce Clause.

IV

On its face, the Indiana Control Share Acquisitions Chapter evenhandedly determines the voting rights of shares of Indiana corporations. The Act does not conflict with the provisions or purposes of the Williams Act. To the limited extent that the Act affects interstate commerce, this is justified by the State's interests in defining the attributes of shares in its corporations and in protecting shareholders. Congress has never questioned the need for state regulation of these matters. Nor do we think such regulation offends the Constitution. Accordingly, we reverse the judgment of the Court of Appeals.

It is so ordered.

JUSTICE SCALIA, concurring in part and concurring in the judgment.

I join Parts I, III-A, and III-B of the Court's opinion. However, having found, as those Parts do, that the Indiana [95] Control Share Acquisitions Chapter neither "discriminates against interstate commerce," *ante,* at 88, nor "create[s] an impermissible risk of inconsistent regulation by different States," *ante*, at 89, I would conclude without further analysis that it is not invalid under the dormant Commerce Clause. While it has become standard practice at least since *Pike* v. *Bruce Church, Inc.*, 397 U. S. 137 (1970), to consider, in addition to these factors, whether the burden on commerce imposed by a state statute "is clearly excessive in relation to the putative local benefits," *id.*, at 142, such an inquiry is ill suited to the judicial function and should be undertaken rarely if at all. This case is a good illustration of the point. Whether the control shares statute "protects shareholders of Indiana corporations," Brief for Appellant in No. 86-97, p. 88, or protects incumbent management seems to me a highly debatable question, but it is extraordinary to think that the constitutionality of the Act should depend on the answer. [...]

I also agree with the Court that the Indiana Control Share Acquisitions Chapter is not pre-empted by the Williams Act, but I reach that conclusion without entering into the debate over the purposes of the two statutes. [...]

I do not share the Court's apparent high estimation of the beneficence of the state statute at issue here. But a law can [97] be both economic folly and constitutional. The Indiana Control Share Acquisitions Chapter is at least the latter. I therefore concur in the judgment of the Court.

JUSTICE WHITE, with whom JUSTICE BLACKMUN and JUSTICE STEVENS join as to Part II, dissenting.

The majority today upholds Indiana's Control Share Acquisitions Chapter, a statute which will predictably foreclose completely some tender offers for stock in Indiana corporations. I disagree with the conclusion that the Chapter is neither pre-empted by the Williams Act nor in conflict with the Commerce Clause. The Chapter undermines the policy of the Williams Act by effectively preventing minority shareholders, in some circumstances, from acting in their own best interests by selling their stock. In addition, the Chapter will substantially burden the interstate market in corporate ownership, particularly if other States follow Indiana's lead as many already have done. The Chapter, therefore, directly inhibits interstate commerce, the very economic consequences the Commerce Clause was intended to prevent. The opinion of the Court of Appeals is far more persuasive than that of the majority today, and the judgment of that court should be affirmed. [...]

B. VantagePoint v. Examen Inc. (Del. 2005)

This Delaware case deals with the only sustained challenge to the internal affairs doctrine in the U.S.: section 2115 of the California Corporations Code.

Questions

1. By its own terms, does section 2115 apply in this case?

2. Why does the Delaware Supreme Court not apply section 2115?

3. Does the Delaware Supreme Court hold that the internal affairs doctrine is embodied in the U.S. constitution?

4. What is better for Delaware's business – section 2115 or strict adherence to the internal affairs doctrine?

5. As a policy matter, did the party arguing for application of section 2115, VantagePoint, deserve its protection in this case?

871 A.2d 1108 (2005)

VANTAGEPOINT VENTURE PARTNERS 1996, a Delaware limited partnership, Defendant Below, Appellant,

v.

EXAMEN, INC., a Delaware corporation, Plaintiff Below, Appellee.

No. 127, 2005.

Supreme Court of Delaware.

Submitted: April 13, 2005.

Decided: May 5, 2005.

J. Travis Laster, Brock E. Czeschin, Philippe Y. Blanchard, Richards, Layton & Finger, Wilmington, DE, for appellant.

Martin P. Tully, David J. Teklits, and Thomas W. Briggs, Jr., Morris, Nichols, Arsht & Tunnell, Wilmington, DE, for appellee.

Before STEELE, Chief Justice, HOLLAND and JACOBS, Justices. [1109]

HOLLAND, Justice:

This is an expedited appeal from the Court of Chancery following the entry of a final judgment on the pleadings. We have concluded that the judgment must be affirmed.

Delaware Action

On March 3, 2005, the plaintiff-appellee, Examen, Inc. ("Examen"), filed a Complaint in the Court of Chancery against VantagePoint Venture Partners, Inc. ("VantagePoint"), a Delaware Limited Partnership and an Examen Series A Preferred shareholder, seeking a judicial declaration that pursuant to the controlling Delaware law and under the Company's Certificate of Designations of Series A Preferred Stock ("Certificate of Designations"), VantagePoint was not entitled to a class vote of the Series A Preferred Stock on the proposed merger between Examen and a Delaware subsidiary of Reed Elsevier Inc.

California Action

On March 8, 2005, VantagePoint filed an action in the California Superior Court seeking: (1) a declaration that Examen was required to identify whether it was a "quasi-California corporation" under section 2115 of the California Corporations Code; (2) a declaration that Examen was [1110] a quasi-California corporation pursuant to California Corporations Code section 2115 and therefore subject to California Corporations Code section 1201(a), and that, as a Series A Preferred shareholder, VantagePoint was entitled to vote its shares as a separate class in connection with the proposed merger; (3) injunctive relief; and (4) damages incurred as the result of alleged violations of California Corporations Code sections 2111(F) and 1201.

Delaware Action Decided

On March 10, 2005, the Court of Chancery granted Examen's request for an expedited hearing on its motion for judgment on the pleadings. On March 21, 2005, the California Superior Court stayed its action pending the ruling of the Court of Chancery. On March 29, 2005, the Court of Chancery ruled that the case was governed by the internal affairs doctrine as explicated by this Court in *McDermott v. Lewis*. In applying that doctrine, the Court of Chancery held that Delaware law governed the vote that was required to approve a merger between two Delaware corporate entities.

On April 1, 2005, VantagePoint filed a notice of appeal with this Court. On April 4, 2005, VantagePoint sought to enjoin the merger from closing pending its appeal. On April 5, 2005, this Court denied VantagePoint's request to enjoin the merger from closing, but granted its request for an expedited appeal [eds: to address the question of post-closing damages].

Facts

Examen was a Delaware corporation engaged in the business of providing web-[1111] based legal expense management solutions to a growing list of Fortune 1000 customers throughout the United States. Following consummation of the merger on April 5, 2005, LexisNexis Examen, also a Delaware corporation, became the surviving entity. VantagePoint is a Delaware Limited Partnership organized and existing under the laws of Delaware. VantagePoint, a major venture capital firm that purchased Examen Series A Preferred Stock in a negotiated transaction, owned eighty-three percent of Examen's outstanding Series A Preferred Stock (909,091 shares) and no shares of Common Stock.

On February 17, 2005, Examen and Reed Elsevier executed the Merger Agreement, which was set to expire on April 15, 2005, if the merger had not closed by that date. Under the Delaware General Corporation Law and Examen's Certificate of Incorporation, including the Certificate of Designations for the Series A Preferred Stock, adoption of the Merger Agreement required the affirmative vote of the holders of a majority of the issued and outstanding shares of the Common Stock and Series A Preferred Stock, *voting together as a single class.* Holders of Series A Preferred Stock had the number of votes equal to the number of shares of Common Stock they would have held if their Preferred Stock was converted. Thus, VantagePoint, which owned 909,091 shares of Series A Preferred Stock and no shares of Common Stock, was entitled to vote based on a converted number of 1,392,727 shares of stock.

There were 9,717,415 total outstanding shares of the Company's capital stock (8,626,826 shares of Common Stock and 1,090,589 shares of Series A Preferred Stock), representing 10,297,608 votes on an as-converted basis. An affirmative vote of at least 5,148,805 shares, constituting a majority of the outstanding voting power on an as-converted basis, was required to approve the merger. If the stockholders were to vote by class, VantagePoint would have controlled 83.4 percent of the Series A Preferred Stock, which would have permitted VantagePoint to block the merger. VantagePoint acknowledges that, if Delaware law applied, it would not have a class vote.

[...]

Internal Affairs Doctrine

In *CTS Corp. v. Dynamics Corp. of Am.,* the United States Supreme Court stated that it is "an accepted part of the business landscape in this country for States to create corporations, to prescribe their powers, and to define the rights that are acquired by purchasing their shares." In *CTS,* it was also recognized that "[a] State has an interest in promoting stable relationships among parties involved in the corporations it charters, as well as in ensuring that investors in such corporations have an effective voice in corporate affairs." The internal affairs doctrine is a long-standing choice of law principle which recognizes that only one state should have the authority to regulate a corporation's internal affairs — the state of incorporation.

The internal affairs doctrine developed on the premise that, in order to prevent corporations from being subjected to inconsistent legal standards, the authority to regulate a corporation's internal affairs should not rest with multiple jurisdictions. [1113] It is now well established that only the law of the state of incorporation governs and determines issues relating to a corporation's internal affairs. By providing certainty and predictability, the internal affairs doctrine protects the justified expectations of the parties with interests in the corporation.

The internal affairs doctrine applies to those matters that pertain to the relationships among or between the corporation and its officers, directors, and shareholders. The Restatement (Second) of Conflict of Laws § 301 provides: "application of the local law of the state of incorporation will usually be supported by those choice-of-law factors favoring the need of the interstate and international systems, certainty, predictability and uniformity of result, protection of the justified expectations of the parties and ease in the application of the law to be applied." Accordingly, the conflicts practice of both state and federal courts has consistently been to apply the law of the state of incorporation to "the entire gamut of internal corporate affairs."

The internal affairs doctrine is not, however, only a conflicts of law principle. Pursuant to the Fourteenth Amendment Due Process Clause, directors and officers of corporations "have a significant right ... to know what law will be applied to their actions" and "[s]tockholders ... have a right to know by what standards of accountability they may hold those managing the corporation's business and affairs." Under the Commerce Clause, a state "has no interest in regulating the internal affairs of foreign corporations." Therefore, this Court has held that an "application of the internal affairs doctrine is mandated by constitutional principles, except in the "rarest situations,'" *e.g.,* when "the law of the state of incorporation is inconsistent with a national policy on foreign or interstate commerce."

California Section 2115

[...] Section 2115 [...] requires certain foreign corporations to conform to a broad range of internal affairs provisions. Section 2115 defines the foreign corporations for which the California statute has an outreach effect as those foreign [1114] corporations, half of whose voting securities are held of record by persons with California addresses, that also conduct half of their business in California as measured by a formula weighing assets, sales and payroll factors.

[...] If the factual conditions precedent for triggering section 2115 are established, many aspects of a corporation's internal affairs are purportedly governed by California corporate law to the exclusion of the law of the state of incorporation.[22]

In her comprehensive analysis of the internal affairs doctrine, Professor Deborah A. DeMott examined section 2115. As she astutely points out:

> In contrast to the certainty with which the state of incorporation may be determined, the criteria upon which the applicability of section 2115 hinges are not constants. For example, whether half of a corporation's business is derived from California and whether half of its voting securities have record holders with California addresses may well vary from year to year (and indeed throughout any given year). Thus, a corporation might be subject to section 2115 one year but not the next, depending on its situation at the time of filing the annual statement required by section 2108.

Internal Affairs Require Uniformity

In *McDermott*, this Court noted that application of local internal affairs law (here California's section 2115) to a foreign corporation (here Delaware) is "apt to produce inequalities, intolerable confusion, and uncertainty, and intrude into the domain of other states that have a superior claim to regulate the same subject matter [1115] ...." Professor DeMott's review of the differences and conflicts between the Delaware and California corporate statutes with regard to internal affairs, illustrates why it is imperative that only the law of the state of incorporation regulate the relationships among a corporation and its officers, directors, and shareholders. To require a factual determination to decide which of two conflicting state laws governs the internal affairs of a corporation at any point in time, completely contravenes the importance of stability within inter-corporate relationships that the United States Supreme Court recognized in *CTS*.

---

[22] If Section 2115 applies, California law is deemed to control the following: the annual election of directors; removal of directors without cause; removal of directors by court proceedings; the filing of director vacancies where less than a majority in office are elected by shareholders; the director's standard of care; the liability of directors for unlawful distributions; indemnification of directors, officers, and others; limitations on corporate distributions in cash or property; the liability of shareholders who receive unlawful distributions; the requirement for annual shareholders' meetings and remedies for the same if not timely held; shareholder's entitlement to cumulative voting; the conditions when a supermajority vote is required; limitations on the sale of assets; limitations on mergers; limitations on conversions; requirements on conversions; the limitations and conditions for reorganization (including the requirement for class voting); dissenter's rights; records and reports; actions by the Attorney General and inspection rights. *See* Cal. Corp.Code § 2115(b) (1977 & Supp.1984).

[...]

State Law of Incorporation Governs Internal Affairs

In *McDermott*, this Court held that the "internal affairs doctrine is a major tenet of Delaware corporation law having important federal constitutional underpinnings." Applying Delaware's well-established choice-of-law rule — the internal affairs doctrine — the Court of Chancery recognized that Delaware courts must apply the law of the state of incorporation to issues involving corporate internal affairs, and that disputes concerning a shareholder's right to vote fall squarely within the purview of the internal affairs doctrine.

Examen is a Delaware corporation. The legal issue in this case — whether a [1116] preferred shareholder of a Delaware corporation had the right, under the corporation's Certificate of Designations, to a Series A Preferred Stock class vote on a merger — clearly involves the relationship among a corporation and its shareholders. As the United States Supreme Court held in *CTS*, "[n]o principle of corporation law and practice is more firmly established than a *State's authority* to regulate domestic corporations, including the authority to *define the voting rights of shareholders.*"

In *CTS*, the Supreme Court held that the Commerce Clause "prohibits States from regulating subjects that 'are in their nature national, or admit only of one uniform system, or plan of regulation,'" and acknowledged that the internal affairs of a corporation are subjects that require one uniform system of regulation. In *CTS*, the Supreme Court concluded that "[s]o long as each State regulates voting rights *only in the corporations it has created,* each corporation will be subject to the law of only one State." Accordingly, we hold Delaware's well-established choice of law rules and the federal constitution mandated that Examen's internal affairs, and in particular, VantagePoint's voting rights, be adjudicated exclusively in accordance with the law of its state of incorporation, in this case, the law of Delaware.

Any Forum — Internal Affairs — Same Law

VantagePoint acknowledges that the courts of Delaware, as the forum state, may apply Delaware's own substantive choice of law rules. VantagePoint argues, however, that Delaware's "choice" to apply the law of the state of incorporation to internal affairs issues — notwithstanding California's enactment of section 2115 — will result in future forum shopping races to the courthouse. VantagePoint submits that, if the California action in these proceedings had been decided first, the California Superior Court would have enjoined the merger until it was factually determined whether section 2115 is applicable. If the statutory prerequisites were found to be factually satisfied, VantagePoint submits that the California Superior Court would have applied the internal affairs law reflected in section 2115, "to the exclusion" of the law of Delaware — the state where Examen is incorporated.

In support of those assertions, VantagePoint relies primarily upon a 1982 decision by the California Court of Appeals in *Wilson v. Louisiana-Pacific Resources, Inc.* In *Wilson v. Louisiana-Pacific Resources, Inc.*, a panel of the California Court of Appeals held that section 2115 did not violate the federal constitution by applying the California Code's mandatory cumulative [1117] voting provision to a Utah corporation that had not provided for cumulative voting but instead had elected the straight voting structure set forth in the Utah corporation statute. [...]

Wilson was decided before the United States Supreme Court's decision in *CTS* and before this Court's decision in *McDermott*. Ten years after *Wilson*, the California Supreme Court cited with approval this Court's analysis of the internal affairs doctrine in *McDermott*, in particular, our holding that corporate voting rights disputes are governed by the law of the state of incorporation. [...]

Conclusion

The judgment of the Court of Chancery is affirmed. The Clerk of this Court is directed to issue the mandate immediately.

C. Lidow v. Superior Court (Cal. 2012)

This California decision accepts the internal affairs doctrine in principle. Nevertheless, in this case it applies California law to a dispute between a Delaware corporation and its officer.

Questions

1. How does the Court of Appeals of California determine the scope of the internal affairs doctrine?

2. Looking beyond this particular case, what scope of the internal affairs doctrine increases the application of California law – a narrow scope or a broad scope?

3. What can corporations—or rather those who control them—do to escape application of California law under section 2115 or under *Lidow*, and are they likely to do that? What can corporations do to escape

application of Delaware law under the internal affairs doctrine, and are they likely to do that?

206 Cal.App.4th 351 (2012)

ALEXANDER LIDOW, Petitioner,

v.

THE SUPERIOR COURT OF LOS ANGELES COUNTY,
Respondent;
INTERNATIONAL RECTIFIER CORP., Real Party in Interest.

No. B239042.

Court of Appeals of California, Second District, Division Two.

May 23, 2012.

[353] Sullivan & Cromwell, Robert A. Sacks, Adam S. Paris, Diane L. McGimsey and Edward E. Johnson for Petitioner.

No appearance for Respondent.

Robins, Kaplan, Miller & Ciresi, Roman M. Silberfeld, Michael A. Geibelson and Rebecka M. Biejo for Real Party in Interest.

[…]

OPINION

BOREN, P. J.—

The novel question presented in this case is whether, under a conflict of laws principle known as the internal affairs doctrine, California law or foreign law applies to a claim brought by an officer of a foreign corporation for wrongful termination in violation of public policy. We hold that under the circumstances alleged here, specifically where a foreign corporation has removed or constructively discharged a corporate officer in retaliation for that person's complaints of possible harmful or unethical activity, California law applies.

BACKGROUND

The parties do not dispute the following facts for the purposes of summary adjudication:

Petitioner, Alexander Lidow, has a Ph.D. in applied physics. Real party in interest, International Rectifier Corporation (IR), is incorporated in Delaware and based in El Segundo, California. IR is a semiconductor company founded by petitioner's father.

Petitioner began working for IR in 1977 after graduating from Stanford University. Petitioner became a member of IR's board of directors (Board) in 1994, co-chief executive officer (CEO) in 1995, and sole CEO in 1999. At no point in time did petitioner have a written employment contract with IR. IR's bylaws provided at all relevant times that the corporation's officers (including the CEO) "shall be chosen annually by, and shall serve at the pleasure of, the Board, and shall hold their respective offices until their resignation, removal, or other disqualification from service." Removal of an officer, according to IR's bylaws, may be "with or without cause, by the Board at any time."

In early 2007, IR commenced an internal investigation after accounting irregularities surfaced at IR's subsidiary in Japan. In late August 2007, the Board placed petitioner on paid administrative leave. Prior to being placed on administrative leave, petitioner had not received any negative criticisms or negative reviews about his performance as CEO. Petitioner stepped down as CEO and Board member in October 2007 pursuant to a negotiated separation agreement entered into by petitioner and IR. Although the separation agreement did not include a release of liability for either party, it did specify that petitioner's resignation was "[a]t the Company's request," and that petitioner had signed the agreement "freely and voluntarily."

[355] Approximately 18 months later, petitioner sued IR in superior court, alleging causes of action for (1) breach of contract; (2) wrongful termination in violation of public policy; (3) breach of employment contract; (4) failure to pay outstanding wages at the time of termination (Lab. Code, §§ 201, 203); (5) failure to make personnel records available in a timely manner (Lab. Code, §§ 226, 1198.5); (6) tortious interference; and (7) unfair business practices (Bus. & Prof. Code, § 17200). After IR prevailed on several pleading motions, only petitioner's second, fourth, and fifth causes of action remained.

IR moved for summary adjudication of petitioner's cause of action for wrongful termination on three grounds: First, pursuant to the "internal affairs doctrine," Delaware law governed petitioner's wrongful termination claim. Under Delaware law, a CEO serves at the pleasure of the corporation's board of directors and is barred from bringing a wrongful termination claim (unless authorized by specific statutory enactments) as a matter of law. [...]

The superior court granted IR's motion for summary adjudication on the first ground raised by IR. [...] Based on our de novo review, we conclude the superior court erred by granting summary adjudication in favor of IR. [...]

DISCUSSION

I. *Overview*

[... W]e hold that a claim for wrongful termination of public policy brought by an officer of a foreign corporation [357] falls outside the scope of the internal affairs doctrine, and thus is governed by California law. [...]

II. *Internal Affairs Doctrine*

A. *Allegations*

As related to the claim for wrongful termination in violation of public policy, petitioner alleged the following events took place:[3]

In October 2006, IR's internal finance department raised concerns that possible accounting improprieties were taking place at the corporation's subsidiary in Japan. In response, the Board's audit committee, which was comprised of all the Board members except for petitioner and his father, and IR's general counsel hired the law firm of Sheppard Mullin Richter & Hampton LLP (Sheppard Mullin) to conduct an investigation into the possible accounting improprieties. Sheppard Mullin had a long-standing relationship with the general counsel and had advised him on past occasions when he had received negative performance reviews from petitioner.

Sheppard Mullin outsourced the accounting investigation to a private company made up predominantly of ex-law enforcement officers from the United States and the United Kingdom. The investigators conducted interrogations during which they physically intimidated employees at IR's Japanese subsidiary, lied to these employees in an attempt to coerce inconsistent statements, and failed to advise these employees that they could, or should, retain independent counsel, despite the possibility that the employees could be criminally prosecuted based on the statements they gave during the interrogations. As a result of the investigators' aggressive and coercive tactics, employees at the Japanese subsidiary filed multiple complaints and threatened to resign in mass numbers. Productivity at the Japanese subsidiary came to a halt.

[358] Concerned about the deteriorating situation, petitioner travelled to Japan in order to convince the remaining employees to cooperate with the investigation, and to ensure, that going forward, the employees were treated with fairness and respect. Petitioner called for the implementation of protocols that would restore integrity to the investigation

---

[3] We emphasize that these are petitioner's allegations and for this reason entirely one sided. At this juncture, a trier of fact has made no findings about the truth or falsity of these allegations, and our discussion of these allegations should not be interpreted as lending any credibility to them.

process and stem the loss of Japanese personnel. At the same time, petitioner spoke out against the tactics used by the investigators, and criticized how Sheppard Mullin, the general counsel, and the audit committee were overseeing the investigation. Additionally, petitioner criticized the audit committee for failing to control the mounting legal and accounting fees associated with the investigation, which were already in the millions of dollars.

When news broke that IR was investigating possible accounting improprieties at its Japanese subsidiary, a class action securities lawsuit was filed against IR. IR's general counsel decided to retain Sheppard Mullin to defend the lawsuit. Petitioner protested Sheppard Mullin's retention, complaining that it would be a conflict of interest for Sheppard Mullin to defend a lawsuit based on accounting irregularities and to conduct a purportedly independent investigation into the irregularities at the same time.

Because of petitioner's complaints about the manner in which employees were being treated in Japan, his critical remarks about how the investigation was progressing, and his protestations over Sheppard Mullin's retention to defend the securities lawsuit, petitioner became a target of Sheppard Mullin, the general counsel, and the audit committee. Approximately 10 months after the investigation commenced, Sheppard Mullin issued a report to the audit committee implicating petitioner in the alleged accounting irregularities. According to the report, which petitioner claims is pure conjecture, petitioner either ordered employees at the Japanese subsidiary to create false accounting documents, or knew that the employees were creating false accounting documents and turned a blind eye to the fraud.

Based on the report, the audit committee, which was now acting as the de facto Board, placed petitioner on administrative leave without giving him an opportunity to respond to the charges. Shortly after the audit committee placed petitioner on administrative leave, it informed him that if he did not resign as CEO in seven days, he would be removed. Petitioner entered in a separation agreement with IR wherein he agreed to step down as CEO and Board member at IR's request.

B. *Legal Framework*

(1) "'The internal affairs doctrine is a conflict of laws principle which recognizes that only one State should have the authority to regulate a [359] corporation's internal affairs— matters peculiar to the relationships among or between the corporation and its current officers, directors, and shareholders— because otherwise a corporation could be faced with conflicting demands.' (*Edgar v. MITE Corp.* (1982) 457 U.S. 624, 645 [73 L.Ed.2d 269, 102 S.Ct. 2629] [citation].)" (*Vaughn v. LJ Internat., Inc.* (2009) 174 Cal.App.4th 213, 223 [94 Cal.Rptr.3d 166] (*Vaughn*).) "'States normally look to the State of a

business' incorporation for the law that provides the relevant corporate governance general standard of care."' (*Vaughn, supra,* at p. 223.)

"Matters falling within the scope of the [internal affairs doctrine] and which involve primarily a corporation's relationship to its shareholders include steps taken in the course of the original incorporation, the election or appointment of directors and officers, the adoption of by-laws, the issuance of corporate shares, preemptive rights, the holding of directors' and shareholders' meetings, methods of voting including any requirement for cumulative voting, shareholders' rights to examine corporate records, charter and by-law amendments, mergers, consolidations and reorganizations and the reclassification of shares." (Rest.2d Conf. of Laws, § 302, com. a, p. 307; see *State Farm Mutual Automobile Ins. Co. v. Superior Court* (2003) 114 Cal.App.4th 434, 442 [8 Cal.Rptr.3d 56] (*State Farm*) [adopting the Restatement's definition of "internal affairs"].) "[I]t would be impractical to have matters of the sort mentioned in the previous paragraph, which involve a corporation's organic structure or internal administration, governed by different laws." (Rest.2d Conf. of Laws, § 302, com. e, p. 310.)

(2) "'The policy underlying the internal affairs doctrine is an important one ...: "Under the prevailing conflicts practice, neither courts nor legislatures have maximized the imposition of local corporate policy on foreign corporations but have consistently applied the law of the state of incorporation to the entire gamut of internal corporate affairs."' (*State Farm, supra,* 114 Cal.App.4th at p. 443.) Applying local law to the internal affairs of a foreign corporation '""produce[s] inequalities, intolerable confusion, and uncertainty, and intrude[s] into the domain of other states that have a superior claim to regulate the same subject matter."'' (*Id.* at p. 444.)

There is, however, a vital limitation to the internal affairs doctrine: "The local law of the state of incorporation will be applied ... *except where, with respect to the particular issue, some other state has a more significant relationship ... to the parties and the transaction ....*" (Rest.2d Conf. of Laws, § 309, italics added.) Indeed, "[t]here is no reason why corporate acts" involving "the making of contracts, the commission of torts and the transfer of property" "should not be governed by the local law of different states." (*Id.,* § 302, com. e, p. 309.)

[360] The issue of whether the termination of a corporate officer for reasons that allegedly violate public policy falls within the scope of a corporation's internal affairs is one of first impression. For guidance, we turn to those cases in which courts of this state have applied, or not applied, the internal affairs doctrine to particular claims.

In *Western Air Lines, Inc. v. Sobieski* (1961) 191 Cal.App.2d 399 [12 Cal.Rptr. 719] (*Western*), the plaintiff, a Delaware corporation with its principal place of business in

California, sought to amend its bylaws to eliminate cumulative voting rights for its shareholders. California's Commissioner of Corporations took the position that this proposed change in voting rights would constitute a "sale" of securities under California law, and thus petitioner would have to apply for and obtain a permit authorizing such action from the commissioner. After petitioner filed the requisite application, the commissioner declined to issue a permit, finding that the proposed elimination of cumulative voting "would be "... unfair, unjust and inequitable to the great number of security holders residing in California.'" (191 Cal.App.2d at p. 403.)

The plaintiff sought review of the commissioner's decision through a petition for writ of administrative mandate before the superior court. The superior court granted the petition and ruled that the commissioner had acted without jurisdiction because the amendment of the plaintiff's articles of incorporation was an "internal affair" of the corporation and its shareholders. (*Western, supra,* 191 Cal.App.2d at p. 405.) The Court of Appeal reversed the superior court's order. It reasoned, in part, that '"ordinarily speaking the issuance of capital stock or the stock structure of a corporation is an internal affair, yet the issuance and sale of stock within a state other than that of its organization may be regulated *in order to protect the residents and citizens of the former state.*"' (*Id.* at p. 410, italics added.)

In *Friese v. Superior Court* (2005) 134 Cal.App.4th 693 [36 Cal.Rptr.3d 558] (*Friese*), the plaintiff, the successor in interest to a Delaware corporation headquartered in California, sued a group of former directors and officers under Corporations Code section 25502.5 (part of California's Corporate Securities Law of 1968 (Corp. Code, § 25000 et seq.)), a statute that gives an issuer of securities standing to sue its own directors and officers for insider trading. The former directors and officers demurred to the plaintiff's complaint, arguing that because their actions violated internal duties owed to the [361] corporation, Delaware law applied under the internal affairs doctrine. And because Delaware did not have a statute analogous to Corporations Code section 25502.5,♦ they were entitled to judgment as a matter of law. (*Friese, supra,* at p. 698.) The superior court agreed and sustained the demurrer.

♦ It is true that Delaware does not have an explicit statute, but Delaware courts have allowed so-called *Brophy* claims by shareholders against insider-trading directors and officers. In this respect, the *Friese* trial court thus probably erred

The Court of Appeal granted writ relief. It explained that "California's corporate securities laws are designed to protect participants in California's securities marketplace and deter unlawful conduct which takes place [in California]." (*Friese, supra,* 134 Cal.App.4th at p. 698; see *id.* at p. 710 ["California's corporate securities regulation scheme ... serves broad public interests rather than the more narrow interests of a corporation's shareholders."].) Although the scope of a director's or officer's duties to a corporation is ordinarily an internal affair of that corporation, the appellate court reasoned that where the conduct in question also implicates the broader public interest of securities regulation, California has a greater stake in applying its law (as opposed to Delaware law) to maintain a fair and equitable marketplace for its shareholder citizens. Thus, the appellate court concluded, the internal affairs doctrine could not be used to shield the directors and officers from liability for insider trading. (134 Cal.App.4th at pp. 706-708.)

The Court of Appeal's decisions in *Western* and *Friese* serve as instructional contrasts to the decisions in *State Farm, supra,* 114 Cal.App.4th 434, and *Vaughn, supra,* 174 Cal.App.4th 213. In *State Farm,* insurance policy holders residing in California sued an insurance company incorporated and headquartered in Illinois, alleging that the company's board of directors did not pay promised dividends. The policyholders framed their claim as an alleged breach of contract [...] The Court of Appeal rejected this argument. [...]

In *Vaughn, supra,* 174 Cal.App.4th 213, the defendant corporation, LJ, was incorporated in the British Virgin Islands (BVI), headquartered in Hong Kong, and had a "few employees" based in California. (*Id.* at p. 216.) A [362] shareholder (who did not reside in Cal.) brought a derivative suit against the corporation based on allegedly false and misleading financial statements that it had issued in Los Angeles. The corporation demurred to the complaint, arguing that BVI law applied under the internal affairs doctrine, and that the shareholder had failed to comply with a BVI statute requiring approval from the high court of that jurisdiction before a shareholder could sue derivatively. (*Id.* at p. 217.) The superior court sustained the demurrer without leave to amend, and the Court of Appeal affirmed, reasoning that the BVI statute in question "establish[ed] a condition precedent to the right of a shareholder to derivatively sue corporate directors on behalf of the company," which "most definitely [implicated] the internal affairs of the corporation." (*Id.* at p. 225.) The appellate court noted that California had "no extraordinary interest" in an international corporation that was not headquartered in the state, and the shareholder had failed to show that a "significant California public policy" would "be offended" if he were forced to bring the derivative suit under BVI law. (*Id.* at p. 226.)

(3) What we learn from the decisions in *Friese* and *Western* is that courts are less apt to apply the internal affairs doctrine when vital statewide interests are at stake, such as maintaining the integrity of California security markets and protecting its citizens from harmful conduct. In contrast, what we learn from the decisions in *State Farm* and *Vaughn* is that when less vital state interests are at stake (e.g., whether a foreign corporation headquartered in another state pays promised dividends to its shareholders, or whether the shareholder of a foreign corporation must fulfill certain procedural requirements set before bringing a derivative suit), courts are more apt to apply the internal affairs doctrine.

(4) We now turn to the situation presented in this case. Certainly, the removal of a CEO for any number of reasons (e.g., the corporation is not performing well, the CEO did not meet certain financial expectations set by the board of directors) falls within the scope of a corporation's internal governance, thus triggering the application of the internal affairs doctrine. This case, however, presents an entirely different set of allegations. Removing an officer in retaliation for his complaints about possible illegal or harmful activity (e.g., witness intimidation, physical threats to employees, etc.) and breaches of ethical conduct (e.g., defending a client against allegations of accounting irregularities and conducting an independent investigation in the same irregularities) goes beyond internal governance and touches upon broader public interest concerns that California has a vital interest in protecting. (Accord, Rest.2d Conf. of Laws, § 6, subd. (2)(b); *id.*, com. c. p. 12 [under general choice-of-law principles, one factor to consider is the relevant public policies of the forum state].)

[363] At oral argument, counsel for IR relied heavily on *VantagePoint Venture Partners 1996 v. Examen, Inc.* (Del. 2005) 871 A.2d 1108 (*VantagePoint*), a decision issued by the Delaware Supreme Court. The reasoning articulated in that case, however, only supports our conclusion in this case. [...]

The Delaware Supreme Court held that Delaware law applied in that case because "courts must apply the law of the state of incorporation to issues involving corporate internal affairs, and ... disputes concerning a shareholder's right to vote fall squarely within the purview of the internal affairs doctrine." (*VantagePoint, supra,* 871 A.2d at p. 1115, fn. omitted.) [...]

This court agrees that the voting rights of shareholders, just like the payment of dividends to shareholders (see *State Farm, supra,* 114 Cal.App.4th 434) and the procedural requirements of shareholder derivative suits (see *Vaughn, supra,* 174 Cal.App.4th 213), involve matters of internal corporate governance and thus, fall within a corporation's internal affairs. But, as stated above, the allegations made by petitioner involve circumstances that go beyond internal corporate governance.

(5) Our Supreme Court has long recognized that claims for wrongful termination in violation of public policy serve vital interests insofar as they impose liability on employers who coerce their employees to engage in [364] criminal or other harmful conduct, or employers who retaliate against their employees for speaking out against such conduct. [...]

(6) For these reasons, we conclude that under the circumstances presented here, i.e., where there are allegations made by a corporate officer that he was removed for

complaining about possible illegal or harmful activity, the internal affairs doctrine is inapplicable and California law governs the claim. [...]

DISPOSITION

[...] Let a peremptory writ of mandate issue directing the superior court to vacate its order of February 6, 2012, granting real party in interest's motion for summary adjudication of petitioner's claim [365] for wrongful termination in violation of public policy, and to enter a new order denying said motion. [...]

Chapter 17. What is the Point of Corporate Law?

We are now ready to tackle the ultimate question: What is the point of corporate law? Is it merely to facilitate contracting? If so, what is the best way to do it? If not, what other goals should corporate law aim to advance?

In this context, commentators like to contrast the so-called contractarian and entity views of the corporation. As its name suggests, the contractarian view emphasizes the contractual aspects of the corporation, from drafting the initial charter to executive compensation contracts to customer relationships. By contrast, the entity view emphasizes the importance of the (large) corporation for the life of its constituents and beyond. Commentators tend to associate the contractarian view with an argument for contractual freedom, and the entity view with an argument for more mandatory rules.

In truth, this is a false dichotomy. The views are two sides of the same coin. A corporation is *both* one or more contracts (the charter above all) and an entity. Contracts can be regulated, and often are — for example, in the criminalization of cartels. And the mere fact that the corporate entity is important for people does not necessarily mean that we think the state should regulate how people organize it.

What the two views do, however, is illustrate the different *rationales* for corporate law-making. One rationale is to remedy contracting imperfections even between the contracting parties. Another rationale is to prevent externalities on non-contracting parties. U.S. corporate law tends to downplay the latter, perhaps because its perspective has been narrowed by the internal affairs doctrine and the doctrine's limiting effects on regulation through corporate law. Implicitly, however, U.S. law also seems to fear externalities arising specifically from incorporation. If not, why would a law firm not be allowed to organize as a corporation? We will approach such questions through *Citizens United*.

Questions

1. *Should* a law firm be allowed to organize as a corporation?

1. The corporation as a contract

As we have seen, U.S. corporate law grants very extensive contractual freedom. Choose your state. Choose your corporate charter (cf. DGCL 102(b)(1) – read!). Even choose your entity type. For example, anyone not satisfied with DGCL 102(b)(7)'s restrictions on eliminating corporate fiduciary duties can choose a Delaware Limited Liability Company instead, where "[fiduciary] duties may be ... eliminated by provisions in the LLC agreement; provided, that the LLC agreement may not eliminate the implied contractual covenant of good faith and fair dealing." Del. LLC Act § 1101(c). If that is still not enough, the Delaware statutory trust may help. *Cf.* Del. Code title 12, ch. 38.

Indeed, why limit permissible charter provisions at all? Once we rely on contracting to get the right result, why stop at particular provisions? In fact, if law is a "product" why not allow *private* providers to supply it? That is, why require election of any state law for incorporation? Private providers might be better at generating and maintaining private contract forms, registries, and arbitration — instead of, for example, the Delaware General Corporation Law, Secretary of State, and Chancery Court respectively. If the contractual model holds, people's self-interest will ensure that they choose the most suitable package. The more options, the better.

Perhaps having so many options would make contracting too complex and confusing? That can hardly be a good argument because the existing options allow for plenty of confusion — for example the offer of non-voting shares and complicated voting structures. Many financial contracts are extremely complex, much more complex than we could reasonably expect charters to be — at present, public corporation charters are generally short, overwhelmingly boilerplate, and show very little variation. And the difficulty of evaluating a charter term pales in comparison to that of valuing a business.

Of course, human fallibility can undermine the contractual model (careful, though — it undermines faith in regulation as well). For example, if gullible investors do not price charter provisions correctly, savvy founders will produce bad charters. This might warrant prohibiting certain charter terms. But why stop there? Why not stop investors from investing in bad businesses? In other words, should some agency review the "investment worthiness" of securities before they can be issued to the public? Such review did exist in many states for a long time.

Perhaps the best argument for why charter freedom may not produce optimal results even if people generally contract well is charters' long life. Drafters cannot foresee everything, and corporations can be around for a very long time. Then again, drafters know this, so they could build whatever flexibility they desire into their charter.

2. The corporation as a social entity

Of course, the contractarian view of the corporation is not the only possible view. In fact, for most of the 20th century, a different view prevailed in the U.S. and elsewhere. This was the view of the corporation as a social entity. This view saw a much larger role for mandatory law in structuring the entity and in regulating the entity's interaction with the world. For example, the most famous account of large U.S. corporations in the 20th century, Adolf Berle & Gardiner Means' "The Modern Corporation & Private Property" (1932; 1968) reviewed the dispersion of (family) ownership and the rise of professional management to conclude (pp. 310-313):

> Observable throughout the world ... is this insistence that power in economic organization shall be subjected to the same tests of public benefit which have been applied in their turn to power otherwise located. ...

> By tradition, a corporation 'belongs' to its shareholders ... and theirs is the only interest to be recognized as the object of corporate activity. Following this tradition, and without regard for the changed character of ownership, it would be possible to apply in the interests of the *passive* property owner [i.e., shareholders] the doctrine of strict property rights ... . Were this course followed, the bulk of American industry might soon be operated by trustees for the sole benefit of inactive and irresponsible security owners. ...

> [Another] possibility exists, however. On the one hand, the owners of passive property, by surrendering control and responsibility over the active property, have surrendered the right that the corporation should be operated in their sole interest ... At the same time, the controlling groups [i.e., managers], by means of the extension of corporate powers, have in their own interest broken the bars of tradition which require that the corporation be operated solely for the benefit of the owners of passive property. ... The control groups have ... cleared the way for the claims of a group far wider than either the owners or the control. They have placed the community in a position to demand that the modern corporation serve not alone the owners or the control but all society. ...

> In still larger view, the modern corporation may be regarded not simply as one form of social organization but potentially (if not yet actually) as the dominant institution of the modern world. ...

> The rise of the modern corporation has brought a concentration of economic power which can compete on equal terms with the modern

state — economic power versus political power, each strong in its own field. The state seeks in some aspects to regulate the corporation, while the corporation, steadily becoming more powerful, makes every effort to avoid such regulation. … The future may see the economic organism, now typified by the corporation, not only on an equal plane with the state, but possibly even superseding it as the dominant form of social organization. The law of corporations, accordingly, might well be considered as a potential constitutional law for the new economic state. …

A. KKR & Co. L.P.

Let's make the discussion of corporate charter freedom more concrete by looking at KKR's publicly traded "common units." We have already encountered KKR in the *MetLife v RJR* case, doing what it usually does: LBOs (and subsequent resale). KKR is a private equity firm that is in the business of buying entire companies, managing them for a couple of years, and then reselling them, hopefully at a higher price. To leverage their returns, KKR and other private equity firms tend to finance the acquisitions with a lot of debt, as KKR did in its purchase of RJR Nabisco. Beyond financial engineering and tax savings (because debt is tax-advantaged), private equity firms promise to generate returns through superior management.

It's a bit too simplistic to say that KKR or other private equity firms buy companies (from here on, we will just talk about KKR). In truth, KKR raises and manages funds that buy the companies. The investors in these funds tend to be large institutional investors, above all pension funds. In return for its services, KKR charges the funds an annual management fee (generally around 2% of the money invested), a performance fee (a/k/a carried interest, roughly 20% of profits generated), and various service fees.

The funds tend to be organized as Limited Partnerships, or L.P.s. A limited partnership is a statutory creation that is treated as a partnership for tax purposes and yet offers limited liability to the so-called limited partners. Partnerships do not pay corporate income tax. Instead, any partnership income is treated as income of the partners. In addition to its limited partners, an L.P. must have at least one so-called general partner. Like a partner in a traditional partnership, the general partner has management authority (the limited partners have none) and unlimited liability for the L.P.'s debts. In practice, and in KKR, the general partner of the fund is another limited liability vehicle, be it a corporation, a limited liability company (L.L.C.), or another L.P. (whose general partner will be another limited liability vehicle).

KKR has three layers of limited partnerships: the funds, their general partners, and the general partners' general partner, KKR & Co. L.P. Public investors own "common units" a/k/a limited partnership interests in KKR & Co. L.P. KKR's founders maintain control of KKR & Co. L.P. through full ownership of its "Managing Partner," i.e., general partner, KKR Management LLC. The founders and KKR's senior managers also maintain 70% of the economic equity as limited partners of the funds' general partners. In sum, common unitholders own 30% of KKR's equity and no control. (The actual structure of KKR is even more complicated, but the preceding sketch suffices for present purposes.)

The reasons to structure the publicly traded vehicle as a limited partnership reside mostly in tax law. KKR & Co. L.P.'s prospectus describes its tax treatment as follows:

> … an entity that is treated as a partnership for U.S. federal income tax purposes is not a taxable entity for U.S. federal income tax purposes and incurs no U.S. federal income tax liabilities. Each partner of a partnership is required to take into account its allocable share of items of income, gain, loss and deduction of the partnership in computing its U.S. federal income tax liability, regardless of the extent to which, or whether, it receives cash distributions from the partnership …

> An entity that would otherwise be classified as a partnership for U.S. federal income tax purposes may nonetheless be taxable as a corporation if it is a "publicly traded partnership," unless an exception applies. …. We are a publicly traded partnership.

> However, an exception to taxation as a corporation, referred to as the "Qualifying Income Exception," exists if at least 90% of the partnership's gross income for every taxable year consists of "qualifying income" and the partnership is not required to register under the Investment Company Act. Qualifying income includes certain interest income, dividends, real property rents, gains from the sale or other disposition of real property, and any gain from the sale or disposition of a capital asset or other property held for the production of income that otherwise constitutes qualifying income. [Eds: These types of income also tend to be taxed at a lower rate than ordinary income, making it especially valuable not to subject them to corporate income tax.]

> Our Managing Partner has adopted a set of investment policies and procedures that will govern the types of investments we can make (and income we can earn), including structuring certain investments through entities, such as our intermediate holding company, classified as corporations for U.S. federal income tax purposes (as discussed further below), to ensure that we will meet the Qualifying Income Exception in each taxable year. …

In addition, the limited partnership offers governance flexibility. Among other things, section 17-1101 of the Delaware Limited Partnership Act provides

> (c) It is the policy of this chapter to give maximum effect to the principle of freedom of contract and to the enforceability of partnership agreements.
>
> (d) To the extent that, at law or in equity, a partner or other person has duties (including fiduciary duties) to a limited partnership or to another partner or to another person that is a party to or is otherwise bound by a partnership agreement, the partner's or other person's duties may be expanded or restricted or eliminated by provisions in the partnership agreement; provided that the partnership agreement may not eliminate the implied contractual covenant of good faith and fair dealing.

Utilizing this flexibility, section 7.9 of KKR & Co. L.P.'s limited partnership agreement provides:

> (a) Unless otherwise expressly provided in this Agreement, whenever a potential conflict of interest exists or arises between the Managing Partner ... and the Partnership ... or any Partner ..., any resolution or course of action by the Managing Partner ... in respect of such conflict of interest shall be permitted and deemed approved by all Partners, and shall not constitute a breach of this Agreement ... or of any duty hereunder or existing at law, in equity or otherwise, if the resolution or course of action in respect of such conflict of interest is (i) approved by Special Approval,[11] (ii) on terms which are, in the aggregate, no less

---

[11] Section 1.1 defines, *inter alia*:

> 'Special Approval' means either (a) approval by a majority of the members of the Conflicts Committee or, if there is only one member of the Conflicts Committee, approval by the sole member of the Conflicts Committee, or (b) approval by the vote of the Record Holders representing a majority of the voting power of the Voting Units (excluding Voting Units owned by the Managing Partner and its Affiliates).
>
> 'Conflicts Committee' means a committee of the Board of Directors of the Managing Partner composed entirely of one or more directors or managers who meet the independence standards (but not, for the avoidance of doubt, the financial literacy or financial expert qualifications) required to serve on an audit committee of a board of directors established by the Securities Exchange Act and the rules and regulations of the Commission thereunder and by the National Securities Exchange on which the Common Units are listed for trading."

favorable to the Partnership than those generally being provided to or available from unrelated third parties or (iii) fair and reasonable to the Partnership, taking into account the totality of the relationships between the parties involved (including other transactions that may be or have been particularly favorable or advantageous to the Partnership). The Managing Partner and the Conflicts Committee[12] (in connection with any Special Approval by the Conflicts Committee) each shall be authorized in connection with its resolution of any conflict of interest to consider such factors as it determines in its sole discretion to be relevant, reasonable or appropriate under the circumstances. The Managing Partner shall be authorized but not required in connection with its resolution of any conflict of interest to seek Special Approval of such resolution, and the Managing Partner may also adopt a resolution or course of action that has not received Special Approval. Failure to seek Special Approval shall not be deemed to indicate that a conflict of interest exists or that Special Approval could not have been obtained. If Special Approval is not sought and the Managing Partner determines that the resolution or course of action taken with respect to a conflict of interest satisfies either of the standards set forth in clauses (ii) or (iii) above, then it shall be presumed that, in making its determination, the Managing Partner acted in good faith and in any proceeding brought by or on behalf of any Limited Partner, the Partnership or any other Person bound by this Agreement challenging such determination, the Person bringing or prosecuting such proceeding shall have the burden of overcoming such presumption. Notwithstanding anything to the contrary in this Agreement or any duty otherwise existing at law or equity, and ... to the fullest extent permitted by the Delaware Limited Partnership Act, the existence of the conflicts of interest described in or contemplated by the Registration Statement [eds: i.e., the prospectus] are hereby approved, and all such conflicts of interest are waived, by all Partners and shall not constitute a breach of this Agreement or any duty existing at Law or otherwise.

(e) Except as expressly set forth in this Agreement, to the fullest extent permitted by law, ... the Managing Partner ... shall [not] have any duties or liabilities, including fiduciary duties, to the Partnership, any Limited Partner or any other Person bound by this Agreement, and the provisions of this Agreement, to the extent that they restrict or otherwise modify or eliminate the duties and liabilities, including fiduciary duties, of the Managing Partner ... otherwise existing at law or

---

[12] See definition in previous note.

in equity, are agreed by the Partners to replace such other duties and
liabilities of the Managing Partner ....

Questions

1. Are you troubled by KKR's contracting out of:

(a) the corporate income tax, and/or

(b) corporate fiduciary duties?

2. By the way, on July 1, 2018, KKR & Co. L.P. converted to a corporation.
    Can you guess why? (Hint: What does a unitholder tax return look like?)

B. Citizens United v. Federal Election Com'n (US 2010)

In this very controversial decision, the Supreme Court's conservative majority
held that a prohibition of corporate expenditures on certain types of speech violates
the First Amendment. The decision implicates important legal issues of free speech,
stare decisis, and judicial restraint. For our purposes, however, we have edited the case
down to the passages dealing directly with the constitutionality of, and rationale for,
distinguishing corporate from non-corporate speech. Please focus on this distinction.

The First Amendment reads, in relevant part:

> Congress shall make no law ... abridging the freedom of speech, or of
> the press.

Questions

As a preliminary matter, consider the following questions:

1. Does a literal reading of the First Amendment protect corporate
    expenditures?

2. Does an originalist reading of the First Amendment, adopted in 1791,
    protect corporate expenditures? You may recall that incorporation
    required a special act of the legislature well into the 19th century. Cf.
    Justice Scalia's concurrence and Justice Stevens' dissent.

In answering the latter question, you may want to distinguish between different
types of corporations. In particular, many of the arguments and precedents that the

Justices discuss relate to news, media, and political organizations, and the petitioner in the case is a non-profit advocacy organization funded mostly by donations from individuals. In this class, we are primarily interested in business corporations.

The main questions to consider are:

3. Do the Justices treat the corporation as an abstraction—a convenient way of summarizing legal relationships between individual human beings? Or as a "concentration of economic power which can compete on equal terms with the modern state" (Berle and Means)? Or as something different altogether?

4. Do the "the procedures of shareholder democracy" protect dissenting shareholders when they disagree with speech approved by (a) boards and managers or (b) majority shareholders? Should they? What would be the contractarian answer?

5. What other arguments for distinguishing corporate and individual speech do the Justices consider?

130 S.Ct. 876 (2010)

CITIZENS UNITED, Appellant,

v.

FEDERAL ELECTION COMMISSION.

[...]

Justice KENNEDY delivered the opinion of the Court.

Federal law prohibits corporations and unions from using their general treasury funds to make independent expenditures for speech defined as an "electioneering communication" or for speech expressly advocating the election or defeat of a candidate. 2 U.S.C. § 441b. Limits on electioneering communications were upheld in *McConnell v. Federal Election Comm'n*, 540 U.S. 93, 203-209, 124 S.Ct. 619, 157 L.Ed.2d 491 (2003). The holding of *McConnell* rested to a large extent on an earlier case, *Austin v. Michigan Chamber of Commerce*, 494 U.S. 652, 110 S.Ct. 1391, 108 L.Ed.2d 652 (1990). *Austin* had held that political speech may be banned based on the speaker's corporate identity.

In this case we are asked to reconsider *Austin* and, in effect, *McConnell*. It has been noted that "*Austin* was a significant departure from ancient First Amendment principles,"

Federal Election Comm'n v. Wisconsin Right to Life, Inc., 551 U.S. 449, 490, 127 S.Ct. 2652, 168 L.Ed.2d 329 (2007) *(WRTL)* (SCALIA, J., concurring in part and concurring in judgment). We agree with that conclusion and hold that *stare decisis* does not compel the continued acceptance of *Austin.* The Government may regulate corporate political speech through disclaimer and disclosure requirements, but it may not suppress that speech altogether. We turn to the case now before us.

I

A

Citizens United is a nonprofit corporation. It brought this action in the United States District Court for the District of [887] Columbia. A three-judge court later convened to hear the cause. The resulting judgment gives rise to this appeal.

Citizens United has an annual budget of about $12 million. Most of its funds are from donations by individuals; but, in addition, it accepts a small portion of its funds from for-profit corporations.

In January 2008, Citizens United released a film entitled *Hillary: The Movie.* We refer to the film as *Hillary.* It is a 90-minute documentary about then-Senator Hillary Clinton, who was a candidate in the Democratic Party's 2008 Presidential primary elections. *Hillary* mentions Senator Clinton by name and depicts interviews with political commentators and other persons, most of them quite critical of Senator Clinton. *Hillary* was released in theaters and on DVD, but Citizens United wanted to increase distribution by making it available through video-on-demand.

Video-on-demand allows digital cable subscribers to select programming from various menus, including movies, television shows, sports, news, and music. The viewer can watch the program at any time and can elect to rewind or pause the program. In December 2007, a cable company offered, for a payment of $1.2 million, to make *Hillary* available on a video-on-demand channel called "Elections '08." App. 255a-257a. Some video-on-demand services require viewers to pay a small fee to view a selected program, but here the proposal was to make *Hillary* available to viewers free of charge.

To implement the proposal, Citizens United was prepared to pay for the video-on-demand; and to promote the film, it produced two 10-second ads and one 30-second ad for *Hillary.* Each ad includes a short (and, in our view, pejorative) statement about Senator Clinton, followed by the name of the movie and the movie's Website address. *Id.,* at 26a-27a. Citizens United desired to promote the video-on-demand offering by running advertisements on broadcast and cable television.

B

Before the Bipartisan Campaign Reform Act of 2002 (BCRA), federal law prohibited— and still does prohibit— corporations and unions from using general treasury funds to make direct contributions to candidates or independent expenditures that expressly advocate the election or defeat of a candidate, through any form of media, in connection with certain qualified federal elections. 2 U.S.C. § 441b (2000 ed.); see *McConnell*, *supra*, at 204, and n. 87, 124 S.Ct. 619; *Federal Election Comm'n v. Massachusetts Citizens for Life, Inc.*, 479 U.S. 238, 249, 107 S.Ct. 616, 93 L.Ed.2d 539 (1986) *(MCFL)*. BCRA § 203 amended § 441b to prohibit any "electioneering communication" as well. 2 U.S.C. § 441b(b)(2) (2006 ed.). An electioneering communication is defined as "any broadcast, cable, or satellite communication" that "refers to a clearly identified candidate for Federal office" and is made within 30 days of a primary or 60 days of a general election. § 434(f)(3)(A). The Federal Election Commission's (FEC) regulations further define an electioneering communication as a communication that is "publicly distributed." 11 CFR § 100.29(a)(2) (2009). "In the case of a candidate for nomination for President ... *publicly distributed* means" that the communication "[c]an be received by 50,000 or more persons in a State where a primary election ... is being held within 30 days." § 100.29(b)(3)(ii). Corporations and unions are barred from using their general treasury funds for express advocacy or electioneering communications. They may establish, however, a "separate segregated fund" (known as a political action committee, or PAC) for these purposes. 2 U.S.C. [888] § 441b(b)(2). The moneys received by the segregated fund are limited to donations from stockholders and employees of the corporation or, in the case of unions, members of the union. *Ibid.*

C

Citizens United wanted to make *Hillary* available through video-on-demand within 30 days of the 2008 primary elections. It feared, however, that both the film and the ads would be covered by § 441b's ban on corporate-funded independent expenditures, thus subjecting the corporation to civil and criminal penalties under § 437g. In December 2007, Citizens United sought declaratory and injunctive relief against the FEC. It argued that (1) § 441b is unconstitutional as applied to *Hillary*; and (2) BCRA's disclaimer and disclosure requirements, BCRA §§ 201 and 311, are unconstitutional as applied to *Hillary* and to the three ads for the movie.

The District Court denied Citizens United's motion for a preliminary injunction, 530 F.Supp.2d 274 (D.D.C.2008) *(per curiam),* and then granted the FEC's motion for summary judgment, App. 261a-262a. See *id.,* at 261a ("Based on the reasoning of our prior opinion, we find that the [FEC] is entitled to judgment as a matter of law. *See Citizen[s] United v. FEC,* 530 F.Supp.2d 274 (D.D.C.2008) (denying Citizens United's request for a preliminary injunction)"). The court held that § 441b was facially constitutional under *McConnell,* and that § 441b was constitutional as applied to *Hillary* because it was "susceptible of no other interpretation than to inform the electorate that Senator Clinton is unfit for office, that the United States would be a dangerous place in a President Hillary Clinton world, and that viewers should vote against her." 530 F.Supp.2d, at 279. The court also rejected Citizens United's challenge to BCRA's disclaimer and disclosure requirements. It noted that "the Supreme Court has written approvingly of disclosure provisions triggered by political speech even though the speech itself was constitutionally protected under the First Amendment." *Id.,* at 281.

We noted probable jurisdiction. 555 U.S. ___, 128 S.Ct. 1471, 170 L.Ed.2d 294 (2008). The case was reargued in this Court after the Court asked the parties to file supplemental briefs addressing whether we should overrule either or both *Austin* and the part of *McConnell* which addresses the facial validity of 2 U.S.C. § 441b. See 557 U.S. ___, 128 S.Ct. 1732, 170 L.Ed.2d 511 (2009).

[...]

III

The First Amendment provides that "Congress shall make no law ... abridging the freedom of speech." [...]

The law before us is an outright ban, backed by criminal sanctions. Section 441b makes it a felony for all corporations—including nonprofit advocacy corporations—either to expressly advocate the election or defeat of candidates or to broadcast electioneering communications within 30 days of a primary election and 60 days of a general election. [...]

We find no basis for the proposition that, in the context of political speech, the Government may impose restrictions on certain disfavored speakers. Both history and logic lead us to this conclusion.

A

1

The Court has recognized that First Amendment protection extends to corporations. *Bellotti, supra,* at 778, n. 14, 98 S.Ct. 1407 (citing *Linmark Associates, Inc. v. Willingboro,* 431 U.S. 85, 97 S.Ct. 1614, 52 L.Ed.2d 155 (1977); *Time, Inc. v. Firestone,* 424 U.S. 448, 96 S.Ct. 958, 47 L.Ed.2d 154 (1976); *Doran v. Salem Inn, Inc.,* 422 U.S. 922, 95 S.Ct. 2561, 45 L.Ed.2d 648 (1975); *Southeastern Promotions, Ltd. v. Conrad,* 420 U.S. 546, 95 S.Ct. 1239, 43 L.Ed.2d 448 (1975); *Cox Broadcasting Corp. v. Cohn,* 420 U.S. 469, 95 S.Ct. 1029, 43 L.Ed.2d 328 (1975); *Miami Herald Publishing Co. v.*

Tornillo, 418 U.S. 241, 94 S.Ct. 2831, 41 L.Ed.2d 730 (1974); *New York Times Co. v. United States,* 403 U.S. 713, 91 S.Ct. 2140, 29 L.Ed.2d 822 (1971) *(per curiam); Time, Inc. v. Hill,* 385 U.S. 374, 87 S.Ct. 534, 17 L.Ed.2d 456 (1967); *New York Times Co. v. Sullivan,* 376 U.S. 254, 84 S.Ct. 710, 11 L.Ed.2d 686; *Kingsley Int'l Pictures Corp.* [900] *v. Regents of Univ. of N. Y.,* 360 U.S. 684, 79 S.Ct. 1362, 3 L.Ed.2d 1512 (1959); *Joseph Burstyn, Inc. v. Wilson,* 343 U.S. 495, 72 S.Ct. 777, 96 L.Ed. 1098 (1952)); see, *e.g., Turner Broadcasting System, Inc. v. FCC,* 520 U.S. 180, 117 S.Ct. 1174, 137 L.Ed.2d 369 (1997); *Denver Area Ed. Telecommunications Consortium, Inc. v. FCC,* 518 U.S. 727, 116 S.Ct. 2374, 135 L.Ed.2d 888 (1996); *Turner,* 512 U.S. 622, 114 S.Ct. 2445, 129 L.Ed.2d 497; *Simon & Schuster,* 502 U.S. 105, 112 S.Ct. 501, 116 L.Ed.2d 476; *Sable Communications of Cal., Inc. v. FCC,* 492 U.S. 115, 109 S.Ct. 2829, 106 L.Ed.2d 93 (1989); *Florida Star v. B.J. F.,* 491 U.S. 524, 109 S.Ct. 2603, 105 L.Ed.2d 443 (1989); *Philadelphia Newspapers, Inc. v. Hepps,* 475 U.S. 767, 106 S.Ct. 1558, 89 L.Ed.2d 783 (1986); *Landmark Communications, Inc. v. Virginia,* 435 U.S. 829, 98 S.Ct. 1535, 56 L.Ed.2d 1 (1978); *Young v. American Mini Theatres, Inc.,* 427 U.S. 50, 96 S.Ct. 2440, 49 L.Ed.2d 310 (1976); *Gertz v. Robert Welch, Inc.,* 418 U.S. 323, 94 S.Ct. 2997, 41 L.Ed.2d 789 (1974); *Greenbelt Cooperative Publishing Assn., Inc. v. Bresler,* 398 U.S. 6, 90 S.Ct. 1537, 26 L.Ed.2d 6 (1970).

This protection has been extended by explicit holdings to the context of political speech. See, *e.g., Button,* 371 U.S., at 428-429, 83 S.Ct. 328; *Grosjean v. American Press Co.,* 297 U.S. 233, 244, 56 S.Ct. 444, 80 L.Ed. 660 (1936). Under the rationale of these precedents, political speech does not lose First Amendment protection "simply because its source is a corporation." *Bellotti, supra,* at 784, 98 S.Ct. 1407; see *Pacific Gas & Elec. Co. v. Public Util. Comm'n of Cal.,* 475 U.S. 1, 8, 106 S.Ct. 903, 89 L.Ed.2d 1 (1986) (plurality opinion) ("The identity of the speaker is not decisive in determining whether speech is protected. Corporations and other associations, like individuals, contribute to the "discussion, debate, and the dissemination of information and ideas' that the First Amendment seeks to foster" (quoting *Bellotti,* 435 U.S., at 783, 98 S.Ct. 1407)). The Court has thus rejected the argument that political speech of corporations or other associations should be treated differently under the First Amendment simply because such associations are not "natural persons." *Id.,* at 776, 98 S.Ct. 1407; see *id.,* at 780, n. 16, 98 S.Ct. 1407. Cf. *id.,* at 828, 98 S.Ct. 1407 (Rehnquist, J., dissenting).

At least since the latter part of the 19th century, the laws of some States and of the United States imposed a ban on corporate direct contributions to candidates. See B. Smith, Unfree Speech: The Folly of Campaign Finance Reform 23 (2001). Yet not until 1947 did Congress first prohibit independent expenditures by corporations and labor unions in § 304 of the Labor Management Relations Act 1947, 61 Stat. 159 (codified at 2 U.S.C. § 251 (1946 ed., Supp. I)). In passing this Act Congress overrode the veto of President Truman, who warned that the expenditure ban was a "dangerous intrusion on free speech." Message from the President of the United States, H.R. Doc. No. 334, 89th Cong., 1st Sess., 9 (1947).

[...]

2

[...]

Bellotti, 435 U.S. 765, 98 S.Ct. 1407, 55 L.Ed.2d 707, reaffirmed the First Amendment principle that the Government cannot restrict political speech based on the speaker's corporate identity. *Bellotti* could not have been clearer when it struck down a state-law prohibition on corporate independent expenditures related to referenda issues:

> "We thus find no support in the First ... Amendment, or in the decisions of this Court, for the proposition that speech that otherwise would be within the protection of the First Amendment loses that protection simply because its source is a corporation that cannot prove, to the satisfaction of a court, a material effect on its business or property. ... [That proposition] amounts to an impermissible legislative prohibition of speech based on the identity of the interests that spokesmen may represent in public debate over controversial issues and a requirement that the speaker have a sufficiently great interest in the subject to justify communication.

[...]

3

Thus the law stood until *Austin*. *Austin* "uph[eld] a direct restriction on the independent expenditure of funds for political speech for the first time in [this Court's] history." 494 U.S., at 695, 110 S.Ct. 1391 (KENNEDY, J., dissenting). There, the Michigan Chamber of Commerce sought to use general treasury funds to run a newspaper ad supporting a specific candidate. Michigan law, however, prohibited corporate independent expenditures that supported or opposed any candidate for state office. A violation of the law was punishable as a felony. The Court sustained the speech prohibition.

To bypass *Buckley* and *Bellotti*, the *Austin* Court identified a new governmental interest in limiting political speech: an antidistortion interest. *Austin* found a compelling governmental interest in preventing "the corrosive and distorting effects of immense aggregations of wealth that are accumulated with the help of the corporate form and that have little or no correlation to the public's support for the corporation's political ideas." 494 U.S., at 660, 110 S.Ct. 1391; see *id.*, at 659, 110 S.Ct. 1391 (citing *MCFL*, 479 U.S., at 257, 107 S.Ct. 616; *NCPAC*, 470 U.S., at 500-501, 105 S.Ct. 1459).

B

The Court is thus confronted with conflicting lines of precedent: a pre-*Austin* line that forbids restrictions on political speech based on the speaker's corporate identity and a post-*Austin* line that permits them. [...]

In its defense of the corporate-speech restrictions in § 441b, the Government notes the antidistortion rationale on which *Austin* and its progeny rest in part, yet it all but abandons reliance upon it. It argues instead that two other compelling interests support *Austin*'s holding that corporate expenditure restrictions are constitutional: an anticorruption interest, see 494 U.S., at 678, 110 S.Ct. 1391 (STEVENS, J., concurring), and a shareholder-protection interest, see *id.*, at 674-675, 110 S.Ct. 1391 (Brennan, J., concurring). We consider the three points in turn. [904]

1

As for *Austin*'s antidistortion rationale, the Government does little to defend it. See Tr. of Oral Arg. 45-48 (Sept. 9, 2009). And with good reason, for the rationale cannot support § 441b.

If the First Amendment has any force, it prohibits Congress from fining or jailing citizens, or associations of citizens, for simply engaging in political speech. If the antidistortion rationale were to be accepted, however, it would permit Government to ban political speech simply because the speaker is an association that has taken on the corporate form. [...]

This protection for speech is inconsistent with *Austin*'s antidistortion rationale. *Austin* sought to defend the antidistortion rationale as a means to prevent corporations from obtaining "'an unfair advantage in the political marketplace'" by using "'resources amassed in the economic marketplace.'" 494 U.S., at 659, 110 S.Ct. 1391 (quoting *MCFL, supra,* at 257, 107 S.Ct. 616). But *Buckley* rejected the premise that the Government has an interest "in equalizing the relative ability of individuals and groups to influence the outcome of elections." 424 U.S., at 48, 96 S.Ct. 612; see *Bellotti, supra,* at 791, n. 30, 98 S.Ct. 1407. *Buckley* was specific in stating that "the skyrocketing cost of political campaigns" could not sustain the governmental prohibition. 424 U.S., at 26, 96 S.Ct. 612. The First Amendment's protections do not depend on the speaker's "financial ability to engage in public discussion." *Id.*, at 49, 96 S.Ct. 612.

[...]

Either as support for its antidistortion rationale or as a further argument, the *Austin* majority undertook to distinguish wealthy individuals from corporations on the ground that "[s]tate law grants corporations special advantages—such as limited liability, perpetual life, and favorable treatment of the accumulation and distribution of assets." 494 U.S., at 658-659, 110 S.Ct. 1391. This does not suffice, however, to allow laws prohibiting speech. "It is rudimentary that the State cannot exact as the price of those special advantages the forfeiture of First Amendment rights." *Id.*, at 680, 110 S.Ct. 1391 (SCALIA, J., dissenting).

It is irrelevant for purposes of the First Amendment that corporate funds may "have little or no correlation to the public's support for the corporation's political ideas." *Id.*, at 660, 110 S.Ct. 1391 (majority opinion). All speakers, including individuals and the media, use money amassed from the economic marketplace to fund their speech. The First Amendment protects the resulting speech, even if it was enabled by economic transactions with persons or entities who disagree with the speaker's ideas. See *id.*, at 707, 110 S.Ct. 1391 (KENNEDY, J., dissenting) ("Many persons can trace their funds to corporations, if not in the form of donations, then in the form of dividends, interest, or salary").

Austin's antidistortion rationale would produce the dangerous, and unacceptable, consequence that Congress could ban political speech of media corporations. [...]

The law's exception for media corporations is, on its own terms, all but an admission of the invalidity of the antidistortion rationale. And the exemption results in a further, separate reason for finding this law invalid: Again by its own terms, the law exempts some corporations but covers others, even though both have the need or the motive to communicate their views. [...]

There is simply no support for the view that the First Amendment, as originally understood, would permit the suppression of political speech by media corporations. The Framers may not have anticipated modern business and media corporations. See *McIntyre v. Ohio Elections Comm'n*, 514 U.S. 334, 360-361, 115 S.Ct. 1511, 131 L.Ed.2d 426 (1995) (Thomas, J., concurring in judgment). Yet television networks and major newspapers owned by media corporations have become the most important means of mass communication in modern times. [...]

Austin interferes with the "open marketplace" of ideas protected by the First Amendment. *New York State Bd. of Elections v. Lopez Torres*, 552 U.S. 196, 208, 128 S.Ct. 791, 169 L.Ed.2d 665 (2008); see *ibid.* (ideas "may compete" in this marketplace "without government interference"); *McConnell, supra*, at 274, 124 S.Ct. 619 (opinion of THOMAS, J.). It permits the [907] Government to ban the political speech of millions of associations of citizens. See Statistics of Income 2 (5.8 million for-profit corporations filed 2006 tax returns). Most of these are small corporations without large amounts of wealth. See Supp. Brief for Chamber of Commerce of the United States of America as *Amicus Curiae* 1, 3 (96% of the 3 million businesses that belong to the U.S. Chamber of

Commerce have fewer than 100 employees); M. Keightley, Congressional Research Service Report for Congress, Business Organizational Choices: Taxation and Responses to Legislative Changes 10 (2009) (more than 75% of corporations whose income is taxed under federal law, see 26 U.S.C. § 301, have less than $1 million in receipts per year). This fact belies the Government's argument that the statute is justified on the ground that it prevents the "distorting effects of immense aggregations of wealth." *Austin*, 494 U.S., at 660, 110 S.Ct. 1391. It is not even aimed at amassed wealth.

[...]

[908] Even if § 441b's expenditure ban were constitutional, wealthy corporations could still lobby elected officials, although smaller corporations may not have the resources to do so. And wealthy individuals and unincorporated associations can spend unlimited amounts on independent expenditures. See, *e.g.*, *WRTL*, 551 U.S., at 503-504, 127 S.Ct. 2652 (opinion of SCALIA, J.) ("In the 2004 election cycle, a mere 24 individuals contributed an astounding total of $142 million to [26 U.S.C. § 527 organizations]"). Yet certain disfavored associations of citizens—those that have taken on the corporate form—are penalized for engaging in the same political speech.

[...]

2

What we have said also shows the invalidity of other arguments made by the Government. For the most part relinquishing the antidistortion rationale, the Government falls back on the argument that corporate political speech can be banned in order to prevent corruption or its appearance. In *Buckley*, the Court found this interest "sufficiently important" to allow limits on contributions but did not extend that reasoning to expenditure limits. 424 U.S., at 25, 96 S.Ct. 612. When *Buckley* examined an expenditure ban, it found "that the governmental interest in preventing corruption and the appearance of corruption [was] inadequate to justify [the ban] on independent expenditures." *Id.*, at 45, 96 S.Ct. 612.

With regard to large direct contributions, *Buckley* reasoned that they could be given "to secure a political *quid pro quo*," *id.*, at 26, 96 S.Ct. 612, and that "the scope of such pernicious practices can never be reliably ascertained," *id.*, at 27, 96 S.Ct. 612. The practices *Buckley* noted would be covered by bribery laws, see, *e.g.*, 18 U.S.C. § 201, if a *quid pro quo* arrangement were proved. See *Buckley*, *supra*, at 27, and n. 28, 96 S.Ct. 612 (citing *Buckley v. Valeo*, 519 F.2d 821, 839-840, and nn. 36-38 (CADC 1975) (en banc) (*per curiam*)). The Court, in consequence, has noted that restrictions on direct contributions are preventative, because few if any contributions to candidates will involve *quid pro quo* arrangements. *MCFL*, 479 U.S., at 260, 107 S.Ct. 616; *NCPAC*, 470 U.S., at 500, 105 S.Ct. 1459; *Federal Election Comm'n v. National Right to Work Comm.*,

459 U.S. 197, 210, 103 S.Ct. 552, 74 L.Ed.2d 364 (1982) *(NRWC)*. The *Buckley* Court, nevertheless, sustained limits on direct contributions in order to ensure against the reality or appearance of corruption. That case did not extend this rationale to independent expenditures, and the Court does not do so here.

"The absence of prearrangement and coordination of an expenditure with the candidate or his agent not only undermines the value of the expenditure to the candidate, but also alleviates the danger that expenditures will be given as a *quid pro quo* for improper commitments from the candidate." *Buckley,* 424 U.S., at 47, 96 S.Ct. 612; see *ibid.* (independent expenditures have a "substantially diminished potential for abuse"). Limits on independent expenditures, such as § 441b, have a chilling effect extending well beyond the Government's interest in preventing *quid pro quo* corruption. The anticorruption interest is not sufficient to displace the speech here in question. Indeed, 26 States do not restrict independent expenditures [909] by for-profit corporations. The Government does not claim that these expenditures have corrupted the political process in those States. [...]

3

The Government contends further that corporate independent expenditures can be limited because of its interest in protecting dissenting shareholders from being compelled to fund corporate political speech. This asserted interest, like *Austin*'s antidistortion rationale, would allow the Government to ban the political speech even of media corporations. See *supra,* at 905-906. Assume, for example, that a shareholder of a corporation that owns a newspaper disagrees with the political views the newspaper expresses. See *Austin,* 494 U.S., at 687, 110 S.Ct. 1391 (SCALIA, J., dissenting). Under the Government's view, that potential disagreement could give the Government the authority to restrict the media corporation's political speech. The First Amendment does not allow that power. There is, furthermore, little evidence of abuse that cannot be corrected by shareholders "through the procedures of corporate democracy." *Bellotti,* 435 U.S., at 794, 98 S.Ct. 1407; see *id.,* at 794, n. 34, 98 S.Ct. 1407.

Those reasons are sufficient to reject this shareholder-protection interest; and, moreover, the statute is both underinclusive and overinclusive. As to the first, if Congress had been seeking to protect dissenting shareholders, it would not have banned corporate speech in only certain media within 30 or 60 days before an election. A dissenting shareholder's interests would be implicated by speech in any media at any time. As to the second, the statute is overinclusive because it covers all corporations, including nonprofit corporations and for-profit corporations with only single shareholders. As to other corporations, the remedy is not to restrict speech but to consider and explore other regulatory mechanisms. The regulatory mechanism here, based on speech, contravenes the First Amendment.

4

We need not reach the question whether the Government has a compelling interest in preventing foreign individuals or associations from influencing our Nation's political process. Cf. 2 U.S.C. § 441e (contribution and expenditure ban applied to "foreign national[s]"). Section 441b is not limited to corporations or associations that were created in foreign countries or funded predominately by foreign shareholders. Section 441b therefore would be overbroad even if we assumed, *arguendo*, that the Government has a compelling interest in limiting foreign influence over our political process. See *Broadrick*, 413 U.S., at 615, 93 S.Ct. 2908.

C

Our precedent is to be respected unless the most convincing of reasons demonstrates that adherence to it puts us [912] on a course that is sure error. "Beyond workability, the relevant factors in deciding whether to adhere to the principle of *stare decisis* include the antiquity of the precedent, the reliance interests at stake, and of course whether the decision was well reasoned." *Montejo v. Louisiana*, 556 U.S. ___, ___, 129 S.Ct. 2079, 2088-2089, 173 L.Ed.2d 955 (2009) (overruling *Michigan v. Jackson*, 475 U.S. 625, 106 S.Ct. 1404, 89 L.Ed.2d 631 (1986)). We have also examined whether "experience has pointed up the precedent's shortcomings." *Pearson v. Callahan*, 555 U.S. ___, ___, 129 S.Ct. 808, 816, 172 L.Ed.2d 565 (2009) (overruling *Saucier v. Katz*, 533 U.S. 194, 121 S.Ct. 2151, 150 L.Ed.2d 272 (2001)).

These considerations counsel in favor of rejecting *Austin*, which itself contravened this Court's earlier precedents in *Buckley* and *Bellotti*. "This Court has not hesitated to overrule decisions offensive to the First Amendment." *WRTL*, 551 U.S., at 500, 127 S.Ct. 2652 (opinion of SCALIA, J.). "*[S]tare decisis* is a principle of policy and not a mechanical formula of adherence to the latest decision." *Helvering v. Hallock*, 309 U.S. 106, 119, 60 S.Ct. 444, 84 L.Ed. 604 (1940).

[...]

Chief Justice ROBERTS, with whom Justice ALITO joins, concurring.

The Government urges us in this case to uphold a direct prohibition on political speech. It asks us to embrace a theory of the First Amendment that would allow censorship not only of television and radio broadcasts, but of pamphlets, posters, the Internet, and virtually any other medium that corporations and unions might find useful in expressing their views on matters of public concern. Its theory, if accepted, would empower the Government to prohibit newspapers from running editorials or opinion pieces supporting or opposing candidates for office, so long as the newspapers were owned by corporations—as the major ones are. First Amendment rights could be confined to individuals, subverting the vibrant public discourse that is at the foundation of our democracy.

The Court properly rejects that theory, and I join its opinion in full. The First Amendment protects more than just the individual on a soapbox and the lonely pamphleteer. I write separately to address the important principles of judicial restraint and *stare decisis* implicated in this case.

[...]

Justice SCALIA, with whom Justice ALITO joins, and with whom Justice THOMAS joins in part, concurring.

I join the opinion of the Court.

I write separately to address Justice STEVENS' discussion of *"Original Understandings,"* *post*, at 948 (opinion concurring in part and dissenting in part) (hereinafter referred to as the dissent). This section of the dissent purports to show that today's decision is not supported by the original understanding of the First Amendment. The dissent attempts this demonstration, however, in splendid isolation from the text of the First Amendment. It never shows why "the freedom of speech" that was the right of Englishmen did not include the freedom to speak in association with other individuals, including association in the corporate form. To be sure, in 1791 (as now) corporations could pursue only the objectives set forth in their charters; but the dissent provides no evidence that their speech in the pursuit of those objectives could be censored.

Instead of taking this straightforward approach to determining the Amendment's meaning, the dissent embarks on a detailed exploration of the Framers' views about the "role of corporations in society." *Post*, at 949. The Framers didn't like corporations, the dissent concludes, and therefore it follows (as night the day) that corporations had no rights of free speech. Of course the Framers' personal affection or disaffection for corporations is relevant only insofar as it can be thought to be reflected in the understood meaning of the text they enacted—not, as the dissent suggests, as a freestanding substitute for that text. But the dissent's distortion of proper analysis is even worse than that. Though faced with a constitutional text that makes no distinction between types of speakers, the dissent feels no necessity to provide even an isolated statement from the founding era to the effect that corporations are *not* covered, but places the burden on petitioners to bring forward statements showing that they *are* ("there is not a scintilla of evidence to support the notion that anyone believed [the First Amendment] would preclude regulatory distinctions based on the corporate form," *post*, at 948).

Despite the corporation-hating quotations the dissent has dredged up, it is far from clear that by the end of the 18th century corporations were despised. If so, how came there to be so many of them? The dissent's statement that there were few business corporations during the eighteenth century—"only a few hundred during all of the 18th century"—is misleading. *Post,* at 949, n. 53. There were approximately 335 charters issued to business corporations in the United States by the end of the 18th century. See 2 J. & Davis, [926] Essays in the Earlier History of American Corporations 24 (1917) (reprint 2006) (hereinafter Davis). This was a "considerable extension of corporate enterprise in the field of business," Davis 8, and represented "unprecedented growth," *id.,* at 309. Moreover, what seems like a small number by today's standards surely does not indicate the relative importance of corporations when the Nation was considerably smaller. As I have previously noted, "[b]y the end of the eighteenth century the corporation was a familiar figure in American economic life." *McConnell v. Federal Election Comm'n,* 540 U.S. 93, 256, 124 S.Ct. 619, 157 L.Ed.2d 491 (2003) (SCALIA, J., concurring in part, concurring in judgment in part, and dissenting in part) (quoting C. Cooke, Corporation Trust and Company 92 (1951) (hereinafter Cooke)).

Even if we thought it proper to apply the dissent's approach of excluding from First Amendment coverage what the Founders disliked, and even if we agreed that the Founders disliked founding-era corporations; modern corporations might not qualify for exclusion. Most of the Founders' resentment towards corporations was directed at the state-granted monopoly privileges that individually chartered corporations enjoyed. Modern corporations do not have such privileges, and would probably have been favored by most of our enterprising Founders—excluding, perhaps, Thomas Jefferson and others favoring perpetuation of an agrarian society. Moreover, if the Founders' specific intent with respect to corporations is what matters, why does the dissent ignore the Founders' views about other legal entities that have more in common with modern business corporations than the founding-era corporations? At the time of the founding, religious, educational, and literary corporations were incorporated under general incorporation statutes, much as business corporations are today. See Davis 16-17; R. Seavoy, Origins of the American Business Corporation, 1784-1855, p. 5 (1982); Cooke 94. There were also small unincorporated business associations, which some have argued were the "'true progenitors'" of today's business corporations. Friedman 200 (quoting S. Livermore, Early American Land Companies: Their Influence on Corporate Development 216 (1939)); see also Davis 33. Were all of these silently excluded from the protections of the First Amendment?

The lack of a textual exception for speech by corporations cannot be explained on the ground that such organizations did not exist or did not speak. To the contrary, colleges, towns and cities, religious institutions, and guilds had long been organized as corporations at common law and under the King's charter, see 1 W. Blackstone, Commentaries on the

Laws of England 455-473 (1765); 1 S. Kyd, A [927] Treatise on the Law of Corporations 1-32, 63 (1793) (reprinted 2006), and as I have discussed, the practice of incorporation only expanded in the United States. Both corporations and voluntary associations actively petitioned the Government and expressed their views in newspapers and pamphlets. For example: An antislavery Quaker corporation petitioned the First Congress, distributed pamphlets, and communicated through the press in 1790. W. diGiacomantonio, "For the Gratification of a Volunteering Society": Antislavery and Pressure Group Politics in the First Federal Congress, 15 J. Early Republic 169 (1995). The New York Sons of Liberty sent a circular to colonies farther south in 1766. P. Maier, From Resistance to Revolution 79-80 (1972). And the Society for the Relief and Instruction of Poor Germans circulated a biweekly paper from 1755 to 1757. Adams, The Colonial German-language Press and the American Revolution, in The Press & the American Revolution 151, 161-162 (B. Bailyn & J. Hench eds.1980). The dissent offers no evidence—none whatever—that the First Amendment's unqualified text was originally understood to exclude such associational speech from its protection.

Historical evidence relating to the textually similar clause "the freedom of ... the press" also provides no support for the proposition that the First Amendment excludes conduct of artificial legal entities from the scope of its protection. The freedom of "the press" was widely understood to protect the publishing activities of individual editors and printers. See McIntyre v. Ohio Elections Comm'n, 514 U.S. 334, 360, 115 S.Ct. 1511, 131 L.Ed.2d 426 (1995) (THOMAS, J., concurring in judgment); see also McConnell, 540 U.S., at 252-253, 124 S.Ct. 619 (opinion of SCALIA, J.). But these individuals often acted through newspapers, which (much like corporations) had their own names, outlived the individuals who had founded them, could be bought and sold, were sometimes owned by more than one person, and were operated for profit. See generally F. [928] Mott, American Journalism: A History of Newspapers in the United States Through 250 Years 3-164 (1941); J. Smith, Freedom's Fetters (1956). Their activities were not stripped of First Amendment protection simply because they were carried out under the banner of an artificial legal entity. And the notion which follows from the dissent's view, that modern newspapers, since they are incorporated, have free-speech rights only at the sufferance of Congress, boggles the mind.[...]

The dissent says that when the Framers "constitutionalized the right to free speech in the First Amendment, it was the free speech of individual Americans that they had in mind." Post, at 950. That is no doubt true. All the provisions of the Bill of Rights set forth the rights of individual men and women—not, for example, of trees or polar bears. But the individual person's right to speak includes the right to speak in association with other individual persons. Surely the dissent does not believe that speech by the Republican Party or the Democratic Party can be censored because it is not the speech of "an individual American." It is the speech of many individual Americans, who have associated in a common cause, giving the leadership of the party the right to speak on their behalf. The association of individuals in a business corporation is no different—or at least it cannot be denied the right to speak on the simplistic ground that it is not "an individual American."

[929] But to return to, and summarize, my principal point, which is the conformity of today's opinion with the original meaning of the First Amendment. The Amendment is written in terms of "speech," not speakers. Its text offers no foothold for excluding any category of speaker, from single individuals to partnerships of individuals, to unincorporated associations of individuals, to incorporated associations of individuals— and the dissent offers no evidence about the original meaning of the text to support any such exclusion. We are therefore simply left with the question whether the speech at issue in this case is "speech" covered by the First Amendment. No one says otherwise. A documentary film critical of a potential Presidential candidate is core political speech, and its nature as such does not change simply because it was funded by a corporation. Nor does the character of that funding produce any reduction whatever in the "inherent worth of the speech" and "its capacity for informing the public," *First Nat. Bank of Boston v. Bellotti,* 435 U.S. 765, 777, 98 S.Ct. 1407, 55 L.Ed.2d 707 (1978). Indeed, to exclude or impede corporate speech is to muzzle the principal agents of the modern free economy. We should celebrate rather than condemn the addition of this speech to the public debate.

Justice STEVENS, with whom Justice GINSBURG, Justice BREYER, and Justice SOTOMAYOR join, concurring in part and dissenting in part.

The real issue in this case concerns how, not if, the appellant may finance its electioneering. Citizens United is a wealthy nonprofit corporation that runs a political action committee (PAC) with millions of dollars in assets. Under the Bipartisan Campaign Reform Act of 2002 (BCRA), it could have used those assets to televise and promote *Hillary: The Movie* wherever and whenever it wanted to. It also could have spent unrestricted sums to broadcast *Hillary* at any time other than the 30 days before the last primary election. Neither Citizens United's nor any other corporation's speech has been "banned," *ante,* at 886. All that the parties dispute is whether Citizens United had a right to use the funds in its general treasury to pay for broadcasts during the 30-day period. The notion that the First Amendment dictates an affirmative answer to that question is, in my judgment, profoundly misguided. Even more misguided is the notion that the Court must rewrite [930] the law relating to campaign expenditures by *for-profit* corporations and unions to decide this case.

The basic premise underlying the Court's ruling is its iteration, and constant reiteration, of the proposition that the First Amendment bars regulatory distinctions based on a speaker's identity, including its "identity" as a corporation. While that glittering generality has rhetorical appeal, it is not a correct statement of the law. Nor does it tell us when a corporation may engage in electioneering that some of its shareholders oppose. It does not even resolve the specific question whether Citizens United may be required to finance some of its messages with the money in its PAC. The conceit that corporations must be treated identically to natural persons in the political sphere is not only inaccurate but also inadequate to justify the Court's disposition of this case.

In the context of election to public office, the distinction between corporate and human speakers is significant. Although they make enormous contributions to our society, corporations are not actually members of it. They cannot vote or run for office. Because they may be managed and controlled by nonresidents, their interests may conflict in fundamental respects with the interests of eligible voters. The financial resources, legal structure, and instrumental orientation of corporations raise legitimate concerns about their role in the electoral process. Our lawmakers have a compelling constitutional basis, if not also a democratic duty, to take measures designed to guard against the potentially deleterious effects of corporate spending in local and national races.

The majority's approach to corporate electioneering marks a dramatic break from our past. Congress has placed special limitations on campaign spending by corporations ever since the passage of the Tillman Act in 1907, ch. 420, 34 Stat. 864. We have unanimously concluded that this "reflects a permissible assessment of the dangers posed by those entities to the electoral process," *FEC v. National Right to Work Comm.*, 459 U.S. 197, 209, 103 S.Ct. 552, 74 L.Ed.2d 364 (1982) *(NRWC)*, and have accepted the "legislative judgment that the special characteristics of the corporate structure require particularly careful regulation," *id.*, at 209-210, 103 S.Ct. 552. The Court today rejects a century of history when it treats the distinction between corporate and individual campaign spending as an invidious novelty born of *Austin v. Michigan Chamber of Commerce*, 494 U.S. 652, 110 S.Ct. 1391, 108 L.Ed.2d 652 (1990). Relying largely on individual dissenting opinions, the majority blazes through our precedents, [...]

III

The novelty of the Court's procedural dereliction and its approach to *stare decisis* is matched by the novelty of its ruling on the merits. The ruling rests on several premises. First, the Court claims that *Austin* and *McConnell* have "banned" corporate speech. Second, it claims that the First Amendment precludes regulatory distinctions based on speaker identity, including the speaker's identity as a corporation. Third, it claims that *Austin* and *McConnell* were radical outliers in our First Amendment tradition and our campaign finance jurisprudence. Each of these claims is wrong.

[...]

Identity-Based Distinctions

The second pillar of the Court's opinion is its assertion that "the Government cannot restrict political speech based on the speaker's ... identity." *Ante,* at 902; accord, *ante,* at 886, 898, 900, 902-904, 912-913. The case on which it relies for this proposition is *First Nat. Bank of Boston v. Bellotti,* 435 U.S. 765, 98 S.Ct. 1407, 55 L.Ed.2d 707 (1978). As I shall explain, *infra,* at 958-960, the holding in that case was far narrower than the Court implies. Like its paeans to unfettered discourse, the Court's denunciation of identity-based distinctions may have rhetorical appeal but it obscures reality.

"Our jurisprudence over the past 216 years has rejected an absolutist interpretation" of the First Amendment. *WRTL,* 551 U.S., at 482, 127 S.Ct. 2652 (opinion of ROBERTS, C.J.). The First Amendment provides that "Congress shall make no law... abridging the freedom of speech, or of the press." Apart perhaps from measures designed to protect the press, that text might seem to permit no distinctions of any kind. Yet in a variety of contexts, we have held that speech can be regulated differentially on account of the speaker's identity, when identity is understood in categorical or institutional terms. The Government routinely places special restrictions on the speech rights of students, prisoners, members of the Armed Forces, foreigners, and its own employees. When such restrictions are justified by a legitimate governmental interest, [946] they do not necessarily raise constitutional problems. [...]

The same logic applies to this case with additional force because it is the identity of corporations, rather than individuals, that the Legislature has taken into account. As we have unanimously observed, legislatures are entitled to decide "that the special characteristics of the corporate structure require particularly careful regulation" in an electoral context. *NRWC,* 459 U.S., at 209-210, 103 S.Ct. 552. Not only has the distinctive potential of corporations to corrupt the electoral process long been recognized, but within the area of campaign finance, corporate spending is also "furthest from the core of political expression, since corporations' First Amendment speech and association interests are derived largely from those of their members and of the public in receiving information," *Beaumont,* 539 U.S., at 161, n. 8, 123 S.Ct. 2200 (citation omitted). Campaign finance distinctions based on corporate identity tend to be less worrisome, in other words, because the "speakers" are not natural persons, much less members of our political community, and the governmental interests are of the highest order. Furthermore, when corporations, as a class, are distinguished from noncorporations, as a class, there is a lesser risk that regulatory distinctions will reflect invidious discrimination or political favoritism.

If taken seriously, our colleagues' assumption that the identity of a speaker has *no* relevance to the Government's ability to regulate political speech would lead to some remarkable conclusions. Such an assumption would have accorded the propaganda broadcasts to our troops by "Tokyo Rose" during World War II the same protection as speech by Allied commanders. More pertinently, it would appear to afford the same protection to multinational corporations [948] controlled by foreigners as to individual Americans: To do otherwise, after all, could "'enhance the relative voice'" of some (*i.e.,* humans) over others (*i.e.,* nonhumans). *Ante,* at 904 (quoting *Buckley,* 424 U.S., at 49, 96 S.Ct. 612). Under the majority's view, I suppose it may be a First Amendment problem that corporations are not permitted to vote, given that voting is, among other things, a form of speech.

In short, the Court dramatically overstates its critique of identity-based distinctions, without ever explaining why corporate identity demands the same treatment as individual identity. Only the most wooden approach to the First Amendment could justify the unprecedented line it seeks to draw.

Our First Amendment Tradition

A third fulcrum of the Court's opinion is the idea that *Austin* and *McConnell* are radical outliers, "aberration[s]," in our First Amendment tradition. *Ante,* at 907; see also *ante,* at 910, 916-917 (professing fidelity to "our law and our tradition"). The Court has it exactly backwards. It is today's holding that is the radical departure from what had been settled First Amendment law. To see why, it is useful to take a long view.

1. Original Understandings

Let us start from the beginning. The Court invokes "ancient First Amendment principles," *ante,* at 886 (internal quotation marks omitted), and original understandings, *ante,* at 906-907, to defend today's ruling, yet it makes only a perfunctory attempt to ground its analysis in the principles or understandings of those who drafted and ratified the Amendment. Perhaps this is because there is not a scintilla of evidence to support the notion that anyone believed it would preclude regulatory distinctions based on the corporate form. To the extent that the Framers' views are discernible and relevant to the disposition of this case, they would appear to cut strongly against the majority's position.

This is not only because the Framers and their contemporaries conceived of speech more narrowly than we now think of it, see Bork, Neutral Principles and Some First Amendment Problems, 47 Ind. [949] L.J. 1, 22 (1971), but also because they held very different views about the nature of the First Amendment right and the role of corporations in society. Those few corporations that existed at the founding were authorized by grant of a special legislative charter. Corporate sponsors would petition the legislature, and the legislature, if amenable, would issue a charter that specified the corporation's powers and purposes and "authoritatively fixed the scope and content of corporate organization," including "the internal structure of the corporation." J. Hurst, The Legitimacy of the Business

Corporation in the Law of the United States 1780-1970, pp. 15-16 (1970) (reprint 2004). Corporations were created, supervised, and conceptualized as quasi-public entities, "designed to serve a social function for the state." Handlin & Handlin, Origin of the American Business Corporation, 5 J. Econ. Hist. 1, 22 (1945). It was "assumed that [they] were legally privileged organizations that had to be closely scrutinized by the legislature because their purposes had to be made consistent with public welfare." R. Seavoy, Origins of the American Business Corporation, 1784-1855, p. 5 (1982).

[...] General incorporation statutes, and widespread acceptance of business corporations as socially useful actors, did not emerge until the 1800's. [...]

The Framers thus took it as a given that corporations could be comprehensively [950] regulated in the service of the public welfare. Unlike our colleagues, they had little trouble distinguishing corporations from human beings, and when they constitutionalized the right to free speech in the First Amendment, it was the free speech of individual Americans that they had in mind. While individuals might join together to exercise their speech rights, business corporations, at least, were plainly not seen as facilitating such associational or expressive ends. Even "the notion that business corporations could invoke the First Amendment would probably have been quite a novelty," given that "at the time, the legitimacy of every corporate activity was thought to rest entirely in a concession of the sovereign." Shelledy, Autonomy, Debate, and Corporate Speech, 18 Hastings Const. L.Q. 541, 578 (1991); cf. *Trustees of Dartmouth College v. Woodward*, 4 Wheat. 518, 636, 4 L.Ed. 629 (1819) (Marshall, C.J.) [...] In light of these background practices and understandings, it seems to me implausible that the Framers believed "the freedom of speech" would extend equally to all corporate speakers, much less that it would preclude legislatures from taking limited measures to guard against corporate capture of elections.

[...]

This case sheds a revelatory light on the assumption of some that an impartial judge's application of an originalist methodology is likely to yield more determinate answers, or to play a more decisive role in the decisional process, than his or her views about sound policy.

[...]

2. Legislative and Judicial Interpretation

A century of more recent history puts to rest any notion that today's ruling is faithful to our First Amendment tradition. At the federal level, the express distinction between corporate and individual political spending on elections stretches back to 1907, when

Congress passed the Tillman Act, ch. 420, 34 Stat. 864, banning all corporate contributions to candidates. [...]

By the time Congress passed FECA in 1971, the bar on corporate contributions and expenditures had become such an accepted part of federal campaign finance regulation that when a large number of plaintiffs, including several nonprofit corporations, challenged virtually every aspect of the Act in *Buckley*, 424 U.S. 1, 96 S.Ct. 612, 46 L.Ed.2d 659, no one even bothered to argue that the bar as such was unconstitutional. [...]

Thus, it was unremarkable, in a 1982 case holding that Congress could bar nonprofit corporations from soliciting nonmembers for PAC funds, that then-Justice Rehnquist wrote for a unanimous Court [955] that Congress' "careful legislative adjustment of the federal electoral laws, in a cautious advance, step by step, to account for the particular legal and economic attributes of corporations ... warrants considerable deference," and "reflects a permissible assessment of the dangers posed by those entities to the electoral process." *NRWC*, 459 U.S., at 209 [...]

The corporate/individual distinction was not questioned by the Court's disposition, in 1986, of a challenge to the expenditure restriction as applied to a distinctive type of nonprofit corporation. In *MCFL*, 479 U.S. 238, 107 S.Ct. 616, 93 L.Ed.2d 539, we stated again "that "the special characteristics of the corporate structure require particularly careful regulation,'" *id.*, at 256, 107 S.Ct. 616 (quoting *NRWC*, 459 U.S., at 209-210, 103 S.Ct. 552), and again we acknowledged that the Government has a legitimate interest in "regulat[ing] the substantial aggregations of wealth amassed by the special advantages which go with the corporate form" [...]

Four years later, in *Austin*, 494 U.S. 652, 110 S.Ct. 1391, 108 L.Ed.2d 652, we considered whether corporations falling outside the *MCFL* exception could be barred from using general treasury funds to make independent expenditures in support of, or in opposition to, candidates. We held they could be. Once again recognizing the importance of "the integrity of the marketplace of political ideas" in candidate elections, *MCFL*, 479 U.S., at 257, 107 S.Ct. 616, we noted that corporations have "special advantages—such as limited liability, perpetual life, and favorable treatment of the accumulation and distribution of assets," 494 U.S., at 658-659, 110 S.Ct. 1391—that allow them to spend prodigious general treasury sums on campaign messages that have "little or no correlation" with the beliefs held by actual persons, *id.*, at 660, 110 S.Ct. 1391. In light of the corrupting effects such spending might have on the political process, *ibid.*, we permitted the State of Michigan to limit corporate expenditures on candidate elections to corporations' PACs, which rely on voluntary contributions and thus "reflect actual public support for the political ideals espoused by corporations," *ibid.* [...]

3. Buckley and Bellotti

Against this extensive background of congressional regulation of corporate campaign spending, and our repeated affirmation of this regulation as constitutionally sound, the majority dismisses *Austin* as "a significant departure from ancient First Amendment principles," *ante,* at 886 (internal quotation marks omitted). How does the majority attempt to justify this claim? Selected passages from two cases, *Buckley,* 424 U.S. 1, 96 S.Ct. 612, 46 L.Ed.2d 659, and *Bellotti,* 435 U.S. 765, 98 S.Ct. 1407, 55 L.Ed.2d 707, do all of the work. [...]

IV

Having explained why this is not an appropriate case in which to revisit *Austin* and *McConnell* and why these decisions sit perfectly well with "First Amendment principles," *ante,* at 886, 912, I come at last to the interests that are at stake. The majority recognizes that *Austin* and *McConnell* may be defended on anticorruption, antidistortion, and shareholder protection rationales. *Ante,* at 903-911. It badly errs both in explaining the nature of these rationales, which overlap and complement each other, and in applying them to the case at hand.

The Anticorruption Interest

[...]

Corporations, as a class, tend to be more attuned to the complexities of the legislative process and more directly affected by tax and appropriations measures that receive little public scrutiny; they also have vastly more money with which to try to buy access and votes. See Supp. Brief for Appellee 17 (stating that the Fortune 100 companies earned revenues of $13.1 trillion during the last election cycle). Business corporations must engage the political process in instrumental terms if they are to maximize shareholder value. The unparalleled resources, professional lobbyists, and single-minded focus they bring to this effort, I believed, make *quid pro quo* corruption and its appearance inherently more likely when they (or their conduits or trade groups) spend unrestricted sums on elections.

[...]

Austin and Corporate Expenditures

Just as the majority gives short shrift to the general societal interests at stake in campaign finance regulation, it also overlooks the distinctive considerations raised by the regulation of *corporate* expenditures. The majority fails to appreciate that *Austin's* antidistortion rationale is itself an anticorruption rationale, see 494 U.S., at 660, 110 S.Ct. 1391 (describing "a different type of corruption"), tied to the special concerns raised by corporations. Understood properly, "antidistortion" is simply a variant on the classic governmental interest in protecting against improper influences on officeholders that debilitate the democratic process. It is manifestly not just an "'equalizing'" ideal in disguise. *Ante,* at 904 (quoting *Buckley,* 424 U.S., at 48, 96 S.Ct. 612). [971]

1. *Antidistortion*

The fact that corporations are different from human beings might seem to need no elaboration, except that the majority opinion almost completely elides it. *Austin* set forth some of the basic differences. Unlike natural persons, corporations have "limited liability" for their owners and managers, "perpetual life," separation of ownership and control, "and favorable treatment of the accumulation and distribution of assets ... that enhance their ability to attract capital and to deploy their resources in ways that maximize the return on their shareholders' investments." 494 U.S., at 658-659, 110 S.Ct. 1391. Unlike voters in U.S. elections, corporations may be foreign controlled. Unlike other interest groups, business corporations have been "effectively delegated responsibility for ensuring society's economic welfare"; they inescapably structure the life of every citizen. "'[T]he resources in the treasury of a business corporation,'" furthermore, "'are not an indication of popular support for the corporation's political ideas.'" *Id.,* at 659, 110 S.Ct. 1391 (quoting *MCFL,* 479 U.S., at 258, 107 S.Ct. 616). "'They reflect instead the economically motivated decisions of investors and customers. The availability of these resources may make a corporation a formidable political presence, even though the power of the corporation may be no reflection of the power of its ideas.'" 494 U.S., at 659, 110 S.Ct. 1391 (quoting *MCFL,* 479 U.S., at 258, 107 S.Ct. 616).

[972] It might also be added that corporations have no consciences, no beliefs, no feelings, no thoughts, no desires. Corporations help structure and facilitate the activities of human beings, to be sure, and their "personhood" often serves as a useful legal fiction. But they are not themselves members of "We the People" by whom and for whom our Constitution was established.

[...]

It is an interesting question "who" is even speaking when a business corporation places an advertisement that endorses or attacks a particular candidate. Presumably it is not the customers or employees, who typically have no say in such matters. It cannot realistically be said to be the shareholders, who tend to be far removed from the day-to-day decisions of the firm and whose political preferences may be opaque to management. Perhaps the officers or directors of the corporation have the best claim to be the ones speaking, except their fiduciary duties generally prohibit them from using corporate funds for personal ends. Some individuals associated with the corporation must make the decision to place the ad, but the idea that these individuals are thereby fostering their self-expression or cultivating their critical faculties is fanciful. It is entirely possible that the corporation's electoral message will *conflict* with their personal convictions. Take away the ability to use general treasury funds for some of those ads, and no one's autonomy, dignity, or political equality has been impinged upon in the least.

[...]

Corporate "domination" of electioneering, *Austin,* 494 U.S., at 659, 110 S.Ct. 1391, can generate the impression that corporations dominate our democracy. When citizens turn on their televisions and radios before an election and hear only corporate electioneering, they may lose faith in their capacity, as citizens, to influence public policy. A Government captured by corporate interests, they may come to believe, will be neither responsive to their needs nor willing to give their views a fair hearing. The predictable result is cynicism and disenchantment: an increased perception that large spenders "'call the tune'" and a reduced "'willingness of voters to take part in democratic governance.'" *McConnell,* 540 U.S., at 144, 124 S.Ct. 619 (quoting *Shrink Missouri,* 528 U.S., at 390, 120 S.Ct. 897). [...]

The majority's unwillingness to distinguish between corporations and humans similarly blinds it to the possibility that corporations' "war chests" and their special "advantages" in the legal realm, *Austin,* 494 U.S., at 659, 110 S.Ct. 1391, may translate into special advantages in the market for legislation. When large numbers of citizens have a common stake in a measure that is under consideration, it may be very difficult for them to coordinate resources on behalf of their position. The corporate form, by contrast, "provides a simple way to channel rents to only those who have paid their dues, as it were. If you do not own stock, you do not benefit from the larger dividends or appreciation in the stock price caused by the passage of private interest legislation." Sitkoff, Corporate Political Speech, Political Extortion, and the Competition for Corporate Charters, 69 U. Chi. L.Rev. 1103, 1113 (2002). Corporations, that is, are uniquely equipped to seek laws that favor their owners, not simply because they have a lot of money but because of their legal and organizational structure. Remove all restrictions on their electioneering, and the door may be opened to a type of rent seeking that is "far more destructive" than what noncorporations are capable of. *Ibid.* It is for reasons such as these that our campaign finance jurisprudence has long appreciated that "the 'differing structures and purposes' of different entities "may require different forms of regulation in order to protect the integrity of the electoral process.'" *NRWC,* 459 U.S., at 210, 103 S.Ct. 552 (quoting *California Medical Assn.,* 453 U.S., at 201, 101 S.Ct. 2712).

[...]

In critiquing *Austin*'s antidistortion rationale and campaign finance regulation more generally, our colleagues place tremendous weight on the example of media corporations. See *ante*, at 905-907, 911; *ante*, at 917, 923 (opinion of ROBERTS, C.J.); *ante*, at 927-928 (opinion of SCALIA, J.). Yet it is not at all clear that *Austin* would permit § 203 to be applied to them. The press plays a unique role not only in the text, history, and structure of the First Amendment but also in facilitating public discourse; as the *Austin* Court explained, "media corporations differ significantly from other corporations in that their resources are devoted to the collection of information and its dissemination to the public," 494 U.S., at 667, 110 S.Ct. 1391. Our colleagues have raised some interesting and difficult questions about Congress' authority to regulate electioneering by the press, and about how to define what constitutes the press. *But that is not the case before us.* Section 203 does not apply to media corporations, and even if it did, Citizens United is not a media corporation. [...]

2. Shareholder Protection

There is yet another way in which laws such as § 203 can serve First Amendment values. Interwoven with *Austin*'s concern to protect the integrity of the electoral process is a concern to protect the rights of shareholders from a kind of coerced speech: electioneering expenditures that do not "reflec[t] [their] support." 494 U.S., at 660-661, 110 S.Ct. 1391. When corporations use general treasury funds to praise or attack a particular candidate for office, it is the shareholders, as the residual claimants, who are effectively footing the bill. Those shareholders who disagree with the corporation's electoral message may find their financial investments being used to undermine their political convictions.

[...]

The Court dismisses this interest on the ground that abuses of shareholder money can be corrected "through the procedures of corporate democracy," *ante*, at 911 (internal quotation marks omitted), and, it seems, through Internet-based disclosures, *ante*, at 916. I fail to understand how this addresses the concerns of dissenting union members, who will also be affected by today's ruling, and I fail to understand why the Court is so confident in these mechanisms. By "corporate democracy," presumably the Court means the rights of shareholders to vote and to bring derivative suits for breach of fiduciary duty. In practice, however, many corporate lawyers will tell you that "these rights are so limited as to be almost nonexistent," given the internal authority wielded by boards and managers and the expansive protections afforded by the business judgment rule. Blair & Stout 320; see also *id.*, at 298-315; Winkler, 32 Loyola (LA) L.Rev., at 165-166, 199-200. Modern technology may help make it easier to track corporate activity, including electoral advocacy, but it is utopian to believe that it solves the problem. Most American households that own stock do so through intermediaries such as mutual funds and pension plans, see Evans, A Requiem for the Retail Investor? 95 Va. L.Rev. 1105 (2009), which makes it more difficult both to monitor and to alter particular holdings. Studies show that a majority of individual investors make no trades at all during a given year. [...]

If and when shareholders learn that a corporation has been spending general treasury money on objectionable electioneering, they can divest. Even assuming that they reliably learn as much, however, this solution is only partial. The injury to the shareholders' expressive rights has already occurred; they might have preferred to keep that corporation's stock in their portfolio for any number of economic reasons; and they may incur a capital gains tax or other penalty from selling their shares, changing their pension plan, or the like. The shareholder protection rationale has been criticized as underinclusive, in that corporations also spend money on lobbying and charitable contributions in ways that any particular shareholder might disapprove. But those expenditures do not implicate the selection of public officials, an area in which "the interests of unwilling ... corporate shareholders [in not being] forced to subsidize that speech" "are at their zenith." [...]

Appendices

A. Apple Inc.'s Restated Articles of Incorporation

I

The name of the corporation is Apple Inc.

II

The purpose of this corporation is to engage in any lawful act or activity for which a corporation may be organized under the General Corporation Law of California other than the banking business, the trust company business or the practice of a profession permitted to be incorporated by the California Corporations Code.

III

This corporation is authorized to issue one class of shares designated "Common Stock," par value $0.00001 per share. The number of shares of Common Stock that this corporation is authorized to issue is 50,400,000,000. As of 5:00 p.m., Pacific Daylight Time, on August 28, 2020, each share of Common Stock outstanding shall be automatically, and with no further action by the holder of such share, split into four shares of Common Stock.

IV

Section 1. *Limitation of Directors' Liability.* The liability of the directors of this corporation for monetary damages shall be eliminated to the fullest extent permissible under California law.

Section 2. *Indemnification of Corporate Agents.* The corporation is authorized to provide indemnification of agents (as defined in Section 317 of the California Corporations Code) through bylaw provisions, agreements with agents, vote of shareholders or disinterested directors or otherwise, in excess of the indemnification otherwise permitted by Section 317 of the California Corporations Code, subject only to the applicable limits set forth in Section 204 of the California Corporations Code with respect to actions for breach of duty to the corporation and its shareholders.

Section 3. *Repeal or Modification.* Any repeal or modification of the foregoing provisions of this Article IV by the shareholders of this corporation shall not adversely affect any right or protection of an agent of this corporation existing at the time of such repeal or modification.

V

There shall be no right with respect to shares of stock of this corporation to cumulate votes in the election of directors.

B. Apple Inc.'s Amended and Restated Bylaws

ARTICLE I
CORPORATE OFFICES

1.1   Principal Office

The Board of Directors shall fix the location of the principal executive office of Apple Inc. (the "Corporation") at any place within or outside the State of California. If the principal executive office is located outside California and the Corporation has one or more business offices in California, then the Board of Directors shall fix and designate a principal business office in California.

1.2   Other Offices

The Board of Directors may at any time establish branch or subordinate offices at any place or places.

ARTICLE II
DIRECTORS

2.1   Powers

Subject to the provisions of the California General Corporation Law (the "Code"), any limitations in the Restated Articles of Incorporation of the Corporation (the "Articles of Incorporation") and these Amended and Restated Bylaws (these "Bylaws") relating to action required to be approved by the shareholders or by the outstanding shares, the business and affairs of the Corporation shall be managed and all corporate powers shall be exercised by or under the direction of the Board of Directors. The Board of Directors may delegate the management of the day-to-day operation of the business of the Corporation to a management company or other person provided that the business and affairs of the Corporation shall be managed and all corporate powers shall be exercised under the ultimate direction of the Board of Directors.

2.2   Number

The number of directors of the Corporation shall be not less than five (5) nor more than nine (9). The exact number of directors shall be nine (9) until changed within the limits specified above, by a bylaw amending this Section 2.2, duly adopted by the Board of Directors or by the shareholders. The indefinite number of directors may be changed, or a definite number fixed without provision for an indefinite number, by a duly adopted amendment to the Articles of Incorporation or by amendment to these Bylaws duly adopted by the vote or written consent of holders of a majority of the outstanding shares entitled to vote; provided, however, that an amendment reducing the fixed number or the minimum number of directors to a number less than five (5) cannot be adopted if the votes cast against its adoption at a meeting of the shareholders, or the shares not consenting in the case of action by written consent, are equal to more than sixteen and two-thirds percent (16-2/3%) of the outstanding shares entitled to vote. No amendment may change the stated maximum number of authorized directors to a number greater than two (2) times the stated minimum number of directors minus one (1).

2.3   Compensation

Directors and members of committees may receive such compensation, if any, for their services, and may be reimbursed for expenses, as fixed or determined by resolution of the Board of Directors. This Section 2.3 shall not be construed to preclude any director from serving the Corporation in any other capacity and receiving compensation for those services.

2.4   Election and Term of Office

Each director shall be elected to serve until the annual meeting of shareholders held in the following fiscal year and until such director's successor shall have been duly elected and qualified. Notwithstanding the foregoing, the term of any incumbent director who fails to be elected by "approval of the shareholders" as defined in Section 153 of the Code in an Uncontested Election (as such term is defined below) and who has not earlier resigned will end on the date that is the earlier of (a) ninety (90) days after the date on which the voting results are determined pursuant to Section 707 of the Code and (b) the date on which the Board of Directors selects a person to fill the office held by that director in accordance with the procedures set forth in Section 2.5. For purposes of these Bylaws, an "Uncontested Election" means an election of directors in which, at the expiration of the later of the time fixed for nomination of director candidates pursuant to (x) Section 5.14 regarding advance notice and (y) Section 5.15 regarding proxy access, the number of candidates for election does not exceed the number of directors to be elected by the shareholders at that election.

2.5   Vacancies and Resignations

(a)   A vacancy or vacancies on the Board of Directors shall be deemed to exist (i) in the event of the death, resignation or removal of any director, (ii) if the authorized number of directors is increased, (iii) if the shareholders fail, at any meeting of shareholders at which any director or directors are elected, to elect the full authorized number of directors to be elected at that meeting, (iv) if the Board of Directors declares vacant the office of a director who has been declared of unsound mind by an order of court or convicted of a felony, or (v) at the end of the term of an incumbent director who fails to be elected by approval of the shareholders as set forth in Section 2.4.

(b)   Except for a vacancy caused by the removal of a director as provided in Section 2.7, a vacancy may be filled by approval of the board, or if the number of directors then in office is less than a quorum by (i) the unanimous written consent of the directors then in office, (ii) the affirmative vote of a majority of the directors then in office, or (iii) a sole remaining director. Vacancies created by the removal of a director shall be filled only by approval of the shareholders, or by the unanimous written consent of all shares entitled to vote.

(c)   The shareholders may elect a director at any time to fill a vacancy or vacancies not filled by the directors, but any such election by written consent, other than to fill a vacancy created by removal, shall require the consent of a majority of the outstanding shares entitled to vote thereon. A director may not be elected by written consent to fill a vacancy created by removal except by unanimous consent of all shares entitled to vote for the election of directors.

(d)   Any director may resign effective upon giving written notice to the Secretary of the Corporation, unless the notice specifies a later time for the effectiveness of such resignation. If the resignation of a director is effective at a future time, the Board of Directors may elect a successor to take office when the resignation becomes effective. A reduction of the authorized number of directors shall not remove any director prior to the expiration of such director's term of office.

2.6   Chair of the Board and Lead Directors

The Corporation may have at the discretion of the Board of Directors, a Chair of the Board of Directors and/or one or more Lead Directors. The Chair of the Board of Directors, if there is one, or a Lead Director, shall have the power to preside at all meetings of the Board of Directors and shall have such other powers and shall be subject to such other duties as the Board of Directors may from time to time prescribe or as may be prescribed by these Bylaws. If there is more than one Lead Director, the Board of Directors may prescribe different responsibilities to each Lead Director.

2.7   Removal

The entire Board of Directors or any individual director may be removed without cause from office by an affirmative vote of a majority of the outstanding shares entitled to vote; provided that, unless the entire Board of Directors is removed, no director shall be removed when the votes cast against removal, or not consenting in writing to such removal, would be sufficient to elect such director if voted cumulatively (without regard to whether such shares may be voted cumulatively) at an election at which the same total number of votes were cast, or, if such action is taken by written consent, all shares entitled to vote were voted, and either the number of directors elected at the most recent annual meeting of shareholders, or if greater, the number of directors for whom removal is being sought, were then being elected. If any or all directors are so removed, new directors may be elected at the same meeting or at a subsequent meeting. If at any time a class or series of shares is entitled to elect one or more directors under authority granted by the Articles of Incorporation, the provisions of this Section 2.7 shall apply to the vote of that class or series and not to the vote of the outstanding shares as a whole.

ARTICLE III
OFFICERS

3.1 Officers

The officers of the Corporation shall be a Chief Executive Officer, a Secretary and a Chief Financial Officer. The Chief Executive Officer shall be deemed the president of the Corporation for purposes of the Code. The Corporation may also have, at the discretion of the Board of Directors, a Chair of the Board of Directors, one or more Vice Presidents, a Treasurer, one or more Assistant Secretaries and one or more Assistant Treasurers and such officers as may be appointed in accordance with the provisions of Section 3.3. Any number of offices may be held by the same person.

3.2 Appointment of Officers

The officers of the Corporation, except such officers as may be appointed in accordance with the provisions of Section 3.3, shall be chosen by the Board of Directors and serve at the pleasure of the Board of Directors, subject to the rights, if any, of an officer under any contract of employment.

3.3 Subordinate Officers

[...]

3.4 Term of Office and Compensation

The term of office and salary of each of said officers and the manner and time of the payment of such salaries shall be fixed and determined by the Board of Directors and may be altered by the Board of Directors from time to time at its pleasure, subject to the rights, if any, of an officer under any contract of employment.

3.5 Removal or Resignation

(a) Subject to the rights, if any, of an officer under any contract of employment, all officers serve at the pleasure of the Board of Directors and any officer may be removed, either with or without cause, by the Board of Directors at any regular or special meeting of the Board of Directors, or, except in the case of an officer chosen by the Board of

Directors, by any officer upon whom such power of removal may be conferred by the Board of Directors.

[...]

3.6   Vacancies

[...]

3.7   Chief Executive Officer

[...]

3.8   President Pro Tem

[...]

3.9   Vice President

[...]

3.10   Secretary

[...]

3.11   Chief Financial Officer

[...]

3.12   Divisional and Other Officers Appointed by the Chief Executive Officer

[...]

ARTICLE IV
COMMITTEES

4.1   Committees of the Board of Directors

The Board of Directors may, by resolution adopted by a majority of the authorized number of directors, designate one (1) or more committees, each consisting of two (2) or more directors, to serve at the pleasure of the Board of Directors. The Board of Directors may designate one (1) or more directors as alternate members of any committee, who may replace any absent member at any meeting of the committee. The appointment of members or alternate members of a committee requires the vote of a majority of the authorized number of directors. Any such committee shall have authority to act in a manner and to the extent provided in the resolution of the Board of Directors and may have all the authority of the Board of Directors, except with respect to:

(a)   the approval of any action which, under the Code, also requires shareholders' approval or approval of the outstanding shares;

(b)   the filling of vacancies on the Board of Directors or in any committee;

(c)   the fixing of compensation of any director or directors for serving on the Board of Directors or on any committee;

(d)   the amendment or repeal of these Bylaws or the adoption of new bylaws;

(e)   the amendment or repeal of any resolution of the Board of Directors which by its express terms is not so amendable or repealable;

(f)   a distribution to the shareholders of the Corporation, except at a rate, in a periodic amount or within a price range set forth in the Articles of Incorporation or determined by the Board of Directors; and

(g)   the appointment or designation of any other committee of the Board of Directors or the members thereof.

ARTICLE V
MEETINGS OF SHAREHOLDERS

5.1   Place of Meetings

(a)   Meetings (whether regular, special, adjourned, or postponed) of the shareholders of the Corporation may be held at the principal executive office for the transaction of business of the Corporation, or at any place within or without the State, in each case as designated by resolution of the Board of Directors or a duly authorized committee thereof.

(b)   At the sole discretion of the Board of Directors, and subject to applicable provisions under the Code and any guidelines and procedures that the Board of Directors may adopt, a meeting of the shareholders may be conducted in whole or in part by electronic transmission by and to the Corporation, electronic video screen communication, conference telephone, or other means of remote communication.

5.2   Annual Meetings

An annual meeting of shareholders shall be held each year on a date and at a time designated by the Board of Directors or a duly authorized committee thereof. The annual meeting shall be held for the purpose of electing directors and for making reports of the affairs of the Corporation. Any other business properly brought before the meeting may be transacted at the annual meeting of shareholders. The Board of Directors may postpone, reschedule, or cancel any previously scheduled annual meeting of shareholders for any reason.

5.3   Special Meetings

(a)   Special meetings of shareholders for any purpose may be called at any time only by (i) the Board of Directors, the Chair of the Board of Directors, or the Chief Executive Officer or (ii) one or more holders of shares entitled to cast not less than ten percent (10%) (the "Requisite Percentage") of the votes on the Requested Record Date (as such term is defined below) if a timely request in proper written form is delivered to the Secretary in compliance with this Section 5.3 (such request, a "Special Meeting Request"). The Board of Directors may postpone, reschedule, or cancel any previously scheduled special meeting of shareholders called pursuant to the foregoing clause (i) for any reason.

[...]

5.4   Notice of Meetings

Notice of any meeting of shareholders shall be given in writing not less than ten (10) nor more than sixty (60) days before the date of the meeting to each shareholder entitled to vote thereat by the Secretary or an Assistant Secretary, or other person charged with that duty, or if there is no such officer or person, or in case of such officer's or person's neglect or refusal, by any director or shareholder. [...]

5.5   Manner of Giving Notice; Affidavit of Notice

[...]

5.6   Consent to Shareholders' Meetings

[...]

5.7   Quorum

The presence in person or by proxy of the holders of a majority of the shares entitled to vote at any meeting of shareholders shall constitute a quorum for the transaction of business. Shares shall not be counted to make up a quorum for a meeting if voting of such shares at the meeting has been enjoined or if for any reason they cannot be lawfully voted at the meeting. The shareholders present at a duly called or held meeting at which a quorum is present may continue to transact business until adjournment, notwithstanding the withdrawal of enough shareholders to leave less than a quorum, if any action taken (other than adjournment) is approved by at least a majority of the shares required to constitute a quorum or, if required by the Code, the vote of a greater number or voting by classes.

5.8   Adjourned Meetings

[...]

5.9   Record Date for Shareholder Notice; Voting; Giving Consents

(a)   In order that the Corporation may determine the shareholders entitled to notice of any meeting or to vote, the Board of Directors may fix, in advance, a record date, which shall not be more than sixty (60) days nor less than ten (10) days prior to the date of such meeting nor more than sixty (60) days before any other action. Only shareholders of record at the close of business on the record date are entitled to notice of, and to vote at, a meeting of shareholders, notwithstanding any transfer of any shares on the books of the Corporation after the record date, except as otherwise provided in the Articles of Incorporation or the Code. In the absence of any contrary provision in the Articles of Incorporation or in any applicable statute relating to the election of directors or to other particular matters, each such person shall be entitled to one (1) vote for each share.

[...]

5.10   Action by Written Consent

(a)   Any action which may be taken at any annual or special meeting of shareholders may be taken without a meeting and without prior notice, if a consent in writing, setting forth the action so taken, shall be provided by the holders of outstanding shares having not less than the minimum number of votes that would be necessary to authorize or take such action at a meeting at which all shares entitled to vote thereon were present and voted.

[...]

5.11   Election of Directors

Approval of the shareholders is required to elect a director in any Uncontested Election of directors. In any other election of directors by the shareholders, the candidates receiving the highest number of affirmative votes of the shares entitled to be voted for them up to the number of directors to be elected by such shares are elected; votes against the directors and votes withheld with respect to the election of the directors shall have no legal effect. Elections of directors need not be by ballot except upon demand made by a shareholder at the meeting and before the voting begins.

5.12   Proxies

[…]

5.13   Inspectors of Elections

[…]

5.14   Advance Notice of Shareholder Business and Nominations

(a)   Annual Meetings of Shareholders.

(i)   Nominations of persons for election to the Board of Directors and the proposal of business to be considered by the shareholders may be made at an annual meeting of shareholders only (1) pursuant to the Corporation's notice of meeting (or any supplement thereto) given by or at the direction of the Board of Directors or any duly authorized committee thereof, (2) as otherwise properly brought before such annual meeting by or at the direction of the Board of Directors or any duly authorized committee thereof, (3) by any shareholder of the Corporation who was a shareholder of record of the Corporation at the time the notice provided for in this Section 5.14 is delivered to the Secretary and through the time of the annual meeting, who is entitled to vote at the meeting, and who complies with the notice procedures set forth in this Section 5.14, or (4) by one or more Eligible Shareholders (as such term is defined below) pursuant to and in accordance with Section 5.15.

[Eds: Here, we omit ~6pages of rules concerning director nominations and other shareholder proposals at annual meetings and another ~3 pages of rules concerning the nominations/proposals at special meetings.]

5.15   Proxy Access for Director Nominations

(a)   Subject to the terms and conditions of these Bylaws, the Corporation shall include in its proxy materials for an annual meeting of shareholders the name and other Required Information (as such term is defined below) of any Shareholder Nominee (as such term is defined below) nominated for election or reelection to the Board of Directors at such annual meeting of shareholders in accordance with this Section 5.15. Capitalized terms used in this Section 5.15 shall have the meanings indicated in this Section 5.15. This Section 5.15 shall be the exclusive method for shareholders to require that the Corporation include nominees for election as a director in the Corporation's proxy materials.

[Eds: The provisions governing proxy access span ~9 pages.]

5.16 Conduct of Meeting

[…]

ARTICLE VI
MEETINGS OF DIRECTORS

6.1 Place of Meetings

[…]

6.2 Regular Annual Meeting; Regular Meetings

[…]

6.3 Special Meetings

[…]

6.4 Notice of Special Meetings

[…]

6.5 Quorum

[…]

6.6 Adjournment

[…]

6.7 Waiver and Notice of Consent

[….]

6.8 Action without a Meeting

Any action required or permitted by law to be taken by the Board of Directors may be taken without a meeting, if all members of the Board of Directors shall individually or collectively consent in writing to such action. Such written consent or consents shall be filed with the minutes of the proceedings of the Board of Directors. Such action by written consent shall have the same force and effect as the unanimous vote of such directors.

6.9 Committees

The provisions of this Article VI also apply to committees of the Board of Directors and action by such committees, mutatis mutandis.

ARTICLE VII
GENERAL MATTERS

7.1   Record Date for Purposes Other than Notice and Voting

[...]

7.2   Instruments in Writing

[...]

7.3   Shares Held by the Corporation

[...]

7.4   Certificated and Uncertificated Shares

[...]

7.5   Lost Certificates

[...]

7.6   Certification and Inspection of Bylaws

The Corporation shall keep at its principal executive or business office the original or a copy of these Bylaws as amended or otherwise altered to date, which shall be open to inspection by the shareholders at all reasonable times during office hours.

7.7   Interpretation

Reference in these Bylaws to any provision of the Code shall be deemed to include all amendments thereof.

7.8   Construction

Unless the context requires otherwise, the general provisions, rules of construction, and definitions in the Code shall govern the construction of these Bylaws. Without limiting the generality of the provision, the singular number includes the plural, the plural number includes the singular, and the term "person" includes both a corporation and a natural person.

ARTICLE VIII
CONSTRUCTION OF BYLAWS WITH REFERENCE TO PROVISIONS OF LAW

8.1   Bylaw Provisions Additional and Supplemental to Provisions of Law

All restrictions, limitations, requirements, and other provisions of these Bylaws shall be construed, insofar as possible, as supplemental and additional to all provisions of law applicable to the subject matter thereof and shall be fully complied with in addition to the said provisions of law unless such compliance shall be illegal.

8.2   Bylaw Provisions Contrary to or Inconsistent with Provisions of Law

Any article, section, subsection, subdivision, sentence, clause, or phrase of these Bylaws which, upon being construed in the manner provided in Section 8.1, shall be contrary to or inconsistent with any applicable provision of law, shall not apply so long as said provisions of law shall remain in effect, but such result shall not affect the validity or applicability of any other portions of these Bylaws, it being hereby declared that these Bylaws, and each article, section, subsection, subdivision, sentence, clause, or phrase thereof, would have been adopted irrespective of the fact that any one or more articles, sections, subsections, subdivisions, sentences, clauses or phrases is or are illegal.

8.3   Definitions

Unless the context requires otherwise or as otherwise defined in these Bylaws, the general provisions, rules of construction, and definitions in the Code and Sections 1-21 of the California Corporations Code govern the construction of these Bylaws. Without limiting the generality of the provision, the singular number includes the plural, the plural number includes the singular, the word "including" is not a term of limitation, the terms "approval of the outstanding shares" and "approved by (or approval of) the shareholders" have the meanings set forth in Sections 152 and 153 of the Code, respectively, and the terms "electronic transmission by the corporation" and "electronic transmission to corporation" have the meanings set forth in Sections 20 and 21 of the California Corporations Code, respectively.

ARTICLE IX
ADOPTION, AMENDMENT OR REPEAL OF BYLAWS

9.1   By Shareholders

These Bylaws may be adopted, amended, or repealed by the vote or written consent of holders of a majority of the outstanding shares entitled to vote. Any bylaws specifying or changing a fixed number of directors or the maximum or minimum number or changing from a fixed to a variable board or vice versa may only be adopted by the shareholders; provided, however, that a bylaw or amendment of the Articles of Incorporation reducing the number or the minimum number of directors to a number less than five (5) cannot be adopted if the votes cast against its adoption at a meeting or the shares not consenting in the case of action by written consent are equal to more than sixteen and two-thirds percent (16 2/3%) of the outstanding shares entitled to vote.

9.2   By the Board of Directors

Subject to the right of shareholders to adopt, amend, or repeal these Bylaws, other than a bylaw or amendment thereof specifying or changing a fixed number of directors or the maximum or minimum number or changing from a fixed to a variable board or vice versa, these Bylaws may be adopted, amended, or repealed by the Board of Directors. A bylaw adopted by the shareholders may restrict or eliminate the power of the Board of Directors to adopt, amend, or repeal these Bylaws.

ARTICLE X
INDEMNIFICATION

10.1   Indemnification of Directors and Officers

The Corporation shall, to the maximum extent and in the manner permitted by the Code, indemnify each of its directors and officers against expenses (as defined in Section 317(a) of the Code), judgments, fines, settlements, and other amounts actually and reasonably incurred in connection with any proceeding (as defined in Section 317(a) of the Code), arising by reason of the fact that such person is or was an agent (as defined in Section 317(a) of the Code) of the Corporation. For purposes of this Article X, a "director" or "officer" of the Corporation includes any person (a) who is or was a director or officer of the Corporation, (b) who is or was serving at the request of the Corporation as a director or officer of another foreign or domestic corporation, partnership, limited liability company, joint venture, trust, or other enterprise, or (c) who was a director or officer of a corporation which was a predecessor corporation of the Corporation or of another enterprise at the request of such predecessor corporation.

10.2   Indemnification of Others

The Corporation shall have the power, to the extent and in the manner permitted by the Code, to indemnify each of its employees and agents (other than directors and officers) against expenses (as defined in Section 317(a) of the Code), judgments, fines, settlements, and other amounts actually and reasonably incurred in connection with any proceeding (as defined in Section 317(a) of the Code), arising by reason of the fact that such person is or was an agent (as defined in Section 317(a) of the Code) of the Corporation. For purposes of this Article X, an "employee" or "agent" of the Corporation (other than a director or officer) includes any person (a) who is or was an employee or agent of the Corporation, (b) who is or was serving at the request of the Corporation as an employee or agent of another foreign or domestic corporation, partnership, limited liability company, joint venture, trust, or other enterprise, or (c) who was an employee or agent of a corporation which was a predecessor corporation of the Corporation or of another enterprise at the request of such predecessor corporation.

10.3   Payment of Expenses in Advance

Expenses incurred in defending any proceeding for which indemnification is required pursuant to Section 10.1, or for which indemnification is permitted pursuant to Section 10.2 following authorization thereof by the Board of Directors, may be advanced by the Corporation prior to the final disposition of the proceeding upon receipt of an undertaking by or on behalf of the indemnified party to repay that amount if it shall be determined ultimately that the indemnified person is not entitled to be indemnified as authorized by this Article X.

10.4   Indemnification not Exclusive

The indemnification provided by this Article X for acts, omissions, or transactions while acting in the capacity of, or while serving as, a director or officer of the Corporation but not involving a breach of duty to the Corporation and its shareholders shall not be deemed exclusive of any other rights to those seeking indemnification may be entitled under any bylaw, agreement, vote of shareholders or disinterested directors, or otherwise, to the extent the additional rights to indemnification are authorized in the Articles of Incorporation.

10.5   Insurance Indemnification

The Corporation shall have the power to purchase and maintain insurance on behalf of any agent of the Corporation against any liability asserted against or incurred by the agent in that capacity or arising out of that agent's status as such, whether or not the Corporation would have the power to indemnify the agent against that liability under the provisions of this Article X.

10.6   Conflicts

Subject to the requirements of Section 317 of the Code, no indemnification or advance shall be made under this Article X, except as provided in Section 317(d) or Section 317(e)(4) of the Code, in any circumstance where it appears:

(a)   that it would be inconsistent with a provision of the Articles of Incorporation, these Bylaws, a resolution of the shareholders or an agreement in effect at the time of the accrual of the alleged cause of the action asserted in the proceeding in which the expenses were incurred or other amounts were paid, which prohibits or otherwise limits indemnification; or

(b)   that it would be inconsistent with any condition expressly imposed by a court in approving a settlement.

ARTICLE XI
EMERGENCY PROVISIONS

11.1   General

The provisions of this Article XI shall be operative only during any emergency as such term is defined in Section 207 of the Code (each, an "emergency"). During an emergency, the provisions of this Article XI shall override all other Bylaws of the Corporation in conflict with any provisions of this Article XI, and shall remain effective during the emergency, and shall not be effective after the emergency ends; provided that all actions taken in good faith pursuant to such provisions shall thereafter remain in full force and effect unless and until revoked by action taken pursuant to the provisions of these Bylaws other than those contained in this Article XI.

11.2   Meetings; Notice of Meetings

[…]

11.3   Unavailable Directors

[…]

11.4   Authorized Number of Directors

[…]

11.5   Quorum

[…]